TIME-SAVER STANDARDS
Site Construction Details Manual

TIME-SAVER STANDARDS
Site Construction Details Manual

Nicholas T. Dines
& Kyle D. Brown

McGraw-Hill Publishing Company

New York ▪ Washington, D.C. ▪ Auckland ▪ Bogotá ▪ Caracas ▪ Lisbon
London ▪ Madrid ▪ Mexico City ▪ Milan ▪ Montreal ▪ New Delhi ▪ San Juan
Singapore ▪ Sydney ▪ Tokyo ▪ Toronto

McGraw-Hill

*A Division of The **McGraw·Hill** Companies*

7 8 9 0 KGP/KGP 0 8 7

DESIGN & PRODUCTION

Suzi Gierman-Clark / Suzani Design

Jeff Potter / Potter Publishing Studio

ISBN 0-07-017039-8

The sponsoring editor for this book was Wendy Lochner.

Printed and bound by Quebecor/Kingsport.

McGraw-Hill books are available at special quantity discounts to use as premiums and sales promotions, or for use in corporate training programs. For more information, please write to Director of Special Sales, McGraw-Hill, 11 West 19th Street, New York, NY 10011. Or contact your local bookstore.

This book is dedicated
to our daughters,
Emily, Eleni, and Mattea.

Table of Contents

Preface

The primary purpose of this Site Construction Details Manual is to provide a desk reference companion for *Time-Saver Standards Landscape Construction Details CD-ROM*. It contains all of the 350 details and their associated cost, application, climate, maintenance, and subgrade rating files included in the CD-ROM, as well as photographs of built landscapes that are representative of each detail. Additionally, this manual is intended to assist the designer in making design decisions prior to construction drawing preparation as part of the usual design process in a professional office or academic classroom setting.

Both the CD-ROM and this manual prompt the designer to consider the proposed level of service and maintenance requirements, the subgrade and climate conditions, cost parameters, and limitations of selected materials with regard to planned use, weathering, and other factors. This Manual is aimed at providing a framework for thinking about appropriate site detail selection and design, and therefore contains a limited number of details types and applications to demonstrate how details may be grouped, sorted, and modified as site conditions and applications indicate. Many details are shown in light, medium, and heavy-duty versions to indicate how each detail type may be modified to accommodate an array of site conditions.

It is intended that the details shown, are to serve as initial templates which require modification to meet local codes and construction practices. All details are dimensioned in both metric and US units to allow for broad application and modification to suit a particular circumstance. As of this printing, metric practices are still evolving in the US and currently, there are still customs that are at odds with both Canadian and Standard International practices. Local dimensioning practices should be followed. All structural calculations and site soil conditions must be verified by appropriate regulatory authorities, or certified professional consultants.

Acknowledgments

The authors wish to acknowledge with gratitude those who contributed ideas, time and effort towards the publishing of this book, and its companion CD-ROM. The Department of Landscape Architecture and Regional Planning at the University of Massachusetts provided space and facilities for this project. Thanks go to Dr. Meir Gross, Department Head, for his enthusiastic support and to Dr. Robert Helgesen, Dean of the College of Food and Natural Resources who through his support of the Department, indirectly assisted this project. The Department's Office Manager, Ms. Dale Morrow, deserves special thanks for her role in administering project funds.

The following individuals deserve specific thanks for their contributions to the project:

- Jeffrey D. Blankenship, for his critical perspective, coordination of the final CAD work and preparation of graphics for publication.

- Xiaoxin Zhang, for her work as CAD manager and careful attention to detail.

- Sarah Gronquist, Michael Davidsohn, John Martin, RIBA and David Bloniarz for contributing photographs from their personal libraries.

- Vesna Maneva and Hongbing Tang for CAD drawing.

- Suzi Gierman-Clark and Jeff Potter for their creative and organizational efforts in the design and production of this book.

A number of firms and product manufacturers are to be thanked for providing photographs for this book. Specific contributions are acknowledged in the Photographic Sources section at the back of the book.

The authors are indebted to many professional firms and individuals for contributing and reviewing this book's content. These individuals include: Mark Brown, Simpson, Gumperts & Heger, Inc.; Steven P. Ellberg & Associates; John Kissida, Camp, Dresser & McKee; Teresa Law, Belt Collins, Hawaii, LTD.; Thomas Papandrew, Belt Collins, Hawaii, LTD.; Robert Sykes, University of Minnesota; Lindsey Thorpe, Belt Collins, Australia; Shavaun Towers, Rolland/Towers, L.L.C.; Mark Zarillo, Symmes, Maini & McKee, Associates.

We wish to further acknowledge the leadership and support extended to the project by McGraw-Hill Publishing Company and especially the vice president and group publisher Michael Hays, past publisher Sybil Parker, editor Wendy Lochner, and manager of electronic product development, Bouqui Moeller, for their vision, encouragement and trust.

Finally, we wish to thank our families and friends who supported us greatly in this effort.

Introduction

To paraphrase the 1st Century architect, Vitruvius, the designer's challenge is to create a site design which is useful, stable, durable, and beautiful in equal measure. In other words, a design should be functional, carefully constructed of durable materials, and possess intrinsic beauty due to the care and craftsmanship evident in its form and aesthetic expression. However, in the pursuit of aesthetic expression of the moment, site design details often fail to match the requirements of local conditions and long term care to maintain the desired performance over time. The text and illustrations in this manual are aimed at helping the designer to make more informed decisions with regard to selecting the most appropriate materials and method of construction for specific site and use requirements.

Design details together with written specifications illustrate and describe how design elements are to be furnished, assembled, installed or placed on the site by the contractor. Generally, a construction detail is required to describe ground plane changes in elevation and material, or at architectural structure foundations or thresholds.

Additionally, details are required to describe site system components such as utilities, stormwater devices, lighting and other site improvements.

Effective site construction details are typically designed to accommodate the intended use intensities, the local climate stresses, subgrade conditions, and subsequent maintenance practices associated with seasonal effects and care requirements. They must be constructed of materials with appropriate physical properties and be sufficiently reinforced and coated or finished in a manner that will withstand sustained use over a specified period of time. Properly designed, the detail should have a predictable service lifespan if maintained in a suitable manner.

It is strongly advised that recycled materials be specified first whenever available, and that materials imported from other regions be limited to those closest to the work site. In addition, local labor practices (often influenced by cultural adaptations to local climate and tastes), codes, and materials should play an important role in selecting details for a particular project.

How to Use this Book

DETAIL TITLE ⎯⎯

FIELD STONE PAVERS WITH MORTAR SETTING BED ON CONCRETE BASE — HEAVY DUTY

DETAIL DRAWING ⎯⎯

100mm (4") FIELD STONE WITH
25mm (1") MORTAR JOINTS

50mm (2") MORTAR SETTING BED

150mm (6") CONCRETE BASE
REINFORCED AS REQUIRED

200mm (8")
AGGREGATE BASE

PREPARED SUBGRADE

APPLICATION RATINGS ⎯⎯

CLIMATE RATINGS

APPLICATION   **CLIMATE**   **SUBGRADE**

LIGHT   MED.   HEAVY   ARID   HUMID   TEMP.   COLD   PERM.   CLAY   ROCK

SUBGRADE RATINGS

CSI MASTER-FORMAT AND DRAWING FILES ⎯⎯

CSI MASTERFORMAT: 04420
DRAWING FILE: PAV33-07

• This drawing is a template for preliminary design only, and is not intended for bid purposes. It is subject to modification based on design calculations, local practices, and all applicable codes and regulations.

• This detail is rated as heavy-duty based on concrete base and aggregate subbase thickness, although the surface stone has a very high strength. It is typically found in dense residential, urban park, and commercial settings. Due to its irregular surface, it is not suitable as a main walk surface and is often used as a transition pavement.

• Subgrade conditions have a significant impact on the longevity of rigid pavements, such as concrete. The subgrade should be uniform to prevent pavement failure due to uneven soil expansion and contraction. This detail provides a well-drained aggregate base to drain sub-surface moisture and increase uniformity.

• This detail is not designed for cold climates, where the use of mortar is discour-

aged. Flexible adhesives, such as bituminous or elastomeric materials are recommended in these conditions.

• Reinforcing practices vary widely. Local codes and practices should be consulted before specifying any type of reinforcing for the base. All steel should be covered by at least 50mm (2") of concrete.

• Expansion joints should be filled, and sealed in temperate and cold climates. These joints require periodic cleaning and resealing.

• A 50mm (2") mortar setting bed is needed to accommodate the irregular shape of field stone, and may vary due to irregularity of stone sizes. Igneous or metamorphic stones of uniform size and color are typically preferred.

• Stone pavers provide a very durable surface highly resistant to abrasion resulting from normal wear and maintenance.

• It is recommended that recycled and regionally available materials and products be given high priority in determining final design and specifications.

Installation Cost (per Square Foot)
LOW ■ ■ ■ ■ ■ ■ ■ ■ HIGH
$13.31

INSTALLATION COSTS

Maintenance
LOW ■ ■ ■ ■ ■ ■ ■ ■ HIGH

MAINTENANCE LEVEL

KEY POINT TEXT ⎯⎯

PHOTOGRAPH

This section provides a detailed explanation of the information contained in this book. The sample page illustrated above labels the components and supporting data included for each detail template, and the following text describes each element.

Detail Title. The index at the back of the book may be used to search for specific construction details by name.

Detail Drawing. Each drawing includes metric dimensions, with US equivalents shown in parentheses. Generic terminology is used, which may be replaced with proprietary specifications. This drawing is a template for preliminary design only, and is subject to modification based on site conditions and all applicable codes and regulations.

Application Ratings. The active icons illustrate the types of applications suitable for the construction detail as drawn. Modifications may be required for the detail to meet the standards for other types of applications. Three types of applications are identified:

Light-Duty: Intended for residential and private garden settings. Vertical loading consists primarily of pedestrian traffic, lateral loading is considered light, and storm water management capacity requirements are minimal. Lighter materials are typically used because they are not subject to persistent wearing or intensive use. Vandalism is not a concern, and a high level of maintenance is often required. Most small-scale private work falls into this category.

Medium-Duty: Intended for dense residential and commercial settings. Vertical loading consists of pedestrian traffic and light vehicular use. Lateral loading may be a concern, and storm water management capacity requirements are moderate. Vandalism may be a concern, and materials must withstand wearing associated with group settings. Examples include small public plazas and courtyards, public recreation and commercial facilities, and low-intensity parking lots and driveways.

Heavy-duty: Intended for public and institutional settings. Vertical loading typically includes heavy vehicular traffic. Lateral loading from high winds or vehicular impact is a concern, and storm water management capacity requirements are high. Vandal-proofing is typically a necessity, and these landscapes are subject to wearing from very intensive use and maintenance. Examples Include highways, large urban parks and plazas, and professional athletic facilities.

Climate Ratings. The active icons illustrate the appropriate climate for the construction detail. Four broad climate ranges are identified. and are intended to serve as a guide for preliminary planning purposes only. Consult detailed site information for climate information pertaining to actual project design. Characteristics of each category include:

Hot-Arid: Characterized by hot summer temperatures [>20°C (68°F)] and mild to cool winters [>0°C (32°F)]. Annual precipitation is low, however seasonal flash-floods may occur. While freezing temperatures are uncommon, extreme diurnal temperature fluctuations are often typical.

Hot-Humid: Characterized by hot summer temperatures [>20°C (68°F)] and mild to cool winters [>0°C (32°F)]. Annual precipitation and humidity are high, with frequent rain showers. Freezing temperatures are uncommon and relatively minor diurnal temperature fluctuations are typical.

Temperate: Characterized by hot summer temperatures [>20°C (68°F)] and cold winters [<0°C (32°F)]. Annual precipitation is fairly high. The region is subject to repetitive freezing/thawing action, and significant seasonal temperature fluctuations are common.

Cold: Characterized by mild summer temperatures [>10°–20°C (50°–68°F)] and very cold winters [<0°C (32°F)]. Annual precipitation is typically low. Region is subject to extreme freezing/thawing action.

Subgrade Ratings. The active icons illustrate the type of subgrade suitable for the construction detail as drawn. Modifications may be required for the detail to meet the standards for other subgrades. Three subgrade types are identified:

Permeable Soils: Soils that are well-drained and provide little expansion and contraction due to moisture retention. Well-drained soils are optimal for construction and typically do not require special modifications.

Expansive Clays: Colloidal soils that shrink or swell considerably as a result of changes in moisture content. Seasonal changes in moisture levels causes heaving. The design must recognize this potential and compensate for movement of materials, diminished bearing capacity of soil, and low permeability.

On-Structure: Landscapes placed directly on top of built structures, such as building rooftops or underground parking garages. The design must ensure proper drainage of the structure, while seeking to minimize the weight of materials.

CSI MasterFormat and Drawing File. CSI MasterFormat identifies the corresponding code number for the detail, as outlined by the Construction Specifications Institute. The drawing file lists the name of the corresponding DWG, DXF and PICT files in the *Time-Saver Standards Landscape Construction Details CD-ROM.*

Key Point Text. A list of important issues for the designer to consider prior to using the construction detail as a template for project design.

Installation Costs. The graphic illustrates the relative installation costs of the detail in comparison to other construction alternatives. Specific dollar amounts shown are intended to serve as a guide for preliminary planning and comparison purposes only, and are not to be used for construction project estimation. Actual construction costs are subject to regional variation and local business practices. Costs shown are per square foot, linear foot, or unit, depending on the component. Prices are based on published U.S. cost data.

Maintenance Level. Illustrates the relative maintenance requirements of the detail in comparison to other construction alternatives.

Photograph. An example of the construction detail in the built landscape. Photos are intended to be representative of the type of detail, and not necessarily an exact record of the drawing.

Athletic Surfaces

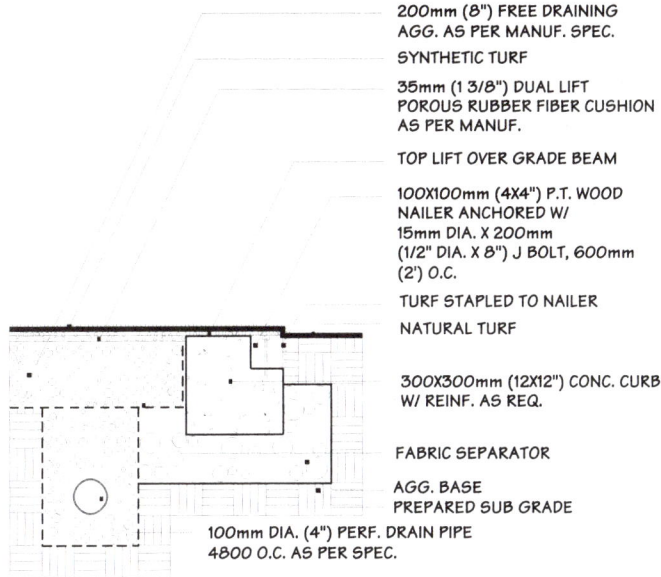

200mm (8") FREE DRAINING
AGG. AS PER MANUF. SPEC.

SYNTHETIC TURF

35mm (1 3/8") DUAL LIFT
POROUS RUBBER FIBER CUSHION
AS PER MANUF.

TOP LIFT OVER GRADE BEAM

100X100mm (4X4") P.T. WOOD
NAILER ANCHORED W/
15mm DIA. X 200mm
(1/2" DIA. X 8") J BOLT, 600mm
(2') O.C.

TURF STAPLED TO NAILER

NATURAL TURF

300X300mm (12X12") CONC. CURB
W/ REINF. AS REQ.

FABRIC SEPARATOR

AGG. BASE
PREPARED SUB GRADE

100mm DIA. (4") PERF. DRAIN PIPE
4800 O.C. AS PER SPEC.

APPLICATION

CLIMATE

SUBGRADE

CSI MASTERFORMAT: 02790
DRAWING FILE: ATH08-05

• This drawing is a template for preliminary design only, and is not intended for bid purposes. It is subject to modification based on design calculations, local practices, and all applicable codes and regulations.

• This artificial turf with resilient pad on aggregate base detail is rated as heavy-duty due to resilient base and aggregate subbase thickness and is typically found in professional sports arenas and stadia. It will support activities typically associated with league athletic events and special function theatrical events.

• If used in outdoor arenas or stadia, base may be crowned to shed water. Porous nature of pad and base allows a flat option in some regions. If soil is poorly drained, a network of subdrainage pipes are trenched into the subgrade. A perimeter concrete grade beam is used to attach the turf at the edge, with care being taken to cushion the beam and to provide smooth grade transition from adjacent surfaces.

• A highly resilient two course porous rubber monolithic pad with proprietary binders is placed under the artificial turf mat directly on the specially graded aggregate subbase. The artificial turf typically has a nap of 15 mm (1/2 "). This process is also useful for retro-fitting an existing paved stadium.

• This surface provides a superior playing field which is much more resilient and therefore safer than artificial turf surfaces of the recent past.

• It is recommended that recycled and regionally available materials and products be given high priority in determining final design and specifications.

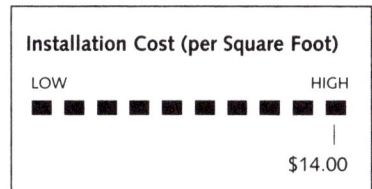

Installation Cost (per Square Foot)

LOW   HIGH

$14.00

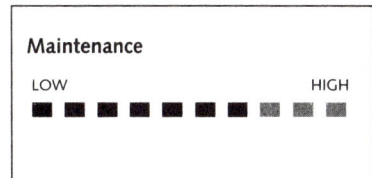

Maintenance

LOW   HIGH

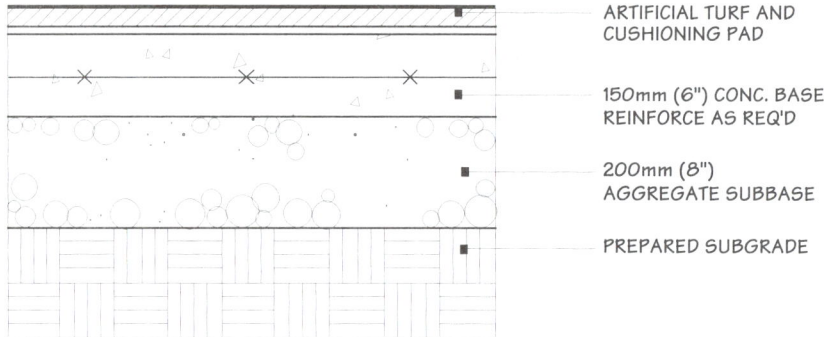

ARTIFICIAL TURF AND CUSHIONING PAD

150mm (6") CONC. BASE REINFORCE AS REQ'D

200mm (8") AGGREGATE SUBBASE

PREPARED SUBGRADE

APPLICATION

CLIMATE

SUBGRADE

CSI MASTERFORMAT: 02790
DRAWING FILE: ATH08-01

• This drawing is a template for preliminary design only, and is not intended for bid purposes. It is subject to modification based on design calculations, local practices, and all applicable codes and regulations.

• This artificial turf on a concrete base detail is rated as heavy-duty due to concrete base and aggregate subbase thickness and is typically found in indoor arenas and multi-purpose exhibition halls. It will support professional athletic events and special function theatrical events. The turf is usually covered with a protective layer.

• If used in an exhibition hall with flat profile, turf and pad are typically laid in 4500 mm (15') strips and held together with "velcro" or other such pressure/friction attachment devices.

• If used outdoors, concrete base must be crowned to shed water. If soil is poorly drained, a network of subdrainage pipes are trenched into the subgrade. A perimeter concrete grade beam is used to attach the turf at the edge, with care being take to provide smooth grade transition from adjacent surfaces.

• Concrete base requires an extra thick pad to be placed under the artificial turf mat which typically has a nap of 15 mm (1/2").

• Subgrade conditions have a significant impact on the longevity of rigid pavements, such as concrete. The subgrade should be uniform to prevent pavement failure due to uneven soil expansion and contraction.

• Rigid pavement design must accommodate movement of materials by providing adequate expansion and control joints, particularly in regions of extreme temperature fluctuations. If designed for temperate or cold climates, air-entrained concrete is typically recommended.

• Reinforcing practices vary widely by region. Local codes and practices should be consulted prior to specifying any type of reinforcing.

• It is recommended that recycled and regionally available materials and products be given high priority in determining final design and specifications.

Installation Cost (per Square Foot)

LOW   HIGH

$9.84

Maintenance

LOW   HIGH

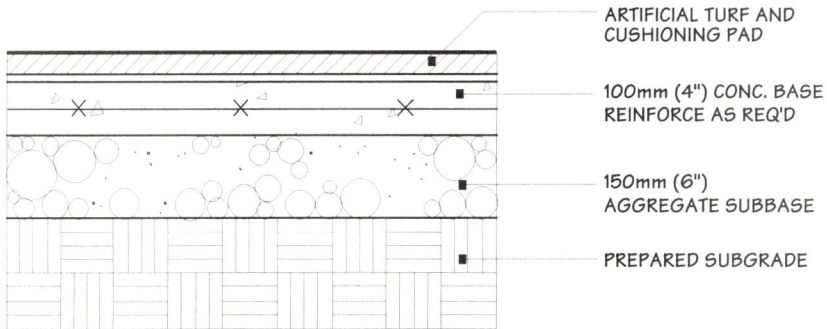

ARTIFICIAL TURF AND CUSHIONING PAD

100mm (4") CONC. BASE REINFORCE AS REQ'D

150mm (6") AGGREGATE SUBBASE

PREPARED SUBGRADE

APPLICATION

CLIMATE

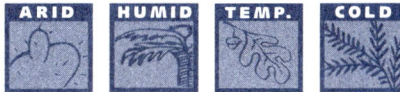

SUBGRADE

CSI MASTERFORMAT: 02790
DRAWING FILE: ATH08-02

• This drawing is a template for preliminary design only, and is not intended for bid purposes. It is subject to modification based on design calculations, local practices, and all applicable codes and regulations.

• This artificial turf on a concrete base detail is rated as medium-duty due to concrete base and aggregate subbase thickness and is typically found in indoor arenas and multi-purpose exhibition halls. It will support activities typically associated with college athletic events and special function theatrical events. The turf is usually covered with a protective layer.

• If used in outdoor arenas or stadia, concrete base must be crowned to shed water. If soil is poorly drained, a network of subdrainage pipes are trenched into the subgrade. A perimeter concrete grade beam is used to attach the turf at the edge, with care being taken to cushion the beam and to provide smooth grade transition from adjacent surfaces.

• Concrete base requires an extra thick pad to be placed under the artificial turf mat which typically has a nap of 15 mm (1/2 ").

• Subgrade conditions have a significant impact on the longevity of rigid pavements, such as concrete. The subgrade should be uniform to prevent pavement failure due to uneven soil expansion and contraction. This detail provides a well-drained aggregate base to drain sub-surface moisture and increase uniformity.

• Rigid pavement design must accommodate movement of materials by providing adequate expansion and control joints, particularly in regions of extreme temperature fluctuations. If designed for temperate or cold climates, air-entrained concrete is typically recommended due to freezing/thawing action.

• Reinforcing practices vary widely by region. Local codes and practices should be consulted prior to specifying any type of reinforcing.

• It is recommended that recycled and regionally available materials and products be given high priority in determining final design and specifications.

Installation Cost (per Square Foot)

LOW   HIGH

$9.22

Maintenance

LOW   HIGH

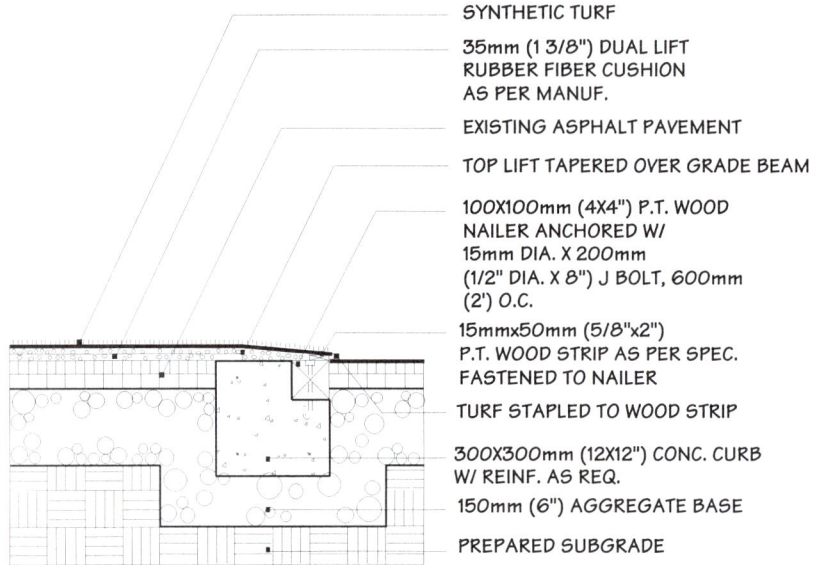

SYNTHETIC TURF

35mm (1 3/8") DUAL LIFT
RUBBER FIBER CUSHION
AS PER MANUF.

EXISTING ASPHALT PAVEMENT

TOP LIFT TAPERED OVER GRADE BEAM

100X100mm (4X4") P.T. WOOD
NAILER ANCHORED W/
15mm DIA. X 200mm
(1/2" DIA. X 8") J BOLT, 600mm
(2') O.C.

15mmx50mm (5/8"x2")
P.T. WOOD STRIP AS PER SPEC.
FASTENED TO NAILER

TURF STAPLED TO WOOD STRIP

300X300mm (12X12") CONC. CURB
W/ REINF. AS REQ.

150mm (6") AGGREGATE BASE

PREPARED SUBGRADE

APPLICATION

CLIMATE

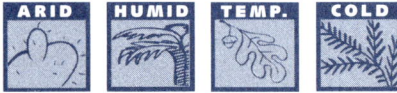

SUBGRADE

CSI MASTERFORMAT: 02790
DRAWING FILE: ATH08-06

• This drawing is a template for preliminary design only, and is not intended for bid purposes. It is subject to modification based on design calculations, local practices, and all applicable codes and regulations.

• This artificial turf with resilient pad on existing base detail is rated as heavy-duty due to resilient base, asphalt, and aggregate subbase thickness and is typically found in professional sports arenas and stadia. It will support activities typically associated with league athletic events and special function theatrical events.

• If used in outdoor arenas or stadia, base must be crowned to shed water. If soil is poorly drained, a network of subdrainage pipes are trenched into the subgrade. A perimeter concrete grade beam is used to attach the turf at the edge, with care being taken to cushion the beam and to provide smooth grade transition from adjacent surfaces.

• A highly resilient two course porous rubber monolithic pad with proprietary binders is placed under the artificial turf mat directly on the specially graded aggregate subbase. The artificial turf typically has a nap of 15 mm (1/2"). This process is also useful for retro-fitting an existing paved stadium.

• This surface provides a superior playing field which is much more resilient and therefore safer than artificial turf surfaces of the recent past.

• It is recommended that recycled and regionally available materials and products be given high priority in determining final design and specifications.

Installation Cost (per Square Foot)

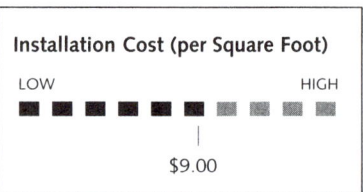

LOW   HIGH

$9.00

Maintenance

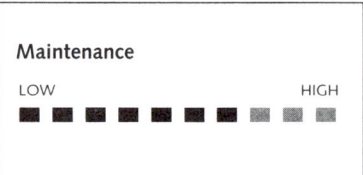

LOW   HIGH

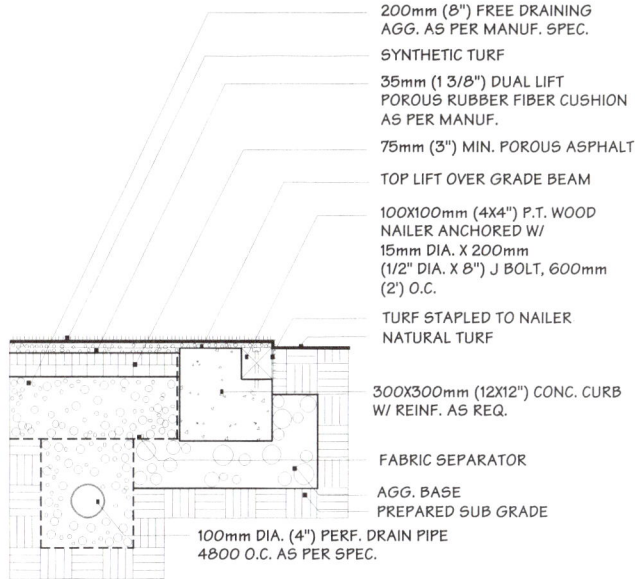

200mm (8") FREE DRAINING AGG. AS PER MANUF. SPEC.

SYNTHETIC TURF

35mm (1 3/8") DUAL LIFT POROUS RUBBER FIBER CUSHION AS PER MANUF.

75mm (3") MIN. POROUS ASPHALT

TOP LIFT OVER GRADE BEAM

100X100mm (4X4") P.T. WOOD NAILER ANCHORED W/ 15mm DIA. X 200mm (1/2" DIA. X 8") J BOLT, 600mm (2') O.C.

TURF STAPLED TO NAILER
NATURAL TURF

300X300mm (12X12") CONC. CURB W/ REINF. AS REQ.

FABRIC SEPARATOR

AGG. BASE
PREPARED SUB GRADE

100mm DIA. (4") PERF. DRAIN PIPE 4800 O.C. AS PER SPEC.

APPLICATION

CLIMATE

SUBGRADE

CSI MASTERFORMAT: 02790
DRAWING FILE: ATH08-04

• This drawing is a template for preliminary design only, and is not intended for bid purposes. It is subject to modification based on design calculations, local practices, and all applicable codes and regulations.

• This artificial turf with resilient pad on porous asphalt base detail is rated as heavy-duty due to asphalt base, and aggregate sub-base thickness, and is typically found in professional sports arenas and stadia. It will support activities typically associated with league athletic events and special function theatrical events.

• If used in outdoor arenas or stadia, base may be crowned to shed water. If soil is poorly drained, a network of subdrainage pipes are trenched into the subgrade. A perimeter concrete grade beam is used to attach the turf at the edge, with care being taken to cushion the beam and to provide smooth grade transition from adjacent surfaces.

• A highly resilient two course porous rubber monolithic pad with proprietary binders is placed under the artificial turf mat directly on the porous asphalt base. The artificial turf typically has a nap of 15 mm (1/2").

• This surface provides a superior playing field which is much more resilient and therefore safer than artificial turf surfaces of the recent past.

• It is recommended that recycled and regionally available materials and products be given high priority in determining final design and specifications.

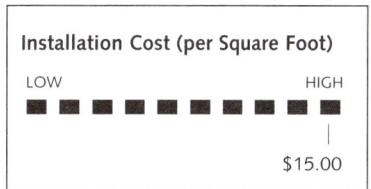

Installation Cost (per Square Foot)

LOW   HIGH

$15.00

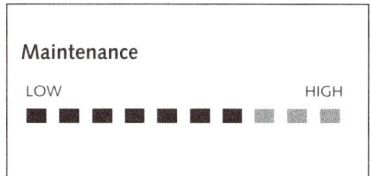

Maintenance

LOW   HIGH

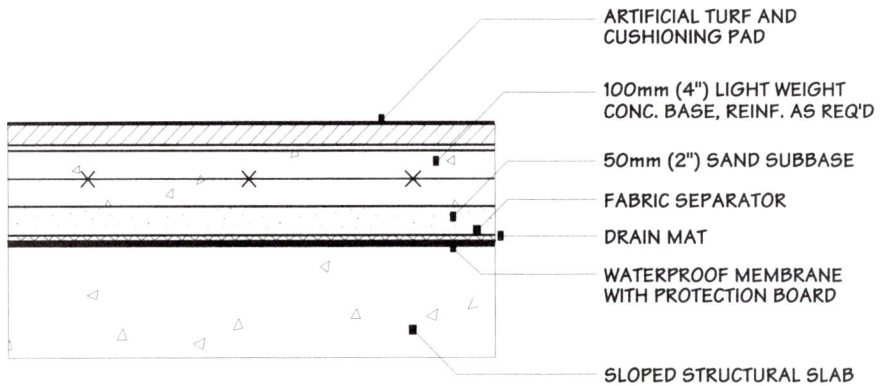

ARTIFICIAL TURF AND CUSHIONING PAD

100mm (4") LIGHT WEIGHT CONC. BASE, REINF. AS REQ'D

50mm (2") SAND SUBBASE

FABRIC SEPARATOR

DRAIN MAT

WATERPROOF MEMBRANE WITH PROTECTION BOARD

SLOPED STRUCTURAL SLAB

APPLICATION

CLIMATE

SUBGRADE

CSI MASTERFORMAT: 02790
DRAWING FILE: ATH08-03

• This drawing is a template for preliminary design only, and is not intended for bid purposes. It is subject to modification based on design calculations, local practices, and all applicable codes and regulations.

• This artificial turf on a concrete base detail is rated as medium-duty due to light-weight concrete base and loading limitations of structural decking. It will support athletic events and special function theatrical events. Due to the absence of rigid insulation and the placement of a heavy-duty drain mat, light vehicular loading may be allowed on this surface.

• A perimeter concrete grade beam is used to attach the turf at the edge, with care being taken to cushion the beam and to provide smooth grade transition from adjacent surfaces.

• Concrete base must be crowned to shed water. Concrete base requires an extra thick pad to be placed under the artificial turf mat which typically has a nap of 15 mm (1/2"). Alternate porous base and proprietary porous

rubber fiber cushion may allow for flat installation in some settings.

• Subgrade conditions have a significant impact on the longevity of rigid pavements, such as concrete. The subgrade should be uniform to prevent pavement failure due to uneven soil expansion and contraction. This detail provides a well-drained aggregate base to drain sub-surface moisture and increase uniformity.

• Rigid pavement design must accommodate movement of materials by providing adequate expansion and control joints, particularly in regions of extreme temperature fluctuations. If designed for temperate or cold climates, air-entrained concrete is typically recommended.

• Reinforcing practices vary widely by region. Local codes and practices should be consulted prior to specifying any type of reinforcing.

• It is recommended that recycled and regionally available materials and products be given high priority in determining final design and specifications.

Installation Cost (per Square Foot)

LOW   HIGH

$9.10

Maintenance

LOW   HIGH

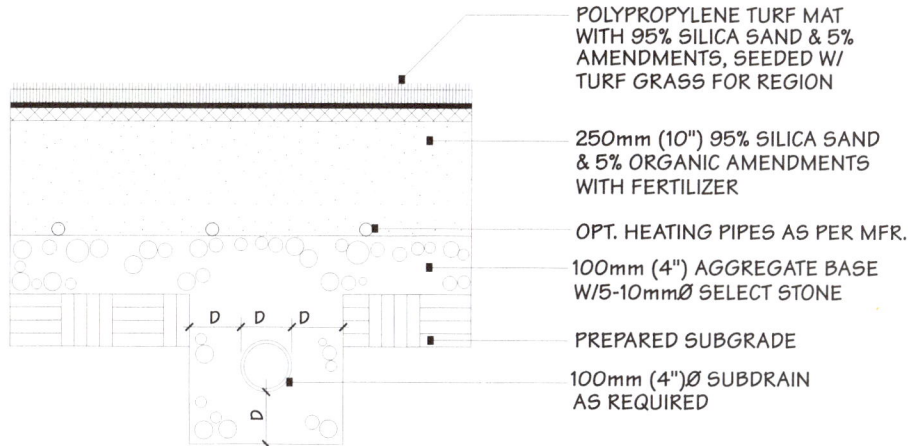

POLYPROPYLENE TURF MAT WITH 95% SILICA SAND & 5% AMENDMENTS, SEEDED W/ TURF GRASS FOR REGION

250mm (10") 95% SILICA SAND & 5% ORGANIC AMENDMENTS WITH FERTILIZER

OPT. HEATING PIPES AS PER MFR.

100mm (4") AGGREGATE BASE W/5-10mmØ SELECT STONE

PREPARED SUBGRADE

100mm (4")Ø SUBDRAIN AS REQUIRED

APPLICATION

CLIMATE

SUBGRADE

CSI MASTERFORMAT: 02920
DRAWING FILE: ATH00-07

• This drawing is a template for preliminary design only, and is not intended for bid purposes. It is subject to modification based on design calculations, local practices, and all applicable codes and regulations.

• This detail is rated as heavy-duty due to the sand content of planting soil and aggregate base which supports the polypropylene reinforced turf layer. It will support major service vehicle loading and is typical of athletic fields for college, and professional league play in stadia or arenas.

• This proprietary product is an actual mat of plastic turf fibers which is filled with sand and amendments and seeded to create an interwoven matrix of turf and artificial matting.

• Heating cables or hot water pipes rest below the growing medium and above the aggregate base drainage layer.

• The crushed stone aggregate base is placed on a fabric separator to bind the base

and to screen infiltration water as it enters the subdrainage system. Subdrain spacing is determined by rainfall data, and soil texture. Place drains below frost where required.

• This reinforced turf detail requires regular irrigation and aeration to achieve the design objective.

• It is recommended that recycled and regionally available materials and products be given high priority in determining final design and specifications.

Installation Cost (per Square Foot)

LOW   HIGH

$10.50

Maintenance

LOW   HIGH

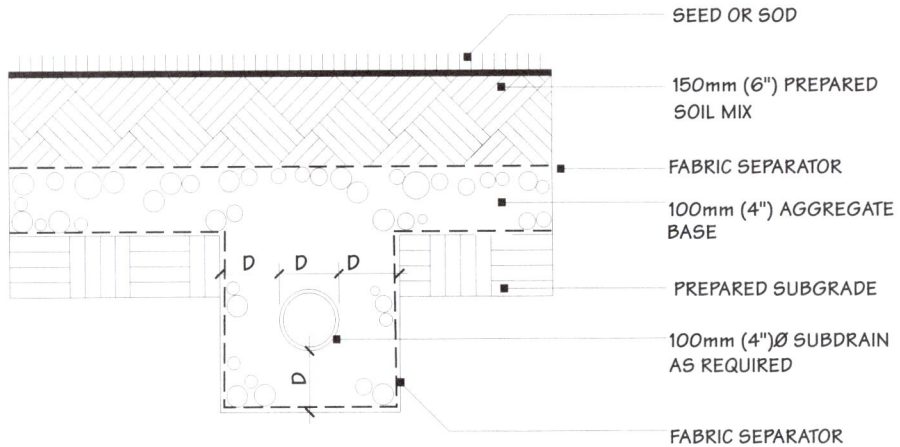

SEED OR SOD

150mm (6") PREPARED SOIL MIX

FABRIC SEPARATOR

100mm (4") AGGREGATE BASE

PREPARED SUBGRADE

100mm (4")Ø SUBDRAIN AS REQUIRED

FABRIC SEPARATOR

APPLICATION

CLIMATE

SUBGRADE

CSI MASTERFORMAT: 02920
DRAWING FILE: ATH00-06

• This drawing is a template for preliminary design only, and is not intended for bid purposes. It is subject to modification based on design calculations, local practices, and all applicable codes and regulations.

• This grass tennis court surface detail is rated as medium-duty due to surface and aggregate base thickness. It is typically found in dense residential, park, and institutional settings in all climates.

• The subgrade is typically trenched to receive perforated drain pipes spaced according to soil texture and infiltration rate. A fabric separator is often placed on the subgrade to bind aggregate base and filter fines from drain grid. An amended topsoil layer is placed over dense graded aggregate base material to complete the installation. Soil is either sodded or fertilized and seeded with selected turf grasses.

• This surface is highly labor intensive to maintain and requires regular irrigation and aeration.

• It is recommended that recycled and regionally available materials and products be given high priority in determining final design and specifications.

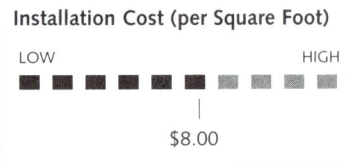

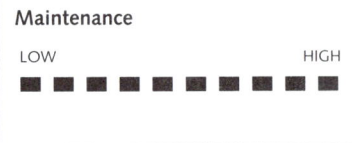

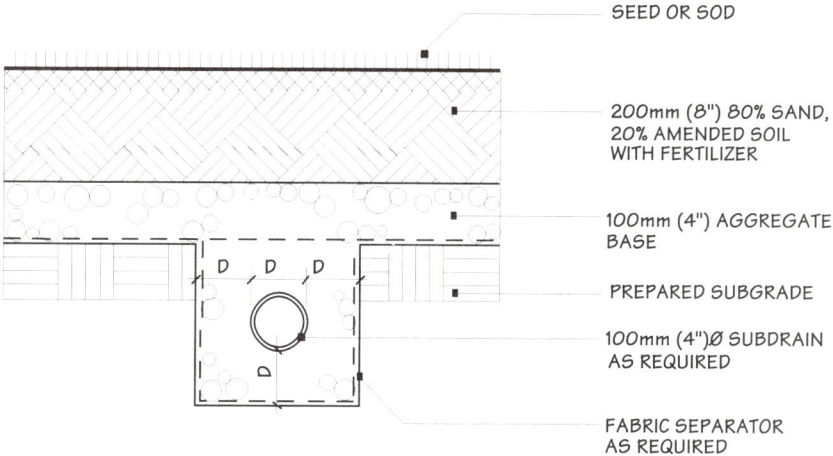

SEED OR SOD

200mm (8") 80% SAND, 20% AMENDED SOIL WITH FERTILIZER

100mm (4") AGGREGATE BASE

PREPARED SUBGRADE

100mm (4")Ø SUBDRAIN AS REQUIRED

FABRIC SEPARATOR AS REQUIRED

APPLICATION

CLIMATE

SUBGRADE

CSI MASTERFORMAT: 02920
DRAWING FILE: ATH00-04

• This drawing is a template for preliminary design only, and is not intended for bid purposes. It is subject to modification based on design calculations, local practices, and all applicable codes and regulations.

• This detail is rated as medium-duty due to the sand content of planting soil and aggregate base which supports the turf layer. It will support light service vehicle loading and is typical of athletic fields for high school, small college, and public park league play. The detail has been designed to accommodate a colloidal subsoil.

• The crushed stone aggregate base is placed on a fabric separator to bind the base and to screen infiltration water as it enters the subdrainage system. Subdrain spacing is determined by rainfall data, and soil texture. Place drains below frost where required.

• This reinforced turf detail requires regular irrigation and aeration to achieve the design objective.

• It is recommended that recycled and regionally available materials and products be given high priority in determining final design and specifications.

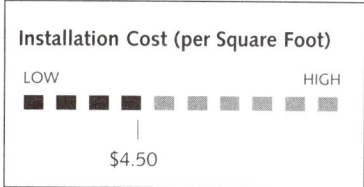

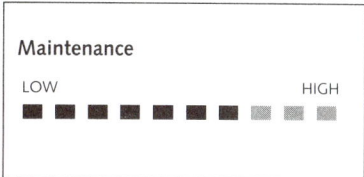

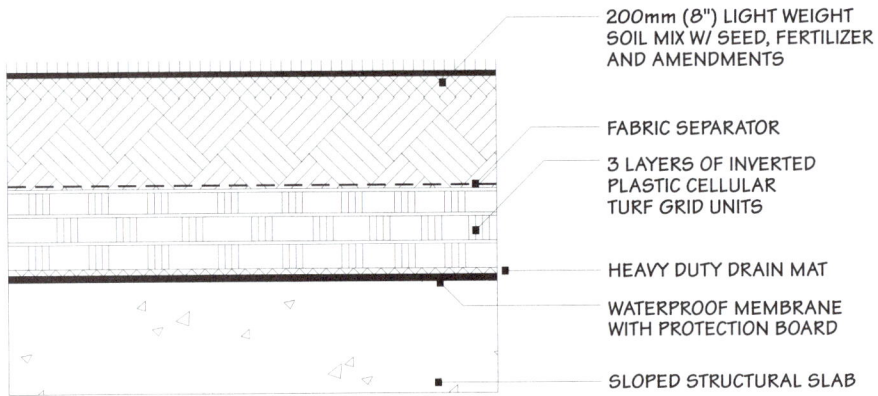

200mm (8") LIGHT WEIGHT SOIL MIX W/ SEED, FERTILIZER AND AMENDMENTS

FABRIC SEPARATOR

3 LAYERS OF INVERTED PLASTIC CELLULAR TURF GRID UNITS

HEAVY DUTY DRAIN MAT

WATERPROOF MEMBRANE WITH PROTECTION BOARD

SLOPED STRUCTURAL SLAB

APPLICATION

CLIMATE

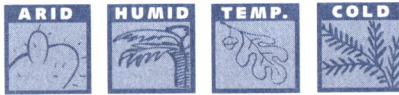

SUBGRADE

CSI MASTERFORMAT: 02920
DRAWING FILE: ATH00-05

• This drawing is a template for preliminary design only, and is not intended for bid purposes. It is subject to modification based on design calculations, local practices, and all applicable codes and regulations.

• This detail is rated for heavy-duty applications due to soil thickness and bearing capabilities of inverted plastic cellular grids upon which it rests. It shows the minimum depth of soil required, but 300 mm (12") would be a better depth if loading and design conditions permit.

• This detail is often found in public and institutional roof deck settings and typically employed as a game lawn or strolling surface.

• A three layer base of inverted plastic celluar turf grids is placed on fabric separator over heavy-duty drain mat, on sloping protection board and waterproof membrane. The normal rigid insulation is eliminated to achieve required bearing.

• This detail allows for free drainage and air circulation, but requires regular irrigation and aeration, as in most roof deck installations. Most soil mixes for roof deck installations are light weight, well drained, but are designed to retain capillarity to sustain root growth.

• It is recommended that recycled and regionally available materials and products be given high priority in determining final design and specifications.

Installation Cost (per Square Foot)

LOW   HIGH

$7.80

Maintenance

LOW   HIGH

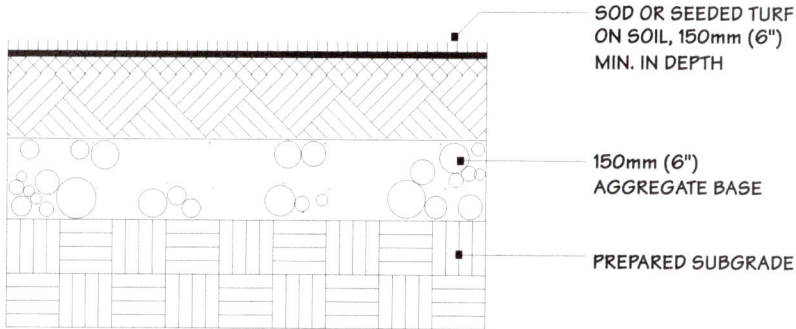

SOD OR SEEDED TURF ON SOIL, 150mm (6") MIN. IN DEPTH

150mm (6") AGGREGATE BASE

PREPARED SUBGRADE

APPLICATION

CLIMATE

SUBGRADE

CSI MASTERFORMAT: 02920
DRAWING FILE: ATH00-01

• This drawing is a template for preliminary design only, and is not intended for bid purposes. It is subject to modification based on design calculations, local practices, and all applicable codes and regulations.

• This game lawn detail is rated for medium-duty applications due to soil thickness and fine aggregate base upon which it rests. It shows the minimum depth of soil required, but 200 mm (8") would be a better depth if loading and design conditions require.

• This detail is often found in public and institutional settings and typically employed as a game lawn or playfield surface.

• A fine aggregate base allows the turf to bear light vehicular loading such as service vehicles, temporary parking, or ceremonies. Aggregate layer may vary from coarse sand to fine dense graded aggregate.

• This detail allows for free drainage, but requires regular irrigation and aeration. Most soil mixes for play field surfaces are

specially designed for local moisture conditions and are usually heavily amended for best results.

• It is recommended that recycled and regionally available materials and products be given high priority in determining final design and specifications.

Installation Cost (per Square Foot)

LOW   HIGH

$1.36

Maintenance

LOW   HIGH

SOD OR SEEDED TURF ON LIGHT WEIGHT SOIL MIX, 150mm (6") MIN. IN DEPTH

FABRIC SEPARATOR

40mm (1 1/2") INVERTED PLASTIC CELLULAR TURFGRID

RIGID INSULATION WITH OPEN JOINTS FOR DRAINAGE

DRAIN MAT

WATERPROOF MEMBRANE WITH PROTECTION BOARD

SLOPED STRUCTURAL SLAB

APPLICATION

LIGHT   MED.   HEAVY

CLIMATE

ARID   HUMID   TEMP.   COLD

SUBGRADE

PERM.   CLAY   ROOF

CSI MASTERFORMAT: 02920
DRAWING FILE: ATH00-03

• This drawing is a template for preliminary design only, and is not intended for bid purposes. It is subject to modification based on design calculations, local practices, and all applicable codes and regulations.

• This detail is rated for light-duty applications due to soil thickness and bearing limitations of the rigid insulation upon which it rests. It shows the minimum depth of soil required, but 300 mm (12") would be a better depth if loading and design conditions permit.

• An inverted layer of plastic celluar turf grid is placed on fabric separator over open jointed rigid insulation. A drain mat is placed over sloping protection board and waterproof membrane.

• This detail allows for free drainage and air circulation, but requires regular irrigation and aeration in most roof deck installations. Most soil mixes for roof deck installations are light weight and well drained, but are designed to retain capillarity to sustain root growth.

• It is recommended that recycled and regionally available materials and products be given high priority in determining final design and specifications.

Installation Cost (per Square Foot)

LOW   HIGH

$5.00

Maintenance

LOW   HIGH

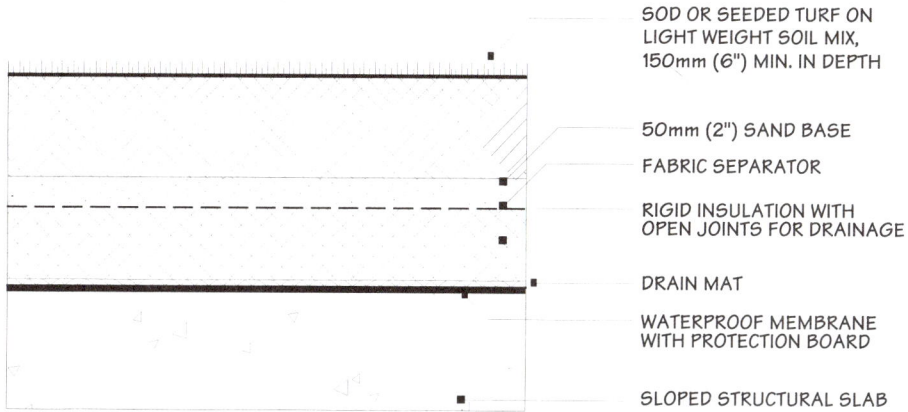

SOD OR SEEDED TURF ON LIGHT WEIGHT SOIL MIX, 150mm (6") MIN. IN DEPTH

50mm (2") SAND BASE

FABRIC SEPARATOR

RIGID INSULATION WITH OPEN JOINTS FOR DRAINAGE

DRAIN MAT

WATERPROOF MEMBRANE WITH PROTECTION BOARD

SLOPED STRUCTURAL SLAB

APPLICATION

CLIMATE

SUBGRADE

CSI MASTERFORMAT: 02920
DRAWING FILE: ATH00-02

• This drawing is a template for preliminary design only, and is not intended for bid purposes. It is subject to modification based on design calculations, local practices, and all applicable codes and regulations.

• This detail is rated for light-duty applications due to soil thickness and bearing limitations of the rigid insulation upon which it rests. It shows the minimum depth of soil required, but 300 mm (12") would be a better depth if loading and design conditions permit.

• This detail is often found in private, public, and institutional roof deck settings and typically employed as a game lawn or strolling surface.

• A sand layer is placed on fabric separator over open jointed rigid insulation. A drain mat is placed over sloping protection board and waterproof membrane.

• This detail allows for free drainage, but requires regular irrigation and aeration as in

most roof deck installations. Most soil mixes for roof deck installations are light weight, well drained, but are designed to retain capillarity to sustain root growth.

• It is recommended that recycled and regionally available materials and products be given high priority in determining final design and specifications.

Installation Cost (per Square Foot)

LOW   HIGH

$1.84

Maintenance

LOW   HIGH

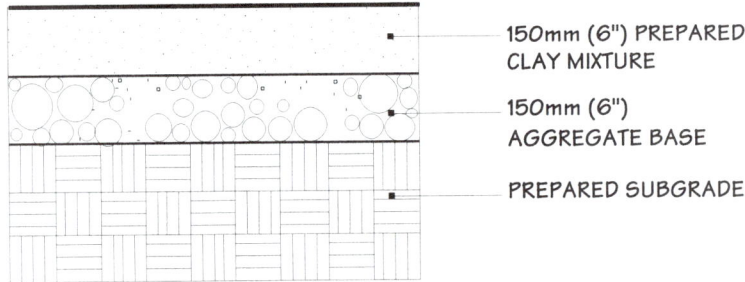

150mm (6") PREPARED CLAY MIXTURE

150mm (6") AGGREGATE BASE

PREPARED SUBGRADE

APPLICATION

CLIMATE

SUBGRADE

CSI MASTERFORMAT: 02790
DRAWING FILE: PAV27-01

• This drawing is a template for preliminary design only, and is not intended for bid purposes. It is subject to modification based on design calculations, local practices, and all applicable codes and regulations.

• This detail illustrates a typical infield surface found in league play facilities associated with public parks and institutions. It is rated as medium-duty due to its base course bearing capacity and ability to support light service vehicles in the course of routine maintenance.

• The subgrade conditions have a significant impact on the design of flexible pavements, such as clay augmented infields. Loads are transferred more directly to the base, requiring well-drained soils with adequate bearing capacity.

• Base course and surface course should be well-prepared for uniformity and to prevent deformation.

• Finish grade must be uniform and sloped to drain.

• Prepared clay topping should be periodically replenished and re-graded to ensure continued performance.

• Fabric, chemical, or manual methods may be needed to remove unwanted vegetative growth from the paved surface.

• It is recommended that recycled and regionally available materials and products be given high priority in determining final design and specifications.

Installation Cost (per Square Foot)

LOW   HIGH

$1.78

Maintenance

LOW   HIGH

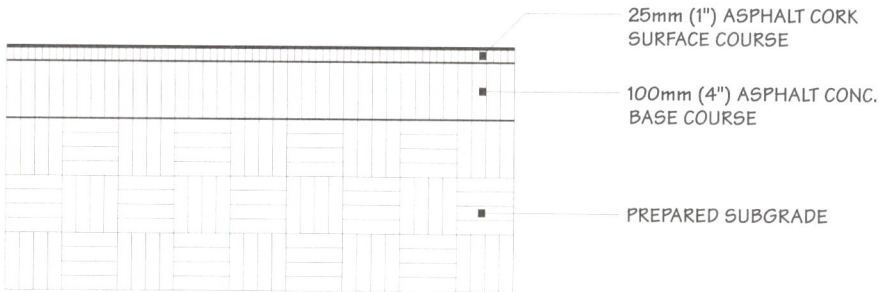

25mm (1") ASPHALT CORK
SURFACE COURSE

100mm (4") ASPHALT CONC.
BASE COURSE

PREPARED SUBGRADE

APPLICATION

CLIMATE

SUBGRADE

CSI MASTERFORMAT: 02790
DRAWING FILE: PAV21-01

• This drawing is a template for preliminary design only, and is not intended for bid purposes. It is subject to modification based on design calculations, local practices, and all applicable codes and regulations.

• This detail is rated for light-duty applications based on thickness of paving course and may support primarily pedestrian loading associated with athletic playing surfaces, walks, and light service access in parks and residential settings.

• Full-Depth asphalt paving is a viable alternative in areas where aggregates are costly, and the subgrade is extremely well-drained and uniform. It is not recommended for cold climates, or regions with colloidal subsoils.

• Rough grading of subgrade in large-area applications should move parallel to the slope direction to avoid blade and machine tracks running perpendicular to the flow of infiltrated water.

• Periodic surface sealing is recommended for longer pavement life. In most circumstances, this is a low maintenance pavement.

• It is recommended that recycled and regionally available materials and products be given high priority in determining final design and specifications. Alternative aggregates, such as recycled glass, may be mixed with aggregate in the bituminous concrete mix.

Installation Cost (per Square Foot)

LOW   HIGH

$3.70

Maintenance

LOW   HIGH

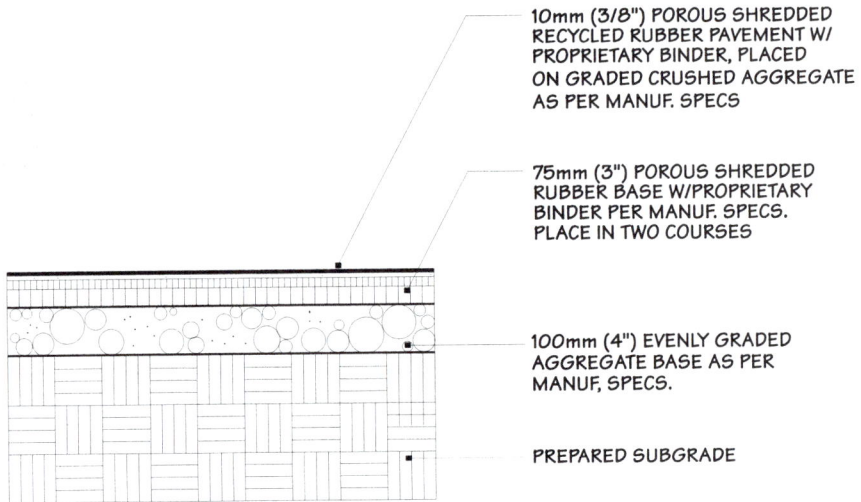

10mm (3/8") POROUS SHREDDED RECYCLED RUBBER PAVEMENT W/ PROPRIETARY BINDER, PLACED ON GRADED CRUSHED AGGREGATE AS PER MANUF. SPECS

75mm (3") POROUS SHREDDED RUBBER BASE W/PROPRIETARY BINDER PER MANUF. SPECS. PLACE IN TWO COURSES

100mm (4") EVENLY GRADED AGGREGATE BASE AS PER MANUF. SPECS.

PREPARED SUBGRADE

APPLICATION

CLIMATE

SUBGRADE

CSI MASTERFORMAT: 02790
DRAWING FILE: PAV28-03

• This drawing is a template for preliminary design only, and is not intended for bid purposes. It is subject to modification based on design calculations, local practices, and all applicable codes and regulations.

• This detail is rated for light-duty applications based on paving course thickness and intended use, and may support primarily pedestrian loading associated with play surfaces in parks and institutional settings.

• The subgrade conditions have a significant impact on the design of flexible pavements, such as asphalt. Loads are transferred more directly to the base, requiring well-drained soils with adequate bearing capacity.

• A wide variety of proprietary resilient surfaces are available. Consult manufacturer's advice for proper installation. This surface requires a dense graded crushed stone aggregate base for proper adhesion of proprietary binder.

• Surface may be subject to abrasion and color fading, unless EPDM topping material is used. All edges must be secured with appropriate curbing or wedges of cast-in-place material for barrier free access.

• It is recommended that recycled and regionally available materials and products be given high priority in determining final design and specifications.

Installation Cost (per Square Foot)

LOW   HIGH

$8.50

Maintenance

LOW   HIGH

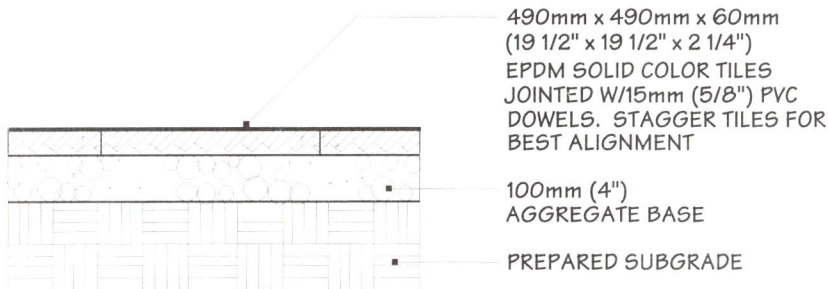

490mm x 490mm x 60mm
(19 1/2" x 19 1/2" x 2 1/4")
EPDM SOLID COLOR TILES
JOINTED W/15mm (5/8") PVC
DOWELS. STAGGER TILES FOR
BEST ALIGNMENT

100mm (4")
AGGREGATE BASE

PREPARED SUBGRADE

APPLICATION

CLIMATE

SUBGRADE

CSI MASTERFORMAT: 02790
DRAWING FILE: PAV28-02

• This drawing is a template for preliminary design only, and is not intended for bid purposes. It is subject to modification based on design calculations, local practices, and all applicable codes and regulations.

• This resilient interlocking play surface detail is rated for light-duty applications based on paving course thickness and intended use, and may support primarily pedestrian loading associated with walks and light service access in parks and residential settings in all climates.

• This detail shows resilient tiles rated for a 1800 mm (6') fall placed on a specially formulated dense graded aggregate base using lateral dowels and proprietary edging to maintain tile alignment. A heavier duty may be achieved using a porous asphalt base for the tiles.

• A wide variety of proprietary resilient surfaces are available. Consult manufacturer's advice for proper installation.

• Surface may be subject to abrasion and color fading, unless EPDM topping material is used.

• It is recommended that recycled and regionally available materials and products be given high priority in determining final design and specifications.

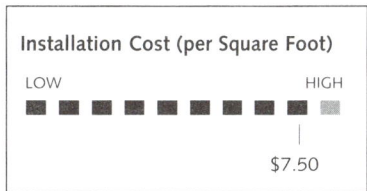

Installation Cost (per Square Foot)

LOW   HIGH

$7.50

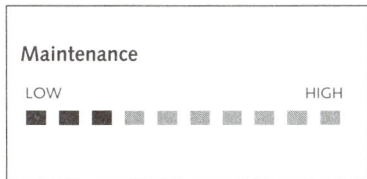

Maintenance

LOW   HIGH

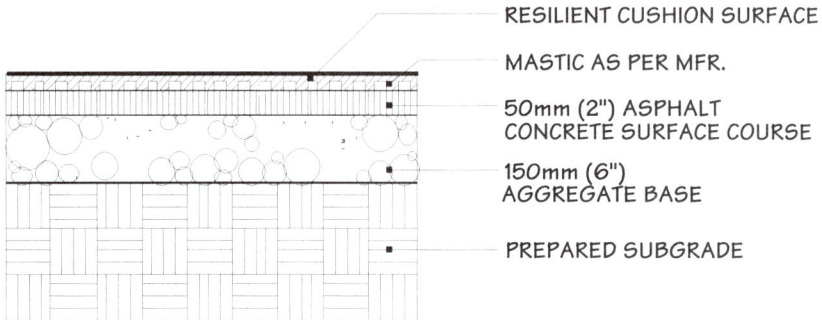

RESILIENT CUSHION SURFACE

MASTIC AS PER MFR.

50mm (2") ASPHALT
CONCRETE SURFACE COURSE

150mm (6")
AGGREGATE BASE

PREPARED SUBGRADE

APPLICATION

CLIMATE

SUBGRADE

CSI MASTERFORMAT: 02790
DRAWING FILE: PAV28-01

• This drawing is a template for preliminary design only, and is not intended for bid purposes. It is subject to modification based on design calculations, local practices, and all applicable codes and regulations.

• This detail is rated for light-duty applications based on paving course thickness and intended use, and may support primarily pedestrian loading associated with walks and light service access in parks and residential settings.

• The subgrade conditions have a significant impact on the design of flexible pavements, such as asphalt. Loads are transferred more directly to the base, requiring well-drained soils with adequate bearing capacity.

• A wide variety of proprietary resilient surfaces are available. Consult manufacturer's advice for proper installation.

• Surface may be subject to abrasion and color fading, unless EPDM topping material is used.

• It is recommended that recycled and regionally available materials and products be given high priority in determining final design and specifications.

Installation Cost (per Square Foot)

LOW  HIGH

$2.82

Maintenance

LOW  HIGH

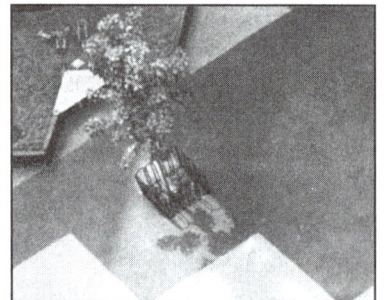

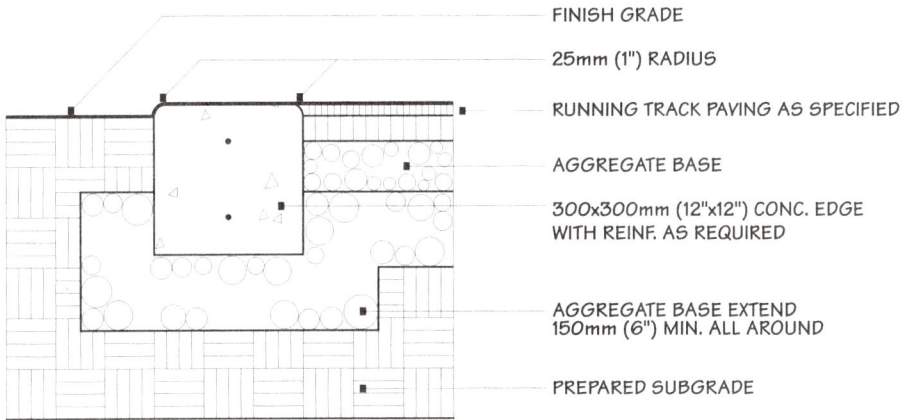

- FINISH GRADE
- 25mm (1") RADIUS
- RUNNING TRACK PAVING AS SPECIFIED
- AGGREGATE BASE
- 300x300mm (12"x12") CONC. EDGE WITH REINF. AS REQUIRED
- AGGREGATE BASE EXTEND 150mm (6") MIN. ALL AROUND
- PREPARED SUBGRADE

APPLICATION

CLIMATE

SUBGRADE

CSI MASTERFORMAT: 02770
DRAWING FILE: EDG02-04

- This drawing is for preliminary design only, and is not intended for bid purposes. It is subject to modification based on design calculations, local practices, and all applicable codes and regulations.

- This detail is typical of competitive running track design. The concrete edge provides added reinforcement and prevents undermining of the pavement turf roots.

- The grade beam is typically cast in place, or in cold climates may be precast and installed by digging a trench and backfilling with well-draining aggregate material.

- This detail is rated for heavy-duty applications due to the use of a large grade beam, capable of supporting heavy vehicular loading.

- Reinforcing practices vary widely by region. Local codes and practices should be consulted prior to specifying any type of reinforcing.

- Concrete grade beams provide a well-defined edge and require only moderate maintenance, consisting of occasional cleaning and re-sealing of expansion joints.

- It is recommended that recycled and regionally available materials and products be given high priority in determining final design and specifications.

Installation Cost (per Linear Foot)

LOW   HIGH

$8.44

Maintenance

LOW   HIGH

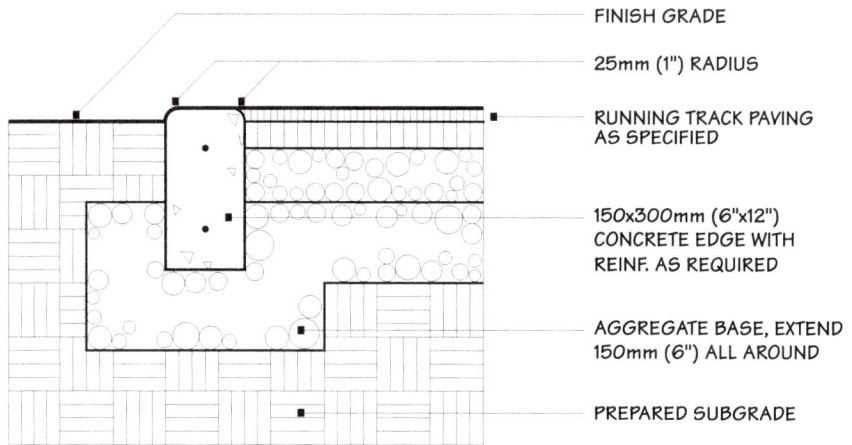

FINISH GRADE

25mm (1") RADIUS

RUNNING TRACK PAVING
AS SPECIFIED

150x300mm (6"x12")
CONCRETE EDGE WITH
REINF. AS REQUIRED

AGGREGATE BASE, EXTEND
150mm (6") ALL AROUND

PREPARED SUBGRADE

APPLICATION

CLIMATE

SUBGRADE

CSI MASTERFORMAT: 02770
DRAWING FILE: EDG02-03

• This drawing is for preliminary design only, and is not intended for bid purposes. It is subject to modification based on design calculations, local practices, and all applicable codes and regulations.

• This detail is typical of competitive running track design. The concrete edge provides added reinforcement and prevents undermining of the pavement by turf roots.

• The grade beam is typically cast in place, or in cold climates may be precast and installed by digging a trench and backfilling with well-draining aggregate material.

• This detail is rated for medium-duty applications due to the use of a moderate-sized grade beam, capable of supporting light vehicular loading.

• Reinforcing practices vary widely by region. Local codes and practices should be consulted prior to specifying any type of reinforcing.

• Concrete grade beams provide a well-defined edge and require only moderate maintenance, consisting of occasional cleaning and re-sealing of expansion joints.

• It is recommended that recycled and regionally available materials and products be given high priority in determining final design and specifications.

Installation Cost (per Linear Foot)

LOW   HIGH

$5.28

Maintenance

LOW   HIGH

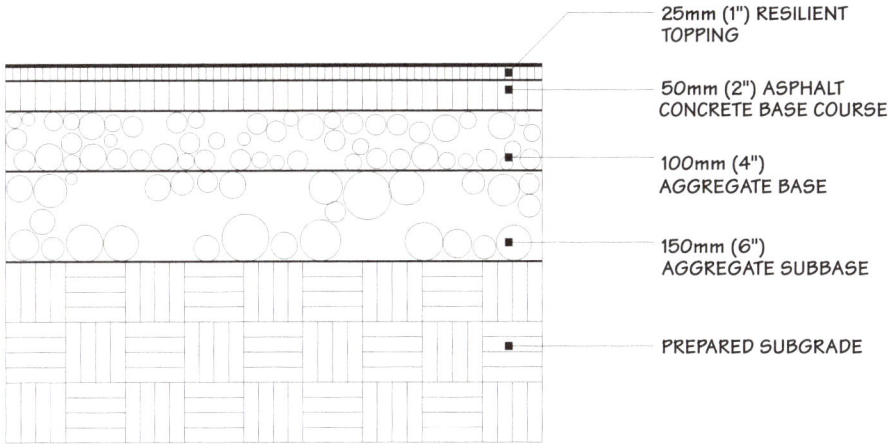

25mm (1") RESILIENT TOPPING

50mm (2") ASPHALT CONCRETE BASE COURSE

100mm (4") AGGREGATE BASE

150mm (6") AGGREGATE SUBBASE

PREPARED SUBGRADE

APPLICATION

CLIMATE

SUBGRADE

CSI MASTERFORMAT: 02790
DRAWING FILE: PAV21-03

• This drawing is a template for preliminary design only, and is not intended for bid purposes. It is subject to modification based on design calculations, local practices, and all applicable codes and regulations.

• This detail is rated for medium-duty applications based on paving course and base thickness, and may support primarily athletic and light service vehicle access associated with public parks dense residential and institutional settings.

• The subgrade conditions have a significant impact on the design of flexible pavements, such as asphalt. Loads are transferred more directly to the base, requiring well-drained soils with adequate bearing capacity.

• Running tracks require a high degree of smoothness and uniformity. The base should be placed in two lifts, a processed aggregate base and an aggregate subbase, to ensure adequate bearing and smoothness.

• The base should extend beyond the pavement edge past the load bearing angle (33°-45°) so the edge will be structurally reinforced.

• Pavement may require subdrains in colloidal soil conditions.

• Various color coat systems are available. Consult local practices to determine the most suitable system. Color coat may require periodic re-surfacing to provide continued performance.

• It is recommended that recycled and regionally available materials and products be given high priority in determining final design and specifications.

Installation Cost (per Square Foot)

LOW   HIGH

$2.78

Maintenance

LOW   HIGH

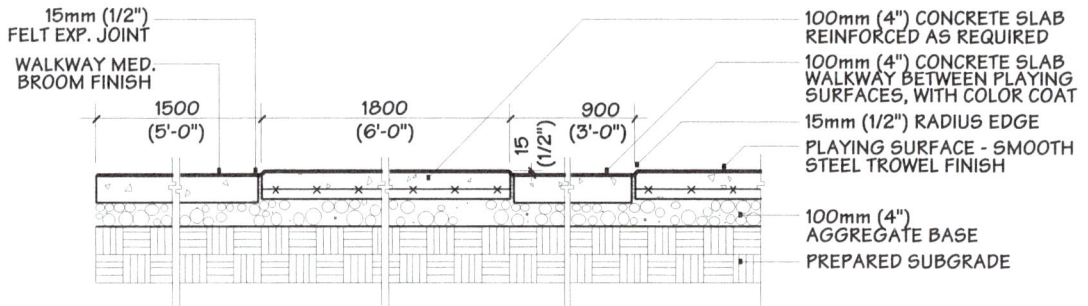

15mm (1/2")
FELT EXP. JOINT

WALKWAY MED.
BROOM FINISH

1500
(5'-0")

1800
(6'-0")

900
(3'-0")

15
(1/2")

100mm (4") CONCRETE SLAB
REINFORCED AS REQUIRED

100mm (4") CONCRETE SLAB
WALKWAY BETWEEN PLAYING
SURFACES, WITH COLOR COAT

15mm (1/2") RADIUS EDGE

PLAYING SURFACE - SMOOTH
STEEL TROWEL FINISH

100mm (4")
AGGREGATE BASE

PREPARED SUBGRADE

APPLICATION

CLIMATE

SUBGRADE

CSI MASTERFORMAT: 03360
DRAWING FILE: PAV22-01

• This drawing is a template for preliminary design only, and is not intended for bid purposes. It is subject to modification based on design calculations, local practices, and all applicable codes and regulations.

• This detail is rated for light-duty applications based on thickness of concrete and aggregate base, and may support primarily pedestrian loading typically associated with residential, park, and light commercial settings.

• Subgrade conditions have a significant impact on the longevity of rigid pavements, such as concrete. The subgrade should be uniform to prevent pavement failure due to uneven soil expansion and contraction. This detail provides a well-drained aggregate base to drain sub-surface moisture and increase uniformity.

• Rigid pavement design must accommodate movement of materials by providing adequate expansion and control joints, particularly in regions of extreme temperature

fluctuations. If designed for temperate or cold climates, air-entrained concrete is typically recommended due to freezing/thawing action.

• Reinforcing practices vary widely by region. Local codes and practices should be consulted prior to specifying any type of reinforcing.

• Finishes should conform to all shuffleboard requirements.

• Sealing of the paving surface with clear sealants can lengthen the life of the pavement, and preserve its appearance over time.

• It is recommended that recycled and regionally available materials and products be given high priority in determining final design and specifications.

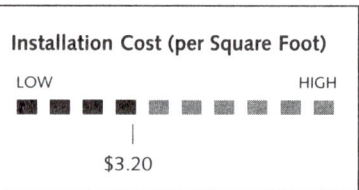

Installation Cost (per Square Foot)

LOW   HIGH

$3.20

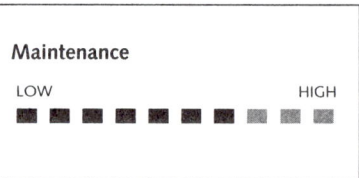

Maintenance

LOW   HIGH

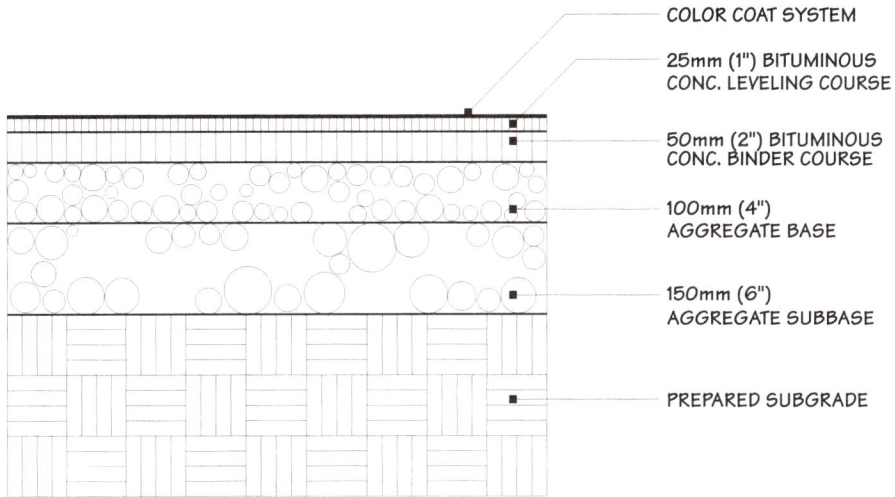

COLOR COAT SYSTEM

25mm (1") BITUMINOUS
CONC. LEVELING COURSE

50mm (2") BITUMINOUS
CONC. BINDER COURSE

100mm (4")
AGGREGATE BASE

150mm (6")
AGGREGATE SUBBASE

PREPARED SUBGRADE

APPLICATION

CLIMATE

SUBGRADE

CSI MASTERFORMAT: 02790
DRAWING FILE: PAV21-02

• This drawing is a template for preliminary design only, and is not intended for bid purposes. It is subject to modification based on design calculations, local practices, and all applicable codes and regulations.

• This detail is rated for medium-duty applications based on thickness of asphalt and aggregate base, and may support intensity of uses typically associated with public park, and institutional settings.

• The subgrade conditions have a significant impact on the design of flexible pavements, such as asphalt. Loads are transferred more directly to the base, requiring well-drained soils with adequate bearing capacity.

• Tennis courts require a high degree of smoothness, with a typical maximum irregularity of 3 mm (1/8") over a 3 m (10') distance.

• Rough grading of subgrade should move parallel to the slope direction to avoid blade and machine tracks running perpendicular to the flow of infiltrated subbase water. This

avoids excessive differential swelling in clay soils, and heaving in frost/thaw climates.

• The base should be placed in two lifts, a processed aggregate base and a compacted gravel subbase, to ensure adequate support and smoothness.

• The base should extend beyond the pavement edge past the load bearing angle (33°-45°) so the edge will be structurally reinforced.

• Pavement may require subdrains in colloidal soil conditions.

• An oil penetration tack coat is recommended on crushed stone bases to seal top interstitial aggregate spaces and to ensure proper bonding.

• Various color coat systems are available. Consult local practices to determine the most suitable system. Color coat may require periodic re-surfacing to provide continued performance.

• It is recommended that recycled and regionally available materials and products be given high priority in determining final design and specifications.

Installation Cost (per Square Foot)

LOW   HIGH

$2.16

Maintenance

LOW   HIGH

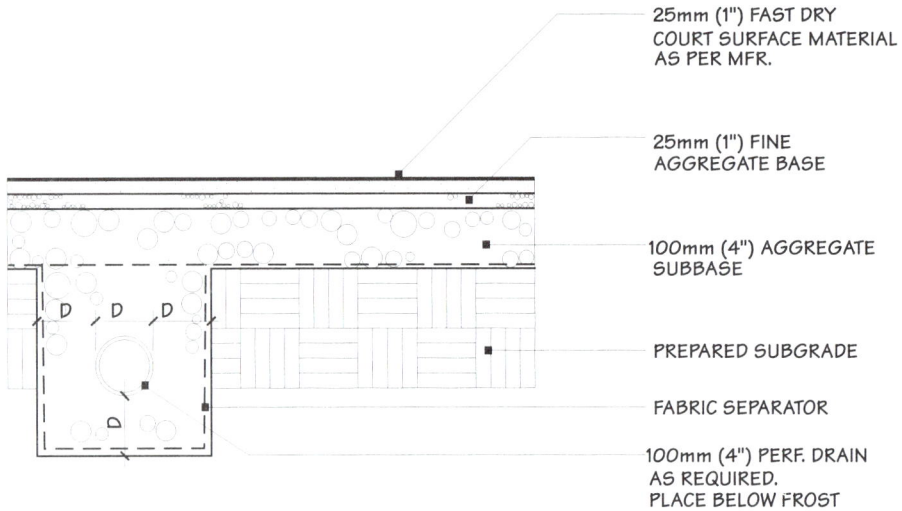

25mm (1") FAST DRY
COURT SURFACE MATERIAL
AS PER MFR.

25mm (1") FINE
AGGREGATE BASE

100mm (4") AGGREGATE
SUBBASE

PREPARED SUBGRADE

FABRIC SEPARATOR

100mm (4") PERF. DRAIN
AS REQUIRED.
PLACE BELOW FROST

APPLICATION

CLIMATE

SUBGRADE

CSI MASTERFORMAT: 02790
DRAWING FILE: PAV27-02

• This drawing is a template for preliminary design only, and is not intended for bid purposes. It is subject to modification based on design calculations, local practices, and all applicable codes and regulations.

• This clay tennis court surface detail is rated as light-duty due to surface and aggregate base thickness. It is typically found in dense residential, park, and institutional settings in all climates.

• The subgrade is typically trenched to receive perforated drain pipes spaced according to soil texture and infiltration rate. A fabric separator is often placed on the subgrade to bind aggregate base and filter fines from drain grid. A fine aggregate course receives a proprietary fast drying court surface material to complete the installation.

• This surface is highly labor intensive to maintain.

• It is recommended that recycled and regionally available materials and products be given high priority in determining final design and specifications.

Installation Cost (per Square Foot)

LOW   HIGH

$2.60

Maintenance

LOW   HIGH

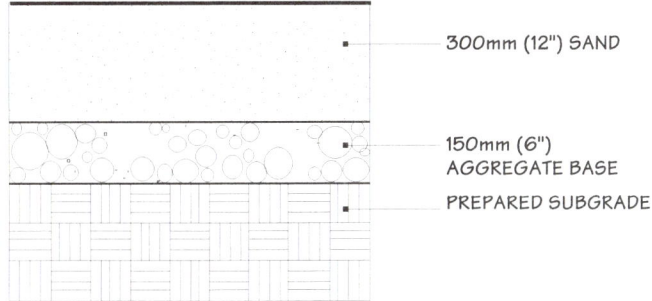

300mm (12") SAND

150mm (6") AGGREGATE BASE

PREPARED SUBGRADE

APPLICATION

CLIMATE

SUBGRADE

CSI MASTERFORMAT: 02790
DRAWING FILE: PAV27-03

• This drawing is a template for preliminary design only, and is not intended for bid purposes. It is subject to modification based on design calculations, local practices, and all applicable codes and regulations.

• This detail illustrates a typical volleyball surface found in league play facilities associated with public parks and institutions. It is rated as medium-duty due to its base course bearing capacity.

• Sand topping should be periodically replenished and re-graded to ensure continued performance.

• Fabric, chemical, or manual methods may be needed to remove unwanted vegetative growth from the paved surface. Proper edging or curbing is required to contain the sand surface.

• It is recommended that recycled and regionally available materials and products be given high priority in determining final design and specifications.

Installation Cost (per Square Foot)

LOW   HIGH

$1.62

Maintenance

LOW   HIGH

Curbs

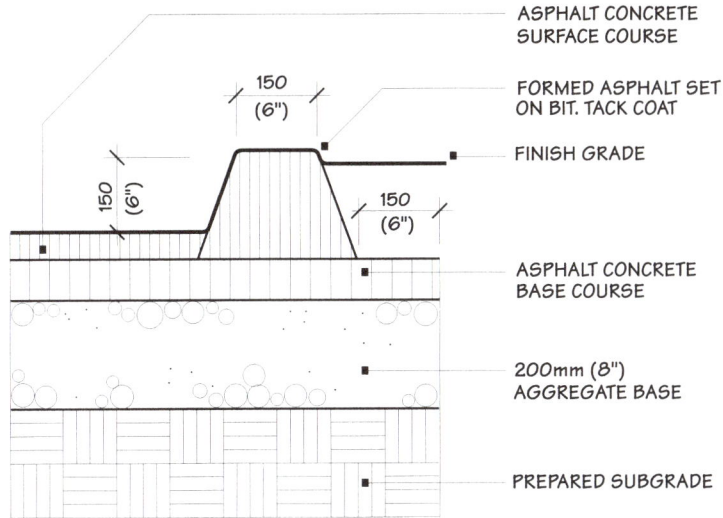

ASPHALT CONCRETE
SURFACE COURSE

FORMED ASPHALT SET
ON BIT. TACK COAT

FINISH GRADE

150
(6")

150
(6")

150
(6")

ASPHALT CONCRETE
BASE COURSE

200mm (8")
AGGREGATE BASE

PREPARED SUBGRADE

APPLICATION

CSI MASTERFORMAT: 02770
DRAWING FILE: CRB21-01

• This drawing is a template for preliminary design only, and is not intended for bid purposes. It is subject to modification based on design calculations, local practices, and all applicable codes and regulations.

• This extruded asphalt curb is rated as medium-duty due to aggregate subbase thickness. It is typically found in residential streets, parks, and institutional settings.

• It can be used in all climates, but becomes brittle when cold, and pliable when hot, and is subject to damage during routine maintenance. It is inexpensive, utilitarian, and has a short service life.

• The subgrade conditions have a significant impact on the design of flexible pavements, such as asphalt. Loads are transferred more directly to the base, requiring well-drained soils with adequate bearing capacity.

• Curb is installed on base course of pavement and usually bonded with a tack coat. Base course is typically extended 150 mm

CLIMATE

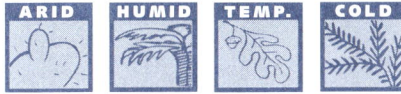

(6") beyond the curb to provide support. Many profiles are available to account for varying wearing course depths, and finished curb heights.

• It is recommended that recycled and regionally available materials and products be given high priority in determining final design and specifications.

SUBGRADE

Installation Cost (per Linear Foot)

LOW   HIGH

$2.76

Maintenance

LOW   HIGH

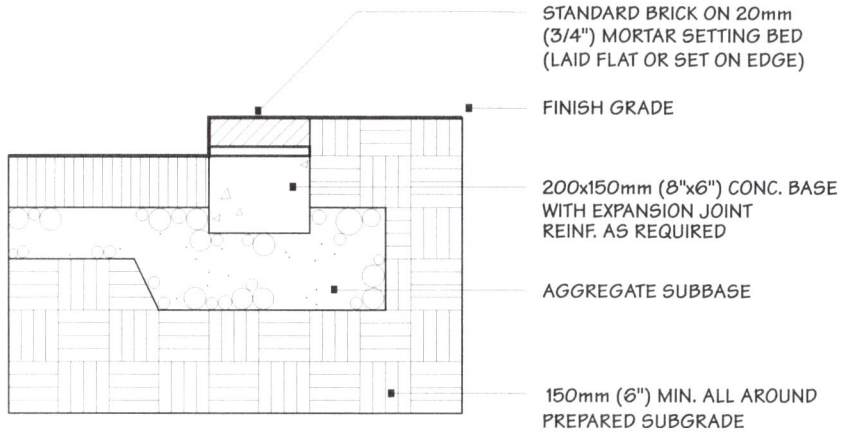

STANDARD BRICK ON 20mm (3/4") MORTAR SETTING BED (LAID FLAT OR SET ON EDGE)

FINISH GRADE

200x150mm (8"x6") CONC. BASE WITH EXPANSION JOINT REINF. AS REQUIRED

AGGREGATE SUBBASE

150mm (6") MIN. ALL AROUND PREPARED SUBGRADE

APPLICATION

CLIMATE

SUBGRADE

CSI MASTERFORMAT: 02770
DRAWING FILE: CRB24-02

• This drawing is a template for preliminary design only, and is not intended for bid purposes. It is subject to modification based on design calculations, local practices, and all applicable codes and regulations.

• This mortared brick curb on concrete base detail is rated as medium-duty due to its concrete base and aggregate subbase thickness. It is typically found in residential, park, or garden settings.

• Brick is mortared to concrete base to resist lateral forces due to routine use impacts. This detail is best applied to building entrance courts and confined areas where maintenance may be practiced with care.

• Rigid pavement design must accommodate movement of materials by providing adequate expansion and control joints, particularly in regions of extreme temperature fluctuations. If designed for temperate or cold climates, air-entrained concrete is typically recommended due to freezing/thawing action. Expansion and butt joints should be sealed with elastomeric compounds.

• Subgrade conditions have a significant impact on the longevity of rigid pavements, such as concrete. The subgrade should be uniform to prevent pavement failure due to uneven soil expansion and contraction. This detail provides a well-drained aggregate base to drain sub-surface moisture and increase uniformity.

• This detail is not designed for cold climates, where the use of mortar is discouraged. Solid stone or concrete grade beam set in aggregate base may be a better alternative.

• It is recommended that recycled and regionally available materials and products be given high priority in determining final design and specifications.

Installation Cost (per Linear Foot)

LOW   HIGH

$8.07

Maintenance

LOW   HIGH

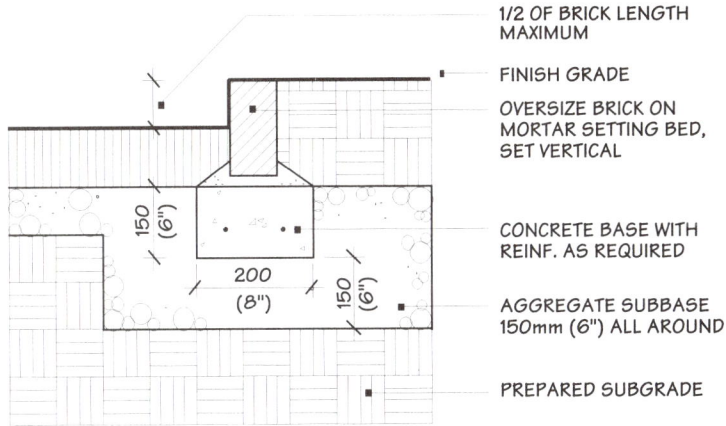

1/2 OF BRICK LENGTH MAXIMUM

FINISH GRADE

OVERSIZE BRICK ON MORTAR SETTING BED, SET VERTICAL

CONCRETE BASE WITH REINF. AS REQUIRED

AGGREGATE SUBBASE 150mm (6") ALL AROUND

PREPARED SUBGRADE

150 (6")

200 (8")

150 (6")

APPLICATION

CSI MASTERFORMAT: 02770
DRAWING FILE: CRB24-01

• This drawing is a template for preliminary design only, and is not intended for bid purposes. It is subject to modification based on design calculations, local practices, and all applicable codes and regulations.

• This brick curb is rated as light-duty due to the nature of brick structure. It is typically found in residential driveways, parks, gardens, and light institutional settings.

• It can be used in all climates, but mortar joints may require re-pointing in cold climates due to freeze/thaw action. It requires special maintenance considerations to avoid abrasive or high impact procedures.

• Subgrade conditions have a significant impact on the longevity of rigid and mortared pavements and curbs. The subgrade should be uniform to prevent pavement failure due to uneven soil expansion and contraction. This detail provides a well-drained aggregate base to drain sub-surface moisture and increase uniformity

CLIMATE

• Rigid pavement design must accommodate movement of materials by providing adequate expansion and control joints, particularly in regions of extreme temperature fluctuations. If designed for temperate or cold climates, air-entrained concrete is typically recommended due to freezing/thawing action.

• Reinforcing practices vary widely by region. Local codes and practices should be consulted prior to specifying any type of reinforcing.

• This residential scaled curb is often used at entrance drop-off areas and as edging for lawns and raised plant beds at the edge of driveways.

• It is recommended that recycled and regionally available materials and products be given high priority in determining final design and specifications.

SUBGRADE

Installation Cost (per Linear Foot)

LOW   HIGH

$9.62

Maintenance

LOW   HIGH

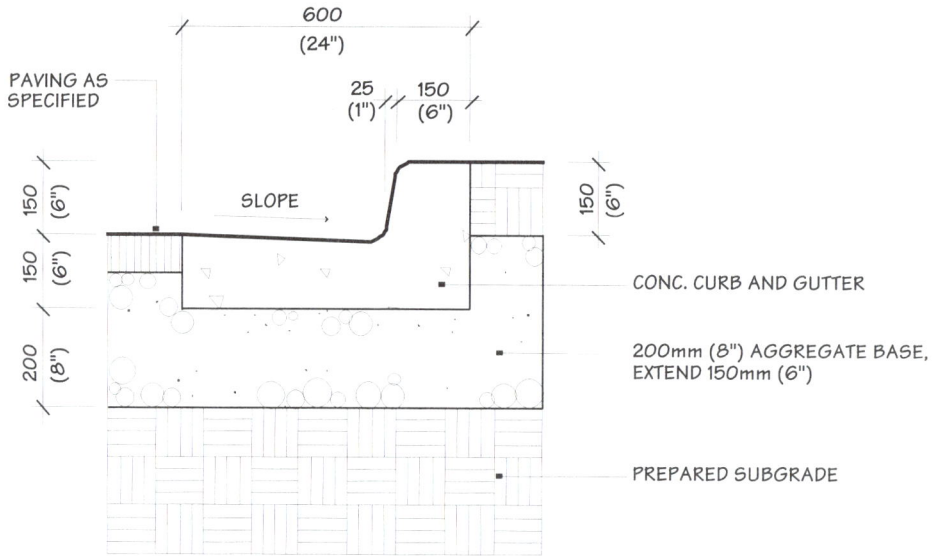

PAVING AS SPECIFIED

600 (24")

25 (1") 150 (6")

150 (6")

150 (6")

150 (6")

200 (8")

SLOPE

CONC. CURB AND GUTTER

200mm (8") AGGREGATE BASE, EXTEND 150mm (6")

PREPARED SUBGRADE

APPLICATION

HEAVY

CLIMATE

ARID HUMID TEMP. COLD

SUBGRADE

PERM. CLAY ROOF

CSI MASTERFORMAT: 02770
DRAWING FILE: CRB12-04

• This drawing is a template for preliminary design only, and is not intended for bid purposes. It is subject to modification based on design calculations, local practices, and all applicable codes and regulations.

• This concrete curb and gutter is rated as heavy-duty due to aggregate subbase and concrete thickness. It is typically found in dense residential and urban streets, parks, and institutional roads and parking area settings.

• It can be used in all climates, but performs best in well-drained soils. This detail illustrates an adaptation to cold climates showing aggregate backfill at back of curb to guard against frost uplift.

• Rigid pavement and curbs must accommodate movement of materials by providing adequate expansion and control joints, particularly in regions of extreme temperature fluctuations. If designed for temperate or cold climates, air-entrained concrete is typically recommended due to freezing/thawing action.

• Reinforcing practices vary widely by region. Most slip-form cast concrete is not reinforced, especially in cold climates due to chemical assault on steel due to infiltration. Local codes and practices should be consulted prior to specifying any type of reinforcing.

• It is recommended that recycled and regionally available materials and products be given high priority in determining final design and specifications.

Installation Cost (per Linear Foot)

LOW HIGH

$10.02

Maintenance

LOW HIGH

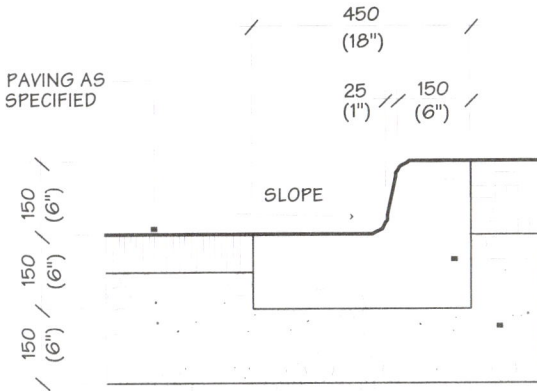

PAVING AS
SPECIFIED

450
(18")

25
(1")

150
(6")

SLOPE

150
(6")

150
(6")

150
(6")

CONC. CURB AND GUTTER

AGGREGATE BASE
150mm (6") TYP.

PREPARED SUBGRADE

APPLICATION

CLIMATE

SUBGRADE

CSI MASTERFORMAT: 02770
DRAWING FILE: CRB12-03

• This drawing is a template for preliminary design only, and is not intended for bid purposes. It is subject to modification based on design calculations, local practices, and all applicable codes and regulations.

• This concrete curb and gutter is rated as medium-duty due to aggregate subbase and concrete thickness. It is typically found in residential streets, parks, and institutional parking area settings.

• It can be used in all climates, but performs best in well-drained soils. This detail illustrates an adaptation to cold climates showing aggregate backfill at back of curb to guard against frost uplift.

• Rigid pavement and curbs must accommodate movement of materials by providing adequate expansion and control joints, particularly in regions of extreme temperature fluctuations. If designed for temperate cr cold climates, air-entrained concrete is typically recommended due to freezing/thawing action.

• Reinforcing practices vary widely by region. Most slip-form cast concrete is not reinforced, especially in cold climates due to chemical assault on steel due to infiltration. Local codes and practices should be consulted prior to specifying any type of reinforcing.

• It is recommended that recycled and regionally available materials and products be given high priority in determining final design and specifications.

Installation Cost (per Linear Foot)

LOW   HIGH

$8.59

Maintenance

LOW   HIGH

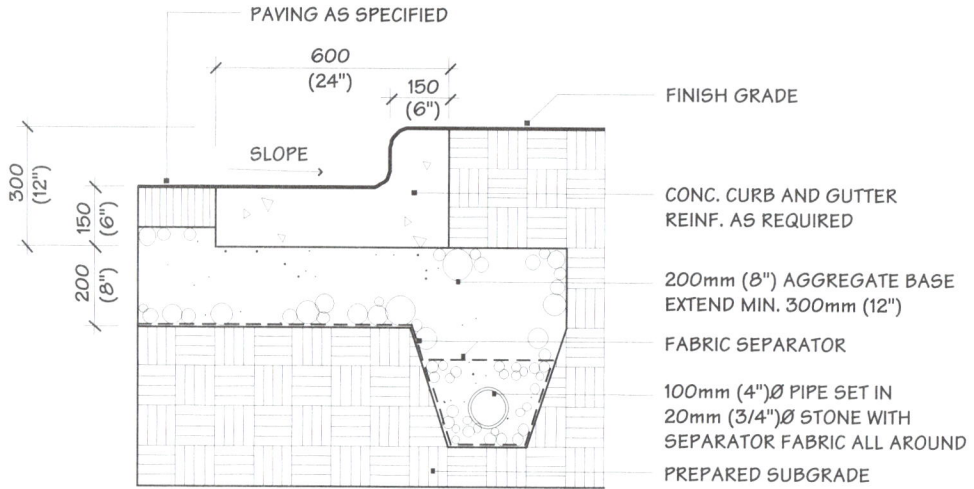

PAVING AS SPECIFIED

600 (24")

150 (6")

300 (12")

150 (6")

200 (8")

SLOPE

FINISH GRADE

CONC. CURB AND GUTTER REINF. AS REQUIRED

200mm (8") AGGREGATE BASE EXTEND MIN. 300mm (12")

FABRIC SEPARATOR

100mm (4")Ø PIPE SET IN 20mm (3/4")Ø STONE WITH SEPARATOR FABRIC ALL AROUND

PREPARED SUBGRADE

APPLICATION

CLIMATE

SUBGRADE

CSI MASTERFORMAT: 02770
DRAWING FILE: CRB12-02

• This drawing is a template for preliminary design only, and is not intended for bid purposes. It is subject to modification based on design calculations, local practices, and all applicable codes and regulations.

• This concrete curb and gutter is rated as heavy-duty due to aggregate subbase and concrete thickness. It is typically found in dense residential and urban streets, parks, and institutional roads and parking area settings.

• It can be used in all climates, but performs best in well-drained soils. This detail shows an adaptation to poorly drained soils using a fabric separator reinforcement and a subdrain pipe set in a stone trench preferably positioned to the back of the curb and away from direct loading.

• Rigid pavement and curbs must accommodate movement of materials by providing adequate expansion and control joints, particularly in regions of extreme temperature

fluctuations. If designed for temperate or cold climates, air-entrained concrete is typically recommended due to freezing/thawing action.

• Reinforcing practices vary widely by region. Most slip-form cast concrete is not reinforced, especially in cold climates due to chemical assault on steel due to infiltration. Local codes and practices should be consulted prior to specifying any type of reinforcing.

• It is recommended that recycled and regionally available materials and products be given high priority in determining final design and specifications.

Installation Cost (per Linear Foot)

LOW   HIGH

$13.47

Maintenance

LOW   HIGH

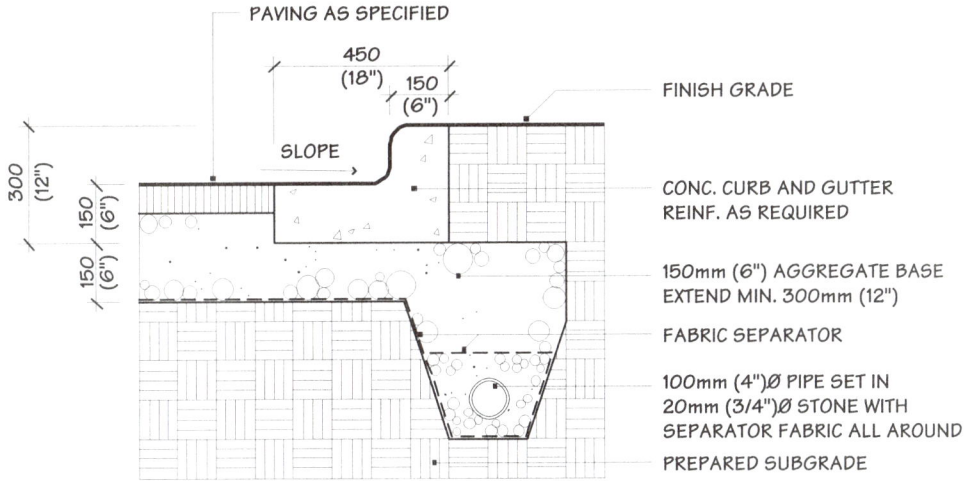

PAVING AS SPECIFIED

450 (18")

150 (6")

SLOPE

300 (12")

150 (6")

150 (6")

FINISH GRADE

CONC. CURB AND GUTTER REINF. AS REQUIRED

150mm (6") AGGREGATE BASE EXTEND MIN. 300mm (12")

FABRIC SEPARATOR

100mm (4")Ø PIPE SET IN 20mm (3/4")Ø STONE WITH SEPARATOR FABRIC ALL AROUND

PREPARED SUBGRADE

APPLICATION

CLIMATE

SUBGRADE

CSI MASTERFORMAT: 02770
DRAWING FILE: CRB12-01

• This drawing is a template for preliminary design only, and is not intended for bid purposes. It is subject to modification based on design calculations, local practices, and all applicable codes and regulations.

• This concrete curb and gutter is rated as medium-duty due to aggregate subbase and concrete thickness. It is typically found in residential streets, parks, and institutional parking area settings.

• It can be used in all climates, but performs best in well-drained soils. This detail shows an adaptation to poorly drained soils using a fabric separator reinforcement and a subdrain pipe set in a stone trench preferably positioned to the back of the curb and away from direct loading.

• Rigid pavement and curbs must accommodate movement of materials by providing adequate expansion and control joints, particularly in regions of extreme temperature fluctuations. If designed for temperate or

cold climates, air-entrained concrete is typically recommended due to freezing/thawing action.

• Reinforcing practices vary widely by region. Most slip-form cast concrete is not reinforced, especially in cold climates due to chemical assault on steel due to infiltration. Local codes and practices should be consulted prior to specifying any type of reinforcing.

• It is recommended that recycled and regionally available materials and products be given high priority in determining final design and specifications.

Installation Cost (per Linear Foot)

LOW   HIGH

$12.10

Maintenance

LOW   HIGH

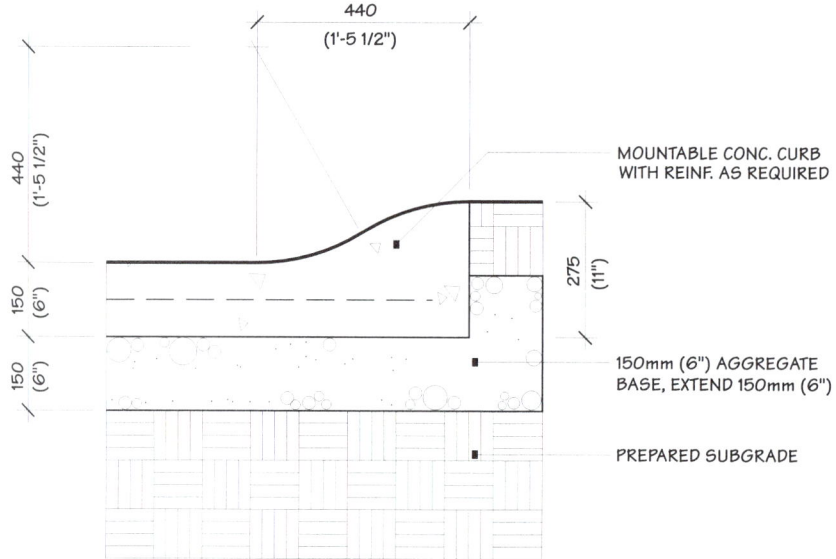

Dimensions shown: 440 (1'-5 1/2") across top; 440 (1'-5 1/2"), 150 (6"), 150 (6") along left side; 275 (11") on right.

MOUNTABLE CONC. CURB WITH REINF. AS REQUIRED

150mm (6") AGGREGATE BASE, EXTEND 150mm (6")

PREPARED SUBGRADE

APPLICATION

CLIMATE

SUBGRADE

CSI MASTERFORMAT: 02770
DRAWING FILE: CRB12-05

• This drawing is a template for preliminary design only, and is not intended for bid purposes. It is subject to modification based on design calculations, local practices, and all applicable codes and regulations.

• This concrete curb and gutter is rated as heavy-duty due to aggregate subbase and concrete thickness. It is typically found in dense residential and urban streets, parks, and institutional roads and parking area settings.

• It can be used in all climates, but performs best in well-drained soils. This detail illustrates an adaptation to cold climates showing aggregate backfill at back of curb to guard against frost uplift.

• Rigid pavement and curbs must accommodate movement of materials by providing adequate expansion and control joints, particularly in regions of extreme temperature fluctuations. If designed for temperate or cold climates, air-entrained concrete is typically recommended due to freezing/thawing action.

• Reinforcing practices vary widely by region. Most slip-form cast concrete is not reinforced, especially in cold climates due to chemical assault on steel due to infiltration. Local codes and practices should be consulted prior to specifying any type of reinforcing.

• It is recommended that recycled and regionally available materials and products be given high priority in determining final design and specifications.

Installation Cost (per Linear Foot)

LOW   HIGH

$7.62

Maintenance

LOW   HIGH

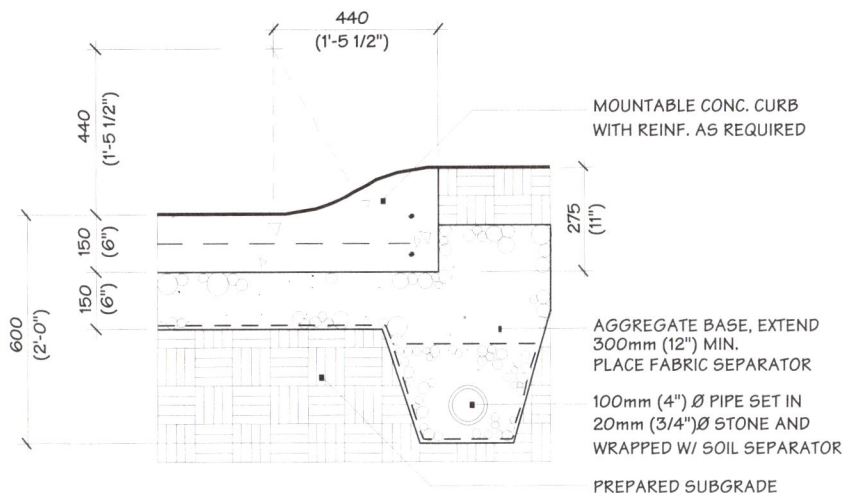

MOUNTABLE CONC. CURB
WITH REINF. AS REQUIRED

440
(1'-5 1/2")

440
(1'-5 1/2")

275
(11")

150
(6")

150
(6")

600
(2'-0")

AGGREGATE BASE, EXTEND
300mm (12") MIN.
PLACE FABRIC SEPARATOR

100mm (4") Ø PIPE SET IN
20mm (3/4")Ø STONE AND
WRAPPED W/ SOIL SEPARATOR

PREPARED SUBGRADE

APPLICATION

CLIMATE

SUBGRADE

CSI MASTERFORMAT: 02770
DRAWING FILE: CRB12-06

• This drawing is a template for preliminary design only, and is not intended for bid purposes. It is subject to modification based on design calculations, local practices, and all applicable codes and regulations.

• This concrete mountable curb and gutter is rated as medium-duty due to aggregate subbase and concrete thickness. It is typically found in residential streets, parks, and institutional parking area settings.

• It can be used in all climates, but performs best in well-drained soils. This detail illustrates an adaptation to cold climates showing aggregate backfill at back of curb to guard against frost uplift. It also shows a fabric separator reinforcement and a subdrain pipe set in a stone filled trench located to the rear of the curb to drain aggregate base.

• In warmer climates, this curb may be cast as an edge of a narrow road. In most cases, it is isolated from the pavement with an expansion joint.

• Rigid pavement and curbs must accommodate movement of materials by providing adequate expansion and control joints, particularly in regions of extreme temperature fluctuations. If designed for temperate or cold climates, air-entrained concrete is typically recommended due to freezing/thawing action.

• Reinforcing practices vary widely by region. Most slip-form cast concrete is not reinforced, especially in cold climates due to chemical assault on steel due to infiltration. Local codes and practices should be consulted prior to specifying any type of reinforcing.

• It is recommended that recycled and regionally available materials and products be given high priority in determining final design and specifications.

Installation Cost (per Linear Foot)

LOW   HIGH

$11.87

Maintenance

LOW   HIGH

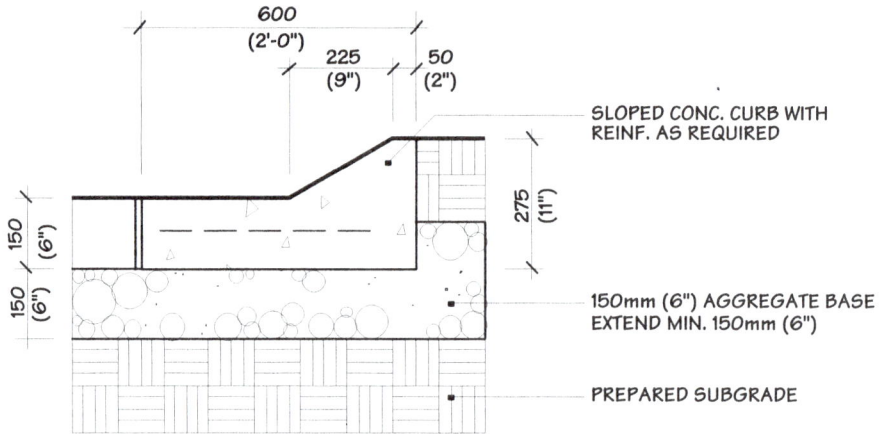

600
(2'-0")

225
(9")

50
(2")

SLOPED CONC. CURB WITH
REINF. AS REQUIRED

275
(11")

150
(6")

150
(6")

150
(6")

150mm (6") AGGREGATE BASE
EXTEND MIN. 150mm (6")

PREPARED SUBGRADE

APPLICATION

CLIMATE

SUBGRADE

CSI MASTERFORMAT: 02770
DRAWING FILE: CRB12-07

• This drawing is a template for preliminary design only, and is not intended for bid purposes. It is subject to modification based on design calculations, local practices, and all applicable codes and regulations.

• This concrete curb and gutter is rated as medium-duty due to aggregate subbase and concrete thickness. It is typically found in dense residential and urban streets, parks, and institutional roads and parking area settings.

• It can be used in all climates, but performs best in well-drained soils. This detail illustrates an adaptation to cold climates showing aggregate backfill at back of curb to guard against frost uplift.

• Rigid pavement and curbs must accommodate movement of materials by providing adequate expansion and control joints, particularly in regions of extreme temperature fluctuations. If designed for temperate or cold climates, air-entrained concrete is typi-

cally recommended due to freezing/thawing action.

• Reinforcing practices vary widely by region. Most slip-form cast concrete is not reinforced, especially in cold climates due to chemical assault on steel due to infiltration. Local codes and practices should be consulted prior to specifying any type of reinforcing.

• It is recommended that recycled and regionally available materials and products be given high priority in determining final design and specifications.

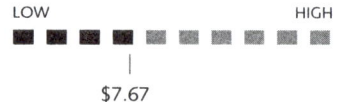

Installation Cost (per Linear Foot)

LOW   HIGH

$7.67

Maintenance

LOW   HIGH

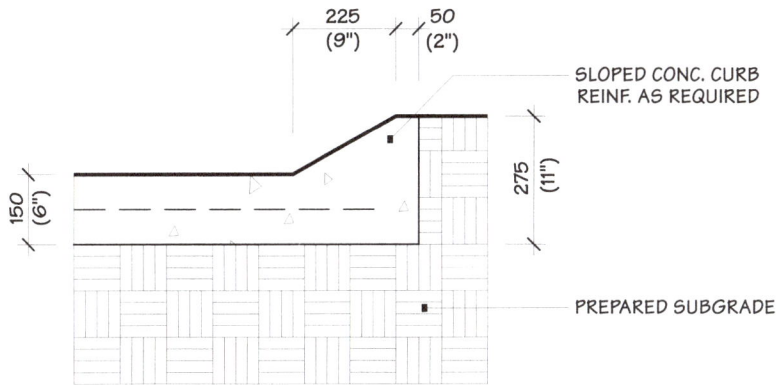

225 (9")　50 (2")

SLOPED CONC. CURB
REINF. AS REQUIRED

275 (11")

150 (6")

PREPARED SUBGRADE

APPLICATION

LIGHT　MED.　HEAVY

CLIMATE

ARID　HUMID　TEMP.　COLD

SUBGRADE

PERM.　CLAY　ROOF

CSI MASTERFORMAT: 02770
DRAWING FILE: CRB12-08

• This drawing is a template for preliminary design only, and is not intended for bid purposes. It is subject to modification based on design calculations, local practices, and all applicable codes and regulations.

• This concrete mountable curb and gutter is rated as medium-duty due to concrete thickness. It is typically found in residential streets, parks, and institutional parking area settings. This detail is not suitable for cold climates due to lack of aggregate base, and is typically found only in warmer climates with uniform subsoils of adequate bearing. Consult local practices.

• In warmer climates, this curb may be cast as an edge of a narrow road. In most cases, it is isolated from the pavement with an expansion joint.

• Rigid pavement and curbs must accommodate movement of materials by providing adequate expansion and control joints, particularly in regions of extreme temperature

fluctuations. If designed for temperate climates, air-entrained concrete is typically recommended due to freezing/thawing action.

• Reinforcing practices vary widely by region. Most slip-form cast concrete is not reinforced. Local codes and practices should be consulted prior to specifying any type of reinforcing.

• It is recommended that recycled and regionally available materials and products be given high priority in determining final design and specifications.

Installation Cost (per Linear Foot)

LOW　　　　　　　　HIGH

$7.12

Maintenance

LOW　　　　　　　　HIGH

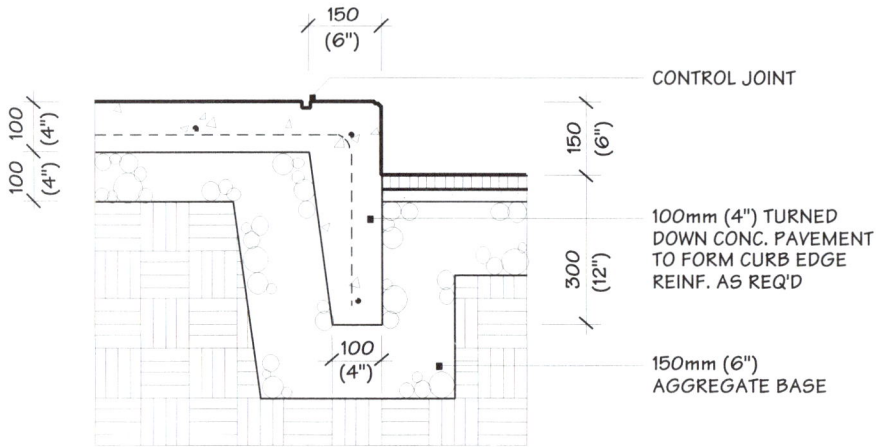

150 (6")

CONTROL JOINT

100 100 100 (4") (4") (4")

150 (6")

100mm (4") TURNED DOWN CONC. PAVEMENT TO FORM CURB EDGE REINF. AS REQ'D

300 (12")

100 (4")

150mm (6") AGGREGATE BASE

APPLICATION

CLIMATE

SUBGRADE

CSI MASTERFORMAT: 02770
DRAWING FILE: CRB22-06

• This drawing is a template for preliminary design only, and is not intended for bid purposes. It is subject to modification based on design calculations, local practices, and all applicable codes and regulations.

• This turn-down concrete slab curb is rated as light-duty due to concrete and aggregate base thickness. It is typically found in residential driveways, schools, parks, and light institutional settings.

• It can be used in all climates, but expansion joints may require sealing to avoid deterioration in cold climates due to freeze/thaw action. Curb is formed and placed in forms with the adjacent pavement slab.

• Rigid pavement and curbs must accommodate movement of materials by providing adequate expansion and control joints, particularly in regions of extreme temperature fluctuations. If designed for temperate or cold climates, air-entrained concrete is typi-

cally recommended due to freezing/thawing action.

• Reinforcing practices vary widely by region. Local codes and practices should be consulted prior to specifying any type of reinforcing.

• This curb is an economical alternative in light-duty applications. Repair requires cutting at the control joint. Long term care may require replacement of entire slab sections if damage is severe.

• It is recommended that recycled and regionally available materials and products be given high priority in determining final design and specifications.

Installation Cost (per Linear Foot)

LOW   HIGH

$4.37

Maintenance

LOW   HIGH

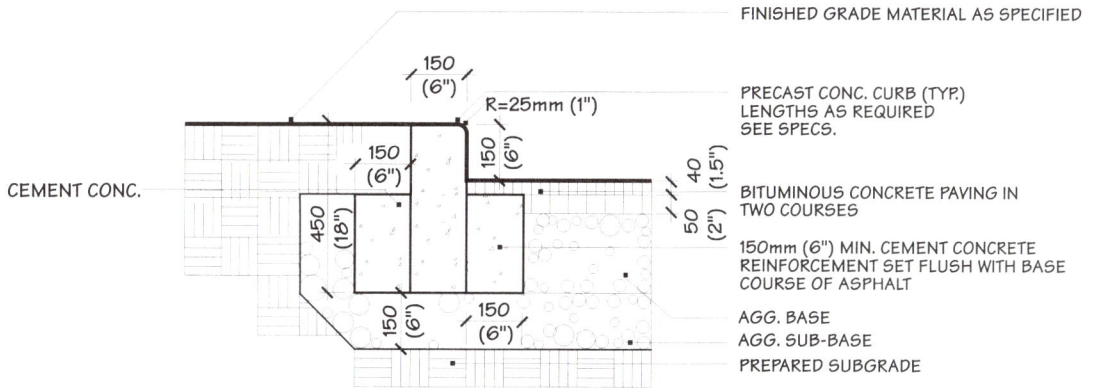

FINISHED GRADE MATERIAL AS SPECIFIED

150 (6")

R=25mm (1")

150 (6")

150 (6")

CEMENT CONC.

150 (6")

450 (18")

40 (1.5")

50 (2")

150 (6")

150 (6")

PRECAST CONC. CURB (TYP.) LENGTHS AS REQUIRED SEE SPECS.

BITUMINOUS CONCRETE PAVING IN TWO COURSES

150mm (6") MIN. CEMENT CONCRETE REINFORCEMENT SET FLUSH WITH BASE COURSE OF ASPHALT

AGG. BASE
AGG. SUB-BASE
PREPARED SUBGRADE

APPLICATION

CLIMATE

SUBGRADE

CSI MASTERFORMAT: 02770
DRAWING FILE: CRB22-07

• This drawing is a template for preliminary design only, and is not intended for bid purposes. It is subject to modification based on design calculations, local practices, and all applicable codes and regulations.

• This precast concrete curb is rated as heavy-duty due to aggregate subbase and concrete reinforcement both front and back. It is typically found in urban streets, parks, and institutional settings.

• It can be used in all climates, but performs best in well-drained soils.

• Rigid pavement and curbs must accommodate movement of materials by providing adequate expansion and control joints, particularly in regions of extreme temperature fluctuations. If designed for temperate or cold climates, air-entrained concrete is typically recommended due to freezing/thawing action.

• In severe cold conditions, longer units are used and butt joints are left open to avoid mortar and to allow maximum drainage. Curb should be backfilled with aggregate to lessen frost uplift.

• It is recommended that recycled and regionally available materials and products be given high priority in determining final design and specifications.

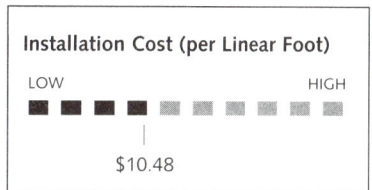

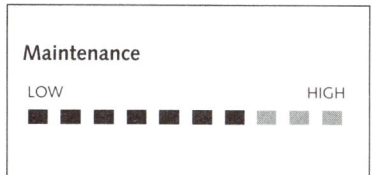

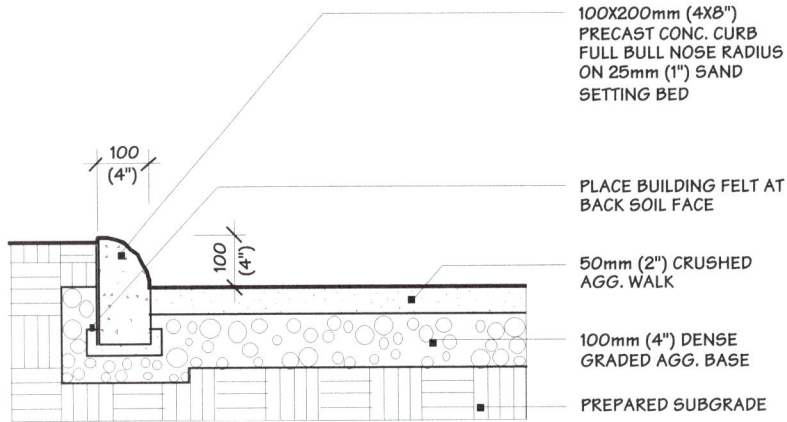

100 (4")

100 (4")

100X200mm (4X8")
PRECAST CONC. CURB
FULL BULL NOSE RADIUS
ON 25mm (1") SAND
SETTING BED

PLACE BUILDING FELT AT
BACK SOIL FACE

50mm (2") CRUSHED
AGG. WALK

100mm (4") DENSE
GRADED AGG. BASE

PREPARED SUBGRADE

APPLICATION

CLIMATE

SUBGRADE

CSI MASTERFORMAT: 02770
DRAWING FILE: CRB22-08

• This drawing is a template for preliminary design only, and is not intended for bid purposes. It is subject to modification based on design calculations, local practices, and all applicable codes and regulations.

• This precast concrete curb is rated as light-duty and typically serves as a raised edge to contain aggregate or unit pavers in pedestrian walkways associated with residential, light park, and garden settings. It provides an informal pedestrian scaled curbing.

• It is best used in well drained soils and is simply butt jointed. When serving as a garden edge containing active cultivation on the retained side, a strip of building paper, or filter fabric helps to contain soil fines.

• This detail is not suitable for vehicular uses due to lack of resistance to significant lateral forces. It is placed on a tamped stone dust setting bed to achieve an even top elevation. A mortar setting bed may be used in warmer climates to stabilize the curb in more active settings.

• This detail is ideal for warmer climates, but with seasonal maintenance it can be effective in colder climates as well.

• This residential scale application is often used where natural stone is not available.

• It is recommended that recycled and regionally available materials and products be given high priority in determining final design and specifications.

Installation Cost (per Linear Foot)

LOW   HIGH

$3.00

Maintenance

LOW   HIGH

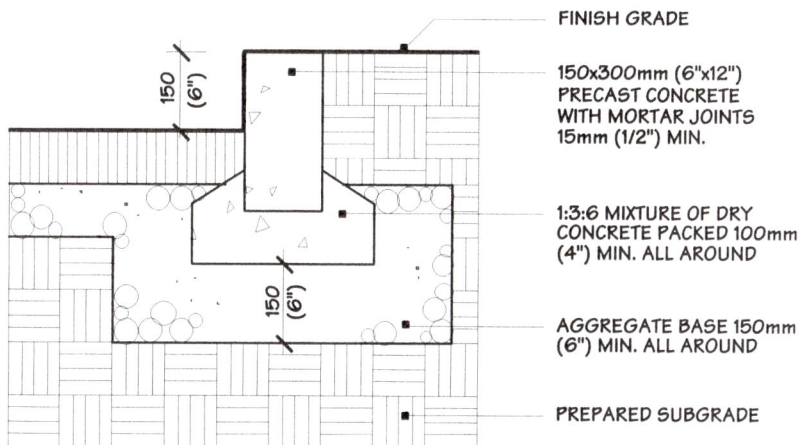

FINISH GRADE

150x300mm (6"x12")
PRECAST CONCRETE
WITH MORTAR JOINTS
15mm (1/2") MIN.

1:3:6 MIXTURE OF DRY
CONCRETE PACKED 100mm
(4") MIN. ALL AROUND

AGGREGATE BASE 150mm
(6") MIN. ALL AROUND

PREPARED SUBGRADE

APPLICATION

CSI MASTERFORMAT: 02770
DRAWING FILE: CRB22-03

• This drawing is a template for preliminary design only, and is not intended for bid purposes. It is subject to modification based on design calculations, local practices, and all applicable codes and regulations.

• This precast concrete curb is rated as medium-duty due to aggregate subbase and mortar reinforcement. It is typically found in residential driveways, parks, and institutional settings.

• It can be used in all climates, but mortar joints may deteriorate in cold climates due to chemical assault during snow and ice clearing.

• Rigid pavement and curbs must accommodate movement of materials by providing adequate expansion and control joints, particularly in regions of extreme temperature fluctuations. If designed for temperate or cold climates, air-entrained concrete is typically recommended due to freezing/thawing action.

CLIMATE

• This medium scale application is often used where natural stone is not available.

• It is recommended that recycled and regionally available materials and products be given high priority in determining final design and specifications.

SUBGRADE

Installation Cost (per Linear Foot)

LOW   HIGH

$9.39

Maintenance

LOW   HIGH

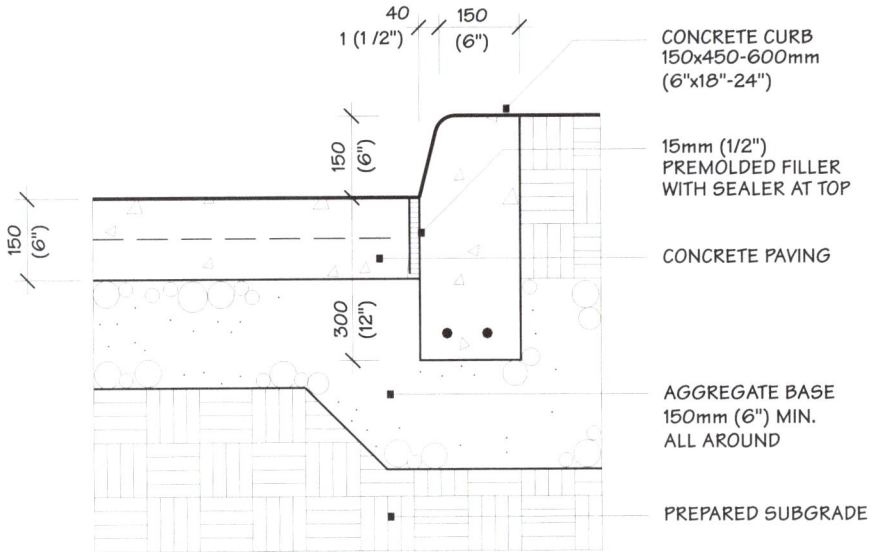

CONCRETE CURB
150x450-600mm
(6"x18"-24")

15mm (1/2")
PREMOLDED FILLER
WITH SEALER AT TOP

CONCRETE PAVING

AGGREGATE BASE
150mm (6") MIN.
ALL AROUND

PREPARED SUBGRADE

40
1 (1/2")

150
(6")

150 (6")

150 (6")

300 (12")

APPLICATION

CLIMATE

SUBGRADE

CSI MASTERFORMAT: 02770
DRAWING FILE: CRB22-05

• This drawing is a template for preliminary design only, and is not intended for bid purposes. It is subject to modification based on design calculations, local practices, and all applicable codes and regulations.

• This concrete curb is rated as medium-duty due to concrete and aggregate base thickness. It is typically found in residential driveways, parks, and institutional settings.

• It can be used in all climates, but expansion joints may require sealing to avoid deterioration in cold climates due to freeze/thaw action.

• Rigid pavement and curbs must accommodate movement of materials by providing adequate expansion and control joints, particularly in regions of extreme temperature fluctuations. If designed for temperate or cold climates, air-entrained concrete is typically recommended due to freezing/thawing action.

• This medium scale application is often used where natural stone is not available. A concrete base reinforcement may be added in heavy loading conditions.

• It is recommended that recycled and regionally available materials and products be given high priority in determining final design and specifications.

Installation Cost (per Linear Foot)

LOW   HIGH

$10.00

Maintenance

LOW   HIGH

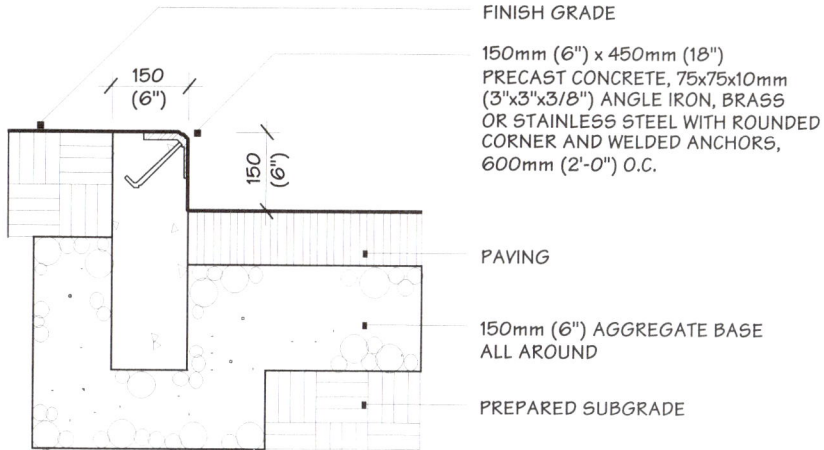

FINISH GRADE

150mm (6") x 450mm (18") PRECAST CONCRETE, 75x75x10mm (3"x3"x3/8") ANGLE IRON, BRASS OR STAINLESS STEEL WITH ROUNDED CORNER AND WELDED ANCHORS, 600mm (2'-0") O.C.

PAVING

150mm (6") AGGREGATE BASE ALL AROUND

PREPARED SUBGRADE

APPLICATION

CLIMATE

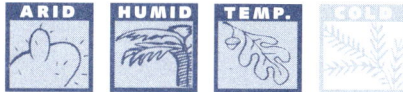

SUBGRADE

CSI MASTERFORMAT: 02770
DRAWING FILE: CRB22-01

• This drawing is a template for preliminary design only, and is not intended for bid purposes. It is subject to modification based on design calculations, local practices, and all applicable codes and regulations.

• This precast concrete curb with steel guard is rated as heavy-duty due to aggregate base and steel reinforcement. It is typically found in urban streets, parks, and institutional settings. It is often associated with heavy service and transportation terminals. It may require additional concrete reinforcement at base of curb.

• It can be used in all climates, but deteriorates in cold climates due to expansion coefficient differentials and chemical assault due to snow clearing. For ornamental effect, brass or stainless steel may be used.

• Rigid pavement and curbs must accommodate movement of materials by providing adequate expansion and control joints, particularly in regions of extreme temperature fluctuations. If designed for temperate or cold climates, air-entrained concrete is typically recommended due to freezing/thawing action.

• It is recommended that recycled and regionally available materials and products be given high priority in determining final design and specifications.

Installation Cost (per Linear Foot)

LOW   HIGH

$19.38

Maintenance

LOW   HIGH

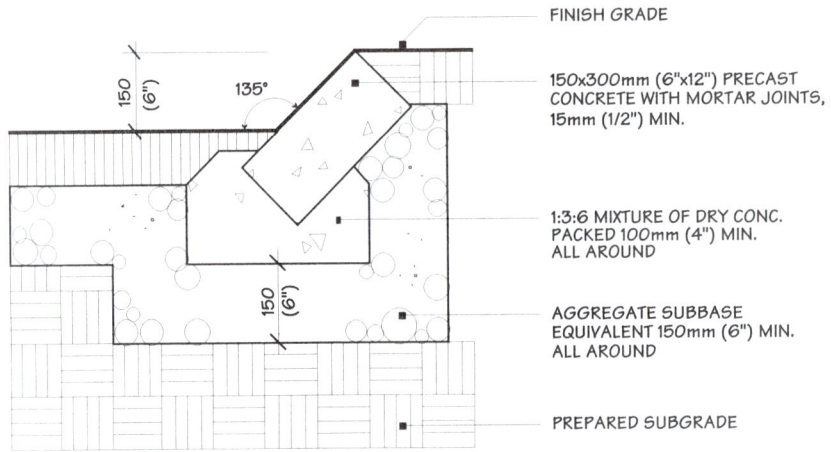

FINISH GRADE

150x300mm (6"x12") PRECAST CONCRETE WITH MORTAR JOINTS, 15mm (1/2") MIN.

1:3:6 MIXTURE OF DRY CONC. PACKED 100mm (4") MIN. ALL AROUND

AGGREGATE SUBBASE EQUIVALENT 150mm (6") MIN. ALL AROUND

PREPARED SUBGRADE

APPLICATION

CLIMATE

SUBGRADE

CSI MASTERFORMAT: 02770
DRAWING FILE: CRB22-04

• This drawing is a template for preliminary design only, and is not intended for bid purposes. It is subject to modification based on design calculations, local practices, and all applicable codes and regulations.

• This precast sloping concrete curb is rated as medium-duty due to aggregate subbase and mortar reinforcement. It is typically found in residential driveways, parks, and institutional settings.

• It can be used in all climates, but mortar joints may deteriorate in cold climates due to chemical assault during snow and clearing.

• Rigid pavement and curbs must accommodate movement of materials by providing adequate expansion and control joints, particularly in regions of extreme temperature fluctuations. If designed for temperate or cold climates, air-entrained concrete is typically recommended due to freezing/thawing action.

• This medium scale application is often used where natural stone is not available. It should not be used as a mountable curb due to load distribution at top. A cast sloped curb would serve better as a mountable curb.

• It is recommended that recycled and regionally available materials and products be given high priority in determining final design and specifications.

Installation Cost (per Linear Foot)

LOW   HIGH

$9.39

Maintenance

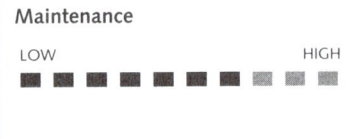

LOW   HIGH

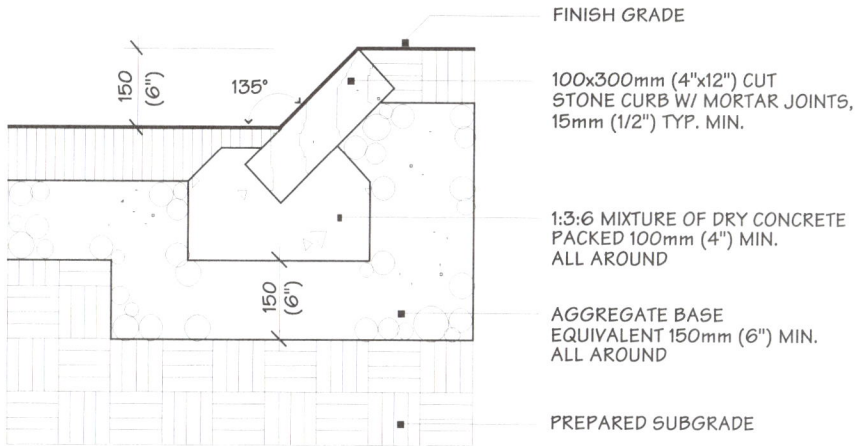

FINISH GRADE

100x300mm (4"x12") CUT STONE CURB W/ MORTAR JOINTS, 15mm (1/2") TYP. MIN.

1:3:6 MIXTURE OF DRY CONCRETE PACKED 100mm (4") MIN. ALL AROUND

AGGREGATE BASE EQUIVALENT 150mm (6") MIN. ALL AROUND

PREPARED SUBGRADE

150 (6")

135°

150 (6")

APPLICATION

CLIMATE

SUBGRADE

CSI MASTERFORMAT: 02770
DRAWING FILE: CRB23-02

• This drawing is a template for preliminary design only, and is not intended for bid purposes. It is subject to modification based on design calculations, local practices, and all applicable codes and regulations.

• This sloped cut stone curb is rated as medium-duty due to stone and aggregate base thickness and concrete setting bed. It is typically found in residential driveways, parks, and institutional settings.

• It can be used in all climates, but mortar joints may require re-pointing in cold climates due to freeze/thaw action.

• Subgrade conditions have a significant impact on the longevity of rigid and mortared units pavements and curbs. The subgrade should be uniform to prevent pavement failure due to uneven soil expansion and contraction. This detail provides a well-drained aggregate base to drain sub-surface moisture and increase uniformity

• Cut stone provides a very durable surface highly resistant to abrasion resulting from normal wear and maintenance. Metamorphic and igneous stone is preferred.

• This residential scaled curb is often used at entrance drop-off areas and as edging for lawns and raised plant beds at the edge of driveways.

• It should not be used as a mountable curb. A thicker stone section and a more generous aggregate and mortar base is required for such an application.

• It is recommended that recycled and regionally available materials and products be given high priority in determining final design and specifications.

Installation Cost (per Linear Foot)

LOW HIGH

$14.30

Maintenance

LOW HIGH

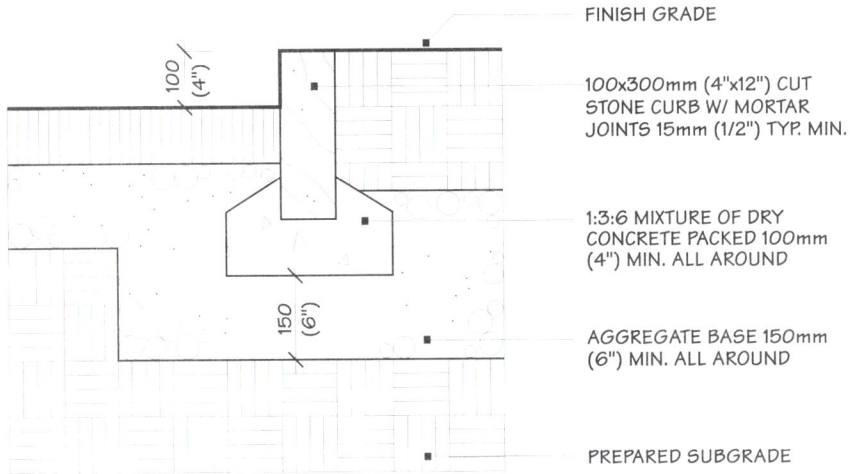

FINISH GRADE

100x300mm (4"x12") CUT STONE CURB W/ MORTAR JOINTS 15mm (1/2") TYP. MIN.

1:3:6 MIXTURE OF DRY CONCRETE PACKED 100mm (4") MIN. ALL AROUND

AGGREGATE BASE 150mm (6") MIN. ALL AROUND

PREPARED SUBGRADE

APPLICATION

CLIMATE

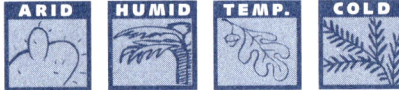

SUBGRADE

CSI MASTERFORMAT: 02770
DRAWING FILE: CRB23-01

• This drawing is a template for preliminary design only, and is not intended for bid purposes. It is subject to modification based on design calculations, local practices, and all applicable codes and regulations.

• This cut stone curb is rated as light-duty due to stone and aggregate base thickness. It is typically found in residential driveways, parks, and institutional settings.

• It can be used in all climates, but mortar joints may require re-pointing in cold climates due to freeze/thaw action.

• Subgrade conditions have a significant impact on the longevity of rigid and mortared pavements and curbs. The subgrade should be uniform to prevent pavement failure due to uneven soil expansion and contraction. This detail provides a well-drained aggregate base to drain sub-surface moisture and increase uniformity

• Cut stone provides a very durable surface highly resistant to abrasion resulting from normal wear and maintenance. Metamorphic and igneous stone is preferred.

• This residential scaled curb is often used at entrance drop-off areas and as edging for lawns and raised plant beds at the edge of driveways.

• It is recommended that recycled and regionally available materials and products be given high priority in determining final design and specifications.

Installation Cost (per Linear Foot)

LOW   HIGH

$14.70

Maintenance

LOW   HIGH

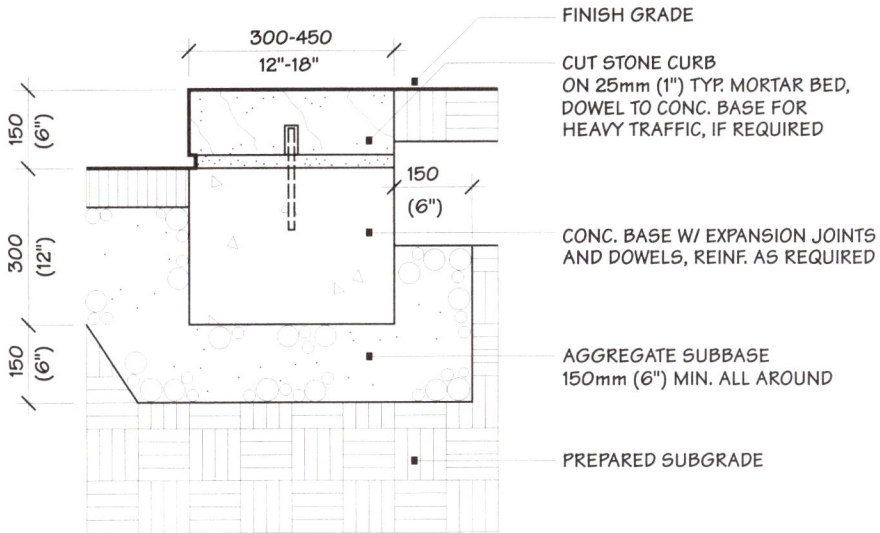

FINISH GRADE

CUT STONE CURB
ON 25mm (1") TYP. MORTAR BED,
DOWEL TO CONC. BASE FOR
HEAVY TRAFFIC, IF REQUIRED

CONC. BASE W/ EXPANSION JOINTS
AND DOWELS, REINF. AS REQUIRED

AGGREGATE SUBBASE
150mm (6") MIN. ALL AROUND

PREPARED SUBGRADE

300-450
12"-18"

150 (6")

150 (6")

300 (12")

150 (6")

APPLICATION

CLIMATE

SUBGRADE

CSI MASTERFORMAT: 02770
DRAWING FILE: CRB22-02

• This drawing is a template for preliminary design only, and is not intended for bid purposes. It is subject to modification based on design calculations, local practices, and all applicable codes and regulations.

• This cut stone curb on concrete base detail is rated as heavy duty due to its concrete base and aggregate subbase thickness. It is typically found in dense residential, urban park, or institutional settings.

• Stone is doweled to concrete base to resist lateral forces due to routine use impacts. This detail is best applied to building entrance courts and confined areas where maintenance may be practiced with care.

• Cut stone provides a very durable surface highly resistant to abrasion resulting from normal wear and maintenance. Metamorphic and igneous stone is preferred.

• Rigid pavement design must accommodate movement of materials by providing adequate expansion and control joints, par-

ticularly in regions of extreme temperature fluctuations. If designed for temperate or cold climates, air-entrained concrete is typically recommended due to freezing/thawing action. Expansion and butt joints should be sealed with elastomeric compounds.

• It is recommended that recycled and regionally available materials and products be given high priority in determining final design and specifications.

Installation Cost (per Linear Foot)

LOW   HIGH

$26.31

Maintenance

LOW   HIGH

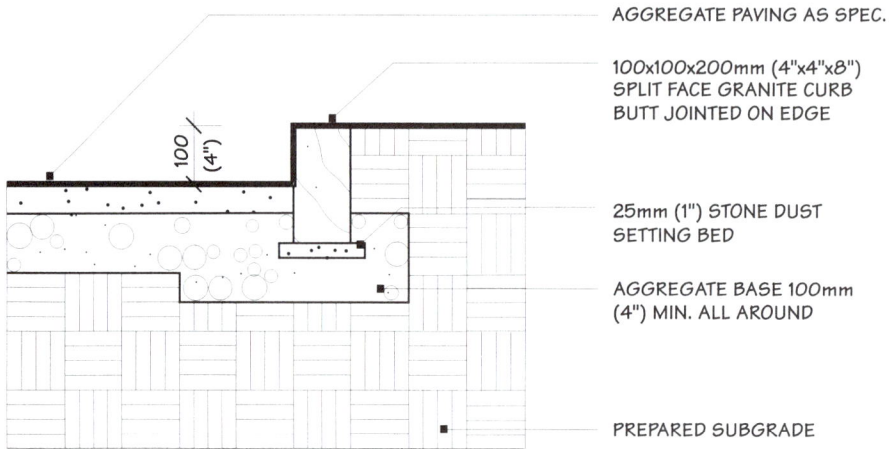

AGGREGATE PAVING AS SPEC.

100x100x200mm (4"x4"x8")
SPLIT FACE GRANITE CURB
BUTT JOINTED ON EDGE

25mm (1") STONE DUST
SETTING BED

AGGREGATE BASE 100mm
(4") MIN. ALL AROUND

PREPARED SUBGRADE

APPLICATION

CLIMATE

SUBGRADE

CSI MASTERFORMAT: 02770
DRAWING FILE: CRB23-04

• This drawing is a template for preliminary design only, and is not intended for bid purposes. It is subject to modification based on design calculations, local practices, and all applicable codes and regulations.

• This granite block curb is rated as light-duty and typically serves as a raised edge to contain aggregate or unit pavers in pedestrian walkways associated with residential, light park, and garden settings. It provides an informal pedestrian scaled curbing.

• It is best used in well drained soils and is simply butt jointed. When serving as a garden edge containing active cultivation on the retained side, a strip of building paper, or filter fabric helps to contain soil fines.

• This detail is not suitable for vehicular uses due to lack of resistance to significant lateral forces. It is placed on a tamped stone dust setting bed to achieve an even top elevation and to account for irregularities in the cut or split stone.

• Stone curbing provides a very durable surface highly resistant to abrasion resulting from normal wear and maintenance. Metamorphic and igneous stone is preferred.

• This detail is ideal for warmer climates, but with seasonal maintenance it can be effective in colder climates as well.

• It is recommended that recycled and regionally available materials and products be given high priority in determining final design and specifications.

Installation Cost (per Linear Foot)

LOW   HIGH

$11.33

Maintenance

LOW   HIGH

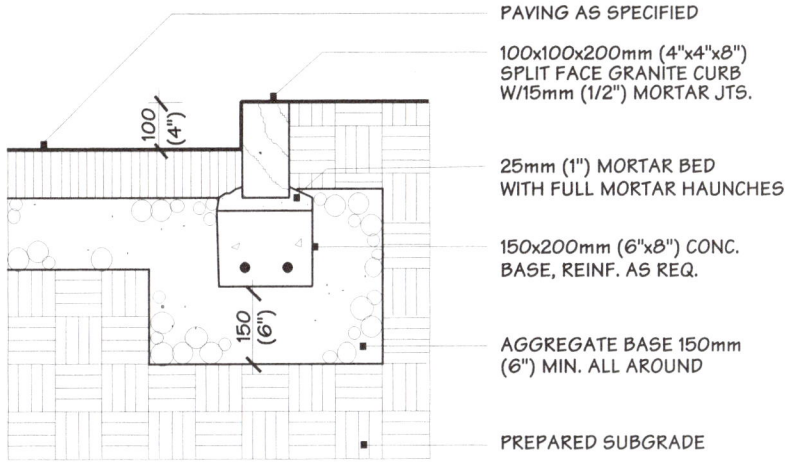

PAVING AS SPECIFIED

100x100x200mm (4"x4"x8")
SPLIT FACE GRANITE CURB
W/15mm (1/2") MORTAR JTS.

25mm (1") MORTAR BED
WITH FULL MORTAR HAUNCHES

150x200mm (6"x8") CONC.
BASE, REINF. AS REQ.

AGGREGATE BASE 150mm
(6") MIN. ALL AROUND

PREPARED SUBGRADE

APPLICATION

CLIMATE

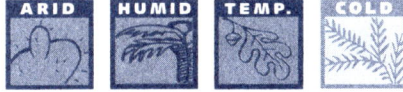

SUBGRADE

CSI MASTERFORMAT: 02770
DRAWING FILE: CRB23-03

• This drawing is a template for preliminary design only, and is not intended for bid purposes. It is subject to modification based on design calculations, local practices, and all applicable codes and regulations.

• This mortared granite block curb is rated as medium-duty and typically serves as a raised edge to contain aggregate, unit pavers, or other flexible paving in driveways and roads associated with residential, urban park, and garden settings. It provides an informal but durable small curb.

• It is best used in well drained soils and is placed on a mortar setting bed, on a concrete grade beam sized to accommodate soil bearing and design load. Joints are mortared and tooled for strength and drainage.

• This detail is suitable for vehicular uses, but should not be used as a mountable structure.

• Stone curbing provides a very durable surface highly resistant to abrasion resulting

from normal wear and maintenance. Metamorphic and igneous stone is preferred.

• This detail is ideal for warmer climates, but with seasonal maintenance and proper installation, it can be effective in mild temperate climates as well.

• It is recommended that recycled and regionally available materials and products be given high priority in determining final design and specifications.

Installation Cost (per Linear Foot)

LOW   HIGH

$13.52

Maintenance

LOW   HIGH

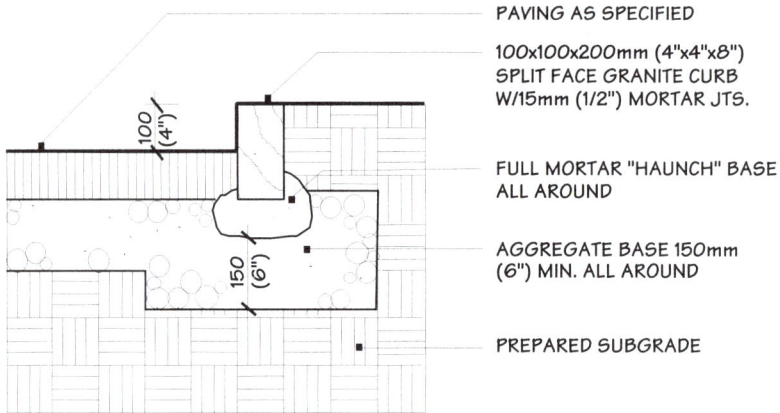

PAVING AS SPECIFIED

100x100x200mm (4"x4"x8")
SPLIT FACE GRANITE CURB
W/15mm (1/2") MORTAR JTS.

FULL MORTAR "HAUNCH" BASE
ALL AROUND

AGGREGATE BASE 150mm
(6") MIN. ALL AROUND

PREPARED SUBGRADE

APPLICATION

CLIMATE

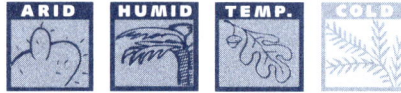

SUBGRADE

CSI MASTERFORMAT: 02770
DRAWING FILE: CRB23-05

• This drawing is a template for preliminary design only, and is not intended for bid purposes. It is subject to modification based on design calculations, local practices, and all applicable codes and regulations.

• This mortared granite block curb is rated as medium-duty and typically serves as a raised edge to contain aggregate, unit pavers, or other flexible paving in pedestrian walkways or light driveways associated with residential, light park, and garden settings. It provides an informal pedestrian scaled curbing.

• It is best used in well drained soils and is placed on a mortar setting bed, which may be reinforced with mesh if required. Joints are mortared and tooled for strength and drainage.

• This detail is not suitable for heavy vehicular uses, but is sufficiently reinforced to serve as an edge in residential settings.

• Stone curbing provides a very durable surface highly resistant to abrasion resulting from normal wear and maintenance. Metamorphic and igneous stone is preferred.

• This detail is ideal for warmer climates, but with seasonal maintenance and proper installation, it can be effective in mild temperate climates as well.

• It is recommended that recycled and regionally available materials and products be given high priority in determining final design and specifications.

Installation Cost (per Linear Foot)

LOW   HIGH

$12.93

Maintenance

LOW   HIGH

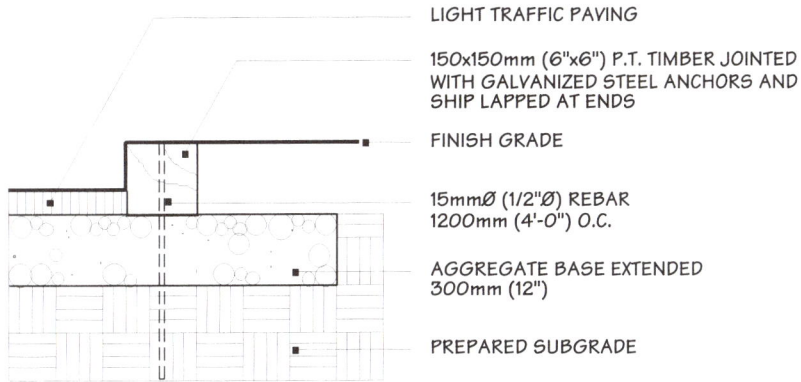

LIGHT TRAFFIC PAVING

150x150mm (6"x6") P.T. TIMBER JOINTED
WITH GALVANIZED STEEL ANCHORS AND
SHIP LAPPED AT ENDS

FINISH GRADE

15mmØ (1/2"Ø) REBAR
1200mm (4'-0") O.C.

AGGREGATE BASE EXTENDED
300mm (12")

PREPARED SUBGRADE

APPLICATION

CLIMATE

SUBGRADE

CSI MASTERFORMAT: 02945
DRAWING FILE: CRB25-02

• This drawing is a template for preliminary design only, and is not intended for bid purposes. It is subject to modification based on design calculations, local practices, and all applicable codes and regulations.

• This detail is typical of paved areas in residential and garden settings. Wood provides a well-defined edge and prevents spreading of flexible paving systems.

• This detail is rated for light-duty applications and is intended to support primarily pedestrian loading.

• Wood is typically pressure-treated to resist decay, and all metal fasteners should be corrosion-resistant.

• This detail is designed for cold climates and clay soils through the use of extended aggregate base and steel pins drilled through the wood timbers. Wood stakes may be subject to heaving in both clay soils and extreme frost conditions. Steel stakes are preferred under these conditions.

• Timbers may be joined with nailed metal plates at back, or with alternate ship-lap end joints, pinned by steel rods for secure unit construction.

• Wood edging requires only minimal maintenance, but it provides a relatively short term of service due to decay.

• It is recommended that recycled and regionally available materials and products be given high priority in determining final design and specifications.

Installation Cost (per Linear Foot)

LOW   HIGH

$5.64

Maintenance

LOW   HIGH

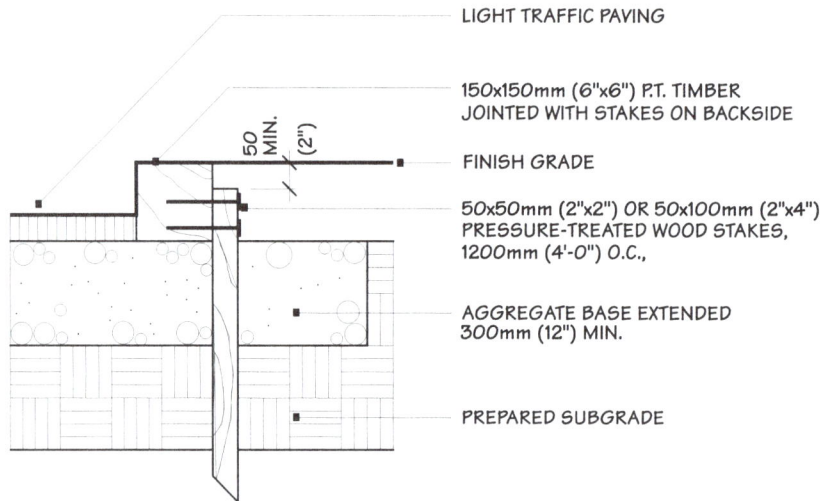

LIGHT TRAFFIC PAVING

150x150mm (6"x6") P.T. TIMBER
JOINTED WITH STAKES ON BACKSIDE

50 MIN. (2")

FINISH GRADE

50x50mm (2"x2") OR 50x100mm (2"x4")
PRESSURE-TREATED WOOD STAKES,
1200mm (4'-0") O.C.,

AGGREGATE BASE EXTENDED
300mm (12") MIN.

PREPARED SUBGRADE

APPLICATION

CLIMATE

SUBGRADE

CSI MASTERFORMAT: 02945
DRAWING FILE: CRB25-01

•   This drawing is a template for preliminary design only, and is not intended for bid purposes. It is subject to modification based on design calculations, local practices, and all applicable codes and regulations.

•   This detail is typical of paved areas in residential and garden settings. Wood provides a well-defined edge and prevents spreading of flexible paving systems.

•   This detail is rated for light-duty applications and is intended to support primarily pedestrian loading.

•   Wood is typically pressure-treated to resist decay, and all metal fasteners should be corrosion-resistant.

•   This detail is not designed for cold climates. Wood stakes may be subject to heaving in both clay soils and extreme frost conditions. Steel stakes are preferred under these conditions.

•   Wood edging requires only minimal maintenance, but it provides a relatively short term of service due to decay.

•   It is recommended that recycled and regionally available materials and products be given high priority in determining final design and specifications.

Installation Cost (per Linear Foot)

LOW   HIGH

$6.82

Maintenance

LOW   HIGH

Drainage Inlets

FRAME AND GRATE

FINISH GRADE, SLOPE TO DRAIN

MORTAR

2-3 COURSES OF BRICK

OPTIONAL MORTAR COAT

200mm (8")
CONC. MASONRY UNITS

200mm (8") AGG. FILL

VARIES 600mm (2'-0") MIN.

CONCRETE FILL, 1:5 SLOPE

OUTLET PIPE

CONC. BASE, REINF. AS REQ'D

PREPARED SUBGRADE

VARIES (FROST DEPTH MIN.)

100 (4")

200 (8")

APPLICATION

LIGHT   MED.   HEAVY

CLIMATE

ARID   HUMID   TEMP.   COLD

SUBGRADE

PERM.   CLAY   ROOF

CSI MASTERFORMAT: 02630
DRAWING FILE: DRN12-02

• This drawing is a template for preliminary design only, and is not intended for bid purposes. It is subject to modification based on design calculations, local practices, and all applicable codes and regulations.

• This concrete masonry drain inlet detail is rated as medium-duty due to bearing capacity and diameter. It is typically found in parks, small courtyards, and garden settings.

• Grate is usually set with mortar on masonry leveling shims typically consisting of three courses of brick. Mortar collar seals grate to masonry. Collar should be smooth due to contact with adjacent soil or backfill, especially in frost/thaw climates. In such conditions, smooth mortar parging on the outside may be indicated.

• Basin rests on a concrete footing which usually bears on subgrade below frost, or deep enough to allow sufficient pipe cover. In warmer climates, aggregate subbase may be used to level subgrade for footing.

• Pipe openings are typically site built and sealed with mortar. Backfill with aggregate material to insure against settlement.

• Cost note: Typically calculated by diameter, material, and depth.

• It is recommended that recycled and regionally available materials and products be given high priority in determining final design and specifications.

Installation Cost (per Unit)

LOW ▪▪▪▪▪▪▪▪▪ HIGH

$1545.00

Maintenance

LOW ▪▪▪▪▪▪▪ HIGH

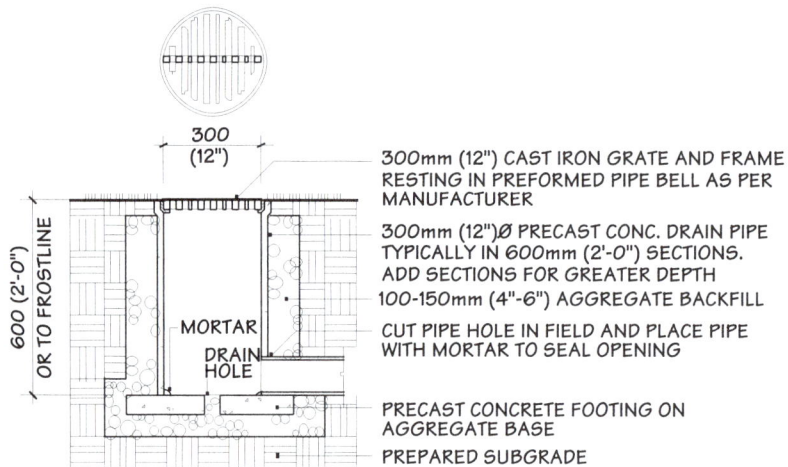

300
(12")

600 (2'-0")
OR TO FROSTLINE

MORTAR
DRAIN HOLE

300mm (12") CAST IRON GRATE AND FRAME RESTING IN PREFORMED PIPE BELL AS PER MANUFACTURER

300mm (12")Ø PRECAST CONC. DRAIN PIPE TYPICALLY IN 600mm (2'-0") SECTIONS. ADD SECTIONS FOR GREATER DEPTH

100-150mm (4"-6") AGGREGATE BACKFILL

CUT PIPE HOLE IN FIELD AND PLACE PIPE WITH MORTAR TO SEAL OPENING

PRECAST CONCRETE FOOTING ON AGGREGATE BASE

PREPARED SUBGRADE

APPLICATION

CLIMATE

SUBGRADE

CSI MASTERFORMAT: 02630
DRAWING FILE: DRN12-05

• This drawing is a template for preliminary design only, and is not intended for bid purposes. It is subject to modification based on design calculations, local practices, and all applicable codes and regulations.

• This precast concrete pipe inlet detail is rated as light-duty due to drain capacity and material. It is typically found in small paved courts, yards, or patios associated with residential, park, or garden settings.

• Precast concrete drain pipe is placed on masonry unit leveling blocks and aggregate base. Drain pipe is cut-in and mortared to pipe on-site. Extension units may be added to achieve desired depth. In cold climates, base and drain pipe must be below frost.

• Grates range from plastic to cast iron.

• Alternate plastic bell pipe can be substituted using proprietary rim and grate combinations. For heavier loading, a concrete slab base may be required.

• It is recommended that recycled and regionally available materials and products be given high priority in determining final design and specifications.

Installation Cost (per Unit)

LOW   HIGH

$500.00

Maintenance

LOW   HIGH

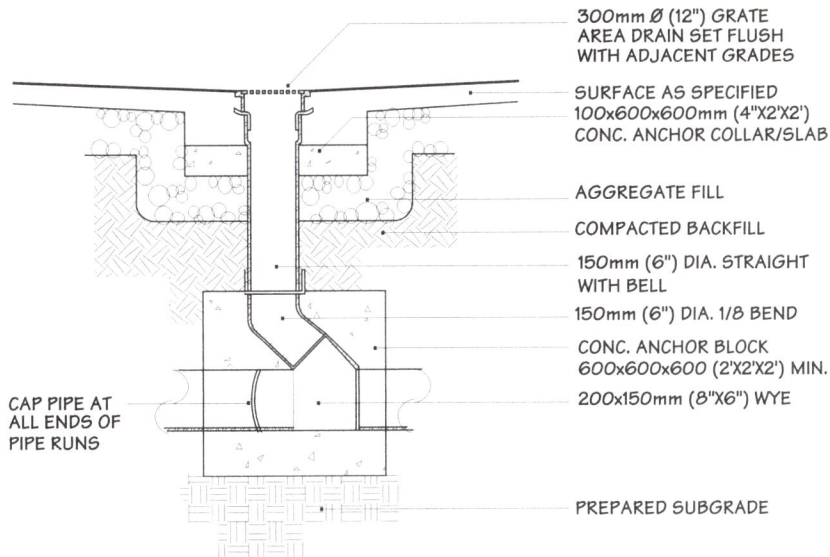

300mm Ø (12") GRATE
AREA DRAIN SET FLUSH
WITH ADJACENT GRADES

SURFACE AS SPECIFIED
100x600x600mm (4"X2'X2')
CONC. ANCHOR COLLAR/SLAB

AGGREGATE FILL

COMPACTED BACKFILL

150mm (6") DIA. STRAIGHT
WITH BELL

150mm (6") DIA. 1/8 BEND

CONC. ANCHOR BLOCK
600x600x600 (2'X2'X2') MIN.

200x150mm (8"X6") WYE

CAP PIPE AT
ALL ENDS OF
PIPE RUNS

PREPARED SUBGRADE

APPLICATION

CLIMATE

SUBGRADE

CSI MASTERFORMAT: 02630
DRAWING FILE: DRN18-01

• This drawing is a template for preliminary design only, and is not intended for bid purposes. It is subject to modification based on design calculations, local practices, and all applicable codes and regulations.

• This small area drain detail is rated as medium-duty due to bearing capacity and concrete reinforcement. It is typically found in small paved courts, yards, or patios associated with residential, park, or garden settings. It will bear light vehicular loading.

• Grate frame is usually cast into finish concrete. This detail performs better in warmer climates where extreme frost is absent. In cold climates, surrounding concrete should be coated and sealed with liquid topping to prevent degradation due to snow melting chemicals and abrasive snow clearing practices. If placed in lawn, a finish ring of concrete is recommended for best results.

• Drain rests on an aggregate base upon which a concrete collar pipe support is placed. Pipe is joined to lateral pipe and encased in concrete all around to act as a bearing base for surface grate.

• If designed for temperate or cold climates, air-entrained concrete is typically recommended due to freezing/thawing action.

• Cost note: Typically calculated by width, material, and length.

• It is recommended that recycled and regionally available materials and products be given high priority in determining final design and specifications.

Installation Cost (per Unit)

LOW   HIGH

$300.00

Maintenance

LOW   HIGH

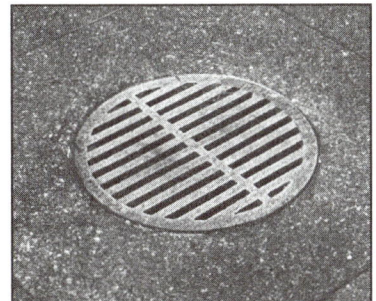

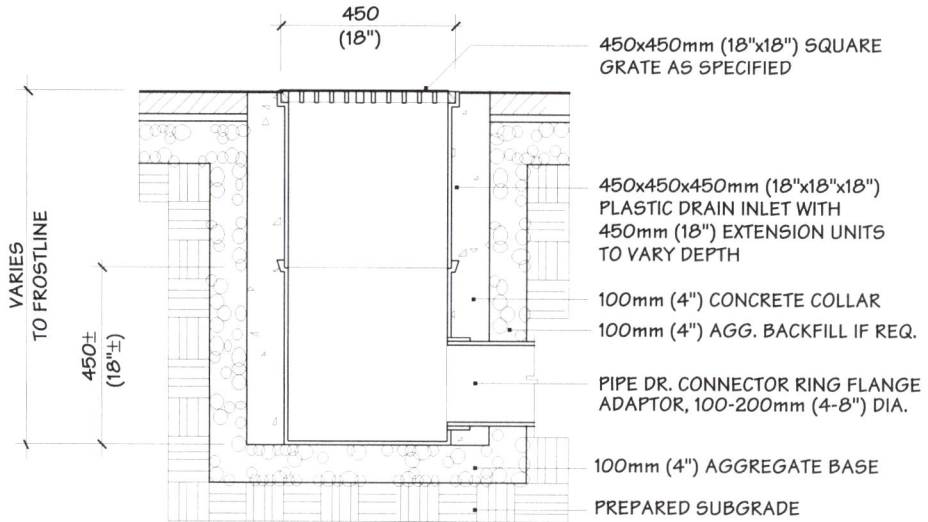

450
(18")

450x450mm (18"x18") SQUARE
GRATE AS SPECIFIED

450x450x450mm (18"x18"x18")
PLASTIC DRAIN INLET WITH
450mm (18") EXTENSION UNITS
TO VARY DEPTH

100mm (4") CONCRETE COLLAR
100mm (4") AGG. BACKFILL IF REQ.

PIPE DR. CONNECTOR RING FLANGE
ADAPTOR, 100-200mm (4-8") DIA.

100mm (4") AGGREGATE BASE

PREPARED SUBGRADE

VARIES
TO FROSTLINE

450±
(18"±)

APPLICATION

CLIMATE

SUBGRADE

CSI MASTERFORMAT: 02630
DRAWING FILE: DRN18-03

• This drawing is a template for preliminary design only, and is not intended for bid purposes. It is subject to modification based on design calculations, local practices, and all applicable codes and regulations.

• This plastic drain inlet in concrete detail is rated as medium-duty due to drain capacity and material. It is typically found in small paved courts, yards, or patios associated with residential, park, or garden settings.

• Plastic inlet boxes are installed on aggregate base and connected to drain pipe through universal pipe adapter rings. Extension units may be added to achieve desired depth. A concrete collar reinforces this drain and allows for use in all climates. In cold climates, concrete collar must be smooth to avoid frost uplift, and drain pipe must be below frost.

• Grates range from plastic to cast iron.

• As shown, this detail is best for warm climates.

• It is recommended that recycled and regionally available materials and products be given high priority in determining final design and specifications.

Installation Cost (per Unit)

LOW   HIGH

$300.00

Maintenance

LOW   HIGH

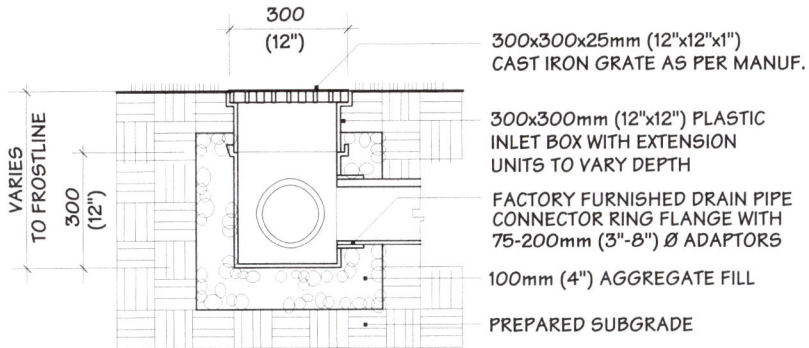

300
(12")

300x300x25mm (12"x12"x1")
CAST IRON GRATE AS PER MANUF.

300x300mm (12"x12") PLASTIC
INLET BOX WITH EXTENSION
UNITS TO VARY DEPTH

FACTORY FURNISHED DRAIN PIPE
CONNECTOR RING FLANGE WITH
75-200mm (3"-8") Ø ADAPTORS

100mm (4") AGGREGATE FILL

PREPARED SUBGRADE

VARIES TO FROSTLINE

300 (12")

APPLICATION

LIGHT   MED.   HEAVY

CLIMATE

ARID   HUMID   TEMP.   COLD

SUBGRADE

PERM.   CLAY   ROOF

CSI MASTERFORMAT: 02630
DRAWING FILE: DRN18-02

• This drawing is a template for preliminary design only, and is not intended for bid purposes. It is subject to modification based on design calculations, local practices, and all applicable codes and regulations.

• This plastic drain inlet in turf detail is rated as light-duty due to drain capacity and material. It is typically found in small paved courts, yards, or patios associated with residential, park, or garden settings.

• Plastic inlet boxes are installed on aggregate base and connected to drain pipe through universal pipe adapter rings. Extension units may be added to achieve desired depth.

• Grates range from plastic to cast iron.

• As shown, this detail is best for warm climates.

• It is recommended that recycled and regionally available materials and products be given high priority in determining final design and specifications.

Installation Cost (per Unit)

LOW   HIGH

$200.00

Maintenance

LOW   HIGH

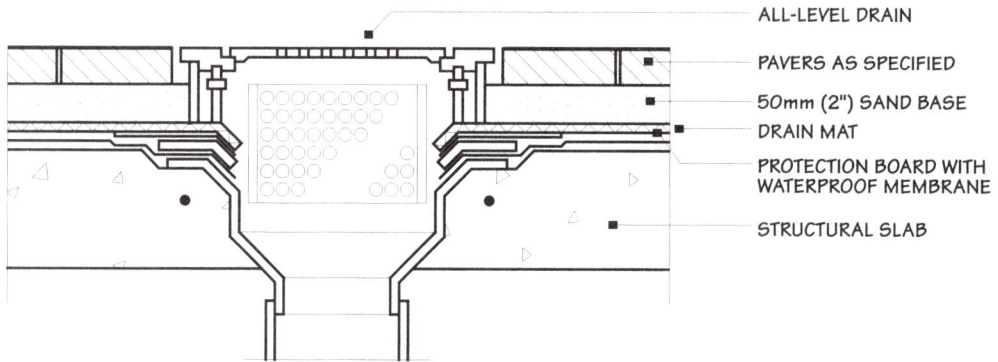

ALL-LEVEL DRAIN

PAVERS AS SPECIFIED

50mm (2") SAND BASE

DRAIN MAT

PROTECTION BOARD WITH
WATERPROOF MEMBRANE

STRUCTURAL SLAB

APPLICATION

CLIMATE

SUBGRADE

CSI MASTERFORMAT: 02630
DRAWING FILE: DRN39-01

• This drawing is a template for preliminary design only, and is not intended for bid purposes. It is subject to modification based on design calculations, local practices, and all applicable codes and regulations.

• This surface drain on structure detail is rated as light-duty due to capacity and diameter. It is typically associated with pavements on structural roof decks.

• Flared casing is cast into structural slab and held into place by integral flanges. A compression ring seals waterproof membrane, side sieves drain lateral infiltration water from drain mats and aggregates, while top grate drains surface water.

• Metal is non-corrosive.

• Cost note: Typically calculated per unit.

• It is recommended that recycled and regionally available materials and products be given high priority in determining final design and specifications.

Installation Cost (per Unit)

LOW   HIGH

$300.00

Maintenance

LOW   HIGH

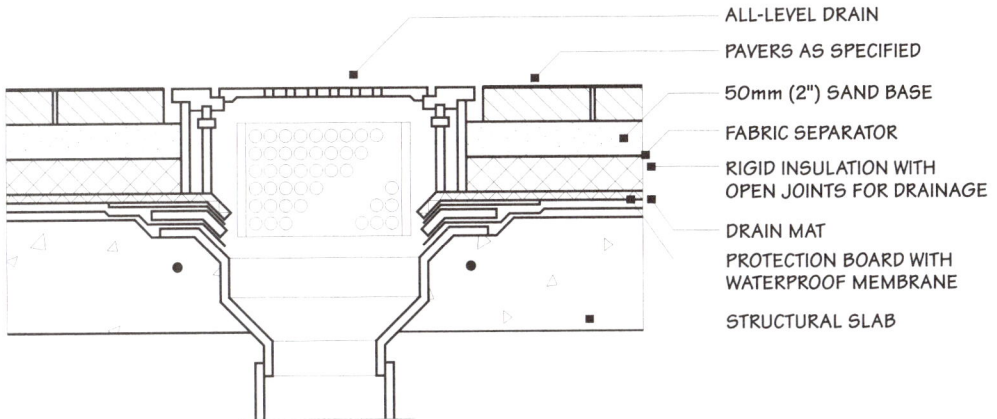

ALL-LEVEL DRAIN

PAVERS AS SPECIFIED

50mm (2") SAND BASE

FABRIC SEPARATOR

RIGID INSULATION WITH
OPEN JOINTS FOR DRAINAGE

DRAIN MAT

PROTECTION BOARD WITH
WATERPROOF MEMBRANE

STRUCTURAL SLAB

APPLICATION

CLIMATE

SUBGRADE

CSI MASTERFORMAT: 02630
DRAWING FILE: DRN39-02

• This drawing is a template for preliminary design only, and is not intended for bid purposes. It is subject to modification based on design calculations, local practices, and all applicable codes and regulations.

• This insulated surface drain on structure detail is rated as medium-duty due to capacity and diameter. It is typically associated with insulated pavements on structural roof decks.

• Flared casing is cast into structural slab and held into place by integral flanges. A compression ring seals waterproof membrane, side sieves drain lateral infiltration water from drain mats and aggregates, while top grate drains surface water.

• Metal is non-corrosive.

• Cost note: Typically calculated per unit.

• It is recommended that recycled and regionally available materials and products be given high priority in determining final design and specifications.

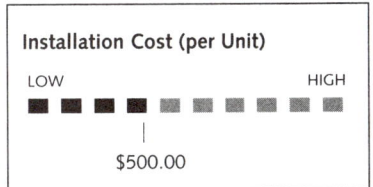

Installation Cost (per Unit)

LOW   HIGH

$500.00

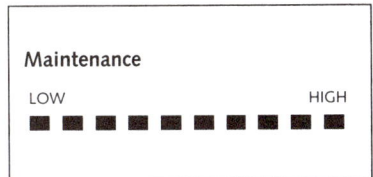

Maintenance

LOW   HIGH

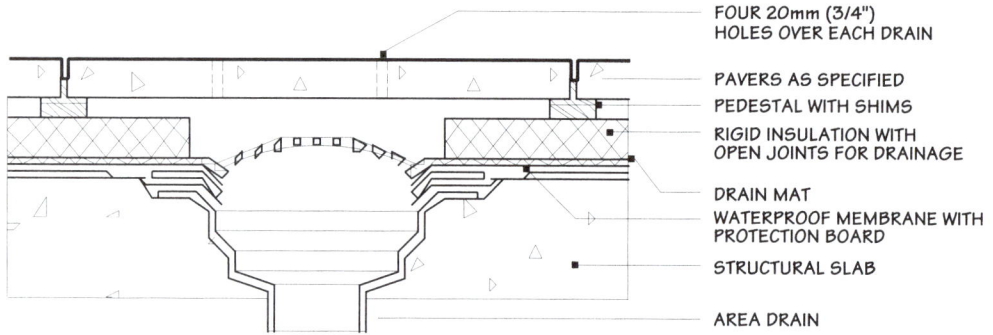

FOUR 20mm (3/4")
HOLES OVER EACH DRAIN

PAVERS AS SPECIFIED

PEDESTAL WITH SHIMS

RIGID INSULATION WITH
OPEN JOINTS FOR DRAINAGE

DRAIN MAT

WATERPROOF MEMBRANE WITH
PROTECTION BOARD

STRUCTURAL SLAB

AREA DRAIN

APPLICATION

CLIMATE

SUBGRADE

CSI MASTERFORMAT: 02630
DRAWING FILE: DRN39-03

• This drawing is a template for preliminary design only, and is not intended for bid purposes. It is subject to modification based on design calculations, local practices, and all applicable codes and regulations.

• This roof drain under suspended pavers on structure detail is rated as light-duty due to capacity and diameter. It is typically associated with suspended pavers on structural roof decks.

• Flared casing is cast into structural slab and held into place by integral flanges. A compression ring seals waterproof membrane, and domed grate strainer drains lateral infiltration water membrane protection board. Suspended paver is usually marked in some fashion to designate location of drain for routine inspection and maintenance.

• Metal is non-corrosive.

• Cost note: Typically calculated per unit.

• It is recommended that recycled and regionally available materials and products be given high priority in determining final design and specifications.

Installation Cost (per Unit)

LOW   HIGH

$300.00

Maintenance

LOW   HIGH

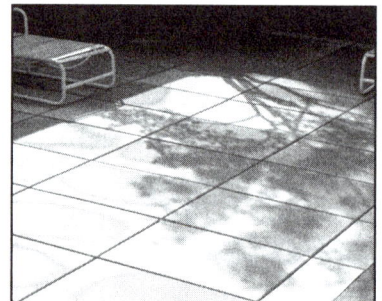

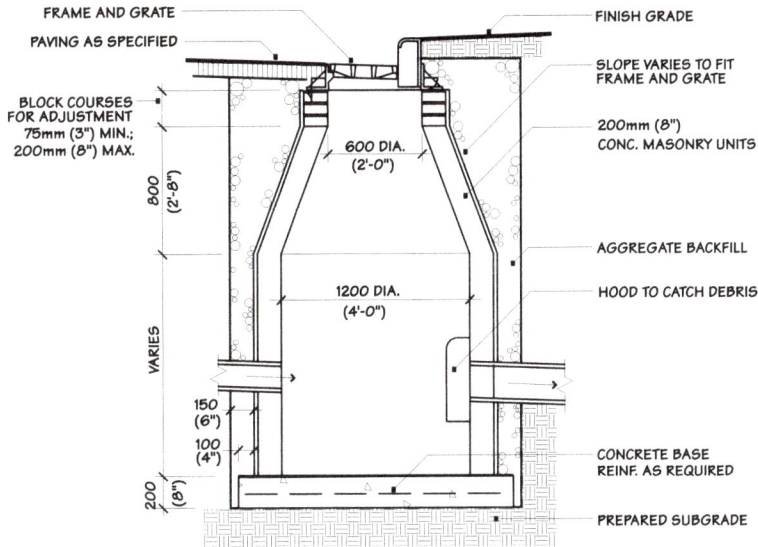

FRAME AND GRATE
PAVING AS SPECIFIED
BLOCK COURSES FOR ADJUSTMENT 75mm (3") MIN.; 200mm (8") MAX.
800 (2'-8")
VARIES
600 DIA. (2'-0")
1200 DIA. (4'-0")
150 (6")
100 (4")
200 (8")

FINISH GRADE
SLOPE VARIES TO FIT FRAME AND GRATE
200mm (8") CONC. MASONRY UNITS
AGGREGATE BACKFILL
HOOD TO CATCH DEBRIS
CONCRETE BASE REINF. AS REQUIRED
PREPARED SUBGRADE

APPLICATION

LIGHT MED. HEAVY

CLIMATE

ARID HUMID TEMP. COLD

SUBGRADE

PERM. CLAY ROOF

CSI MASTERFORMAT: 02630
DRAWING FILE: DRN12-06

• This drawing is a template for preliminary design only, and is not intended for bid purposes. It is subject to modification based on design calculations, local practices, and all applicable codes and regulations.

• This concrete masonry catch basin with cast iron curb grate detail is rated as heavy-duty due to bearing capacity, diameter, and wall thickness. It is typically found in urban streets, highways and large parking areas.

• It is built with concrete radius block and mortar as specified. Reduction cone is created using sloped radius block. In cold climates, outside is often parged to create smooth surface and to lessen adhesion of surrounding frozen soils.

• Grate is usually set with mortar on masonry leveling shims typically consisting of three courses of brick. Concrete collar may be placed around grate after base course of paving has been placed.

• Basin rests on a reinforced concrete footing which usually bears on subgrade below frost, or deep enough to allow sufficient pipe cover. In warmer climates, aggregate subbase may be used to level subgrade for footing.

• Pipe openings are typically site built and sealed with mortar. Backfill with aggregate material to insure against settlement under pavement.

• Cost note: Typically calculated by diameter, material, and depth.

• It is recommended that recycled and regionally available materials and products be given high priority in determining final design and specifications.

Installation Cost (per Unit)

LOW   HIGH

$1600.00

Maintenance

LOW   HIGH

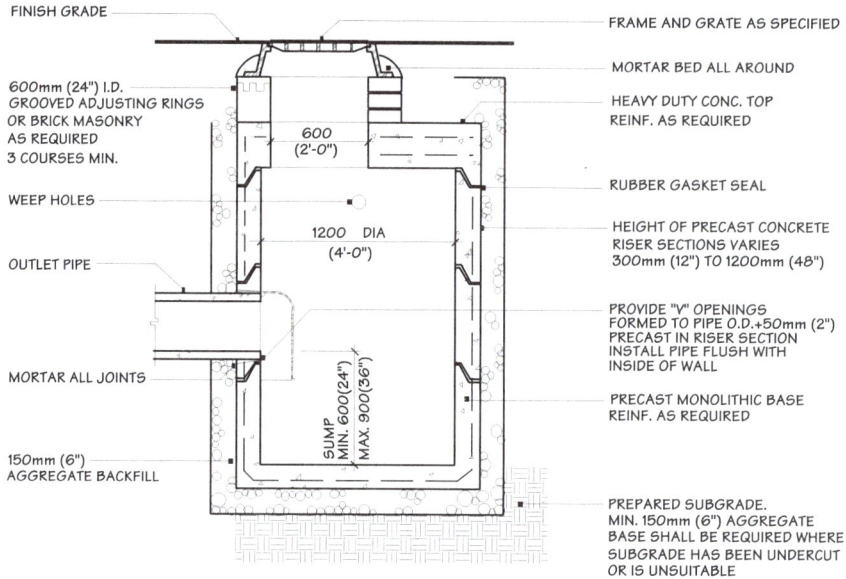

FINISH GRADE

FRAME AND GRATE AS SPECIFIED

MORTAR BED ALL AROUND

600mm (24") I.D.
GROOVED ADJUSTING RINGS
OR BRICK MASONRY
AS REQUIRED
3 COURSES MIN.

HEAVY DUTY CONC. TOP
REINF. AS REQUIRED

600
(2'-0")

WEEP HOLES

RUBBER GASKET SEAL

1200   DIA
(4'-0")

HEIGHT OF PRECAST CONCRETE
RISER SECTIONS VARIES
300mm (12") TO 1200mm (48")

OUTLET PIPE

PROVIDE "V" OPENINGS
FORMED TO PIPE O.D.+50mm (2")
PRECAST IN RISER SECTION
INSTALL PIPE FLUSH WITH
INSIDE OF WALL

MORTAR ALL JOINTS

SUMP MIN. 600(24")
MAX. 900(36")

PRECAST MONOLITHIC BASE
REINF. AS REQUIRED

150mm (6")
AGGREGATE BACKFILL

PREPARED SUBGRADE.
MIN. 150mm (6") AGGREGATE
BASE SHALL BE REQUIRED WHERE
SUBGRADE HAS BEEN UNDERCUT
OR IS UNSUITABLE

APPLICATION

CLIMATE

SUBGRADE

CSI MASTERFORMAT: 02630
DRAWING FILE: DRN12-03

• This drawing is a template for preliminary design only, and is not intended for bid purposes. It is subject to modification based on design calculations, local practices, and all applicable codes and regulations.

• This precast concrete catch basin detail is rated as heavy-duty due to bearing capacity, diameter, and wall thickness. It is typically found in urban streets, highways and large parking areas. It often contains a metal hood to filter debris, and a sump to settle suspended particles.

• Grate is usually set with mortar on masonry leveling shims, typically consisting of three courses of brick. Concrete collar may be placed around grate after base course of paving has been placed.

• Basin rests on a reinforced concrete footing which usually bears on subgrade below frost, or deep enough to allow sufficient pipe cover. In warmer climates, aggregate subbase

may be used to level subgrade for footing (often integral with first base ring).

• Pipe openings are typically factory cast with beveled forms to allow mortar to seal pipe into basin. Backfill with aggregate material to insure against settlement under pavement. Rings come in various 300 mm (12") increments.

• Cost note: Typically calculated by diameter, material, and depth.

• It is recommended that recycled and regionally available materials and products be given high priority in determining final design and specifications.

Installation Cost (per Unit)

LOW   HIGH

$1500.00

Maintenance

LOW   HIGH

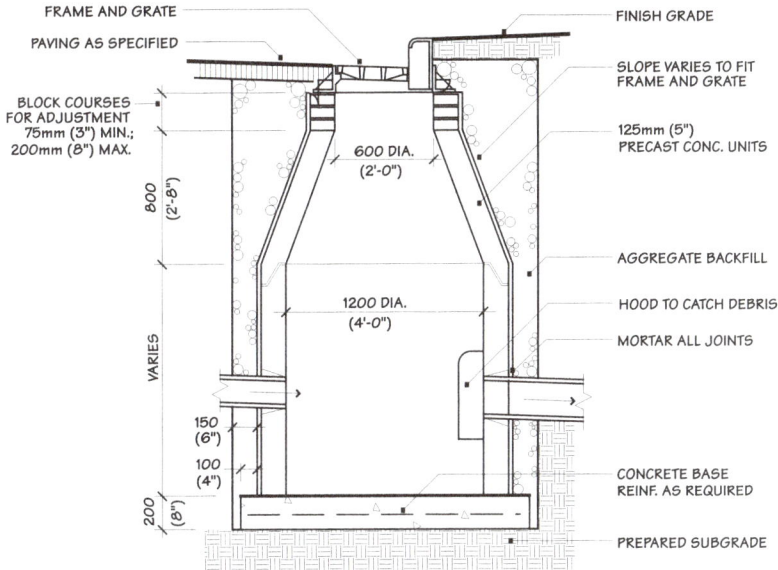

FRAME AND GRATE

PAVING AS SPECIFIED

BLOCK COURSES
FOR ADJUSTMENT
75mm (3") MIN.;
200mm (8") MAX.

800 (2'-8")

VARIES

600 DIA.
(2'-0")

1200 DIA.
(4'-0")

150 (6")

100 (4")

200 (8")

FINISH GRADE

SLOPE VARIES TO FIT
FRAME AND GRATE

125mm (5")
PRECAST CONC. UNITS

AGGREGATE BACKFILL

HOOD TO CATCH DEBRIS

MORTAR ALL JOINTS

CONCRETE BASE
REINF. AS REQUIRED

PREPARED SUBGRADE

APPLICATION

CLIMATE

SUBGRADE

CSI MASTERFORMAT: 02630
DRAWING FILE: DRN12-01

• This drawing is a template for preliminary design only, and is not intended for bid purposes. It is subject to modification based on design calculations, local practices, and all applicable codes and regulations.

• This precast concrete catch basin with cast iron curb grate detail is rated as heavy-duty due to bearing capacity, diameter, and wall thickness. It is typically found in urban streets, highways and large parking areas.

• Grate is usually set with mortar on masonry leveling shims typically consisting of three courses of brick. Concrete collar may be placed around grate after base course of paving has been placed.

• Basin rests on a reinforced concrete footing which usually bears on subgrade below frost, or deep enough to allow sufficient pipe cover. In warmer climates, aggregate subbase may be used to level subgrade for footing.

• Pipe openings are typically factory cast with beveled forms to allow mortar to seal

pipe into basin. Backfill with aggregate material to insure against settlement under pavement. Rings come in various 300 mm (12") increments.

• Cost note: Typically calculated by diameter, material, and depth.

• It is recommended that recycled and regionally available materials and products be given high priority in determining final design and specifications.

Installation Cost (per Unit)

LOW   HIGH

$1535.00

Maintenance

LOW   HIGH

FINISH GRADE

FRAME AND GRATE AS SPECIFIED

MORTAR BED ALL AROUND

600mm (24") I.D.
GROOVED ADJUSTING RINGS
OR BRICK MASONRY
AS REQUIRED
3 COURSES MIN.

SLAB TOP OR 900mm (3'-0")
ECCENTRIC CONE AS REQUIRED

600
(2'-0")

STEPS - 300mm
(12") O.C.

RUBBER GASKET SEAL

HEIGHT OF PRECAST
CONC. RISER SECTIONS
VARIES 300mm (12")
TO 1200mm (48")

1200   DIA
(4'-0")

OUTLET PIPE

PROVIDE "V" OPENINGS
FORMED TO PIPE O.D.+50mm (2")
PRECAST IN RISER SECTION
INSTALL PIPE FLUSH WITH
INSIDE OF WALL

25 (1")
WASH

PRECAST MONOLITHIC BASE
REINF. AS REQUIRED

MORTAR ALL JOINTS

CEMENT CONC. (CLASS "A")
PAVED INVERT & BENCH

150mm (6")
AGGREGATE BACKFILL

PREPARED SUBGRADE.
MIN. 150mm (6") AGGREGATE
BASE SHALL BE REQUIRED WHERE
SUBGRADE HAS BEEN UNDERCUT
OR IS UNSUITABLE

APPLICATION

LIGHT   MED.   HEAVY

CLIMATE

ARID   HUMID   TEMP.   COLD

SUBGRADE

PERM.   CLAY   ROCK

CSI MASTERFORMAT: 02630
DRAWING FILE: DRN12-04

• This drawing is a template for preliminary design only, and is not intended for bid purposes. It is subject to modification based on design calculations, local practices, and all applicable codes and regulations.

• This precast concrete drain manhole detail is rated as heavy-duty due to bearing capacity, diameter, and wall thickness. It is typically found in urban streets, highways and large parking areas. It contains metal steps for clean-out access.

• Grate is usually set with mortar on masonry leveling shims, typically consisting of three courses of brick. Concrete collar may be placed around grate after base course of paving has been placed.

• Basin rests on a reinforced concrete footing which usually bears on subgrade below frost, or deep enough to allow sufficient pipe cover. In warmer climates, aggregate subbase may be used to level subgrade for footing (often integral with the first base ring).

• Pipe openings are typically factory cast with beveled forms to allow mortar to seal pipe into basin. Backfill with aggregate material to insure against settlement under pavement. Rings come in various 300 mm (12") increments.

• Cost note: Typically calculated by diameter, material, and depth.

• It is recommended that recycled and regionally available materials and products be given high priority in determining final design and specifications.

Installation Cost (per Unit)

LOW   HIGH

$1600.00

Maintenance

LOW   HIGH

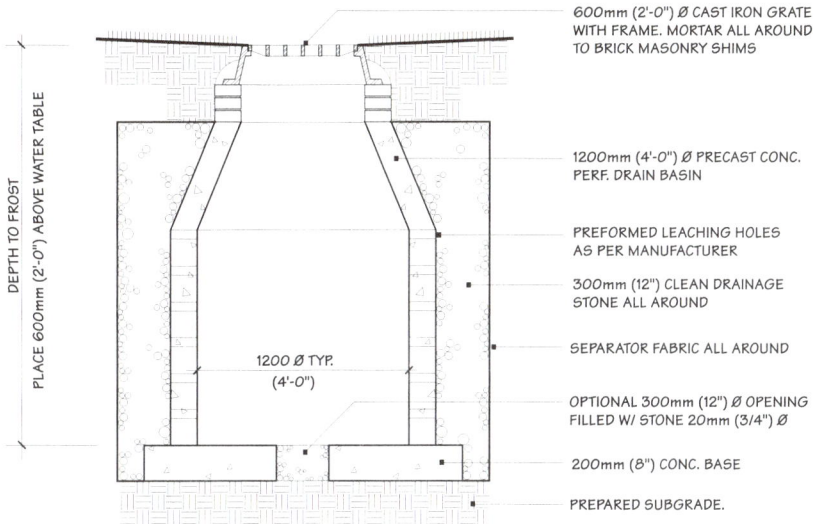

600mm (2'-0") Ø CAST IRON GRATE WITH FRAME. MORTAR ALL AROUND TO BRICK MASONRY SHIMS

1200mm (4'-0") Ø PRECAST CONC. PERF. DRAIN BASIN

PREFORMED LEACHING HOLES AS PER MANUFACTURER

300mm (12") CLEAN DRAINAGE STONE ALL AROUND

SEPARATOR FABRIC ALL AROUND

OPTIONAL 300mm (12") Ø OPENING FILLED W/ STONE 20mm (3/4") Ø

200mm (8") CONC. BASE

PREPARED SUBGRADE.

DEPTH TO FROST
PLACE 600mm (2'-0") ABOVE WATER TABLE

1200 Ø TYP. (4'-0")

APPLICATION

CLIMATE

SUBGRADE

CSI MASTERFORMAT: 02630
DRAWING FILE: DRN12-08

•   This drawing is a template for preliminary design only, and is not intended for bid purposes. It is subject to modification based on design calculations, local practices, and all applicable codes and regulations.

•   This precast concrete infiltration basin detail is rated as medium-duty due to drain capacity. It is typically found in lawns and adjacent to parking areas associated with residential, park, or garden settings.

•   Precast concrete perforated rings are placed on concrete base. Extension units may be added to achieve desired depth. In cold climates, base must be below frost. Excavated area is lined with fabric separator and backfilled with free draining stone.

•   Grates are typically cast iron.

•   Soil texture and local runoff data must be determined to calculate capacity.

•   It is recommended that recycled and regionally available materials and products be given high priority in determining final design and specifications.

Installation Cost (per Unit)

LOW   HIGH

$1500.00

Maintenance

LOW   HIGH

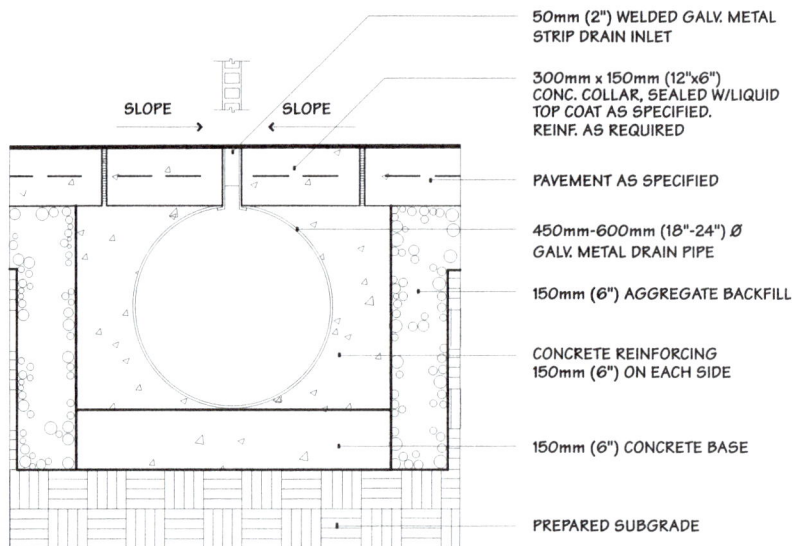

SLOPE

SLOPE

50mm (2") WELDED GALV. METAL
STRIP DRAIN INLET

300mm x 150mm (12"x6")
CONC. COLLAR, SEALED W/LIQUID
TOP COAT AS SPECIFIED.
REINF. AS REQUIRED

PAVEMENT AS SPECIFIED

450mm-600mm (18"-24") Ø
GALV. METAL DRAIN PIPE

150mm (6") AGGREGATE BACKFILL

CONCRETE REINFORCING
150mm (6") ON EACH SIDE

150mm (6") CONCRETE BASE

PREPARED SUBGRADE

APPLICATION

CLIMATE

SUBGRADE

CSI MASTERFORMAT: 02630
DRAWING FILE: DRN22-02

• This drawing is a template for preliminary design only, and is not intended for bid purposes. It is subject to modification based on design calculations, local practices, and all applicable codes and regulations.

• This galvanized metal trench drain detail is rated as heavy-duty due to bearing capacity and diameter. It is typically found at the edge of vehicular parking areas.

• Grate frame is usually cast into concrete. This detail performs better in warmer climates where extreme frost is absent. In cold climates, surrounding concrete should be coated and sealed with liquid topping to prevent degradation due to snow melting chemicals and abrasive snow clearing practices. Embedded heating cables are another alternative to add to the length of service.

• Drain rests on a concrete base of sufficient depth to bear the expected loads and to bear on frost-free subgrade. Metal pipe is

encased in concrete, and inlet strip is encased in a concrete collar.

• Concrete design must accommodate movement of materials by providing adequate expansion and control joints, particularly in regions of extreme temperature fluctuations. If designed for temperate or cold climates, air-entrained concrete is typically recommended due to freezing/thawing action.

• Reinforcing practices vary widely by region. Local codes and practices should be consulted prior to specifying any type of reinforcing.

• Cost note: Typically calculated by width, material, and length.

• It is recommended that recycled and regionally available materials and products be given high priority in determining final design and specifications.

Installation Cost (per Unit)

LOW   HIGH

$120.00

Maintenance

LOW   HIGH

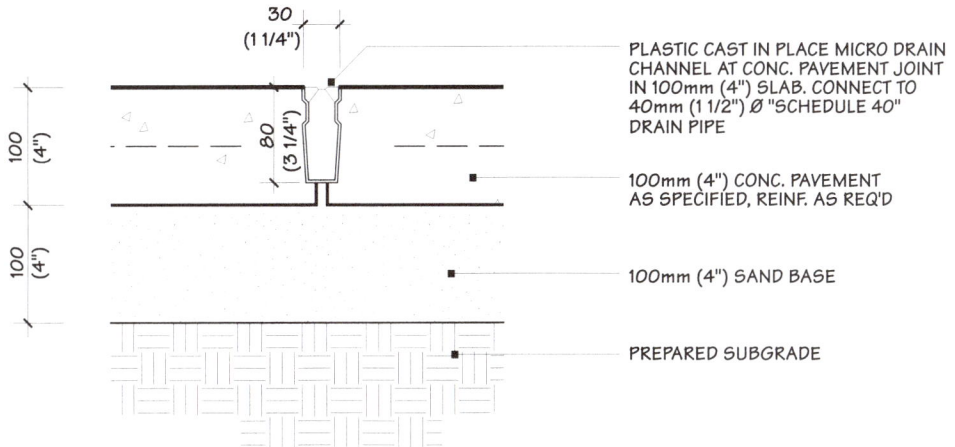

30
(1 1/4")

100 (4")

80 (3 1/4")

100 (4")

PLASTIC CAST IN PLACE MICRO DRAIN CHANNEL AT CONC. PAVEMENT JOINT IN 100mm (4") SLAB. CONNECT TO 40mm (1 1/2") Ø "SCHEDULE 40" DRAIN PIPE

100mm (4") CONC. PAVEMENT AS SPECIFIED, REINF. AS REQ'D

100mm (4") SAND BASE

PREPARED SUBGRADE

APPLICATION

CLIMATE

SUBGRADE

CSI MASTERFORMAT: 02630
DRAWING FILE: DRN28-03

• This drawing is a template for preliminary design only, and is not intended for bid purposes. It is subject to modification based on design calculations, local practices, and all applicable codes and regulations.

• This polymer stip drain detail is rated as light-duty due to bearing capacity and depth. It is typically found at the top and bottom of ramps, and at the edge of single plane pavements such as pool decks.

• This detail performs better in warmer climates where extreme frost is absent. In cold climates, surrounding concrete should be coated and sealed with liquid topping to prevent degradation due to snow melting chemicals and abrasive snow clearing practices. Embedded heating cables are another alternative to add to the length of service.

• Drain is embedded in concrete surround and held into position by attaching to the form of the initial pavement slab. Concrete is

placed on a sand or aggregate base of sufficient depth to bear the expected loads.

• Pipe openings are typically factory supplied in a number of configurations. Their are numerous types of polymer trench drains which vary in depth and width. Most snap together.

• Concrete design must accommodate movement of materials by providing adequate expansion and control joints, particularly in regions of extreme temperature fluctuations. If designed for temperate or cold climates, air-entrained concrete is typically recommended due to freezing/thawing action.

• Reinforcing practices vary widely by region. Local codes and practices should be consulted prior to specifying any type of reinforcing.

• Cost note: Typically calculated by width, material, and length.

• It is recommended that recycled and regionally available materials and products be given high priority in determining final design and specifications.

Installation Cost (per Unit)

LOW   HIGH

$14.00

Maintenance

LOW   HIGH

CENTER OF TRENCH DRAIN
SHALL BE CENTERLINE OF SWALE

150mm (6") AMENDED TOPSOIL

50mm (2") SAND BASE

FABRIC SEPARATOR
LINING FOR ENTIRE TRENCH
OVERLAP 300mm (12") MIN.
AT TOP OF TRENCH

WASHED STONE
AGGREGATE
15-20mm (1/2"-3/4") Ø

PERFORATED 100mm (4")
WRAPPED PVC. PIPE

PREPARED SUBGRADE

DEPTH BY SOIL POROSITY
OR BELOW FROST

300-450
(12"-18")

APPLICATION

LIGHT | MED. | HEAVY

CLIMATE

ARID | HUMID | TEMP. | COLD

SUBGRADE

PERM. | CLAY | ROOF

CSI MASTERFORMAT: 02620
DRAWING FILE: DRN28-01

• This drawing is a template for preliminary design only, and is not intended for bid purposes. It is subject to modification based on design calculations, local practices, and all applicable codes and regulations.

• This perforated pipe curtain drain detail is rated as light-duty due to its volume and infiltration rate characteristics, and is typically found in residential, park, institutional, and garden settings. It is found in all climate zones.

• The trench is lined with fabric separator and filled with a base layer of clean stone aggregate, perforated pipe, more aggregate, and finally topped with fabric over-fold and sand filter.

• If pipe is collecting water, place pipe at bottom of trench.

• Perforated pipe should be set below frost and set to discharge into stream, pond, or drainage structure. This is an effective

means to delay the impact of site runoff, or of gathering water from saturated soils.

• It is recommended that recycled and regionally available materials and products be given high priority in determining final design and specifications.

Installation Cost (per Unit)

LOW   HIGH

$15.00

Maintenance

LOW   HIGH

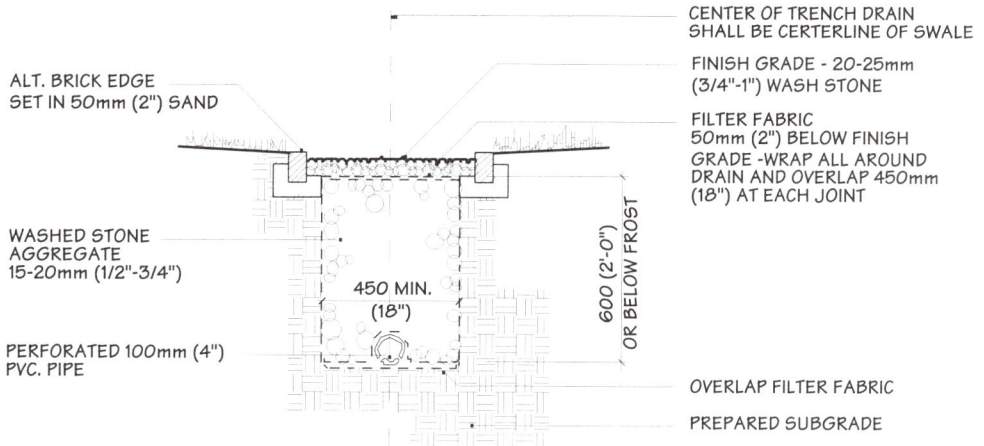

ALT. BRICK EDGE
SET IN 50mm (2") SAND

WASHED STONE
AGGREGATE
15-20mm (1/2"-3/4")

PERFORATED 100mm (4")
PVC. PIPE

450 MIN.
(18")

CENTER OF TRENCH DRAIN
SHALL BE CERTERLINE OF SWALE

FINISH GRADE - 20-25mm
(3/4"-1") WASH STONE

FILTER FABRIC
50mm (2") BELOW FINISH
GRADE -WRAP ALL AROUND
DRAIN AND OVERLAP 450mm
(18") AT EACH JOINT

600 (2'-0")
OR BELOW FROST

OVERLAP FILTER FABRIC

PREPARED SUBGRADE

APPLICATION

CLIMATE

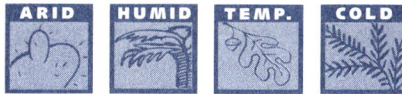

SUBGRADE

CSI MASTERFORMAT: 02620
DRAWING FILE: DRN27-01

• This drawing is a template for preliminary design only, and is not intended for bid purposes. It is subject to modification based on design calculations, local practices, and all applicable codes and regulations.

• This stone lined trench with infiltration drain is rated as medium-duty due to its volume and infiltration rate characteristics, and is typically found in residential, urban park, institutional, and commercial settings.

• Stone is placed, on an aggregate base over a fabric separator, which binds aggregate base and inhibits downward migration of fines into the subdrain trench. The aggregate is edged with brick or stone to serve as a mowing strip. The trench is lined with fabric separator to protect pipe.

• If pipe is collecting water, place pipe at bottom of trench. If dispersing water, place pipe in the middle of the trench.

• It is found in all climate zones, but requires well drained subsoil to be effective as a dispersal device.

• Perforated pipe should be set below frost and set to discharge into stream, pond, or drainage structure. This is an effective means to delay the impact of site runoff, or of gathering water from saturated soils.

• It is recommended that recycled and regionally available materials and products be given high priority in determining final design and specifications.

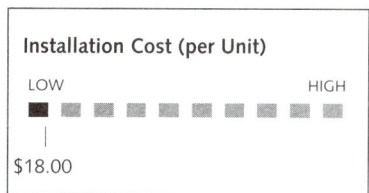

Installation Cost (per Unit)

LOW   HIGH

$18.00

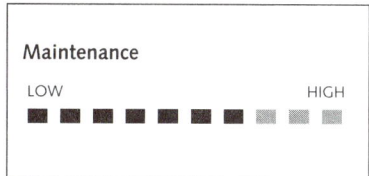

Maintenance

LOW   HIGH

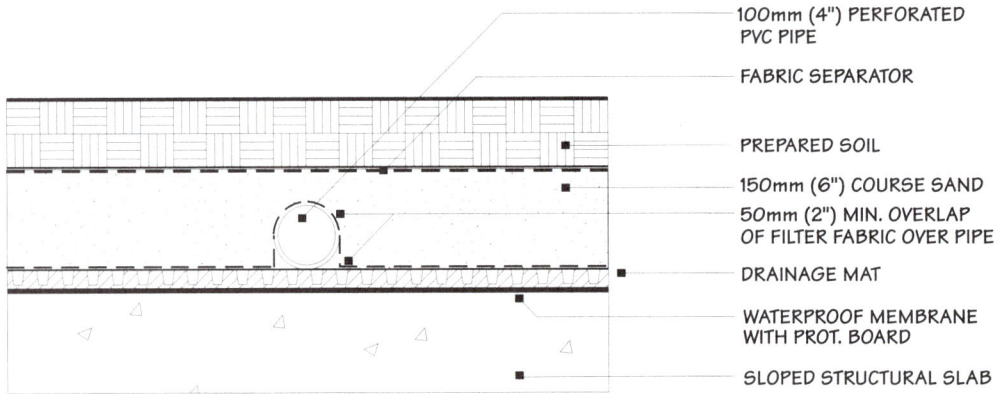

100mm (4") PERFORATED
PVC PIPE

FABRIC SEPARATOR

PREPARED SOIL

150mm (6") COURSE SAND

50mm (2") MIN. OVERLAP
OF FILTER FABRIC OVER PIPE

DRAINAGE MAT

WATERPROOF MEMBRANE
WITH PROT. BOARD

SLOPED STRUCTURAL SLAB

APPLICATION

CLIMATE

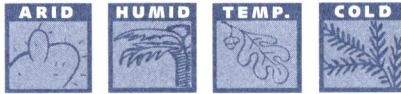

SUBGRADE

CSI MASTERFORMAT: 02630
DRAWING FILE: DRN39-04

• This drawing is a template for preliminary design only, and is not intended for bid purposes. It is subject to modification based on design calculations, local practices, and all applicable codes and regulations.

• This perforated pipe drain on structure detail is rated as light-duty due to capacity, loading, and diameter. It is typically associated with draining planting areas on structural roof decks.

• Perforated pipe rests on sloping drain mat within a free-draining aggregate under augmented planting soil and fabric separator.• Pipe may be integrally wrapped or covered on-site with fabric separator to prevent clogging.

• It is recommended that recycled and regionally available materials and products be given high priority in determining final design and specifications.

Installation Cost (per Unit)

LOW   HIGH

|

$3.75

Maintenance

LOW   HIGH

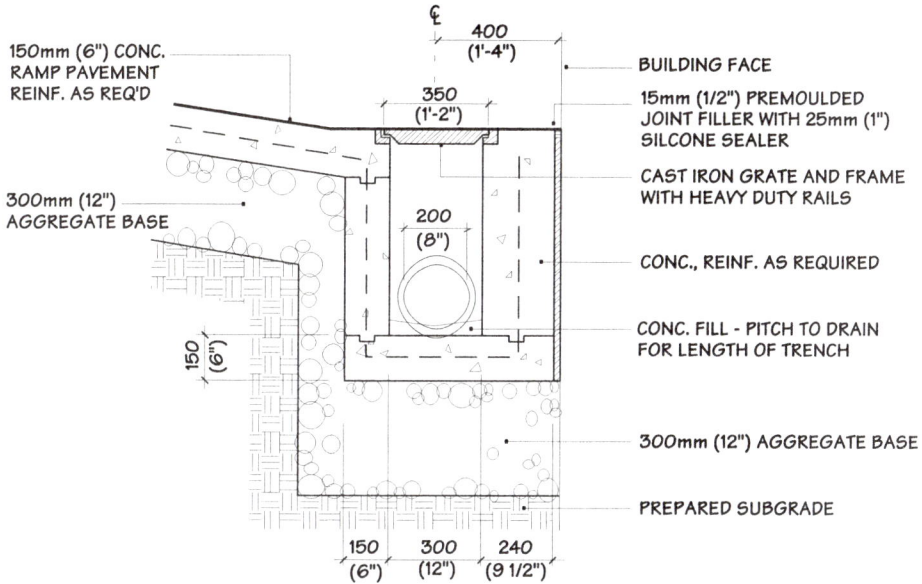

150mm (6") CONC.
RAMP PAVEMENT
REINF. AS REQ'D

300mm (12")
AGGREGATE BASE

400 (1'-4")

350 (1'-2")

200 (8")

150 (6")

150 (6")   300 (12")   240 (9 1/2")

BUILDING FACE

15mm (1/2") PREMOULDED
JOINT FILLER WITH 25mm (1")
SILCONE SEALER

CAST IRON GRATE AND FRAME
WITH HEAVY DUTY RAILS

CONC., REINF. AS REQUIRED

CONC. FILL - PITCH TO DRAIN
FOR LENGTH OF TRENCH

300mm (12") AGGREGATE BASE

PREPARED SUBGRADE

APPLICATION

CLIMATE

SUBGRADE

CSI MASTERFORMAT: 02630
DRAWING FILE: DRN22-01

• This drawing is a template for preliminary design only, and is not intended for bid purposes. It is subject to modification based on design calculations, local practices, and all applicable codes and regulations.

• This concrete trench drain with cast iron grate detail is rated as heavy-duty due to bearing capacity and diameter. It is typically found at the top and bottom of vehicular ramps, especially at loading docks and service door openings.

• Grate frame is usually cast into concrete. This detail performs better in warmer climates where extreme frost is absent. In cold climates, surrounding concrete should be coated and sealed with liquid topping to prevent degradation due to snow melting chemicals and abrasive snow clearing practices. Embedded heating cables are another alternative to add to the length of service.

• Drain rests on an aggregate base of sufficient depth to bear the expected loads and

to bear on frost-free subgrade. Aggregate is typically applied in two lifts.

• Pipe openings are typically site built and sealed with mortar. Backfill with aggregate material to insure against settlement.

• Concrete design must accommodate movement of materials by providing adequate expansion and control joints, particularly in regions of extreme temperature fluctuations. If designed for temperate or cold climates, air-entrained concrete is typically recommended due to freezing/thawing action.

• Reinforcing practices vary widely by region. Local codes and practices should be consulted prior to specifying any type of reinforcing.

• Cost note: Typically calculated by width, material, and length.

• It is recommended that recycled and regionally available materials and products be given high priority in determining final design and specifications.

Installation Cost (per Unit)

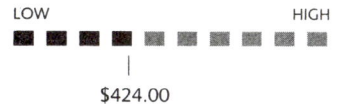

LOW .... HIGH

$424.00

Maintenance

LOW .... HIGH

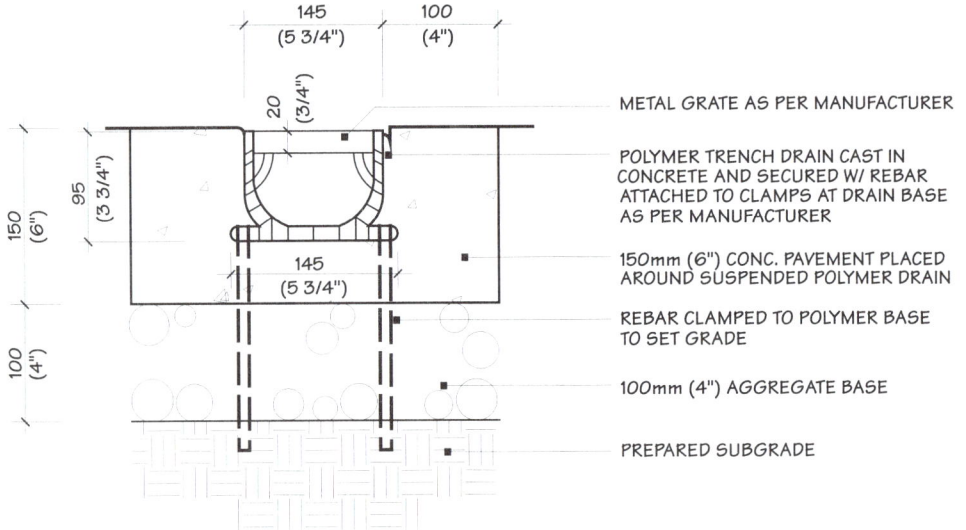

145
(5 3/4")   100
(4")

20
(3/4")

95
(5 3/4")

150
(6")

145
(5 3/4")

100
(4")

METAL GRATE AS PER MANUFACTURER

POLYMER TRENCH DRAIN CAST IN
CONCRETE AND SECURED W/ REBAR
ATTACHED TO CLAMPS AT DRAIN BASE
AS PER MANUFACTURER

150mm (6") CONC. PAVEMENT PLACED
AROUND SUSPENDED POLYMER DRAIN

REBAR CLAMPED TO POLYMER BASE
TO SET GRADE

100mm (4") AGGREGATE BASE

PREPARED SUBGRADE

APPLICATION

CLIMATE

SUBGRADE

CSI MASTERFORMAT: 02630
DRAWING FILE: DRN28-02

• This drawing is a template for preliminary design only, and is not intended for bid purposes. It is subject to modification based on design calculations, local practices, and all applicable codes and regulations.

• This polymer trench drain detail is rated as light-duty due to bearing capacity and depth. It is typically found at the top and bottom of ramps, or at the edge of single plane pavements adjacent to pools or fountains.

• This detail performs better in warmer climates, but will perform adequately in temperate and cold climates with sufficient maintenance and care in installation. Embedded heating cables may add to the length of service in cold climates.

• Drain is embedded in concrete surround and held into position by means of steel rods clamped to unit, which suspend the unit within form edges. Concrete is placed on an aggregate base of sufficient depth to bear the expected loads. Rigid pavements require

sealed expansion joints at edge of drain encasement.

• Pipe openings are typically factory supplied in a number of configurations. Their are numerous types of polymer trench drains which vary in depth and width. Most snap together, while others are bolted together to achieve the desired length.

• Concrete design must accommodate movement of materials by providing adequate expansion and control joints, particularly in regions of extreme temperature fluctuations. If designed for temperate or cold climates, air-entrained concrete is typically recommended due to freezing/thawing action.

• Cost note: Typically calculated by width, material, and length.

• It is recommended that recycled and regionally available materials and products be given high priority in determining final design and specifications.

Installation Cost (per Unit)

LOW   HIGH

$24.00

Maintenance

LOW   HIGH

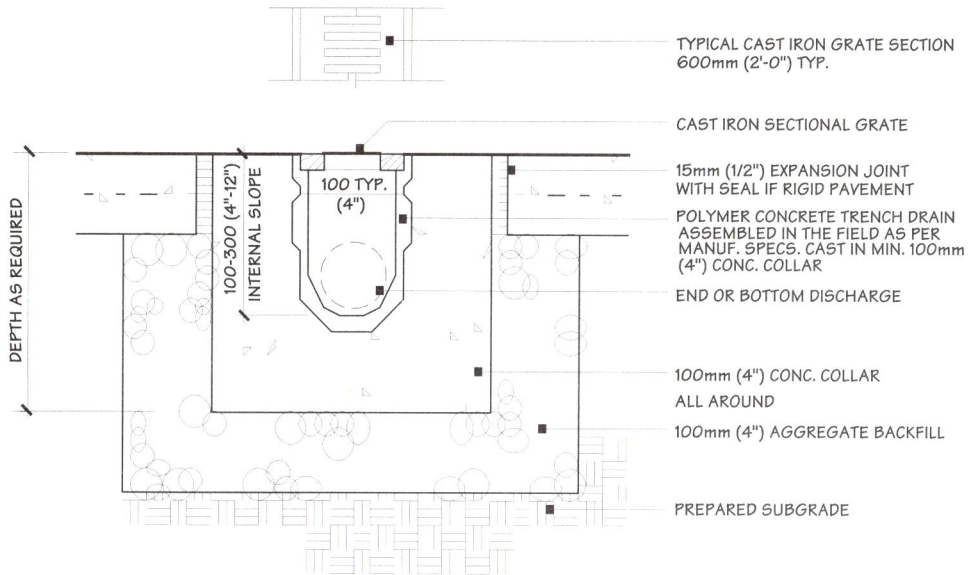

TYPICAL CAST IRON GRATE SECTION 600mm (2'-0") TYP.

CAST IRON SECTIONAL GRATE

15mm (1/2") EXPANSION JOINT WITH SEAL IF RIGID PAVEMENT

POLYMER CONCRETE TRENCH DRAIN ASSEMBLED IN THE FIELD AS PER MANUF. SPECS. CAST IN MIN. 100mm (4") CONC. COLLAR

END OR BOTTOM DISCHARGE

100mm (4") CONC. COLLAR ALL AROUND

100mm (4") AGGREGATE BACKFILL

PREPARED SUBGRADE

DEPTH AS REQUIRED

100-300 (4"-12") INTERNAL SLOPE

100 TYP. (4")

APPLICATION

CLIMATE

SUBGRADE

CSI MASTERFORMAT: 02630
DRAWING FILE: DRN28-04

• This drawing is a template for preliminary design only, and is not intended for bid purposes. It is subject to modification based on design calculations, local practices, and all applicable codes and regulations.

• This polymer trench drain detail is rated as medium-duty due to bearing capacity and depth. It is typically found at the edge of single plane pavements. This drain is often composed of polymer concrete and is capable of receiving cast iron or brass grates.

• This detail performs better in warmer climates, but due to its stable composition will perform adequately in temperate and cold climates with sufficient maintenance and care in installation. Embedded heating cables may add to the length of service in cold climates.

• Drain is embedded in concrete and held into position by means of integral flanges and clamps which suspend the unit within form edges. Concrete is placed on an aggregate base of sufficient depth to bear the expected loads. Rigid pavements require sealed expansion joints at edge of drain encasement.

• Pipe openings are typically factory supplied in a number of configurations. Their are numerous types of polymer trench drains which vary in depth and width. Most snap together, while others are bolted.

• Concrete design must accommodate movement of materials by providing adequate expansion and control joints, particularly in regions of extreme temperature fluctuations. If designed for temperate or cold climates, air-entrained concrete is typically recommended.

• Cost note: Typically calculated by width, material, and length.

• It is recommended that recycled and regionally available materials and products be given high priority in determining final design and specifications.

Installation Cost (per Unit)

LOW   HIGH

$24.00

Maintenance

LOW   HIGH

Drainage Swales

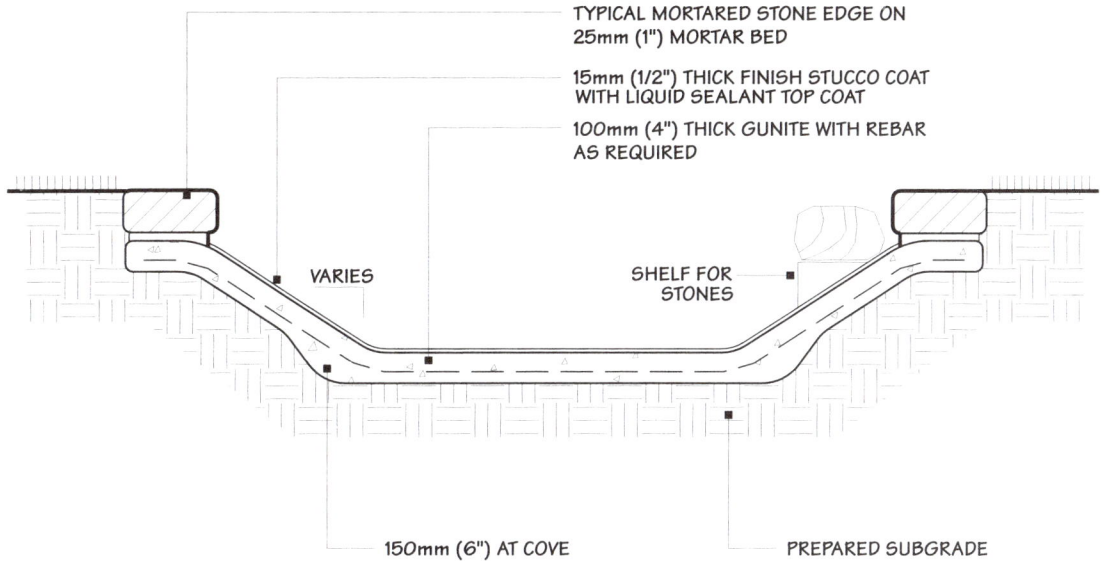

TYPICAL MORTARED STONE EDGE ON
25mm (1") MORTAR BED

15mm (1/2") THICK FINISH STUCCO COAT
WITH LIQUID SEALANT TOP COAT

100mm (4") THICK GUNITE WITH REBAR
AS REQUIRED

VARIES

SHELF FOR
STONES

150mm (6") AT COVE

PREPARED SUBGRADE

APPLICATION

CLIMATE

SUBGRADE

CSI MASTERFORMAT: 02370
DRAWING FILE: SWA02-01

• This drawing is a template for preliminary design only, and is not intended for bid purposes. It is subject to modification based on design calculations, local practices, and all applicable codes and regulations.

• This gunite stream channel swale detail is rated as heavy-duty due to its volume and velocity characteristics, and is typically found in dense residential, urban park, institutional, and commercial settings.

• Subgrade is prepared to receive aggregate (required in temperate zones), reinforcing steel, and gunite concrete. Ornamental stone is typically incorporated by means of concrete pedestals and mortar. Large stones require thicker concrete base and drain mat to cushion the weight.

• It is found in warm climate zones and is employed as a main channel, typically associated with a water feature adjacent to human use areas, or as part of a water garden. However, gunite properties will allow for

higher velocities and may be used for main discharge swales.

• Side slopes range from 1:1.5 to 1:2. Periodic debris removal may be required.

• It is recommended that recycled and regionally available materials and products be given high priority in determining final design and specifications.

Installation Cost (per Square Foot)

LOW   HIGH

$10.00

Maintenance

LOW   HIGH

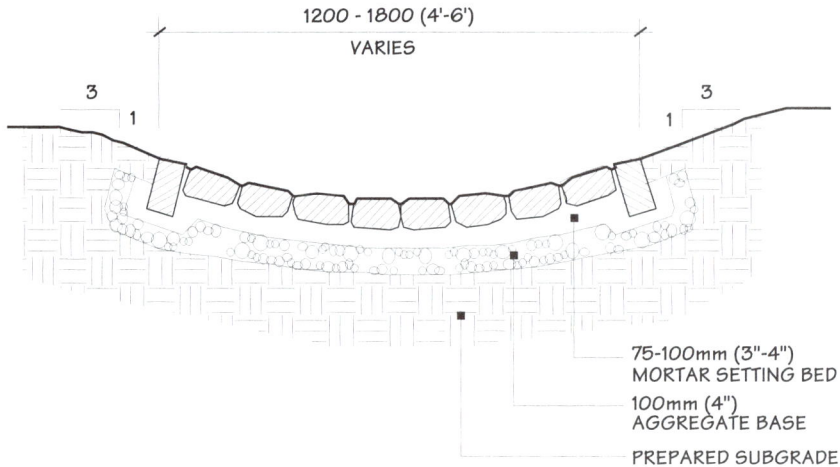

1200 - 1800 (4'-6')
VARIES

3
1

3
1

75-100mm (3"-4")
MORTAR SETTING BED

100mm (4")
AGGREGATE BASE

PREPARED SUBGRADE

APPLICATION

LIGHT   MED.   HEAVY

CLIMATE

ARID   HUMID   TEMP.   COLD

SUBGRADE

PERM.   CLAY   ROOF

CSI MASTERFORMAT: 02370
DRAWING FILE: SWA03-04

• This drawing is a template for preliminary design only, and is not intended for bid purposes. It is subject to modification based on design calculations, local practices, and all applicable codes and regulations.

• This mortared stone lined swale is rated as heavy-duty due to its volume and velocity characteristics, and is typically found in dense residential, urban park, institutional, and commercial settings. Mortared stone creates a smooth channel capable of sustaining relatively high velocities. Volume may be increased by either widening the wetted perimeter, or by deepening the swale.

• Stone is placed and mortared by hand in a roughly parabolic section, on a stiff reinforced mortar bed on an aggregate base.

• It is found in all climate zones, except cold due to the mortar joints.

• It is cost effective and useful as a means of both conveying storm run-off and of increasing time-of-concentration through broad cross-section design and minimal longitudinal slopes. It also helps to dissipate hydraulic energy of channel flow at point of dispersal.

• Side slopes range from 1:3 to 1:4. Periodic debris removal may be required.

• Pipe should be set below frost and set to discharge into stream, pond, or drainage structure. This is an effective means to delay the impact of site runoff.

• It is recommended that recycled and regionally available materials and products be given high priority in determining final design and specifications.

Installation Cost (per Square Foot)

LOW   HIGH

$7.39

Maintenance

LOW   HIGH

450mm (18") DEEP MACHINE SPREAD OR DUMPED STONE RIP RAP

FINISHED GRADE

900 MIN.
(3' - 0")

1-1/2
1

1-1/2
1

600 TYP.
(2'-0")

450
(18")

150 MIN.
(6")

150mm (6") MIN. AGGREGATE BASE

SEPARATOR FABRIC

PREPARED SUBGRADE

APPLICATION

LIGHT   MED.   HEAVY

CLIMATE

ARID   HUMID   TEMP.   COLD

SUBGRADE

PERM.   CLAY   ROOF

CSI MASTERFORMAT: 02370
DRAWING FILE: SWA03-01

• This drawing is a template for preliminary design only, and is not intended for bid purposes. It is subject to modification based on design calculations, local practices, and all applicable codes and regulations.

• This stone rip-rap swale is rated as heavy-duty due to its volume and velocity characteristics, and is typically found in dense residential, urban park, institutional, and commercial settings.

• Stone is placed by mechanical means in a roughly trapezoidal section. In deep channels, a fabric separator is recommended to bind aggregate base and inhibit upward migration of fines in colloidal soils.

• It is found in all climate zones and is employed as a main channel, usually away from human use areas. Broad cross-sections may be used to infiltrate water in appropriate subsoil conditions.

• It is cost effective and useful as a means of both conveying high volume storm run-off

and of increasing time-of-concentration through broad cross-section design and minimal longitudinal slopes. It also helps to dissipate hydraulic energy of channel flow at point of dispersal.

• Side slopes range from 1:1.5 to 1:2. Periodic debris removal may be required.

• It is recommended that recycled and regionally available materials and products be given high priority in determining final design and specifications.

Installation Cost (per Square Foot)

LOW   HIGH

$5.41

Maintenance

LOW   HIGH

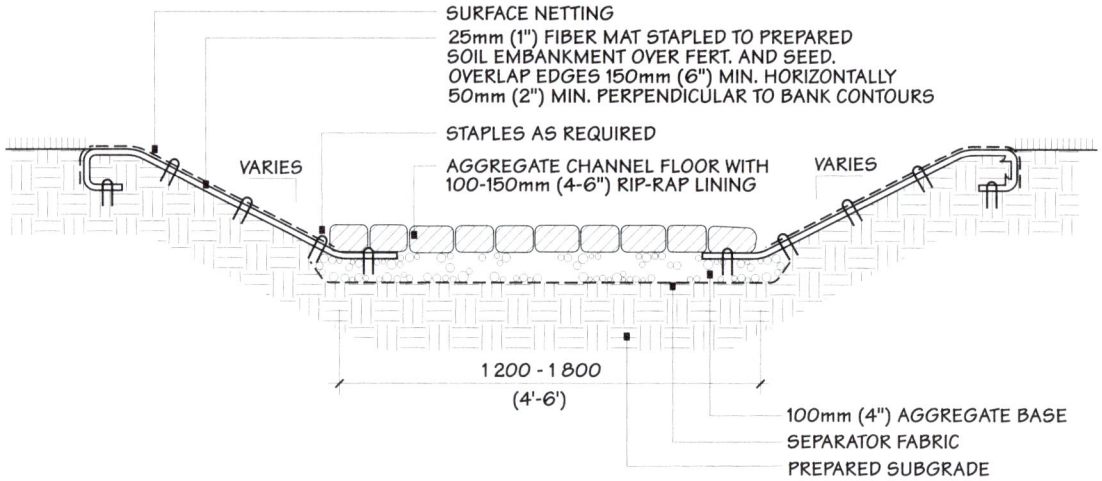

SURFACE NETTING
25mm (1") FIBER MAT STAPLED TO PREPARED
SOIL EMBANKMENT OVER FERT. AND SEED.
OVERLAP EDGES 150mm (6") MIN. HORIZONTALLY
50mm (2") MIN. PERPENDICULAR TO BANK CONTOURS

STAPLES AS REQUIRED

VARIES

AGGREGATE CHANNEL FLOOR WITH
100-150mm (4-6") RIP-RAP LINING

VARIES

1 200 - 1 800
(4'-6')

100mm (4") AGGREGATE BASE
SEPARATOR FABRIC
PREPARED SUBGRADE

APPLICATION

CLIMATE

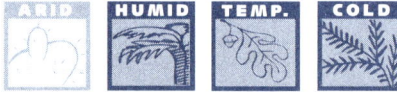

SUBGRADE

CSI MASTERFORMAT: 02370
DRAWING FILE: SWA00-04

• This drawing is a template for preliminary design only, and is not intended for bid purposes. It is subject to modification based on design calculations, local practices, and all applicable codes and regulations.

• This fiber mat swale reinforcing is rated as heavy-duty due to its volume and velocity characteristics, and is typically found in dense residential, urban park, institutional, and commercial settings.

• Fiber mat is stapled to prepared and seeded swale as per manufacturer. Matting cross seams are trenched, stapled, and filled with stone to serve as check slots to both secure matting and to reduce velocity. Side slopes range from 1:2 to 1:3.

• It is found in most climate zones and is employed as a main channel, usually away from human use areas. Seed requires suitable climate.

• It is cost effective and useful as a means of both conveying high volume storm run-off and of increasing time-of-concentration through broad cross-section design and minimal longitudinal slopes, while at the same time providing effective cover while vegetation is established.

• It is recommended that recycled and regionally available materials and products be given high priority in determining final design and specifications.

Installation Cost (per Square Foot)

LOW   HIGH

$2.80

Maintenance

LOW   HIGH

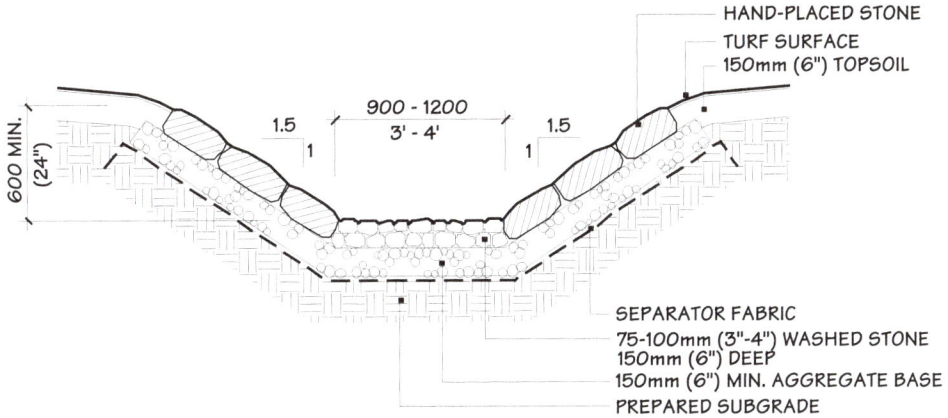

HAND-PLACED STONE
TURF SURFACE
150mm (6") TOPSOIL

900 - 1200
3' - 4'

1.5
1

1.5
1

600 MIN.
(24")

SEPARATOR FABRIC
75-100mm (3"-4") WASHED STONE
150mm (6") DEEP
150mm (6") MIN. AGGREGATE BASE
PREPARED SUBGRADE

APPLICATION

CLIMATE

SUBGRADE

CSI MASTERFORMAT: 02370
DRAWING FILE: SWA03-02

• This drawing is a template for preliminary design only, and is not intended for bid purposes. It is subject to modification based on design calculations, local practices, and all applicable codes and regulations.

• This stone lined infiltration swale is rated as heavy-duty due to its volume and velocity characteristics, and is typically found in dense residential, urban park, institutional, and commercial settings.

• Stones are placed by mechanical means in a roughly trapezoidal section, but if a more refined appearance is required, they may be hand placed on the aggregate base. A fabric separator is recommened to bind aggregate base and inhibit upward migration of fines in fine soils.

• It is found in all climate zones and is often employed as a main channel, but requires well drained subsoil to be effective. Often located away from human use areas, but if

hand placed and edged, it may be part of a human landscape.

• It is cost effective and useful as a means of both conveying high volume storm run-off and of increasing time-of-concentration through broad cross-section design and minimal longitudinal slopes. It also helps to dissipate hydraulic energy of channel flow at point of dispersal.

• Side slopes range from 1:1.5 to 1:2. Periodic debris removal may be required.

• It is recommended that recycled and regionally available materials and products be given high priority in determining final design and specifications.

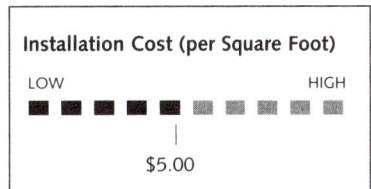

Installation Cost (per Square Foot)

LOW   HIGH

$5.00

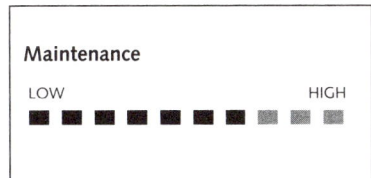

Maintenance

LOW   HIGH

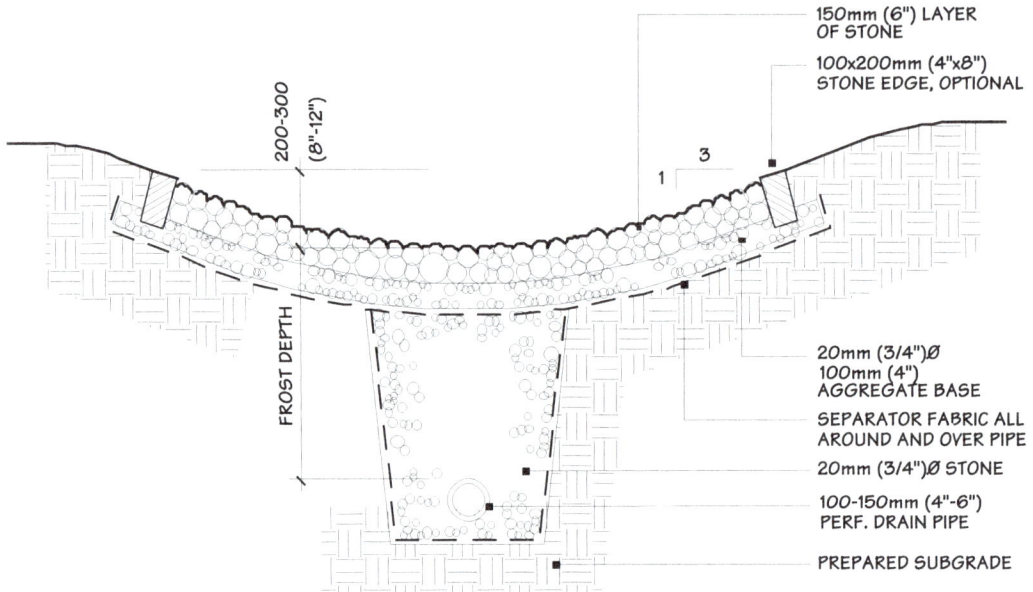

150mm (6") LAYER OF STONE

100x200mm (4"x8") STONE EDGE, OPTIONAL

200-300 (8"-12")

FROST DEPTH

3

1

20mm (3/4")Ø 100mm (4") AGGREGATE BASE

SEPARATOR FABRIC ALL AROUND AND OVER PIPE

20mm (3/4")Ø STONE

100-150mm (4"-6") PERF. DRAIN PIPE

PREPARED SUBGRADE

APPLICATION

LIGHT   MED.   HEAVY

CLIMATE

ARID   HUMID   TEMP.   COLD

SUBGRADE

PERM.   CLAY   ROOF

CSI MASTERFORMAT: 02370
DRAWING FILE: SWA03-03

• This drawing is a template for preliminary design only, and is not intended for bid purposes. It is subject to modification based on design calculations, local practices, and all applicable codes and regulations.

• This stone lined swale with infiltration drain is rated as medium-duty due to its volume and velocity characteristics, and is typically found in residential, urban park, institutional, and commercial settings.

• Stone is placed by mechanical means in a roughly parabolic section, on an aggregate base over a fabric separator, which binds aggregate base and inhibits downward migration of fines into the subdrain trench.

• It is found in all climate zones and is often employed as a main channel, but requires well drained subsoil to be effective. Often located away from human use areas, but if hand placed and edged, it may be part of a human landscape.

• It is cost effective and useful as a means of both conveying storm run-off and of increasing time-of-concentration through broad cross-section design and minimal longitudinal slopes. It also helps to dissipate hydraulic energy of channel flow at point of dispersal.

• Side slopes range from 1:3 to 1:4. Periodic debris removal may be required.

• Pipe should be set below frost and set to discharge into stream, pond, or drainage structure. This is an effective means to delay the impact of site runoff.

• It is recommended that recycled and regionally available materials and products be given high priority in determining final design and specifications.

Installation Cost (per Square Foot)

LOW   HIGH

$2.25

Maintenance

LOW   HIGH

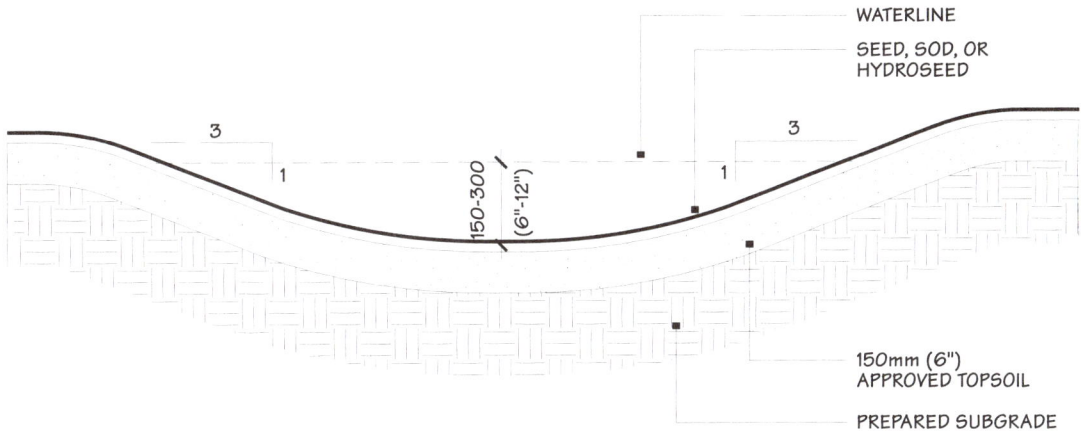

WATERLINE

SEED, SOD, OR HYDROSEED

150-300 (6"-12")

150mm (6") APPROVED TOPSOIL

PREPARED SUBGRADE

APPLICATION

CLIMATE

SUBGRADE

CSI MASTERFORMAT: 02920
DRAWING FILE: SWA00-01

• This drawing is a template for preliminary design only, and is not intended for bid purposes. It is subject to modification based on design calculations, local practices, and all applicable codes and regulations.

• This parabolic turf swale is rated as medium-duty due to its volume and velocity characteristics, and is typically found in residential, urban park, institutional, and commercial settings. Maximum velocity varies by soil type, with colloidal soils requiring reinforcement or slow velocities.

• Parabolic cross-section mimics natural soil deposition in streams and rills, and is self-cleaning if slope is set correctly.

• It is found in all climate zones, but may be limited to riverine contexts in hot-arid regions. To remain effective, the region must support natural turf during dry periods to avoid seasonal outwashes and periodic erosion during heavy rains.

• It is cost effective and useful as a means of both conveying storm run-off and of increasing time-of-concentration through broad cross-section design and minimal longitudinal slopes, but requires regular mowing and cleaning.

• Ideal side slopes range from 1:3 to 1:4.

• It is recommended that recycled and regionally available materials and products be given high priority in determining final design and specifications.

Installation Cost (per Square Foot)

LOW   HIGH

$0.30

Maintenance

LOW   HIGH

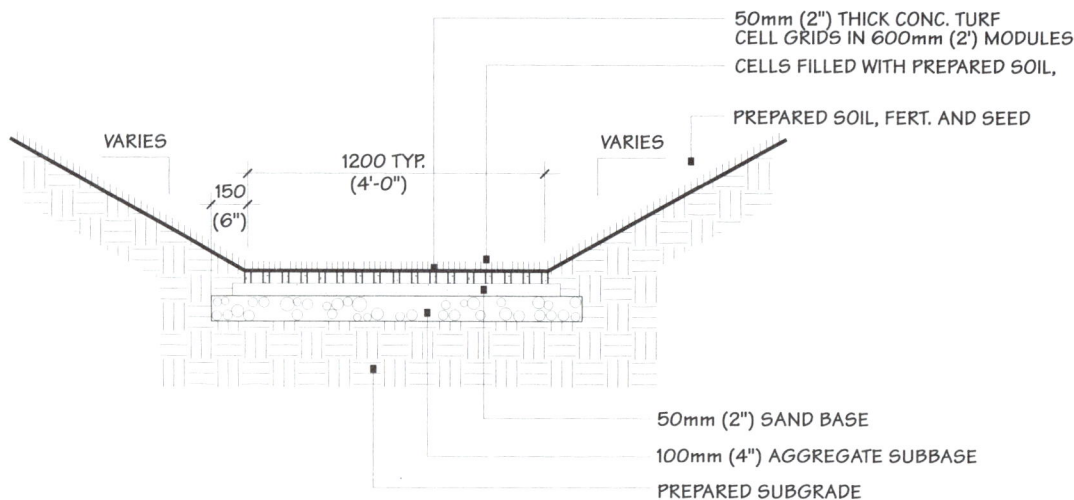

50mm (2") THICK CONC. TURF CELL GRIDS IN 600mm (2') MODULES
CELLS FILLED WITH PREPARED SOIL,

PREPARED SOIL, FERT. AND SEED

VARIES

VARIES

1200 TYP.
(4'-0")

150
(6")

50mm (2") SAND BASE

100mm (4") AGGREGATE SUBBASE

PREPARED SUBGRADE

APPLICATION

CLIMATE

SUBGRADE

CSI MASTERFORMAT: 02370
DRAWING FILE: SWA03-05

• This drawing is a template for preliminary design only, and is not intended for bid purposes. It is subject to modification based on design calculations, local practices, and all applicable codes and regulations.

• This concrete cellular turf grid swale is rated as heavy-duty due to its volume and velocity characteristics, and is typically found in dense residential, urban park, institutional, and commercial settings.

• Swale subgrade is machine shaped and aggregate base and sand setting bed is placed on the swale bottom in preparation for receiving concrete turf grid inits, amended soil, fertilizer, and seed. Side slopes may be seeded, hydrocast, or sodded for a more immediate effect. Side slopes range from 1:3 to 1:4.

• Finer soils may require a soil separator under aggregate base.

• It is found in all climate zones and is employed as a main channel, usually away from human use areas. Broad cross-sections may be used to infiltrate water in appropriate subsoil conditions.

• It is cost effective and useful as a means of both conveying high volume storm run-off and of increasing time-of-concentration through broad cross-section design and minimal longitudinal slopes. It also helps to dissipate hydraulic energy of channel flow at point of dispersal.

• It is recommended that recycled and regionally available materials and products be given high priority in determining final design and specifications.

Installation Cost (per Square Foot)

LOW   HIGH

$6.00

Maintenance

LOW   HIGH

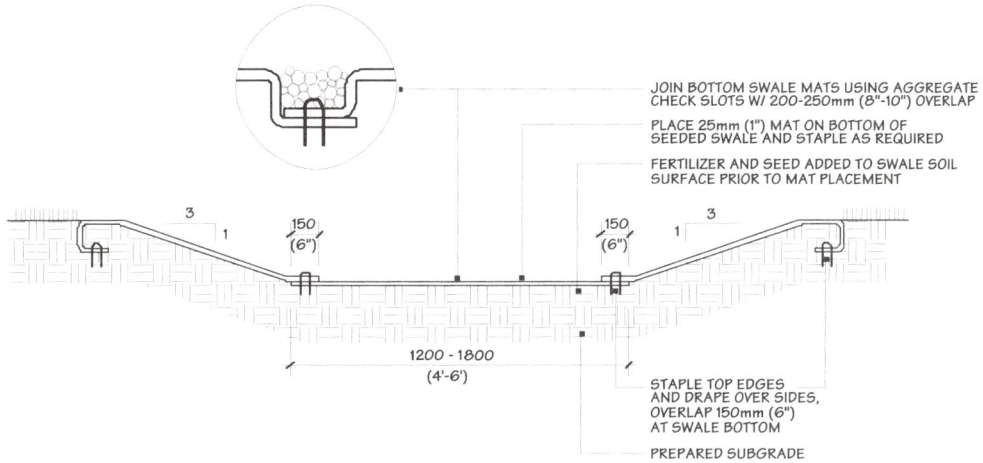

JOIN BOTTOM SWALE MATS USING AGGREGATE
CHECK SLOTS W/ 200-250mm (8"-10") OVERLAP

PLACE 25mm (1") MAT ON BOTTOM OF
SEEDED SWALE AND STAPLE AS REQUIRED

FERTILIZER AND SEED ADDED TO SWALE SOIL
SURFACE PRIOR TO MAT PLACEMENT

STAPLE TOP EDGES
AND DRAPE OVER SIDES,
OVERLAP 150mm (6")
AT SWALE BOTTOM

PREPARED SUBGRADE

APPLICATION

CLIMATE

SUBGRADE

CSI MASTERFORMAT: 02370
DRAWING FILE: SWA00-03

• This drawing is a template for preliminary design only, and is not intended for bid purposes. It is subject to modification based on design calculations, local practices, and all applicable codes and regulations.

• This fiber mat swale reinforcing is rated as heavy-duty due to its volume and velocity characteristics, and is typically found in dense residential, urban park, institutional, and commercial settings.

• Fiber mat is stapled to prepared and seeded swale as per manufacturer. Matting cross seams are trenched, stapled, and filled with stone to serve as check slots to both secure matting and to reduce velocity. Side slopes range from 1:2 to 1:3.

• It is found in most climate zones and is employed as a main channel, usually away from human use areas. Seed requires suitable climate.

• It is cost effective and useful as a means of both conveying high volume storm run-off

and of increasing time-of-concentration through broad cross-section design and minimal longitudinal slopes, while at the same time providing effective cover while vegetation is established.

• It is recommended that recycled and regionally available materials and products be given high priority in determining final design and specifications.

Installation Cost (per Square Foot)

LOW   HIGH

$2.30

Maintenance

LOW   HIGH

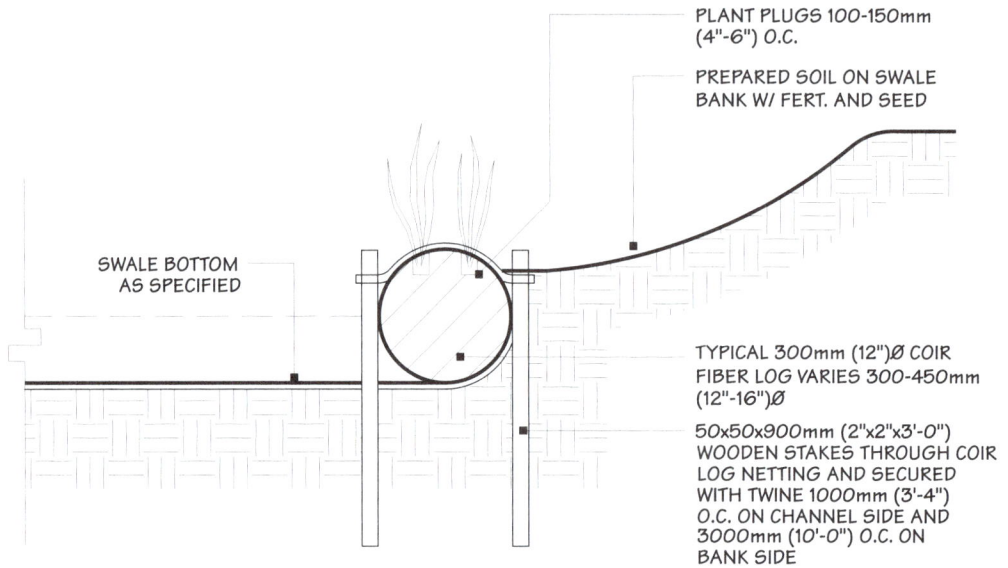

PLANT PLUGS 100-150mm (4"-6") O.C.

PREPARED SOIL ON SWALE BANK W/ FERT. AND SEED

SWALE BOTTOM AS SPECIFIED

TYPICAL 300mm (12")Ø COIR FIBER LOG VARIES 300-450mm (12"-16")Ø

50x50x900mm (2"x2"x3'-0") WOODEN STAKES THROUGH COIR LOG NETTING AND SECURED WITH TWINE 1000mm (3'-4") O.C. ON CHANNEL SIDE AND 3000mm (10'-0") O.C. ON BANK SIDE

APPLICATION

CLIMATE

SUBGRADE

CSI MASTERFORMAT: 02370
DRAWING FILE: SWA00-02

• This drawing is a template for preliminary design only, and is not intended for bid purposes. It is subject to modification based on design calculations, local practices, and all applicable codes and regulations.

• This fiber log reinforced swale is rated as heavy-duty due to its volume and velocity characteristics, and is typically found in dense residential, urban park, institutional, and commercial settings.

• Fiber log is staked as per manufacturer, and plugged with selected plant species to eventually tie the log to bank with natural roots. Planting requires shallow stream channel to preserve mat capillarity. Log is backfilled with prepared soil which is seeded.

• It is found in most climate zones and is employed as a main channel, usually away from human use areas. Seed or plant plugs require suitable climate.

• It is cost effective and useful as a means of both conveying high volume storm run-off, and of increasing time-of-concentration through broad cross-section design and minimal longitudinal slopes. It also helps to naturalize the new construction with quick plant cover.

• It is recommended that recycled and regionally available materials and products be given high priority in determining final design and specifications.

Installation Cost (per Square Foot)

LOW   HIGH

$2.50

Maintenance

LOW   HIGH

Fences

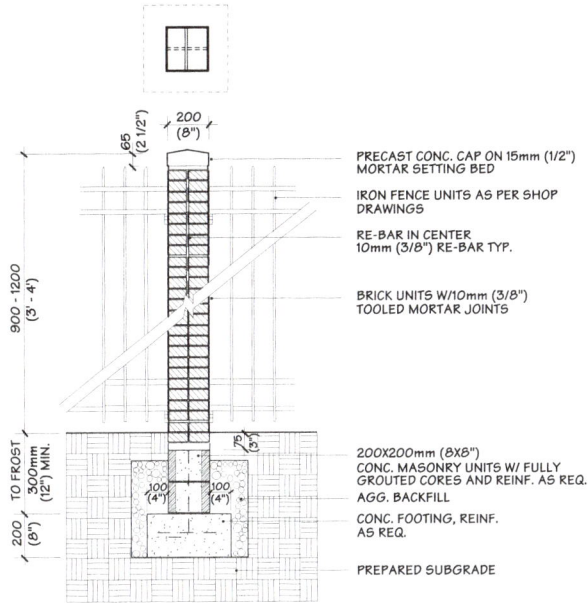

PRECAST CONC. CAP ON 15mm (1/2")
MORTAR SETTING BED

IRON FENCE UNITS AS PER SHOP
DRAWINGS

RE-BAR IN CENTER
10mm (3/8") RE-BAR TYP.

BRICK UNITS W/10mm (3/8")
TOOLED MORTAR JOINTS

200X200mm (8X8")
CONC. MASONRY UNITS W/ FULLY
GROUTED CORES AND REINF. AS REQ.

AGG. BACKFILL

CONC. FOOTING, REINF.
AS REQ.

PREPARED SUBGRADE

APPLICATION

CLIMATE

SUBGRADE

CSI MASTERFORMAT: 04810
DRAWING FILE: FEN04-03

- This drawing is a template for preliminary design only, and is not intended for bid purposes. It is subject to modification based on design calculations, local practices, and all applicable codes and regulations.

- This solid brick reinforced pier detail is rated as light-duty due to its height potential, strength, and durability, and is typically found in residential, urban park, or institutional settings in all climates.

- The footing is typically reinforced and often bears on prepared subgrade in most soils. Aggregate leveling course may be used in warmer climates or in finer soils.

- Fully grouted and reinforced concrete masonry units are mortared to the footing to act as sill for the reinforced solid brick pier.

- Cap may be precast concrete or cut stone, sloped to drain.

- Metal fence sections are attached with masonry screws to brick face. Alternate methods include grouting slotted bar into masonry and bolting fence units to slotted bar.

- Reinforcing practices vary widely by region. Local codes and practices should be consulted prior to specifying any type of reinforcing.

- It is recommended that recycled and regionally available materials and products be given high priority in determining final design and specifications.

Installation Cost (per Linear Foot)

LOW .... HIGH

$22.89

Maintenance

LOW .... HIGH

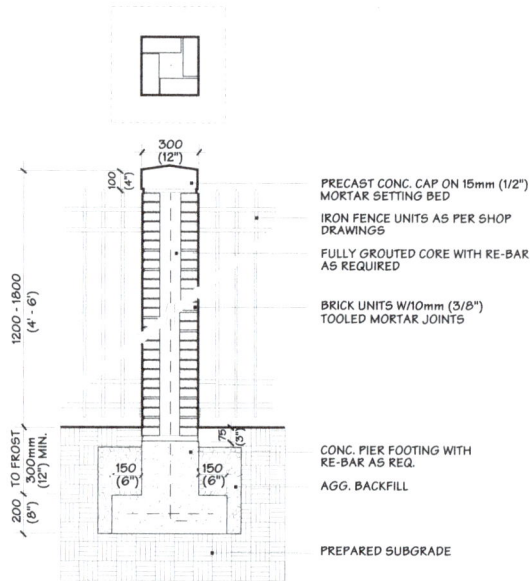

300
(12")

100
(4")

PRECAST CONC. CAP ON 15mm (1/2")
MORTAR SETTING BED

IRON FENCE UNITS AS PER SHOP
DRAWINGS

FULLY GROUTED CORE WITH RE-BAR
AS REQUIRED

1200 - 1800
(4' - 6')

BRICK UNITS W/10mm (3/8")
TOOLED MORTAR JOINTS

200 TO FROST
(8") 300mm (12") MIN.

150
(6")

150
(6")

CONC. PIER FOOTING WITH
RE-BAR AS REQ.

AGG. BACKFILL

PREPARED SUBGRADE

APPLICATION

CLIMATE

SUBGRADE

CSI MASTERFORMAT: 04810
DRAWING FILE: FEN04-02

• This drawing is a template for preliminary design only, and is not intended for bid purposes. It is subject to modification based on design calculations, local practices, and all applicable codes and regulations.

• This brick pier with grouted core detail is rated as medium-duty due to its height potential, strength, and durability, and is typically found in residential, commercial, urban park, or institutional settings in all climates.

• The footing is typically reinforced and often bears on prepared subgrade in most soils. Aggregate leveling course may be used in warmer climates or in finer soils.

• Fully grouted and reinforced concrete masonry units are mortared to the footing to act as sill for the reinforced fully grouted masonry block core, and the brick faces. This detail shows alternate solid concrete pier base. Lateral reinforcing may be required in heavy wind load circumstances and when wall is above 1800 mm (6') to tie structure together.

• Cap may be precast concrete or cut stone, sloped to drain.

• Metal fence sections are attached with masonry screws to brick face. Alternate methods include grouting slotted bar into masonry and bolting fence units to slotted bar.

• Reinforcing practices vary widely by region. Local codes and practices should be consulted prior to specifying any type of reinforcing.

• It is recommended that recycled and regionally available materials and products be given high priority in determining final design and specifications.

Installation Cost (per Linear Foot)

LOW   HIGH

$32.80

Maintenance

LOW   HIGH

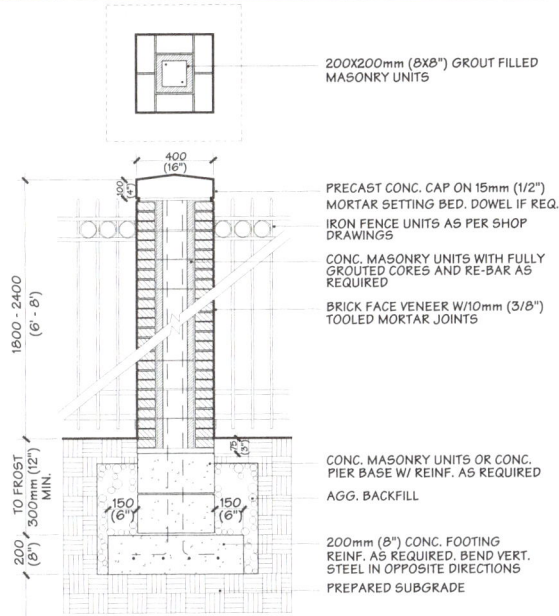

200X200mm (8X8") GROUT FILLED
MASONRY UNITS

PRECAST CONC. CAP ON 15mm (1/2")
MORTAR SETTING BED. DOWEL IF REQ.

IRON FENCE UNITS AS PER SHOP
DRAWINGS

CONC. MASONRY UNITS WITH FULLY
GROUTED CORES AND RE-BAR AS
REQUIRED

BRICK FACE VENEER W/10mm (3/8")
TOOLED MORTAR JOINTS

CONC. MASONRY UNITS OR CONC.
PIER BASE W/ REINF. AS REQUIRED

AGG. BACKFILL

200mm (8") CONC. FOOTING
REINF. AS REQUIRED. BEND VERT.
STEEL IN OPPOSITE DIRECTIONS

PREPARED SUBGRADE

400 (16")

1800 - 2400 (6' - 8')

200 (8") TO FROST 300mm (12") MIN.

150 (6")   150 (6")

APPLICATION

CLIMATE

SUBGRADE

CSI MASTERFORMAT: 04810
DRAWING FILE: FEN04-01

• This drawing is a template for preliminary design only, and is not intended for bid purposes. It is subject to modification based on design calculations, local practices, and all applicable codes and regulations.

• This brick pier with masonry core fence post detail is rated as heavy-duty due to its height potential, strength, and durability, and is typically found in commercial, urban park, or institutional settings in all climates.

• The footing is typically reinforced and often bears on prepared subgrade in most soils. Aggregate leveling course may be used in warmer climates or in finer soils.

• Fully grouted and reinforced concrete masonry units are mortared to the footing to act as sill for the fully grouted and reinforced concrete masonry block core, and the brick veneer faces. Lateral reinforcing may be required in heavy wind load circumstances and when wall is above 1800 mm (6') to tie structure together.

• Cap may be precast concrete or cut stone, sloped to drain.

• Metal fence sections are attached with masonry screws to brick face. Alternate methods include grouting slotted bar into masonry and bolting fence units to slotted bar.

• Reinforcing practices vary widely by region. Local codes and practices should be consulted prior to specifying any type of reinforcing.

• It is recommended that recycled and regionally available materials and products be given high priority in determining final design and specifications.

Installation Cost (per Linear Foot)

LOW   HIGH

$52.10

Maintenance

LOW   HIGH

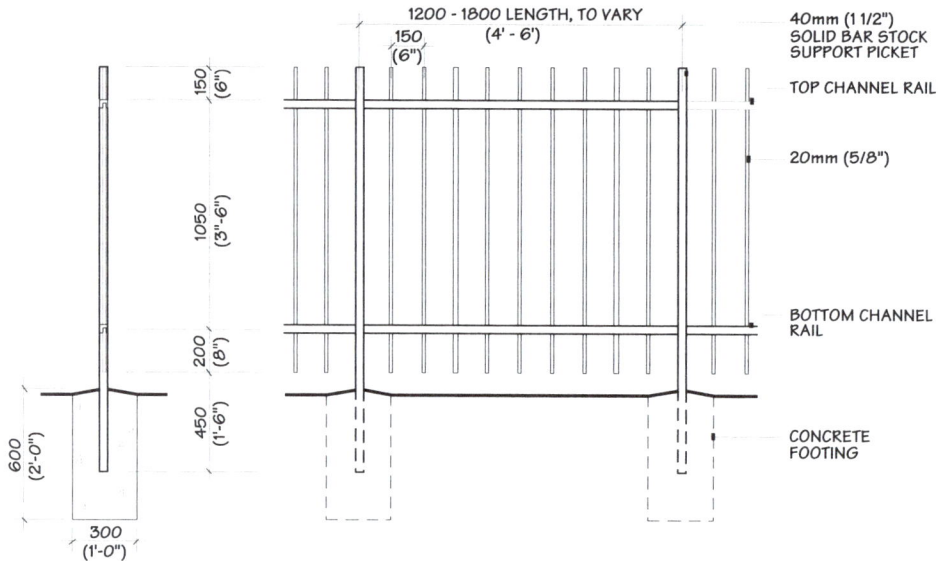

1200 - 1800 LENGTH, TO VARY
(4' - 6')
150
(6")

40mm (1 1/2")
SOLID BAR STOCK
SUPPORT PICKET

TOP CHANNEL RAIL

20mm (5/8")

BOTTOM CHANNEL
RAIL

CONCRETE
FOOTING

150
(6")

1050
(3"-6")

200
(8")

450
(1'-6")

600
(2'-0")

300
(1'-0")

APPLICATION

LIGHT MED. HEAVY

CLIMATE

ARID HUMID TEMP. COLD

SUBGRADE

PERM. CLAY ROOF

CSI MASTERFORMAT: 02820
DRAWING FILE: FEN06-01

• This drawing is a template for preliminary design only, and is not intended for bid purposes. It is subject to modification based on design calculations, local practices, and all applicable codes and regulations.

• This metal picket fence on concrete pier detail is rated as heavy-duty due to its height and structural system. It is typically found in dense residential, urban park, institutional, and light commercial settings.

• The welded picket fence sections are either site welded or bolted to steel bars which are embedded in a concrete pier for permanent placement. Bars must be covered by a minimum of 50 mm (2") of concrete. This detail is especially effective in cold climates, where footing must be placed below local frost depth.

• Posts may also be made of heavy tubular steel stock with welded cap seals.

• This fence has a long life span of service if routinely maintained with appropriate finish coating.

• It is recommended that recycled and regionally available materials and products be given high priority in determining final design and specifications.

Installation Cost (per Linear Foot)

LOW   HIGH

$29.39

Maintenance

LOW   HIGH

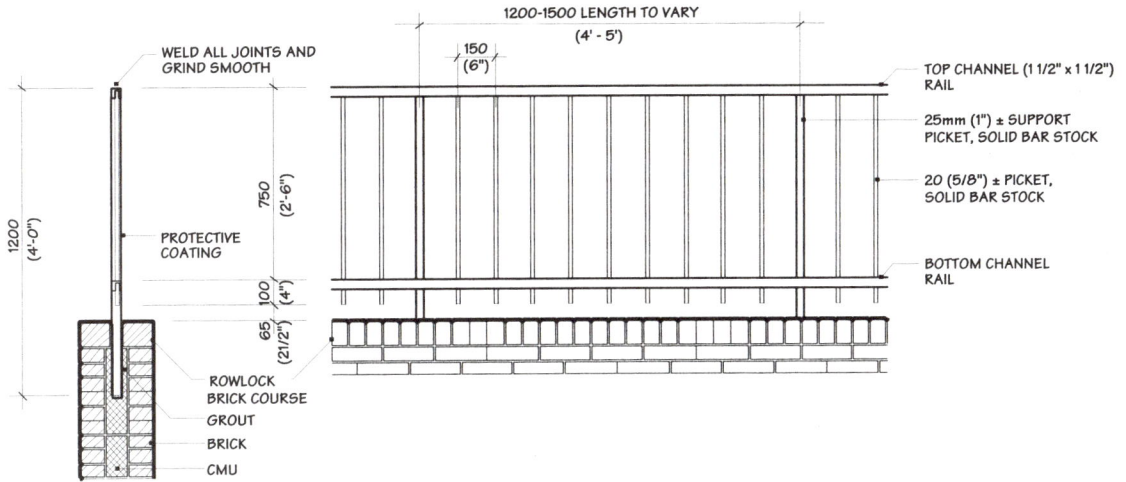

APPLICATION

LIGHT | MED. | HEAVY

CLIMATE

ARID | HUMID | TEMP. | COLD

SUBGRADE

PERM. | CLAY | ROOF

CSI MASTERFORMAT: 02820
DRAWING FILE: FEN06-02

• This drawing is a template for preliminary design only, and is not intended for bid purposes. It is subject to modification based on design calculations, local practices, and all applicable codes and regulations.

• This closed metal picket fence on masonry wall detail is rated as light-duty due to its height and structural system. It is typically found in residential, urban park, institutional, and light commercial settings.

• The welded fence sections are either site welded or bolted to steel bars, which are embedded in preformed holes atop a masonry wall using high strength epoxy cement for permanent placement.

• This fence has a long life span of service if routinely maintained with appropriate finish coating. Joint at bar post and masonry wall may need periodic sealing to prevent moisture penetration.

• It is recommended that recycled and regionally available materials and products be given high priority in determining final design and specifications.

Installation Cost (per Linear Foot)

LOW   HIGH

$19.27

Maintenance

LOW   HIGH

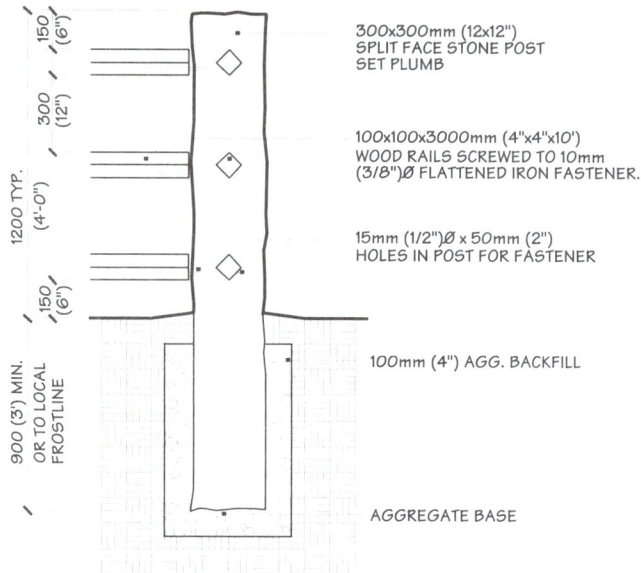

300x300mm (12x12")
SPLIT FACE STONE POST
SET PLUMB

100x100x3000mm (4"x4"x10')
WOOD RAILS SCREWED TO 10mm
(3/8")Ø FLATTENED IRON FASTENER.

15mm (1/2")Ø x 50mm (2")
HOLES IN POST FOR FASTENER

100mm (4") AGG. BACKFILL

AGGREGATE BASE

APPLICATION

CLIMATE

SUBGRADE

CSI MASTERFORMAT: 04810
DRAWING FILE: FEN03-01

• This drawing is a template for preliminary design only, and is not intended for bid purposes. It is subject to modification based on design calculations, local practices, and all applicable codes and regulations.

• This stone post and rail fence detail is rated as light-duty due to its height, and is typically found in residential, commercial, urban park, or institutional settings in all climates.

• Stone posts are lowered into auger dug holes and placed on aggregate base to achieve proper height, and backfilled with soil if appropriate. In softer soils, aggregate backfill may be required. Rails are attached to metal pins which rest in holes which are pre-bored in the stone posts as per spacing requirements.

• Rails are standard 100x100 mm (4x4") set on the diagonal as shown.

• This is a very simple fence of great durability.

• It is recommended that recycled and regionally available materials and products be given high priority in determining final design and specifications.

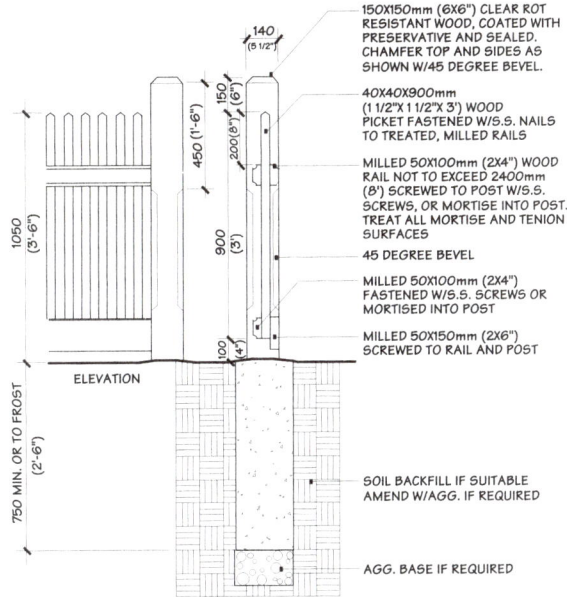

150X150mm (6X6") CLEAR ROT RESISTANT WOOD, COATED WITH PRESERVATIVE AND SEALED. CHAMFER TOP AND SIDES AS SHOWN W/45 DEGREE BEVEL.

40X40X900mm (1 1/2"X 1 1/2"X 3') WOOD PICKET FASTENED W/S.S. NAILS TO TREATED, MILLED RAILS

MILLED 50X100mm (2X4") WOOD RAIL NOT TO EXCEED 2400mm (8') SCREWED TO POST W/S.S. SCREWS, OR MORTISE INTO POST. TREAT ALL MORTISE AND TENION SURFACES

45 DEGREE BEVEL

MILLED 50X100mm (2X4") FASTENED W/S.S. SCREWS OR MORTISED INTO POST

MILLED 50X150mm (2X6") SCREWED TO RAIL AND POST

ELEVATION

SOIL BACKFILL IF SUITABLE AMEND W/AGG. IF REQUIRED

AGG. BASE IF REQUIRED

140 (5 1/2")
150 (6")
200 (8")
450 (1'-6")
900 (3')
100 (4")
1050 (3'-6")
750 MIN. OR TO FROST (2'-6")

APPLICATION

CLIMATE

SUBGRADE

CSI MASTERFORMAT: 02820
DRAWING FILE: FEN05-07

• This drawing is a template for preliminary design only, and is not intended for bid purposes. It is subject to modification based on design calculations, local practices, and all applicable codes and regulations.

• This square picket wood fence is rated as light-duty due to its height and structural system. It is typically found in residential, park, and light commercial settings in all climates.

• The treated or rot resistant wood post is buried directly into auger dug hole and backfilled firmly. Direct burial requires well drained soils.

• Rails are attached by means of treated mortise and tenon joints. All surfaces are milled to shed water. Caps and mouldings should be caulked and sealed.

• This fence has a long life span of service if routinely maintained with sealer or coatings. Service life is limited to degradation rate of buried posts.

• It is recommended that recycled and regionally available materials and products be given high priority in determining final design and specifications.

Installation Cost (per Linear Foot)

LOW   HIGH

$15.00

Maintenance

LOW   HIGH

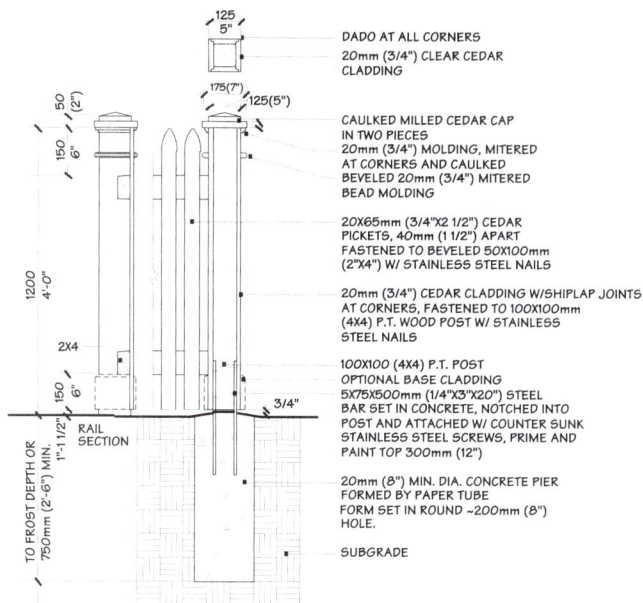

DADO AT ALL CORNERS

20mm (3/4") CLEAR CEDAR CLADDING

CAULKED MILLED CEDAR CAP IN TWO PIECES
20mm (3/4") MOLDING, MITERED AT CORNERS AND CAULKED BEVELED 20mm (3/4") MITERED BEAD MOLDING

20X65mm (3/4"X2 1/2") CEDAR PICKETS, 40mm (1 1/2") APART FASTENED TO BEVELED 50X100mm (2"X4") W/ STAINLESS STEEL NAILS

20mm (3/4") CEDAR CLADDING W/SHIPLAP JOINTS AT CORNERS, FASTENED TO 100X100mm (4X4) P.T. WOOD POST W/ STAINLESS STEEL NAILS

100X100 (4X4) P.T. POST OPTIONAL BASE CLADDING 5X75X500mm (1/4"X3"X20") STEEL BAR SET IN CONCRETE, NOTCHED INTO POST AND ATTACHED W/ COUNTER SUNK STAINLESS STEEL SCREWS, PRIME AND PAINT TOP 300mm (12")

20mm (8") MIN. DIA. CONCRETE PIER FORMED BY PAPER TUBE FORM SET IN ROUND ~200mm (8") HOLE.

SUBGRADE

RAIL SECTION

APPLICATION

CLIMATE

SUBGRADE

CSI MASTERFORMAT: 02820
DRAWING FILE: FEN05-04

• This drawing is a template for preliminary design only, and is not intended for bid purposes. It is subject to modification based on design calculations, local practices, and all applicable codes and regulations.

• This wood picket fence on concrete pier is rated as light-duty due to its height and structural system. It is typically found in residential, park, and light commercial settings.

• The treated wood post is fastened to steel bars which are embedded in a concrete pier for permanent placement. This detail is especially effective in cold climates, and for use as a gate post on both hinge and latch ends. The post is clad in clear wood and painted or stained. This adds bulk to the post and covers metal attachments.

• Rails are attached with stainless steel screws for ease of repair and longevity. All surfaces are milled to shed water. Caps and mouldings should be caulked and sealed.

• This fence has a long life span of service if routinely maintained with sealer or coatings.

• It is recommended that recycled and regionally available materials and products be given high priority in determining final design and specifications.

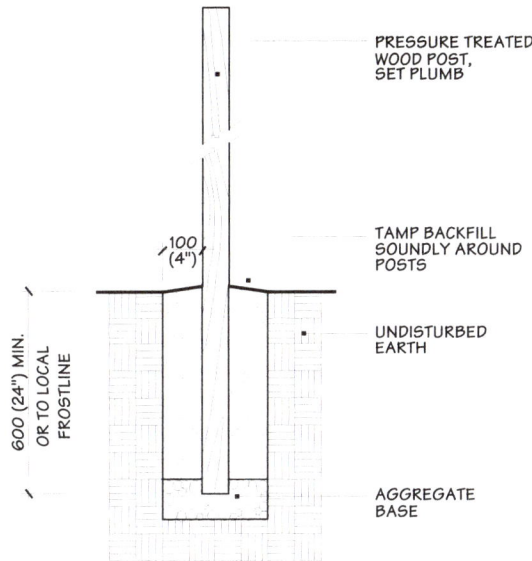

PRESSURE TREATED
WOOD POST,
SET PLUMB

TAMP BACKFILL
SOUNDLY AROUND
POSTS

100
(4")

UNDISTURBED
EARTH

600 (24") MIN.
OR TO LOCAL
FROSTLINE

AGGREGATE
BASE

APPLICATION

LIGHT MED HEAVY

CLIMATE

ARID HUMID TEMP. COLD

SUBGRADE

PERM. CLAY ROOF

CSI MASTERFORMAT: 02820
DRAWING FILE: FEN05-01

• This drawing is a template for preliminary design only, and is not intended for bid purposes. It is subject to modification based on design calculations, local practices, and all applicable codes and regulations.

• This wood fence post detail is rated as light-duty due to its height and direct burial installation system. It is typically found in residential, park, and light commercial settings. It is not intended to receive vertical loads from decks or major pergolas. Such loads require concrete footings.

• The treated wood post is positioned in an auger dug hole on an aggregate base to provide firm footing and adequate drainage. It also lessens the chance of settlement due to weight or lateral movement. If well-drained, excavated soil may be backfilled and tamped to secure the post, true and plumb.

• This detail is not suitable for wet clay soils, or poorly drained sites in cold climates due to periodic uplift movement.

• Rails may be attached with stainless steel screws for ease of repair and longevity of fence. All surfaces should be milled to shed water, even if treated wood is used.

• This fence post has a moderate life span of service due to eventual leaching of preservatives. Warm dry climates provide longer service potential.

• It is recommended that recycled and regionally available materials and products be given high priority in determining final design and specifications.

Installation Cost (per Linear Foot)

LOW   HIGH

$12.00

Maintenance

LOW   HIGH

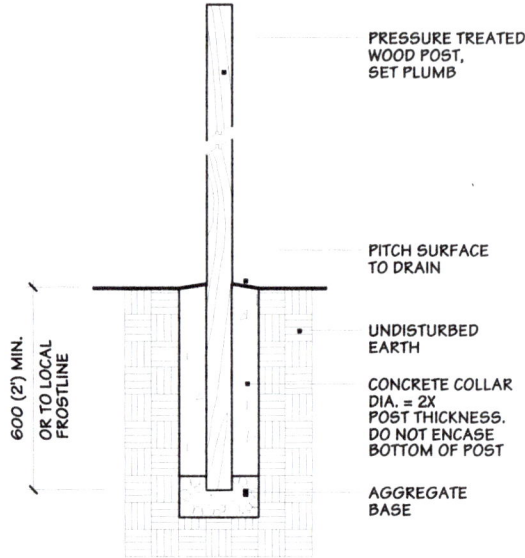

PRESSURE TREATED
WOOD POST,
SET PLUMB

PITCH SURFACE
TO DRAIN

UNDISTURBED
EARTH

CONCRETE COLLAR
DIA. = 2X
POST THICKNESS.
DO NOT ENCASE
BOTTOM OF POST

AGGREGATE
BASE

600 (2') MIN.
OR TO LOCAL
FROSTLINE

APPLICATION

CLIMATE

SUBGRADE

CSI MASTERFORMAT: 02820
DRAWING FILE: FEN05-02

• This drawing is a template for preliminary design only, and is not intended for bid purposes. It is subject to modification based on design calculations, local practices, and all applicable codes and regulations.

• This wood fence post detail is rated as medium-duty due to its height and direct burial installation system. It is typically found in residential, park, and light commercial settings. It is not intended to receive vertical loads from decks or major pergolas. Such loads require concrete footings.

• The treated wood post in concrete is positioned in an auger dug hole on an aggregate base to provide firm footing and adequate drainage. It also lessens the chance of settlement due to weight or lateral movement. In warm climates, hole may be filled with concrete, setting post true and plumb, taking care to slope top of concrete away from wood. Bottom of post should rest in aggregate to allow for drainage, and concrete should not engulf post bottom.

• If used in wet clay soils, or poorly drained sites in cold climates, more aggregate base should be used, and concrete should be placed within a smooth tubular paper form to prevent frost or soil expansion from lifting post.

• Rails may be attached with stainless steel screws for ease of repair and longevity of fence. All surfaces should be milled to shed water, even if treated wood is used.

• This fence post has a moderate life span of service due to eventual leaching of preservatives. Warm dry climates provide longer service potential. Annual preservative treatment at concrete line will help to prolong life in cold and wet climates.

• It is recommended that recycled and regionally available materials and products be given high priority in determining final design and specifications.

Installation Cost (per Linear Foot)

LOW   HIGH

$14.00

Maintenance

LOW   HIGH

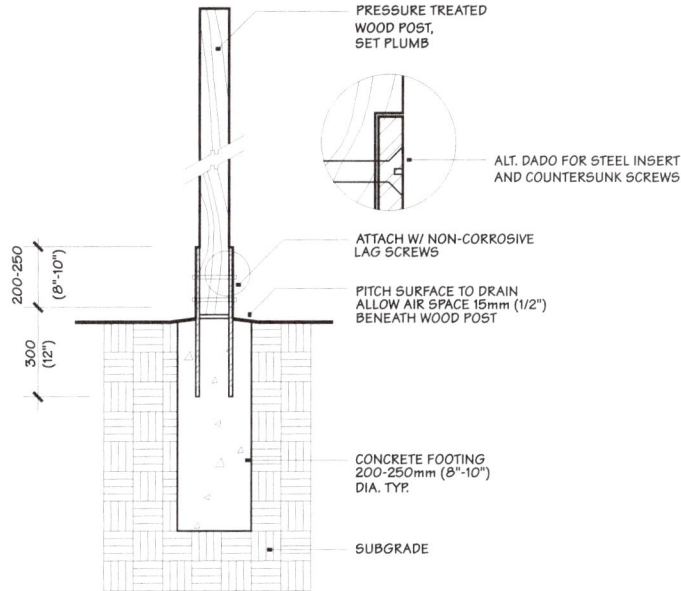

PRESSURE TREATED
WOOD POST,
SET PLUMB

ALT. DADO FOR STEEL INSERT
AND COUNTERSUNK SCREWS

ATTACH W/ NON-CORROSIVE
LAG SCREWS

PITCH SURFACE TO DRAIN
ALLOW AIR SPACE 15mm (1/2")
BENEATH WOOD POST

200-250
(8"-10")

300
(12")

CONCRETE FOOTING
200-250mm (8"-10")
DIA. TYP.

SUBGRADE

APPLICATION

CLIMATE

SUBGRADE

CSI MASTERFORMAT: 02820
DRAWING FILE: FEN05-03

• This drawing is a template for preliminary design only, and is not intended for bid purposes. It is subject to modification based on design calculations, local practices, and all applicable codes and regulations.

• This wood fence post on concrete pier is rated as heavy-duty due to its height and structural system. It is typically found in residential, park, and light commercial settings.

• The treated wood post is fastened to steel bars which are embedded in a concrete pier for permanent placement. This detail is especially effective in cold climates, and for use as a gate post on both hinge and latch ends. The post may be clad in clear wood and painted or stained.

• The post may be routed to receive flush alignment of steel bars attached with counter-sunk wood screws. If vertical loading is used, weld horizontal steel to vertical bars to create a stirrup support at post base.

• Rails may be attached with stainless steel screws for ease of repair and longevity. All surfaces are milled to shed water.

• This fence post has a long life span of service if routinely maintained with sealer or coatings, and is easily replaced if damage does occur.

• It is recommended that recycled and regionally available materials and products be given high priority in determining final design and specifications.

Installation Cost (per Linear Foot)

LOW   HIGH

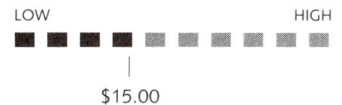

$15.00

Maintenance

LOW   HIGH

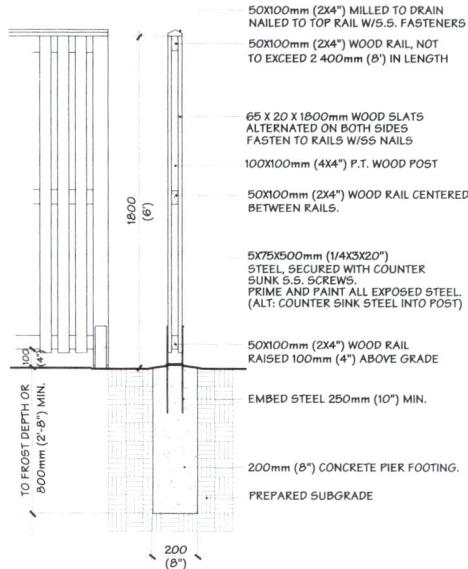

50X100mm (2X4") MILLED TO DRAIN
NAILED TO TOP RAIL W/S.S. FASTENERS

50X100mm (2X4") WOOD RAIL, NOT
TO EXCEED 2 400mm (8') IN LENGTH

65 X 20 X 1800mm WOOD SLATS
ALTERNATED ON BOTH SIDES
FASTEN TO RAILS W/SS NAILS

100X100mm (4X4") P.T. WOOD POST

50X100mm (2X4") WOOD RAIL CENTERED
BETWEEN RAILS.

5X75X500mm (1/4X3X20")
STEEL, SECURED WITH COUNTER
SUNK S.S. SCREWS.
PRIME AND PAINT ALL EXPOSED STEEL.
(ALT: COUNTER SINK STEEL INTO POST)

50X100mm (2X4") WOOD RAIL
RAISED 100mm (4") ABOVE GRADE

EMBED STEEL 250mm (10") MIN.

200mm (8") CONCRETE PIER FOOTING.

PREPARED SUBGRADE

1800 (6')

TO FROST DEPTH OR
800mm (2'-8") MIN.

100 4"

200 (8")

APPLICATION

CLIMATE

SUBGRADE

CSI MASTERFORMAT: 02820
DRAWING FILE: FEN05-05

• This drawing is a template for preliminary design only, and is not intended for bid purposes. It is subject to modification based on design calculations, local practices, and all applicable codes and regulations.

• This wood alternate board slat fence on concrete pier is rated as medium-duty due to its height and structural system. It is typically found in residential, park, and light commercial settings.

• The treated wood post is fastened to steel bars which are embedded in a concrete pier for permanent placement. This detail is especially effective in cold climates.

• The fence posts may be routed to receive flush alignment of steel bars attached with counter-sunk wood screws.

• Rails may be attached with stainless steel screws for ease of repair and longevity. All surfaces are milled to shed water.

• This fence has a long life span of service if routinely maintained with sealer or coatings, and is easily replaced if damage does occur.

• It is recommended that recycled and regionally available materials and products be given high priority in determining final design and specifications.

Installation Cost (per Linear Foot)

LOW   HIGH

$15.00

Maintenance

LOW   HIGH

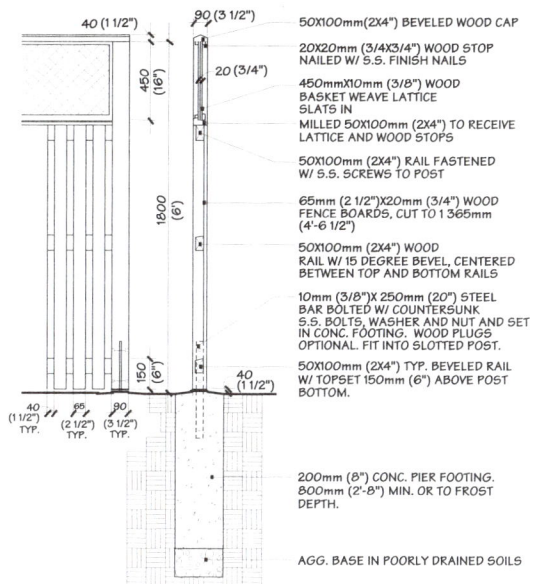

40 (1 1/2")
90 (3 1/2")
450 (16")
20 (3/4")
1800 (6')
150 (6")
40 (1 1/2")

40 (1 1/2") TYP.
65 (2 1/2") TYP.
90 (3 1/2") TYP.

50X100mm(2X4") BEVELED WOOD CAP

20X20mm (3/4X3/4") WOOD STOP NAILED W/ S.S. FINISH NAILS

450mmX10mm (3/8") WOOD BASKET WEAVE LATTICE SLATS IN

MILLED 50X100mm (2X4") TO RECEIVE LATTICE AND WOOD STOPS

50X100mm (2X4") RAIL FASTENED W/ S.S. SCREWS TO POST

65mm (2 1/2")X20mm (3/4") WOOD FENCE BOARDS, CUT TO 1 365mm (4'-6 1/2")

50X100mm (2X4") WOOD RAIL W/ 15 DEGREE BEVEL, CENTERED BETWEEN TOP AND BOTTOM RAILS

10mm (3/8")X 250mm (20") STEEL BAR BOLTED W/ COUNTERSUNK S.S. BOLTS, WASHER AND NUT AND SET IN CONC. FOOTING. WOOD PLUGS OPTIONAL. FIT INTO SLOTTED POST.

50X100mm (2X4") TYP. BEVELED RAIL W/ TOPSET 150mm (6") ABOVE POST BOTTOM.

200mm (8") CONC. PIER FOOTING. 800mm (2'-8") MIN. OR TO FROST DEPTH.

AGG. BASE IN POORLY DRAINED SOILS

APPLICATION

CLIMATE

SUBGRADE

CSI MASTERFORMAT: 02820
DRAWING FILE: FEN05-06

• This drawing is a template for preliminary design only, and is not intended for bid purposes. It is subject to modification based on design calculations, local practices, and all applicable codes and regulations.

• This wood slat fence with lattice on concrete pier is rated as medium-duty due to its height and structural system. It is typically found in residential, park, and light commercial settings.

• The treated wood post is fastened to a steel bar which is bolted into a centered slot and embedded in a concrete pier for permanent placement. This detail is especially effective in cold climates. Posts so installed should not be vertically loaded.

• Rails may be attached with stainless steel screws for ease of repair and longevity. All surfaces are milled as shown to shed water.

• Lattice units are tacked between bead stops nailed to posts and milled rails.

• This fence has a long life span of service if routinely maintained with sealer or coatings, and is easily replaced if damage does occur.

• It is recommended that recycled and regionally available materials and products be given high priority in determining final design and specifications.

Installation Cost (per Linear Foot)
LOW ... HIGH
$15.00

Maintenance
LOW ... HIGH

Lighting

350
(1'-2")

LIGHT FIXTURE W/LOUVER
AS SPECIFIED

20mm (3/4") L.T.F.M. CONDUIT
TO ALLOW 90° VERTICAL ROTATION

MOUNTING PLATE

FOUR 15x150mm (3/8"x6") LONG
S.S. VANDAL RESISTANT EXP. BOLTS

FINISH GRADE

40
(1 1/2")

600 MIN.
(2'-0")

900
(3'-0")

20mm (3/4") DIA. G.S. CONDUIT

150
(6")

THREE #12 FLEXIBLE CABLE
TYPE U.S.E.

CONC. FOUNDATION, REINF. AS REQ.
20mm (3/4") CHAMFERED TOP,
DEPTH VARIES WITH FROSTLINE

450
(1'-6")

APPLICATION

LIGHT | MED. | HEAVY

CLIMATE

ARID | HUMID | TEMP. | COLD

SUBGRADE

PERM. | CLAY | ROOF

CSI MASTERFORMAT: 16520
DRAWING FILE: LGT16-02

• This drawing is a template for preliminary design only, and is not intended for bid purposes. It is subject to modification based on design calculations, local practices, and all applicable codes and regulations.

• This above grade up-light detail is rated as medium-duty due to material strength, and application. It is typically found in planting beds and used to illuminate buildings, plants, and signs in public park, commercial, and institutional settings.

• Fixture requires a concrete footing which rests on subgrade below frost depth in cold and temperate climates. Air-entrained concrete is typically recommended due to freezing/thawing action.

• This fixture is best suited for warmer climates, or on raised pedestals in cold climates.

• Waterproof light fixture is attached to concrete with bolts and leveling plate and connected to standard waterproof junction box. Conduit is required for all connections.

• Fixture usually requires a protective planting or structure to guard against accidental damage or unsightly exposure in open lawns.

• It is recommended that recycled and regionally available materials and products be given high priority in determining final design and specifications.

Installation Cost (per Unit)

LOW ▪▫▫▫▫▫▫▫▫▫ HIGH

$250.00

Maintenance

LOW ▪▪▪▫▫▫▫▫▫▫ HIGH

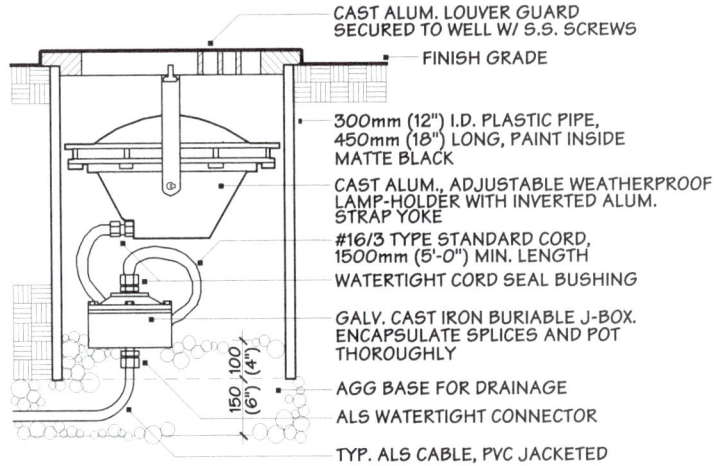

CAST ALUM. LOUVER GUARD
SECURED TO WELL W/ S.S. SCREWS

FINISH GRADE

300mm (12") I.D. PLASTIC PIPE,
450mm (18") LONG, PAINT INSIDE
MATTE BLACK

CAST ALUM., ADJUSTABLE WEATHERPROOF
LAMP-HOLDER WITH INVERTED ALUM.
STRAP YOKE

#16/3 TYPE STANDARD CORD,
1500mm (5'-0") MIN. LENGTH
WATERTIGHT CORD SEAL BUSHING

GALV. CAST IRON BURIABLE J-BOX.
ENCAPSULATE SPLICES AND POT
THOROUGHLY

AGG BASE FOR DRAINAGE
ALS WATERTIGHT CONNECTOR
TYP. ALS CABLE, PVC JACKETED

APPLICATION

CLIMATE

SUBGRADE

CSI MASTERFORMAT: 16520
DRAWING FILE: LGT16-01

• This drawing is a template for preliminary design only, and is not intended for bid purposes. It is subject to modification based on design calculations, local practices, and all applicable codes and regulations.

• This below grade up-light detail is rated as medium-duty due to material strength, grate, and application. It is typically found in planting beds and used to illuminate buildings, plants, and signs in public park, commercial, and institutional settings.

• This fixture is best suited for warmer climates, or under canopies in cold climates.

• Waterproof light fixture is suspended from grate, or casing clips and connected to standard waterproof junction box. Conduit is required for all connections. Plastic casing rests on an dense aggregate base.

• Open grating requires periodic cleaning of debris. Units are best located away from swales and natural low points to avoid an

excess of surface water. Clay soil sites may require sealed or on-grade fixtures.

• It is recommended that recycled and regionally available materials and products be given high priority in determining final design and specifications.

Installation Cost (per Unit)

LOW   HIGH

$200.00

Maintenance

LOW   HIGH

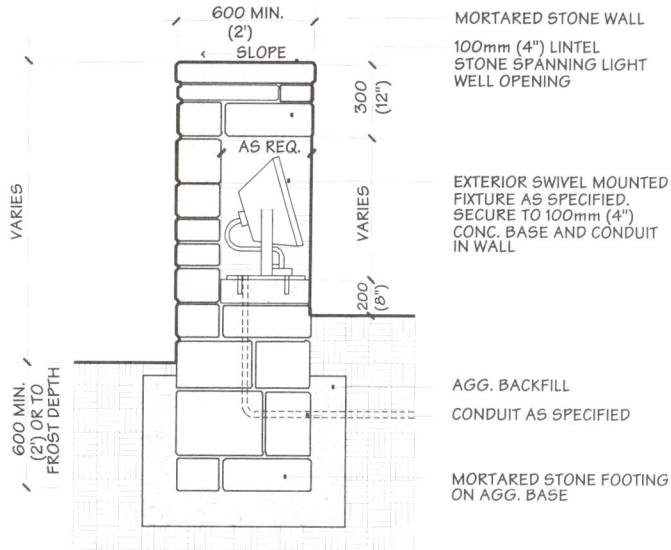

600 MIN. (2')
SLOPE

MORTARED STONE WALL

100mm (4") LINTEL STONE SPANNING LIGHT WELL OPENING

300 (12")

AS REQ.

EXTERIOR SWIVEL MOUNTED FIXTURE AS SPECIFIED. SECURE TO 100mm (4") CONC. BASE AND CONDUIT IN WALL

VARIES

200 (8")

VARIES

600 MIN. (2') OR TO FROST DEPTH

AGG. BACKFILL

CONDUIT AS SPECIFIED

MORTARED STONE FOOTING ON AGG. BASE

APPLICATION

CLIMATE

SUBGRADE

CSI MASTERFORMAT: 16520
DRAWING FILE: LGT16-04

• This drawing is a template for preliminary design only, and is not intended for bid purposes. It is subject to modification based on design calculations, local practices, and all applicable codes and regulations.

• This wall wash light detail is rated as heavy-duty due to material strength, and application. It is typically found in commercial and institutional settings used to illuminate buildings, monuments and other structures.

• This fixture is mounted on a concrete slab built into a stone wall which acts as a housing and conceals the light from view. Air-entrained concrete is typically recommended due to freezing/thawing action. This fixture is suited for all climates.

• Waterproof light fixture is attached to concrete with bolts and leveling plate and connected to standard waterproof junction box. Conduit is required for all connections.

• This detail provides excellent protection for the light and integrates it into the designed landscape.

• It is recommended that recycled and regionally available materials and products be given high priority in determining final design and specifications.

Installation Cost (per Unit)

LOW _____ HIGH

$500.00

Maintenance

LOW _____ HIGH

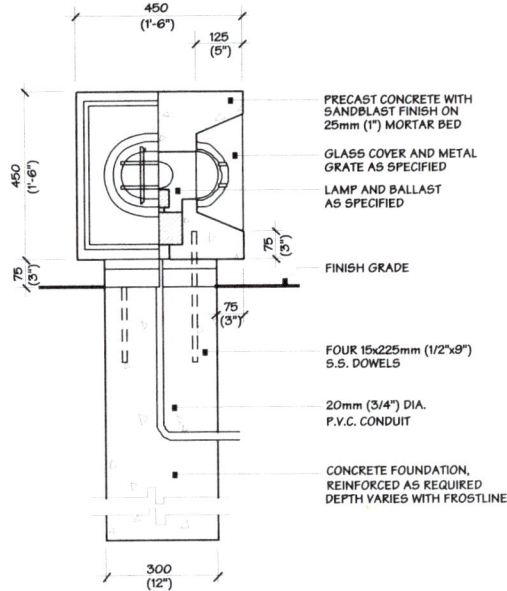

PRECAST CONCRETE WITH
SANDBLAST FINISH ON
25mm (1") MORTAR BED

GLASS COVER AND METAL
GRATE AS SPECIFIED

LAMP AND BALLAST
AS SPECIFIED

FINISH GRADE

FOUR 15x225mm (1/2"x9")
S.S. DOWELS

20mm (3/4") DIA.
P.V.C. CONDUIT

CONCRETE FOUNDATION,
REINFORCED AS REQUIRED
DEPTH VARIES WITH FROSTLINE

APPLICATION

CLIMATE

SUBGRADE

CSI MASTERFORMAT: 16520
DRAWING FILE: LGT13-02

• This drawing is a template for preliminary design only, and is not intended for bid purposes. It is subject to modification based on design calculations, local practices, and all applicable codes and regulations.

• This concrete on-grade area light detail is rated as heavy-duty due to material strength, base, and application. It is typically found along public walkways associated with public parks, commercial, and institutional settings. Although custom designed, it represents a family of precast concrete fixtures typical of institutional applications.

• Reinforcing practices vary widely by region. Local codes and practices should be consulted prior to specifying any type of reinforcing.

• If designed for temperate or cold climates, air-entrained concrete is typically recommended due to freezing/thawing action. Footing must bear on subgrade below frost depth in this circumstance.

• Concrete unit is attached with dowels and mortared to concrete base, or alternately set with polymer adhesive. Conduit is required for all connections.

• It is recommended that recycled and regionally available materials and products be given high priority in determining final design and specifications.

Installation Cost (per Unit)

LOW   HIGH

$500.00

Maintenance

LOW   HIGH

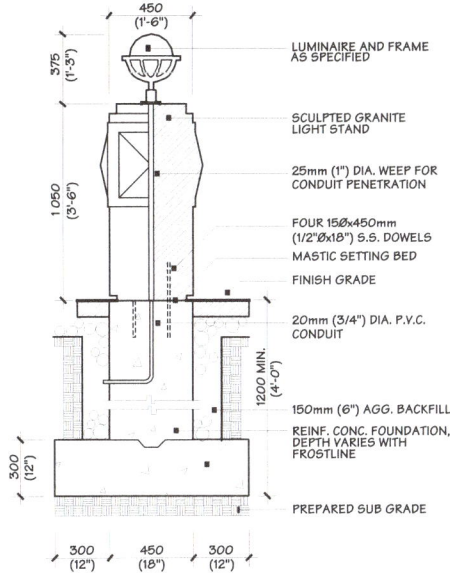

450 (1'-6")

575 (1'-3")

1,050 (3'-6")

1,200 MIN. (4'-0")

300 (12")

300 (12")   450 (18")   300 (12")

LUMINAIRE AND FRAME AS SPECIFIED

SCULPTED GRANITE LIGHT STAND

25mm (1") DIA. WEEP FOR CONDUIT PENETRATION

FOUR 150x450mm (1/2"Øx18") S.S. DOWELS

MASTIC SETTING BED

FINISH GRADE

20mm (3/4") DIA. P.V.C. CONDUIT

150mm (6") AGG. BACKFILL

REINF. CONC. FOUNDATION, DEPTH VARIES WITH FROSTLINE

PREPARED SUB GRADE

APPLICATION

CLIMATE

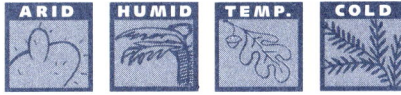

SUBGRADE

CSI MASTERFORMAT: 16520
DRAWING FILE: LGT13-03

• This drawing is a template for preliminary design only, and is not intended for bid purposes. It is subject to modification based on design calculations, local practices, and all applicable codes and regulations.

• This sculpted granite stand area light is rated as heavy-duty due to material strength, base, and application. It is typically found along public walkways associated with public parks, commercial, and institutional settings. Although custom designed, it represents a family of cut stone bases typical of institutional applications.

• Reinforcing practices vary widely by region. Local codes and practices should be consulted prior to specifying any type of reinforcing.

• If designed for temperate or cold climates, air-entrained concrete is typically recommended due to freezing/thawing action.

• Stone is attached with dowels and mortared to concrete base, or alternately set

with polymer adhesive. Conduit is required for all connections.

• It is recommended that recycled and regionally available materials and products be given high priority in determining final design and specifications.

Installation Cost (per Unit)

LOW   HIGH

$500.00

Maintenance

LOW   HIGH

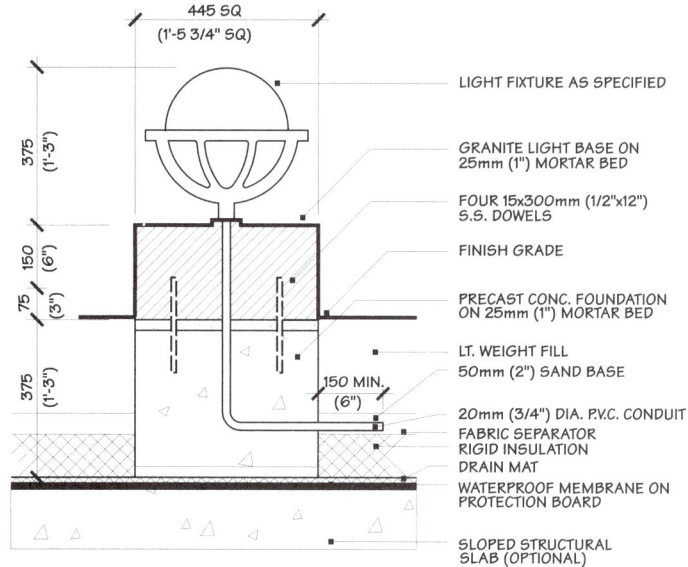

445 SQ
(1'-5 3/4" SQ)

375 (1'-3")
150 (6")
75 (3")
375 (1'-3")
150 MIN. (6")

LIGHT FIXTURE AS SPECIFIED

GRANITE LIGHT BASE ON
25mm (1") MORTAR BED

FOUR 15x300mm (1/2"x12")
S.S. DOWELS

FINISH GRADE

PRECAST CONC. FOUNDATION
ON 25mm (1") MORTAR BED

LT. WEIGHT FILL
50mm (2") SAND BASE

20mm (3/4") DIA. P.V.C. CONDUIT
FABRIC SEPARATOR
RIGID INSULATION
DRAIN MAT
WATERPROOF MEMBRANE ON
PROTECTION BOARD

SLOPED STRUCTURAL
SLAB (OPTIONAL)

APPLICATION

CLIMATE

SUBGRADE

CSI MASTERFORMAT: 16520
DRAWING FILE: LGT13-01

• This drawing is a template for preliminary design only, and is not intended for bid purposes. It is subject to modification based on design calculations, local practices, and all applicable codes and regulations.

• This granite stand area light is rated as heavy-duty due to material strength, base, and application. It is typically found along public walkways, in pedestrian areas on structural roof deck. Although custom designed, it represents a family of cut stone bases typical of institutional applications.

• Concrete base is placed directly onto heavy-duty drainage mat on sloping protection board, waterproof membrane, and structural slab.

• Reinforcing practices vary widely by region. Local codes and practices should be consulted prior to specifying any type of reinforcing.

• If designed for temperate or cold climates, air-entrained concrete is typically recommended due to freezing/thawing action.

• Stone is attached with dowels and mortared to concrete base, or alternately set with polymer adhesive. Conduit is required for all connections.

• It is recommended that recycled and regionally available materials and products be given high priority in determining final design and specifications.

Installation Cost (per Unit)

LOW   HIGH

$500.00

Maintenance

LOW   HIGH

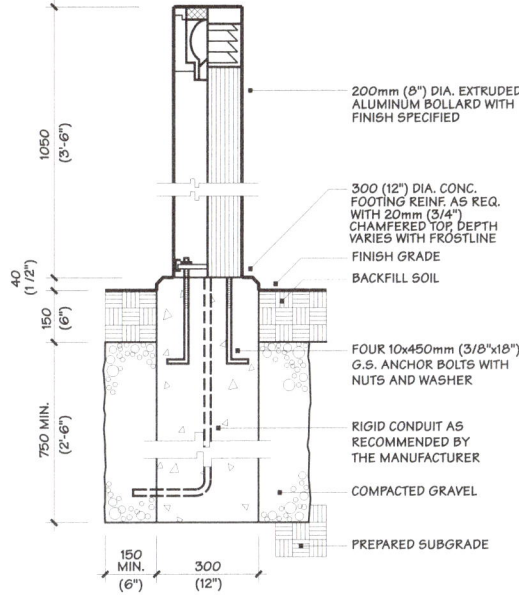

200mm (8") DIA. EXTRUDED ALUMINUM BOLLARD WITH FINISH SPECIFIED

300 (12") DIA. CONC. FOOTING REINF. AS REQ. WITH 20mm (3/4") CHAMFERED TOP, DEPTH VARIES WITH FROSTLINE

FINISH GRADE

BACKFILL SOIL

FOUR 10x450mm (3/8"x18") G.S. ANCHOR BOLTS WITH NUTS AND WASHER

RIGID CONDUIT AS RECOMMENDED BY THE MANUFACTURER

COMPACTED GRAVEL

PREPARED SUBGRADE

1050 (3'-6")
40 (1 1/2")
150 (6")
750 MIN. (2'-6")
150 MIN. (6")
300 (12")

APPLICATION

CLIMATE

SUBGRADE

CSI MASTERFORMAT: 16520
DRAWING FILE: LGT16-03

- This drawing is a template for preliminary design only, and is not intended for bid purposes. It is subject to modification based on design calculations, local practices, and all applicable codes and regulations.

- This metal bollard walkway light is rated as medium-duty due to material strength, height and application. It is typically found along public walkways, in pedestrian areas.

- Concrete footing depth is determined by soil type, and pole height, and is typically 10% of pole height plus 600 mm (2') in depth, under normal conditions. Footings should extend beyond frost line in cold climates regardless of minimal calculation.

- Reinforcing practices vary widely by region. Local codes and practices should be consulted prior to specifying any type of reinforcing.

- If designed for temperate or cold climates, air-entrained concrete is typically recommended due to freezing/thawing action.

- Most fixtures are non-glare types using reflective indirect configurations and are appropriate for public settings. Concrete bolt pattern jig is usually provided by manufacturer.

- It is recommended that recycled and regionally available materials and products be given high priority in determining final design and specifications.

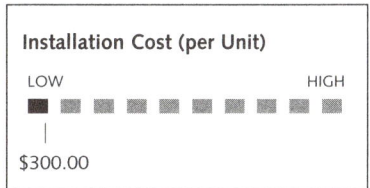

Installation Cost (per Unit)

LOW   HIGH

$300.00

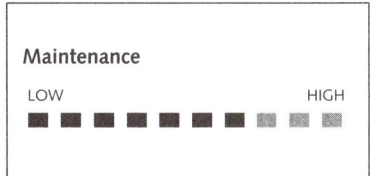

Maintenance

LOW   HIGH

40
(1/2")

ROUT POST TO RECEIVE
JUNCTION BOX

925
(3'-1")

600
(2'-0")

LIGHT FIXTURE
AS SPECIFIED

CONDUIT SET INTO POST,
COVERED WITH WOOD STRIP

200X200mm (8"x8")
PRESSURE-TREATED
WOOD POST WITH 20mm
(3/4") CHAMFERED TOP

FINISH GRADE

150 MIN.
(6")

COMPACTED SUBGRADE

300
(12")

CONC. COLLAR FOOTING,
DEPTH VARIES WITH
FROSTLINE

25-30
(1-2")

100
(4")

100
(4")

APPLICATION

LIGHT   MED.   HEAVY

CLIMATE

ARID   HUMID   TEMP.   COLD

SUBGRADE

PERM.   CLAY   ROOF

CSI MASTERFORMAT: 16520
DRAWING FILE: LGT15-01

• This drawing is a template for preliminary design only, and is not intended for bid purposes. It is subject to modification based on design calculations, local practices, and all applicable codes and regulations.

• This wood bollard walkway light is rated as light-duty due to material strength, height, and application. It is typically found along public walkways, in pedestrian areas in school, park, or garden settings.

• Footing depth is determined by soil type, and post height, and is typically 10% of post height plus 600 mm (2') in depth, under normal conditions. Footings should extend beyond frost line in cold climates regardless of minimal calculation.

• Wood is rot resistant or treated and directly buried with a concrete collar at bottom of post. Post is milled, drilled, and routed to receive conduit, box, and fixture. Wood strip typically covers conduit slot in rear of post.

• This detail is economical, but has a limited service life due to wood deterioration. It is more suited to warmer drier settings.

• Most fixtures are non-glare types, often using low voltage power systems.

• It is recommended that recycled and regionally available materials and products be given high priority in determining final design and specifications.

Installation Cost (per Unit)

LOW   HIGH

$100.00

Maintenance

LOW   HIGH

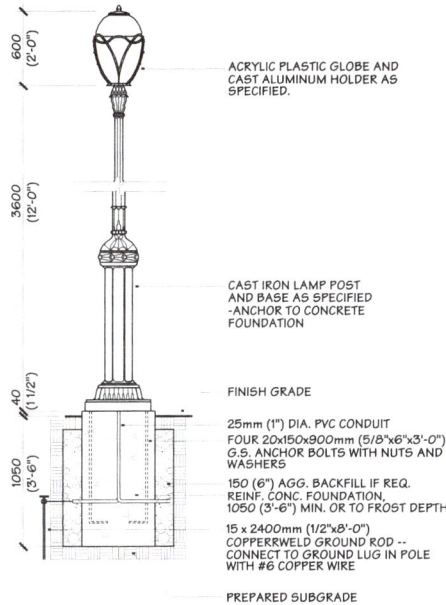

Diagram labels:

600 (2'-0")
3600 (12'-0")
40 (1 1/2")
1050 (3'-6")

ACRYLIC PLASTIC GLOBE AND CAST ALUMINUM HOLDER AS SPECIFIED.

CAST IRON LAMP POST AND BASE AS SPECIFIED -ANCHOR TO CONCRETE FOUNDATION

FINISH GRADE

25mm (1") DIA. PVC CONDUIT

FOUR 20x150x900mm (5/8"x6"x3'-0") G.S. ANCHOR BOLTS WITH NUTS AND WASHERS

150 (6") AGG. BACKFILL IF REQ. REINF. CONC. FOUNDATION, 1050 (3'-6") MIN. OR TO FROST DEPTH

15 x 2400mm (1/2"x8'-0") COPPERRWELD GROUND ROD -- CONNECT TO GROUND LUG IN POLE WITH #6 COPPER WIRE

PREPARED SUBGRADE

APPLICATION	CLIMATE	SUBGRADE

CSI MASTERFORMAT: 16520
DRAWING FILE: LGT26-01

• This drawing is a template for preliminary design only, and is not intended for bid purposes. It is subject to modification based on design calculations, local practices, and all applicable codes and regulations.

• This cast iron historic replica walkway light is rated as heavy-duty due to material strength, concrete footing attachment, and finish. It is typically found in public street, urban park, and institutional settings.

• Concrete footing depth is determined by soil type, pole height, and wind loads, and is typically 10% of pole height plus 600 mm (2') in depth, under in normal conditions.

• Reinforcing practices vary widely by region. Local codes and practices should be consulted prior to specifying any type of reinforcing.

• If designed for temperate or cold climates, air-entrained concrete is typically recommended due to freezing/thawing action.

• Cast iron is very expensive but it is very durable and appropriate for public settings.

• It is recommended that recycled and regionally available materials and products be given high priority in determining final design and specifications.

Installation Cost (per Unit)

LOW   HIGH

$1000.00

Maintenance

LOW   HIGH

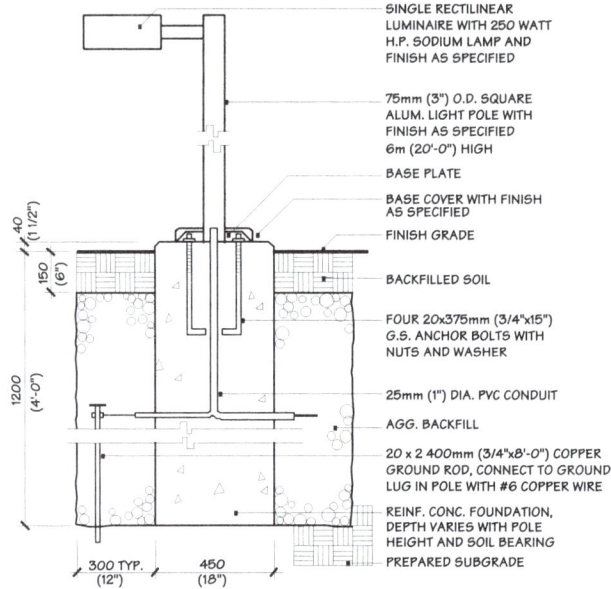

SINGLE RECTILINEAR LUMINAIRE WITH 250 WATT H.P. SODIUM LAMP AND FINISH AS SPECIFIED

75mm (3") O.D. SQUARE ALUM. LIGHT POLE WITH FINISH AS SPECIFIED 6m (20'-0") HIGH

BASE PLATE

BASE COVER WITH FINISH AS SPECIFIED

FINISH GRADE

BACKFILLED SOIL

FOUR 20x375mm (3/4"x15") G.S. ANCHOR BOLTS WITH NUTS AND WASHER

25mm (1") DIA. PVC CONDUIT

AGG. BACKFILL

20 x 2 400mm (3/4"x8'-0") COPPER GROUND ROD, CONNECT TO GROUND LUG IN POLE WITH #6 COPPER WIRE

REINF. CONC. FOUNDATION, DEPTH VARIES WITH POLE HEIGHT AND SOIL BEARING

PREPARED SUBGRADE

40 (1 1/2")
150 (6")
1200 (4'-0")
300 TYP. (12")
450 (18")

APPLICATION

CLIMATE

SUBGRADE

CSI MASTERFORMAT: 16520
DRAWING FILE: LGT36-01

• This drawing is a template for preliminary design only, and is not intended for bid purposes. It is subject to modification based on design calculations, local practices, and all applicable codes and regulations.

• This typical cutoff light is rated as medium-duty due to material strength, concrete footing attachment, and finish. It is typically found in public street, urban park, and institutional road settings.

• Concrete footing depth is determined by soil type, pole height, and wind loads, and is typically 10% of pole height plus 600 mm (2') in depth, under normal conditions. Bolt spacing jig is often supplied by manufacturer.

• Reinforcing practices vary widely by region. Local codes and practices should be consulted prior to specifying any type of reinforcing.

• If designed for temperate or cold climates, air-entrained concrete is typically recommended due to freezing/thawing action.

• Aluminum pole is durable and is available in a number of finishes. Maintenance is relatively low.

• It is recommended that recycled and regionally available materials and products be given high priority in determining final design and specifications.

Installation Cost (per Unit)

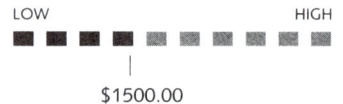

LOW   HIGH

$1500.00

Maintenance

LOW   HIGH

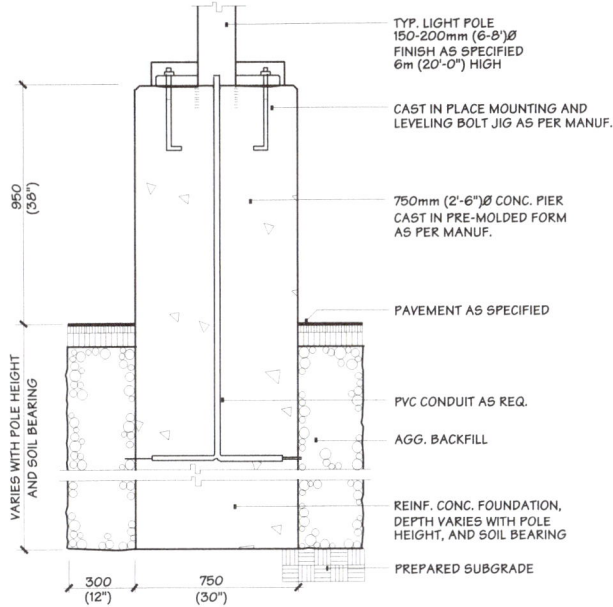

TYP. LIGHT POLE
150-200mm (6-8')Ø
FINISH AS SPECIFIED
6m (20'-0") HIGH

CAST IN PLACE MOUNTING AND
LEVELING BOLT JIG AS PER MANUF.

750mm (2'-6")Ø CONC. PIER
CAST IN PRE-MOLDED FORM
AS PER MANUF.

PAVEMENT AS SPECIFIED

PVC CONDUIT AS REQ.

AGG. BACKFILL

REINF. CONC. FOUNDATION,
DEPTH VARIES WITH POLE
HEIGHT, AND SOIL BEARING

PREPARED SUBGRADE

950 (38")

VARIES WITH POLE HEIGHT AND SOIL BEARING

300 (12")   750 (30")

APPLICATION

CLIMATE

SUBGRADE

CSI MASTERFORMAT: 16520
DRAWING FILE: LGT36-02

• This drawing is a template for preliminary design only, and is not intended for bid purposes. It is subject to modification based on design calculations, local practices, and all applicable codes and regulations.

• This vehicular light with raised footing detail is rated as heavy-duty due to material strength, concrete footing attachment, and finish. It is typically found in public street, urban park, and institutional road settings.

• This detail shows the application of a proprietary form designed to fit over a standard fiber form for a smooth ornamental effect. Many style options are available.

• Concrete footing depth is determined by soil type, pole height, and wind loads, and is typically 10% of pole height plus 600 mm (2') in depth, under normal conditions. Bolt spacing jig is often supplied by manufacturer.

• Reinforcing practices vary widely by region. Local codes and practices should be consulted prior to specifying any type of reinforcing.

• If designed for temperate or cold climates, air-entrained concrete is typically recommended due to freezing/thawing action.

• It is recommended that recycled and regionally available materials and products be given high priority in determining final design and specifications.

Installation Cost (per Unit)

LOW   HIGH

$2500.00

Maintenance

LOW   HIGH

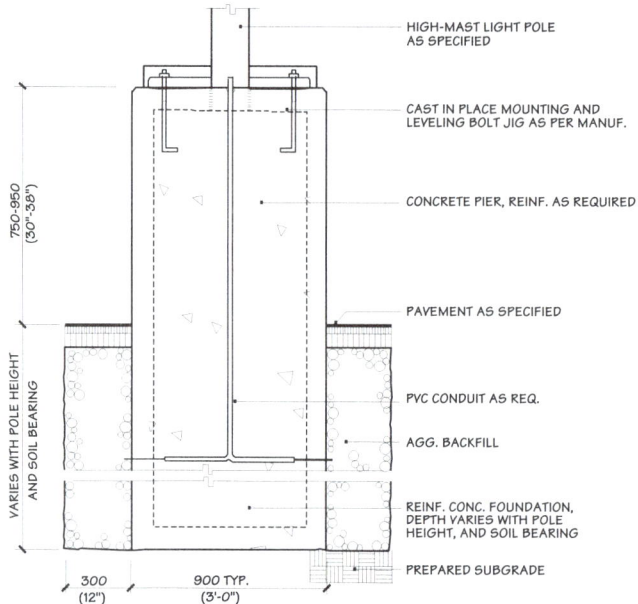

HIGH-MAST LIGHT POLE AS SPECIFIED

CAST IN PLACE MOUNTING AND LEVELING BOLT JIG AS PER MANUF.

CONCRETE PIER, REINF. AS REQUIRED

PAVEMENT AS SPECIFIED

PVC CONDUIT AS REQ.

AGG. BACKFILL

REINF. CONC. FOUNDATION, DEPTH VARIES WITH POLE HEIGHT, AND SOIL BEARING

PREPARED SUBGRADE

750-950 (30"-38")

VARIES WITH POLE HEIGHT AND SOIL BEARING

300 (12")

900 TYP. (3'-0")

APPLICATION

CLIMATE

SUBGRADE

CSI MASTERFORMAT: 16520
DRAWING FILE: LGT46-01

• This drawing is a template for preliminary design only, and is not intended for bid purposes. It is subject to modification based on design calculations, local practices, and all applicable codes and regulations.

• This high mast light base detail is rated as heavy-duty due to material strength, concrete footing attachment, and finish. It is typically found in public street, urban park, and institutional road settings.

• This detail shows typical dimensions of high mast light footings. Soils play a critical role in determining final diameter and depth base on bearing and shearing characteristics.

• Concrete footing depth is determined by soil type, pole height, and wind loads, and is typically 10% of pole height plus 600 mm (2') in depth, under normal conditions. Bolt spacing jig is often supplied by manufacturer.

• Reinforcing practices vary widely by region. Local codes and practices should be consulted prior to specifying any type of reinforcing.

• If designed for temperate or cold climates, air-entrained concrete is typically recommended due to freezing/thawing action.

• It is recommended that recycled and regionally available materials and products be given high priority in determining final design and specifications.

Installation Cost (per Unit)

LOW   HIGH

$5000.00

Maintenance

LOW   HIGH

Paving

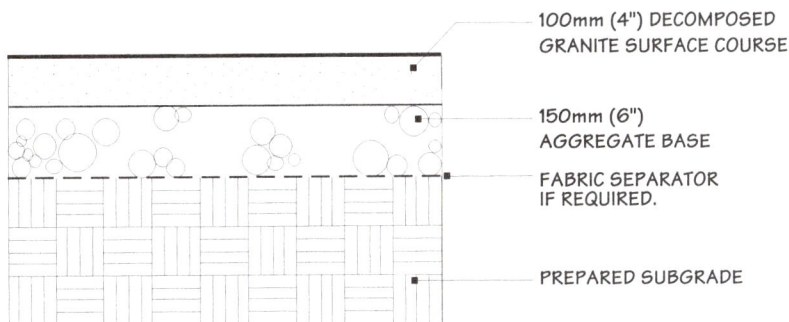

100mm (4") DECOMPOSED GRANITE SURFACE COURSE

150mm (6") AGGREGATE BASE

FABRIC SEPARATOR IF REQUIRED.

PREPARED SUBGRADE

APPLICATION

CLIMATE

SUBGRADE

CSI MASTERFORMAT: 02730
DRAWING FILE: PAV17-03

• This drawing is a template for preliminary design only, and is not intended for bid purposes. It is subject to modification based on design calculations, local practices, and all applicable codes and regulations.

• This detail is rated for medium-duty applications based on paving course and base thickness, and may support pedestrian loading associated with walks and light service access in parks, residential, and light institutional settings such as outdoor sculpture courts.

• The subgrade conditions have a significant impact on the design of flexible pavements, such as aggregate finish courses. Loads are transferred more directly to the base, requiring well-drained soils with adequate bearing capacity. Use a fabric separator reinforcing layer on the subgrade if existing soil requires or if loading is uneven.

• Fabric may be used as a separator to prevent migration of aggregates between base and subbase.

• Aggregate pavements usually require a secure edge containment to prevent migration and to ease maintenance.

• While this is a low installation cost paving alternative, it may require moderate maintenance. Aggregate should be periodically replenished and re-graded to ensure continued performance. Decomposed granite is usually found in hot-humid regions. Graded crushed stone screenings may be substituted in cold and temperate regions.

• Fabric, chemical, or manual methods may be needed to remove unwanted vegetative growth from the paved surface.

• It is recommended that recycled and regionally available materials and products be given high priority in determining final design and specifications.

Installation Cost (per Square Foot)

LOW   HIGH

$1.66

Maintenance

LOW   HIGH

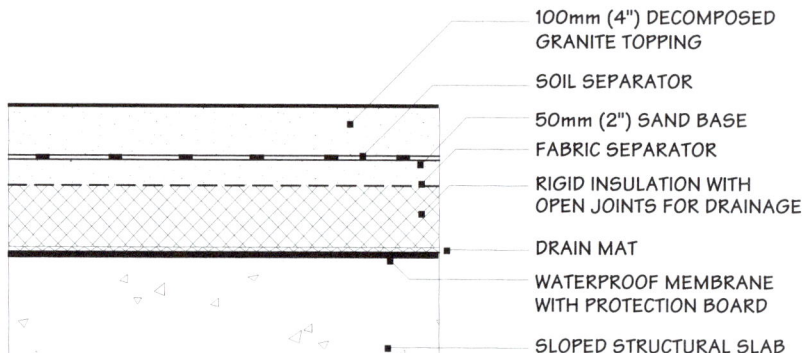

100mm (4") DECOMPOSED
GRANITE TOPPING

SOIL SEPARATOR

50mm (2") SAND BASE
FABRIC SEPARATOR

RIGID INSULATION WITH
OPEN JOINTS FOR DRAINAGE

DRAIN MAT

WATERPROOF MEMBRANE
WITH PROTECTION BOARD

SLOPED STRUCTURAL SLAB

APPLICATION

CLIMATE

SUBGRADE

CSI MASTERFORMAT: 02730
DRAWING FILE: PAV17-04

• This drawing is a template for preliminary design only, and is not intended for bid purposes. It is subject to modification based on design calculations, local practices, and all applicable codes and regulations.

• This detail is rated for light-duty applications due to pavement thickness and bearing limitations of the rigid insulation upon which it rests, and may support pedestrian loading associated with walks and light institutional settings such as outdoor sculpture courts on structural roof decks.

• A sand base is placed on fabric separator over open jointed rigid insulation. A drain mat is placed over sloping protection board and waterproof membrane.

• Fabric may be used as a separator both to prevent migration of aggregates between surface and sand base, and to bind the surface as well.

• Aggregate pavements usually require a secure edge containment to prevent migration and to ease maintenance.

• While this is a low installation cost paving alternative, it may require moderate maintenance. Aggregate should be periodically replenished and re-graded to ensure continued performance. Decomposed granite is usually found in hot-humid regions. Graded crushed stone screenings may be substituted in cold and temperate regions.

• Fabric, chemical, or manual methods may be needed to remove unwanted vegetative growth from the paved surface.

• It is recommended that recycled and regionally available materials and products be given high priority in determining final design and specifications.

Installation Cost (per Square Foot)

LOW   HIGH

$3.40

Maintenance

LOW   HIGH

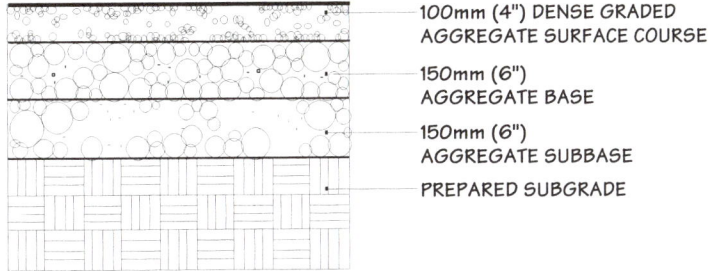

100mm (4") DENSE GRADED
AGGREGATE SURFACE COURSE

150mm (6")
AGGREGATE BASE

150mm (6")
AGGREGATE SUBBASE

PREPARED SUBGRADE

APPLICATION

CLIMATE

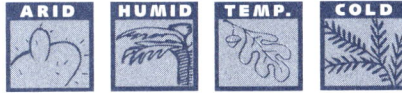

SUBGRADE

CSI MASTERFORMAT: 02730
DRAWING FILE: PAV37-02

• This drawing is a template for preliminary design only, and is not intended for bid purposes. It is subject to modification based on design calculations, local practices, and all applicable codes and regulations.

• This detail is rated for heavy-duty applications based on paving course and base thickness, and may support vehicular access in parks, residential, and institutional settings.

• The subgrade conditions have a significant impact on the design of flexible porous pavements, such as dense graded aggregates. Loads are transferred more directly to the base, requiring well-drained soils with adequate bearing capacity. This detail uses an aggregate subbase for additional pavement support.

• Surface course should consist of dense graded aggregate to create uniform surface and promote an interlocking of aggregates to resist shear forces. A binding material, such as clay, may also be used to help support loads.

• While this is a low installation cost paving alternative, it may require moderate maintenance. Aggregate may need periodical replenishment and re-grading to ensure continued performance.

• Fabric, chemical, or manual methods may be needed to remove unwanted vegetative growth from the surface.

• Edging is usually required to contain aggregates and ease maintenance.

• It is recommended that recycled and regionally available materials and products be given high priority in determining final design and specifications.

Installation Cost (per Square Foot)

LOW   HIGH

$2.41

Maintenance

LOW   HIGH

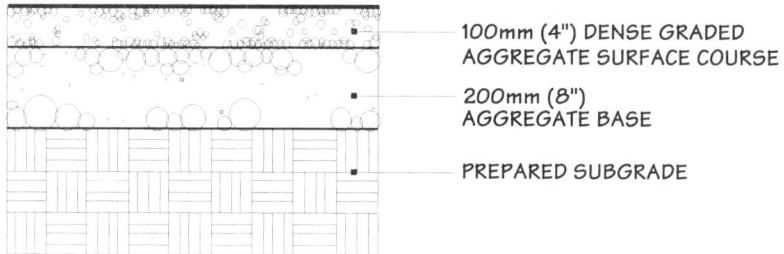

100mm (4") DENSE GRADED
AGGREGATE SURFACE COURSE

200mm (8")
AGGREGATE BASE

PREPARED SUBGRADE

APPLICATION

CLIMATE

SUBGRADE

CSI MASTERFORMAT: 02730
DRAWING FILE: PAV37-01

• This drawing is a template for preliminary design only, and is not intended for bid purposes. It is subject to modification based on design calculations, local practices, and all applicable codes and regulations.

• This detail is rated for medium-duty applications based on paving course and base thickness, and may support significant pedestrian loading associated with park walkways, and vehicular access in parks and residential settings.

• The subgrade conditions have a significant impact on the design of flexible porous pavements, such as dense graded aggregates. Loads are transferred more directly to the base, requiring well-drained soils with adequate bearing capacity.

• Surface course should consist of dense graded aggregate to create uniform surface and promote an interlocking of aggregates to resist shear forces. A binding material, such as clay, may also be used to help support loads.

• While this is a low installation cost paving alternative, it may require moderate maintenance. Aggregate may need periodical replenishment and re-grading to ensure continued performance.

• Fabric, chemical, or manual methods may be needed to remove unwanted vegetative growth from the surface.

• Edging is usually required to contain aggregates and ease maintenance.

• It is recommended that recycled and regionally available materials and products be given high priority in determining final design and specifications.

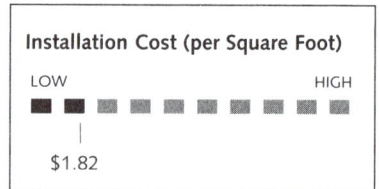

Installation Cost (per Square Foot)

LOW   HIGH

$1.82

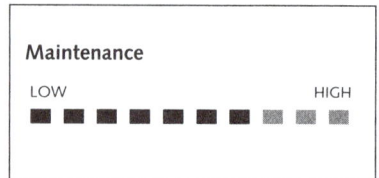

Maintenance

LOW   HIGH

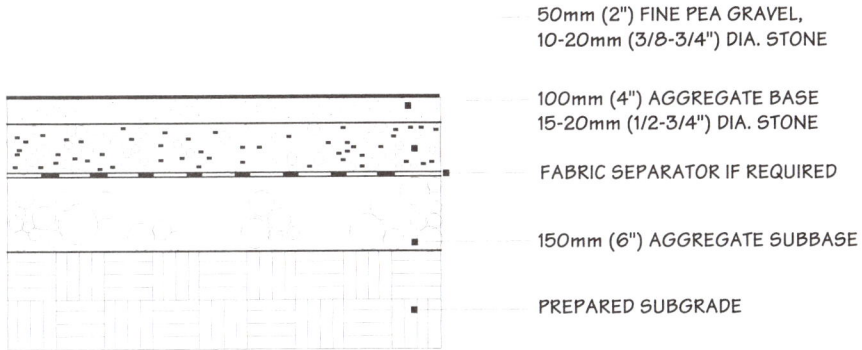

50mm (2") FINE PEA GRAVEL,
10-20mm (3/8-3/4") DIA. STONE

100mm (4") AGGREGATE BASE
15-20mm (1/2-3/4") DIA. STONE

FABRIC SEPARATOR IF REQUIRED

150mm (6") AGGREGATE SUBBASE

PREPARED SUBGRADE

APPLICATION

CLIMATE

SUBGRADE

CSI MASTERFORMAT: 02730
DRAWING FILE: PAV17-01

• This drawing is a template for preliminary design only, and is not intended for bid purposes. It is subject to modification based on design calculations, local practices, and all applicable codes and regulations.

• This detail is rated for light-duty applications based on paving course and base thickness, and may support primarily pedestrian loading associated with walks and light service access in parks, residential, and light institutional settings such as outdoor sculpture courts.

• The subgrade conditions have a significant impact on the design of flexible pavements, such as aggregate finish courses. Loads are transferred more directly to the base, requiring well-drained soils with adequate bearing capacity.

• Fabric may be used as a separator to prevent migration of aggregates between base and subbase.

• Aggregate pavements usually require a secure edge containment to prevent migration and to ease maintenance.

• While this is a low installation cost paving alternative, it may require moderate maintenance. Pea gravel should be periodically replenished and re-graded to ensure continued performance.

• Fabric, chemical, or manual methods may be needed to remove unwanted vegetative growth from the paved surface.

• It is recommended that recycled and regionally available materials and products be given high priority in determining final design and specifications.

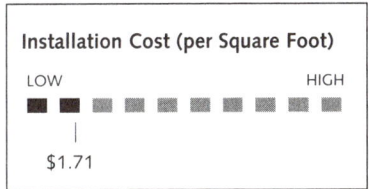

Installation Cost (per Square Foot)

LOW   HIGH

$1.71

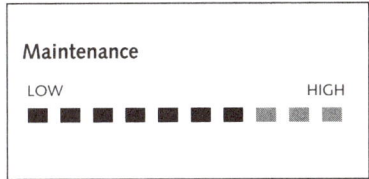

Maintenance

LOW   HIGH

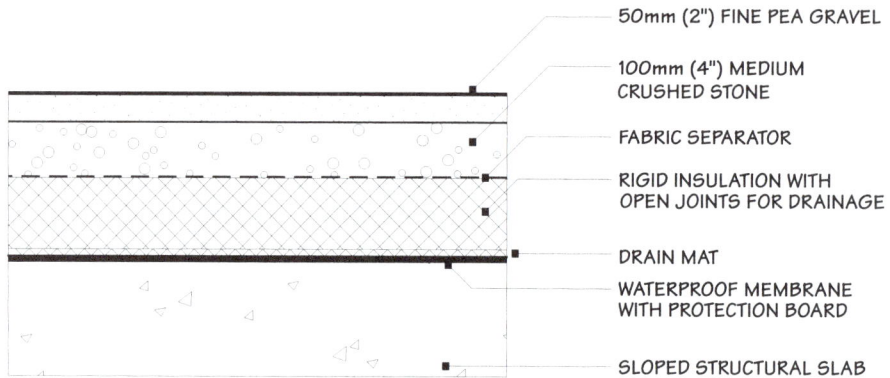

50mm (2") FINE PEA GRAVEL

100mm (4") MEDIUM
CRUSHED STONE

FABRIC SEPARATOR

RIGID INSULATION WITH
OPEN JOINTS FOR DRAINAGE

DRAIN MAT

WATERPROOF MEMBRANE
WITH PROTECTION BOARD

SLOPED STRUCTURAL SLAB

APPLICATION

CLIMATE

SUBGRADE

CSI MASTERFORMAT: 02730
DRAWING FILE: PAV17-02

• This drawing is a template for preliminary design only, and is not intended for bid purposes. It is subject to modification based on design calculations, local practices, and all applicable codes and regulations.

• This detail is rated for light-duty applications due to pavement thickness and bearing limitations of the rigid insulation upon which it rests, and may support primarily pedestrian loading associated with walks and light institutional settings such as outdoor sculpture courts on roof decks.

• A crushed stone aggregate base is placed on fabric separator over open jointed rigid insulation. A drain mat is placed over sloping protection board and waterproof membrane.

• Aggregate pavements usually require a secure edge containment to prevent migration and to ease maintenance.

• While this is a low installation cost paving alternative, it may require moderate mainte-nance. Pea gravel should be periodically replenished and re-graded to ensure continued performance.

• It is recommended that recycled and regionally available materials and products be given high priority in determining final design and specifications.

Installation Cost (per Square Foot)

LOW   HIGH

$3.36

Maintenance

LOW   HIGH

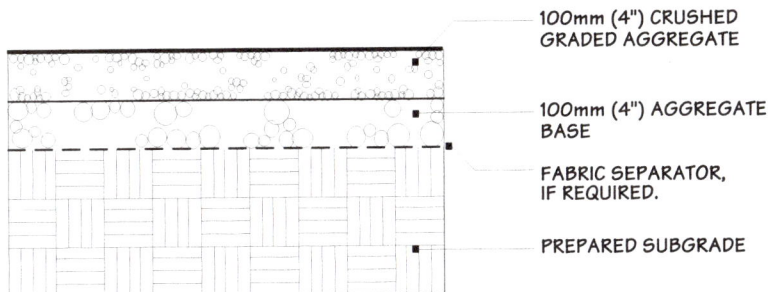

100mm (4") CRUSHED
GRADED AGGREGATE

100mm (4") AGGREGATE
BASE

FABRIC SEPARATOR,
IF REQUIRED.

PREPARED SUBGRADE

APPLICATION

CLIMATE

SUBGRADE

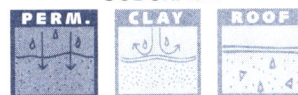

CSI MASTERFORMAT: 02740
DRAWING FILE: PAV11-01

• This drawing is a template for preliminary design only, and is not intended for bid purposes. It is subject to modification based on design calculations, local practices, and all applicable codes and regulations.

• This detail is rated for light-duty applications based on paving course and base thickness, and may support primarily pedestrian loading associated with walks and light service access in parks, residential, and light institutional settings such as outdoor sculpture courts.

• The subgrade conditions have a significant impact on the design of flexible pavements, such as aggregate finish courses. Loads are transferred more directly to the base, requiring well-drained soils with adequate bearing capacity.

• Fabric may be used to bind the base and to contain edges in low bearing or colloidal soils.

• Aggregate pavements usually require a secure edge containment to prevent migration and to ease maintenance.

• While this is a low installation cost paving alternative, it may require moderate maintenance. Crushed stone may require periodic re-grading to ensure continued performance.

• Fabric, chemical, or manual methods may be needed to remove unwanted vegetative growth from the paved surface.

• It is recommended that recycled and regionally available materials and products be given high priority in determining final design and specifications.

Installation Cost (per Square Foot)

LOW   HIGH

$2.26

Maintenance

LOW   HIGH

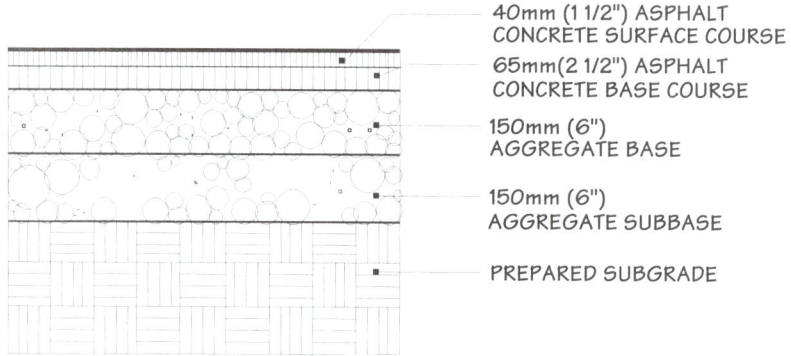

40mm (1 1/2") ASPHALT CONCRETE SURFACE COURSE

65mm(2 1/2") ASPHALT CONCRETE BASE COURSE

150mm (6") AGGREGATE BASE

150mm (6") AGGREGATE SUBBASE

PREPARED SUBGRADE

APPLICATION

CLIMATE

SUBGRADE

CSI MASTERFORMAT: 02740
DRAWING FILE: PAV31-05

• This drawing is a template for preliminary design only, and is not intended for bid purposes. It is subject to modification based on design calculations, local practices, and all applicable codes and regulations.

• This detail is rated for heavy-duty applications based on thickness of pavement courses and aggregate base, and may support vehicular loading typically associated with dense residential, urban park, and commercial settings.

• The subgrade conditions have a significant impact on the design of flexible pavements, such as asphalt. Loads are transferred more directly to the base, requiring adequate bearing capacity. This detail provides a well-drained aggregate subbase to drain subsurface moisture and increase uniformity, and a dense graded aggregate base for uniform structural support.

• The base should be placed in two lifts to ensure adequate compaction.

• The base should extend beyond the pavement edge past the load bearing angle (33°-45°) so the edge will be structurally reinforced.

• An oil penetration tack coat is recommended on crushed stone bases to seal top interstitial aggregate spaces and to ensure proper bonding.

• Frequent surface sealing is recommended for longer pavement life.

• It is recommended that recycled and regionally available materials and products be given high priority in determining final design and specifications.

Installation Cost (per Square Foot)

LOW   HIGH

$2.26

Maintenance

LOW   HIGH

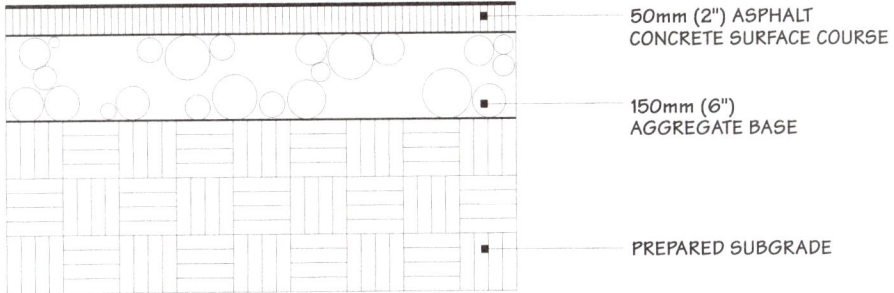

50mm (2") ASPHALT
CONCRETE SURFACE COURSE

150mm (6")
AGGREGATE BASE

PREPARED SUBGRADE

APPLICATION

CLIMATE

SUBGRADE

CSI MASTERFORMAT: 02740
DRAWING FILE: PAV11-03

• This drawing is a template for preliminary design only, and is not intended for bid purposes. It is subject to modification based on design calculations, local practices, and all applicable codes and regulations.

• This detail is typically associated with pedestrian walks and light service access in residential and park settings. With ideal subgrade bearing capacity, it may serve as a light duty driveway.

• This detail is rated for light-duty applications due to its single asphalt course and the base thickness.

• Rough grading of subgrade in large-area applications should move parallel to the slope direction to avoid blade and machine tracks running perpendicular to the flow of infiltrated subbase water. This avoids excessive differential swelling in clay soils, and heaving in frost/thaw climates.

• The subgrade conditions have a significant impact on the design of flexible pavements, such as asphalt. Loads are transferred more directly to the base, requiring well-drained soils with adequate bearing capacity.

• The base should extend beyond the pavement edge past the load bearing angle (33°-45°) so that the edge will be structurally reinforced.

• An oil penetration tack coat is recommended on crushed stone bases to seal top interstitial aggregate spaces and to ensure proper bonding.

• A layer thickness must be at least twice the thickness of the largest aggregate particle size specified.

• Alternative aggregates, such as recycled glass, may be mixed with aggregate in the bituminous concrete mix, and ground asphalt paving may be used as an aggregate base.

• Initial and periodic surface sealing is recommended for single course asphalt, especially if coarser stone is specified for strength. This pavement has low maintenance requirements.

Installation Cost (per Square Foot)

LOW   HIGH

$1.31

Maintenance

LOW   HIGH

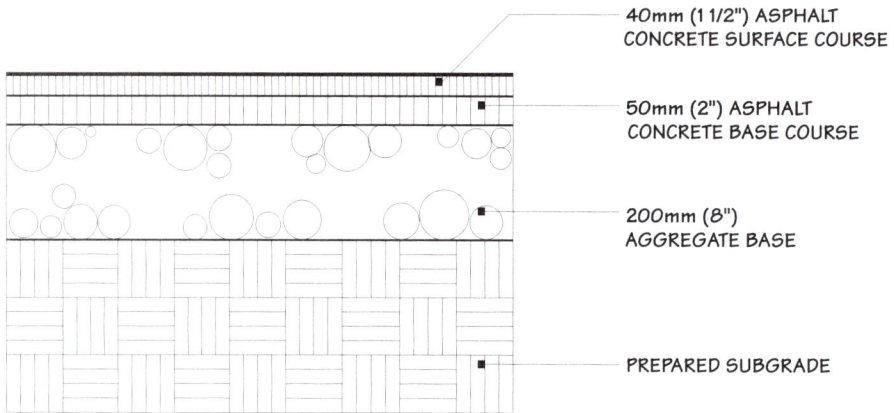

40mm (1 1/2") ASPHALT
CONCRETE SURFACE COURSE

50mm (2") ASPHALT
CONCRETE BASE COURSE

200mm (8")
AGGREGATE BASE

PREPARED SUBGRADE

APPLICATION

LIGHT   MED.   HEAVY

CLIMATE

ARID   HUMID   TEMP.   COLD

SUBGRADE

PERM.   CLAY   ROOF

CSI MASTERFORMAT: 02740
DRAWING FILE: PAV31-01

• This drawing is a template for preliminary design only, and is not intended for bid purposes. It is subject to modification based on design calculations, local practices, and all applicable codes and regulations.

• This detail is rated for medium-duty applications based on thickness of pavement courses and aggregate base, and may support vehicular loading typically associated with residential, park, and light commercial settings.

• Subgrade conditions have a significant impact on the longevity of rigid pavements, such as concrete. The subgrade should be uniform to prevent pavement failure due to uneven soil expansion and contraction. This detail provides a well-drained aggregate base to drain sub-surface moisture and increase uniformity.

• The base should be placed in two lifts to ensure adequate compaction.

• The base should extend beyond the pavement edge past the load bearing angle (33°-45°) so the edge will be structurally reinforced.

• An oil penetration tack coat is recommended on crushed stone bases to seal top interstitial aggregate spaces and to ensure proper bonding.

• Frequent surface sealing is recommended for longer pavement life.

• It is recommended that recycled and regionally available materials and products be given high priority in determining final design and specifications.

Installation Cost (per Square Foot)

LOW   HIGH

$2.12

Maintenance

LOW   HIGH

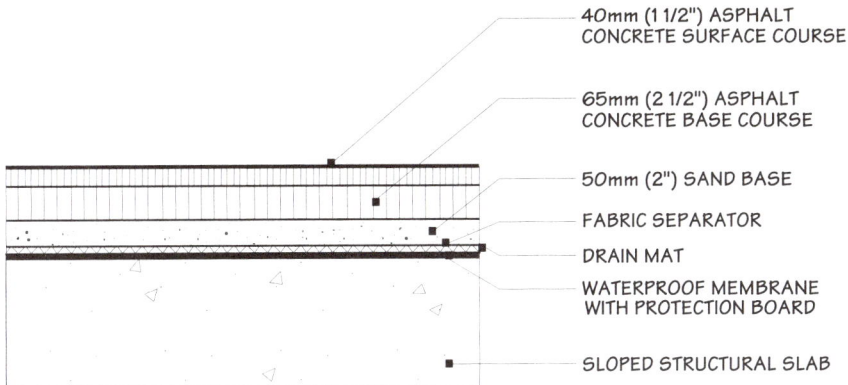

40mm (1 1/2") ASPHALT
CONCRETE SURFACE COURSE

65mm (2 1/2") ASPHALT
CONCRETE BASE COURSE

50mm (2") SAND BASE

FABRIC SEPARATOR

DRAIN MAT

WATERPROOF MEMBRANE
WITH PROTECTION BOARD

SLOPED STRUCTURAL SLAB

APPLICATION

CLIMATE

SUBGRADE

CSI MASTERFORMAT: 02740
DRAWING FILE: PAV31-04

• This drawing is a template for preliminary design only, and is not intended for bid purposes. It is subject to modification based on design calculations, local practices, and all applicable codes and regulations.

• This detail is rated for heavy-duty applications due to its multiple asphalt courses and the use of a heavy-duty drain mat capable of supporting the vehicular loads on structural roof decks. Rigid insulation is typically eliminated under such loading conditions.

• This detail may serve as an emergency access road on a structural roof deck.

• A sand base is placed on fabric separator over a heavy-duty drain mat, placed over sloping protection board and waterproof membrane.

• This surface requires periodic re-sealing to maintain surface integrity. Installation is limited to those areas accessible to installation equipment.

• It is recommended that recycled and regionally available materials and products be given high priority in determining final design and specifications.

Installation Cost (per Square Foot)

LOW   HIGH

$3.05

Maintenance

LOW   HIGH

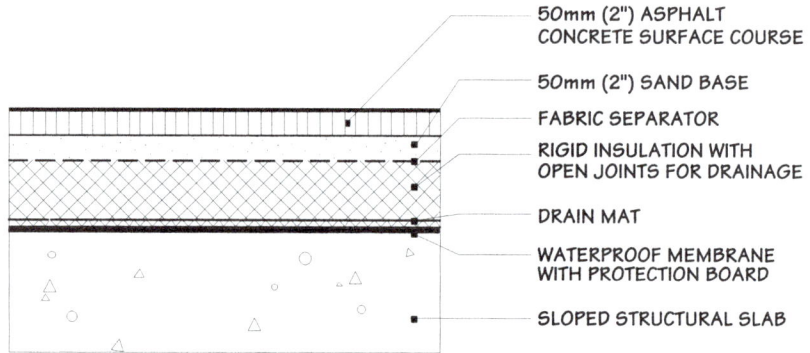

50mm (2") ASPHALT
CONCRETE SURFACE COURSE

50mm (2") SAND BASE

FABRIC SEPARATOR

RIGID INSULATION WITH
OPEN JOINTS FOR DRAINAGE

DRAIN MAT

WATERPROOF MEMBRANE
WITH PROTECTION BOARD

SLOPED STRUCTURAL SLAB

APPLICATION

CLIMATE

SUBGRADE

CSI MASTERFORMAT: 02740
DRAWING FILE: PAV11-04

• This drawing is a template for preliminary design only, and is not intended for bid purposes. It is subject to modification based on design calculations, local practices, and all applicable codes and regulations.

• This detail is typically associated with pedestrian walks and multi-purpose recreation surfaces on structural roof decks. It is often installed manually in small areas. Larger areas may require concrete for ease of installation.

• This detail is rated for light-duty applications due to its single asphalt course and bearing limitations of the rigid insulation upon which it rests.

• A sand base is placed on fabric separator over open jointed rigid insulation. A drain mat is placed over sloping protection board and waterproof membrane.

• It is recommended that recycled and regionally available materials and products be given high priority in determining final design and specifications.

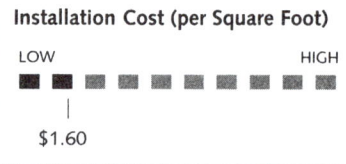

Installation Cost (per Square Foot)

LOW   HIGH

$1.60

Maintenance

LOW   HIGH

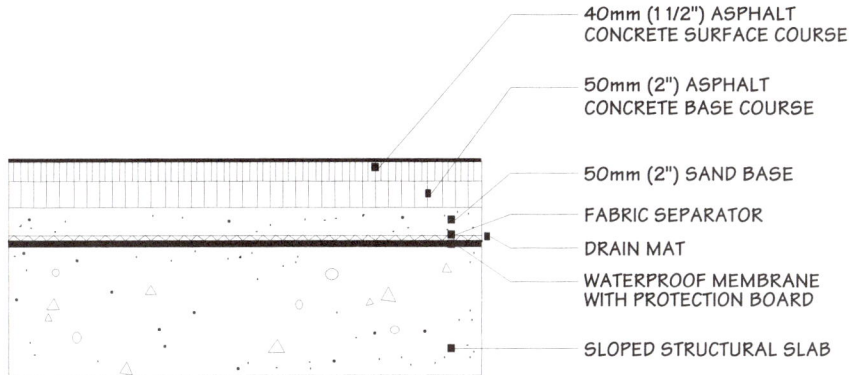

40mm (1 1/2") ASPHALT CONCRETE SURFACE COURSE

50mm (2") ASPHALT CONCRETE BASE COURSE

50mm (2") SAND BASE

FABRIC SEPARATOR

DRAIN MAT

WATERPROOF MEMBRANE WITH PROTECTION BOARD

SLOPED STRUCTURAL SLAB

APPLICATION

CLIMATE

SUBGRADE

CSI MASTERFORMAT: 02740
DRAWING FILE: PAV31-08

• This drawing is a template for preliminary design only, and is not intended for bid purposes. It is subject to modification based on design calculations, local practices, and all applicable codes and regulations.

• This detail is rated for medium-duty applications due to its multiple asphalt courses and the use of a heavy-duty drain mat capable of supporting the vehicular loads on structural roof decks. Rigid insulation is typically eliminated under such loading conditions.

• This detail may serve as a light service access road or parking surface on a structural roof deck.

• A sand base is placed on fabric separator over a heavy-duty drain mat, placed over sloping protection board and waterproof membrane.

• This surface requires periodic re-sealing to maintain surface integrity. Installation is limited to those areas accessible to installation equipment.

• It is recommended that recycled and regionally available materials and products be given high priority in determining final design and specifications.

Installation Cost (per Square Foot)

LOW   HIGH

$1.89

Maintenance

LOW   HIGH

COLOR COAT SYSTEM

40mm (1 1/2") ASPHALT CONC. SURFACE COURSE

65mm (2 1/2") ASPHALT CONC. BASE COURSE

150mm (6") AGGREGATE BASE

150mm (6") AGGREGATE SUBBASE

PREPARED SUBGRADE

APPLICATION

LIGHT   MED.   HEAVY

CLIMATE

ARID   HUMID   TEMP.   COLD

SUBGRADE

PERM.   CLAY   ROOF

CSI MASTERFORMAT: 02780
DRAWING FILE: PAV14-03

• This drawing is a template for preliminary design only, and is not intended for bid purposes. It is subject to modification based on design calculations, local practices, and all applicable codes and regulations.

• This detail is rated for heavy-duty applications based on thickness of pavement courses and aggregate base, and may support vehicular loading typically associated with dense residential, urban park, and commercial settings.

• The subgrade conditions have a significant impact on the design of flexible pavements, such as asphalt. Loads are transferred more directly to the base, requiring adequate bearing capacity. This detail provides a well-drained aggregate subbase to drain subsurface moisture and increase uniformity, and a dense graded aggregate base for uniform structural support.

• The base and subbase should extend beyond the pavement edge past the load bearing angle (33°-45°) so the edge will be structurally reinforced.

• An oil penetration tack coat is recommended on crushed stone bases to seal top interstitial aggregate spaces and to ensure proper bonding.

• Frequent surface sealing is recommended for longer pavement life.

• Various color coat systems are available. Consult local practices to determine the most suitable system. Color coat may require periodic re-surfacing to provide continued performance.

• It is recommended that recycled and regionally available materials and products be given high priority in determining final design and specifications.

Installation Cost (per Square Foot)

LOW   HIGH

$2.26

Maintenance

LOW   HIGH

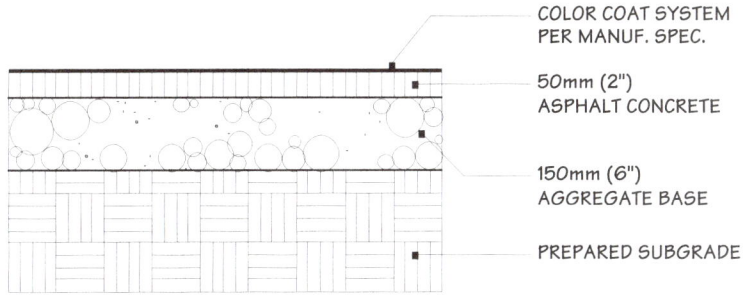

COLOR COAT SYSTEM
PER MANUF. SPEC.

50mm (2")
ASPHALT CONCRETE

150mm (6")
AGGREGATE BASE

PREPARED SUBGRADE

APPLICATION

CLIMATE

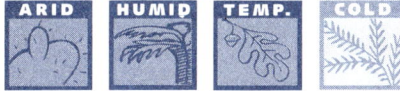

SUBGRADE

CSI MASTERFORMAT: 02780
DRAWING FILE: PAV34-11

• This drawing is a template for preliminary design only, and is not intended for bid purposes. It is subject to modification based on design calculations, local practices, and all applicable codes and regulations.

• This detail is typically associated with pedestrian walks and multi-purpose recreation surfaces in residential and park settings. With ideal subgrade bearing capacity, it may serve as a light-duty driveway.

• This detail is rated for light-duty applications due to its single asphalt course and the base thickness.

• Rough grading of subgrade in large-area applications should move parallel to the slope direction to avoid blade and machine tracks running perpendicular to the flow of infiltrated subbase water. This avoids excessive differential swelling in clay soils, and heaving in frost/thaw climates.

• The subgrade conditions have a significant impact on the design of flexible pavements, such as asphalt. Loads are transferred more directly to the base, requiring well-drained soils with adequate bearing capacity.

• The base should extend beyond the pavement edge past the load bearing angle (33°-45°) so that the edge will be structurally reinforced.

• A layer thickness must be at least twice the thickness of the largest aggregate particle size specified.

• Alternative aggregates may be mixed with aggregate in the bituminous concrete mix, and ground asphalt paving may be used as an aggregate base.

• Various color coat systems are available. Consult local practices to determine the most suitable system. Color coat may require periodic re-surfacing to provide continued performance.

Installation Cost (per Square Foot)

LOW   HIGH

$1.05

Maintenance

LOW   HIGH

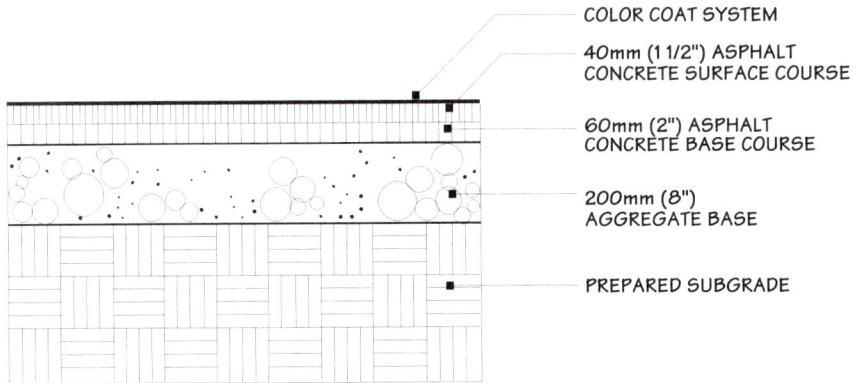

COLOR COAT SYSTEM

40mm (1 1/2") ASPHALT
CONCRETE SURFACE COURSE

60mm (2") ASPHALT
CONCRETE BASE COURSE

200mm (8")
AGGREGATE BASE

PREPARED SUBGRADE

APPLICATION

CLIMATE

SUBGRADE

CSI MASTERFORMAT: 02790
DRAWING FILE: PAV31-10

• This drawing is a template for preliminary design only, and is not intended for bid purposes. It is subject to modification based on design calculations, local practices, and all applicable codes and regulations.

• This detail is rated for medium-duty applications based on thickness of asphalt and aggregate base, and may support intensity of uses typically associated with public park, and institutional settings.

• The subgrade conditions have a significant impact on the design of flexible pavements, such as asphalt. Loads are transferred more directly to the base, requiring well-drained soils with adequate bearing capacity.

• Rough grading of subgrade should move parallel to the slope direction to avoid blade and machine tracks running perpendicular to the flow of infiltrated subbase water. This avoids excessive differential swelling in clay soils, and heaving in frost/thaw climates.

• The base should extend beyond the pavement edge past the load bearing angle (33°-45°) so the edge will be structurally reinforced.

• Pavement may require subdrains in colloidal soil conditions.

• Various color coat systems are available. Consult local practices to determine the most suitable system. Color coat may require periodic re-surfacing to provide continued performance.

• It is recommended that recycled and regionally available materials and products be given high priority in determining final design and specifications.

Installation Cost (per Square Foot)

LOW   HIGH

$2.40

Maintenance

LOW   HIGH

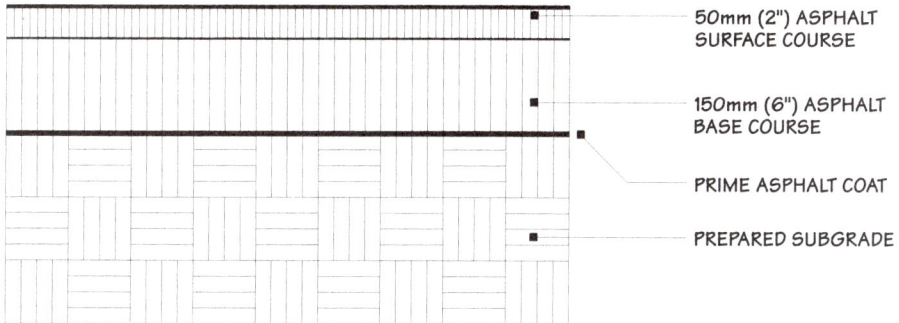

50mm (2") ASPHALT SURFACE COURSE

150mm (6") ASPHALT BASE COURSE

PRIME ASPHALT COAT

PREPARED SUBGRADE

APPLICATION

LIGHT MED. HEAVY

CLIMATE

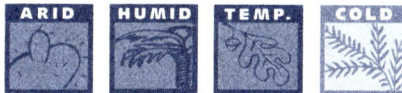

ARID HUMID TEMP. COLD

SUBGRADE

PERM. CLAY ROOF

CSI MASTERFORMAT: 02740
DRAWING FILE: PAV31-03

• This drawing is a template for preliminary design only, and is not intended for bid purposes. It is subject to modification based on design calculations, local practices, and all applicable codes and regulations.

• This detail is rated for heavy-duty applications based on thickness of paving course and may support vehicular loading associated with roads and service access in parks and dense residential settings.

• Full-Depth asphalt paving is a viable alternative in areas where aggregates are costly, and the subgrade is extremely well-drained and uniform.

• Rough grading of subgrade in large-area applications should move parallel to the slope direction to avoid blade and machine tracks running perpendicular to the flow of infiltrated water.

• Bituminous concrete is placed in layers using a coarse base course, and a fine finish course. A layer thickness must be at least twice the thickness of the largest aggregate particle size specified.

• It is recommended that recycled and regionally available materials and products be given high priority in determining final design and specifications. Alternative aggregates, such as recycled glass, may be mixed with aggregate in the bituminous concrete mix.

• Periodic surface sealing is recommended for longer pavement life. In most circumstances, this is a low maintenance pavement.

Installation Cost (per Square Foot)

LOW   HIGH

$2.27

Maintenance

LOW   HIGH

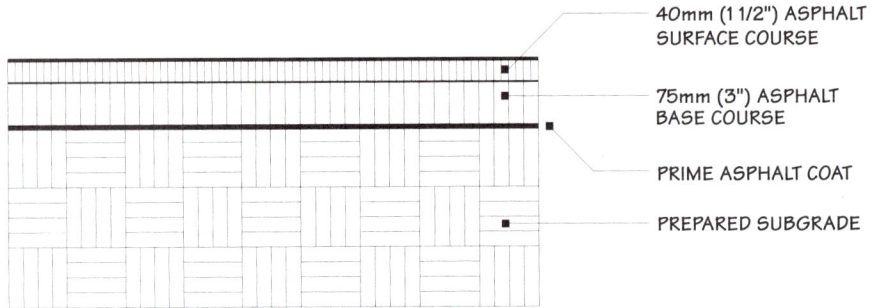

40mm (1 1/2") ASPHALT
SURFACE COURSE

75mm (3") ASPHALT
BASE COURSE

PRIME ASPHALT COAT

PREPARED SUBGRADE

APPLICATION

CLIMATE

SUBGRADE

CSI MASTERFORMAT: 02780
DRAWING FILE: PAV34-03

• This drawing is a template for preliminary design only, and is not intended for bid purposes. It is subject to modification based on design calculations, local practices, and all applicable codes and regulations.

• This detail is rated for light-duty applications based on thickness of paving course and may support primarily pedestrian loading associated with walks and light service access in parks and residential settings.

• Full-Depth asphalt paving is a viable alternative in areas where aggregates are costly, and the subgrade is extremely well-drained and uniform.

• Rough grading of subgrade in large-area applications should move parallel to the slope direction to avoid blade and machine tracks running perpendicular to the flow of infiltrated water.

• Bituminous concrete is placed in layers using a coarse base course, and a fine finish course. A layer thickness must be at least twice the thickness of the largest aggregate particle size specified.

• It is recommended that recycled and regionally available materials and products be given high priority in determining final design and specifications. Alternative aggregates, such as recycled glass, may be mixed with aggregate in the bituminous concrete mix.

• Periodic surface sealing is recommended for longer pavement life. In most circumstances, this is a low maintenance pavement.

Installation Cost (per Square Foot)

LOW   HIGH

$1.64

Maintenance

LOW   HIGH

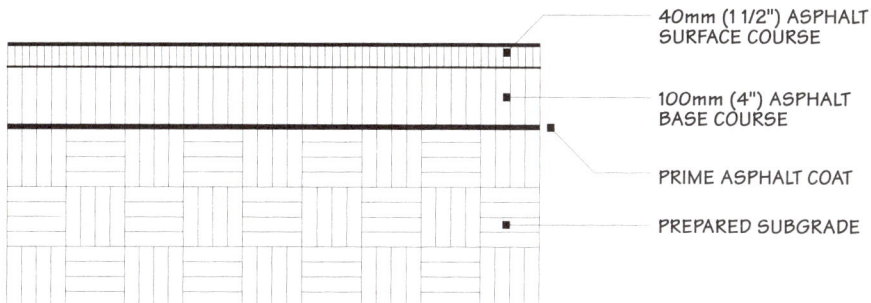

40mm (1 1/2") ASPHALT SURFACE COURSE

100mm (4") ASPHALT BASE COURSE

PRIME ASPHALT COAT

PREPARED SUBGRADE

APPLICATION

LIGHT MED. HEAVY

CLIMATE

ARID HUMID TEMP. COLD

SUBGRADE

PERM. CLAY ROOF

CSI MASTERFORMAT: 02740
DRAWING FILE: PAV31-07

• This drawing is a template for preliminary design only, and is not intended for bid purposes. It is subject to modification based on design calculations, local practices, and all applicable codes and regulations.

• This detail is rated for medium-duty applications based on thickness of paving course and may support vehicular loading associated with driveways and light service access in parks and residential settings.

• Full-Depth asphalt paving is a viable alternative in areas where aggregates are costly, and the subgrade is extremely well-drained and uniform.

• Rough grading of subgrade in large-area applications should move parallel to the slope direction to avoid blade and machine tracks running perpendicular to the flow of infiltrated water.

• Bituminous concrete is placed in layers using a coarse base course, and a fine finish course. A layer thickness must be at least twice the thickness of the largest aggregate particle size specified.

• It is recommended that recycled and regionally available materials and products be given high priority in determining final design and specifications. Alternative aggregates, such as recycled glass, may be mixed with aggregate in the bituminous concrete mix.

• Periodic surface sealing is recommended for longer pavement life. In most circumstances, this is a low maintenance pavement.

Installation Cost (per Square Foot)

LOW   HIGH

$1.81

Maintenance

LOW   HIGH

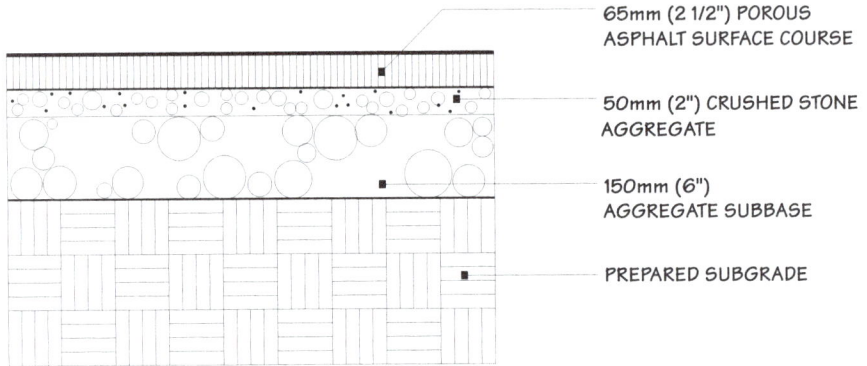

65mm (2 1/2") POROUS ASPHALT SURFACE COURSE

50mm (2") CRUSHED STONE AGGREGATE

150mm (6") AGGREGATE SUBBASE

PREPARED SUBGRADE

APPLICATION

CLIMATE

SUBGRADE

CSI MASTERFORMAT: 02795
DRAWING FILE: PAV11-07

• This drawing is a template for preliminary design only, and is not intended for bid purposes. It is subject to modification based on design calculations, local practices, and all applicable codes and regulations.

• This detail is rated for light-duty applications based on paving course and base thickness, and may support significant pedestrian loading associated with walks and light service access and parking in parks and dense residential settings. Pavement thickness is based on stone size required to achieve the open lattice structure of porous asphalt.

• The subgrade conditions have a significant impact on the design of flexible pavements, such as porous asphalt. Loads are transferred more directly to the base, requiring well-drained soils with adequate bearing capacity.

• This porous asphalt pavement requires a well graded crushed stone base over a free draining aggregate subbase and well drained subgrade. Subbase thickness is determined by drainage requirements and subsoil infiltration rates.

• Due to its open structure, pavement edges typically require containment.

• It is recommended that recycled and regionally available materials and products be given high priority in determining final design and specifications.

Installation Cost (per Square Foot)

LOW   HIGH

$1.46

Maintenance

LOW   HIGH

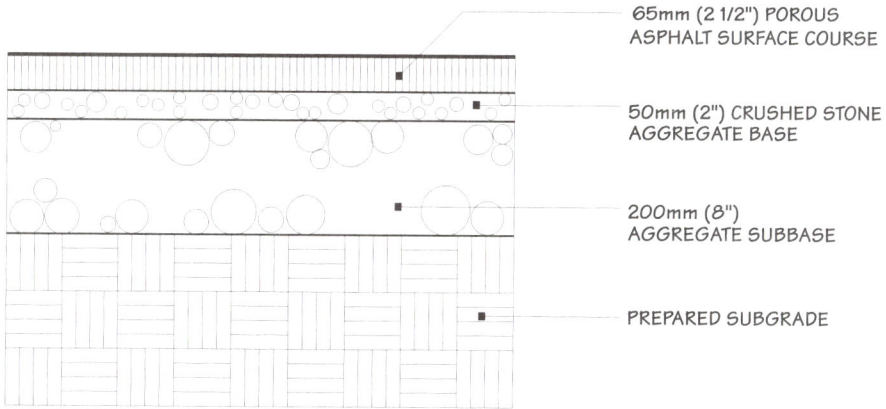

65mm (2 1/2") POROUS
ASPHALT SURFACE COURSE

50mm (2") CRUSHED STONE
AGGREGATE BASE

200mm (8")
AGGREGATE SUBBASE

PREPARED SUBGRADE

APPLICATION

LIGHT · MED. · HEAVY

CLIMATE

ARID · HUMID · TEMP. · COLD

SUBGRADE

PERM. · CLAY · ROOF

CSI MASTERFORMAT: 02795
DRAWING FILE: PAV31-11

• This drawing is a template for preliminary design only, and is not intended for bid purposes. It is subject to modification based on design calculations, local practices, and all applicable codes and regulations.

• This detail is rated for medium-duty applications based on paving course and base thickness, and may support vehicular loading associated with service access and parking in parks and dense residential settings.

• The subgrade conditions have a significant impact on the design of flexible pavements, such as porous asphalt. Loads are transferred more directly to the base, requiring well-drained soils with adequate bearing capacity.

• This porous asphalt pavement requires a well graded crushed stone base over a free draining aggregate subbase and well drained subgrade. The subbase is thickened to accommodate drainage requirements.

• Due to its open structure, pavement edges typically require containment. Over time, surface may require power washing and chemical oxidation treatment.

• It is recommended that recycled and regionally available materials and products be given high priority in determining final design and specifications.

Installation Cost (per Square Foot)

LOW   HIGH

$1.65

Maintenance

LOW   HIGH

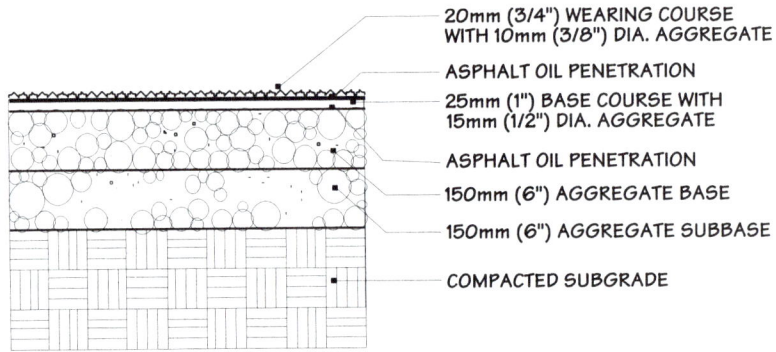

20mm (3/4") WEARING COURSE
WITH 10mm (3/8") DIA. AGGREGATE

ASPHALT OIL PENETRATION

25mm (1") BASE COURSE WITH
15mm (1/2") DIA. AGGREGATE

ASPHALT OIL PENETRATION

150mm (6") AGGREGATE BASE

150mm (6") AGGREGATE SUBBASE

COMPACTED SUBGRADE

APPLICATION

CLIMATE

SUBGRADE

CSI MASTERFORMAT: 02740
DRAWING FILE: PAV31-06

• This drawing is for preliminary design only, and is not intended for bid purposes. It is subject to modification based on design calculations, local practices, and all applicable codes and regulations.

• This detail is typical of asphalt paving serving vehicular traffic in park and dense residential settings. Stone and oil penetration (Macadam) is prepared on site. It is a suitable paving option in remote locations, where bituminous hot-mix is not readily available or affordable.

• This detail is rated for heavy-duty uses due to pavement and base thickness and may support typical road and driveway related loads.

• The subgrade conditions have a significant impact on the design of flexible pavements, such as asphalt. Loads are transferred more directly to the base, requiring adequate bearing capacity.

• The base should be placed in two lifts to ensure adequate compaction. Additional base may be required in clay soils or extremely cold conditions.

• Installation during cold weather is not recommended, due to the need to maintain sufficient oil heat in its liquid form before curing, and to insure adhesion to the stone layers.

• While this is a low installation cost paving alternative, it may require greater maintenance. Snow plowing will remove surface stone if not properly rolled and cured, requiring periodic re-oiling and surfacing with finish stone layer.

• It is recommended that recycled and regionally available materials and products be given high priority in determining final design and specifications.

Installation Cost (per Square Foot)

LOW   HIGH

$1.22

Maintenance

LOW   HIGH

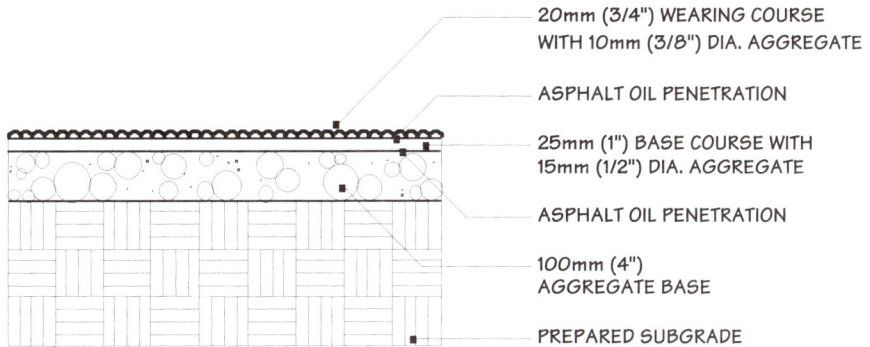

20mm (3/4") WEARING COURSE
WITH 10mm (3/8") DIA. AGGREGATE

ASPHALT OIL PENETRATION

25mm (1") BASE COURSE WITH
15mm (1/2") DIA. AGGREGATE

ASPHALT OIL PENETRATION

100mm (4")
AGGREGATE BASE

PREPARED SUBGRADE

APPLICATION

CLIMATE

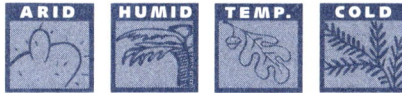

SUBGRADE

CSI MASTERFORMAT: 02730
DRAWING FILE: PAV17-05

• This drawing is for preliminary design only, and is not intended for bid purposes. It is subject to modification based on design calculations, local practices, and all applicable codes and regulations.

• This detail is typical of asphalt paving serving pedestrian traffic in small park and garden settings. Stone and oil penetration (Macadam) is prepared on site. It is a suitable paving option in remote locations, where bituminous hot-mix is not readily available or affordable.

• This detail is rated for light-duty uses due to pavement and base thickness and may support typical pedestrian and related loads.

• The subgrade conditions have a significant impact on the design of flexible pavements, such as asphalt. Loads are transferred more directly to the base, requiring adequate bearing capacity.

• Installation during cold weather is not recommended, due to the need to maintain sufficient oil heat in its liquid form before curing, and to insure adhesion to the stone layers.

• While this is a low installation cost paving alternative, it may require greater maintenance. Snow plowing will remove surface stone if not properly rolled and cured, requiring periodic re-oiling and surfacing with finish stone layer.

• It is recommended that recycled and regionally available materials and products be given high priority in determining final design and specifications.

Installation Cost (per Square Foot)

LOW   HIGH

$0.81

Maintenance

LOW   HIGH

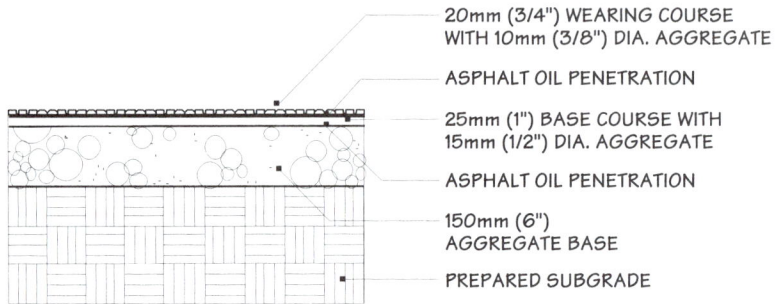

20mm (3/4") WEARING COURSE
WITH 10mm (3/8") DIA. AGGREGATE

ASPHALT OIL PENETRATION

25mm (1") BASE COURSE WITH
15mm (1/2") DIA. AGGREGATE

ASPHALT OIL PENETRATION

150mm (6")
AGGREGATE BASE

PREPARED SUBGRADE

APPLICATION

CLIMATE

SUBGRADE

CSI MASTERFORMAT: 02740
DRAWING FILE: PAV31-02

• This drawing is for preliminary design only, and is not intended for bid purposes. It is subject to modification based on design calculations, local practices, and all applicable codes and regulations.

• This detail is typical of asphalt paving serving vehicular traffic in park and dense residential settings. Stone and oil penetration (Macadam) is prepared on site. It is a suitable paving option in remote locations, where bituminous hot-mix is not readily available or affordable.

• This detail is rated for medium-duty uses due to pavement and base thickness and may support typical road and driveway related loads.

• The subgrade conditions have a significant impact on the design of flexible pavements, such as asphalt. Loads are transferred more directly to the base, requiring adequate bearing capacity.

• A subbase may be required in clay soils or extremely cold conditions to achieve the same performance.

• Installation during cold weather is not recommended, due to the need to maintain sufficient oil heat in its liquid form before curing, and to insure adhesion to the stone layers.

• While this is a low installation cost paving alternative, it may require greater maintenance. Snow plowing will remove surface stone if not properly rolled and cured, requiring periodic re-oiling and surfacing with finish stone layer.

• It is recommended that recycled and regionally available materials and products be given high priority in determining final design and specifications.

Installation Cost (per Square Foot)

LOW   HIGH

$0.97

Maintenance

LOW   HIGH

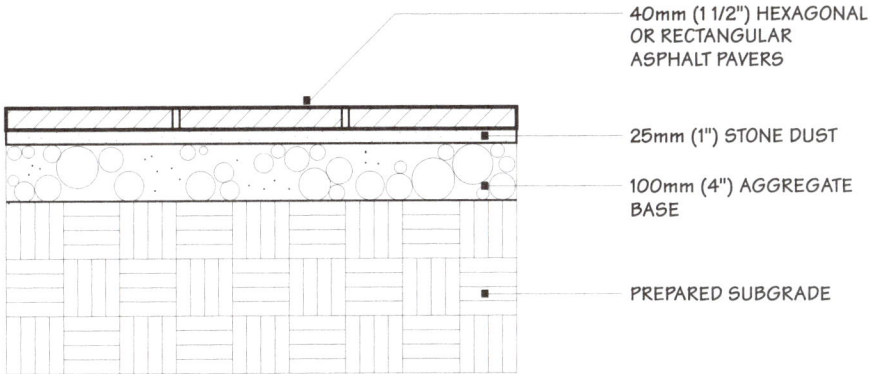

40mm (1 1/2") HEXAGONAL OR RECTANGULAR ASPHALT PAVERS

25mm (1") STONE DUST

100mm (4") AGGREGATE BASE

PREPARED SUBGRADE

APPLICATION

CLIMATE

SUBGRADE

CSI MASTERFORMAT: 02780
DRAWING FILE: PAV11-06

• This drawing is a template for preliminary design only, and is not intended for bid purposes. It is subject to modification based on design calculations, local practices, and all applicable codes and regulations.

• This detail is rated for light-duty applications based on paving course and base thickness, and may support primarily pedestrian loading associated with walks and light service access in parks and residential settings.

• The subgrade conditions have a significant impact on the design of flexible pavements, such as asphalt unit pavers. Loads are transferred more directly to the base, requiring well-drained soils with adequate bearing capacity.

• A well graded aggregate is recommended to achieve a smooth even pavement base to insure a uniform finish surface. Joints are normally butted and swept with setting bed material.

• It is recommended that recycled and regionally available materials and products be given high priority in determining final design and specifications.

Installation Cost (per Square Foot)

LOW   HIGH

$5.59

Maintenance

LOW   HIGH

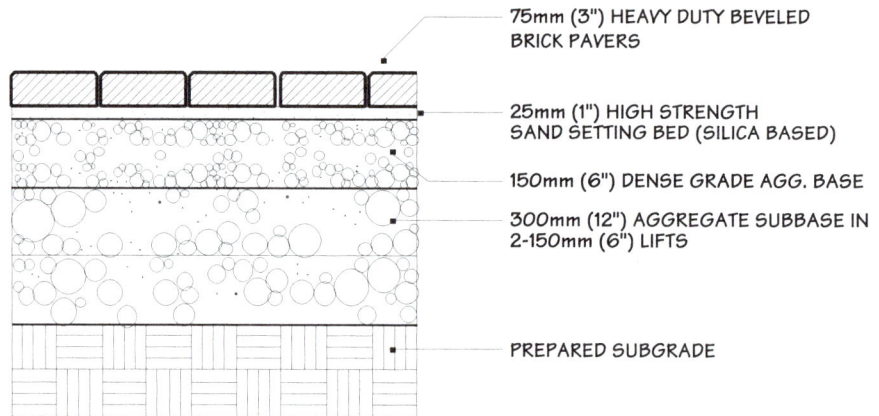

75mm (3") HEAVY DUTY BEVELED BRICK PAVERS

25mm (1") HIGH STRENGTH SAND SETTING BED (SILICA BASED)

150mm (6") DENSE GRADE AGG. BASE

300mm (12") AGGREGATE SUBBASE IN 2-150mm (6") LIFTS

PREPARED SUBGRADE

APPLICATION

CLIMATE

SUBGRADE

CSI MASTERFORMAT: 02740
DRAWING FILE: PAV11-02

• This drawing is a template for preliminary design only, and is not intended for bid purposes. It is subject to modification based on design calculations, local practices, and all applicable codes and regulations.

• This beveled brick paver on sand detail is rated for heavy-duty applications based on paving course and base thickness, and subgrade bearing. Where persistent vehicular loading occurs, use high content silica sand setting bed rather than stone dust or other such processed material.

• This detail may support vehicular loading associated with vehicular access in urban parks, and residential settings. It is typically laid in herring-bone pattern to resist multi-directional lateral movement.

• As with all unit pavers, pavement edges require restraints to prevent creeping, especially if subjected to vehicular access.

• The subgrade conditions have a significant impact on the design of flexible pave-

ments, such as unit pavers. Loads are transferred more directly to the base, requiring well-drained soils with adequate bearing capacity.

• Set brick with light vibrating compactor over sand cushion and final sweep sand to complete installation. Final wash-down will help to set brick sand grout.

• Bricks may require periodic re-setting due to differential settling or deformation of subgrade. Use of sub-drains may lessen the possibility of subgrade deformation. Severe abrasive maintenance in cold climates may damage surface.

• It is recommended that recycled and regionally available materials and products be given high priority in determining final design and specifications.

Installation Cost (per Square Foot)

LOW   HIGH

$9.00

Maintenance

LOW   HIGH

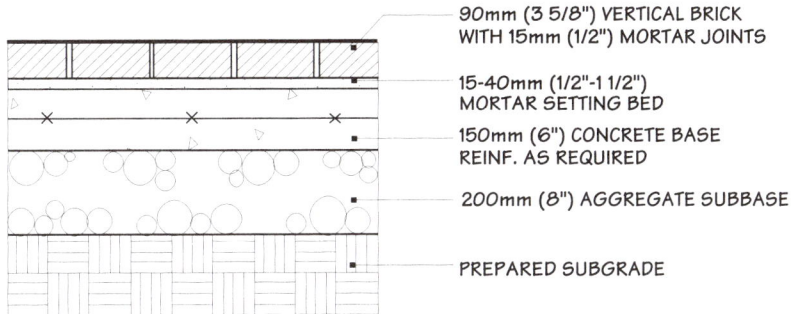

90mm (3 5/8") VERTICAL BRICK
WITH 15mm (1/2") MORTAR JOINTS

15-40mm (1/2"-1 1/2")
MORTAR SETTING BED

150mm (6") CONCRETE BASE
REINF. AS REQUIRED

200mm (8") AGGREGATE SUBBASE

PREPARED SUBGRADE

APPLICATION

CSI MASTERFORMAT: 02790
DRAWING FILE: PAV11-05

• This drawing is a template for preliminary design only, and is not intended for bid purposes. It is subject to modification based on design calculations, local practices, and all applicable codes and regulations.

• This detail is rated for heavy-duty applications based on thickness of concrete and aggregate base, and may support pedestrian and vehicular loading typically associated with dense residential, urban park, and light commercial settings.

• This detail utilizes the full depth of the brick for strength and exposes the narrow edge surface to the elements and to wear. It is typically laid in a herringbone pattern to accentuate its edge proportions.

• This detail is not designed for cold climates, where the use of mortar in pavements is discouraged. Flexible adhesives, such as bituminous or elastomeric materials are recommended in these conditions.

CLIMATE

• Rigid pavement design must accommodate movement of materials by providing adequate expansion and control joints, particularly in regions of extreme temperature fluctuations. If designed for temperate or cold climates, air-entrained concrete is typically recommended due to freezing/thawing action.

• Reinforcing practices vary widely by region. Local codes and practices should be consulted prior to specifying any type of reinforcing.

• Bricks may require periodic re-pointing or re-setting at edges, and requires more bricks per square unit than when laid flat.

• It is recommended that recycled and regionally available materials and products be given high priority in determining final design and specifications.

SUBGRADE

Installation Cost (per Square Foot)

LOW   HIGH

$12.59

Maintenance

LOW   HIGH

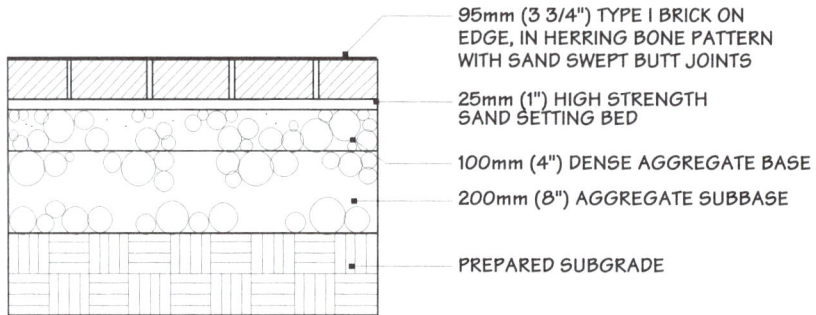

95mm (3 3/4") TYPE I BRICK ON EDGE, IN HERRING BONE PATTERN WITH SAND SWEPT BUTT JOINTS

25mm (1") HIGH STRENGTH SAND SETTING BED

100mm (4") DENSE AGGREGATE BASE

200mm (8") AGGREGATE SUBBASE

PREPARED SUBGRADE

APPLICATION

CLIMATE

SUBGRADE

CSI MASTERFORMAT: 02780
DRAWING FILE: PAV34-02

• This drawing is a template for preliminary design only, and is not intended for bid purposes. It is subject to modification based on design calculations, local practices, and all applicable codes and regulations.

• This brick paver on edge detail is rated for heavy-duty applications based on paving course and base thickness, and subgrade bearing. Where persistent vehicular loading occurs, use high silica content sand setting bed rather than stone dust or other such processed material.

• This detail may support vehicular loading associated with vehicular access in urban parks, and residential settings. It is typically laid in herring-bone pattern to resist multi-directional lateral movement, and to use full dimension of brick strength.

• As with all unit pavers, pavement edges require restraints to prevent creeping, especially if subjected to vehicular access.

• The subgrade conditions have a significant impact on the design of flexible pavements, such as unit pavers. Loads are transferred more directly to the base, requiring well-drained soils with adequate bearing capacity.

• Set brick with light vibrating compactor over sand cushion and final sweep sand to complete installation. Final wash-down will help to set brick sand grout.

• Bricks may require periodic re-setting due to differential settling or deformation of subgrade. Use of sub-drains may lessen the possibility of subgrade deformation. Severe abrasive maintenance in cold climates may damage surface.

• It is recommended that recycled and regionally available materials and products be given high priority in determining final design and specifications.

Installation Cost (per Square Foot)

LOW   HIGH

$12.50

Maintenance

LOW   HIGH

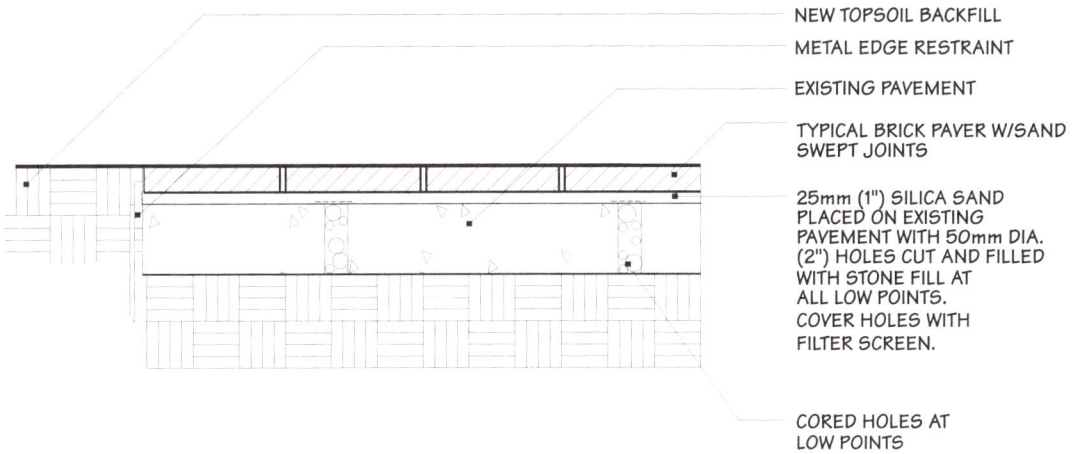

NEW TOPSOIL BACKFILL

METAL EDGE RESTRAINT

EXISTING PAVEMENT

TYPICAL BRICK PAVER W/SAND
SWEPT JOINTS

25mm (1") SILICA SAND
PLACED ON EXISTING
PAVEMENT WITH 50mm DIA.
(2") HOLES CUT AND FILLED
WITH STONE FILL AT
ALL LOW POINTS.
COVER HOLES WITH
FILTER SCREEN.

CORED HOLES AT
LOW POINTS

APPLICATION

CLIMATE

SUBGRADE

CSI MASTERFORMAT: 02780
DRAWING FILE: PAV14-08

• This drawing is a template for preliminary design only, and is not intended for bid purposes. It is subject to modification based on design calculations, local practices, and all applicable codes and regulations.

• This brick paver on existing pavement detail is rated for medium-duty applications based on paving course and base thickness, and may support significant pedestrian loading associated with walks and light vehicular access in parks and residential settings.

• This detail requires that holes be bored into existing pavement low-points and filled with crushed aggregate for drainage as conditions demand. Holes should be covered with a fabric separator to insure proper drainage and to contain setting bed fines. A 25 mm (1") sand cushion is placed over pavement to receive new brick.

• As with all unit pavers, pavement edges require restraints to prevent creeping, especially if subjected to even occasional vehicu-

lar access. Vertical metal edge is shown in this detail.

• Set brick with light vibrating compactor over sand cushion and final sweep sand to complete installation. Final wash-down will help to set brick sand grout.

• Radius edge brick may be required for certain handicapped access circumstances.

• It is recommended that recycled and regionally available materials and products be given high priority in determining final design and specifications.

Installation Cost (per Square Foot)

LOW · HIGH

$6.10

Maintenance

LOW · HIGH

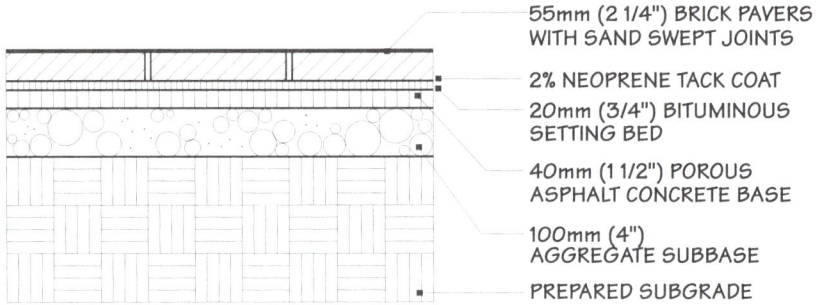

55mm (2 1/4") BRICK PAVERS
WITH SAND SWEPT JOINTS

2% NEOPRENE TACK COAT

20mm (3/4") BITUMINOUS
SETTING BED

40mm (1 1/2") POROUS
ASPHALT CONCRETE BASE

100mm (4")
AGGREGATE SUBBASE

PREPARED SUBGRADE

APPLICATION

CLIMATE

SUBGRADE

CSI MASTERFORMAT: 02790
DRAWING FILE: PAV31-09

• This drawing is a template for preliminary design only, and is not intended for bid purposes. It is subject to modification based on design calculations, local practices, and all applicable codes and regulations.

• This detail is rated for light-duty applications based on paving course and base thickness, and may support significant pedestrian loading associated with walks and light service access in urban parks, plazas, and dense residential settings.

• This detail is useful for cold climates and those with frequent frost-thaw cycles. Asphalt setting bed is used to create a uniform surface to receive the brick. Mastic is often used in urban conditions to insure stability. It requires a minimum slope of 2% in such conditions.

• As with all unit pavers, pavement edges require restraints to prevent creeping, especially if subjected to even occasional vehicular access.

• The subgrade conditions have a significant impact on the design of flexible pavements, such as unit pavers. Loads are transferred more directly to the base, requiring well-drained soils with adequate bearing capacity.

• Final wash-down will help to set brick sand grout.

• Radius edge brick may be required for certain handicapped access circumstances.

• Bricks may require periodic re-setting due to spawling in cold settings.

• It is recommended that recycled and regionally available materials and products be given high priority in determining final design and specifications.

Installation Cost (per Square Foot)

LOW   HIGH

$7.24

Maintenance

LOW   HIGH

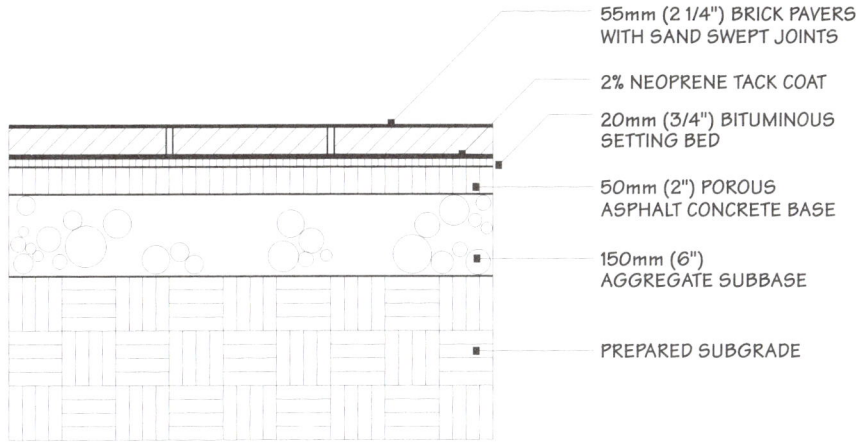

55mm (2 1/4") BRICK PAVERS WITH SAND SWEPT JOINTS

2% NEOPRENE TACK COAT

20mm (3/4") BITUMINOUS SETTING BED

50mm (2") POROUS ASPHALT CONCRETE BASE

150mm (6") AGGREGATE SUBBASE

PREPARED SUBGRADE

APPLICATION

CLIMATE

SUBGRADE

CSI MASTERFORMAT: 02780
DRAWING FILE: PAV34-05

• This drawing is a template for preliminary design only, and is not intended for bid purposes. It is subject to modification based on design calculations, local practices, and all applicable codes and regulations.

• This detail is rated for medium-duty applications based on paving course and base thickness, and may support pedestrian and vehicular loading associated with walks and auto access in urban parks, plazas, and dense residential settings.

• This detail is useful for cold climates and those with frequent frost-thaw cycles. Asphalt setting bed is used to create a uniform surface to receive the brick. Mastic is often used in urban conditions to insure stability. It requires a minimum slope of 2% in such conditions.

• As with all unit pavers, pavement edges require restraints to prevent creeping, especially if subjected to even occasional vehicular access.

• The subgrade conditions have a significant impact on the design of flexible pavements, such as unit pavers. Loads are transferred more directly to the base, requiring well-drained soils with adequate bearing capacity.

• Final wash-down will help to set brick sand grout.

• Radius edge brick may be required for certain handicapped access circumstances.

• Bricks may require periodic re-setting due to spawling in cold settings.

• It is recommended that recycled and regionally available materials and products be given high priority in determining final design and specifications.

Installation Cost (per Square Foot)

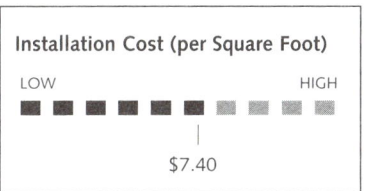

LOW   HIGH

$7.40

Maintenance

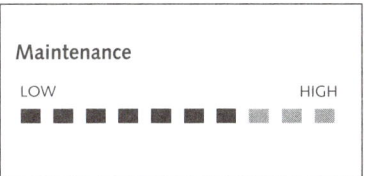

LOW   HIGH

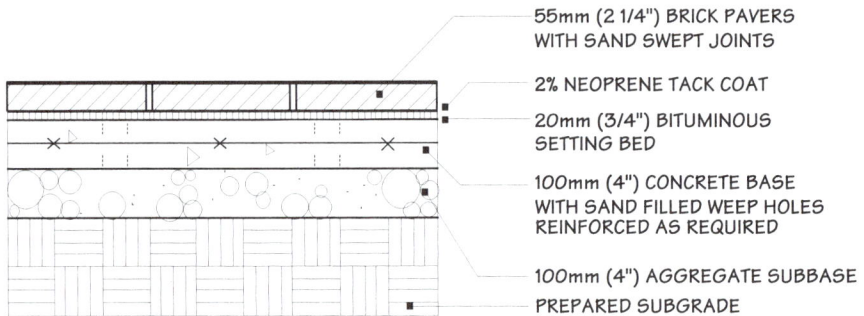

55mm (2 1/4") BRICK PAVERS
WITH SAND SWEPT JOINTS

2% NEOPRENE TACK COAT

20mm (3/4") BITUMINOUS
SETTING BED

100mm (4") CONCRETE BASE
WITH SAND FILLED WEEP HOLES
REINFORCED AS REQUIRED

100mm (4") AGGREGATE SUBBASE

PREPARED SUBGRADE

APPLICATION

CLIMATE

SUBGRADE

CSI MASTERFORMAT: 02780
DRAWING FILE: PAV14-04

• This drawing is a template for preliminary design only, and is not intended for bid purposes. It is subject to modification based on design calculations, local practices, and all applicable codes and regulations.

• This detail is rated for light-duty applications based on thickness of concrete and aggregate base, and may support significant pedestrian loading typically associated with residential, park, and light commercial settings.

• This detail is a useful alternative for cold climates and those with frequent frost-thaw cycles, providing that subgrade is uniform and well drained. Asphalt setting bed is used to create a uniform surface to receive the brick. Mastic is often used in urban conditions to insure stability. It requires a minimum slope of 2% in such conditions.

• As with all unit pavers, pavement edges require restraints to prevent creeping, especially if subjected to even occasional vehicular access.

• Final wash-down will help to set brick sand grout.

• Radius edge brick may be required for certain handicapped access circumstances.

• Bricks may require periodic re-setting due to spawling in cold settings.

• It is recommended that recycled and regionally available materials and products be given high priority in determining final design and specifications.

Installation Cost (per Square Foot)

LOW   HIGH

$8.81

Maintenance

LOW   HIGH

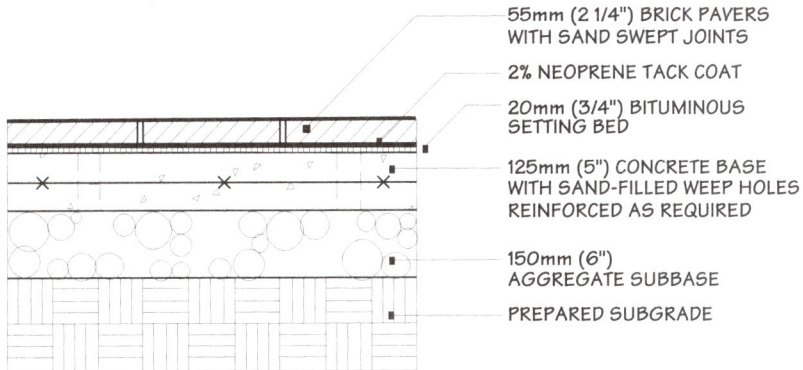

55mm (2 1/4") BRICK PAVERS
WITH SAND SWEPT JOINTS

2% NEOPRENE TACK COAT

20mm (3/4") BITUMINOUS
SETTING BED

125mm (5") CONCRETE BASE
WITH SAND-FILLED WEEP HOLES
REINFORCED AS REQUIRED

150mm (6")
AGGREGATE SUBBASE

PREPARED SUBGRADE

APPLICATION

CLIMATE

SUBGRADE

CSI MASTERFORMAT: 02780
DRAWING FILE: PAV34-06

• This drawing is a template for preliminary design only, and is not intended for bid purposes. It is subject to modification based on design calculations, local practices, and all applicable codes and regulations.

• This detail is rated for medium-duty applications based on thickness of concrete and aggregate base, and may support pedestrian and vehicular loading typically associated with residential, park, and light commercial settings.

• This detail is a useful alternative for cold climates and those with frequent frost-thaw cycles, providing that subgrade is uniform and well drained. Asphalt setting bed is used to create a uniform surface to receive the brick. Mastic is often used in urban conditions to insure stability. It requires a minimum slope of 2% in such conditions.

• As with all unit pavers, pavement edges require restraints to prevent creeping, especially if subjected to even occasional vehicular access.

• Final wash-down will help to set brick sand grout.

• Radius edge brick may be required for certain handicapped access circumstances.

• Bricks may require periodic re-setting due to spawling in cold settings.

• It is recommended that recycled and regionally available materials and products be given high priority in determining final design and specifications.

Installation Cost (per Square Foot)

LOW   HIGH

$9.25

Maintenance

LOW   HIGH

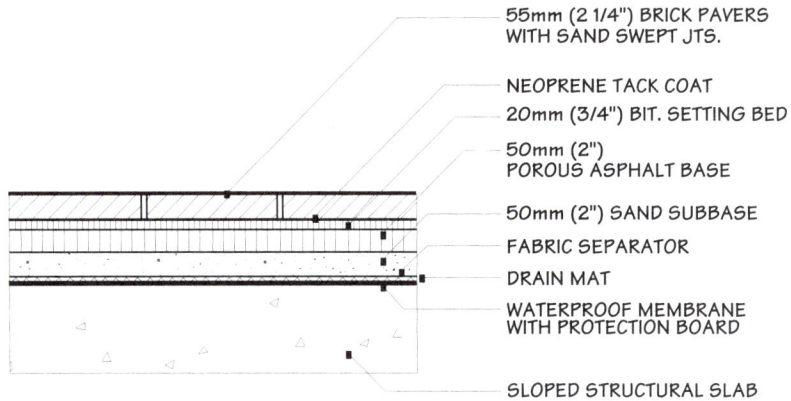

55mm (2 1/4") BRICK PAVERS
WITH SAND SWEPT JTS.

NEOPRENE TACK COAT

20mm (3/4") BIT. SETTING BED

50mm (2")
POROUS ASPHALT BASE

50mm (2") SAND SUBBASE

FABRIC SEPARATOR

DRAIN MAT

WATERPROOF MEMBRANE
WITH PROTECTION BOARD

SLOPED STRUCTURAL SLAB

APPLICATION

CLIMATE

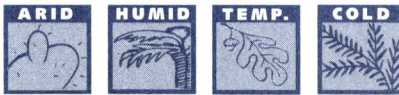

SUBGRADE

CSI MASTERFORMAT: 02780
DRAWING FILE: PAV34-08

• This drawing is a template for preliminary design only, and is not intended for bid purposes. It is subject to modification based on design calculations, local practices, and all applicable codes and regulations.

• This detail is rated for medium-duty applications based on paving course and asphalt base thickness, and may support pedestrian and vehicular loading associated with walks and auto access in urban parks, plazas, and dense residential settings on structural roof decks. This detail requires a heavy-duty drain mat and the elimination of a rigid insulation layer.

• This detail is useful for cold climates and those with frequent frost-thaw cycles. Asphalt setting bed is used to create a uniform surface to receive the brick.

• As with all unit pavers, pavement edges require restraints to prevent creeping, especially if subjected to even occasional vehicular access.

• A sand base is placed on fabric separator over a drain mat, placed over sloping protection board and waterproof membrane.

• Final wash-down will help to set brick sand grout.

• Radius edge brick may be required for certain handicapped access circumstances.

• Bricks may require periodic re-setting due to spawling in cold settings.

• It is recommended that recycled and regionally available materials and products be given high priority in determining final design and specifications.

Installation Cost (per Square Foot)

LOW   HIGH

$8.36

Maintenance

LOW   HIGH

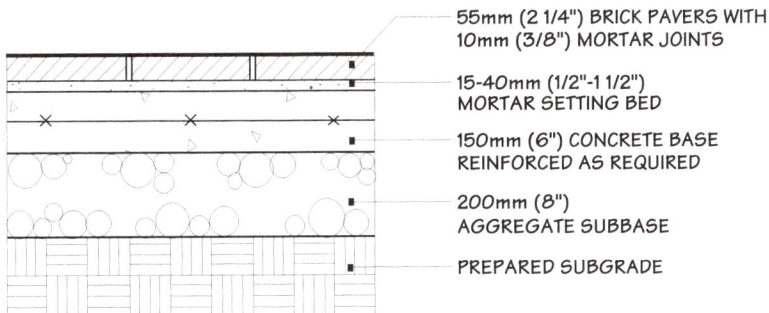

55mm (2 1/4") BRICK PAVERS WITH
10mm (3/8") MORTAR JOINTS

15-40mm (1/2"-1 1/2")
MORTAR SETTING BED

150mm (6") CONCRETE BASE
REINFORCED AS REQUIRED

200mm (8")
AGGREGATE SUBBASE

PREPARED SUBGRADE

APPLICATION

CLIMATE

SUBGRADE

CSI MASTERFORMAT: 02780
DRAWING FILE: PAV34-10

• This drawing is a template for preliminary design only, and is not intended for bid purposes. It is subject to modification based on design calculations, local practices, and all applicable codes and regulations.

• This detail is rated for heavy-duty applications based on thickness of concrete and aggregate base, and may support pedestrian and vehicular loading typically associated with dense residential, urban park, and light commercial settings.

• This detail is not designed for cold climates, where the use of mortar in pavements is discouraged. Flexible adhesives, such as bituminous or elastomeric materials are recommended in these conditions.

• Rigid pavement design must accommodate movement of materials by providing adequate expansion and control joints, particularly in regions of extreme temperature fluctuations. If designed for temperate or cold climates, air-entrained concrete is typi-cally recommended due to freezing/thawing action.

• Reinforcing practices vary widely by region. Local codes and practices should be consulted prior to specifying any type of reinforcing.

• Bricks may require periodic re-pointing or re-setting at edges.

• It is recommended that recycled and regionally available materials and products be given high priority in determining final design and specifications.

Installation Cost (per Square Foot)

LOW   HIGH

$10.80

Maintenance

LOW   HIGH

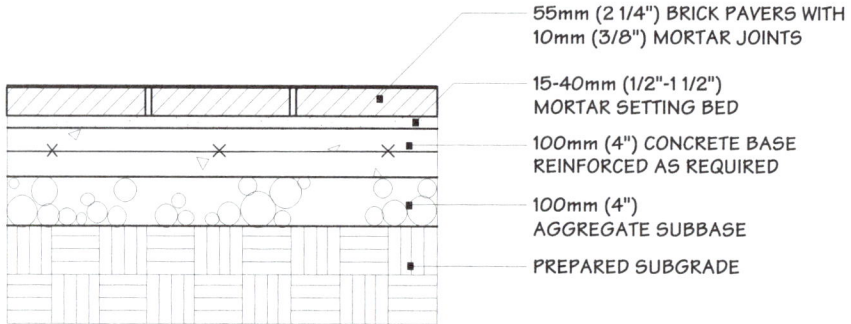

55mm (2 1/4") BRICK PAVERS WITH
10mm (3/8") MORTAR JOINTS

15-40mm (1/2"-1 1/2")
MORTAR SETTING BED

100mm (4") CONCRETE BASE
REINFORCED AS REQUIRED

100mm (4")
AGGREGATE SUBBASE

PREPARED SUBGRADE

APPLICATION

CLIMATE

SUBGRADE

CSI MASTERFORMAT: 02780
DRAWING FILE: PAV14-06

• This drawing is a template for preliminary design only, and is not intended for bid purposes. It is subject to modification based on design calculations, local practices, and all applicable codes and regulations.

• This detail is rated for light-duty applications based on thickness of concrete and aggregate base, and may support significant pedestrian loading typically associated with residential, park, and light commercial settings.

• This detail is not designed for cold climates, where the use of mortar in pavements is discouraged. Flexible adhesives, such as bituminous or elastomeric materials are recommended in these conditions.

• Rigid pavement design must accommodate movement of materials by providing adequate expansion and control joints, particularly in regions of extreme temperature fluctuations. If designed for temperate or cold climates, air-entrained concrete is typically recommended due to freezing/thawing action.

• Reinforcing practices vary widely by region. Local codes and practices should be consulted prior to specifying any type of reinforcing.

• Bricks may require periodic re-pointing or re-setting at edges.

• It is recommended that recycled and regionally available materials and products be given high priority in determining final design and specifications.

Installation Cost (per Square Foot)

LOW   HIGH

$8.55

Maintenance

LOW   HIGH

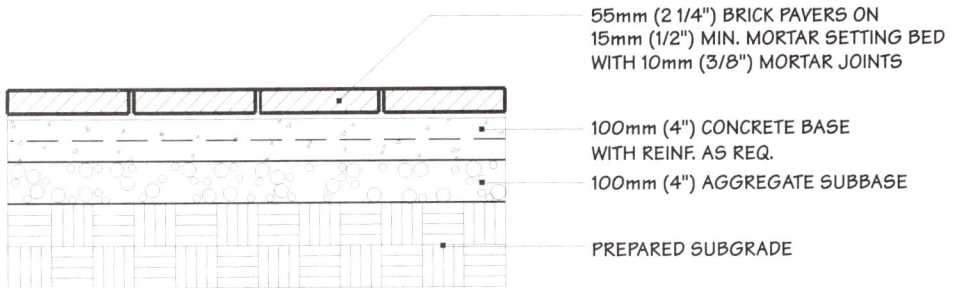

55mm (2 1/4") BRICK PAVERS ON
15mm (1/2") MIN. MORTAR SETTING BED
WITH 10mm (3/8") MORTAR JOINTS

100mm (4") CONCRETE BASE
WITH REINF. AS REQ.

100mm (4") AGGREGATE SUBBASE

PREPARED SUBGRADE

APPLICATION

CLIMATE

SUBGRADE

CSI MASTERFORMAT: 02780
DRAWING FILE: PAV34-09

• This drawing is a template for preliminary design only, and is not intended for bid purposes. It is subject to modification based on design calculations, local practices, and all applicable codes and regulations.

• This mortared brick paver on concrete detail is rated for medium-duty applications based on thickness of concrete and aggregate base, and may support pedestrian and light vehicular loading typically associated with residential, park, and light commercial settings.

• This detail is not designed for cold climates, where the use of mortar in pavements is discouraged. Flexible adhesives, such as bituminous or elastomeric materials are recommended in these conditions.

• Rigid pavement design must accommodate movement of materials by providing adequate expansion and control joints, particularly in regions of extreme temperature fluctuations. If designed for temperate or cold climates, air-entrained concrete is typi-

cally recommended due to freezing/thawing action.

• Reinforcing practices vary widely by region. Local codes and practices should be consulted prior to specifying any type of reinforcing.

• Bricks may require periodic re-pointing or re-setting at edges.

• It is recommended that recycled and regionally available materials and products be given high priority in determining final design and specifications.

Installation Cost (per Square Foot)

LOW   HIGH

$8.48

Maintenance

LOW   HIGH

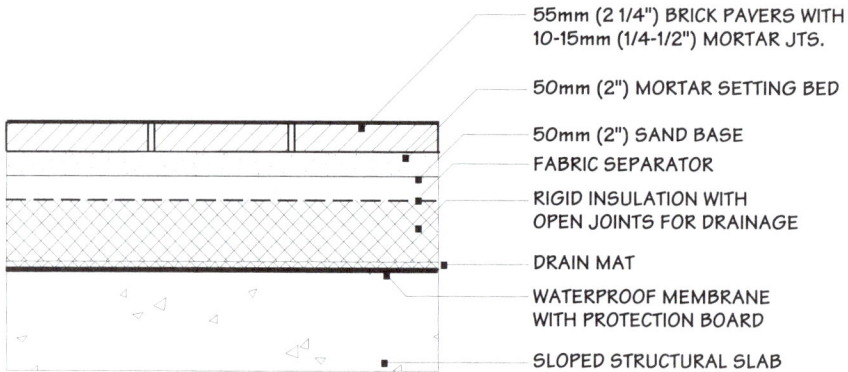

55mm (2 1/4") BRICK PAVERS WITH
10-15mm (1/4-1/2") MORTAR JTS.

50mm (2") MORTAR SETTING BED

50mm (2") SAND BASE
FABRIC SEPARATOR

RIGID INSULATION WITH
OPEN JOINTS FOR DRAINAGE

DRAIN MAT

WATERPROOF MEMBRANE
WITH PROTECTION BOARD

SLOPED STRUCTURAL SLAB

APPLICATION

CLIMATE

SUBGRADE

CSI MASTERFORMAT: 02780
DRAWING FILE: PAV14-07

• This drawing is a template for preliminary design only, and is not intended for bid purposes. It is subject to modification based on design calculations, local practices, and all applicable codes and regulations.

• This detail is rated for light-duty applications due to pavement thickness and bearing limitations of the rigid insulation upon which it rests. It is found on structural roof decks and accommodates pedestrian loading associated with paths and plazas in such settings.

• This detail is limited to warm climates due to its mortar base. It may be strengthened with a light-duty mortar reinforcing mesh of plastic or metal.

• A sand base is placed on fabric separator over open jointed rigid insulation. A drain mat is placed over sloping protection board and waterproof membrane.

• Bricks may require periodic re-pointing.

• It is recommended that recycled and regionally available materials and products be given high priority in determining final design and specifications.

Installation Cost (per Square Foot)

LOW   HIGH

$9.04

Maintenance

LOW   HIGH

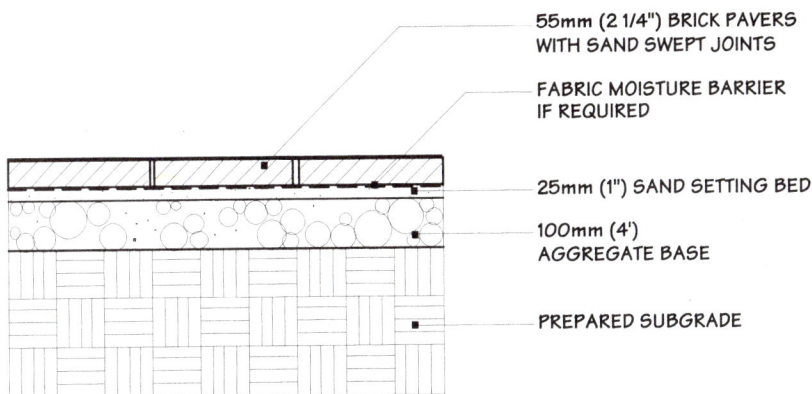

55mm (2 1/4") BRICK PAVERS
WITH SAND SWEPT JOINTS

FABRIC MOISTURE BARRIER
IF REQUIRED

25mm (1") SAND SETTING BED

100mm (4') AGGREGATE BASE

PREPARED SUBGRADE

APPLICATION

CLIMATE

SUBGRADE

CSI MASTERFORMAT: 02780
DRAWING FILE: PAV14-01

• This drawing is a template for preliminary design only, and is not intended for bid purposes. It is subject to modification based on design calculations, local practices, and all applicable codes and regulations.

• This detail is rated for light-duty applications based on paving course and base thickness, and may support primarily pedestrian loading associated with walks and light service access in parks and residential settings.

• As with all unit pavers, pavement edges require restraints to prevent creeping, especially if subjected to even occasional vehicular access.

• The subgrade conditions have a significant impact on the design of flexible pavements, such as unit pavers. Loads are transferred more directly to the base, requiring well-drained soils with adequate bearing capacity.

• Set brick with light vibrating compactor over sand cushion and final sand sweeping to complete installation. Final wash-down will help to set brick sand grout.

• Radius edge brick may be required for certain handicapped access circumstances.

• Bricks may require periodic re-setting due to differential settling or deformation of subgrade.

• It is recommended that recycled and regionally available materials and products be given high priority in determining final design and specifications.

Installation Cost (per Square Foot)

LOW   HIGH

$6.29

Maintenance

LOW   HIGH

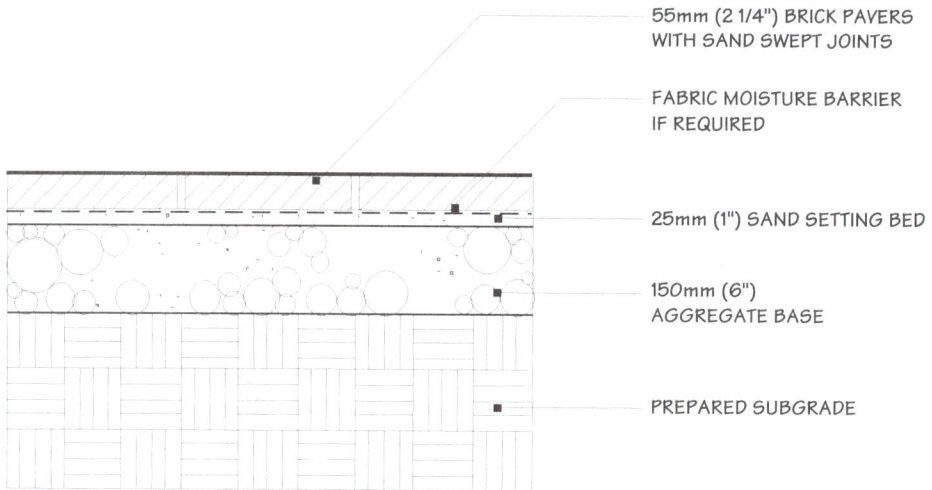

55mm (2 1/4") BRICK PAVERS
WITH SAND SWEPT JOINTS

FABRIC MOISTURE BARRIER
IF REQUIRED

25mm (1") SAND SETTING BED

150mm (6")
AGGREGATE BASE

PREPARED SUBGRADE

APPLICATION

CLIMATE

SUBGRADE

CSI MASTERFORMAT: 02780
DRAWING FILE: PAV34-01

• This drawing is a template for preliminary design only, and is not intended for bid purposes. It is subject to modification based on design calculations, local practices, and all applicable codes and regulations.

• This detail is rated for medium-duty applications based on paving course and base thickness, and subgrade bearing. Where persistent vehicular loading occurs, use high silica sand setting bed rather than stone dust or other such processed material.

• This detail may support pedestrian loading associated with walks and light vehicular access in parks and residential settings.

• As with all unit pavers, pavement edges require restraints to prevent creeping, especially if subjected to even occasional vehicular access.

• The subgrade conditions have a significant impact on the design of flexible pavements, such as unit pavers. Loads are transferred more directly to the base, requiring

well-drained soils with adequate bearing capacity.

• Set brick with light vibrating compactor over sand cushion and final sand sweeping to complete installation. Final wash-down will help to set brick sand grout.

• Radius edge brick may be required for certain handicapped access circumstances.

• Bricks may require periodic re-setting due to differential settling or deformation of subgrade. Use of sub-drains may lessen the possibility of subgrade deformation.

• It is recommended that recycled and regionally available materials and products be given high priority in determining final design and specifications.

Installation Cost (per Square Foot)

LOW   HIGH

$6.34

Maintenance

LOW   HIGH

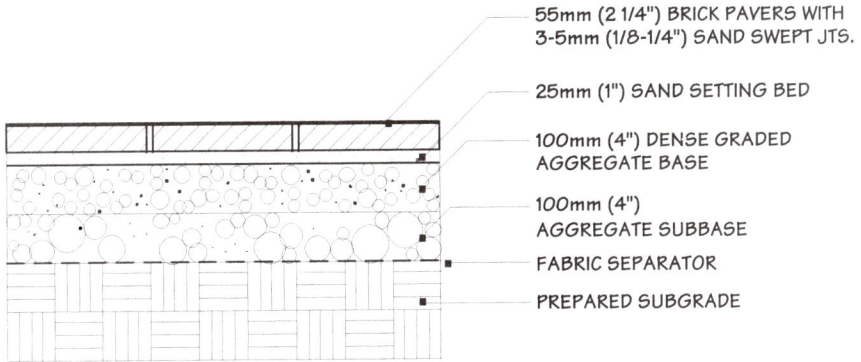

55mm (2 1/4") BRICK PAVERS WITH
3-5mm (1/8-1/4") SAND SWEPT JTS.

25mm (1") SAND SETTING BED

100mm (4") DENSE GRADED
AGGREGATE BASE

100mm (4")
AGGREGATE SUBBASE

FABRIC SEPARATOR

PREPARED SUBGRADE

APPLICATION

CLIMATE

SUBGRADE

CSI MASTERFORMAT: 02780
DRAWING FILE: PAV14-05

• This drawing is a template for preliminary design only, and is not intended for bid purposes. It is subject to modification based on design calculations, local practices, and all applicable codes and regulations.

• This detail is rated for light-duty applications based on paving course and base thickness, and subgrade bearing. It has been adapted for clay soils and includes a subbase and fabric separator to bind the aggregate base.

• This detail may support primarily pedestrian loading associated with walks and light service access in parks and residential settings.

• As with all unit pavers, pavement edges require restraints to prevent creeping, especially if subjected to even occasional vehicular access.

• The subgrade conditions have a significant impact on the design of flexible pavements, such as unit pavers. Loads are transferred more directly to the base, requiring well-drained soils with adequate bearing capacity.

• Set brick with light vibrating compactor over sand cushion and final sand sweeping to complete installation. Final wash-down will help to set brick sand grout.

• Radius edge brick may be required for certain handicapped access circumstances.

• Bricks may require periodic re-setting due to differential settling or deformation of subgrade. Use of sub-drains may lessen the possibility of subgrade deformation.

• It is recommended that recycled and regionally available materials and products be given high priority in determining final design and specifications.

Installation Cost (per Square Foot)

LOW   HIGH

$6.87

Maintenance

LOW   HIGH

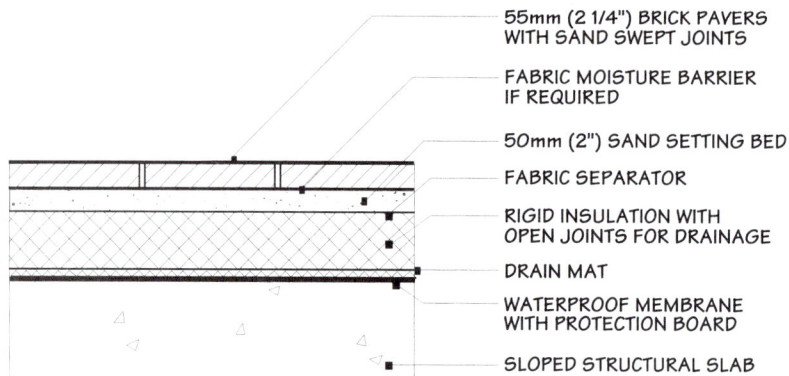

55mm (2 1/4") BRICK PAVERS
WITH SAND SWEPT JOINTS

FABRIC MOISTURE BARRIER
IF REQUIRED

50mm (2") SAND SETTING BED

FABRIC SEPARATOR

RIGID INSULATION WITH
OPEN JOINTS FOR DRAINAGE

DRAIN MAT

WATERPROOF MEMBRANE
WITH PROTECTION BOARD

SLOPED STRUCTURAL SLAB

APPLICATION

CLIMATE

SUBGRADE

CSI MASTERFORMAT: 02780
DRAWING FILE: PAV34-04

• This drawing is a template for preliminary design only, and is not intended for bid purposes. It is subject to modification based on design calculations, local practices, and all applicable codes and regulations.

• This detail is rated for light-duty applications due to pavement thickness and bearing limitations of the rigid insulation upon which it rests.

• This detail may support primarily pedestrian loading associated with walks and plazas on structural roof decks.

• As with all unit pavers, pavement edges require restraints to prevent creeping, especially if subjected to even occasional vehicular access.

• A sand base is placed on fabric separator over open jointed rigid insulation. A drain mat is placed over sloping protection board and waterproof membrane.

• Set brick with light vibrating compactor over sand cushion and final sand sweeping to complete installation. Final wash-down will help to set brick sand grout.

• Radius edge brick may be required for certain handicapped access circumstances.

• It is recommended that recycled and regionally available materials and products be given high priority in determining final design and specifications.

Installation Cost (per Square Foot)

LOW   HIGH

$7.04

Maintenance

LOW   HIGH

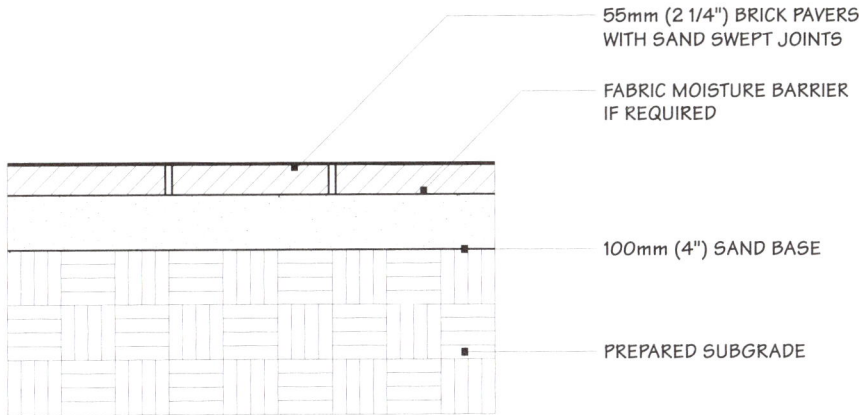

55mm (2 1/4") BRICK PAVERS
WITH SAND SWEPT JOINTS

FABRIC MOISTURE BARRIER
IF REQUIRED

100mm (4") SAND BASE

PREPARED SUBGRADE

APPLICATION

CLIMATE

SUBGRADE

CSI MASTERFORMAT: 02780
DRAWING FILE: PAV14-02

• This drawing is a template for preliminary design only, and is not intended for bid purposes. It is subject to modification based on design calculations, local practices, and all applicable codes and regulations.

• This brick paver on sand detail is rated for light-duty applications based on paving course and base thickness, and may support primarily pedestrian loading associated with walks and light service access in parks and residential settings.

• As with all unit pavers, pavement edges require restraints to prevent creeping, especially if subjected to even occasional vehicular access.

• The subgrade conditions have a significant impact on the design of flexible pavements, such as unit pavers. Loads are transferred more directly to the base, requiring well-drained soils with adequate bearing capacity.

• Set brick with light vibrating compactor over sand cushion and sweep with sand to complete installation. Final wash-down will help to set brick sand grout.

• Radius edge brick may be required for certain handicapped access circumstances.

• Bricks may require periodic re-setting due to differential settling or deformation of subgrade. In softer soils, a layer of dense graded aggregate may be required to prevent subgrade deformation.

• It is recommended that recycled and regionally available materials and products be given high priority in determining final design and specifications.

Installation Cost (per Square Foot)

LOW   HIGH

$6.31

Maintenance

LOW   HIGH

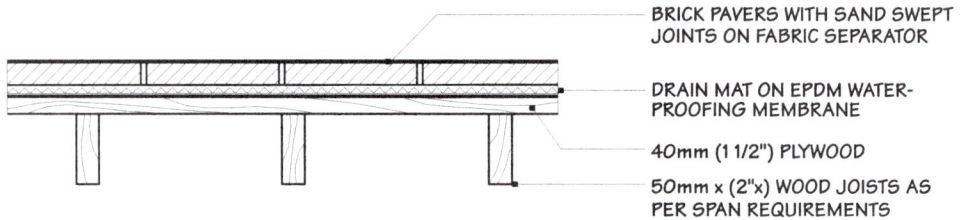

BRICK PAVERS WITH SAND SWEPT
JOINTS ON FABRIC SEPARATOR

DRAIN MAT ON EPDM WATER-
PROOFING MEMBRANE

40mm (1 1/2") PLYWOOD

50mm x (2"x) WOOD JOISTS AS
PER SPAN REQUIREMENTS

APPLICATION

CLIMATE

SUBGRADE

CSI MASTERFORMAT: 02780
DRAWING FILE: PAV34-07

• This drawing is a template for preliminary design only, and is not intended for bid purposes. It is subject to modification based on design calculations, local practices, and all applicable codes and regulations.

• This brick paver on deck structure detail is rated for light-duty applications due to loading limitations of the wood deck upon which it rests. The brick provides an excellent ballast for single ply membranes.

• This detail may support primarily pedestrian loading associated with patios and terraces on structural wood roof decks.

• As with all unit pavers, pavement edges require restraints to prevent creeping.

• A sand base is placed on fabric separator over heavy duty drain mat, which is placed over sloping waterproof membrane and heavy-duty plywood deck.

• Brick is set with rubber mallet over sand cushion and joints are swept with sand to

complete installation. Final gentle wash-down will help to set brick sand grout.

• Radius edge brick may be required for certain handicapped access circumstances.

• It is recommended that recycled and regionally available materials and products be given high priority in determining final design and specifications.

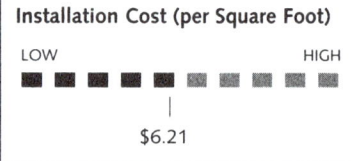

Installation Cost (per Square Foot)

LOW   HIGH

$6.21

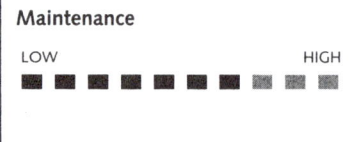

Maintenance

LOW   HIGH

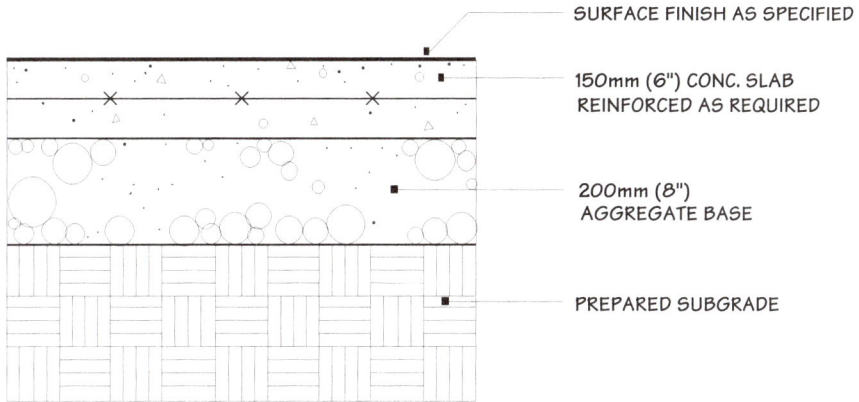

SURFACE FINISH AS SPECIFIED

150mm (6") CONC. SLAB
REINFORCED AS REQUIRED

200mm (8")
AGGREGATE BASE

PREPARED SUBGRADE

APPLICATION

CLIMATE

SUBGRADE

CSI MASTERFORMAT: 02750
DRAWING FILE: PAV32-02

• This drawing is a template for preliminary design only, and is not intended for bid purposes. It is subject to modification based on design calculations, local practices, and all applicable codes and regulations.

• This detail is rated for heavy-duty applications based on thickness of concrete and aggregate base, and may support vehicular loading typically found in dense residential, urban park, or institutional settings.

• Subgrade must be uniform and sloped to drain, usually in a plane parallel to the finished surface. Slabs should not be placed directly on subgrades with extreme porosity (i.e. volcanic pumice).

• Rigid pavement design must accommodate movement of materials by providing adequate expansion and control joints, particularly in regions of extreme temperature fluctuations. If designed for temperate or cold climates, air-entrained concrete is typically recommended due to freezing/thawing action.

• Reinforcing practices vary widely. Local codes and practices should be consulted before specifying any type of reinforcing. All steel should be covered by at least 50mm (2") of concrete.

• Control joints should be tooled or sawn to restrict cracking.

• Expansion joints should be filled, and sealed in temperate and cold climates. These joints require periodic cleaning and re-sealing. Periodic surface sealing may be required.

• It is recommended that recycled and regionally available materials and products be given high priority in determining final design and specifications.

Installation Cost (per Square Foot)

LOW   HIGH

$3.35

Maintenance

LOW   HIGH

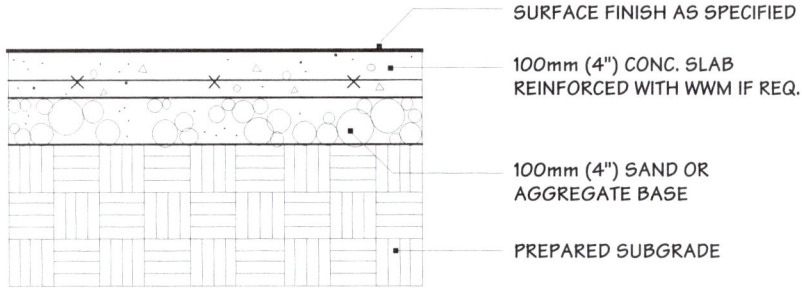

SURFACE FINISH AS SPECIFIED

100mm (4") CONC. SLAB
REINFORCED WITH WWM IF REQ.

100mm (4") SAND OR
AGGREGATE BASE

PREPARED SUBGRADE

APPLICATION

LIGHT · MED. · HEAVY

CLIMATE

ARID · HUMID · TEMP. · COLD

SUBGRADE

PERM. · CLAY · ROOF

CSI MASTERFORMAT: 02750
DRAWING FILE: PAV12-02

• This drawing is a template for preliminary design only, and is not intended for bid purposes. It is subject to modification based on design calculations, local practices, and all applicable codes and regulations.

• This detail is rated for light-duty applications based on thickness of concrete and aggregate base, and may support primarily pedestrian loading typically associated with residential, park, and light commercial settings.

• Subgrade conditions have a significant impact on the longevity of rigid pavements, such as concrete. The subgrade should be uniform to prevent pavement failure due to uneven soil expansion and contraction. This detail provides a well-drained aggregate base to drain sub-surface moisture and increase uniformity.

• Reinforcing practices vary widely. Local codes and practices should be consulted before specifying any type of reinforcing. All steel should be covered by at least 50mm (2") of concrete.

• Rigid pavement design must accommodate movement of materials by providing adequate expansion and control joints, particularly in regions of extreme temperature fluctuations. If designed for temperate or cold climates, air-entrained concrete is typically recommended due to freezing/thawing action.

• Sealing of the paving surface with clear sealants can lengthen the life of the pavement, and preserve its appearance over time. This pavement requires moderate maintenance.

• It is recommended that recycled and regionally available materials and products be given high priority in determining final design and specifications.

Installation Cost (per Square Foot)

LOW ... HIGH

$2.27

Maintenance

LOW ... HIGH

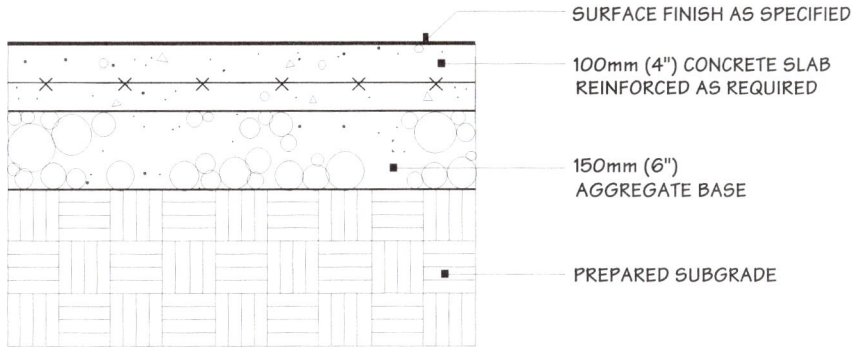

SURFACE FINISH AS SPECIFIED

100mm (4") CONCRETE SLAB
REINFORCED AS REQUIRED

150mm (6")
AGGREGATE BASE

PREPARED SUBGRADE

APPLICATION

CLIMATE

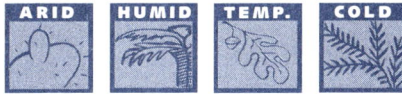

SUBGRADE

CSI MASTERFORMAT: 02750
DRAWING FILE: PAV32-03

• This drawing is a template for preliminary design only, and is not intended for bid purposes. It is subject to modification based on design calculations, local practices, and all applicable codes and regulations.

• This detail is rated for medium-duty applications based on thickness of concrete and aggregate base, and may support significant pedestrian or light vehicular loading typically found in residential, park, or light commercial settings.

• Subgrade must be uniform and sloped to drain, usually in a plane parallel to the finished surface. Slabs should not be placed directly on subgrades with extreme porosity (i.e. volcanic pumice).

• Rigid pavement design must accommodate movement of materials by providing adequate expansion and control joints, particularly in regions of extreme temperature fluctuations. If designed for temperate or cold climates, air-entrained concrete is typi-

cally recommended due to freezing/thawing action.

• Reinforcing practices vary widely. Local codes and practices should be consulted before specifying any type of reinforcing. All steel should be covered by at least 50mm (2") of concrete.

• Control joints should be tooled or sawn to restrict cracking.

• Expansion joints should be filled, and sealed in temperate and cold climates. These joints require periodic cleaning and resealing. Periodic surface sealing may be required.

• It is recommended that recycled and regionally available materials and products be given high priority in determining final design and specifications.

Installation Cost (per Square Foot)

LOW   HIGH

$2.22

Maintenance

LOW   HIGH

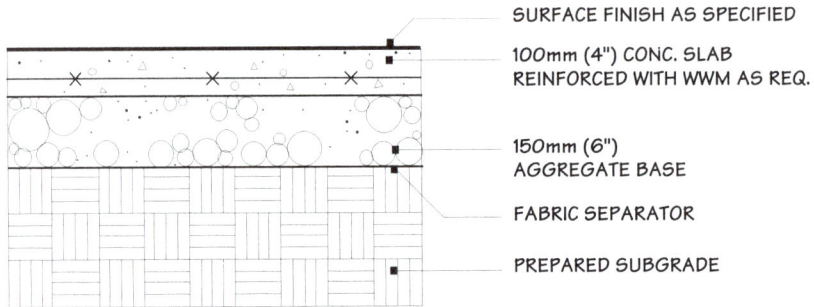

SURFACE FINISH AS SPECIFIED

100mm (4") CONC. SLAB
REINFORCED WITH WWM AS REQ.

150mm (6")
AGGREGATE BASE

FABRIC SEPARATOR

PREPARED SUBGRADE

APPLICATION

CLIMATE

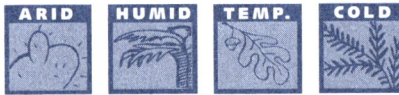

SUBGRADE

CSI MASTERFORMAT: 02750
DRAWING FILE: PAV12-03

• This drawing is a template for preliminary design only, and is not intended for bid purposes. It is subject to modification based on design calculations, local practices, and all applicable codes and regulations.

• This detail is rated for light-duty applications based on thickness of concrete and aggregate base, and may support primarily pedestrian loading typically associated with residential, park, and light commercial settings.

• Subgrade conditions have a significant impact on the longevity of rigid pavements, such as concrete. The subgrade should be uniform to prevent pavement failure due to uneven soil expansion and contraction. This detail provides a thicker well-drained aggregate base to drain sub-surface moisture and increase uniformity, in addition to a fabric separator to bind the aggregate for greater strength in expansive clay soils.

• Reinforcing practices vary widely. Local codes and practices should be consulted

before specifying any type of reinforcing. All steel should be covered by at least 50mm (2") of concrete.

• Rigid pavement design must accommodate movement of materials by providing adequate expansion and control joints, particularly in regions of extreme temperature fluctuations. If designed for temperate or cold climates, air-entrained concrete is typically recommended due to freezing/thawing action.

• Sealing of the paving surface with clear sealants can lengthen the life of the pavement, and preserve its appearance over time. This pavement requires moderate maintenance.

• It is recommended that recycled and regionally available materials and products be given high priority in determining final design and specifications.

Installation Cost (per Square Foot)

LOW   HIGH

$2.17

Maintenance

LOW   HIGH

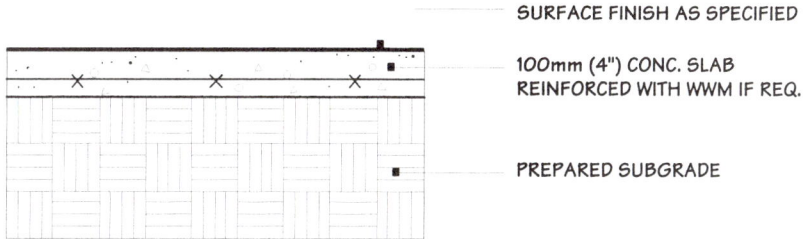

SURFACE FINISH AS SPECIFIED

100mm (4") CONC. SLAB
REINFORCED WITH WWM IF REQ.

PREPARED SUBGRADE

APPLICATION

CLIMATE

SUBGRADE

CSI MASTERFORMAT: 02750
DRAWING FILE: PAV12-01

• This drawing is a template for preliminary design only, and is not intended for bid purposes. It is subject to modification based on design calculations, local practices, and all applicable codes and regulations.

• This detail is rated for light-duty applications based on thickness of concrete and aggregate base, and may support primarily pedestrian loading typically found in residential and park settings.

• Subgrade must be uniform and sloped to drain, usually in a plane parallel to the finished surface. Slabs should not be placed directly on subgrades with extreme porosity (i.e. volcanic pumice).

• Rigid pavement design must accommodate movement of materials by providing adequate expansion and control joints, particularly in regions of extreme temperature fluctuations. If designed for temperate or cold climates, air-entrained concrete is typically recommended due to freezing/thawing action.

• Reinforcing practices vary widely. Local codes and practices should be consulted before specifying any type of reinforcing. All steel should be covered by at least 50mm (2") of concrete.

• Control joints should be tooled or sawn to restrict cracking.

• Expansion joints should be filled, and sealed in temperate and cold climates. These joints require periodic cleaning and resealing. Periodic surface sealing may be required.

• It is recommended that recycled and regionally available materials and products be given high priority in determining final design and specifications.

Installation Cost (per Square Foot)

LOW   HIGH

$1.97

Maintenance

LOW   HIGH

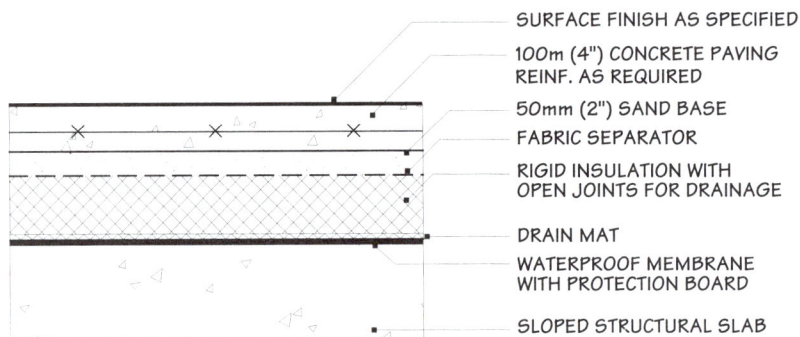

SURFACE FINISH AS SPECIFIED

100m (4") CONCRETE PAVING
REINF. AS REQUIRED

50mm (2") SAND BASE
FABRIC SEPARATOR

RIGID INSULATION WITH
OPEN JOINTS FOR DRAINAGE

DRAIN MAT

WATERPROOF MEMBRANE
WITH PROTECTION BOARD

SLOPED STRUCTURAL SLAB

APPLICATION

CLIMATE

SUBGRADE

CSI MASTERFORMAT: 02775
DRAWING FILE: PAV12-05

• This drawing is a template for preliminary design only, and is not intended for bid purposes. It is subject to modification based on design calculations, local practices, and all applicable codes and regulations.

• This detail is typically associated with pedestrian walks and multi-purpose recreation surfaces on structural roof decks. Light weight concrete is often used in warmer climates.

• This detail is rated for light-duty applications due to pavement thickness and bearing limitations of the rigid insulation upon which it rests. For vehicular loads, rigid insulation is often omitted, and sand cushion is placed on filtered drain mat.

• Rigid pavement design must accommodate movement of materials by providing adequate expansion and control joints, particularly in regions of extreme temperature fluctuations. If designed for temperate or cold climates, air-entrained concrete is typically recommended due to freezing/thawing action.

• Reinforcing practices vary widely by region. Local codes and practices should be consulted prior to specifying any type of reinforcing.

• A sand base is placed on fabric separator over open jointed rigid insulation. A drain mat is placed over sloping protection board and waterproof membrane.

• It is recommended that recycled and regionally available materials and products be given high priority in determining final design and specifications.

Installation Cost (per Square Foot)

LOW   HIGH

$3.05

Maintenance

LOW   HIGH

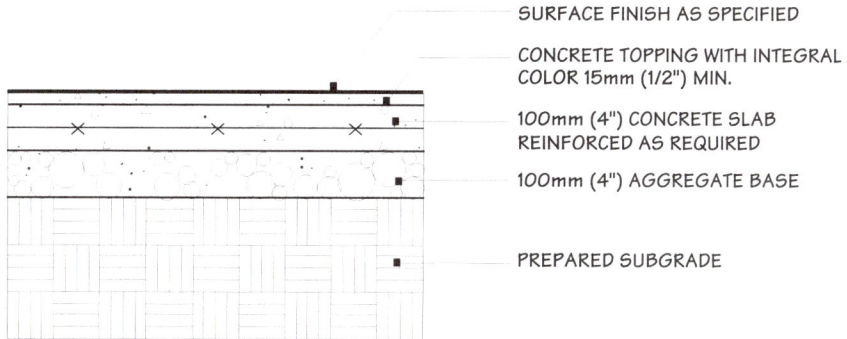

SURFACE FINISH AS SPECIFIED

CONCRETE TOPPING WITH INTEGRAL COLOR 15mm (1/2") MIN.

100mm (4") CONCRETE SLAB REINFORCED AS REQUIRED

100mm (4") AGGREGATE BASE

PREPARED SUBGRADE

APPLICATION

CLIMATE

SUBGRADE

CSI MASTERFORMAT: 03360
DRAWING FILE: PAV12-07

• This drawing is a template for preliminary design only, and is not intended for bid purposes. It is subject to modification based on design calculations, local practices, and all applicable codes and regulations.

• This detail is rated for light-duty applications based on paving course and base thickness, and may support primarily pedestrian loading associated with walks and light service access in parks and residential settings.

• Integral color is applied to the surface of the slab, typically in 15mm (1/2") top coat. Sealing of the paving surface with clear sealants can lengthen the life of the pavement, and preserve its appearance over time.

• Rigid pavement design must accommodate movement of materials by providing adequate expansion and control joints, particularly in regions of extreme temperature fluctuations. If designed for temperate or cold climates, air-entrained concrete is typically recommended due to freezing/thawing action.

• Subgrade conditions have a significant impact on the longevity of rigid pavements, such as concrete. The subgrade should be uniform to prevent pavement failure due to uneven soil expansion and contraction. This detail provides a well-drained aggregate base to drain sub-surface moisture and increase uniformity.

• Reinforcing practices vary widely by region. Local codes and practices should be consulted prior to specifying any type of reinforcing.

• This detail is not recommended for circumstances requiring abrasive maintenance practices.

• It is recommended that recycled and regionally available materials and products be given high priority in determining final design and specifications.

Installation Cost (per Square Foot)

LOW   HIGH

$3.08

Maintenance

LOW   HIGH

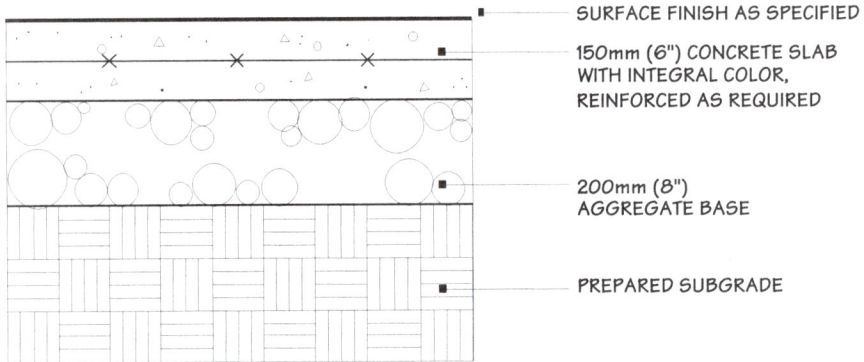

SURFACE FINISH AS SPECIFIED

150mm (6") CONCRETE SLAB WITH INTEGRAL COLOR, REINFORCED AS REQUIRED

200mm (8") AGGREGATE BASE

PREPARED SUBGRADE

APPLICATION

CLIMATE

SUBGRADE

CSI MASTERFORMAT: 03360
DRAWING FILE: PAV32-06

• This drawing is a template for preliminary design only, and is not intended for bid purposes. It is subject to modification based on design calculations, local practices, and all applicable codes and regulations.

• This detail is rated for heavy-duty applications based on thickness of concrete and aggregate base, and may support significant pedestrian or vehicular loading typically found in dense residential, urban park, or commercial settings.

• Subgrade must be uniform and sloped to drain, usually in a plane parallel to the finished surface. Slabs should not be placed directly on subgrades with extreme porosity (i.e. volcanic pumice).

• Rigid pavement design must accommodate movement of materials by providing adequate expansion and control joints, particularly in regions of extreme temperature fluctuations. If designed for temperate or cold climates, air-entrained concrete is typically recommended due to freezing/thawing action.

• Reinforcing practices vary widely. Local codes and practices should be consulted before specifying any type of reinforcing. All steel should be covered by at least 50mm (2") of concrete.

• Control joints should be tooled or sawn to restrict cracking.

• Expansion joints should be filled, and sealed in temperate and cold climates. These joints require periodic cleaning and re-sealing. Periodic surface sealing may be required.

• Color is added to the concrete mix, prior to installation and provides a uniform finish.

• Sealing of the paving surface with clear sealants can lengthen the life of the pavement, and preserve its appearance over time.

• It is recommended that recycled and regionally available materials and products be given high priority in determining final design and specifications.

Installation Cost (per Square Foot)

LOW   HIGH

$3.84

Maintenance

LOW   HIGH

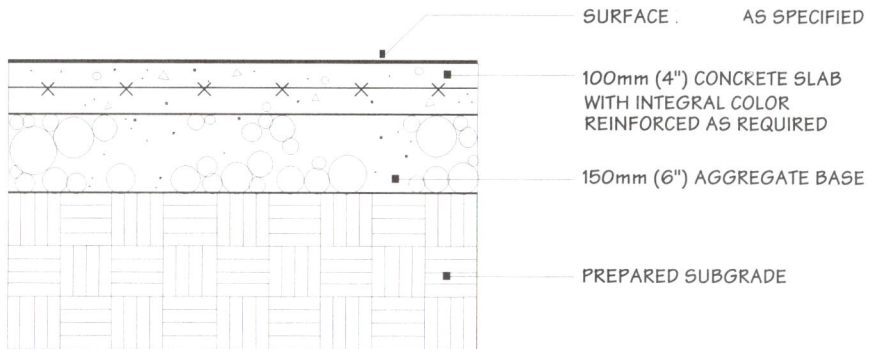

SURFACE . AS SPECIFIED

100mm (4") CONCRETE SLAB WITH INTEGRAL COLOR REINFORCED AS REQUIRED

150mm (6") AGGREGATE BASE

PREPARED SUBGRADE

APPLICATION

CLIMATE

SUBGRADE

CSI MASTERFORMAT: 03360
DRAWING FILE: PAV32-07

• This drawing is a template for preliminary design only, and is not intended for bid purposes. It is subject to modification based on design calculations, local practices, and all applicable codes and regulations.

• This detail is rated for medium-duty applications based on thickness of concrete and aggregate base, and may support significant pedestrian or light vehicular loading typically found in residential, park, or light commercial settings.

• Subgrade must be uniform and sloped to drain, usually in a plane parallel to the finished surface. Slabs should not be placed directly on subgrades with extreme porosity (i.e. volcanic pumice).

• Rigid pavement design must accommodate movement of materials by providing adequate expansion and control joints, particularly in regions of extreme temperature fluctuations. If designed for temperate or cold climates, air-entrained concrete is typically recommended due to freezing/thawing action.

• Reinforcing practices vary widely. Local codes and practices should be consulted before specifying any type of reinforcing. All steel should be covered by at least 50mm (2") of concrete.

• Control joints should be tooled or sawn to restrict cracking.

• Expansion joints should be filled, and sealed in temperate and cold climates. These joints require periodic cleaning and re-sealing. Periodic surface sealing may be required.

• Color is added to the concrete mix, prior to installation and provides a uniform finish.

• Sealing of the paving surface with clear sealants can lengthen the life of the pavement, and preserve its appearance over time.

• It is recommended that recycled and regionally available materials and products be given high priority in determining final design and specifications.

Installation Cost (per Square Foot)

$3.01

Maintenance

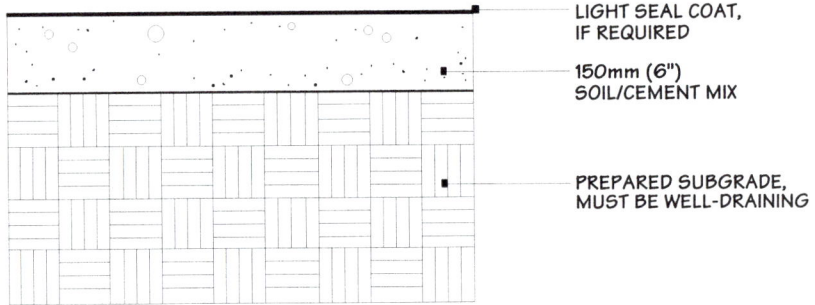

LIGHT SEAL COAT,
IF REQUIRED

150mm (6")
SOIL/CEMENT MIX

PREPARED SUBGRADE,
MUST BE WELL-DRAINING

APPLICATION

CLIMATE

SUBGRADE

CSI MASTERFORMAT: 02710
DRAWING FILE: PAV32-01

• This drawing is a template for preliminary design only, and is not intended for bid purposes. It is subject to modification based on design calculations, local practices, and all applicable codes and regulations.

• This detail is rated for light-duty applications based on thickness of soil cement concrete, and may support primarily pedestrian loading typically associated with residential and recreational settings.

• Soil cement is prepared on site using existing soil and/or aggregates in the cement mix. It is an important alternative in remote locations where ready-mix is not available. It requires a well-drained and uniform subgrade, particularly in frost/thaw conditions. It is restricted to warmer climates in regions with uniform well drained soils, or for temporary purposes in other areas.

• It is recommended that recycled and regionally available materials and products be given high priority in determining final design and specifications.

Installation Cost (per Square Foot)

LOW   HIGH

$0.92

Maintenance

LOW   HIGH

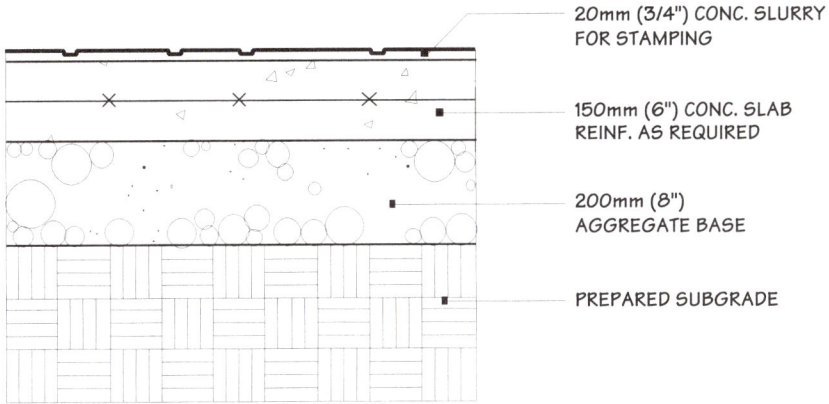

20mm (3/4") CONC. SLURRY
FOR STAMPING

150mm (6") CONC. SLAB
REINF. AS REQUIRED

200mm (8")
AGGREGATE BASE

PREPARED SUBGRADE

APPLICATION

CLIMATE

SUBGRADE

CSI MASTERFORMAT: 02760
DRAWING FILE: PAV32-04

• This drawing is a template for preliminary design only, and is not intended for bid purposes. It is subject to modification based on design calculations, local practices, and all applicable codes and regulations.

• This detail is rated for heavy-duty applications based on thickness of concrete and aggregate base, and may support vehicular loading typically associated with residential, park, and light commercial settings.

• Subgrade conditions have a significant impact on the longevity of rigid pavements, such as concrete. The subgrade should be uniform to prevent pavement failure due to uneven soil expansion and contraction. This detail provides a well-drained aggregate base to drain sub-surface moisture and increase uniformity.

• Reinforcing practices vary widely. Local codes and practices should be consulted before specifying any type of reinforcing. All steel should be covered by at least 50mm (2") of concrete.

• Rigid pavement design must accommodate movement of materials by providing adequate expansion and control joints, particularly in regions of extreme temperature fluctuations. If designed for temperate or cold climates, air-entrained concrete is typically recommended due to freezing/thawing action.

• Sealing of the paving surface with clear sealants can lengthen the life of the pavement, and preserve its appearance over time. This pavement requires moderate maintenance.

• Stamped concrete finishes are more appropriate for warm climates and may include warm temperate zones. Although relatively inexpensive to install, stamped pavements are difficult to repair and are easily damaged by abrasive wear and maintenance practices. Careful placement of expansion joints may allow for easier sectional repair or replacement.

• It is recommended that recycled and regionally available materials and products be given high priority in determining final design and specifications.

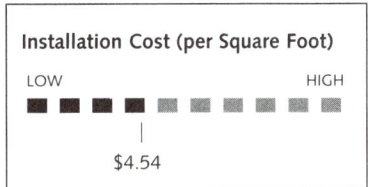

Installation Cost (per Square Foot)

LOW   HIGH

$4.54

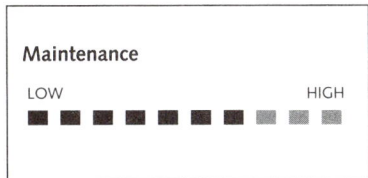

Maintenance

LOW   HIGH

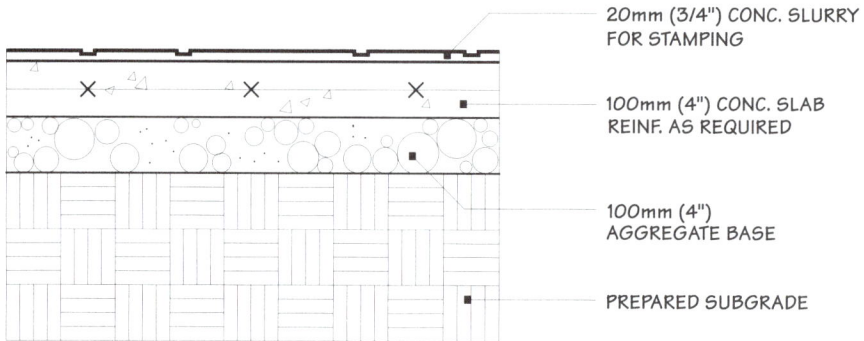

20mm (3/4") CONC. SLURRY FOR STAMPING

100mm (4") CONC. SLAB REINF. AS REQUIRED

100mm (4") AGGREGATE BASE

PREPARED SUBGRADE

APPLICATION

CLIMATE

SUBGRADE

CSI MASTERFORMAT: 02760
DRAWING FILE: PAV12-06

• This drawing is a template for preliminary design only, and is not intended for bid purposes. It is subject to modification based on design calculations, local practices, and all applicable codes and regulations.

• This detail is rated for light-duty applications based on thickness of concrete and aggregate base, and may support primarily pedestrian loading typically associated with residential, park, and light commercial settings.

• Subgrade conditions have a significant impact on the longevity of rigid pavements, such as concrete. The subgrade should be uniform to prevent pavement failure due to uneven soil expansion and contraction. This detail provides a well-drained aggregate base to drain sub-surface moisture and increase uniformity.

• Reinforcing practices vary widely. Local codes and practices should be consulted before specifying any type of reinforcing. All

steel should be covered by at least 50mm (2") of concrete.

• Rigid pavement design must accommodate movement of materials by providing adequate expansion and control joints, particularly in regions of extreme temperature fluctuations. If designed for temperate or cold climates, air-entrained concrete is typically recommended due to freezing/thawing action.

• Sealing of the paving surface with clear sealants can lengthen the life of the pavement, and preserve its appearance over time. This pavement requires moderate maintenance.

• Stamped concrete finishes are more appropriate for warm climates and may include warm temperate zones. Although relatively inexpensive to install, stamped pavements are difficult to repair and are easily damaged by abrasive wear and maintenance practices.

• It is recommended that recycled and regionally available materials and products be given high priority in determining final design and specifications.

Installation Cost (per Square Foot)

LOW   HIGH

$3.84

Maintenance

LOW   HIGH

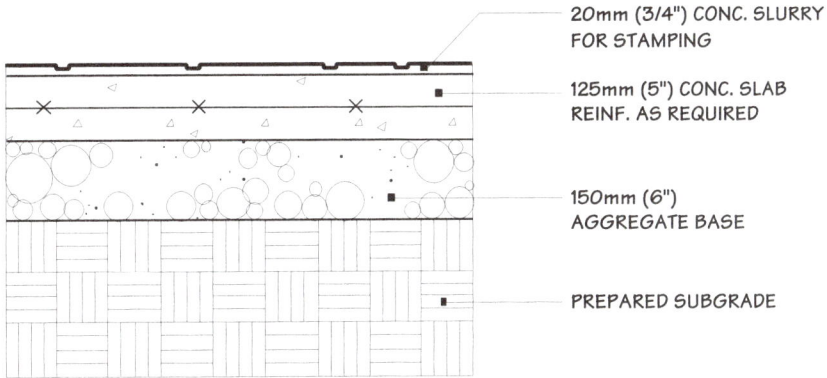

20mm (3/4") CONC. SLURRY
FOR STAMPING

125mm (5") CONC. SLAB
REINF. AS REQUIRED

150mm (6")
AGGREGATE BASE

PREPARED SUBGRADE

APPLICATION

CLIMATE

SUBGRADE

CSI MASTERFORMAT: 02760
DRAWING FILE: PAV32-05

• This drawing is a template for preliminary design only, and is not intended for bid purposes. It is subject to modification based on design calculations, local practices, and all applicable codes and regulations.

• This detail is rated for medium-duty applications based on thickness of concrete and aggregate base, and may support pedestrian and vehicular loading typically associated with residential, park, and light commercial settings.

• Subgrade conditions have a significant impact on the longevity of rigid pavements, such as concrete. The subgrade should be uniform to prevent pavement failure due to uneven soil expansion and contraction. This detail provides a well-drained aggregate base to drain sub-surface moisture and increase uniformity.

• Reinforcing practices vary widely. Local codes and practices should be consulted before specifying any type of reinforcing. All steel should be covered by at least 50mm (2") of concrete.

• Rigid pavement design must accommodate movement of materials by providing adequate expansion and control joints, particularly in regions of extreme temperature fluctuations. If designed for temperate or cold climates, air-entrained concrete is typically recommended due to freezing/thawing action.

• Sealing of the paving surface with clear sealants can lengthen the life of the pavement, and preserve its appearance over time. This pavement requires moderate maintenance.

• Stamped concrete finishes are more appropriate for warm climates and may include warm temperate zones. Although relatively inexpensive to install, stamped pavements are difficult to repair and are easily damaged by abrasive wear and maintenance practices. Careful placement of expansion joints may allow for easier sectional repair or replacement.

• It is recommended that recycled and regionally available materials and products be given high priority in determining final design and specifications.

Installation Cost (per Square Foot)

LOW   HIGH

$4.21

Maintenance

LOW   HIGH

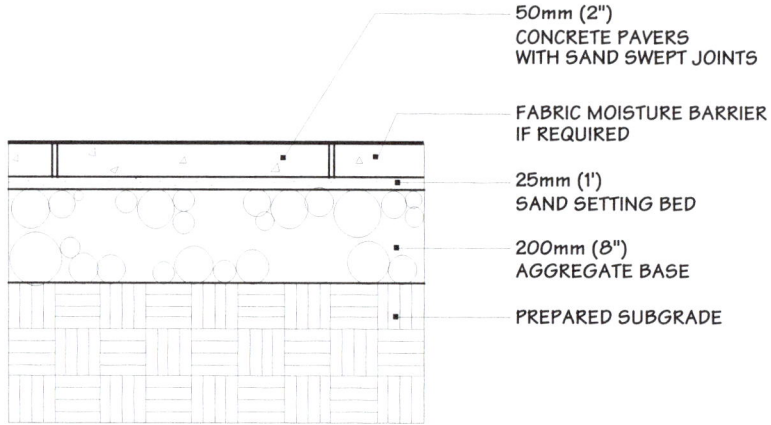

50mm (2")
CONCRETE PAVERS
WITH SAND SWEPT JOINTS

FABRIC MOISTURE BARRIER
IF REQUIRED

25mm (1')
SAND SETTING BED

200mm (8")
AGGREGATE BASE

PREPARED SUBGRADE

APPLICATION

CLIMATE

SUBGRADE

CSI MASTERFORMAT: 02780
DRAWING FILE: PAV12-10

• This drawing is a template for preliminary design only, and is not intended for bid purposes. It is subject to modification based on design calculations, local practices, and all applicable codes and regulations.

• This detail is rated for heavy-duty applications based on concrete design strength and aggregate base thickness, and may support significant pedestrian and associated vehicular loading typically associated with dense residential, urban park, or commercial settings.

• Precast concrete pavers should be specified to handle expected loads. Typical heavy duty design strength is 250 kg per square cm (3,500 psi).

• Sealing of the paving surface with clear sealants can lengthen the life of the pavement, and preserve its appearance over time.

• As with all unit pavers, pavement edges require restraints to prevent creeping, especially in heavy-duty circumstances, where lat-eral pressure can be significant. High silica content sand is recommended as a setting bed to resist breakdown due to vibration and pressure stresses under such sustained loading.

• It is recommended that recycled and regionally available materials and products be given high priority in determining final design and specifications.

Installation Cost (per Square Foot)

LOW   HIGH

$3.05

Maintenance

LOW   HIGH

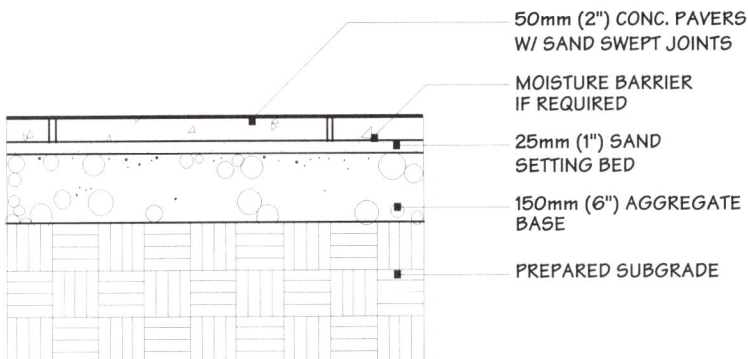

50mm (2") CONC. PAVERS
W/ SAND SWEPT JOINTS

MOISTURE BARRIER
IF REQUIRED

25mm (1") SAND
SETTING BED

150mm (6") AGGREGATE
BASE

PREPARED SUBGRADE

APPLICATION

CLIMATE

SUBGRADE

CSI MASTERFORMAT: 02780
DRAWING FILE: PAV12-08

• This drawing is a template for preliminary design only, and is not intended for bid purposes. It is subject to modification based on design calculations, local practices, and all applicable codes and regulations.

• This detail is rated for medium-duty applications based on concrete design strength and aggregate base thickness, and may support pedestrian and associated vehicular loading typically associated with residential, park, or light commercial settings.

• Precast concrete pavers should be specified to handle expected loads.

• Sealing of the paving surface with clear sealants can lengthen the life of the pavement, and preserve its appearance over time.

• As with all unit pavers, pavement edges require restraints to prevent creeping, especially in heavy-duty circumstances, where lateral pressure can be significant. High silica content sand is recommended as a setting bed to resist breakdown due to vibration and pressure stresses under such sustained loading.

• It is recommended that recycled and regionally available materials and products be given high priority in determining final design and specifications.

Installation Cost (per Square Foot)

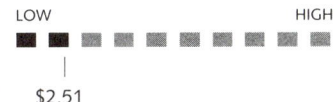

LOW   HIGH

$2.51

Maintenance

LOW   HIGH

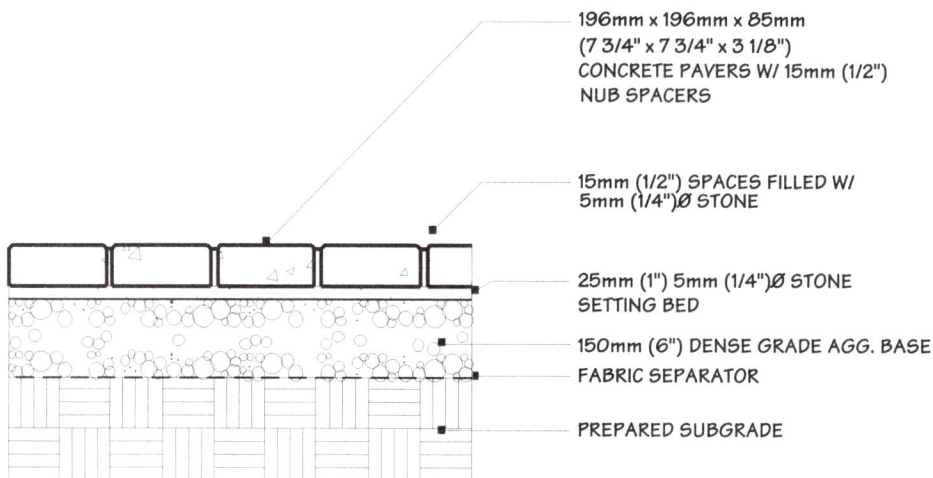

196mm x 196mm x 85mm
(7 3/4" x 7 3/4" x 3 1/8")
CONCRETE PAVERS W/ 15mm (1/2")
NUB SPACERS

15mm (1/2") SPACES FILLED W/
5mm (1/4")Ø STONE

25mm (1") 5mm (1/4")Ø STONE
SETTING BED

150mm (6") DENSE GRADE AGG. BASE

FABRIC SEPARATOR

PREPARED SUBGRADE

APPLICATION

CLIMATE

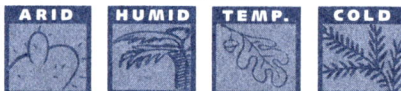

SUBGRADE

CSI MASTERFORMAT: 02795
DRAWING FILE: PAV32-13

• This drawing is a template for preliminary design only, and is not intended for bid purposes. It is subject to modification based on design calculations, local practices, and all applicable codes and regulations.

• This detail is rated as medium-duty due to aggregate subbase thickness and is typically found in residential, park, and institutional settings.

• Precast concrete pavers are spaced by attached nubs to create a 15 mm (1/2") space between paver units. Spaces are filled with small washed stone and swept and washed into the joints. In heavy-duty uses, a fabric separator may be placed beneath the aggregate base.

• Depth of sand base will vary with local soil conditions, typically 25mm — 50mm (1"-2"). Heavy loads require high silica sand content to maintain capilarity and bearing.

• These units may be stagger jointed or aligned in a grid by virtue of variable nub positions.

• This detail is rated for all climates, but requires well drained soils.

• It is recommended that recycled and regionally available materials and products be given high priority in determining final design and specifications.

Installation Cost (per Square Foot)

LOW   HIGH

$3.32

Maintenance

LOW   HIGH

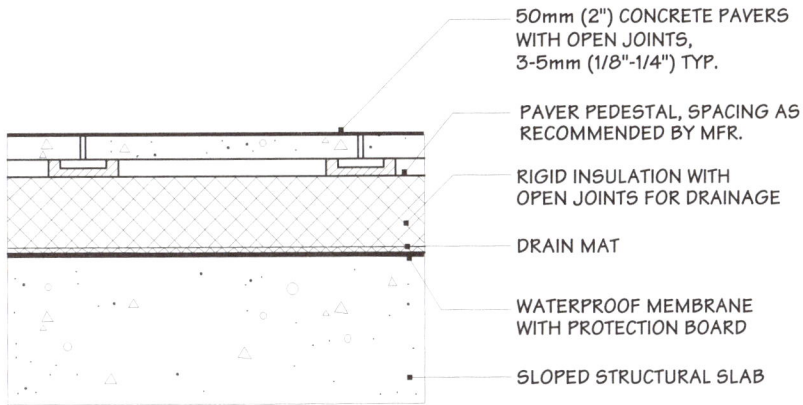

50mm (2") CONCRETE PAVERS
WITH OPEN JOINTS,
3-5mm (1/8"-1/4") TYP.

PAVER PEDESTAL, SPACING AS
RECOMMENDED BY MFR.

RIGID INSULATION WITH
OPEN JOINTS FOR DRAINAGE

DRAIN MAT

WATERPROOF MEMBRANE
WITH PROTECTION BOARD

SLOPED STRUCTURAL SLAB

APPLICATION

CLIMATE

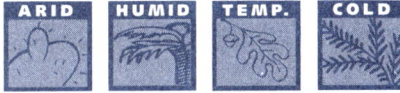

SUBGRADE

CSI MASTERFORMAT: 07760
DRAWING FILE: PAV12-09

• This drawing is a template for preliminary design only, and is not intended for bid purposes. It is subject to modification based on design calculations, local practices, and all applicable codes and regulations.

• This detail is rated for light-duty applications based on paving course and rigid insulation bearing capacity, and may support primarily pedestrian loading associated with plazas on roof structures.

• Waterproof membrane with protection board should be placed on sloped structural slab. Proprietary drain mat should be placed directly on membrane and protection board to ensure proper drainage.

• Rigid insulation may be placed on drain mat in areas of non-vehicular loading. Open joints should be provided in the insulation to allow for proper drainage. Some applications may require a perforated protection board on insulation to support the specified loads.

• Precast concrete pavers should be specified to handle expected loads. Typical light-duty design strength is 175 kg per square cm (2,500 psi). Units may be placed on paver pedestals, as specified by manufacturer.

• Periodic clearing of debris beneath the suspended pavers may be required in regions with heavy precipitation, or on heavily planted plazas.

• It is recommended that recycled and regionally available materials and products be given high priority in determining final design and specifications.

Installation Cost (per Square Foot)

LOW   HIGH

$2.92

Maintenance

LOW   HIGH

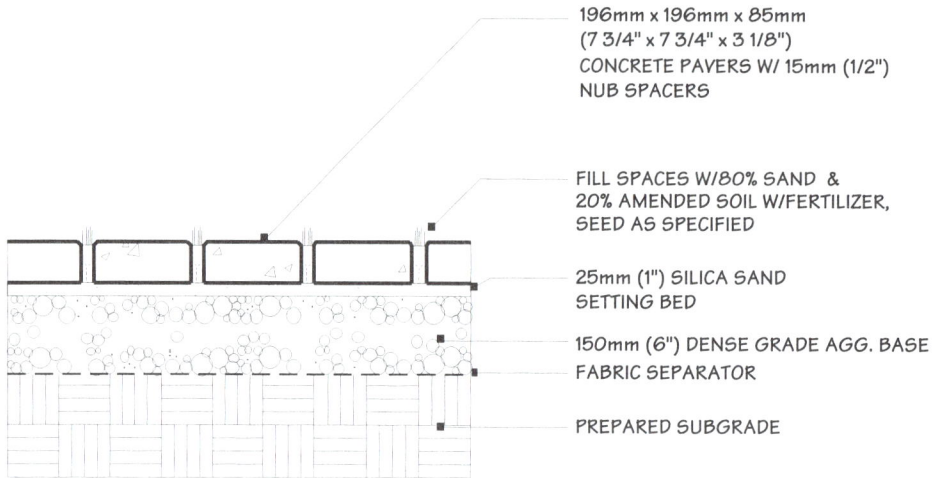

196mm x 196mm x 85mm
(7 3/4" x 7 3/4" x 3 1/8")
CONCRETE PAVERS W/ 15mm (1/2")
NUB SPACERS

FILL SPACES W/80% SAND &
20% AMENDED SOIL W/FERTILIZER,
SEED AS SPECIFIED

25mm (1") SILICA SAND
SETTING BED

150mm (6") DENSE GRADE AGG. BASE
FABRIC SEPARATOR

PREPARED SUBGRADE

APPLICATION

CLIMATE

SUBGRADE

CSI MASTERFORMAT: 02795
DRAWING FILE: PAV32-12

• This drawing is a template for preliminary design only, and is not intended for bid purposes. It is subject to modification based on design calculations, local practices, and all applicable codes and regulations.

• This detail is rated as medium-duty due to aggregate subbase thickness and is typically found in residential, park, and institutional settings.

• Precast concrete pavers are spaced by attached nubs to create a 25 mm (1") space between paver units. Spaces are filled with a sandy amended soil to serve as a growing medium for seeded turf. In heavy-duty uses, a fabric separator may be placed beneath the aggregate base.

• Dense-graded aggregate subbase will prevent excessive drainage of the planting medium.

• Depth of sand base will vary with local soil conditions, typically 25mm — 50mm (1"-2"). Heavy loads require high silica sand content to maintain capilarity and bearing.

• Pavement spaces should be filled with specified soil, mixed with lime and fertilizer, and topped with seed as specified. Water well to settle planting medium.

• It is recommended that recycled and regionally available materials and products be given high priority in determining final design and specifications.

Installation Cost (per Square Foot)

LOW ⬛⬛⬛⬛ ⬛ ⬜⬜⬜⬜⬜ HIGH

$3.50

Maintenance

LOW ⬛⬛⬛⬛⬛⬛⬛ ⬜⬜⬜ HIGH

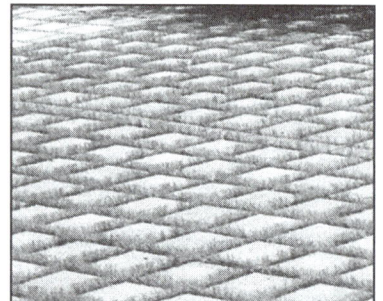

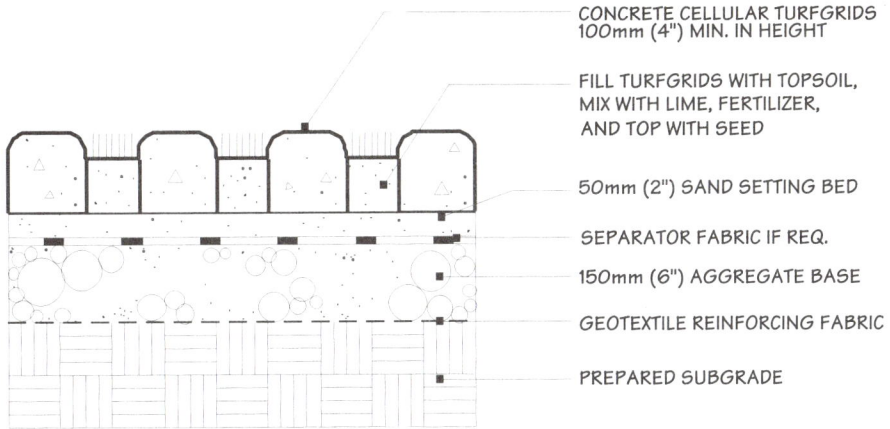

CONCRETE CELLULAR TURFGRIDS
100mm (4") MIN. IN HEIGHT

FILL TURFGRIDS WITH TOPSOIL,
MIX WITH LIME, FERTILIZER,
AND TOP WITH SEED

50mm (2") SAND SETTING BED

SEPARATOR FABRIC IF REQ.

150mm (6") AGGREGATE BASE

GEOTEXTILE REINFORCING FABRIC

PREPARED SUBGRADE

APPLICATION

CLIMATE

SUBGRADE

CSI MASTERFORMAT: 02795
DRAWING FILE: PAV32-08

• This drawing is a template for preliminary design only, and is not intended for bid purposes. It is subject to modification based on design calculations, local practices, and all applicable codes and regulations.

• This detail is rated as heavy-duty due to bearing capacity of aggregate base and the concrete design strength. It is intended to serve as a turf roadway for emergency vehicles or for occasional parking.

• Reinforcing fabric may be placed on top of the prepared subgrade to help bind the aggregate base and support heavy loads.

• Dense-graded aggregate base will prevent excessive drainage of the planting medium.

• Fabric separator may be placed between the aggregate base and sand setting bed, to prevent the migration of fines through the sub-surface.

• Depth of sand setting bed will vary with local soil conditions, typically 25mm—50mm (1"-2").

• Precast concrete cellular turfgrids must be selected that adequately support expected loads. Typical heavy duty design strength is 250 kg per square cm (3,500 psi).

• Turfgrids should be filled with topsoil, mixed with lime and fertilizer, and topped with seed as specified. Water well to settle planting medium.

• It is recommended that recycled and regionally available materials and products be given high priority in determining final design and specifications.

Installation Cost (per Square Foot)

LOW   HIGH

$5.32

Maintenance

LOW   HIGH

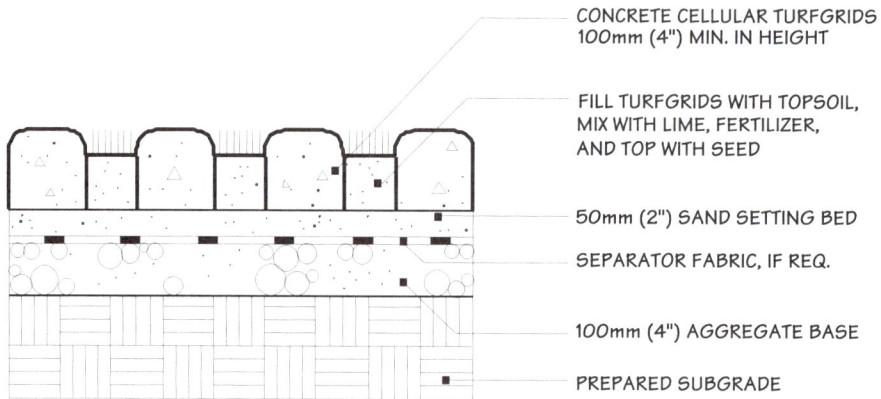

CONCRETE CELLULAR TURFGRIDS
100mm (4") MIN. IN HEIGHT

FILL TURFGRIDS WITH TOPSOIL,
MIX WITH LIME, FERTILIZER,
AND TOP WITH SEED

50mm (2") SAND SETTING BED

SEPARATOR FABRIC, IF REQ.

100mm (4") AGGREGATE BASE

PREPARED SUBGRADE

APPLICATION

CLIMATE

SUBGRADE

CSI MASTERFORMAT: 02795
DRAWING FILE: PAV32-09

• This drawing is a template for preliminary design only, and is not intended for bid purposes. It is subject to modification based on design calculations, local practices, and all applicable codes and regulations.

• This detail is rated as medium-duty due to bearing capacity of aggregate base and the concrete design strength. It is intended to serve as a turf roadway for emergency vehicles or for occasional parking.

• Dense-graded aggregate base will prevent excessive drainage of the planting medium.

• Fabric separator may be placed between the aggregate base and sand setting bed, to prevent the migration of fines through the sub-surface.

• Depth of sand setting bed will vary with local soil conditions, typically 25mm—50mm (1"-2").

• Precast concrete cellular turfgrids must be selected that adequately support expected loads.

• Turfgrids should be filled with topsoil, mixed with lime and fertilizer, and topped with seed as specified. Water well to settle planting medium.

• It is recommended that recycled and regionally available materials and products be given high priority in determining final design and specifications.

Installation Cost (per Square Foot)

LOW   HIGH

$4.96

Maintenance

LOW   HIGH

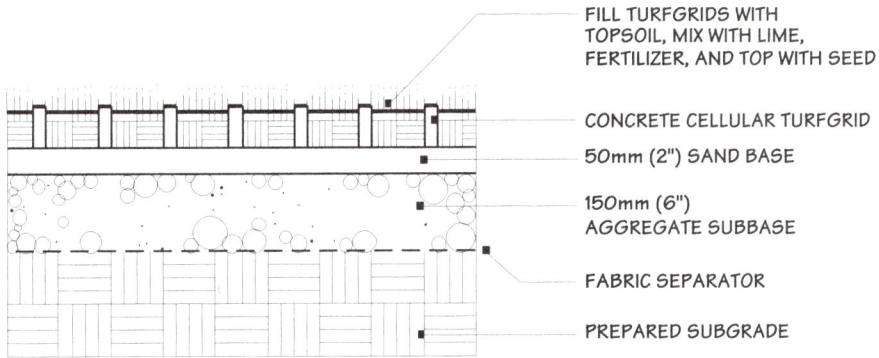

FILL TURFGRIDS WITH TOPSOIL, MIX WITH LIME, FERTILIZER, AND TOP WITH SEED

CONCRETE CELLULAR TURFGRID

50mm (2") SAND BASE

150mm (6") AGGREGATE SUBBASE

FABRIC SEPARATOR

PREPARED SUBGRADE

APPLICATION

CLIMATE

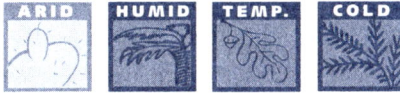

SUBGRADE

CSI MASTERFORMAT: 02795
DRAWING FILE: PAV32-10

• This drawing is a template for preliminary design only, and is not intended for bid purposes. It is subject to modification based on design calculations, local practices, and all applicable codes and regulations.

• This detail is rated as heavy-duty due to aggregate subbase thickness and fabric reinforcement typically found in urban park and institutional settings.

• Fabric separator may be placed on top of the prepared subgrade to help bind the aggregate base and distribute heavy loads.

• Dense-graded aggregate subbase will prevent excessive drainage of the planting medium.

• Depth of sand base will vary with local soil conditions, typically 25mm—50mm (1'–2").

• Precast concrete cellular turfgrids must be selected that adequately support expected loads.

• Turfgrids should be filled with topsoil, mixed with lime and fertilizer, and topped with seed as specified. Water well to settle planting medium.

• It is recommended that recycled and regionally available materials and products be given high priority in determining final design and specifications.

Installation Cost (per Square Foot)

LOW   HIGH

$3.27

Maintenance

LOW   HIGH

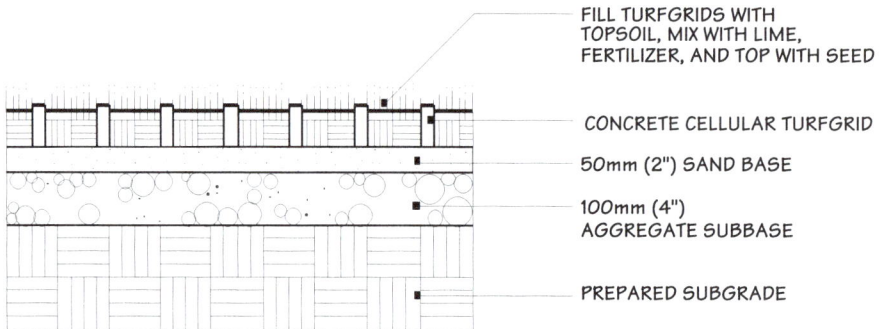

FILL TURFGRIDS WITH TOPSOIL, MIX WITH LIME, FERTILIZER, AND TOP WITH SEED

CONCRETE CELLULAR TURFGRID

50mm (2") SAND BASE

100mm (4") AGGREGATE SUBBASE

PREPARED SUBGRADE

APPLICATION

CLIMATE

SUBGRADE

CSI MASTERFORMAT: 02795
DRAWING FILE: PAV32-11

• This drawing is a template for preliminary design only, and is not intended for bid purposes. It is subject to modification based on design calculations, local practices, and all applicable codes and regulations.

• This detail is rated as medium-duty due to aggregate subbase thickness and typically found in residential, park, and institutional settings.

• Dense-graded aggregate subbase will prevent excessive drainage of the planting medium.

• Depth of sand base will vary with local soil conditions, typically 25mm—50mm (1"–2").

• Precast concrete cellular turfgrids must be selected that adequately support expected loads.

• Turfgrids should be filled with topsoil, mixed with lime and fertilizer, and topped with seed as specified. Water well to settle planting medium.

• It is recommended that recycled and regionally available materials and products be given high priority in determining final design and specifications.

Installation Cost (per Square Foot)

LOW   HIGH

$2.91

Maintenance

LOW   HIGH

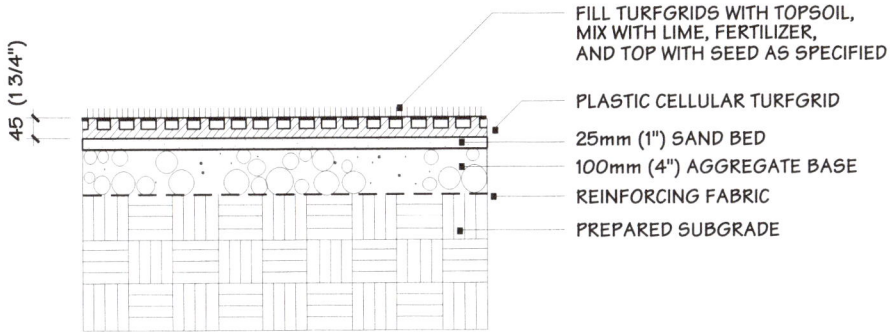

FILL TURFGRIDS WITH TOPSOIL,
MIX WITH LIME, FERTILIZER,
AND TOP WITH SEED AS SPECIFIED

PLASTIC CELLULAR TURFGRID

25mm (1") SAND BED

100mm (4") AGGREGATE BASE

REINFORCING FABRIC

PREPARED SUBGRADE

45 (1 3/4")

APPLICATION

CLIMATE

SUBGRADE

CSI MASTERFORMAT: 02795
DRAWING FILE: PAV18-06

• This drawing is a template for preliminary design only, and is not intended for bid purposes. It is subject to modification based on design calculations, local practices, and all applicable codes and regulations.

• This detail is rated for light-duty applications based on paving course and base thickness, and may support pedestrian loading associated with walks and light service access in parks and residential settings. It is intended to reinforce turf areas subject to occasional vehicular loading.

• The subgrade conditions have a significant impact on the design of flexible pavements, such as cellular turf reinforcing grids. Loads are transferred more directly to the base, requiring well-drained soils with adequate bearing capacity.

• Reinforcing fabric may be placed on top of the prepared subgrade to help bind the aggregate base and support occasional heavy loads.

• Dense-graded aggregate base will prevent excessive drainage of the planting medium.

• Depth of sand setting bed will vary with local soil conditions, typically 25mm— 50mm (1"-2").

• Turfgrids should be filled with prepared topsoil, mixed with lime and fertilizer, and topped with seed as specified. Water well to settle planting medium.

• It is recommended that recycled and regionally available materials and products be given high priority in determining final design and specifications.

Installation Cost (per Square Foot)

LOW   HIGH

$2.97

Maintenance

LOW   HIGH

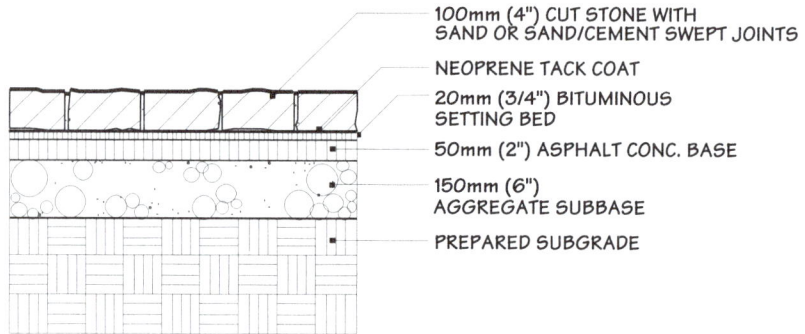

100mm (4") CUT STONE WITH
SAND OR SAND/CEMENT SWEPT JOINTS

NEOPRENE TACK COAT

20mm (3/4") BITUMINOUS
SETTING BED

50mm (2") ASPHALT CONC. BASE

150mm (6")
AGGREGATE SUBBASE

PREPARED SUBGRADE

APPLICATION

CLIMATE

SUBGRADE

CSI MASTERFORMAT: 02780
DRAWING FILE: PAV33-03

• This drawing is a template for preliminary design only, and is not intended for bid purposes. It is subject to modification based on design calculations, local practices, and all applicable codes and regulations.

• This detail is rated for light-duty applications based on thickness of asphalt base and aggregate subbase, and may support pedestrian and light vehicular loading typically associated with dense residential, urban park, and commercial settings.

• This detail is suitable for cold climates due to the absence of mortar joints in the pavement. Flexible adhesives, such as bituminous or elastomeric materials are recommended in these conditions.

• The subgrade conditions have a significant impact on the design of flexible pavements, such as asphalt. Loads are transferred more directly to the base, requiring well-drained soils with adequate bearing capacity.

• As with all unit pavers, pavement edges require restraints to prevent creeping, especially in vehicular loaded circumstances, where lateral pressure can be significant.

• Cut stone pavers provide a very durable surface highly resistant to abrasion resulting from normal wear and maintenance. Metamorphic and igneous stone is preferred.

• It is recommended that recycled and regionally available materials and products be given high priority in determining final design and specifications.

Installation Cost (per Square Foot)

LOW   HIGH

$10.19

Maintenance

LOW   HIGH

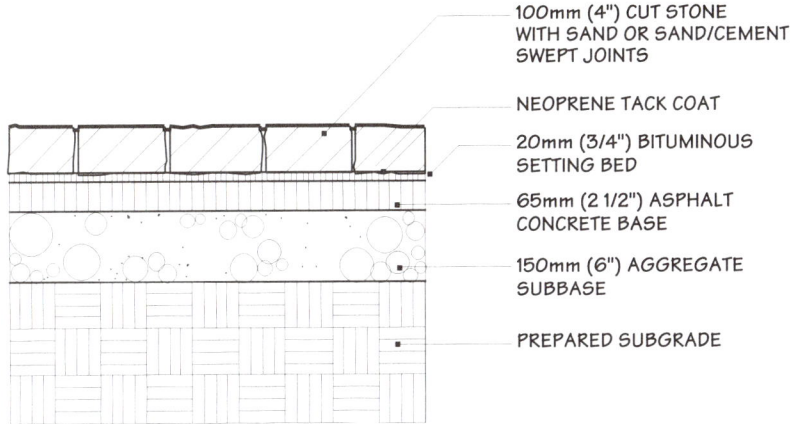

100mm (4") CUT STONE
WITH SAND OR SAND/CEMENT
SWEPT JOINTS

NEOPRENE TACK COAT

20mm (3/4") BITUMINOUS
SETTING BED

65mm (2 1/2") ASPHALT
CONCRETE BASE

150mm (6") AGGREGATE
SUBBASE

PREPARED SUBGRADE

APPLICATION

CLIMATE

SUBGRADE

CSI MASTERFORMAT: 02780
DRAWING FILE: PAV13-05

• This drawing is a template for preliminary design only, and is not intended for bid purposes. It is subject to modification based on design calculations, local practices, and all applicable codes and regulations.

• This detail is rated for medium-duty applications based on thickness of asphalt base and aggregate subbase, and may support vehicular loading and occasional service access typically associated with dense residential, urban park, and commercial settings.

• This detail is suitable for cold climates due to the absence of mortar joints in the pavement. Flexible adhesives, such as bituminous or elastomeric materials are recommended in these conditions.

• The subgrade conditions have a significant impact on the design of flexible pavements, such as asphalt. Loads are transferred more directly to the base, requiring well-drained soils with adequate bearing capacity.

• As with all unit pavers, pavement edges require restraints to prevent creeping, especially in vehicular loaded circumstances, where lateral pressure can be significant.

• Cut stone pavers provide a very durable surface highly resistant to abrasion resulting from normal wear and maintenance. Metamorphic and igneous stone is preferred.

• It is recommended that recycled and regionally available materials and products be given high priority in determining final design and specifications.

Installation Cost (per Square Foot)

LOW   HIGH

$10.40

Maintenance

LOW   HIGH

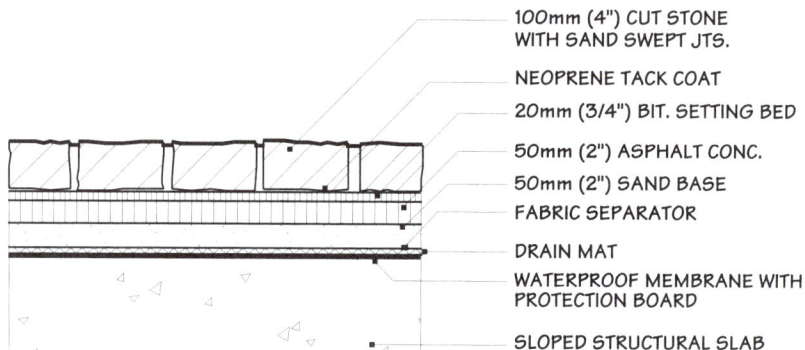

100mm (4") CUT STONE WITH SAND SWEPT JTS.

NEOPRENE TACK COAT

20mm (3/4") BIT. SETTING BED

50mm (2") ASPHALT CONC.

50mm (2") SAND BASE

FABRIC SEPARATOR

DRAIN MAT

WATERPROOF MEMBRANE WITH PROTECTION BOARD

SLOPED STRUCTURAL SLAB

APPLICATION

CLIMATE

SUBGRADE

CSI MASTERFORMAT: 02780
DRAWING FILE: PAV13-06

• This drawing is a template for preliminary design only, and is not intended for bid purposes. It is subject to modification based on design calculations, local practices, and all applicable codes and regulations.

• This detail is rated for medium-duty applications due primarily to bearing capacity of asphalt base and the heavy-duty drain mat upon which it rests. Cut stone pavers are often used as an informal transition paving in dense residential, park, and commercial settings.

• A sand base is placed on a fabric separator over a heavy-duty drain mat, which rests on a sloping protection board and waterproof membrane.

• As with all unit pavers, pavement edges require restraints to prevent creeping, especially if subjected to light vehicular loading.

• Set stones with light vibrating compactor and final sand sweeping to complete installation.

• Cut stone pavers provide a very durable surface highly resistant to abrasion resulting from normal wear and maintenance. Metamorphic and igneous stone is preferred.

• It is recommended that recycled and regionally available materials and products be given high priority in determining final design and specifications.

Installation Cost (per Square Foot)

LOW   HIGH

$10.60

Maintenance

LOW   HIGH

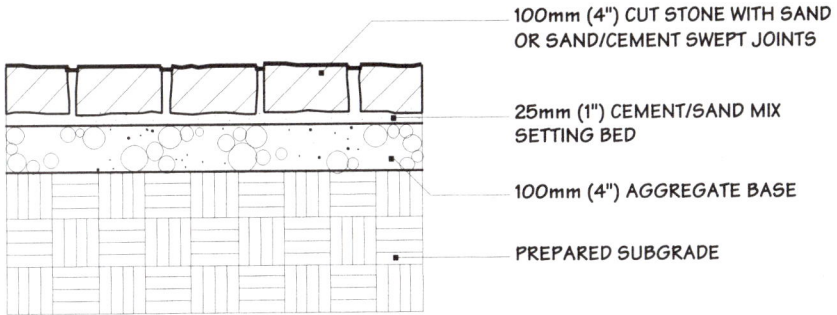

100mm (4") CUT STONE WITH SAND
OR SAND/CEMENT SWEPT JOINTS

25mm (1") CEMENT/SAND MIX
SETTING BED

100mm (4") AGGREGATE BASE

PREPARED SUBGRADE

APPLICATION

CLIMATE

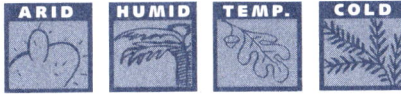

SUBGRADE

CSI MASTERFORMAT: 02780
DRAWING FILE: PAV13-10

• This drawing is a template for preliminary design only, and is not intended for bid purposes. It is subject to modification based on design calculations, local practices, and all applicable codes and regulations.

• This detail is rated for light-duty applications based on paving course and base thickness, and may support primarily pedestrian loading associated with walks and light service access in parks and residential settings. Although rated for all climates, this detail performs best in warmer zones which are not subject to intensive frost-thaw cycles. A well drained subgrade is required in cold climates.

• As with all unit pavers, pavement edges require restraints to prevent creeping, especially if subjected to even occasional vehicular access.

• The subgrade conditions have a significant impact on the design of flexible pavements, such as unit pavers. Loads are transferred more directly to the base, requiring

well-drained soils with adequate bearing capacity.

• Set stones with light vibrating compactor and final sand/cement sweeping to complete installation. Wet down surface with fine spray to slowly activate dry sand/cement setting bed.

• Cut stone pavers provide a very durable surface highly resistant to abrasion resulting from normal wear and maintenance. Metamorphic and igneous stone is preferred.

• It is recommended that recycled and regionally available materials and products be given high priority in determining final design and specifications.

Installation Cost (per Square Foot)

$9.42

Maintenance

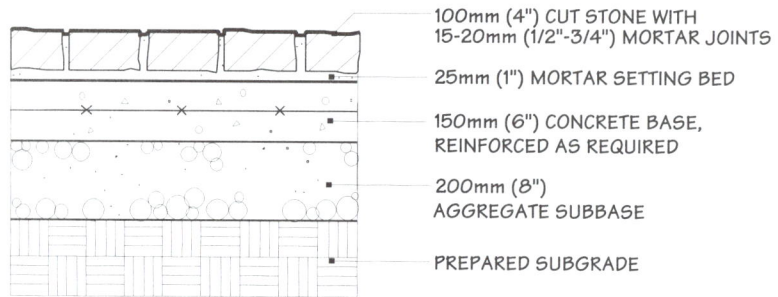

100mm (4") CUT STONE WITH
15-20mm (1/2"-3/4") MORTAR JOINTS

25mm (1") MORTAR SETTING BED

150mm (6") CONCRETE BASE,
REINFORCED AS REQUIRED

200mm (8")
AGGREGATE SUBBASE

PREPARED SUBGRADE

APPLICATION

CLIMATE

SUBGRADE

CSI MASTERFORMAT: 02780
DRAWING FILE: PAV33-05

• This drawing is a template for preliminary design only, and is not intended for bid purposes. It is subject to modification based on design calculations, local practices, and all applicable codes and regulations.

• This detail is rated for heavy-duty applications based on thickness of concrete and aggregate base, and may support significant pedestrian loading and vehicular access typically associated with dense residential, urban park, and commercial settings.

• This detail is not designed for cold climates, where the use of mortar in unit paving is discouraged. Flexible adhesives, such as bituminous or elastomeric materials are recommended in these conditions.

• Rigid pavement design must accommodate movement of materials by providing adequate expansion and control joints, particularly in regions of extreme temperature fluctuations. If designed for temperate or cold climates, air-entrained concrete is typi-

cally recommended due to freezing/thawing action.

• Reinforcing practices vary widely by region. Local codes and practices should be consulted prior to specifying any type of reinforcing.

• Expansion joints should be filled, and sealed in temperate and cold climates. These joints require periodic cleaning and resealing.

• It is recommended that recycled and regionally available materials and products be given high priority in determining final design and specifications.

Installation Cost (per Square Foot)

LOW   HIGH

$13.34

Maintenance

LOW   HIGH

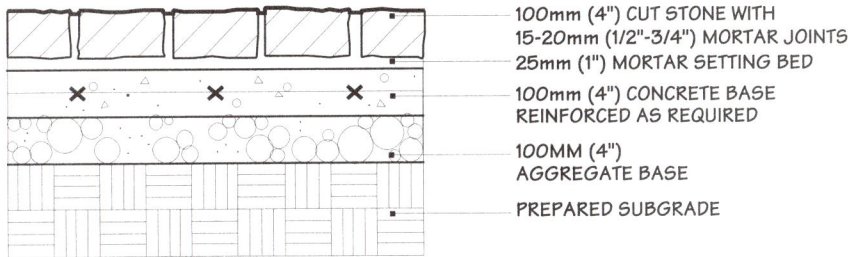

100mm (4") CUT STONE WITH
15-20mm (1/2"-3/4") MORTAR JOINTS
25mm (1") MORTAR SETTING BED
100mm (4") CONCRETE BASE
REINFORCED AS REQUIRED
100MM (4")
AGGREGATE BASE
PREPARED SUBGRADE

APPLICATION

CLIMATE

SUBGRADE

CSI MASTERFORMAT: 02780
DRAWING FILE: PAV13-07

• This drawing is a template for preliminary design only, and is not intended for bid purposes. It is subject to modification based on design calculations, local practices, and all applicable codes and regulations.

• This detail is rated for light-duty applications based on thickness of concrete and aggregate base, and may support primarily pedestrian loading and occasional light service access typically associated with residential, park, and light commercial settings.

• This detail is not designed for cold climates, where the use of mortar in unit paving is discouraged. Flexible adhesives, such as bituminous or elastomeric materials are recommended in these conditions.

• Rigid pavement design must accommodate movement of materials by providing adequate expansion and control joints, particularly in regions of extreme temperature fluctuations. If designed for temperate or cold climates, air-entrained concrete is typi-cally recommended due to freezing/thawing action.

• Reinforcing practices vary widely by region. Local codes and practices should be consulted prior to specifying any type of reinforcing.

• Expansion joints should be filled, and sealed in temperate and cold climates. These joints require periodic cleaning and re-sealing.

• It is recommended that recycled and regionally available materials and products be given high priority in determining final design and specifications.

Installation Cost (per Square Foot)

LOW   HIGH

$12.64

Maintenance

LOW   HIGH

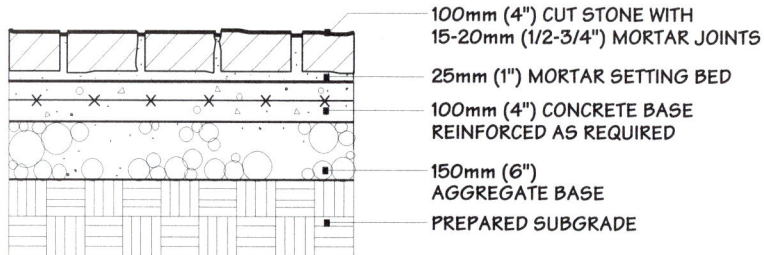

100mm (4") CUT STONE WITH
15-20mm (1/2-3/4") MORTAR JOINTS

25mm (1") MORTAR SETTING BED

100mm (4") CONCRETE BASE
REINFORCED AS REQUIRED

150mm (6")
AGGREGATE BASE

PREPARED SUBGRADE

APPLICATION

CLIMATE

SUBGRADE

CSI MASTERFORMAT: 02780
DRAWING FILE: PAV33-04

• This drawing is a template for preliminary design only, and is not intended for bid purposes. It is subject to modification based on design calculations, local practices, and all applicable codes and regulations.

• This detail is rated for medium-duty applications based on thickness of concrete and aggregate base, and may support significant pedestrian loading and light service access typically associated with residential, urban park, and light commercial settings.

• This detail is not designed for cold climates, where the use of mortar in unit paving is discouraged. Flexible adhesives, such as bituminous or elastomeric materials are recommended in these conditions.

• Rigid pavement design must accommodate movement of materials by providing adequate expansion and control joints, particularly in regions of extreme temperature fluctuations. If designed for temperate or cold climates, air-entrained concrete is typi-

cally recommended due to freezing/thawing action.

• Reinforcing practices vary widely by region. Local codes and practices should be consulted prior to specifying any type of reinforcing.

• Expansion joints should be filled, and sealed in temperate and cold climates. These joints require periodic cleaning and re-sealing.

• It is recommended that recycled and regionally available materials and products be given high priority in determining final design and specifications.

Installation Cost (per Square Foot)

LOW · · · · · · · · · HIGH

|
$12.72

Maintenance

LOW · · · · · · · · · HIGH

100mm (4") CUT STONE WITH
SAND OR SAND/CEMENT
SWEPT IN BUTTED JOINTS

25mm (1") SAND SETTING BED

100mm (4")
AGGREGATE BASE

PREPARED SUBGRADE

APPLICATION

CLIMATE

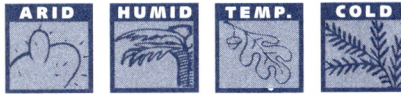

SUBGRADE

CSI MASTERFORMAT: 02780
DRAWING FILE: PAV13-02

• This drawing is a template for preliminary design only, and is not intended for bid purposes. It is subject to modification based on design calculations, local practices, and all applicable codes and regulations.

• This detail is rated for light-duty applications based on paving course and base thickness, and may support primarily pedestrian loading associated with walks and light service access in parks and residential settings.

• As with all unit pavers, pavement edges require restraints to prevent creeping, especially if subjected to even occasional vehicular access.

• The subgrade conditions have a significant impact on the design of flexible pavements, such as unit pavers. Loads are transferred more directly to the base, requiring well-drained soils with adequate bearing capacity.

• Set stones with light vibrating compactor and final sand sweeping to complete installation.

• Cut stone pavers provide a very durable surface highly resistant to abrasion resulting from normal wear and maintenance. Metamorphic and igneous stone is preferred.

• It is recommended that recycled and regionally available materials and products be given high priority in determining final design and specifications.

Installation Cost (per Square Foot)

LOW   HIGH

$9.45

Maintenance

LOW   HIGH

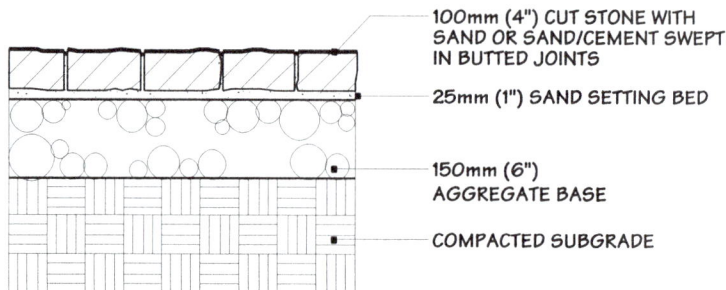

100mm (4") CUT STONE WITH SAND OR SAND/CEMENT SWEPT IN BUTTED JOINTS

25mm (1") SAND SETTING BED

150mm (6") AGGREGATE BASE

COMPACTED SUBGRADE

APPLICATION

CLIMATE

SUBGRADE

CSI MASTERFORMAT: 02780
DRAWING FILE: PAV33-01

• This drawing is a template for preliminary design only, and is not intended for bid purposes. It is subject to modification based on design calculations, local practices, and all applicable codes and regulations.

• This detail is rated for medium-duty applications based on paving course and base thickness, and may support primarily pedestrian loading associated with walks and vehicular access in parks and residential settings.

• As with all unit pavers, pavement edges require restraints to prevent creeping, especially if subjected to even occasional vehicular access.

• The subgrade conditions have a significant impact on the design of flexible pavements, such as unit pavers. Loads are transferred more directly to the base, requiring well-drained soils with adequate bearing capacity.

• Set stones with light vibrating compactor and final sand sweeping to complete installation.

• Cut stone pavers provide a very durable surface highly resistant to abrasion resulting from normal wear and maintenance. Metamorphic and igneous stone is preferred.

• It is recommended that recycled and regionally available materials and products be given high priority in determining final design and specifications.

Installation Cost (per Square Foot)

LOW   HIGH

$9.88

Maintenance

LOW   HIGH

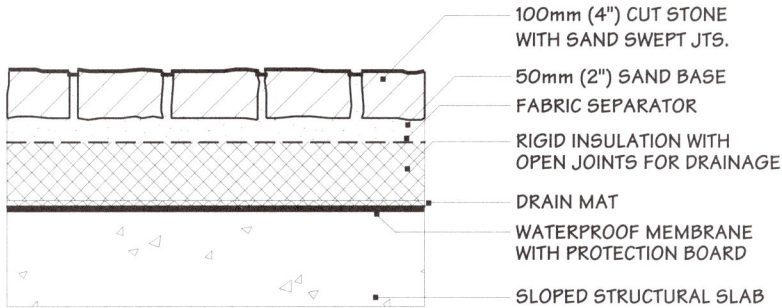

100mm (4") CUT STONE
WITH SAND SWEPT JTS.

50mm (2") SAND BASE
FABRIC SEPARATOR

RIGID INSULATION WITH
OPEN JOINTS FOR DRAINAGE

DRAIN MAT

WATERPROOF MEMBRANE
WITH PROTECTION BOARD

SLOPED STRUCTURAL SLAB

APPLICATION

CLIMATE

SUBGRADE

CSI MASTERFORMAT: 02780
DRAWING FILE: PAV13-03

• This drawing is a template for preliminary design only, and is not intended for bid purposes. It is subject to modification based on design calculations, local practices, and all applicable codes and regulations.

• This detail is rated for light-duty applications due primarily to bearing limitations of the rigid insulation upon which it rests. Cut stone pavers are often used as an informal transition paving in residential and commercial settings.

• A sand base is placed on fabric separator over open jointed rigid insulation. A drain mat is placed over sloping protection board and waterproof membrane.

• As with all unit pavers, pavement edges require restraints to prevent creeping, especially if subjected to even occasional light vehicular access.

• The subgrade conditions have a significant impact on the design of flexible pavements, such as unit pavers. Loads are transferred more directly to the base, requiring well-drained soils with adequate bearing capacity.

• Set stones with light vibrating compactor and final sand sweeping to complete installation.

• Cut stone pavers provide a very durable surface highly resistant to abrasion resulting from normal wear and maintenance. Metamorphic and igneous stone is preferred.

• It is recommended that recycled and regionally available materials and products be given high priority in determining final design and specifications.

Installation Cost (per Square Foot)

LOW   HIGH

$10.00

Maintenance

LOW   HIGH

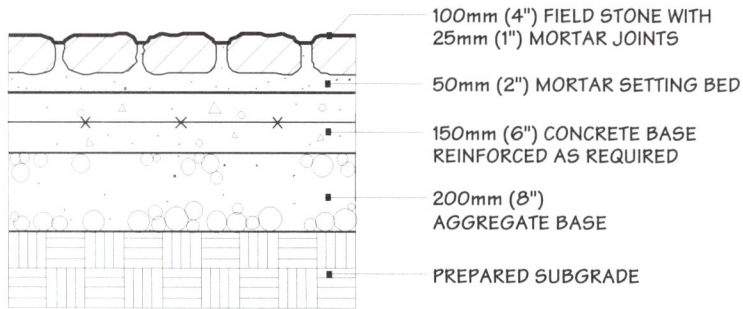

100mm (4") FIELD STONE WITH
25mm (1") MORTAR JOINTS

50mm (2") MORTAR SETTING BED

150mm (6") CONCRETE BASE
REINFORCED AS REQUIRED

200mm (8")
AGGREGATE BASE

PREPARED SUBGRADE

APPLICATION

CLIMATE

SUBGRADE

CSI MASTERFORMAT: 04420
DRAWING FILE: PAV33-07

• This drawing is a template for preliminary design only, and is not intended for bid purposes. It is subject to modification based on design calculations, local practices, and all applicable codes and regulations.

• This detail is rated as heavy-duty based on concrete base and aggregate subbase thickness, although the surface stone has a very high strength. It is typically found in dense residential, urban park, and commercial settings. Due to its irregular surface, it is not suitable as a main walk surface and is often used as a transition pavement.

• Subgrade conditions have a significant impact on the longevity of rigid pavements, such as concrete. The subgrade should be uniform to prevent pavement failure due to uneven soil expansion and contraction. This detail provides a well-drained aggregate base to drain sub-surface moisture and increase uniformity.

• This detail is not designed for cold climates, where the use of mortar is discouraged. Flexible adhesives, such as bituminous or elastomeric materials are recommended in these conditions.

• Reinforcing practices vary widely. Local codes and practices should be consulted before specifying any type of reinforcing for the base. All steel should be covered by at least 50mm (2") of concrete.

• Expansion joints should be filled, and sealed in temperate and cold climates. These joints require periodic cleaning and re-sealing.

• A 50mm (2") mortar setting bed is needed to accommodate the irregular shape of field stone, and may vary due to irregularity of stone sizes. Igneous or metamorphic stones of uniform size and color are typically preferred.

• Stone pavers provide a very durable surface highly resistant to abrasion resulting from normal wear and maintenance.

• It is recommended that recycled and regionally available materials and products be given high priority in determining final design and specifications.

Installation Cost (per Square Foot)

LOW   HIGH

$13.31

Maintenance

LOW   HIGH

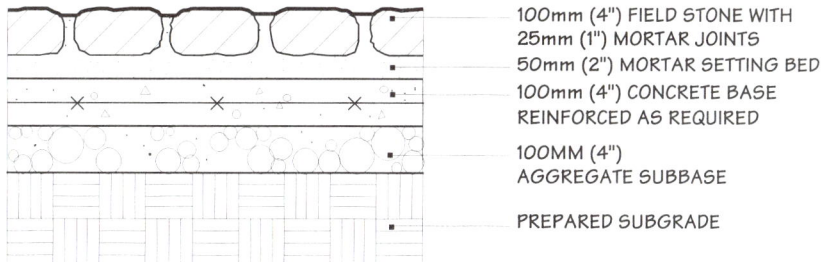

100mm (4") FIELD STONE WITH
25mm (1") MORTAR JOINTS

50mm (2") MORTAR SETTING BED

100mm (4") CONCRETE BASE
REINFORCED AS REQUIRED

100MM (4")
AGGREGATE SUBBASE

PREPARED SUBGRADE

APPLICATION

CLIMATE

SUBGRADE

CSI MASTERFORMAT: 04420
DRAWING FILE: PAV13-08

• This drawing is a template for preliminary design only, and is not intended for bid purposes. It is subject to modification based on design calculations, local practices, and all applicable codes and regulations.

• This detail is rated as light-duty based on concrete base and subbase thickness, although the surface stone has a very high strength. It is typically found in residential and park settings. Due to its irregular surface, it is not suitable as a main walk surface and is often used as a transition pavement.

• Subgrade conditions have a significant impact on the longevity of rigid pavements, such as concrete. The subgrade should be uniform to prevent pavement failure due to uneven soil expansion and contraction. This detail provides a well-drained aggregate base to drain sub-surface moisture and increase uniformity.

• This detail is not designed for cold climates, where the use of mortar is discouraged. Flexible adhesives, such as bituminous or elastomeric materials are recommended in these conditions.

• Reinforcing practices vary widely. Local codes and practices should be consulted before specifying any type of reinforcing for the base. All steel should be covered by at least 50mm (2") of concrete.

• Expansion joints should be filled, and sealed in temperate and cold climates. These joints require periodic cleaning and re-sealing.

• A 50mm (2") mortar setting bed is needed to accommodate the irregular shape of field stone, and may vary due to irregularity of stone sizes. Igneous or metamorphic stones of uniform size and color are typically preferred.

• Stone pavers provide a very durable surface highly resistant to abrasion resulting from normal wear and maintenance.

• It is recommended that recycled and regionally available materials and products be given high priority in determining final design and specifications.

Installation Cost (per Square Foot)

LOW   HIGH

$11.64

Maintenance

LOW   HIGH

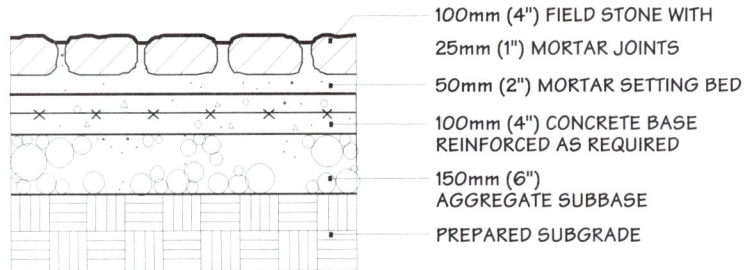

100mm (4") FIELD STONE WITH

25mm (1") MORTAR JOINTS

50mm (2") MORTAR SETTING BED

100mm (4") CONCRETE BASE
REINFORCED AS REQUIRED

150mm (6")
AGGREGATE SUBBASE

PREPARED SUBGRADE

APPLICATION

CLIMATE

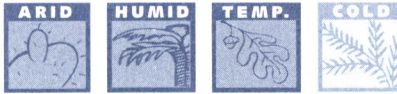

SUBGRADE

CSI MASTERFORMAT: 04420
DRAWING FILE: PAV33-06

• This drawing is a template for preliminary design only, and is not intended for bid purposes. It is subject to modification based on design calculations, local practices, and all applicable codes and regulations.

• This detail is rated as medium-duty based on concrete base and aggregate subbase thickness, although the surface stone has a very high strength. It is typically found in residential and park settings. Due to its irregular surface, it is not suitable as a main walk surface and is often used as a transition pavement.

• Subgrade conditions have a significant impact on the longevity of rigid pavements, such as concrete. The subgrade should be uniform to prevent pavement failure due to uneven soil expansion and contraction. This detail provides a well-drained aggregate base to drain sub-surface moisture and increase uniformity.

• This detail is not designed for cold climates, where the use of mortar is discour-aged. Flexible adhesives, such as bituminous or elastomeric materials are recommended in these conditions.

• Reinforcing practices vary widely. Local codes and practices should be consulted before specifying any type of reinforcing for the base. All steel should be covered by at least 50mm (2") of concrete.

• Expansion joints should be filled, and sealed in temperate and cold climates. These joints require periodic cleaning and re-sealing.

• A 50mm (2") mortar setting bed is need-ed to accommodate the irregular shape of field stone, and may vary due to irregularity of stone sizes. Igneous or metamorphic stones of uniform size and color are typically preferred.

• Stone pavers provide a very durable surface highly resistant to abrasion resulting from normal wear and maintenance.

• It is recommended that recycled and regionally available materials and products be given high priority in determining final design and specifications.

Installation Cost (per Square Foot)

LOW   HIGH

$11.72

Maintenance

LOW   HIGH

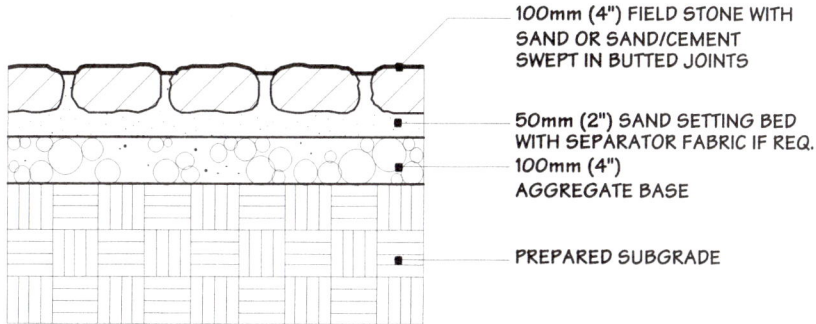

100mm (4") FIELD STONE WITH
SAND OR SAND/CEMENT
SWEPT IN BUTTED JOINTS

50mm (2") SAND SETTING BED
WITH SEPARATOR FABRIC IF REQ.

100mm (4")
AGGREGATE BASE

PREPARED SUBGRADE

APPLICATION

CLIMATE

SUBGRADE

CSI MASTERFORMAT: 04420
DRAWING FILE: PAV13-04

• This drawing is a template for preliminary design only, and is not intended for bid purposes. It is subject to modification based on design calculations, local practices, and all applicable codes and regulations.

• This detail is rated as light-duty based on base thickness, although the surface stone has a very high strength. It is typically found in residential and park settings. Due to its irregular surface, it is not suitable as a main walk surface.

• The subgrade conditions have a significant impact on the design of flexible pavements, such as unit stone pavers. Loads are transferred more directly to the base, requiring well-drained soils with adequate bearing capacity.

• A 50mm (2") sand setting bed is needed to accommodate the irregular shape of field stone, and may vary due to irregularity of stone sizes.

• Igneous or metamorphic stones of uniform size and color are typically preferred.

• Stone pavers provide a very durable surface highly resistant to abrasion resulting from normal wear and maintenance.

• It is recommended that recycled and regionally available materials and products be given high priority in determining final design and specifications.

Installation Cost (per Square Foot)

LOW   HIGH

$7.32

Maintenance

LOW   HIGH

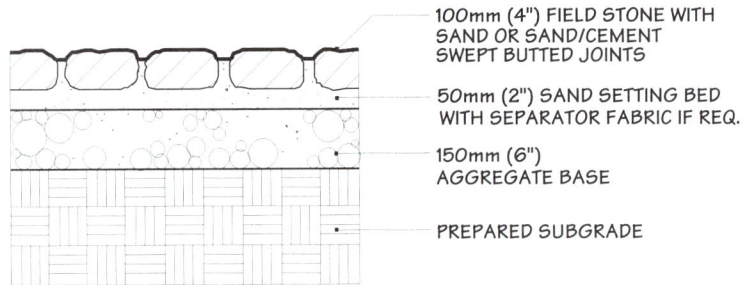

100mm (4") FIELD STONE WITH SAND OR SAND/CEMENT SWEPT BUTTED JOINTS

50mm (2") SAND SETTING BED WITH SEPARATOR FABRIC IF REQ.

150mm (6") AGGREGATE BASE

PREPARED SUBGRADE

APPLICATION

CLIMATE

SUBGRADE

CSI MASTERFORMAT: 04420
DRAWING FILE: PAV33-02

• This drawing is a template for preliminary design only, and is not intended for bid purposes. It is subject to modification based on design calculations, local practices, and all applicable codes and regulations.

• This detail is rated as medium-duty based on base thickness, although the surface stone has a very high strength. It is typically found in dense residential and urban park settings. Due to its irregular surface, it is not suitable as a main walk surface and is usually employed as a transition pavement.

• The subgrade conditions have a significant impact on the design of flexible pavements, such as unit stone pavers. Loads are transferred more directly to the base, requiring well-drained soils with adequate bearing capacity.

• A 50mm (2") sand setting bed is needed to accommodate the irregular shape of field stone, and may vary due to irregularity of stone sizes.

• Igneous or metamorphic stones of uniform size and color are typically preferred.

• Stone pavers provide a very durable surface highly resistant to abrasion resulting from normal wear and maintenance.

• It is recommended that recycled and regionally available materials and products be given high priority in determining final design and specifications.

Installation Cost (per Square Foot)

LOW   HIGH

$7.57

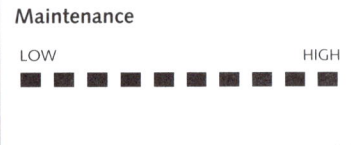

Maintenance

LOW   HIGH

25-40mm (1"-1 1/2") FLAGSTONE WITH SAND SWEPT JOINTS

25mm (1") MORTAR SETTING BED

100mm (4") AGGREGATE BASE

PREPARED SUBGRADE

APPLICATION

CLIMATE

SUBGRADE

CSI MASTERFORMAT: 02780
DRAWING FILE: PAV13-09

• This drawing is a template for preliminary design only, and is not intended for bid purposes. It is subject to modification based on design calculations, local practices, and all applicable codes and regulations.

• This detail is rated for light-duty applications based on paving course and base thickness, and may support primarily pedestrian loading associated with walks in parks and residential settings.

• The subgrade conditions have a significant impact on the design of pavements, such as flag stone patios or walks. Loads are transferred more directly to the base, requiring well-drained soils with adequate bearing capacity.

• Stone should be non-porous in cold climates. Metamorphic and igneous stone is preferred. This detail is more appropriate in warm climates not subject to frost or heavy rains.

• Stones should be carefully fitted to achieve consistant mortar joints. Edge containment and reinforcement is recommended.

• It is recommended that recycled and regionally available materials and products be given high priority in determining final design and specifications.

Installation Cost (per Square Foot)

LOW   HIGH

$8.29

Maintenance

LOW   HIGH

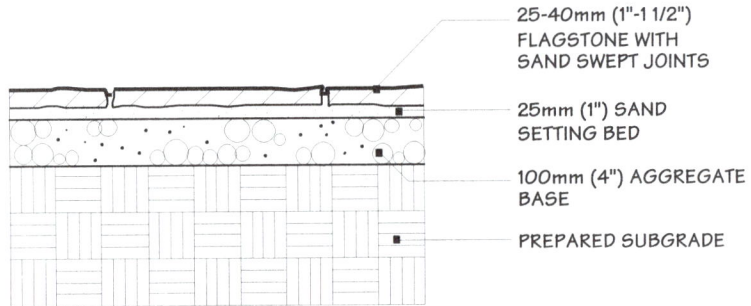

25-40mm (1"-1 1/2")
FLAGSTONE WITH
SAND SWEPT JOINTS

25mm (1") SAND
SETTING BED

100mm (4") AGGREGATE
BASE

PREPARED SUBGRADE

APPLICATION

CLIMATE

SUBGRADE

CSI MASTERFORMAT: 02780
DRAWING FILE: PAV13-01

• This drawing is a template for preliminary design only, and is not intended for bid purposes. It is subject to modification based on design calculations, local practices, and all applicable codes and regulations.

• This detail is rated for light-duty applications based on paving course and base thickness, and may support primarily pedestrian loading associated with walks in parks and residential settings.

• The subgrade conditions have a significant impact on the design of flexible pavements, such as flag stone patios or walks. Loads are transferred more directly to the base, requiring well-drained soils with adequate bearing capacity.

• Stone should be non-porous in cold climates. Metamorphic and igneous stone is preferred.

• Stones should be tightly fitted and butted with sand swept joints. Edging to prevent lateral creeping is recommended.

• It is recommended that recycled and regionally available materials and products be given high priority in determining final design and specifications.

Installation Cost (per Square Foot)

LOW   HIGH

$6.92

Maintenance

LOW   HIGH

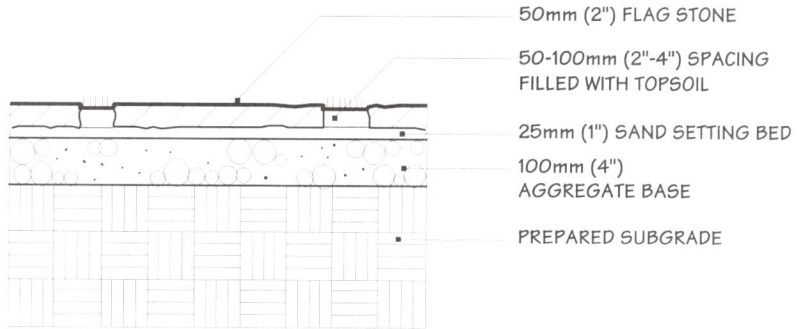

50mm (2") FLAG STONE

50-100mm (2"-4") SPACING
FILLED WITH TOPSOIL

25mm (1") SAND SETTING BED

100mm (4")
AGGREGATE BASE

PREPARED SUBGRADE

APPLICATION

CLIMATE

SUBGRADE

CSI MASTERFORMAT: 02780
DRAWING FILE: PAV13-11

• This drawing is a template for preliminary design only, and is not intended for bid purposes. It is subject to modification based on design calculations, local practices, and all applicable codes and regulations.

• This detail is rated for light-duty applications based on paving course and base thickness, and may support primarily pedestrian loading associated with walks in parks and residential settings.

• The subgrade conditions have a significant impact on the design of flexible pavements, such as flag stone patios or walks. Loads are transferred more directly to the base, requiring well-drained soils with adequate bearing capacity.

• Stone should be non-porous in cold climates.

• Spaces between flag stone should be filled with well drained prepared topsoil and seeded as specified. Custom design may require fitted sod to be placed between stones for a more immediate finished effect.

• It is recommended that recycled and regionally available materials and products be given high priority in determining final design and specifications.

Installation Cost (per Square Foot)

LOW   HIGH

$9.01

Maintenance

LOW   HIGH

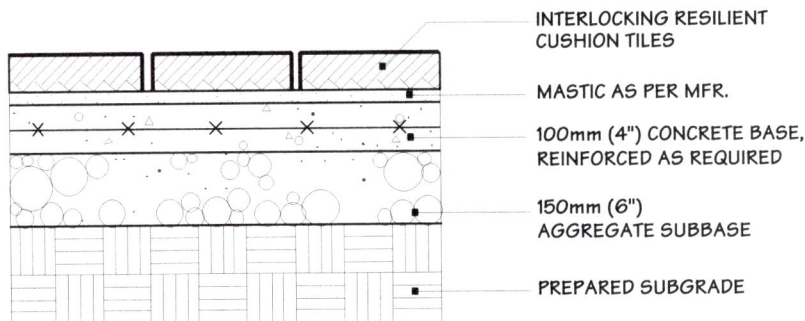

INTERLOCKING RESILIENT CUSHION TILES

MASTIC AS PER MFR.

100mm (4") CONCRETE BASE, REINFORCED AS REQUIRED

150mm (6") AGGREGATE SUBBASE

PREPARED SUBGRADE

APPLICATION

CLIMATE

SUBGRADE

CSI MASTERFORMAT: 02790
DRAWING FILE: PAV18-01

• This drawing is a template for preliminary design only, and is not intended for bid purposes. It is subject to modification based on design calculations, local practices, and all applicable codes and regulations.

• This detail is rated for light-duty applications based on thickness of concrete and aggregate base, and may support primarily pedestrian loading typically associated with residential, park, and light commercial settings.

• Many proprietary resilient cushion tiles are available. Consult manufacturer's advice for proper installation and fall attenuation ratings of various thicknesses and cross-section designs.

• Subgrade conditions have a significant impact on the longevity of rigid pavements, such as concrete. The subgrade should be uniform to prevent pavement failure due to uneven soil expansion and contraction. This detail provides a well-drained aggregate base

to drain sub-surface moisture and increase uniformity.

• Air-entrained concrete should be used for the base in freezing conditions and may be used in milder conditions to improve workability of the mixture.

• Reinforcing practices vary widely. Local codes and practices should be consulted before specifying any type of reinforcing for the base. All steel should be covered by at least 50mm (2") of concrete.

• Expansion joints should be filled, and sealed in temperate and cold climates. These joints require periodic cleaning and re-sealing.

• Surface may be subject to abrasion and color fading, unless EPDM finish material is used. Proprietary edging is usually required.

• It is recommended that recycled and regionally available materials and products be given high priority in determining final design and specifications.

Installation Cost (per Square Foot)

LOW   HIGH

$4.27

Maintenance

LOW   HIGH

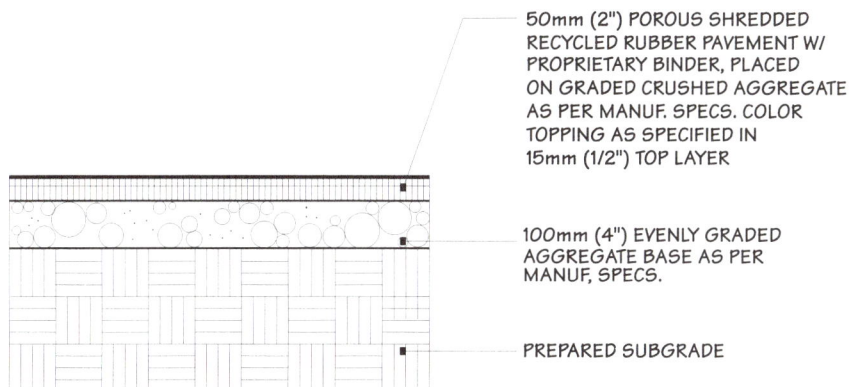

50mm (2") POROUS SHREDDED RECYCLED RUBBER PAVEMENT W/ PROPRIETARY BINDER, PLACED ON GRADED CRUSHED AGGREGATE AS PER MANUF. SPECS. COLOR TOPPING AS SPECIFIED IN 15mm (1/2") TOP LAYER

100mm (4") EVENLY GRADED AGGREGATE BASE AS PER MANUF. SPECS.

PREPARED SUBGRADE

APPLICATION

CLIMATE

SUBGRADE

CSI MASTERFORMAT: 02790
DRAWING FILE: PAV18-05

• This drawing is a template for preliminary design only, and is not intended for bid purposes. It is subject to modification based on design calculations, local practices, and all applicable codes and regulations.

• This rubber fiber emulsion pavement detail is rated for light-duty applications due to pavement and aggregate base thickness, and may support primarily pedestrian loading typically associated with public park or commercial recreation settings in all climates.

• This porous resilient surface is rated for fall attenuation, and is most commonly used in children's play areas associated with parks and commercial recreaton.

• Many proprietary resilient surfaces are available. Consult manufacturer's advice for proper installation and fall attenuation ratings of various thicknesses and cross-section designs. This poured in place surface must be contained with ramped or flush edge to allow for barrier free access.

• This detail applies the rubber fiber emulsion using a proprietary binder over a specially formulated dense graded aggregate base placed on prepared subgrade. Various thicknesses are available for attenuation ratings of up to 9600 mm (12').

• Surface may be subject to abrasion and color fading, unless EPDM finish material is used.

• It is recommended that recycled and regionally available materials and products be given high priority in determining final design and specifications.

Installation Cost (per Square Foot)

LOW  HIGH

$8.50

Maintenance

LOW  HIGH

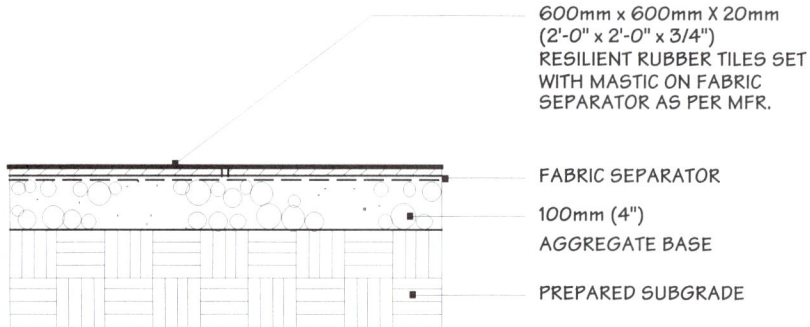

600mm x 600mm X 20mm
(2'-0" x 2'-0" x 3/4")
RESILIENT RUBBER TILES SET
WITH MASTIC ON FABRIC
SEPARATOR AS PER MFR.

FABRIC SEPARATOR

100mm (4")
AGGREGATE BASE

PREPARED SUBGRADE

APPLICATION

CLIMATE

SUBGRADE

CSI MASTERFORMAT: 02790
DRAWING FILE: PAV18-04

• This drawing is a template for preliminary design only, and is not intended for bid purposes. It is subject to modification based on design calculations, local practices, and all applicable codes and regulations.

• This resilient paver detail is rated for light-duty applications due to pavement and aggregate base thickness, and may support primarily pedestrian loading typically associated with public park or commercial recreation settings in all climates.

• This resilient tile surface is not rated for fall attenuation, and is most commonly used in golf course and public dinning areas associated with commercial recreaton.

• Many proprietary resilient cushion tiles are available. Consult manufacturer's advice for proper installation and fall attenuation ratings of various thicknesses and cross-section designs. Most tiles require a mastic and must be contained by ramped or flush edge to allow for barrier free access and to maintain tile alignment after extended use.

• This detail applies the tiles to a fabric separator with a proprietary mastic over a dense graded aggregate base placed on prepared subgrade.

• Interlocking or mastic type tiles are often used over existing pavements. New pavement bases should account for grade differentials at the surface edges for smooth transisitions onto the resilient pavement.

• Surface may be subject to abrasion and color fading, unless EPDM finish material is used. Proprietary edging is usually required.

• It is recommended that recycled and regionally available materials and products be given high priority in determining final design and specifications.

Installation Cost (per Square Foot)

$8.50

Maintenance

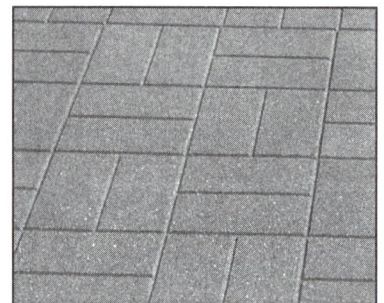

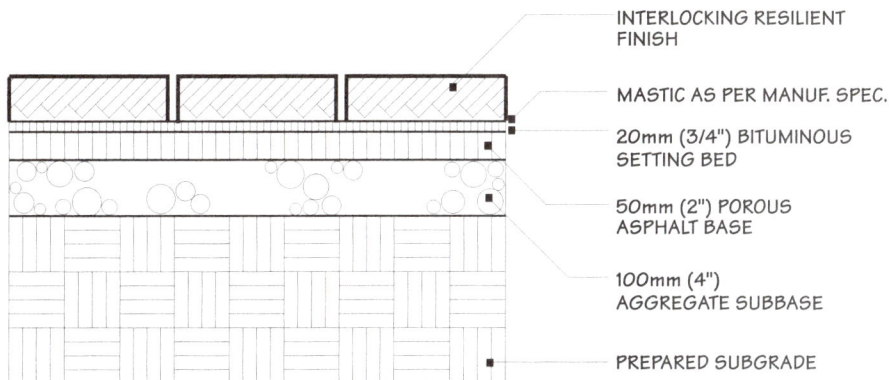

INTERLOCKING RESILIENT FINISH

MASTIC AS PER MANUF. SPEC.

20mm (3/4") BITUMINOUS SETTING BED

50mm (2") POROUS ASPHALT BASE

100mm (4") AGGREGATE SUBBASE

PREPARED SUBGRADE

APPLICATION

CLIMATE

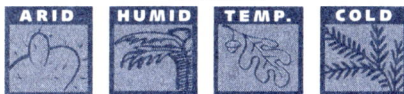

SUBGRADE

CSI MASTERFORMAT: 02790
DRAWING FILE: PAV18-03

• This drawing is a template for preliminary design only, and is not intended for bid purposes. It is subject to modification based on design calculations, local practices, and all applicable codes and regulations.

• This synthetic resilient paver detail is rated for light-duty applications due to pavement and aggregate base thickness, and may support primarily pedestrian loading typically associated with public park or commercial recreation settings.• Many proprietary resilient cushion tiles are available. Consult manufacturer's advice for proper installation and fall attenuation ratings of various thicknesses and cross-section designs. Most tiles require a mastic and must be contained by ramped or flush edge to allow for barrier free access and to maintain tile alignment after extended use.

• The subgrade conditions have a significant impact on the design of flexible pavements, such as asphalt. Loads are transferred

more directly to the base, requiring well-drained soils with adequate bearing capacity.

• Interlocking or mastic type tiles are often used over existing pavements. New pavement bases should account for grade differentials at the surface edges for smooth transitions onto the resilient pavement.• Surface may be subject to abrasion and color fading, unless EPDM finish material is used. Proprietary edging is usually required.

• It is recommended that recycled and regionally available materials and products be given high priority in determining final design and specifications.

Installation Cost (per Square Foot)

LOW   HIGH

$8.37

Maintenance

LOW   HIGH

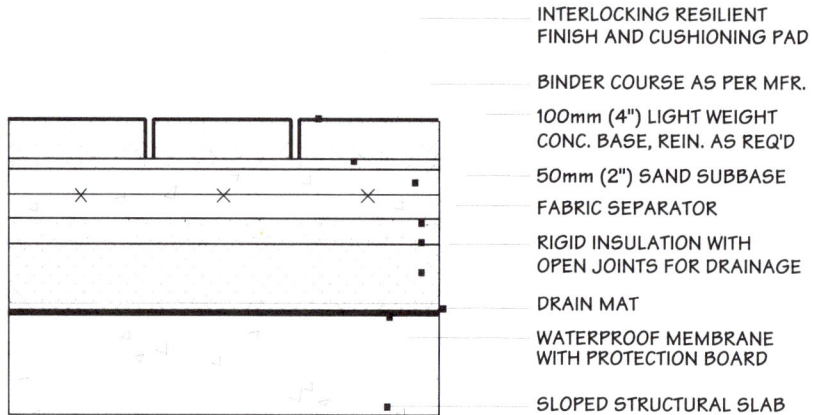

INTERLOCKING RESILIENT
FINISH AND CUSHIONING PAD

BINDER COURSE AS PER MFR.

100mm (4") LIGHT WEIGHT
CONC. BASE, REIN. AS REQ'D

50mm (2") SAND SUBBASE

FABRIC SEPARATOR

RIGID INSULATION WITH
OPEN JOINTS FOR DRAINAGE

DRAIN MAT

WATERPROOF MEMBRANE
WITH PROTECTION BOARD

SLOPED STRUCTURAL SLAB

APPLICATION

CLIMATE

SUBGRADE

CSI MASTERFORMAT: 02790
DRAWING FILE: PAV18-02

• This drawing is a template for preliminary design only, and is not intended for bid purposes. It is subject to modification based on design calculations, local practices, and all applicable codes and regulations.

• This detail is rated for light-duty applications due to pavement thickness and bearing limitations of the rigid insulation upon which it rests, and may support primarily pedestrian loading typically associated with public park, commercial recreation settings.

• Many proprietary resilient cushion tiles are available. Consult manufacturer's advice for proper installation and fall attenuation ratings of various thicknesses and cross-section designs. Most tiles require a mastic, and some are attached with plastic pins glued to holes drilled into concrete base.

• A sand base is placed on fabric separator over open jointed rigid insulation. A drain mat is placed over sloping protection board and waterproof membrane.

• Air-entrained concrete should be used for the base in freezing conditions and may be used in milder conditions to improve workability of the mixture. Light weight concrete may be required to lessen loading on deck.

• Reinforcing practices vary widely. Local codes and practices should be consulted before specifying any type of reinforcing for the base. All steel should be covered by at least 50mm (2") of concrete.

• Surface may be subject to abrasion and color fading, unless EPDM finish material is used. Proprietary edging is usually required.

• It is recommended that recycled and regionally available materials and products be given high priority in determining final design and specifications.

Installation Cost (per Square Foot)

LOW   HIGH
$10.50

Maintenance

LOW   HIGH

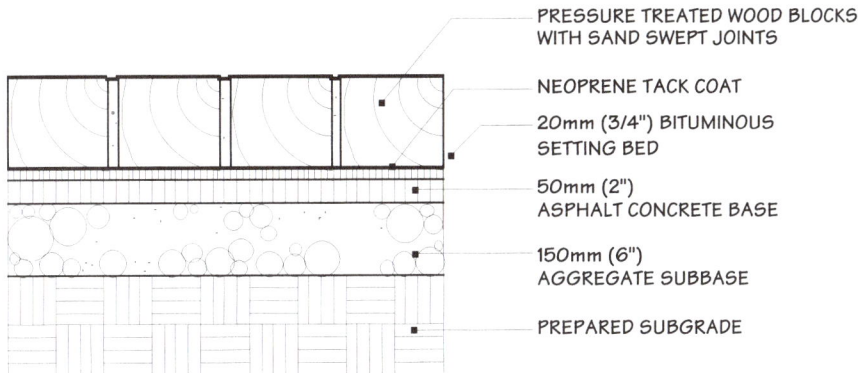

PRESSURE TREATED WOOD BLOCKS
WITH SAND SWEPT JOINTS

NEOPRENE TACK COAT

20mm (3/4") BITUMINOUS
SETTING BED

50mm (2")
ASPHALT CONCRETE BASE

150mm (6")
AGGREGATE SUBBASE

PREPARED SUBGRADE

APPLICATION

CLIMATE

SUBGRADE

CSI MASTERFORMAT: 02945
DRAWING FILE: PAV15-03

• This drawing is a template for preliminary design only, and is not intended for bid purposes. It is subject to modification based on design calculations, local practices, and all applicable codes and regulations.

• This detail is rated for medium-duty applications based on paving course and base thickness, and may support pedestrian and light vehicular loading associated with walks, driveways, and light service access in urban parks, plazas, and dense residential settings. It is limited to warm climate zones and requires rot resistant or treated wood cubes.• Asphalt setting bed is used to create a uniform surface to receive the block. Mastic is often used in urban conditions to insure stability. It requires a minimum slope of 2% in such conditions.

• As with all unit pavers, pavement edges require restraints to prevent creeping, especially if subjected to even occasional vehicular access.

• The subgrade conditions have a significant impact on the design of flexible pavements, such as unit pavers. Loads are transferred more directly to the base, requiring well-drained soils with adequate bearing capacity.

• Final wash-down will help to set brick sand grout.

• Blocks may require periodic re-setting or replacement due to cracking or organic failure. This is not a long term pavement.

• It is recommended that recycled and regionally available materials and products be given high priority in determining final design and specifications.

Installation Cost (per Square Foot)

LOW   HIGH

$4.49

Maintenance

LOW   HIGH

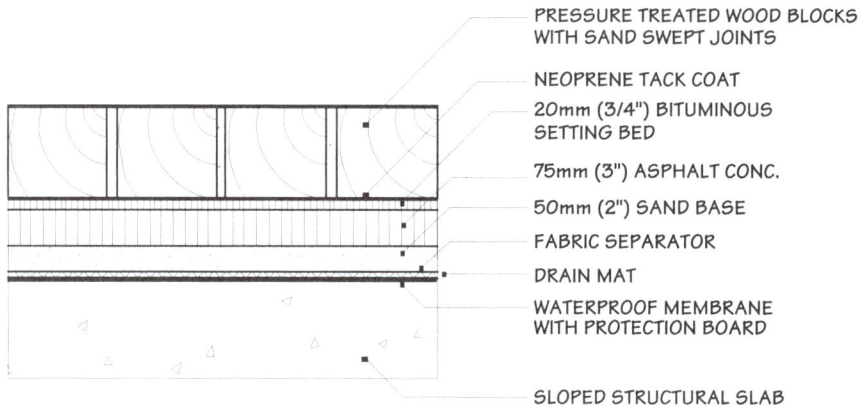

PRESSURE TREATED WOOD BLOCKS
WITH SAND SWEPT JOINTS

NEOPRENE TACK COAT

20mm (3/4") BITUMINOUS
SETTING BED

75mm (3") ASPHALT CONC.

50mm (2") SAND BASE

FABRIC SEPARATOR

DRAIN MAT

WATERPROOF MEMBRANE
WITH PROTECTION BOARD

SLOPED STRUCTURAL SLAB

APPLICATION

CLIMATE

SUBGRADE

CSI MASTERFORMAT: 02945
DRAWING FILE: PAV15-04

• This drawing is a template for preliminary design only, and is not intended for bid purposes. It is subject to modification based on design calculations, local practices, and all applicable codes and regulations.

• This detail is rated for medium-duty applications based on paving course and base thickness, and may support pedestrian and light vehicular loading associated with walks, driveways, and light service access in urban parks, plazas, and dense residential settings on structural roof decks. It is limited to warm climate zones and requires rot resistant or treated wood cubes.• Asphalt setting bed is used to create a uniform surface to receive the block. Mastic is often used in urban conditions to insure stability. It requires a minimum slope of 2% in such conditions.

• A sand base is placed on fabric separator over open jointed rigid insulation. A heavy-duty drain mat is placed over sloping protection board and waterproof membrane.

• As with all unit pavers, pavement edges require restraints to prevent creeping, especially if subjected to even occasional vehicular access.

• The subgrade conditions have a significant impact on the design of flexible pavements, such as unit pavers. Loads are transferred more directly to the base, requiring well-drained soils with adequate bearing capacity.

• Final wash-down will help to set brick sand grout.

• Blocks may require periodic re-setting or replacement due to cracking or organic failure. This is not a long term pavement.

• It is recommended that recycled and regionally available materials and products be given high priority in determining final design and specifications.

Installation Cost (per Square Foot)

LOW   HIGH

$5.32

Maintenance

LOW   HIGH

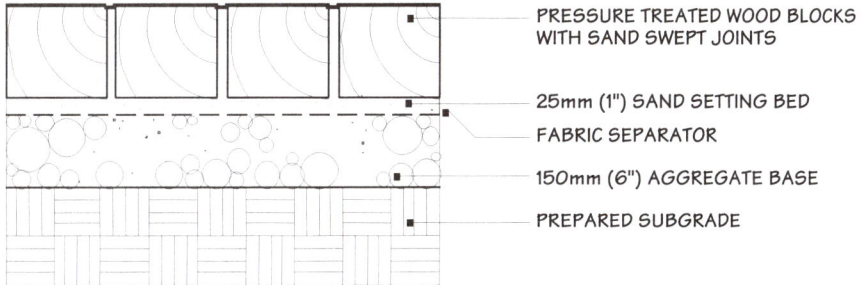

PRESSURE TREATED WOOD BLOCKS
WITH SAND SWEPT JOINTS

25mm (1") SAND SETTING BED

FABRIC SEPARATOR

150mm (6") AGGREGATE BASE

PREPARED SUBGRADE

APPLICATION

CLIMATE

SUBGRADE

CSI MASTERFORMAT: 02945
DRAWING FILE: PAV15-01

• This drawing is a template for preliminary design only, and is not intended for bid purposes. It is subject to modification based on design calculations, local practices, and all applicable codes and regulations.

• This detail is rated for medium-duty applications based on paving course and base thickness, and may support pedestrian and light vehicular loading associated with walks and light service access in parks and dense residential settings. It is limited to warm climate zones and requires rot resistant or treated wood cubes.

• As with all unit pavers, pavement edges require restraints to prevent creeping, especially if subjected to even occasional vehicular access.

• The subgrade conditions have a significant impact on the design of flexible pavements, such as unit pavers. Loads are transferred more directly to the base, requiring well-drained soils with adequate bearing capacity.

• Set uniform wood blocks with light vibrating compactor over sand cushion and final sand sweeping to complete installation. Final wash-down will help to set block sand grout.

• Fabric separator helps to bind the block pavement and contains fines within sand base.

• Blocks may require periodic re-setting or replacement due to cracking or organic failure.

• It is recommended that recycled and regionally available materials and products be given high priority in determining final design and specifications.

Installation Cost (per Square Foot)

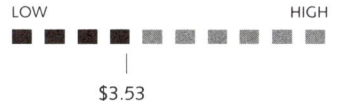

LOW   HIGH

$3.53

Maintenance

LOW   HIGH

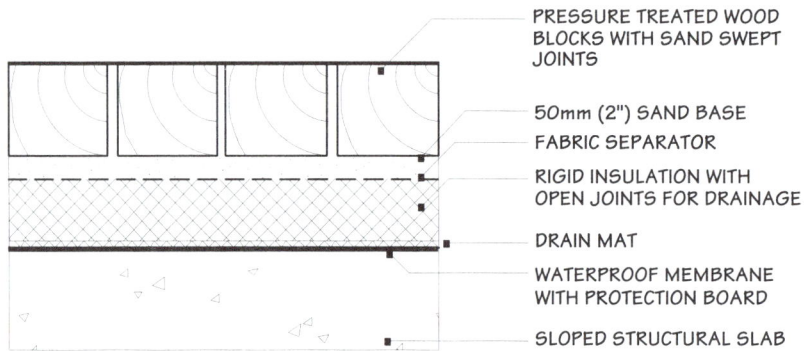

PRESSURE TREATED WOOD
BLOCKS WITH SAND SWEPT
JOINTS

50mm (2") SAND BASE

FABRIC SEPARATOR

RIGID INSULATION WITH
OPEN JOINTS FOR DRAINAGE

DRAIN MAT

WATERPROOF MEMBRANE
WITH PROTECTION BOARD

SLOPED STRUCTURAL SLAB

APPLICATION

CLIMATE

SUBGRADE

CSI MASTERFORMAT: 02945
DRAWING FILE: PAV15-02

• This drawing is a template for preliminary design only, and is not intended for bid purposes. It is subject to modification based on design calculations, local practices, and all applicable codes and regulations.

• This detail is rated for light-duty applications due to pavement thickness and bearing limitations of the rigid insulation upon which it rests. It is limited to warm climate zones and requires rot resistant or treated wood cubes. It typically may serve as a walkway or patio in residential or park settings.

• A sand base is placed on fabric separator over open jointed rigid insulation. A drain mat is placed over sloping protection board and waterproof membrane.

• As with all unit pavers, pavement edges require restraints to prevent creeping, especially if subjected to even occasional vehicular access.

• Set uniform wood blocks with light vibrating compactor over sand cushion and final sand sweeping to complete installation. Final wash-down will help to set block sand grout.

• Blocks may require periodic re-setting or replacement due to cracking or organic failure.

• It is recommended that recycled and regionally available materials and products be given high priority in determining final design and specifications.

Installation Cost (per Square Foot)

LOW   HIGH

$3.97

Maintenance

LOW   HIGH

Paving Dividers

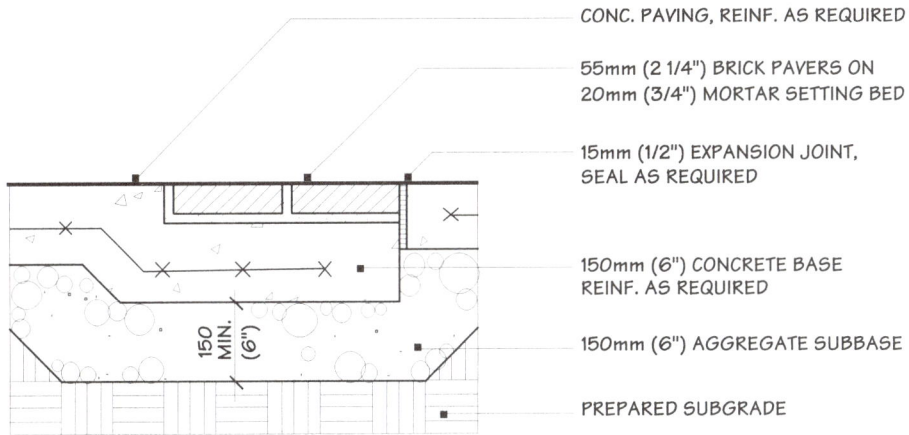

CONC. PAVING, REINF. AS REQUIRED

55mm (2 1/4") BRICK PAVERS ON
20mm (3/4") MORTAR SETTING BED

15mm (1/2") EXPANSION JOINT,
SEAL AS REQUIRED

150mm (6") CONCRETE BASE
REINF. AS REQUIRED

150mm (6") AGGREGATE SUBBASE

PREPARED SUBGRADE

150 MIN. (6")

APPLICATION

LIGHT   MED.   HEAVY

CLIMATE

ARID   HUMID   TEMP.   COLD

SUBGRADE

PERM.   CLAY   ROOF

CSI MASTERFORMAT: 02780
DRAWING FILE: DIV04-01

• This drawing is a template for preliminary design only, and is not intended for bid purposes. It is subject to modification based on design calculations, local practices, and all applicable codes and regulations.

• Brick dividers in concrete paving are typical of public sidewalk and plaza design. This detail illustrates brick inset at the edge of a concrete slab.

• This detail is rated for medium-duty applications based on thickness of concrete and aggregate subbase, and may be required to bear light vehicular loads.

• Reinforcing practices vary widely by region. Local codes and practices should be consulted prior to specifying any type of reinforcing.

• Rigid pavement design must accommodate movement of materials by providing adequate expansion and control joints, particularly in regions of extreme temperature fluctuations.

• This detail is not designed for cold climates, where the use of mortar in pavements is discouraged due to seasonal deterioration. Where unit pavers are desired, placement on an asphalt setting bed with mastic may be more suitable in cold climates.

• Subgrade conditions have a significant impact on the longevity of rigid pavements, such as brick pavers mortared on a concrete base. The subgrade should be uniform to prevent pavement failure due to uneven soil expansion and contraction. This detail provides a well-drained aggregate base to drain sub-surface moisture and increase uniformity.

• Mortared pavements require significant maintenance due to the need for regular pointing and sealing of joints.

• It is recommended that recycled and regionally available materials and products be given high priority in determining final design and specifications.

Installation Cost (per Square Foot)

LOW   HIGH

$8.60

Maintenance

LOW   HIGH

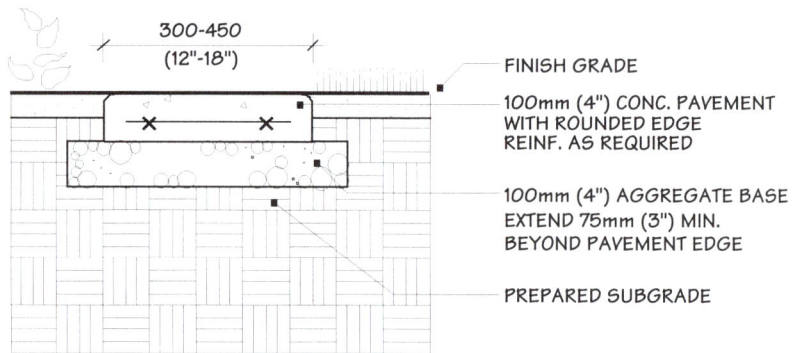

300-450
(12"-18")

FINISH GRADE

100mm (4") CONC. PAVEMENT
WITH ROUNDED EDGE
REINF. AS REQUIRED

100mm (4") AGGREGATE BASE
EXTEND 75mm (3") MIN.
BEYOND PAVEMENT EDGE

PREPARED SUBGRADE

APPLICATION

CLIMATE

SUBGRADE

CSI MASTERFORMAT: 02775
DRAWING FILE: DIV02-01

• This drawing is a template for preliminary design only, and is not intended for bid purposes. It is subject to modification based on design calculations, local practices, and all applicable codes and regulations.

• Mowing strips are typical in residential and garden settings and provide a well-defined edge between turf areas and planting beds. In addition to concrete, they are frequently constructed out of stone and brick pavements.

• This detail is rated for light-duty applications and may support light loads.

• A granular base is provided to minimize movement of materials due to the collection of sub-surface moisture. If designed for temperate or cold climates, air-entrained concrete is typically recommended due to freezing/thawing action.

• Reinforcing practices vary widely by region. Local codes and practices should be consulted prior to specifying any type of reinforcing.

• It is recommended that recycled and regionally available materials and products be given high priority in determining final design and specifications.

Installation Cost (per Square Foot)

LOW   HIGH

$2.18

Maintenance

LOW   HIGH

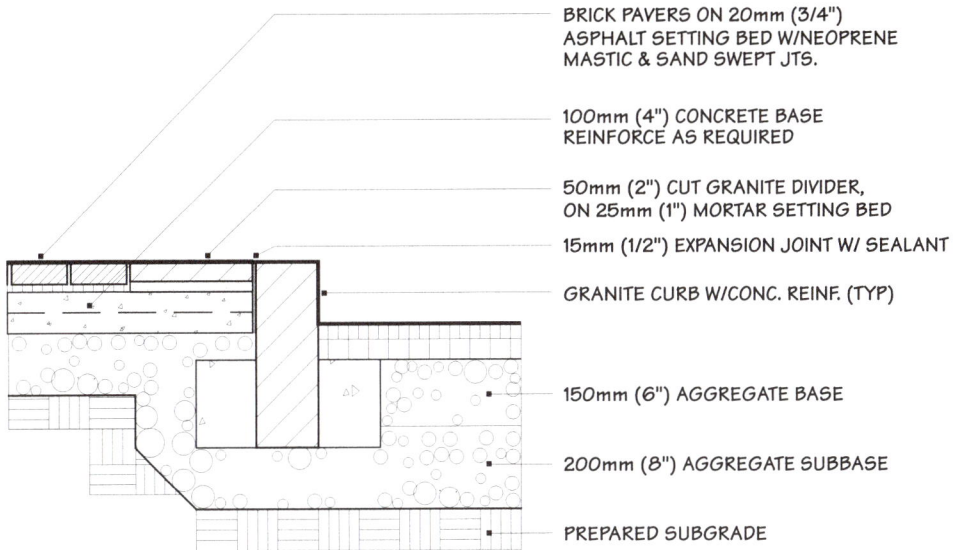

BRICK PAVERS ON 20mm (3/4")
ASPHALT SETTING BED W/NEOPRENE
MASTIC & SAND SWEPT JTS.

100mm (4") CONCRETE BASE
REINFORCE AS REQUIRED

50mm (2") CUT GRANITE DIVIDER,
ON 25mm (1") MORTAR SETTING BED

15mm (1/2") EXPANSION JOINT W/ SEALANT

GRANITE CURB W/CONC. REINF. (TYP)

150mm (6") AGGREGATE BASE

200mm (8") AGGREGATE SUBBASE

PREPARED SUBGRADE

APPLICATION

CLIMATE

SUBGRADE

CSI MASTERFORMAT: 02780
DRAWING FILE: DIV03-02

- This drawing is a template for preliminary design only, and is not intended for bid purposes. It is subject to modification based on design calculations, local practices, and all applicable codes and regulations.

- Granite dividers in brick paving are typical of public sidewalk and plaza design, and represent only a variation in surfacing of pavement construction.

- This detail is rated for heavy-duty applications based on thickness of concrete base and aggregate subbase, and may be required to bear vehicular loads. It is placed on a mortar setting bed adjacent to stone curbing which has been reinforced with concrete front and back.

- Reinforcing practices vary widely by region. Local codes and practices should be consulted prior to specifying any type of reinforcing.

- Rigid pavement design must accommodate movement of materials by providing adequate expansion and control joints, particularly in regions of extreme temperature fluctuations.

- This detail is not designed for cold climates, where the use of mortar in pavements is discouraged due to seasonal deterioration. Where unit pavers are desired, placement on an asphalt setting bed with mastic may be more suitable in cold climates.

- Subgrade conditions have a significant impact on the longevity of rigid pavements, such as pavers mortared on a concrete base. The subgrade should be uniform to prevent pavement failure due to uneven soil expansion and contraction. This detail provides a well-drained aggregate base to drain subsurface moisture and increase uniformity.

- Mortared pavements require significant maintenance due to the need for regular pointing and sealing of joints.

- It is recommended that recycled and regionally available materials and products be given high priority in determining final design and specifications.

Installation Cost (per Square Foot)

LOW   HIGH

$11.91

Maintenance

LOW   HIGH

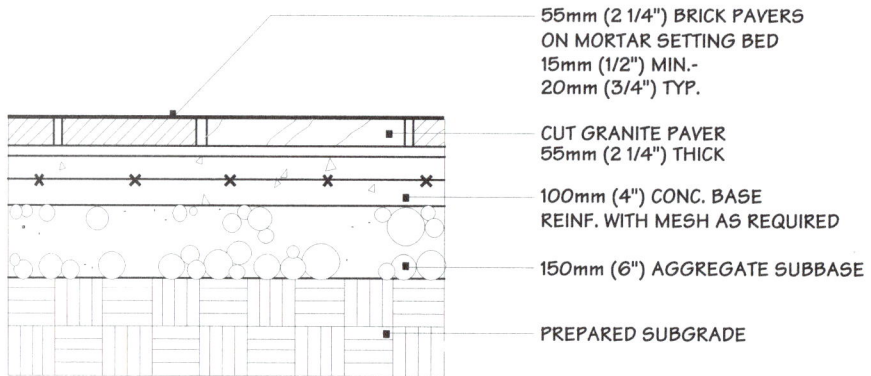

55mm (2 1/4") BRICK PAVERS
ON MORTAR SETTING BED
15mm (1/2") MIN.-
20mm (3/4") TYP.

CUT GRANITE PAVER
55mm (2 1/4") THICK

100mm (4") CONC. BASE
REINF. WITH MESH AS REQUIRED

150mm (6") AGGREGATE SUBBASE

PREPARED SUBGRADE

APPLICATION

CLIMATE

SUBGRADE

CSI MASTERFORMAT: 02780
DRAWING FILE: DIV03-01

• This drawing is a template for preliminary design only, and is not intended for bid purposes. It is subject to modification based on design calculations, local practices, and all applicable codes and regulations.

• Granite dividers in brick paving are typical of public sidewalk and plaza design, and represent only a variation in surfacing of pavement construction.

• This detail is rated for medium-duty applications based on thickness of concrete base and aggregate subbase, and may be required to bear light vehicular loads.

• Reinforcing practices vary widely by region. Local codes and practices should be consulted prior to specifying any type of reinforcing.

• Rigid pavement design must accommodate movement of materials by providing adequate expansion and control joints, particularly in regions of extreme temperature fluctuations.

• This detail is not designed for cold climates, where the use of mortar in pavements is discouraged due to seasonal deterioration. Where unit pavers are desired, placement on an asphalt setting bed with mastic may be more suitable in cold climates.

• Subgrade conditions have a significant impact on the longevity of rigid pavements, such as brick pavers mortared on a concrete base. The subgrade should be uniform to prevent pavement failure due to uneven soil expansion and contraction. This detail provides a well-drained aggregate base to drain subsurface moisture and increase uniformity.

• Mortared pavements require significant maintenance due to the need for regular pointing and sealing of joints.

• It is recommended that recycled and regionally available materials and products be given high priority in determining final design and specifications.

Installation Cost (per Square Foot)

LOW   HIGH

$11.43

Maintenance

LOW   HIGH

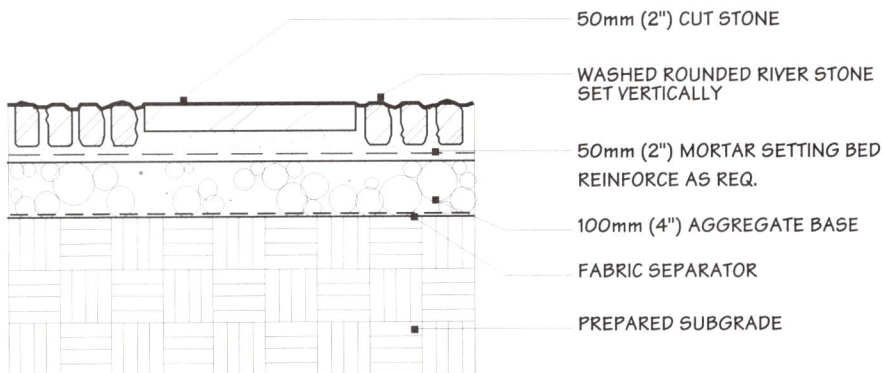

50mm (2") CUT STONE

WASHED ROUNDED RIVER STONE SET VERTICALLY

50mm (2") MORTAR SETTING BED REINFORCE AS REQ.

100mm (4") AGGREGATE BASE

FABRIC SEPARATOR

PREPARED SUBGRADE

APPLICATION

CLIMATE

SUBGRADE

CSI MASTERFORMAT: 02780
DRAWING FILE: DIV03-05

• This drawing is a template for preliminary design only, and is not intended for bid purposes. It is subject to modification based on design calculations, local practices, and all applicable codes and regulations.

• Cut stone dividers are typically found in residential, public park, and large garden settings.

• This detail is rated for light-duty applications based on thickness of mortar base and aggregate subbase and may be used to divide pavements of varying textures, or be used as a walking surface within a highly textured pavement. It is placed on a reinforced mortar setting bed, on an aggregate base.

• This detail is not designed for cold climates, where the use of mortar in pavements is discouraged due to seasonal deterioration. Where unit pavers are desired, placement on an asphalt setting bed with mastic may be more suitable in cold climates.

• Subgrade conditions have a significant impact on the longevity of rigid pavements, such as brick pavers mortared on a concrete base. The subgrade should be uniform to prevent pavement failure due to uneven soil expansion and contraction. This detail provides a well-drained aggregate base to drain sub-surface moisture and increase uniformity.

• Mortared pavements require significant maintenance due to the need for regular pointing and sealing of joints.

• It is recommended that recycled and regionally available materials and products be given high priority in determining final design and specifications.

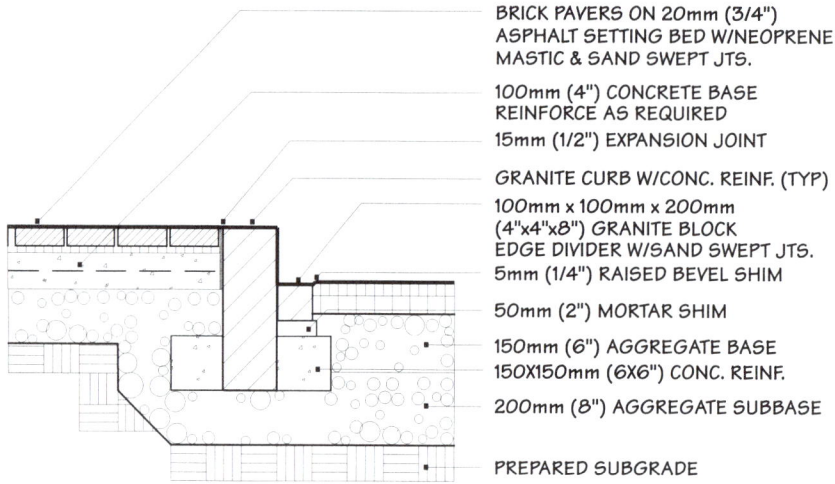

BRICK PAVERS ON 20mm (3/4")
ASPHALT SETTING BED W/NEOPRENE
MASTIC & SAND SWEPT JTS.

100mm (4") CONCRETE BASE
REINFORCE AS REQUIRED

15mm (1/2") EXPANSION JOINT

GRANITE CURB W/CONC. REINF. (TYP)

100mm x 100mm x 200mm
(4"x4"x8") GRANITE BLOCK
EDGE DIVIDER W/SAND SWEPT JTS.

5mm (1/4") RAISED BEVEL SHIM

50mm (2") MORTAR SHIM

150mm (6") AGGREGATE BASE
150X150mm (6X6") CONC. REINF.

200mm (8") AGGREGATE SUBBASE

PREPARED SUBGRADE

APPLICATION

CLIMATE

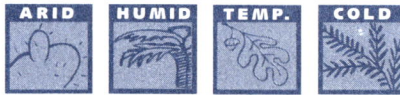

SUBGRADE

CSI MASTERFORMAT: 02780
DRAWING FILE: DIV03-03

• This drawing is a template for preliminary design only, and is not intended for bid purposes. It is subject to modification based on design calculations, local practices, and all applicable codes and regulations.

• Granite dividers in asphalt paving are typical of public roadway and plaza design, and represent only a variation in surfacing of pavement construction.

• This flush granite block gutter detail is rated for heavy-duty applications based on thickness of aggregate base and aggregate subbase, and is required to bear vehicular loads. It is placed on a mortared setting bed adjacent to stone curbing which has been reinforced with concrete front and back.

• Granite blocks are typically set 5 mm (1/4") below the finish asphalt grade to ensure good drainage and appearance.

• Mortared pavements require significant maintenance due to the need for regular pointing and sealing of joints. In more mod-

erate use, blocks may be set on aggregate and butted with sand swept joints.

• It is recommended that recycled and regionally available materials and products be given high priority in determining final design and specifications.

Installation Cost (per Square Foot)

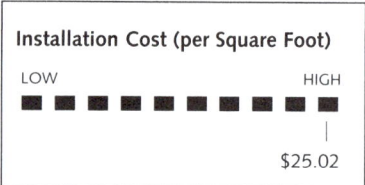

LOW   HIGH

$25.02

Maintenance

LOW   HIGH

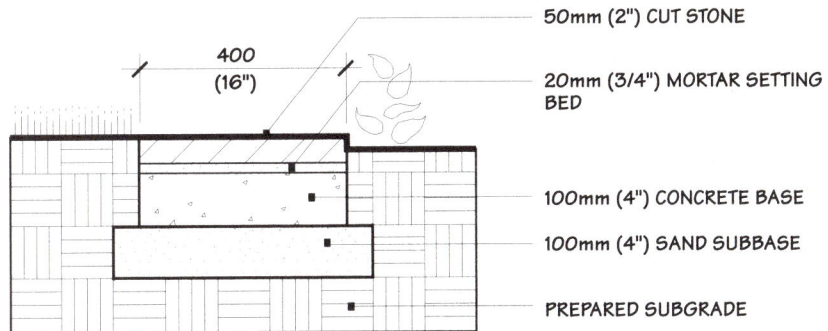

50mm (2") CUT STONE

20mm (3/4") MORTAR SETTING BED

100mm (4") CONCRETE BASE

100mm (4") SAND SUBBASE

PREPARED SUBGRADE

400 (16")

APPLICATION

CLIMATE

SUBGRADE

CSI MASTERFORMAT: 02780
DRAWING FILE: DIV03-04

• This drawing is a template for preliminary design only, and is not intended for bid purposes. It is subject to modification based on design calculations, local practices, and all applicable codes and regulations.

• Granite dividers in lawn and garden design are typically found in public park and large garden settings.

• This detail is rated for light-duty applications based on thickness of concrete base and aggregate subbase and may be used to divide use areas in lawns or botanical gardens. It is placed on a mortared setting bed on a concrete base.

• Rigid pavement design must accommodate movement of materials by providing adequate expansion and control joints, particularly in regions of extreme temperature fluctuations.

• This detail is not designed for cold climates, where the use of mortar in pavements is discouraged due to seasonal deterioration.

Where unit pavers are desired, placement on an asphalt setting bed with mastic may be more suitable in cold climates.

• Subgrade conditions have a significant impact on the longevity of rigid pavements, such as pavers mortared on a concrete base. The subgrade should be uniform to prevent pavement failure due to uneven soil expansion and contraction. This detail provides a well-drained aggregate base to drain subsurface moisture and increase uniformity.

• Mortared pavements require significant maintenance due to the need for regular pointing and sealing of joints.

• It is recommended that recycled and regionally available materials and products be given high priority in determining final design and specifications.

Installation Cost (per Square Foot)

LOW   HIGH

$11.91

Maintenance

LOW   HIGH

Paving Edges

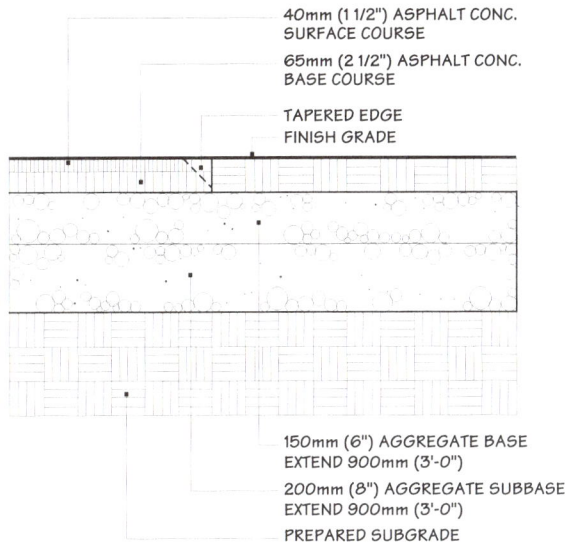

40mm (1 1/2") ASPHALT CONC. SURFACE COURSE

65mm (2 1/2") ASPHALT CONC. BASE COURSE

TAPERED EDGE
FINISH GRADE

150mm (6") AGGREGATE BASE EXTEND 900mm (3'-0")
200mm (8") AGGREGATE SUBBASE EXTEND 900mm (3'-0")
PREPARED SUBGRADE

APPLICATION

CLIMATE

SUBGRADE

CSI MASTERFORMAT: 02740
DRAWING FILE: EDG01-02

• This drawing is for preliminary design only, and is not intended for bid purposes. It is subject to modification based on design calculations, local practices, and all applicable codes and regulations.

• This detail is typical of asphalt roadway design. The tapered design provides added reinforcement and prevents undermining of the pavement by turf roots.

• The tapered edge is created by extending the base course beyond the finished pavement edge. The surface course is typically tamped by mechanical methods to form the tapered edge.

• This detail is rated for heavy-duty applications due to thicker asphalt courses and the addition of an aggregate subbase that provides greater support for heavy loads.

• The base and subbase are extended well beyond the pavement edge, past the load bearing angle, for sufficient reinforcement of both pavement edge and the turf shoulder.

• The subgrade conditions have a significant impact on the design of flexible pavements, such as asphalt. Loads are transferred more directly to the base, requiring well-drained soils with adequate bearing capacity.

• Tapered edges require little or no special maintenance and are not subject to significant wearing, unlike containment edges or curbing, but they do require regular turf trimming to achieve a well-defined edge.

• It is recommended that recycled and regionally available materials and products be given high priority in determining final design and specifications.

Installation Cost (per Linear Foot)

LOW   HIGH
$3.47

Maintenance

LOW   HIGH

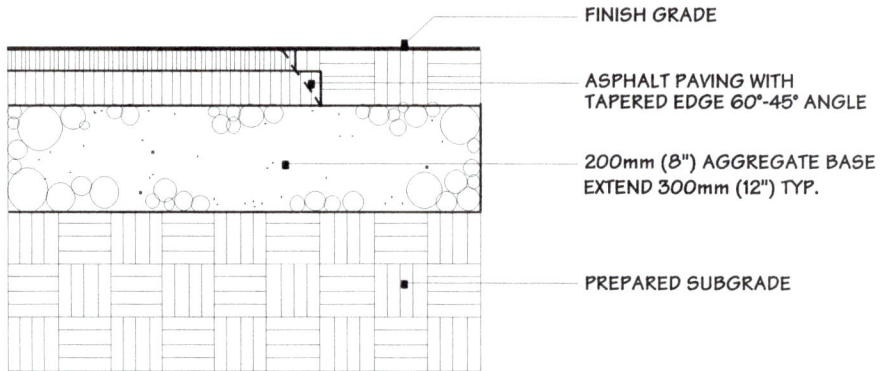

FINISH GRADE

ASPHALT PAVING WITH
TAPERED EDGE 60°-45° ANGLE

200mm (8") AGGREGATE BASE
EXTEND 300mm (12") TYP.

PREPARED SUBGRADE

APPLICATION

LIGHT   MED.   HEAVY

CLIMATE

ARID   HUMID   TEMP.   COLD

SUBGRADE

PERM.   CLAY   ROOF

CSI MASTERFORMAT: 02740
DRAWING FILE: EDG01-03

• This drawing is for preliminary design only, and is not intended for bid purposes. It is subject to modification based on design calculations, local practices, and all applicable codes and regulations.

• This detail is typical of asphalt roadway design. The tapered design provides added reinforcement and prevents undermining of the pavement by turf roots.

• The tapered edge is created by extending the base course beyond the finished pavement edge. The surface course is typically tamped by mechanical methods to form the tapered edge.

• This detail is rated for medium-duty applications due to multiple asphalt courses and a well-drained aggregate base that provides support for moderate loads.

• The base is extended beyond the pavement edge, past the load bearing angle, for sufficient pavement edge reinforcement.

• The subgrade conditions have a significant impact on the design of flexible pavements, such as asphalt. Loads are transferred more directly to the base, requiring well-drained soils with adequate bearing capacity.

• Tapered edges require little or no special maintenance and are not subject to significant wearing, unlike containment edges or curbing, but they do require regular turf trimming to achieve a well-defined edge.

• It is recommended that recycled and regionally available materials and products be given high priority in determining final design and specifications.

Installation Cost (per Linear Foot)

LOW   HIGH

$0.56

Maintenance

LOW   HIGH

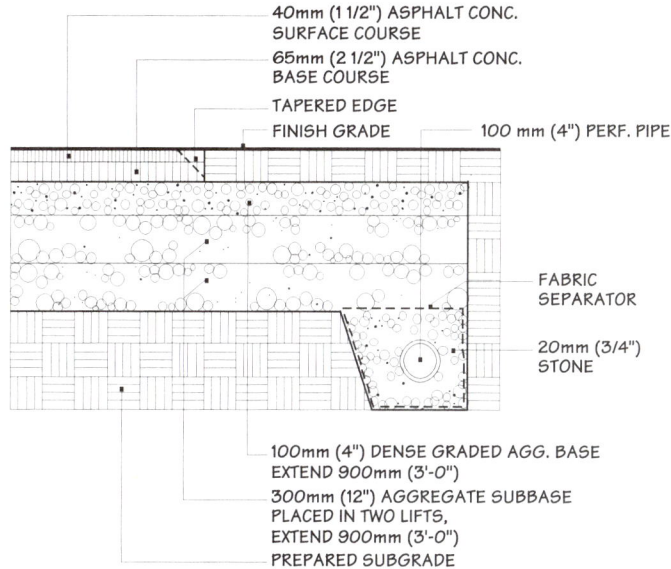

40mm (1 1/2") ASPHALT CONC.
SURFACE COURSE

65mm (2 1/2") ASPHALT CONC.
BASE COURSE

TAPERED EDGE

FINISH GRADE

100 mm (4") PERF. PIPE

FABRIC
SEPARATOR

20mm (3/4")
STONE

100mm (4") DENSE GRADED AGG. BASE
EXTEND 900mm (3'-0")

300mm (12") AGGREGATE SUBBASE
PLACED IN TWO LIFTS,
EXTEND 900mm (3'-0")

PREPARED SUBGRADE

APPLICATION

CLIMATE

SUBGRADE

CSI MASTERFORMAT: 02740
DRAWING FILE: EDG01-04

- This drawing is for preliminary design only, and is not intended for bid purposes. It is subject to modification based on design calculations, local practices, and all applicable codes and regulations.

- This detail is typical of asphalt roadway design. The tapered design provides added reinforcement and prevents undermining of the pavement by turf roots.

- The tapered edge is created by extending the base course beyond the finished pavement edge. The surface course is typically tamped by mechanical methods to form the tapered edge.

- This detail is rated for heavy-duty applications due to thicker asphalt courses and the addition of a subbase that provides support for heavy loads.

- The base and subbase are extended well beyond the pavement edge, past the load bearing angle, for sufficient reinforcement of both the pavement edge and the shoulder.

- The subgrade conditions have a significant impact on the design of flexible pavements, such as asphalt. Loads are transferred more directly to the base, requiring adequate bearing capacity. This detail provides a thicker subbase and fabric separator to bind the aggregate for greater strength in expansive clay soils.

- A perforated drain pipe is provided at the pavement edge to ensure adequate sub-surface drainage in wet soils. The drain is located outside the load bearing angle of the pavement, to avoid crushing.

- Tapered edges require little or no special maintenance and are not subject to significant wearing, unlike containment edges or curbing, but they do require regular turf trimming to achieve a well-defined edge.

Installation Cost (per Linear Foot)

LOW   HIGH

$7.37

Maintenance

LOW   HIGH

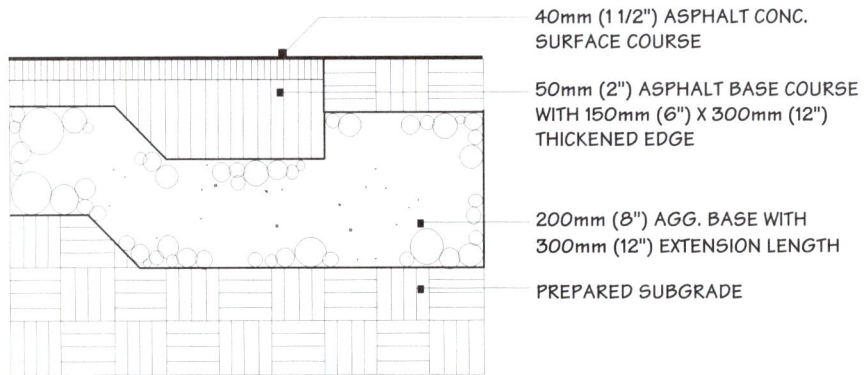

40mm (1 1/2") ASPHALT CONC. SURFACE COURSE

50mm (2") ASPHALT BASE COURSE WITH 150mm (6") X 300mm (12") THICKENED EDGE

200mm (8") AGG. BASE WITH 300mm (12") EXTENSION LENGTH

PREPARED SUBGRADE

APPLICATION

CLIMATE

SUBGRADE

CSI MASTERFORMAT: 02740
DRAWING FILE: EDG01-01

• This drawing is for preliminary design only, and is not intended for bid purposes. It is subject to modification based on design calculations, local practices, and all applicable codes and regulations.

• This detail is typical of asphalt roadway design in sandy coastal soils. The thickened edge provides added reinforcement and prevents undermining of the pavement by turf roots and wind erosion in sandy exposed soils.

• This detail is rated for medium-duty applications due to thicker asphalt courses and the base course thickness.

• The base is extended well beyond the pavement edge, past the load bearing angle, for sufficient reinforcement.

• The subgrade conditions have a significant impact on the design of flexible pavements, such as asphalt. Loads are transferred more directly to the base, requiring adequate

bearing capacity. This detail provides an aggregate base extension for added support.

• Thickened edges require little or no special maintenance and are not subject to significant wearing, unlike containment edges or curbing, but they do require regular turf trimming to achieve a well-defined edge.

• It is recommended that recycled and regionally available materials and products be given high priority in determining final design and specifications.

Installation Cost (per Linear Foot)

LOW   HIGH

$5.82

Maintenance

LOW   HIGH

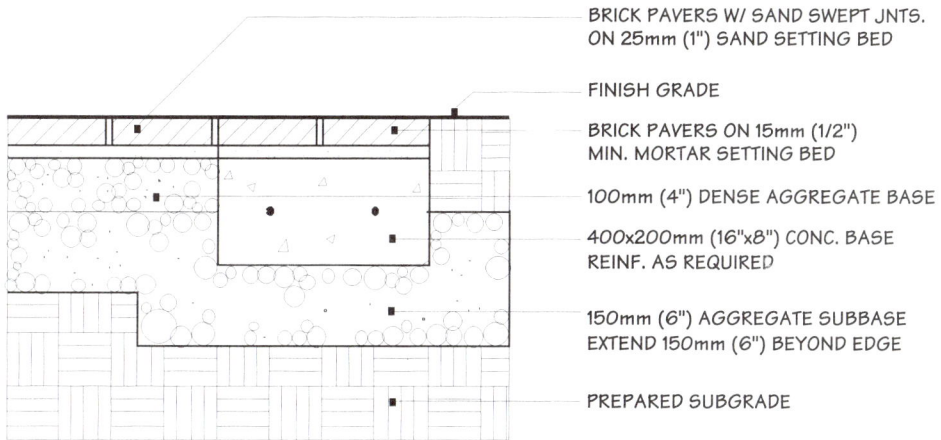

BRICK PAVERS W/ SAND SWEPT JNTS.
ON 25mm (1") SAND SETTING BED

FINISH GRADE

BRICK PAVERS ON 15mm (1/2")
MIN. MORTAR SETTING BED

100mm (4") DENSE AGGREGATE BASE

400x200mm (16"x8") CONC. BASE
REINF. AS REQUIRED

150mm (6") AGGREGATE SUBBASE
EXTEND 150mm (6") BEYOND EDGE

PREPARED SUBGRADE

APPLICATION

CLIMATE

SUBGRADE

CSI MASTERFORMAT: 02780
DRAWING FILE: EDG04-04

• This drawing is a template for preliminary design only, and is not intended for bid purposes. It is subject to modification based on design calculations, local practices, and all applicable codes and regulations.

• This detail is typical of public plaza and roadway design. The concrete grade beam provides added reinforcement and prevents spreading of flexible brick pavers, particularly in dynamic vehicular loading situations.

• This detail is rated for heavy-duty applications due to the size of the grade beam and bearing capacity of pavement base and subbase.

• The base is extended beyond the pavement edge, past the load bearing angle, for sufficient reinforcement.

• Reinforcing practices vary widely by region. Local codes and practices should be consulted prior to specifying any type of reinforcing.

• This detail is not designed for cold climates, where the use of mortar is discouraged. Flexible adhesives are recommended in these conditions.

• Brick mortared on a concrete grade beam is a high maintenance detail due to the need for regular pointing and sealing of expansion joints.

• It is recommended that recycled and regionally available materials and products be given high priority in determining final design and specifications.

Installation Cost (per Linear Foot)

LOW   HIGH

$13.00

Maintenance

LOW   HIGH

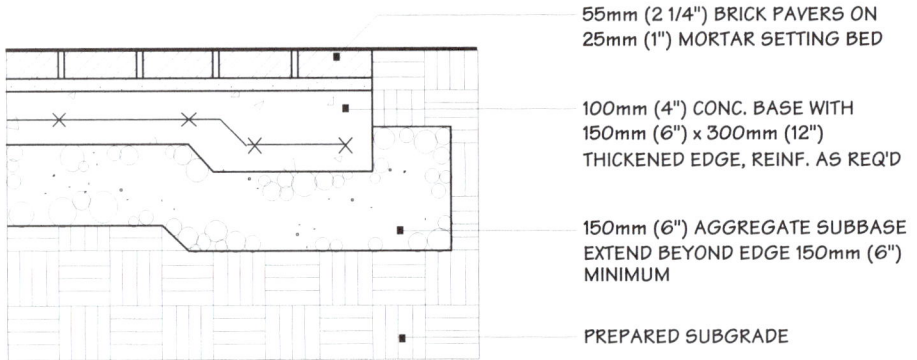

55mm (2 1/4") BRICK PAVERS ON
25mm (1") MORTAR SETTING BED

100mm (4") CONC. BASE WITH
150mm (6") x 300mm (12")
THICKENED EDGE, REINF. AS REQ'D

150mm (6") AGGREGATE SUBBASE
EXTEND BEYOND EDGE 150mm (6")
MINIMUM

PREPARED SUBGRADE

APPLICATION

CLIMATE

SUBGRADE

CSI MASTERFORMAT: 02780
DRAWING FILE: EDG04-03

• This drawing is a template for preliminary design only, and is not intended for bid purposes. It is subject to modification based on design calculations, local practices, and all applicable codes and regulations.

• This detail is typical of pedestrian plaza and driveway design in coastal regions with sandy soils. The thickened concrete base edge provides added reinforcement and prevents undermining of the pavement by plant roots and wind erosion.

• This detail is rated for medium-duty applications due to a thickend edge and a well-drained base that provides uniform support for moderate loads.

• The base is extended beyond the pavement edge, past the load bearing angle, for sufficient reinforcement.

• Reinforcing practices vary widely by region. Local codes and practices should be consulted prior to specifying any type of reinforcing.

• Rigid pavement design must accommodate movement of materials by providing adequate expansion and control joints, particularly in regions of extreme temperature fluctuations.

• This detail is not designed for cold climates, where the use of mortar in pavements is discouraged due to seasonal deterioration. Where unit pavers are desired, placement on an asphalt setting bed with mastic may be more suitable in cold climates.

• Subgrade conditions have a significant impact on the longevity of rigid pavements, such as brick pavers mortared on a concrete base. The subgrade should be uniform to prevent pavement failure due to uneven soil expansion and contraction. This detail provides a well-drained aggregate base to drain sub-surface moisture and increase uniformity.

• Thickened edges do not require special maintenance, however mortared brick is a high maintenance detail due to the need for regular pointing and sealing of joints.

Installation Cost (per Linear Foot)

LOW   HIGH

$10.00

Maintenance

LOW   HIGH

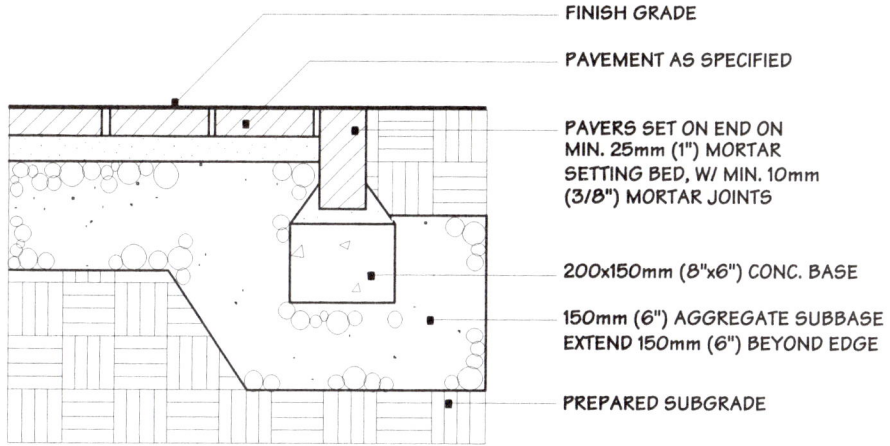

FINISH GRADE

PAVEMENT AS SPECIFIED

PAVERS SET ON END ON
MIN. 25mm (1") MORTAR
SETTING BED, W/ MIN. 10mm
(3/8") MORTAR JOINTS

200x150mm (8"x6") CONC. BASE

150mm (6") AGGREGATE SUBBASE
EXTEND 150mm (6") BEYOND EDGE

PREPARED SUBGRADE

APPLICATION

CLIMATE

SUBGRADE

CSI MASTERFORMAT: 02780
DRAWING FILE: EDG04-07

• This drawing is a template for preliminary design only, and is not intended for bid purposes. It is subject to modification based on design calculations, local practices, and all applicable codes and regulations.

• This detail is typical of public plaza and driveway design. The bricks set on end provide a well-defined edge and prevent spreading of flexible brick pavers. The concrete base provides added reinforcement to handle moderate loads.

• Edge is typically installed by trenching prior to placement of adjacent paving. Bricks are mortared onto concrete base and backfilled with granular material.

• This detail is rated for medium-duty applications and is intended to support pedestrian and light vehicular loading.

• This detail is not designed for cold climates, where the use of mortar is discouraged in pavement design due to seasonal deterioration.

• Mortared brick edging is a moderate maintenance detail due to the need for regular pointing and sealing of joints.

• It is recommended that recycled and regionally available materials and products be given high priority in determining final design and specifications.

Installation Cost (per Linear Foot)

LOW   HIGH

$9.11

Maintenance

LOW   HIGH

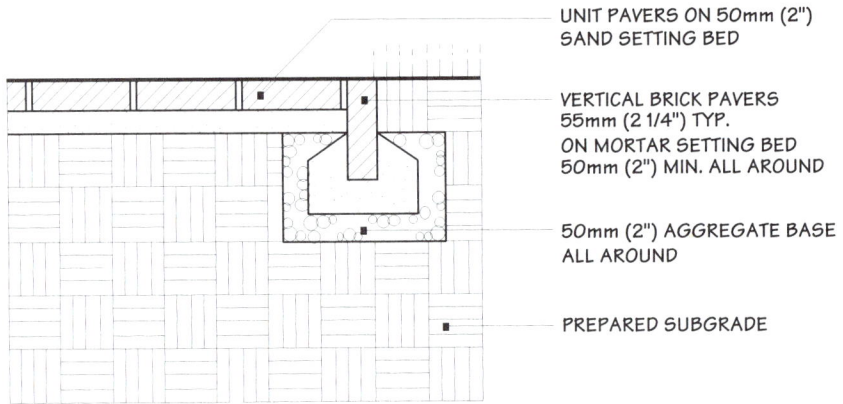

UNIT PAVERS ON 50mm (2")
SAND SETTING BED

VERTICAL BRICK PAVERS
55mm (2 1/4") TYP.
ON MORTAR SETTING BED
50mm (2") MIN. ALL AROUND

50mm (2") AGGREGATE BASE
ALL AROUND

PREPARED SUBGRADE

APPLICATION

CLIMATE

SUBGRADE

CSI MASTERFORMAT: 02780
DRAWING FILE: EDG04-06

• This drawing is a template for preliminary design only, and is not intended for bid purposes. It is subject to modification based on design calculations, local practices, and all applicable codes and regulations.

• This detail is typical of pedestrian path and plaza design in residential and garden settings. The bricks set on end provide a well-defined edge and prevent spreading of flexible brick pavers.

• Edge is typically installed by trenching prior to placement of adjacent paving. Mortar bed is laid on aggregate base, bricks set, and backfilled with granular material.

• This detail is rated for light-duty applications and is intended to support only pedestrian loading.

• This detail is not designed for cold climates, where the use of mortar is discouraged in pavement design due to seasonal deterioration.

• Mortared brick edging is a moderate maintenance detail due to the need for regular pointing and sealing of joints.

• It is recommended that recycled and regionally available materials and products be given high priority in determining final design and specifications.

Installation Cost (per Linear Foot)

LOW  HIGH

$6.08

Maintenance

LOW  HIGH

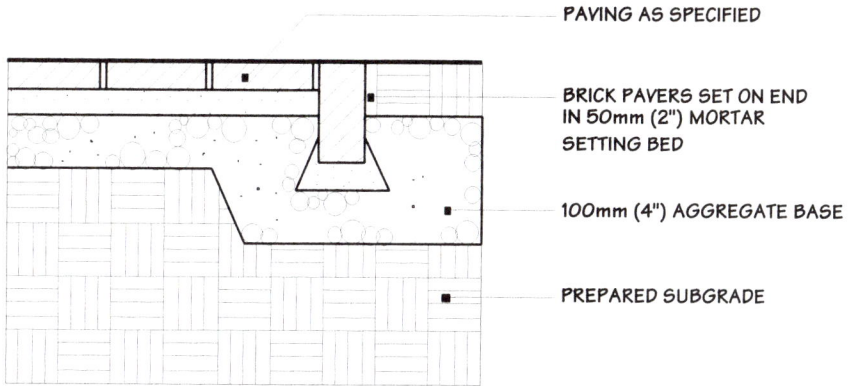

PAVING AS SPECIFIED

BRICK PAVERS SET ON END IN 50mm (2") MORTAR SETTING BED

100mm (4") AGGREGATE BASE

PREPARED SUBGRADE

APPLICATION

CLIMATE

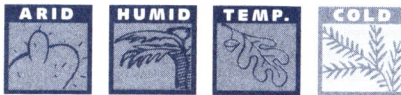

SUBGRADE

CSI MASTERFORMAT: 02780
DRAWING FILE: EDG04-05

• This drawing is a template for preliminary design only, and is not intended for bid purposes. It is subject to modification based on design calculations, local practices, and all applicable codes and regulations.

• This detail is typical of pedestrian path and plaza design in residential and garden settings. The bricks set on end provide a well-defined edge and prevent spreading of flexible brick pavers.

• Edge is typically installed by trenching prior to placement of adjacent paving. Mortar bed is laid on aggregate base, bricks set, and backfilled with granular material.

• This detail is rated for light-duty applications and is intended to support only pedestrian loading.

• This detail is not designed for cold climates, where the use of mortar in paving is discouraged due to seasonal deterioration. Rigid edge restraints may be more appropriate in cold settings.

• Mortared brick edging is a moderate maintenance detail due to the need for regular pointing and sealing of joints.

• It is recommended that recycled and regionally available materials and products be given high priority in determining final design and specifications.

Installation Cost (per Linear Foot)

LOW   HIGH

$7.98

Maintenance

LOW   HIGH

ALT. FLANGE EDGE

FINISH GRADE

"L" METAL STRIP W/SPIKES

BRICK PAVERS WITH SAND OR STONEDUST SWEPT JOINTS

25mm (1") SAND OR STONEDUST SETTING BED

150mm (6") AGGREGATE BASE EXTEND 150mm (6")

PREPARED SUBGRADE

APPLICATION

LIGHT | MED. | HEAVY

CLIMATE

ARID | HUMID | TEMP. | COLD

SUBGRADE

PERM. | CLAY | ROOF

CSI MASTERFORMAT: 02945
DRAWING FILE: EDG04-02

• This drawing is a template for preliminary design only, and is not intended for bid purposes. It is subject to modification based on design calculations, local practices, and all applicable codes and regulations.

• This detail is commonly used for pedestrian paths and paved areas in residential or garden settings. The metal "L" strip prevents lateral creeping of brick pavers due to loading over time.

• A variety of metal edging proprietary products are available, each with its own specifications. Edging is typically installed prior to placement of setting bed and brick pavers.

• This detail is rated for light-duty applications and may support pedestrian loading.

• Metal edging requires little or no special maintenance and is not subject to significant wearing.

• It is recommended that recycled and regionally available materials and products be given high priority in determining final design and specifications.

Installation Cost (per Linear Foot)
LOW HIGH

$3.00

Maintenance
LOW HIGH

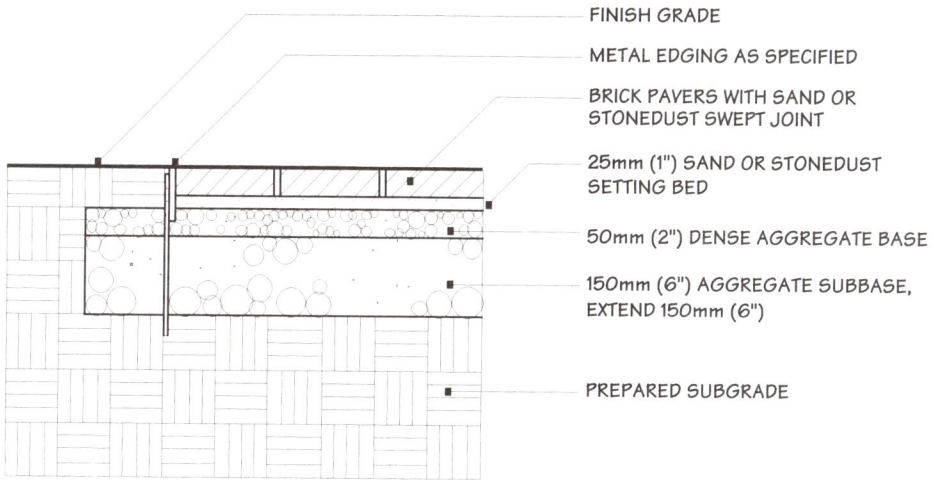

FINISH GRADE

METAL EDGING AS SPECIFIED

BRICK PAVERS WITH SAND OR STONEDUST SWEPT JOINT

25mm (1") SAND OR STONEDUST SETTING BED

50mm (2") DENSE AGGREGATE BASE

150mm (6") AGGREGATE SUBBASE, EXTEND 150mm (6")

PREPARED SUBGRADE

APPLICATION

CLIMATE

SUBGRADE

CSI MASTERFORMAT: 02945
DRAWING FILE: EDG04-01

• This drawing is a template for preliminary design only, and is not intended for bid purposes. It is subject to modification based on design calculations, local practices, and all applicable codes and regulations.

• This detail is commonly used for pedestrian paths and plaza design. The metal edge reinforces the edge and prevents lateral creeping of brick pavers due to loading over time.

• A variety of metal edging proprietary products are available, each with its own specifications. Edging is typically installed prior to placement of setting bed and brick pavers.

• This detail is rated for medium-duty applications and may support light vehicular loading.

• Metal edging requires little or no special maintenance and is not subject to significant wearing, but it does not provide a well-defined edge.

• It is recommended that recycled and regionally available materials and products be given high priority in determining final design and specifications.

Installation Cost (per Linear Foot)

LOW   HIGH

$3.00

Maintenance

LOW   HIGH

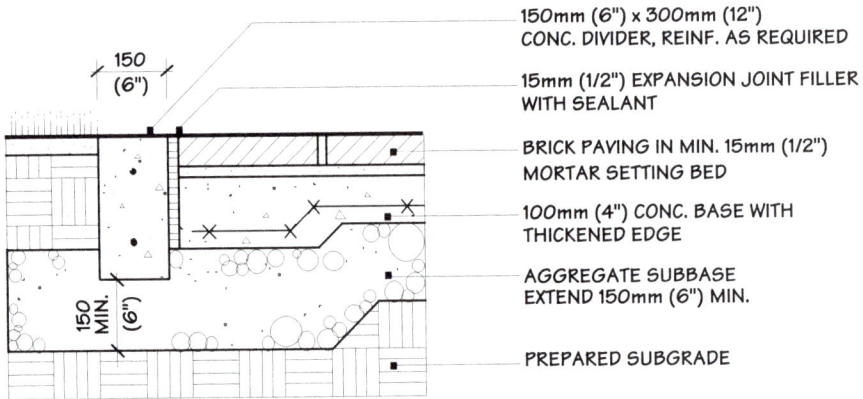

150
(6")

150mm (6") x 300mm (12")
CONC. DIVIDER, REINF. AS REQUIRED

15mm (1/2") EXPANSION JOINT FILLER
WITH SEALANT

BRICK PAVING IN MIN. 15mm (1/2")
MORTAR SETTING BED

100mm (4") CONC. BASE WITH
THICKENED EDGE

AGGREGATE SUBBASE
EXTEND 150mm (6") MIN.

PREPARED SUBGRADE

150 MIN. (6")

APPLICATION

CLIMATE

SUBGRADE

CSI MASTERFORMAT: 02770
DRAWING FILE: EDG02-06

• This drawing is for preliminary design only, and is not intended for bid purposes. It is subject to modification based on design calculations, local practices, and all applicable codes and regulations.

• This detail is typical of driveway or parking lot design. The thickened edge and concrete grade beam provides a well-defined edge and added reinforcement.

• The grade beam is typically a precast unit or may be cast-in-place, installed by backfilling with well-draining aggregate material. The unit is separated from the pavement by expansion joint filler, and is not tied to the concrete pavement base.

• This detail is rated for medium-duty applications due to the use of a moderate-sized grade beam, capable of supporting light vehicular loading.

• Reinforcing practices vary widely by region. Local codes and practices should be consulted prior to specifying any type of reinforcing.

• Subgrade conditions have a significant impact on the longevity of rigid pavements, such as mortared brick. The subgrade should be uniform to prevent pavement failure due to uneven soil expansion and contraction. This detail provides a well-drained aggregate base to drain sub-surface moisture and increase uniformity.

• Rigid pavement design must accommodate movement of materials by providing adequate expansion and control joints, particularly in regions of extreme temperature fluctuations. If designed for temperate or cold climates, air-entrained concrete is typically recommended due to freezing/thawing action.

• Concrete grade beams provide a well-defined edge and require only moderate maintenance, consisting of occasional cleaning and re-sealing of expansion joints.

• It is recommended that recycled and regionally available materials and products be given high priority in determining final design and specifications.

Installation Cost (per Linear Foot)

LOW   HIGH

$5.28

Maintenance

LOW   HIGH

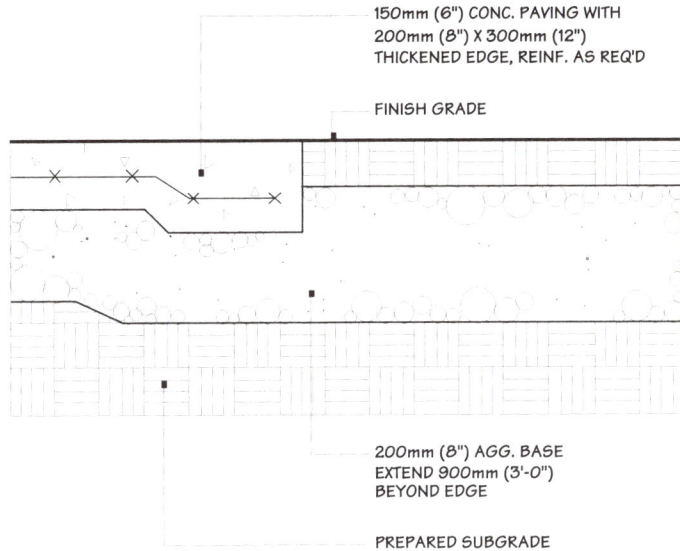

150mm (6") CONC. PAVING WITH
200mm (8") X 300mm (12")
THICKENED EDGE, REINF. AS REQ'D

FINISH GRADE

200mm (8") AGG. BASE
EXTEND 900mm (3'-0")
BEYOND EDGE

PREPARED SUBGRADE

APPLICATION

CLIMATE

SUBGRADE

CSI MASTERFORMAT: 02750
DRAWING FILE: EDG02-02

• This drawing is for preliminary design only, and is not intended for bid purposes. It is subject to modification based on design calculations, local practices, and all applicable codes and regulations.

• This detail is typical of concrete roadway and parking lot design in coastal regions with sandy soils. The thickened edge provides added reinforcement and prevents undermining of the pavement by plant roots and wind erosion.

• This detail is rated for heavy-duty applications due to a thickend edge and a well-drained base that provides uniform support for moderate loads.

• The base is extended well beyond the pavement edge, past the load bearing angle, for sufficient reinforcement.

• Reinforcing practices vary widely by region. Local codes and practices should be consulted prior to specifying any type of reinforcing.

• Rigid pavement design must accommodate movement of materials by providing adequate expansion and control joints, particularly in regions of extreme temperature fluctuations. If designed for temperate or cold climates, air-entrained concrete is typically recommended due to freezing/thawing action.

• Subgrade conditions have a significant impact on the longevity of rigid pavements, such as concrete. The subgrade should be uniform to prevent pavement failure due to uneven soil expansion and contraction. This detail provides a well-drained aggregate base to drain sub-surface moisture and increase uniformity.

• Thickened edges require little or no special maintenance and are not subject to significant wearing, unlike containment edges or curbing.

• It is recommended that recycled and regionally available materials and products be given high priority in determining final design and specifications.

Installation Cost (per Linear Foot)

LOW   HIGH

$6.88

Maintenance

LOW   HIGH

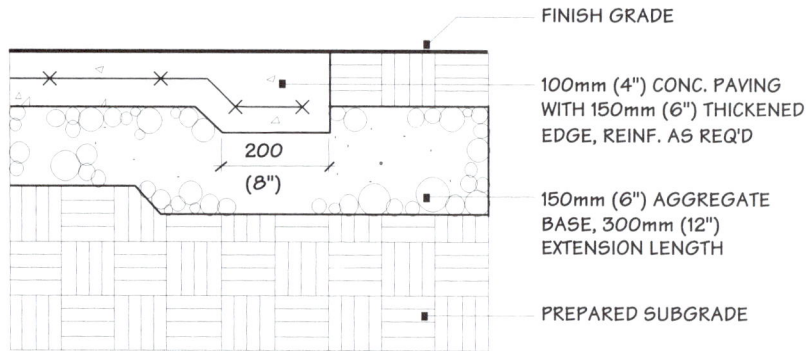

FINISH GRADE

100mm (4") CONC. PAVING WITH 150mm (6") THICKENED EDGE, REINF. AS REQ'D

150mm (6") AGGREGATE BASE, 300mm (12") EXTENSION LENGTH

PREPARED SUBGRADE

200 (8")

APPLICATION

CLIMATE

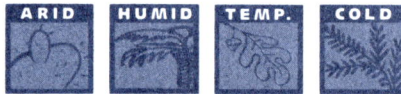

SUBGRADE

CSI MASTERFORMAT: 02750
DRAWING FILE: EDG02-01

• This drawing is for preliminary design only, and is not intended for bid purposes. It is subject to modification based on design calculations, local practices, and all applicable codes and regulations.

• This detail is typical of concrete driveway and parking lot design in coastal regions with sandy soils. The thickened edge provides added reinforcement and prevents undermining of the pavement by plant roots and wind erosion.

• This detail is rated for medium-duty applications due to a thickend edge and a well-drained base that provides uniform support for moderate loads.

• The base is extended beyond the pavement edge, past the load bearing angle, for sufficient reinforcement.

• Reinforcing practices vary widely by region. Local codes and practices should be consulted prior to specifying any type of reinforcing.

• Rigid pavement design must accommodate movement of materials by providing adequate expansion and control joints, particularly in regions of extreme temperature fluctuations. If designed for temperate or cold climates, air-entrained concrete is typically recommended due to freezing/thawing action.

• Subgrade conditions have a significant impact on the longevity of rigid pavements, such as concrete. The subgrade should be uniform to prevent pavement failure due to uneven soil expansion and contraction. This detail provides a well-drained aggregate base to drain sub-surface moisture and increase uniformity.

• Thickened edges require little or no special maintenance and are not subject to significant wearing, unlike containment edges or curbing.

• It is recommended that recycled and regionally available materials and products be given high priority in determining final design and specifications.

Installation Cost (per Linear Foot)

LOW   HIGH

$2.75

Maintenance

LOW   HIGH

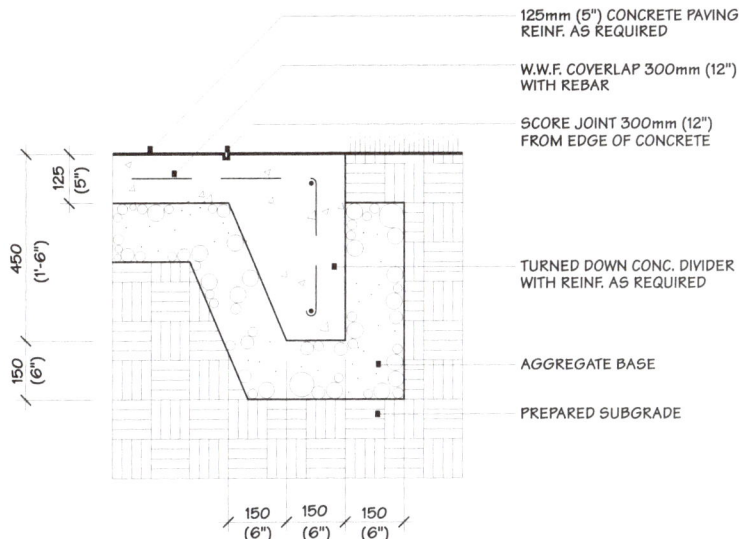

125mm (5") CONCRETE PAVING REINF. AS REQUIRED

W.W.F. COVERLAP 300mm (12") WITH REBAR

SCORE JOINT 300mm (12") FROM EDGE OF CONCRETE

TURNED DOWN CONC. DIVIDER WITH REINF. AS REQUIRED

AGGREGATE BASE

PREPARED SUBGRADE

125 (5") 450 (1'-6") 150 (6")

150 (6") 150 (6") 150 (6")

APPLICATION

CLIMATE

SUBGRADE

CSI MASTERFORMAT: 02770
DRAWING FILE: EDG02-05

• This drawing is for preliminary design only, and is not intended for bid purposes. It is subject to modification based on design calculations, local practices, and all applicable codes and regulations.

• This detail is typical of concrete driveway and parking lot design. The turn-down edge provides added reinforcement.

• This detail is rated for medium-duty applications based on thickness of concrete and aggregate base, and may be required to bear light vehicular loads.

• The edge is trenched, formed, and poured in conjunction with the adjacent pavement.

• Reinforcing practices vary widely by region. Local codes and practices should be consulted prior to specifying any type of reinforcing.

• Rigid pavement design must accommodate movement of materials by providing adequate expansion and control joints, par-

ticularly in regions of extreme temperature fluctuations. If designed for temperate or cold climates, air-entrained concrete is typically recommended due to freezing/thawing action.

• Subgrade conditions have a significant impact on the longevity of rigid pavements, such as concrete. The subgrade should be uniform to prevent pavement failure due to uneven soil expansion and contraction. This detail provides a well-drained aggregate base to drain sub-surface moisture and increase uniformity.

• Turn-down edges require little or no special maintenance and are not subject to significant wearing, unlike containment edges or curbing.

• It is recommended that recycled and regionally available materials and products be given high priority in determining final design and specifications.

Installation Cost (per Linear Foot)

LOW   HIGH

$5.24

Maintenance

LOW   HIGH

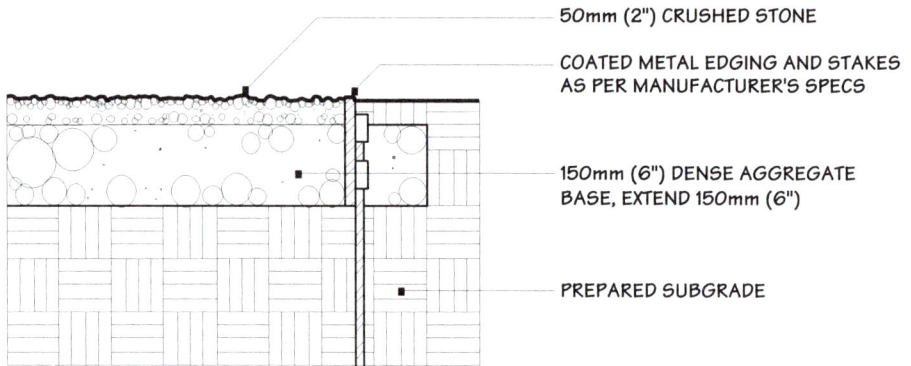

50mm (2") CRUSHED STONE

COATED METAL EDGING AND STAKES
AS PER MANUFACTURER'S SPECS

150mm (6") DENSE AGGREGATE
BASE, EXTEND 150mm (6")

PREPARED SUBGRADE

APPLICATION

CLIMATE

SUBGRADE

CSI MASTERFORMAT: 02945
DRAWING FILE: EDG06-03

• This drawing is a template for preliminary design only, and is not intended for bid purposes. It is subject to modification based on design calculations, local practices, and all applicable codes and regulations.

• This detail is commonly used for pedestrian paths and plaza design. The metal strip serves to contain aggregate paving material.

• A variety of metal edging proprietary products are available, each with its own specifications. Edging is typically installed prior to placement of aggregate paving.

• This detail is rated for medium-duty applications and is capable of supporting light vehicular loading.

• Metal edging is relatively easy to install, but requires moderate maintenance for raking and retrieving of scattered aggregate material.

• It is recommended that recycled and regionally available materials and products be given high priority in determining final design and specifications.

Installation Cost (per Linear Foot)

LOW   HIGH

$3.57

Maintenance

LOW   HIGH

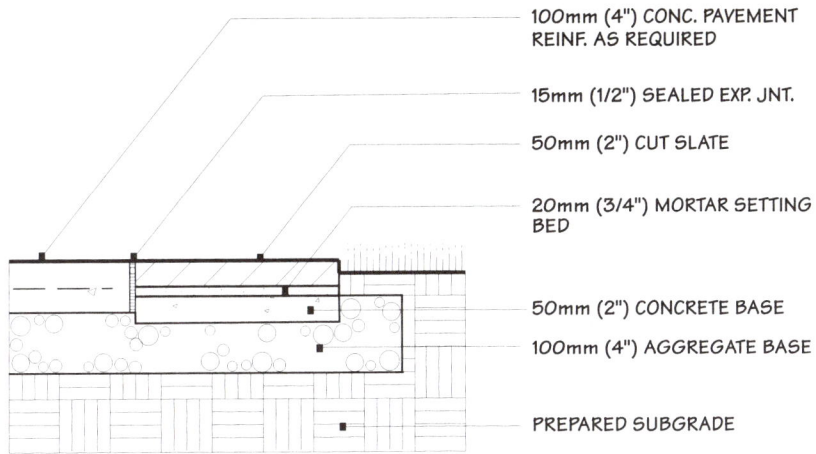

100mm (4") CONC. PAVEMENT REINF. AS REQUIRED

15mm (1/2") SEALED EXP. JNT.

50mm (2") CUT SLATE

20mm (3/4") MORTAR SETTING BED

50mm (2") CONCRETE BASE

100mm (4") AGGREGATE BASE

PREPARED SUBGRADE

APPLICATION

CLIMATE

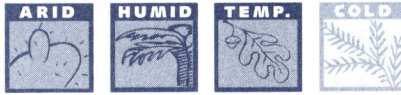

SUBGRADE

CSI MASTERFORMAT: 02780
DRAWING FILE: EDG03-02

• This drawing is a template for preliminary design only, and is not intended for bid purposes. It is subject to modification based on design calculations, local practices, and all applicable codes and regulations.

• This slate edge on concrete base detail is rated as light-duty and is commonly used for pedestrian paths and plaza design in residential, garden, and park settings. The cut stone edge provides a transition between pavement and turf or between turf and garden in mild climate regions.

• Stone units are mortared onto a concrete base on aggregate subbase, which extends beyond the stone edge for reinforcement.

• Cut stone pavers provide a very durable surface highly resistant to abrasion resulting from normal wear and maintenance. Metamorphic and igneous stone is preferred.

• Edge may require periodic re-pointing.

• It is recommended that recycled and regionally available materials and products be given high priority in determining final design and specifications.

Installation Cost (per Linear Foot)

LOW   HIGH

$8.00

Maintenance

LOW   HIGH

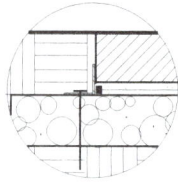

ALT. FLANGE EDGE

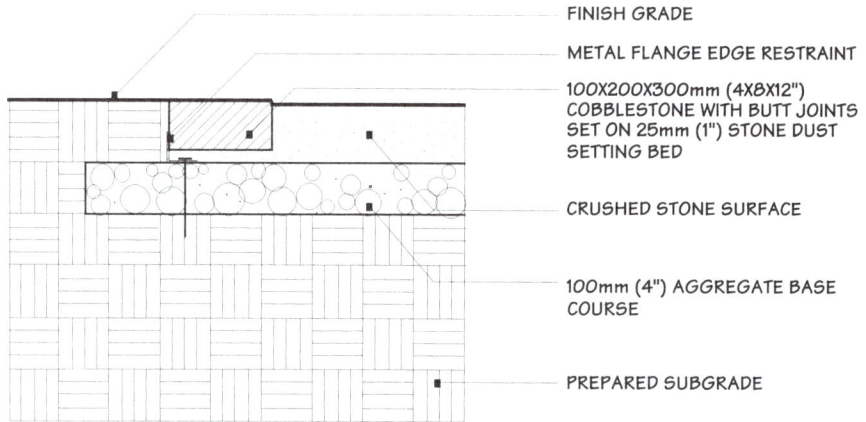

FINISH GRADE

METAL FLANGE EDGE RESTRAINT

100X200X300mm (4X8X12")
COBBLESTONE WITH BUTT JOINTS
SET ON 25mm (1") STONE DUST
SETTING BED

CRUSHED STONE SURFACE

100mm (4") AGGREGATE BASE
COURSE

PREPARED SUBGRADE

APPLICATION

CLIMATE

SUBGRADE

CSI MASTERFORMAT: 02780
DRAWING FILE: EDG03-01

• This drawing is a template for preliminary design only, and is not intended for bid purposes. It is subject to modification based on design calculations, local practices, and all applicable codes and regulations.

• This cobblestone edge detail is rated as light-duty and is commonly used for pedestrian paths and plaza design in residential, garden, and park settings. The metal edge reinforces the pavement and prevents lateral creeping of stone pavement due to loading over time.

• Stone edge units are placed on a 25 mm (1") setting bed to level irregularities in the cobblestones, and butt joints are sand swept and wetted down for final setting.

• A variety of metal edging proprietary products are available, each with its own specifications. Edging is typically installed prior to placement of setting bed and unit pavers.

• Cut stone pavers provide a very durable surface highly resistant to abrasion resulting from normal wear and maintenance. Metamorphic and igneous stone is preferred.

• Edge may require hand, mechanical, or non-toxic chemical weeding (inert compounds and fatty acids, etc.).

• It is recommended that recycled and regionally available materials and products be given high priority in determining final design and specifications.

Installation Cost (per Linear Foot)

LOW   HIGH

$6.00

Maintenance

LOW   HIGH

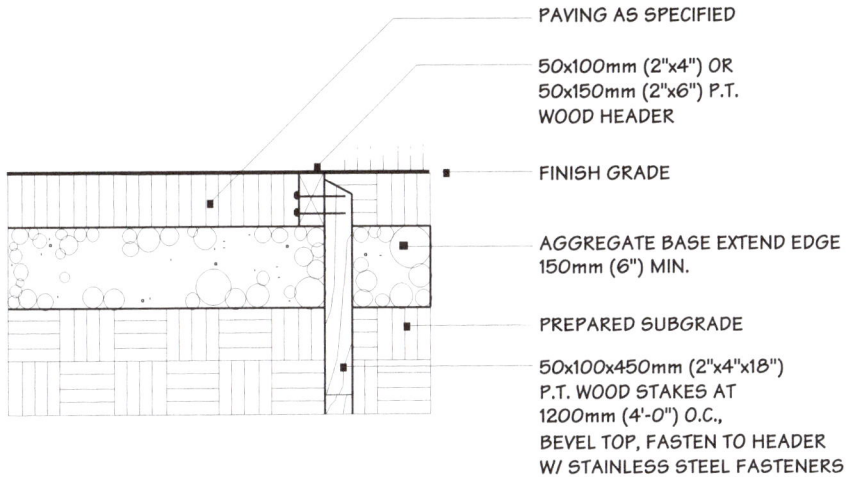

PAVING AS SPECIFIED

50x100mm (2"x4") OR
50x150mm (2"x6") P.T.
WOOD HEADER

FINISH GRADE

AGGREGATE BASE EXTEND EDGE
150mm (6") MIN.

PREPARED SUBGRADE

50x100x450mm (2"x4"x18")
P.T. WOOD STAKES AT
1200mm (4'-0") O.C.,
BEVEL TOP, FASTEN TO HEADER
W/ STAINLESS STEEL FASTENERS

APPLICATION

CLIMATE

SUBGRADE

CSI MASTERFORMAT: 02945
DRAWING FILE: EDG05-01

• This drawing is a template for preliminary design only, and is not intended for bid purposes. It is subject to modification based on design calculations, local practices, and all applicable codes and regulations.

• This detail is typical of paved areas in residential and garden settings. Wood provides a well-defined edge and prevents spreading of flexible paving systems.

• Wood is typically pressure-treated to resist decay, and all metal fasteners should be corrosion-resistant.

• This detail is rated for light-duty applications and is intended to support primarily pedestrian loading.

• This detail is not designed for cold climates. Wood stakes may be subject to heaving in both clay soils and extreme frost conditions. Steel edging is preferred under these conditions.

• Wood edging requires only minimal maintenance, but it provides a relatively short term of service due to decay.

• It is recommended that recycled and regionally available materials and products be given high priority in determining final design and specifications.

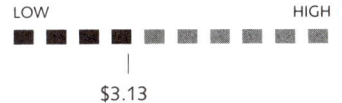

Installation Cost (per Linear Foot)

LOW HIGH

$3.13

Maintenance

LOW HIGH

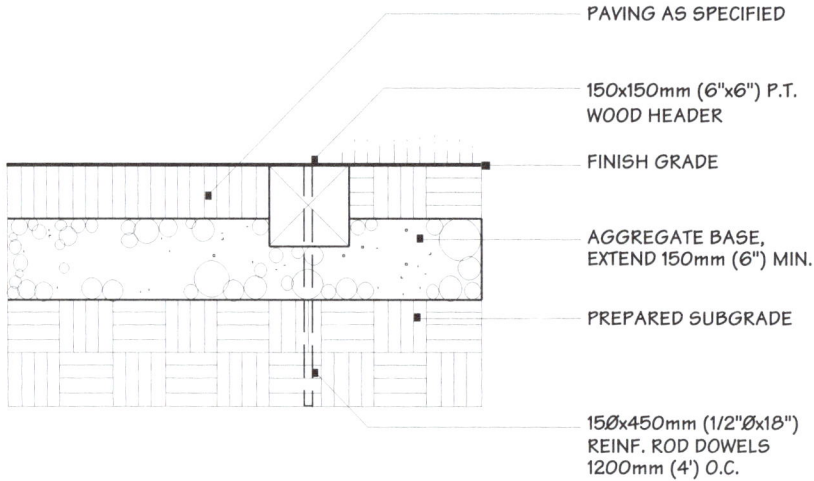

PAVING AS SPECIFIED

150x150mm (6"x6") P.T.
WOOD HEADER

FINISH GRADE

AGGREGATE BASE,
EXTEND 150mm (6") MIN.

PREPARED SUBGRADE

15Øx450mm (1/2"Øx18")
REINF. ROD DOWELS
1200mm (4') O.C.

APPLICATION

CLIMATE

SUBGRADE

CSI MASTERFORMAT: 02945
DRAWING FILE: EDG05-02

• This drawing is a template for preliminary design only, and is not intended for bid purposes. It is subject to modification based on design calculations, local practices, and all applicable codes and regulations.

• This detail is typical of paved areas in residential and garden settings. Wood provides a well-defined edge and prevents spreading of flexible paving systems.

• Wood is typically pressure-treated to resist decay.

• This detail is rated for medium-duty applications and is intended to support pedestrian and light vehicular loading.

• Steel pin anchoring prevents movement of wood edge, and is suitable for clay soils and cold climates.

• Wood edging requires only minimal maintenance, but is subject to eventual decay.

• It is recommended that recycled and regionally available materials and products be given high priority in determining final design and specifications.

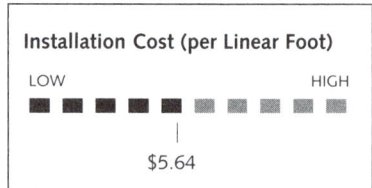

Installation Cost (per Linear Foot)

LOW   HIGH

$5.64

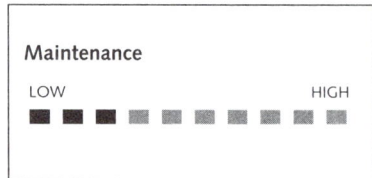

Maintenance

LOW   HIGH

Paving Joints

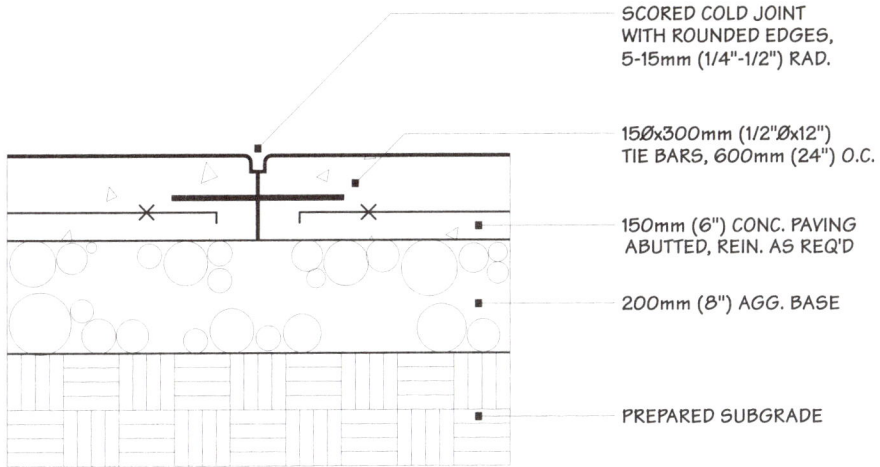

SCORED COLD JOINT
WITH ROUNDED EDGES,
5-15mm (1/4"-1/2") RAD.

15Øx300mm (1/2"Øx12")
TIE BARS, 600mm (24") O.C.

150mm (6") CONC. PAVING
ABUTTED, REIN. AS REQ'D

200mm (8") AGG. BASE

PREPARED SUBGRADE

APPLICATION

LIGHT | MED. | HEAVY

CLIMATE

ARID | HUMID | TEMP. | COLD

SUBGRADE

PERM. | CLAY | ROOF

CSI MASTERFORMAT: 03100
DRAWING FILE: JNT12-03

• This drawing is a template for preliminary design only, and is not intended for bid purposes. It is subject to modification based on design calculations, local practices, and all applicable codes and regulations.

• Cold or butt joints are used to join slabs poured at different times, in climates without significant expansion due to freezing and thawing. Joints may be scored during finishing. Tie bars are used to transfer loads between the slabs.

• This detail is rated for heavy-duty applications, due to the relatively thick concrete slab and aggregate base illustrated. However, control joints are similar for all types of applications. If thinner slabs are used, they may need to be thickened at the joint to provide adequate coverage of tie bars.

• This detail is designed for climates which are not subject to freezing conditions. Keyed joints offer a stronger alternative in temperate and cold climates, where movement of materials is greater.

• Cold or butt joints require no special maintenance practices in hot-arid and hot-humid climates.

• It is recommended that recycled and regionally available materials and products be given high priority in determining final design and specifications.

Installation Cost (per Linear Foot)

LOW   HIGH

|
$1.14

Maintenance

LOW   HIGH

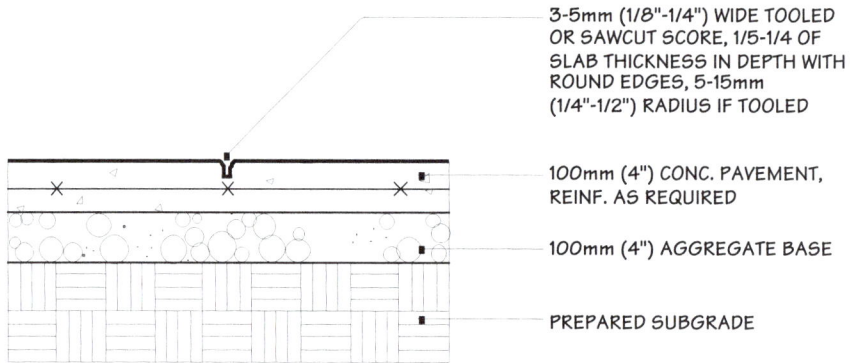

3-5mm (1/8"-1/4") WIDE TOOLED OR SAWCUT SCORE, 1/5-1/4 OF SLAB THICKNESS IN DEPTH WITH ROUND EDGES, 5-15mm (1/4"-1/2") RADIUS IF TOOLED

100mm (4") CONC. PAVEMENT, REINF. AS REQUIRED

100mm (4") AGGREGATE BASE

PREPARED SUBGRADE

APPLICATION

CLIMATE

SUBGRADE

CSI MASTERFORMAT:
DRAWING FILE: JNT12-01

• This drawing is a template for preliminary design only, and is not intended for bid purposes. It is subject to modification based on design calculations, local practices, and all applicable codes and regulations.

• Control joints are designed to restrict the cracking of concrete to predetermined locations due to contraction. Joints may be tooled during finishing, or sawn after the concrete is firm enough to avoid damage, usually 12 to 24 hours after finishing.

• This detail is rated for light-duty applications, due to the relatively thin concrete slab and aggregate base illustrated. However, control joints are similar for all types of applications and are proportional to pavement depth.

• The spacing of control joints is a function of the slab's thickness and the expected shrinkage of the concrete. Typically, concrete slabs 100mm (4") thick or greater should have control joints about every 2.5 to 3M (8-10') apart. Joints may need to be spaced more frequently in areas of rapid temperature change.

• In temperate and cold climates, control joints should be sloped with the pavement surface to prevent ponding and freeze/thaw action.

• It is recommended that recycled and regionally available materials and products be given high priority in determining final design and specifications.

Installation Cost (per Linear Foot)

LOW   HIGH

$0.04

Maintenance

LOW   HIGH

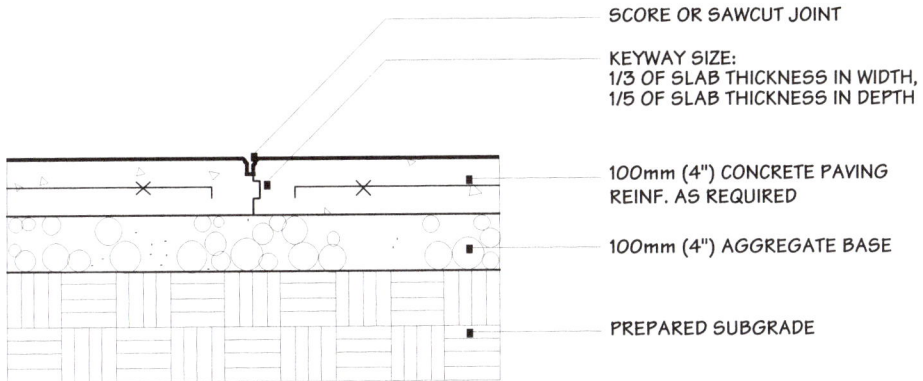

SCORE OR SAWCUT JOINT

KEYWAY SIZE:
1/3 OF SLAB THICKNESS IN WIDTH,
1/5 OF SLAB THICKNESS IN DEPTH

100mm (4") CONCRETE PAVING
REINF. AS REQUIRED

100mm (4") AGGREGATE BASE

PREPARED SUBGRADE

APPLICATION

CLIMATE

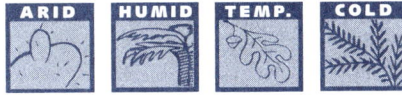

SUBGRADE

CSI MASTERFORMAT: 02775
DRAWING FILE: JNT12-04

• This drawing is a template for preliminary design only, and is not intended for bid purposes. It is subject to modification based on design calculations, local practices, and all applicable codes and regulations.

• Keyed control joints are used to join slabs poured at different times. Joints may be scored during finishing. Keyways are used to transfer loads between the slabs.

• This detail is rated for light-duty applications, due to the relatively thin concrete slab and aggregate base illustrated. However, control joints are similar for all types of applications.

• Keyed joints are particularly useful in temperate and cold climates, where movement of materials is greater. If used as an expansion joint, pre-molded filler is attached to the form to create a sealed expansion seam.

• In temperate and cold climates, control joints require adequate lateral drainage, typically associated with slab cross-slope.

• It is recommended that recycled and regionally available materials and products be given high priority in determining final design and specifications.

Installation Cost (per Linear Foot)

LOW   HIGH

$1.15

Maintenance

LOW   HIGH

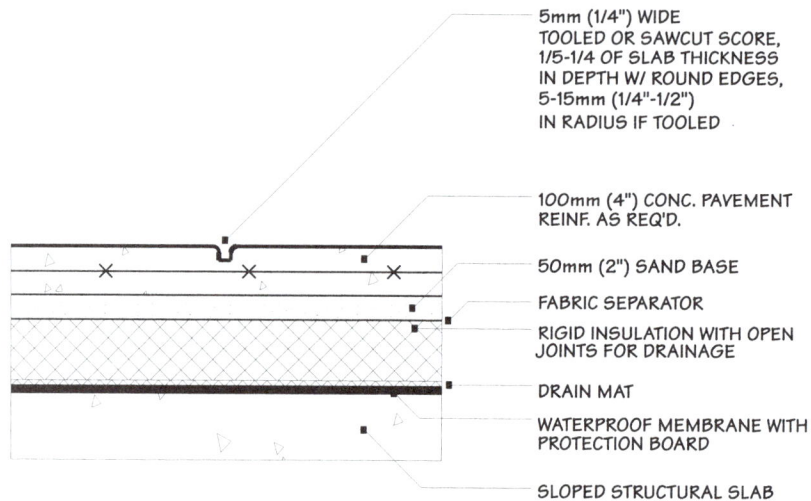

5mm (1/4") WIDE
TOOLED OR SAWCUT SCORE,
1/5-1/4 OF SLAB THICKNESS
IN DEPTH W/ ROUND EDGES,
5-15mm (1/4"-1/2")
IN RADIUS IF TOOLED

100mm (4") CONC. PAVEMENT
REINF. AS REQ'D.

50mm (2") SAND BASE

FABRIC SEPARATOR

RIGID INSULATION WITH OPEN
JOINTS FOR DRAINAGE

DRAIN MAT

WATERPROOF MEMBRANE WITH
PROTECTION BOARD

SLOPED STRUCTURAL SLAB

APPLICATION

CLIMATE

SUBGRADE

CSI MASTERFORMAT: 02775

DRAWING FILE: JNT12-02

• This drawing is a template for preliminary design only, and is not intended for bid purposes. It is subject to modification based on design calculations, local practices, and all applicable codes and regulations.

• Control joints are designed to restrict the cracking of concrete to predetermined locations due to contraction. Joints may be tooled during finishing, or sawn after the concrete is firm enough to avoid damage, usually 12 to 24 hours after finishing.

• This detail is rated for light-duty applications, due to the relatively thin concrete slab and presence of insulation, as illustrated. However, control joints are similar for all types of applications.

• The spacing of control joints is a function of the slab's thickness and the expected shrinkage of the concrete. Typically, concrete slabs 100mm (4") thick or greater should have control joints about every 2.5 to 3M (8-10') apart. Joints may need to be spaced more frequently in areas of rapid temperature change.

• In temperate and cold climates, control joints should be sloped with the pavement surface to prevent ponding and freeze/thaw action.

• It is recommended that recycled and regionally available materials and products be given high priority in determining final design and specifications.

Installation Cost (per Linear Foot)

LOW   HIGH

$0.04

Maintenance

LOW   HIGH

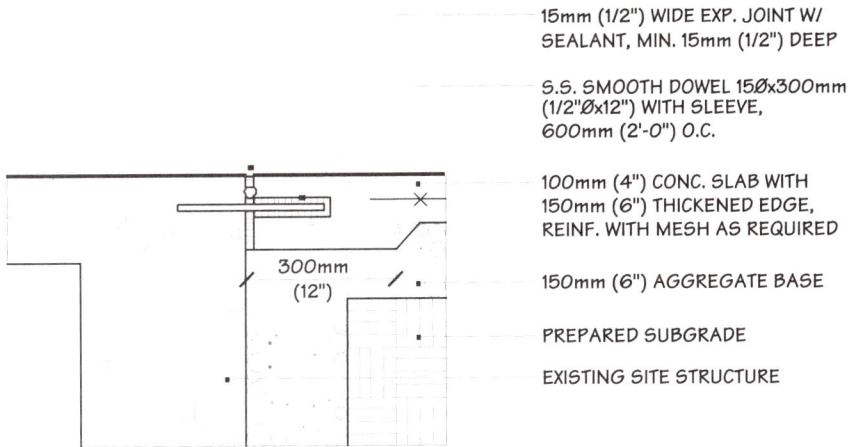

15mm (1/2") WIDE EXP. JOINT W/ SEALANT, MIN. 15mm (1/2") DEEP

S.S. SMOOTH DOWEL 15Øx300mm (1/2"Øx12") WITH SLEEVE, 600mm (2'-0") O.C.

100mm (4") CONC. SLAB WITH 150mm (6") THICKENED EDGE, REINF. WITH MESH AS REQUIRED

150mm (6") AGGREGATE BASE

PREPARED SUBGRADE

EXISTING SITE STRUCTURE

300mm (12")

APPLICATION

CLIMATE

SUBGRADE

CSI MASTERFORMAT: 03150
DRAWING FILE: JNT32-02

• This drawing is a template for preliminary design only, and is not intended for bid purposes. It is subject to modification based on design calculations, local practices, and all applicable codes and regulations.

• Expansion joints are used to accommodate the movement of materials in rigid pavements, such as brick mortared on a concrete base. This joint is placed between concrete pavement and an existing site structure. A thickened edge is provided for added pavement strength.

• Joints are filled with a variety of proprietary filler materials, depending on climate. Backer rods are placed on top of filler material as additional fill, and to prevent the sealant from bonding to the filler material.

• Smooth dowels are used to transfer loads between slab and structure, and to minimize vertical movement, while accommodating lateral movement of materials.

• This detail is rated for light-duty applications, based on the thickness of the concrete slab and aggregate base illustrated. However, expansion joints are similar for all types of applications.

• This detail is not designed for cold climates with extreme freezing conditions. Keyed or sill joints offer a stronger alternative in these climates, where movement of materials is greater.

• In temperate climates, the expansion joint should be caulked or sealed with elastomeric material, to minimize moisture and debris penetration. Occasional re-sealing is typically the only maintenance related to these joints.

• It is recommended that recycled and regionally available materials and products be given high priority in determining final design and specifications.

Installation Cost (per Linear Foot)

LOW   HIGH

$8.80

Maintenance

LOW   HIGH

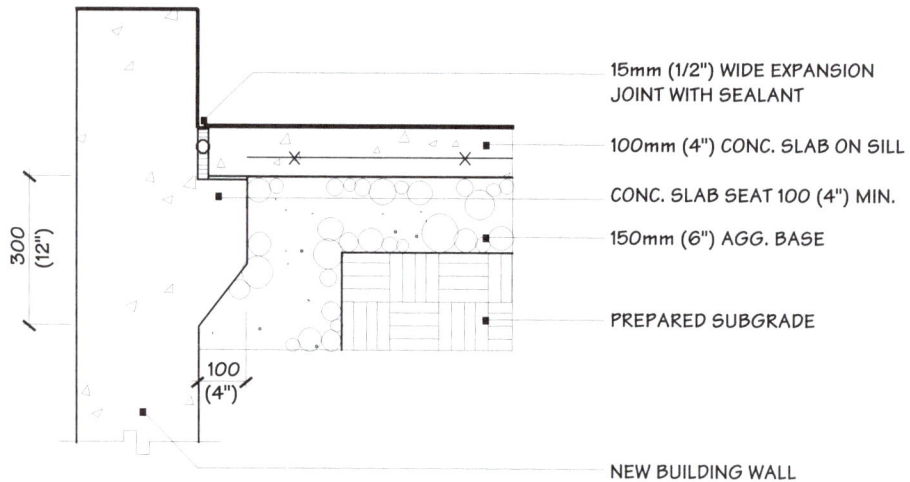

15mm (1/2") WIDE EXPANSION JOINT WITH SEALANT

100mm (4") CONC. SLAB ON SILL

CONC. SLAB SEAT 100 (4") MIN.

150mm (6") AGG. BASE

PREPARED SUBGRADE

NEW BUILDING WALL

300 (12")

100 (4")

APPLICATION

CLIMATE

SUBGRADE

CSI MASTERFORMAT: 03150

DRAWING FILE: JNT32-04

• This drawing is a template for preliminary design only, and is not intended for bid purposes. It is subject to modification based on design calculations, local practices, and all applicable codes and regulations.

• Expansion joints are used to accommodate the movement of materials in rigid pavements, such as brick mortared on a concrete base. This joint is placed between concrete pavement and a new site structure. A concrete sill is provided at the pavement edge for added strength.

• Joints are filled with a variety of proprietary filler materials, depending on climate. Backer rods are placed on top of filler material as additional fill, and to prevent the sealant from bonding to the filler material.

• This detail is rated for light-duty applications based on the thickness of the concrete slab and aggregate base illustrated. However, expansion joints are similar for all types of applications.

• In temperate and cold climates, the expansion joint should be caulked or sealed with elastomeric material, to minimize moisture and debris penetration. Occasional resealing is typically the only maintenance related to these joints.

• It is recommended that recycled and regionally available materials and products be given high priority in determining final design and specifications.

Installation Cost (per Linear Foot)

LOW   HIGH

$3.14

Maintenance

LOW   HIGH

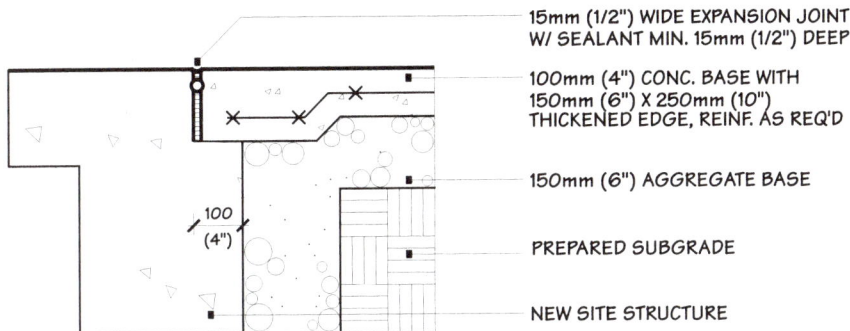

15mm (1/2") WIDE EXPANSION JOINT
W/ SEALANT MIN. 15mm (1/2") DEEP

100mm (4") CONC. BASE WITH
150mm (6") X 250mm (10")
THICKENED EDGE, REINF. AS REQ'D

150mm (6") AGGREGATE BASE

PREPARED SUBGRADE

NEW SITE STRUCTURE

100 (4")

APPLICATION

CLIMATE

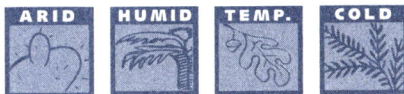

SUBGRADE

CSI MASTERFORMAT: 03150
DRAWING FILE: JNT32-01

• This drawing is a template for preliminary design only, and is not intended for bid purposes. It is subject to modification based on design calculations, local practices, and all applicable codes and regulations.

• Expansion joints are used to accommodate the movement of materials in rigid pavements, such as brick mortared on a concrete base. This joint is placed between concrete pavement and a new site structure. A thickened edge and sill are provided for added pavement strength.

• Joints are filled with a variety of proprietary filler materials, depending on climate. Backer rods are placed on top of filler material as additional fill, and to prevent the sealant from bonding to the filler material.

• This detail is rated for medium-duty applications, based on the thickness of the concrete slab and aggregate base illustrated. However, expansion joints are similar for all types of applications.

• In temperate and cold climates, the expansion joint should be caulked or sealed with elastomeric material, to minimize moisture and debris penetration. Occasional re-sealing is typically the only maintenance related to these joints.

• It is recommended that recycled and regionally available materials and products be given high priority in determining final design and specifications.

Installation Cost (per Linear Foot)

LOW　　　　　　　　　　　　　　HIGH

$1.65

Maintenance

LOW　　　　　　　　　　　　　　HIGH

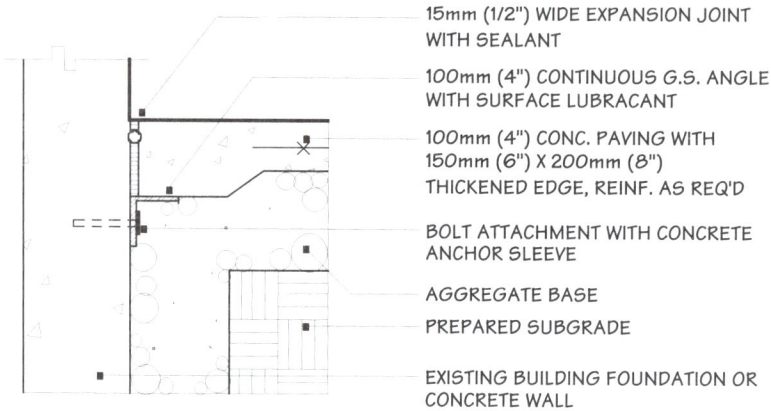

15mm (1/2") WIDE EXPANSION JOINT
WITH SEALANT

100mm (4") CONTINUOUS G.S. ANGLE
WITH SURFACE LUBRACANT

100mm (4") CONC. PAVING WITH
150mm (6") X 200mm (8")
THICKENED EDGE, REINF. AS REQ'D

BOLT ATTACHMENT WITH CONCRETE
ANCHOR SLEEVE

AGGREGATE BASE

PREPARED SUBGRADE

EXISTING BUILDING FOUNDATION OR
CONCRETE WALL

APPLICATION

CLIMATE

SUBGRADE

CSI MASTERFORMAT: 03150
DRAWING FILE: JNT32-03

• This drawing is a template for preliminary design only, and is not intended for bid purposes. It is subject to modification based on design calculations, local practices, and all applicable codes and regulations.

• Expansion joints are used to accommodate the movement of materials in rigid pavements, such as brick mortared on a concrete base. This joint is placed between concrete pavement and an existing site structure. A thickened edge and metal flange sill is provided for added pavement strength.

• Joints are filled with a variety of proprietary filler materials, depending on climate. Backer rods are placed on top of filler material as additional fill, and to prevent the sealant from bonding to the filler material.

• This detail is rated for light-duty applications and is designed to accommodate primarily pedestrian loading. Heavier loading would require greater reinforcement of the edge through use of a grade beam or turndown design.

• This detail is not designed for cold climates with extreme freezing conditions. Keyed or sill joints offer a stronger alternative in these climates, where movement of materials is greater.

• In temperate climates, the expansion joint should be caulked or sealed with elastomeric material, to minimize moisture and debris penetration. Occasional re-sealing is typically the only maintenance related to these joints.

• It is recommended that recycled and regionally available materials and products be given high priority in determining final design and specifications.

Installation Cost (per Linear Foot)

$5.35

Maintenance

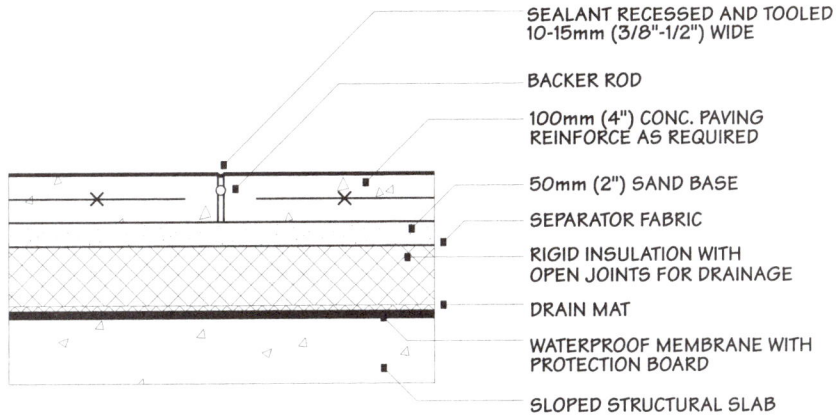

- SEALANT RECESSED AND TOOLED 10-15mm (3/8"-1/2") WIDE
- BACKER ROD
- 100mm (4") CONC. PAVING REINFORCE AS REQUIRED
- 50mm (2") SAND BASE
- SEPARATOR FABRIC
- RIGID INSULATION WITH OPEN JOINTS FOR DRAINAGE
- DRAIN MAT
- WATERPROOF MEMBRANE WITH PROTECTION BOARD
- SLOPED STRUCTURAL SLAB

APPLICATION

CLIMATE

SUBGRADE

CSI MASTERFORMAT: 03150
DRAWING FILE: JNT22-02

- This drawing is a template for preliminary design only, and is not intended for bid purposes. It is subject to modification based on design calculations, local practices, and all applicable codes and regulations.

- Expansion joints are used to accommodate the movement of materials in rigid pavements, such as concrete. Joints are placed between slabs or between site structures and the pavement.

- Joints are filled with a variety of proprietary filler materials, depending on climate. Backer rods are placed on top of filler material as additional fill, and to prevent the sealant from bonding to the filler material.

- This detail is rated for light-duty applications, based on the thickness of the concrete slab and aggregate base illustrated. However, expansion joints are similar for all types of applications.

- In temperate and cold climates, the expansion joint should be caulked or sealed with elastomeric material, to minimize moisture and debris penetration. Occasional resealing is typically the only maintenance related to these joints.

- It is recommended that recycled and regionally available materials and products be given high priority in determining final design and specifications.

Installation Cost (per Linear Foot)

LOW — HIGH

$2.50

Maintenance

LOW — HIGH

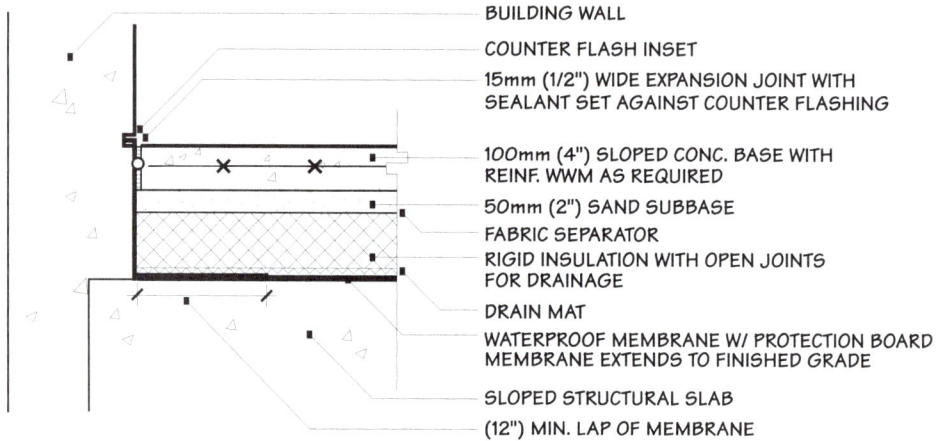

BUILDING WALL

COUNTER FLASH INSET

15mm (1/2") WIDE EXPANSION JOINT WITH
SEALANT SET AGAINST COUNTER FLASHING

100mm (4") SLOPED CONC. BASE WITH
REINF. WWM AS REQUIRED

50mm (2") SAND SUBBASE

FABRIC SEPARATOR

RIGID INSULATION WITH OPEN JOINTS
FOR DRAINAGE

DRAIN MAT

WATERPROOF MEMBRANE W/ PROTECTION BOARD
MEMBRANE EXTENDS TO FINISHED GRADE

SLOPED STRUCTURAL SLAB

(12") MIN. LAP OF MEMBRANE

APPLICATION

CLIMATE

SUBGRADE

CSI MASTERFORMAT: 03150
DRAWING FILE: JNT34-01

• This drawing is a template for preliminary design only, and is not intended for bid purposes. It is subject to modification based on design calculations, local practices, and all applicable codes and regulations.

• Expansion joints are used to accommodate the movement of materials in rigid pavements, such as brick mortared on a concrete base. This joint is placed between concrete pavement and an existing site structure.

• Joints are filled with a variety of proprietary filler materials, depending on climate. Backer rods are placed on top of filler material as additional fill, and to prevent the sealant from bonding to the filler material.

• This detail is rated for medium-duty applications based on the thickness of the concrete slab and presence of insulation, as illustrated. However, expansion joints are similar for all types of applications.

• In temperate and cold climates, the expansion joint should be caulked or sealed

with elastomeric material, to minimize moisture and debris penetration. Occasional resealing is typically the only maintenance related to these joints.

• It is recommended that recycled and regionally available materials and products be given high priority in determining final design and specifications.

Installation Cost (per Linear Foot)

LOW   HIGH

$1.65

Maintenance

LOW   HIGH

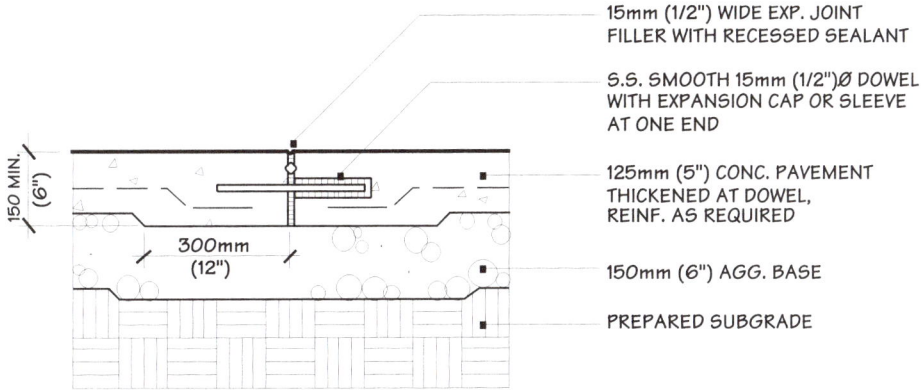

15mm (1/2") WIDE EXP. JOINT FILLER WITH RECESSED SEALANT

S.S. SMOOTH 15mm (1/2")Ø DOWEL WITH EXPANSION CAP OR SLEEVE AT ONE END

125mm (5") CONC. PAVEMENT THICKENED AT DOWEL, REINF. AS REQUIRED

150mm (6") AGG. BASE

PREPARED SUBGRADE

150 MIN. (6")

300mm (12")

APPLICATION

CLIMATE

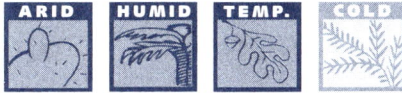

SUBGRADE

CSI MASTERFORMAT: 03150
DRAWING FILE: JNT22-04

• This drawing is a template for preliminary design only, and is not intended for bid purposes. It is subject to modification based on design calculations, local practices, and all applicable codes and regulations.

• Expansion joints are used to accommodate the movement of materials in rigid pavements, such as concrete. Joints are placed between slabs or between site structures and the pavement.

• Joints are filled with a variety of proprietary filler materials, depending on climate. Backer rods are placed on top of filler material as additional fill, and to prevent the sealant from bonding to the filler material.

• Dowels and sleeves are used to transfer loads between slabs and to minimize vertical movement, while accommodating lateral movement of materials.

• This detail is rated for medium-duty applications, based on the thickness of the concrete slab and aggregate base illustrated,

and this detail is commonly associated with larger slabs and medium or heavy-duty loading.

• This detail is not designed for cold climates with extreme freezing conditions. Keyed joints offer a stronger alternative in these climates, where movement of materials is greater.

• In temperate climates, the expansion joint should be caulked or sealed with elastomeric material, to minimize moisture and debris penetration. Occasional re-sealing is typically the only maintenance related to these joints.

• It is recommended that recycled and regionally available materials and products be given high priority in determining final design and specifications.

Installation Cost (per Linear Foot)

LOW   HIGH

$8.00

Maintenance

LOW   HIGH

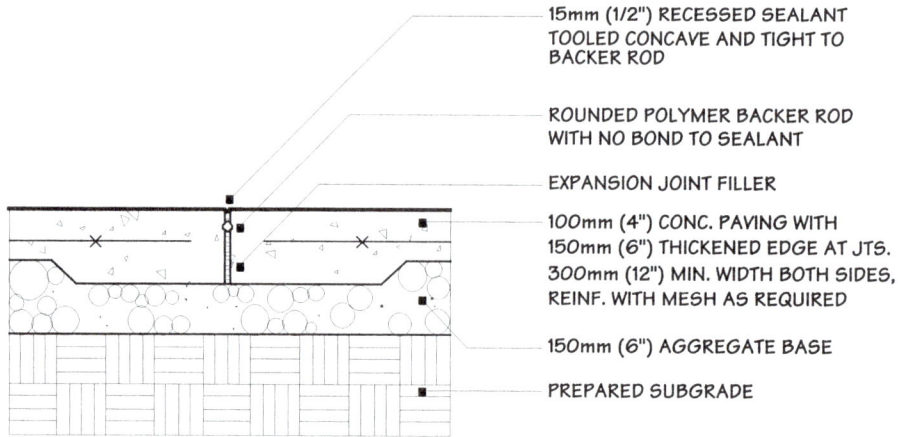

15mm (1/2") RECESSED SEALANT
TOOLED CONCAVE AND TIGHT TO
BACKER ROD

ROUNDED POLYMER BACKER ROD
WITH NO BOND TO SEALANT

EXPANSION JOINT FILLER

100mm (4") CONC. PAVING WITH
150mm (6") THICKENED EDGE AT JTS.
300mm (12") MIN. WIDTH BOTH SIDES,
REINF. WITH MESH AS REQUIRED

150mm (6") AGGREGATE BASE

PREPARED SUBGRADE

APPLICATION

CLIMATE

SUBGRADE

CSI MASTERFORMAT: 03150
DRAWING FILE: JNT22-01

• This drawing is a template for preliminary design only, and is not intended for bid purposes. It is subject to modification based on design calculations, local practices, and all applicable codes and regulations.

• Expansion joints are used to accommodate the movement of materials in rigid pavements, such as concrete. Joints are placed between slabs or between site structures and the pavement.

• Joints are filled with a variety of proprietary filler materials, depending on climate. Backer rods are placed on top of filler material as additional fill, and to prevent the sealant from bonding to the filler material.

• This detail is rated for medium-duty applications, based on the thickness of the concrete slab and aggregate base illustrated. Thickened edges are common in thinner slabs, for added reinforcement. However, expansion joints are similar for all types of applications.

• In temperate and cold climates, the expansion joint should be caulked or sealed with elastomeric material, to minimize moisture and debris penetration. Occasional re-sealing is typically the only maintenance related to these joints.

• It is recommended that recycled and regionally available materials and products be given high priority in determining final design and specifications.

Installation Cost (per Linear Foot)

LOW   HIGH

$3.00

Maintenance

LOW   HIGH

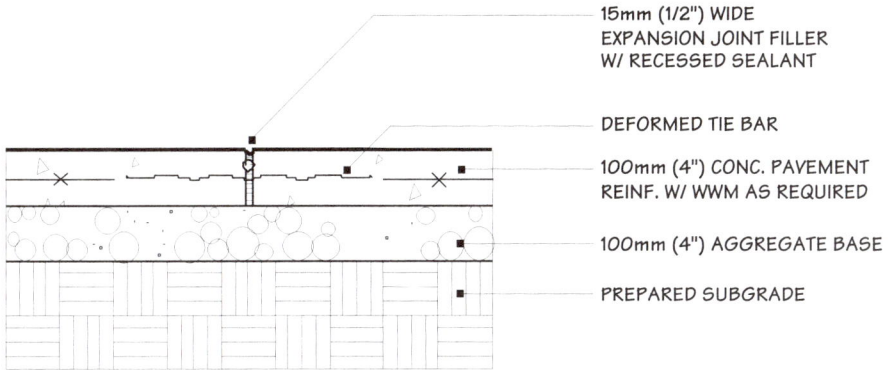

15mm (1/2") WIDE
EXPANSION JOINT FILLER
W/ RECESSED SEALANT

DEFORMED TIE BAR

100mm (4") CONC. PAVEMENT
REINF. W/ WWM AS REQUIRED

100mm (4") AGGREGATE BASE

PREPARED SUBGRADE

APPLICATION

CLIMATE

SUBGRADE

CSI MASTERFORMAT: 03150
DRAWING FILE: JNT22-03

• This drawing is a template for preliminary design only, and is not intended for bid purposes. It is subject to modification based on design calculations, local practices, and all applicable codes and regulations.

• Expansion joints are used to accommodate the movement of materials in rigid pavements, such as concrete. Joints are placed between slabs or between site structures and the pavement.

• Joints are filled with a variety of proprietary filler materials, depending on climate. Backer rods are placed on top of filler material as additional fill, and to prevent the sealant from bonding to the filler material.

• Deformed tie bar is used to transfer loads between slabs with minimal movement.

• This detail is rated for light-duty applications, based on the thickness of the concrete slab and aggregate base illustrated. However, expansion joints are similar for all types of applications.

• This detail is not designed for cold climates with extreme freezing conditions. Keyed joints offer a stronger alternative in these climates, where movement of materials is greater.

• In temperate climates, the expansion joint should be caulked or sealed with elastomeric material, to minimize moisture and debris penetration. Occasional re-sealing is typically the only maintenance related to these joints.

• It is recommended that recycled and regionally available materials and products be given high priority in determining final design and specifications.

Installation Cost (per Linear Foot)

LOW   HIGH

$3.10

Maintenance

LOW   HIGH

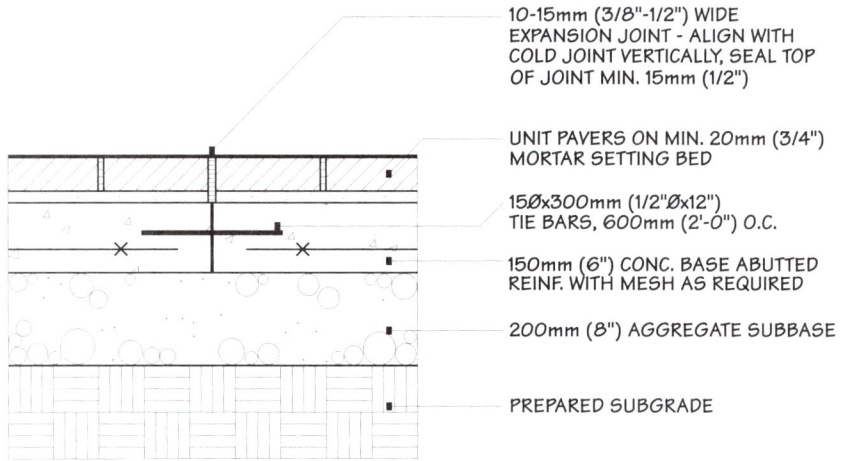

10-15mm (3/8"-1/2") WIDE
EXPANSION JOINT - ALIGN WITH
COLD JOINT VERTICALLY, SEAL TOP
OF JOINT MIN. 15mm (1/2")

UNIT PAVERS ON MIN. 20mm (3/4")
MORTAR SETTING BED

150x300mm (1/2"Øx12")
TIE BARS, 600mm (2'-0") O.C.

150mm (6") CONC. BASE ABUTTED
REINF. WITH MESH AS REQUIRED

200mm (8") AGGREGATE SUBBASE

PREPARED SUBGRADE

APPLICATION

CLIMATE

SUBGRADE

CSI MASTERFORMAT: 03100
DRAWING FILE: JNT14-01

• This drawing is a template for preliminary design only, and is not intended for bid purposes. It is subject to modification based on design calculations, local practices, and all applicable codes and regulations.

• Cold or butt joints are used to join slabs poured at different times, in climates without significant expansion due to freezing and thawing. Expansion joint in the brick paving should be aligned with cold control joint. Tie bars are used to transfer loads between the slabs.

• This detail is rated for heavy-duty applications, due to the relatively thick concrete slab and aggregate base illustrated. However, control joints are similar for all types of applications. If thinner slabs are used, they may need to be thickened at the joint to provide adequate coverage of tie bars.

• This detail is designed for climates which are not subject to freezing conditions. Keyed joints offer a stronger alternative in temper-

ate and cold climates, where movement of materials is greater.

• Cold or butt joints require no special maintenance practices in hot-arid and hot-humid climates. Care should be taken to periodically inspect joint filler and seal in brick pavement.

• It is recommended that recycled and regionally available materials and products be given high priority in determining final design and specifications.

Installation Cost (per Linear Foot)

LOW   HIGH

|
$1.24

Maintenance

LOW   HIGH

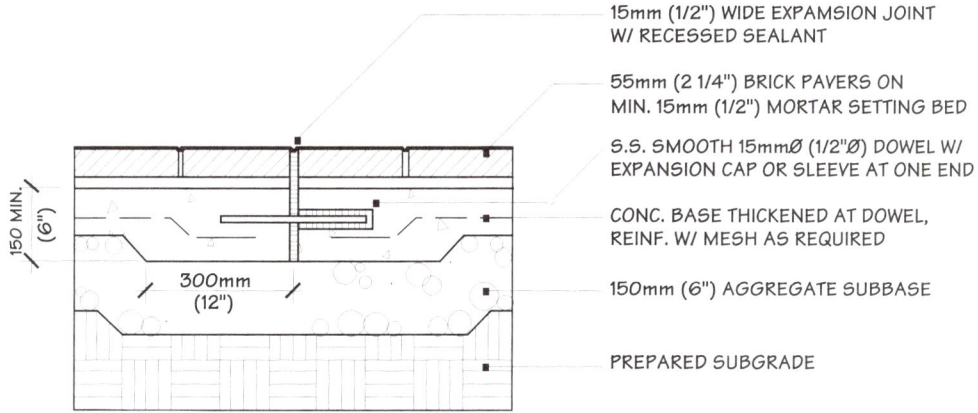

15mm (1/2") WIDE EXPAMSION JOINT W/ RECESSED SEALANT

55mm (2 1/4") BRICK PAVERS ON MIN. 15mm (1/2") MORTAR SETTING BED

S.S. SMOOTH 15mmØ (1/2"Ø) DOWEL W/ EXPANSION CAP OR SLEEVE AT ONE END

CONC. BASE THICKENED AT DOWEL, REINF. W/ MESH AS REQUIRED

150mm (6") AGGREGATE SUBBASE

PREPARED SUBGRADE

150 MIN. (6")

300mm (12")

APPLICATION

CLIMATE

SUBGRADE

CSI MASTERFORMAT: 03150
DRAWING FILE: JNT24-01

• This drawing is a template for preliminary design only, and is not intended for bid purposes. It is subject to modification based on design calculations, local practices, and all applicable codes and regulations.

• Expansion joints are used to accommodate the movement of materials in rigid pavements, such as brick mortared on a concrete base. Joints are placed between slabs or between site structures and the pavement.

• Joints are filled with a variety of proprietary filler materials, depending on climate. Backer rods are placed on top of filler material as additional fill, and to prevent the sealant from bonding to the filler material.

• Dowels and sleeves are used to transfer loads between slabs and minimize vertical movement, while accommodating lateral movement of materials.

• This detail is rated for medium-duty applications, based on the thickness of the concrete slab and aggregate base illustrated,

and this detail is commonly associated with larger slabs and medium or heavy-duty loading.

• This detail is not designed for cold climates, where the use of mortar and metal dowels is discouraged. Where unit pavers are desired, placement on an asphalt setting bed with mastic may be more suitable in cold climates.

• In temperate climates, the expansion joint should be caulked or sealed with elastomeric material, to minimize moisture and debris penetration. Occasional re-sealing is typically the only maintenance related to these joints.

• It is recommended that recycled and regionally available materials and products be given high priority in determining final design and specifications.

Installation Cost (per Linear Foot)

LOW   HIGH

$8.00

Maintenance

LOW   HIGH

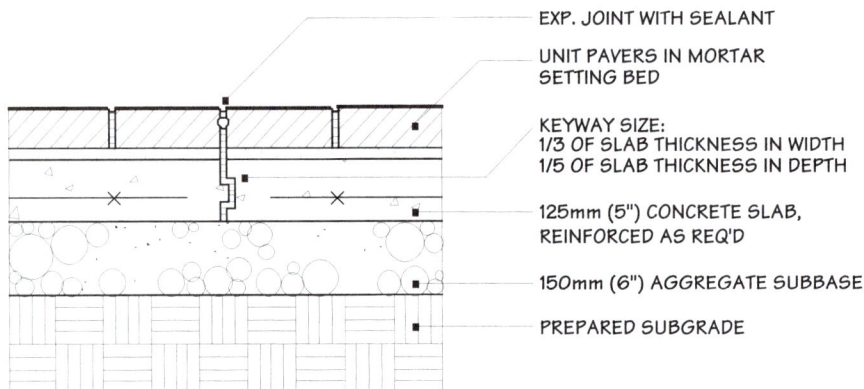

EXP. JOINT WITH SEALANT

UNIT PAVERS IN MORTAR
SETTING BED

KEYWAY SIZE:
1/3 OF SLAB THICKNESS IN WIDTH
1/5 OF SLAB THICKNESS IN DEPTH

125mm (5") CONCRETE SLAB,
REINFORCED AS REQ'D

150mm (6") AGGREGATE SUBBASE

PREPARED SUBGRADE

APPLICATION

CLIMATE

SUBGRADE

CSI MASTERFORMAT: 03150
DRAWING FILE: JNT24-02

• This drawing is a template for preliminary design only, and is not intended for bid purposes. It is subject to modification based on design calculations, local practices, and all applicable codes and regulations.

• Expansion joints are used to accommodate the movement of materials in rigid pavements, such as brick mortared on a concrete base. Joints are placed between slabs or between site structures and the pavement.

• Joints are filled with a variety of proprietary filler materials, depending on climate. Backer rods are placed on top of filler material as additional fill, and to prevent the sealant from bonding to the filler material.

• Keyway is used to transfer loads between slabs and minimize vertical movement of materials.

• This detail is rated for medium-duty applications, based on the thickness of the concrete slab and aggregate base illustrated.

However, expansion joints are similar for all types of applications.

• This detail is not designed for cold climates, where the use of mortar in unit pavers is discouraged. Where unit pavers are desired, placement on an asphalt setting bed with mastic may be more suitable in cold climates.

• In temperate climates, the expansion joint should be caulked or sealed with elastomeric material, to minimize moisture and debris penetration. Occasional re-sealing is typically the only maintenance related to these joints.

• It is recommended that recycled and regionally available materials and products be given high priority in determining final design and specifications.

Pedestrian Ramps

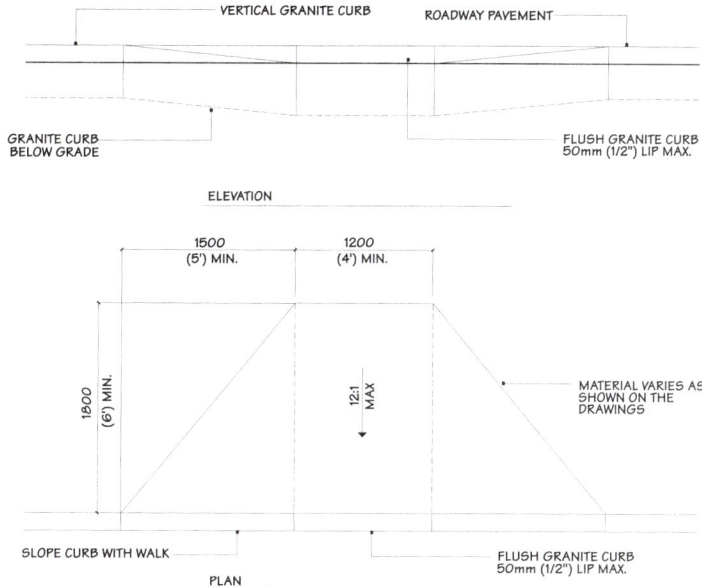

APPLICATION

CLIMATE

SUBGRADE

CSI MASTERFORMAT: 02750
DRAWING FILE: RMP02-03

• This drawing is a template for preliminary design only, and is not intended for bid purposes. It is subject to modification based on design calculations, local practices, and all applicable codes and regulations.

• This concrete curb ramp is rated as medium-duty due to aggregate base and pavement thickness and is typically found in dense residential, park, urban, and institutional settings.

• The concrete ramp may abut a variety of paving materials, and dimensions shown are minimal to achieve maximum allowable slope for barrier free design.

• It is ideal to bury curb fully as shown for maximum durability and load bearing capacity. A thicker slab and heavier aggregate base would result in a heavy-duty rating.

• Rigid pavement design must accommodate movement of materials by providing adequate expansion and control joints, particularly in regions of extreme temperature

fluctuations. If designed for temperate or cold climates, air-entrained concrete is typically recommended due to freezing/thawing action.

• Reinforcing practices vary widely by region. Local codes and practices should be consulted prior to specifying any type of reinforcing.

• It is recommended that recycled and regionally available materials and products be given high priority in determining final design and specifications.

Installation Cost (per Square Foot)

LOW   HIGH

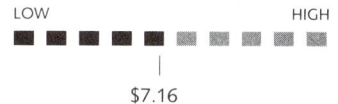

$7.16

Maintenance

LOW   HIGH

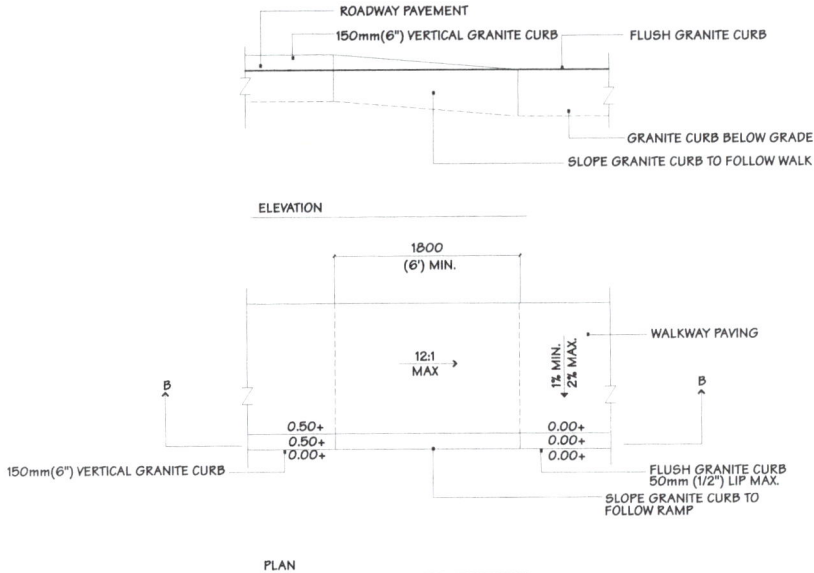

APPLICATION

CLIMATE

SUBGRADE

CSI MASTERFORMAT: 02750
DRAWING FILE: RMP02-04

• This drawing is a template for preliminary design only, and is not intended for bid purposes. It is subject to modification based on design calculations, local practices, and all applicable codes and regulations.

• This concrete curb ramp is rated as medium-duty due to aggregate base and pavement thickness and is typically found in dense residential, park, urban, and institutional settings. This application is typically used to convey a pedestrian path across a street or parking area, or to provide a walkway ramp from a parking place to a doorway.

• The concrete ramp may abut a variety of paving materials and dimensions shown are minimal to achieve maximum allowable slope for barrier free design.

• It is ideal to bury curb fully as shown for maximum durability and load bearing capacity. A thicker slab and heavier aggregate base would result in a heavy-duty rating.

• Rigid pavement design must accommodate movement of materials by providing adequate expansion and control joints, particularly in regions of extreme temperature fluctuations. If designed for temperate or cold climates, air-entrained concrete is typically recommended due to freezing/thawing action.

• Reinforcing practices vary widely by region. Local codes and practices should be consulted prior to specifying any type of reinforcing.

• It is recommended that recycled and regionally available materials and products be given high priority in determining final design and specifications.

Installation Cost (per Square Foot)

$7.16

Maintenance

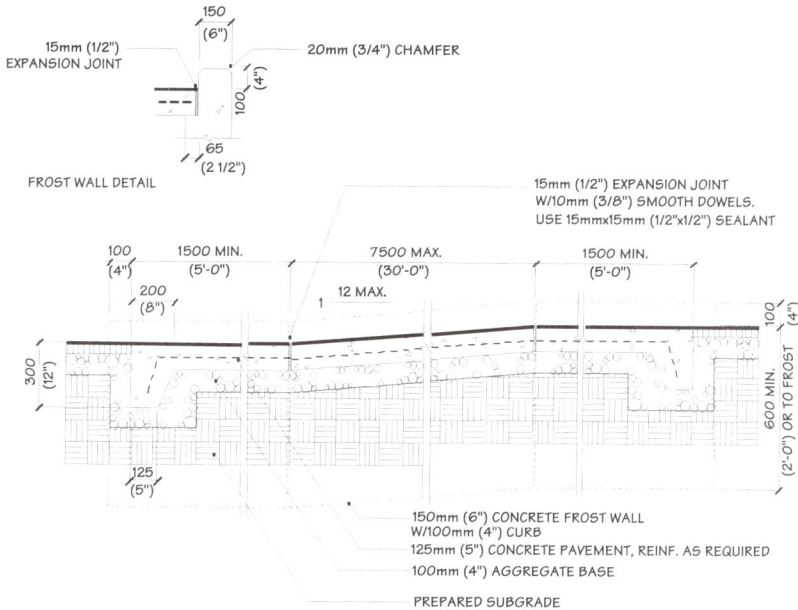

FROST WALL DETAIL

APPLICATION

CLIMATE

SUBGRADE

CSI MASTERFORMAT: 03300
DRAWING FILE: RMP02-01

• This drawing is a template for preliminary design only, and is not intended for bid purposes. It is subject to modification based on design calculations, local practices, and all applicable codes and regulations.

• This concrete ramp detail is rated for heavy-duty applications based on thickness of concrete and aggregate base, and may support significant pedestrian loading typically associated with dense residential, public park, institutional, and commercial settings.

• Rigid pavement design must accommodate movement of materials by providing adequate expansion and control joints, particularly in regions of extreme temperature fluctuations. If designed for temperate or cold climates, air-entrained concrete is typically recommended due to freezing/thawing action.

• Reinforcing practices vary widely by region. Local codes and practices should be consulted prior to specifying any type of reinforcing.

• This detail shows concrete cheek wall for continous support of ramp unit. Ramp rests on a sill and abuts the walls with a continuous expansion joint sealed to prevent moisture penetration.

• Long ramp runs require approved trench drains at landing intervals, or small area drains in landing. Rails as required by regulations. In cold climates, heating cables may be required.

• It is recommended that recycled and regionally available materials and products be given high priority in determining final design and specifications.

Installation Cost (per Square Foot)

LOW   HIGH

$7.00

Maintenance

LOW   HIGH

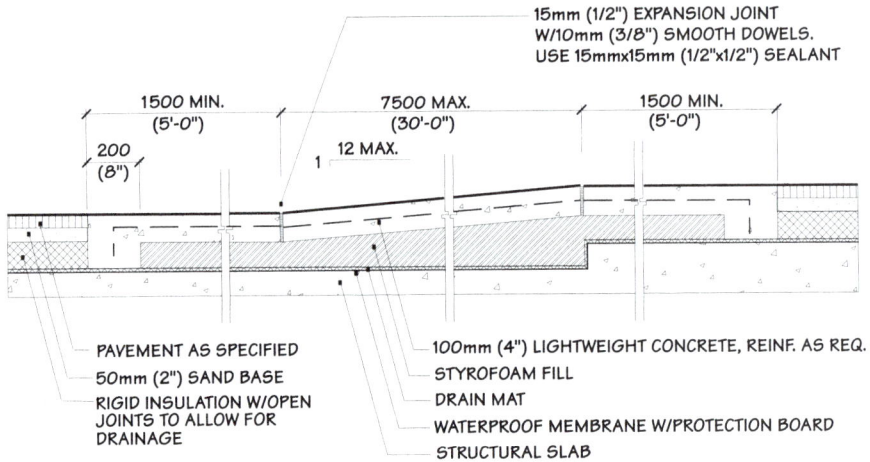

15mm (1/2") EXPANSION JOINT
W/10mm (3/8") SMOOTH DOWELS.
USE 15mmx15mm (1/2"x1/2") SEALANT

1500 MIN. (5'-0")   7500 MAX. (30'-0")   1500 MIN. (5'-0")

200 (8")   12 MAX.   1

PAVEMENT AS SPECIFIED
50mm (2") SAND BASE
RIGID INSULATION W/OPEN JOINTS TO ALLOW FOR DRAINAGE

100mm (4") LIGHTWEIGHT CONCRETE, REINF. AS REQ.
STYROFOAM FILL
DRAIN MAT
WATERPROOF MEMBRANE W/PROTECTION BOARD
STRUCTURAL SLAB

APPLICATION

CLIMATE

SUBGRADE

CSI MASTERFORMAT: 03300
DRAWING FILE: RMP02-02

• This drawing is a template for preliminary design only, and is not intended for bid purposes. It is subject to modification based on design calculations, local practices, and all applicable codes and regulations.

• This concrete ramp on structure detail is rated for light-duty applications based on thickness of concrete and bearing limitations of drain mat on structural roof deck, and may support pedestrian loading typically associated with residential, public park, institutional, and commercial roof deck garden settings.

• Rigid pavement design must accommodate movement of materials by providing adequate expansion and control joints, particularly in regions of extreme temperature fluctuations. If designed for temperate or cold climates, air-entrained concrete is typically recommended due to freezing/thawing action.

• Reinforcing practices vary widely by region. Local codes and practices should be consulted prior to specifying any type of reinforcing.

• Ramp base rests on a heavy-duty drain mat resting on protection board and sloping waterproof membrane. Ramp slap is paced on styrofoam fill to reduce weight. Base of styrofoam is typically grooved for drainage over drain mat.

• Long ramp runs require approved trench drains at landing intervals, or small area drains in landing. Rails as required by regulations. In cold climates, heating cables may be required.

• It is recommended that recycled and regionally available materials and products be given high priority in determining final design and specifications.

Installation Cost (per Square Foot)

LOW   HIGH

$8.00

Maintenance

LOW   HIGH

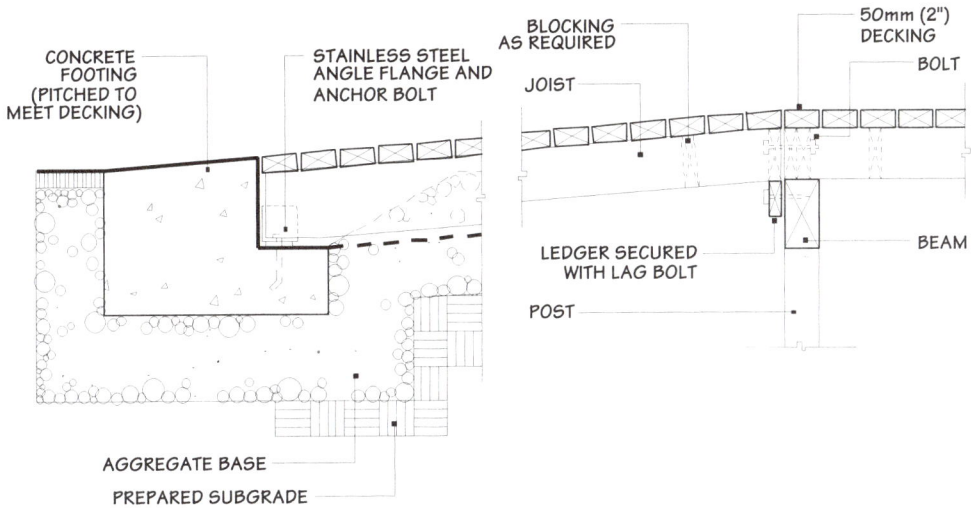

CONCRETE FOOTING (PITCHED TO MEET DECKING)

STAINLESS STEEL ANGLE FLANGE AND ANCHOR BOLT

BLOCKING AS REQUIRED

50mm (2") DECKING

BOLT

JOIST

LEDGER SECURED WITH LAG BOLT

BEAM

POST

AGGREGATE BASE

PREPARED SUBGRADE

APPLICATION

CLIMATE

SUBGRADE

CSI MASTERFORMAT: 06150
DRAWING FILE: RMP05-01

• This drawing is a template for preliminary design only, and is not intended for bid purposes. It is subject to modification based on design calculations, local practices, and all applicable codes and regulations.

• This wood pedestrian ramp with concrete footing is rated as medium-duty due to its bearing capacity, and is typically found in dense residential, public park, and commercial settings.

• Wood should be naturally rot resistant or treated. Concrete footing provides excellent transition from walk to ramp. In cold climates, footing must typically extend below frost line.

• If designed for temperate or cold climates, air-entrained concrete is typically recommended due to freezing/thawing action.

• Stainless steel or corrosion resistant fasteners are recommended for all attachments. Main joist may rest on treated sill bolted to footing as an alternate method of attachment.

• It is recommended that recycled and regionally available materials and products be given high priority in determining final design and specifications.

Installation Cost (per Square Foot)

LOW   HIGH

$15.00

Maintenance

LOW   HIGH

WOOD RAMP WITH FLUSH PAVEMENT

METAL JOIST FLANGE AS REQUIRED

BEVEL FIRST DECK BOARD TO ABUT PAVEMENT CLEANLY

PAVEMENT AS SPEC.

50mm x 150mm (2"x6") P.T. WOOD DECKING ON P.T. WOOD JOIST, SIZED ACCORDING TO LOAD. SECURE W/STAINLESS STEEL FASTENERS

BLOCKING AS REQUIRED

P.T. JOIST

BOLT

LEDGER SECURED WITH LAG BOLT

BEAM

POST

100mm (4") AGG. BASE

P.T. 50x (2"x) RAMP FOOT SECURED W/450mm (18"), 15mm (1/2")Ø STEEL REBAR

PREPARED SUBGRADE

APPLICATION

LIGHT | MED. | HEAVY

CLIMATE

ARID | HUMID | TEMP. | COLD

SUBGRADE

PERM. | CLAY | ROOF

CSI MASTERFORMAT: 06150

DRAWING FILE: RMP05-02

• This drawing is a template for preliminary design only, and is not intended for bid purposes. It is subject to modification based on design calculations, local practices, and all applicable codes and regulations.

• This wood pedestrian ramp with flush pavement detail is rated as light-duty due to its bearing capacity and material, and is typically found in residential, park, and garden settings.

• Wood should be naturally rot resistant or treated. Bottom of ramp rests on wood base, pinned to a dense graded aggregate base. The ramp joist is attached to base plank with metal flange fasteners and abutted to beveled plank header with stainless steel screws. Aggregate base is backfilled against header paved to create transition from walk to ramp.

• This ramp is designed to serve as a temporary transition and requires periodic adjustment of pavement and wood ramp edge if pavement is flexible. Concrete slab would lessen need for adjustments.

• Stainless steel or corrosion resistant fasteners are recommended for all attachments.

• It is recommended that recycled and regionally available materials and products be given high priority in determining final design and specifications.

Installation Cost (per Square Foot)

LOW ... HIGH

$14.00

Maintenance

LOW ... HIGH

Planting

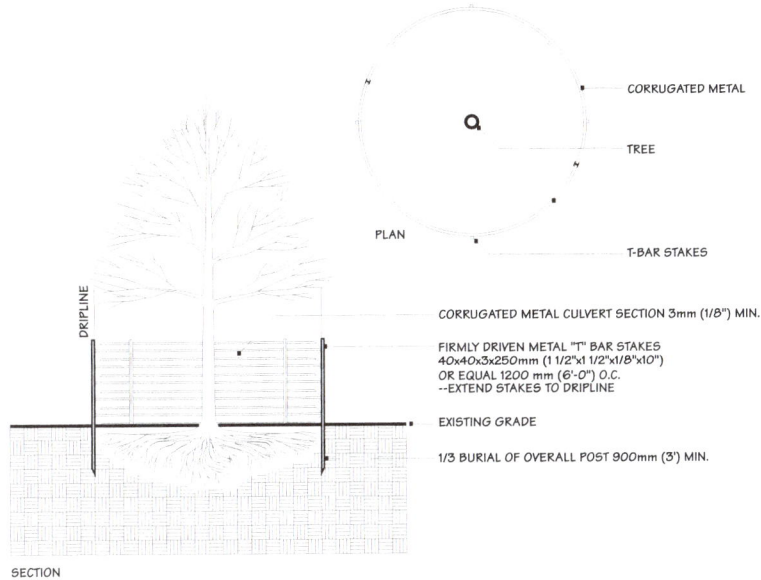

CORRUGATED METAL

TREE

Q

PLAN

T-BAR STAKES

CORRUGATED METAL CULVERT SECTION 3mm (1/8") MIN.

FIRMLY DRIVEN METAL "T" BAR STAKES
40x40x3x250mm (1 1/2"x1 1/2"x1/8"x10")
OR EQUAL 1200 mm (6'-0") O.C.
--EXTEND STAKES TO DRIPLINE

EXISTING GRADE

1/3 BURIAL OF OVERALL POST 900mm (3') MIN.

DRIPLINE

SECTION

APPLICATION

CLIMATE

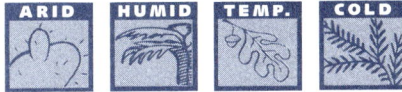

SUBGRADE

CSI MASTERFORMAT: 02930
DRAWING FILE: PLA30-02

• This drawing is a template for preliminary design only, and is not intended for bid purposes. It is subject to modification based on design calculations, local practices, and all applicable codes and regulations.

• This tree protection with metal barrier detail is rated as heavy-duty due to the level of protection afforded, and is typically applied to specimen trees adjacent to dense residential, commercial, or institutional construction. Its main purpose is to avoid damage to vascular system due to equipment abrasion, or root compaction due to heavy vehicle intrusion.

• This detail is used to fully prohibit all construction activity from entering the tree dripline zone.

• An open heavy rail fence is another alternative where aesthetics is an important factor due to site location.

• It is recommended that recycled and regionally available materials and products be given high priority in determining final design and specifications.

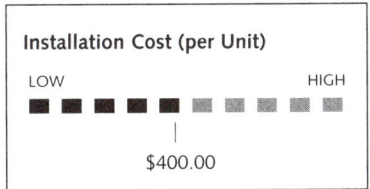

Installation Cost (per Unit)

LOW   HIGH

$400.00

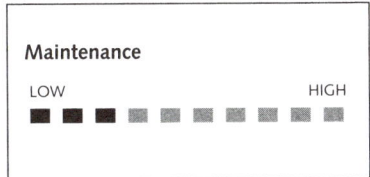

Maintenance

LOW   HIGH

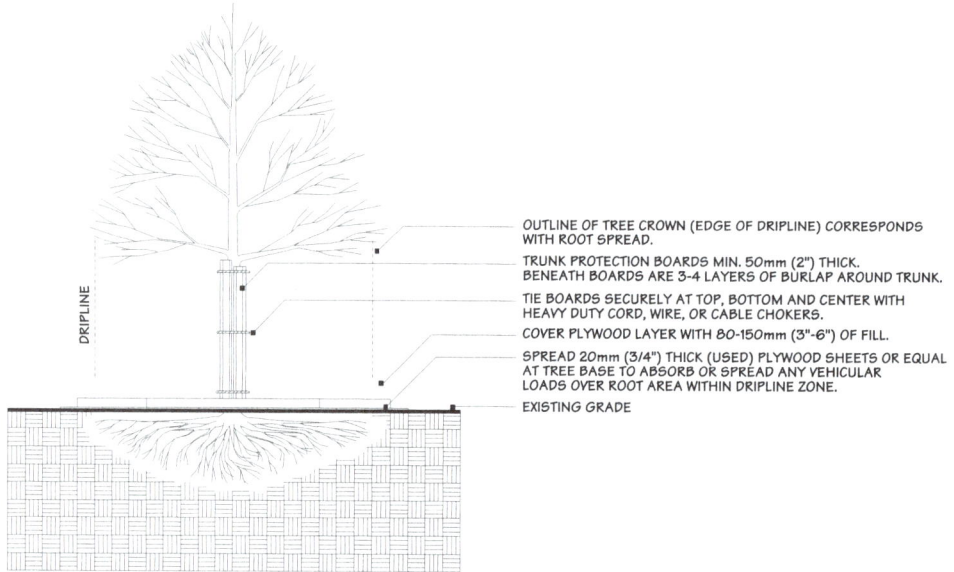

OUTLINE OF TREE CROWN (EDGE OF DRIPLINE) CORRESPONDS WITH ROOT SPREAD.

TRUNK PROTECTION BOARDS MIN. 50mm (2") THICK. BENEATH BOARDS ARE 3-4 LAYERS OF BURLAP AROUND TRUNK.

TIE BOARDS SECURELY AT TOP, BOTTOM AND CENTER WITH HEAVY DUTY CORD, WIRE, OR CABLE CHOKERS.

COVER PLYWOOD LAYER WITH 80-150mm (3"-6") OF FILL.

SPREAD 20mm (3/4") THICK (USED) PLYWOOD SHEETS OR EQUAL AT TREE BASE TO ABSORB OR SPREAD ANY VEHICULAR LOADS OVER ROOT AREA WITHIN DRIPLINE ZONE.

EXISTING GRADE

DRIPLINE

APPLICATION

CLIMATE

SUBGRADE

CSI MASTERFORMAT: 02930
DRAWING FILE: PLA30-01

• This drawing is a template for preliminary design only, and is not intended for bid purposes. It is subject to modification based on design calculations, local practices, and all applicable codes and regulations.

• This tree protection with plywood detail is rated as medium-duty due to the level of protection afforded, and is typically applied to specimen trees adjacent to light residential scale construction. Its main purpose is to avoid damage to vascular system due to equipment abrasion, or root compaction due to light vehicle intrusion.

• This detail is used in close quarters where full vehicular prohibition is not possible.

• Burlap padding under trunk wrap boards is critically important. Remove all protection devices at the earliest opportunity. Aerate root zone and water tree after completion.

• It is recommended that recycled and regionally available materials and products be given high priority in determining final design and specifications.

Installation Cost (per Unit)

LOW   HIGH

$250.00

Maintenance

LOW   HIGH

PRUNE UP TO 1/3 OF BRANCHES DEPENDING ON AMOUNT OF ROOT DAMAGE.

RETAINING WALL NO CLOSER THAN DRIPLINE

EXISTING GRADE TO BE MAINTAINED UNDER TREE CROWN IF POSSIBLE

TOP OF SLOPE AT DRIPLINE OR AS FAR AWAY AS POSSIBLE

FORMER GRADE

NEW GRADE

DRIPLINE

FORMER GRADE

NEW GRADE

APPLICATION

LIGHT   MED.   HEAVY

CLIMATE

ARID   HUMID   TEMP.   COLD

SUBGRADE

PERM.   CLAY   ROOF

CSI MASTERFORMAT: 02930
DRAWING FILE: PLA30-03

• This drawing is a template for preliminary design only, and is not intended for bid purposes. It is subject to modification based on design calculations, local practices, and all applicable codes and regulations.

• This tree protection in cut detail is rated as heavy-duty due to the level of protection afforded, and is typically applied to specimen trees adjacent to dense residential, commercial, or institutional construction. Its main purpose is to avoid damage to tree root system due to grade changes adjacent to the tree.

• Ideally, existing grade should be held constant within the tree branch dripline. Species and root structure determine specific criteria for locating cut or fill line.

• Dry laid or porous walls without frost footings are typically used to form both tree walls and tree wells.

• This detail shows back of stone wall and top of cut embankment at dripline.

• It is recommended that recycled and regionally available materials and products be given high priority in determining final design and specifications.

Installation Cost (per Unit)

LOW   HIGH

$800.00

Maintenance

LOW   HIGH

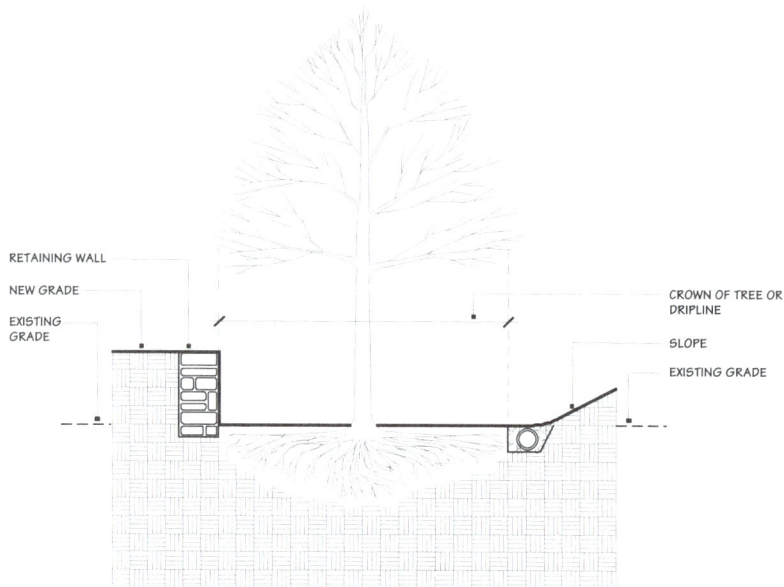

RETAINING WALL
NEW GRADE
EXISTING GRADE
CROWN OF TREE OR DRIPLINE
SLOPE
EXISTING GRADE

APPLICATION

CLIMATE

SUBGRADE

CSI MASTERFORMAT: 02930
DRAWING FILE: PLA30-04

• This drawing is a template for preliminary design only, and is not intended for bid purposes. It is subject to modification based on design calculations, local practices, and all applicable codes and regulations.

• This tree protection in fill detail is rated as heavy-duty due to the level of protection afforded, and is typically applied to specimen trees adjacent to dense residential, commercial, or institutional construction. Its main purpose is to avoid damage to tree root system due to grade changes adjacent to the tree.

• Ideally, existing grade should be held constant within the tree branch dripline. Species and root structure determine specific criteria for locating cut or fill line.

• Dry laid or porous walls without frost footings are typically used to form both tree walls and tree wells.

• This detail shows face of stone wall and toe of fill embankment at dripline, and indi-cates a trench drain at the low point of the newly created well. Generally, it is easier for a tree to adapt to a cut, than to a fill due to potential for flooding and lack of oxygen to the upper roots.

• It is recommended that recycled and regionally available materials and products be given high priority in determining final design and specifications.

Installation Cost (per Unit)

LOW   HIGH

$900.00

Maintenance

LOW   HIGH

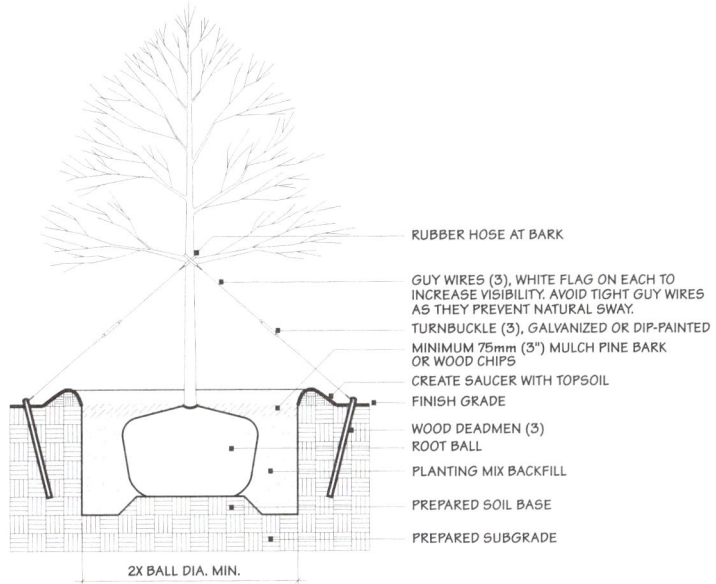

RUBBER HOSE AT BARK

GUY WIRES (3), WHITE FLAG ON EACH TO INCREASE VISIBILITY. AVOID TIGHT GUY WIRES AS THEY PREVENT NATURAL SWAY.

TURNBUCKLE (3), GALVANIZED OR DIP-PAINTED

MINIMUM 75mm (3") MULCH PINE BARK OR WOOD CHIPS

CREATE SAUCER WITH TOPSOIL

FINISH GRADE

WOOD DEADMEN (3)

ROOT BALL

PLANTING MIX BACKFILL

PREPARED SOIL BASE

PREPARED SUBGRADE

2X BALL DIA. MIN.

APPLICATION

CLIMATE

SUBGRADE

CSI MASTERFORMAT: 02930
DRAWING FILE: PLA10-13

• This drawing is a template for preliminary design only, and is not intended for bid purposes. It is subject to modification based on design calculations, local practices, and all applicable codes and regulations.

• This deciduous tree transplanting detail is rated as medium-duty due to the tree size and park or institutional location typically associated with this installation in all climates.

• Tree sits on subgrade pedestal to prevent settlement and is firmly backfilled with amended soil. Transplanted tree requires as broad a hole as possible to allow for recently dug root ball. These trees are often collected stock and require drastic pruning to reduce bio-mass and root feeding demand.

• A soil saucer filled with mulch is used to conserve water and keep roots cool during recovery period of initial growth. Water copiously and plant in spring when possible.

• Tree height should be placed at or above previous existing grade as shown.

• Staking and guying are reserved for windy sites only, and should not be routinely specified. When specified, care should be taken to protect bark and wires should be removed as soon as possible. Initial staking of collected stock is indicated.

• It is recommended that recycled and regionally available materials and products be given high priority in determining final design and specifications.

Installation Cost (per Unit)

LOW   HIGH

$400.00

Maintenance

LOW   HIGH

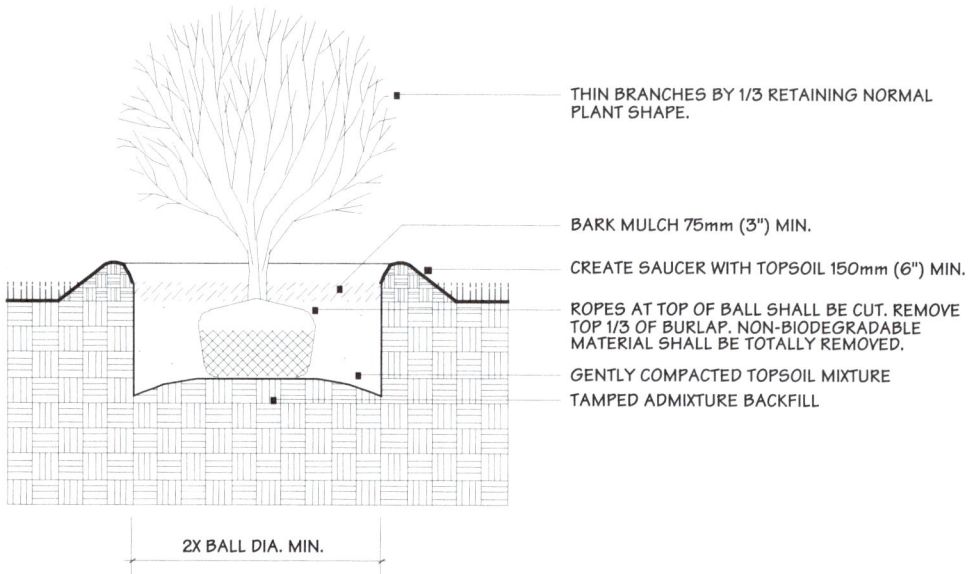

THIN BRANCHES BY 1/3 RETAINING NORMAL PLANT SHAPE.

BARK MULCH 75mm (3") MIN.

CREATE SAUCER WITH TOPSOIL 150mm (6") MIN.

ROPES AT TOP OF BALL SHALL BE CUT. REMOVE TOP 1/3 OF BURLAP. NON-BIODEGRADABLE MATERIAL SHALL BE TOTALLY REMOVED.

GENTLY COMPACTED TOPSOIL MIXTURE

TAMPED ADMIXTURE BACKFILL

2X BALL DIA. MIN.

APPLICATION

CLIMATE

SUBGRADE

CSI MASTERFORMAT: 02930
DRAWING FILE: PLA20-02

• This drawing is a template for preliminary design only, and is not intended for bid purposes. It is subject to modification based on design calculations, local practices, and all applicable codes and regulations.

• This ball and burlap shrub planting detail is rated as medium-duty due to plant size and installation operation. It is typically used on residential, park, and garden settings in all climates.

• This detail calls for tamping amended soil to create a firm base upon which to place the shrub root ball. The amended soil is backfilled carefully around the roots to support the plant and to prevent air pockets from forming, taking care to remove upper burlap wrap, or entire wrap if composed of plastic fabric. Generous soaking is required to remove remaining air pockets around roots.

• Hole diameter should be at least twice the diameter of the shrub ball. Shrub root crown should be placed slightly higher than surrounding finished grade.

• Saucer is formed by a soil berm, which is filled with mulch to conserve water and to cool roots during initial acclimation.

• Prune back 1/3 to stimulate root growth, taking care to retain shape and growth leaders. Avoid high nitrogen fertilizers during the initial growing season. Water well and frequently.

• It is recommended that recycled and regionally available materials and products be given high priority in determining final design and specifications.

Installation Cost (per Unit)

LOW   HIGH

$50.00

Maintenance

LOW   HIGH

THIN BRANCHES BY 1/3 RETAINING NORMAL PLANT SHAPE.

SHRUBS SHALL BE SLIGHTLY HIGHER IN RELATION TO FINISHED GRADE THAN THEY WERE TO PREVIOUS EXISTING GRADE.

PINE BARK MULCH 75mm (3") MIN.

CREATE SAUCER WITH TOPSOIL 150mm (6") MIN.

PRUNE DAMAGED OR DESICCATED ROOTS.

GENTLY COMPACTED TOPSOIL MIXTURE

SCARIFY PIT BOTTOM 150mm (6") MIN.

300 (12")   300 (12")

APPLICATION

LIGHT   MED.   HEAVY

CLIMATE

ARID   HUMID   TEMP.   COLD

SUBGRADE

PERM.   CLAY   ROOF

CSI MASTERFORMAT: 02930
DRAWING FILE: PLA20-01

• This drawing is a template for preliminary design only, and is not intended for bid purposes. It is subject to modification based on design calculations, local practices, and all applicable codes and regulations.

• This bare root shrub planting detail is rated as light-duty due to plant size and installation operation. It is typically used on residential, park, and garden settings in all climates.

• This detail calls for scarifying bottom of hole and tamping amended soil to create a firm base upon which to place the shrub roots. The amended soil is backfilled carefully around the roots to support the plant and to prevent air pockets from forming. Generous soaking is required to remove remaining air pockets around roots.

• Shrub root crown should be placed slightly higher than surrounding finished grade.

• Saucer is formed by a soil berm, which is filled with mulch to conserve water and to cool roots during initial acclimation.

• Prune back 1/3 to stimulate root growth, taking care to retain shape and growth leaders. Avoid high nitrogen fertilizers during the initial growing season. Water well and frequently.

• It is recommended that recycled and regionally available materials and products be given high priority in determining final design and specifications.

Installation Cost (per Unit)

LOW   HIGH

$30.00

Maintenance

LOW   HIGH

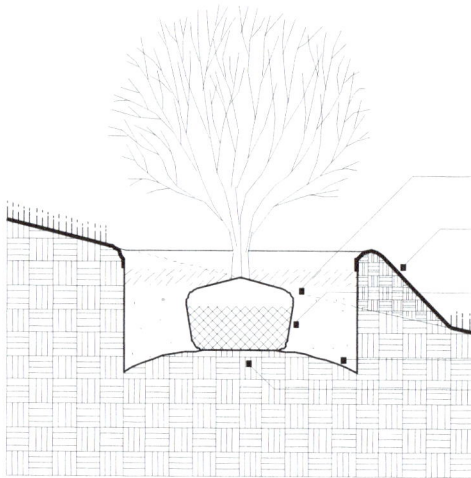

CORNER OF ROOT SYSTEM TO BE AT LINE OF ORIGINAL GRADE

FIRMLY COMPACTED SAUCER (USE TOPSOIL). ANGLE OF REPOSE VARIES WITH STEEPNESS OF SLOPE AND SOIL TYPE.

CUT THE ROPES AT TOP OF BALL. REMOVE TOP 1/3 OF BURLAP. NON-BIODEGRADABLE MATERIAL SHALL BE TOTALLY REMOVED.

GENTLY COMPACTED TOPSOIL MIXTURE, 300mm (12") ALL AROUND BALL, MIN.

TAMPED ADMIXTURE BACKFILL

APPLICATION

CLIMATE

SUBGRADE

CSI MASTERFORMAT: 02930
DRAWING FILE: PLA20-04

• This drawing is a template for preliminary design only, and is not intended for bid purposes. It is subject to modification based on design calculations, local practices, and all applicable codes and regulations.

• This ball and burlap shrub planting on slope detail is rated as medium-duty due to plant size and installation operation. It is typically used on residential, park, and garden settings in all climates.

• This detail calls for tamping amended soil to create a firm base upon which to place the shrub root ball. The amended soil is backfilled carefully around the roots to support the plant and to prevent air pockets from forming, taking care to remove upper burlap wrap, or entire wrap if composed of plastic fabric. Generous soaking is required to remove remaining air pockets around roots.

• Hole diameter should be at least twice the diameter of the shrub ball. Shrub root crown should be placed slightly higher than surrounding finished grade.

• Saucer is formed by a soil berm, which is filled with mulch to conserve water and to cool roots during initial acclimation. Berm should be firmly packed on the down-hill side to avoid washouts during normal rains or irrigation. Mulch cover may protect berm during this period.

• Prune back 1/3 to stimulate root growth, taking care to retain shape and growth leaders. Avoid high nitrogen fertilizers during the initial growing season. Water well and frequently.

• It is recommended that recycled and regionally available materials and products be given high priority in determining final design and specifications.

Installation Cost (per Unit)

LOW   HIGH

$60.00

Maintenance

LOW   HIGH

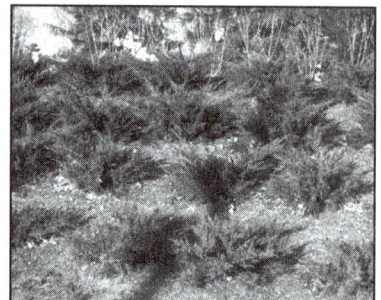

CORNER OF ROOT SYSTEM TO BE AT LINE
OF ORIGINAL GRADE.

FIRMLY COMPACTED SAUCER (USE TOPSOIL).

ANGLE OF REPOSE VARIES WITH STEEPNESS
OF SLOPE AND SOIL TYPE.

PREPARED SOIL MIXTURE.

SCARIFY PIT BOTTOM 150mm (6") MIN.

300
(12")
MIN.

APPLICATION

| LIGHT | MED. | HEAVY |

CLIMATE

| ARID | HUMID | TEMP. | COLD |

SUBGRADE

| PERM. | CLAY | ROOF |

CSI MASTERFORMAT: 02930
DRAWING FILE: PLA20-03

- This drawing is a template for preliminary design only, and is not intended for bid purposes. It is subject to modification based on design calculations, local practices, and all applicable codes and regulations.

- This bare root shrub planting on slope detail is rated as light-duty due to plant size and installation operation. It is typically used on residential, park, and garden settings in all climates.

- This detail calls for scarifying bottom of generous hole and tamping amended soil to create a firm base upon which to place the shrub roots. The amended soil is backfilled carefully around the roots to support the plant and to prevent air pockets from forming. Generous soaking is required to remove remaining air pockets around roots.

- Shrub root crown should be placed slightly higher than surrounding finished grade.

- Saucer is formed by a soil berm, which is filled with mulch to conserve water and to cool roots during initial acclimation. Berm should be firmly packed on the down-hill side to avoid washouts during normal rains or irrigation. Mulch cover may protect berm during this period.

- Prune back 1/3 to stimulate root growth, taking care to retain shape and growth leaders. Avoid high nitrogen fertilizers during the initial growing season. Water well and frequently.

- It is recommended that recycled and regionally available materials and products be given high priority in determining final design and specifications.

Installation Cost (per Unit)

LOW   HIGH

$35.00

Maintenance

LOW   HIGH

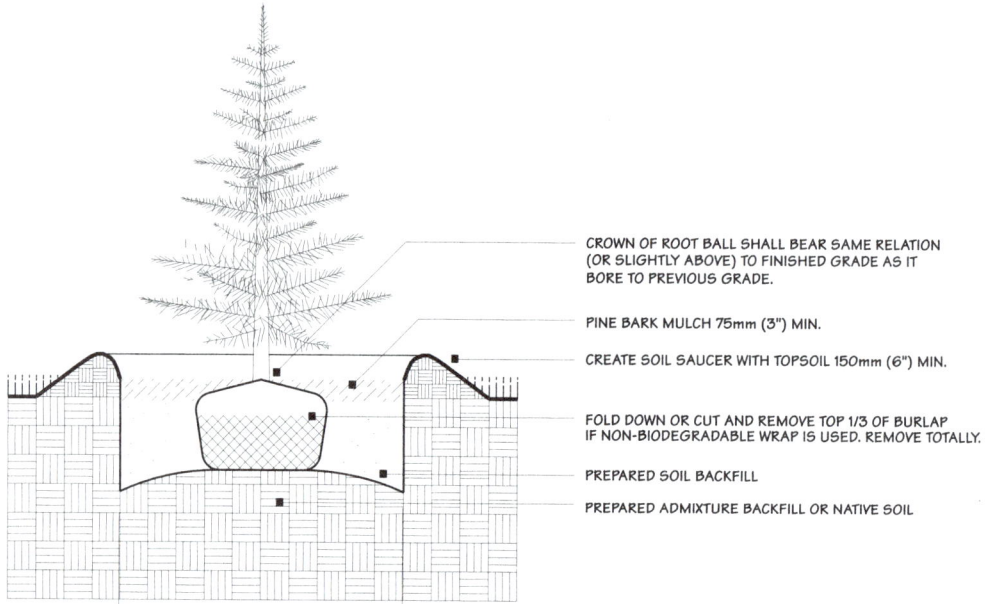

CROWN OF ROOT BALL SHALL BEAR SAME RELATION (OR SLIGHTLY ABOVE) TO FINISHED GRADE AS IT BORE TO PREVIOUS GRADE.

PINE BARK MULCH 75mm (3") MIN.

CREATE SOIL SAUCER WITH TOPSOIL 150mm (6") MIN.

FOLD DOWN OR CUT AND REMOVE TOP 1/3 OF BURLAP IF NON-BIODEGRADABLE WRAP IS USED. REMOVE TOTALLY.

PREPARED SOIL BACKFILL

PREPARED ADMIXTURE BACKFILL OR NATIVE SOIL

APPLICATION

CLIMATE

SUBGRADE

CSI MASTERFORMAT: 02930
DRAWING FILE: PLA10-08

• This drawing is a template for preliminary design only, and is not intended for bid purposes. It is subject to modification based on design calculations, local practices, and all applicable codes and regulations.

• This coniferous tree planting with stake and wire tie detail is rated as heavy-duty due to the tree size and urban or institutional location typically associated with this installation in all climates.

• This detail shows placement of single stake on windward side of tree. If multi-directional winds prevail, select a triangular pattern for stakes.

• Tree sits on subgrade pedestal to prevent settlement and is firmly backfilled with amended soil.

• A soil saucer filled with mulch is used to conserve water and keep roots cool during recovery period of initial growth.

• Tree height should be placed at or above previous existing grade as shown.

• Staking and guying are reserved for windy sites only, and should not be routinely specified. When specified, care should be taken to protect bark and wires should be removed as soon as possible.

• It is recommended that recycled and regionally available materials and products be given high priority in determining final design and specifications.

Installation Cost (per Unit)

LOW   HIGH

$400.00

Maintenance

LOW   HIGH

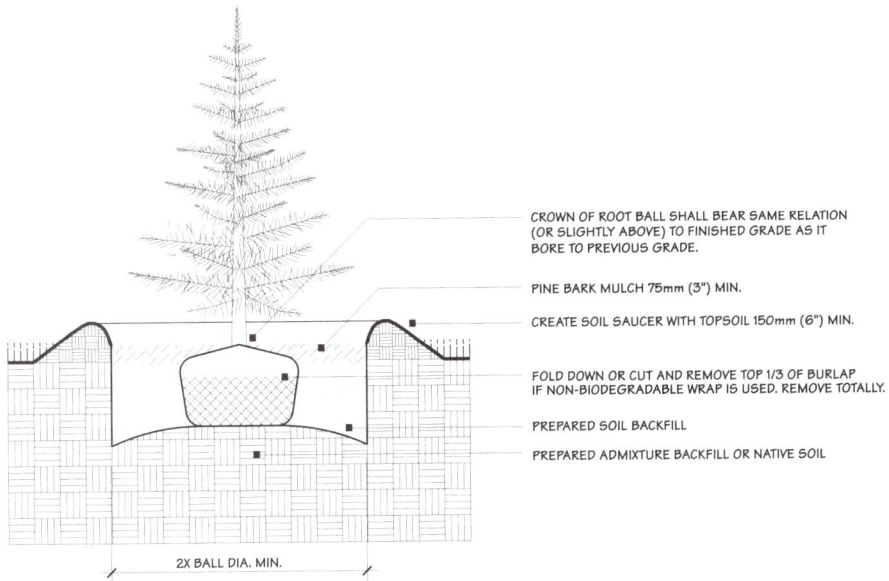

CROWN OF ROOT BALL SHALL BEAR SAME RELATION (OR SLIGHTLY ABOVE) TO FINISHED GRADE AS IT BORE TO PREVIOUS GRADE.

PINE BARK MULCH 75mm (3") MIN.

CREATE SOIL SAUCER WITH TOPSOIL 150mm (6") MIN.

FOLD DOWN OR CUT AND REMOVE TOP 1/3 OF BURLAP IF NON-BIODEGRADABLE WRAP IS USED. REMOVE TOTALLY.

PREPARED SOIL BACKFILL

PREPARED ADMIXTURE BACKFILL OR NATIVE SOIL

2X BALL DIA. MIN.

APPLICATION

CLIMATE

SUBGRADE

CSI MASTERFORMAT: 02930
DRAWING FILE: PLA10-09

• This drawing is a template for preliminary design only, and is not intended for bid purposes. It is subject to modification based on design calculations, local practices, and all applicable codes and regulations.

• This coniferous tree planting detail is rated as medium-duty due to the tree size and residential or garden location typically associated with this installation in all climates.

• Tree sits on prepared admixture pedestal to prevent settlement and is firmly backfilled with amended soil. Smaller trees with less weight may be placed on site-built mound within the hole.

• A soil saucer filled with mulch is used to conserve water and keep roots cool during recovery period of initial growth.

• Tree height should be placed at or above previous existing grade as shown.

• Staking and guying are reserved for windy sites only, and should not be routinely specified. When specified, care should be taken to protect bark and wires should be removed as soon as possible.

• It is recommended that recycled and regionally available materials and products be given high priority in determining final design and specifications.

Installation Cost (per Unit)

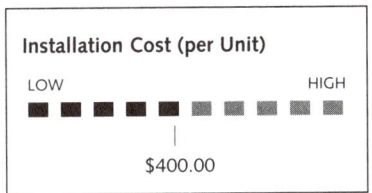

LOW   HIGH

$400.00

Maintenance

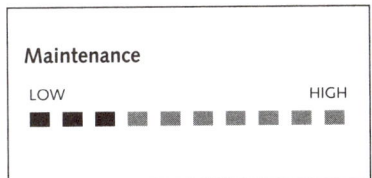

LOW   HIGH

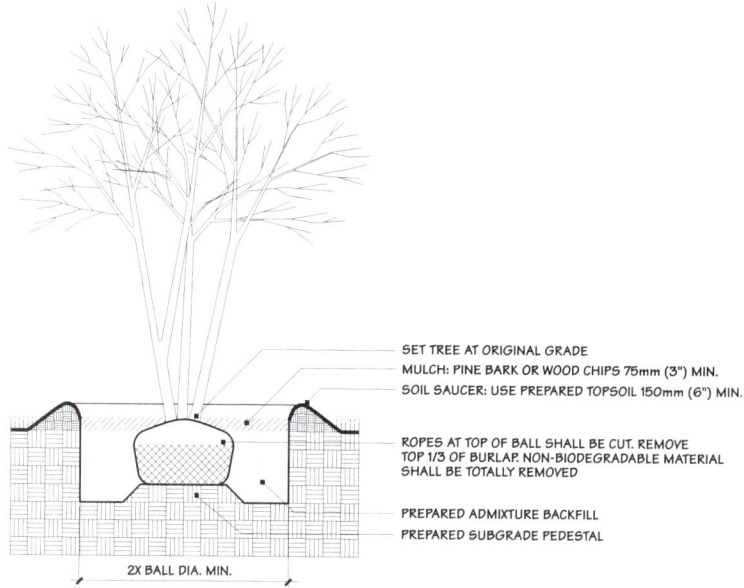

SET TREE AT ORIGINAL GRADE
MULCH: PINE BARK OR WOOD CHIPS 75mm (3") MIN.
SOIL SAUCER: USE PREPARED TOPSOIL 150mm (6") MIN.

ROPES AT TOP OF BALL SHALL BE CUT. REMOVE
TOP 1/3 OF BURLAP. NON-BIODEGRADABLE MATERIAL
SHALL BE TOTALLY REMOVED

PREPARED ADMIXTURE BACKFILL
PREPARED SUBGRADE PEDESTAL

2X BALL DIA. MIN.

APPLICATION

CLIMATE

SUBGRADE

CSI MASTERFORMAT: 02930
DRAWING FILE: PLA10-16

• This drawing is a template for preliminary design only, and is not intended for bid purposes. It is subject to modification based on design calculations, local practices, and all applicable codes and regulations.

• This multi-stem planting detail is rated as medium-duty due to the tree size and urban park or residential location typically associated with this installation in all climates.

• Tree sits on subgrade pedestal to prevent settlement and is firmly backfilled with amended soil.

• A soil saucer filled with mulch is used to conserve water and keep roots cool during recovery period of initial growth.

• Tree height should be placed at or above previous existing grade as shown.

• Staking and guying are reserved for windy sites only, and should not be routinely specified. When specified, care should be taken to protect bark and wires should be removed as soon as possible.

• It is recommended that recycled and regionally available materials and products be given high priority in determining final design and specifications.

Installation Cost (per Unit)

LOW   HIGH

$300.00

Maintenance

LOW   HIGH

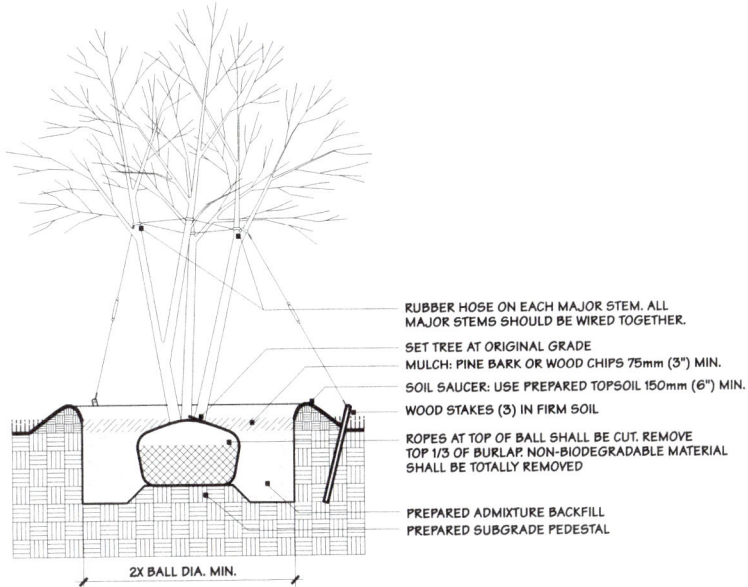

RUBBER HOSE ON EACH MAJOR STEM. ALL MAJOR STEMS SHOULD BE WIRED TOGETHER.

SET TREE AT ORIGINAL GRADE
MULCH: PINE BARK OR WOOD CHIPS 75mm (3") MIN.

SOIL SAUCER: USE PREPARED TOPSOIL 150mm (6") MIN.

WOOD STAKES (3) IN FIRM SOIL

ROPES AT TOP OF BALL SHALL BE CUT. REMOVE TOP 1/3 OF BURLAP. NON-BIODEGRADABLE MATERIAL SHALL BE TOTALLY REMOVED

PREPARED ADMIXTURE BACKFILL
PREPARED SUBGRADE PEDESTAL

2X BALL DIA. MIN.

APPLICATION

CLIMATE

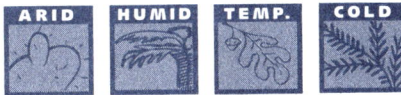

SUBGRADE

CSI MASTERFORMAT: 02930
DRAWING FILE: PLA10-07

• This drawing is a template for preliminary design only, and is not intended for bid purposes. It is subject to modification based on design calculations, local practices, and all applicable codes and regulations.

• This multi-stem planting on windy sites detail is rated as heavy-duty due to the tree size and urban park or institutional location typically associated with this installation in all climates.

• Tree sits on subgrade pedestal to prevent settlement and is firmly backfilled with amended soil.

• This detail shows guying pattern for multi-stem trees on a windy site.

• A soil saucer filled with mulch is used to conserve water and keep roots cool during recovery period of initial growth.

• Tree height should be placed at or above previous existing grade as shown.

• Staking and guying are reserved for windy sites only, and should not be routinely specified. When specified, care should be taken to protect bark and wires should be removed as soon as possible.

• It is recommended that recycled and regionally available materials and products be given high priority in determining final design and specifications.

Installation Cost (per Unit)

LOW   HIGH

$350.00

Maintenance

LOW   HIGH

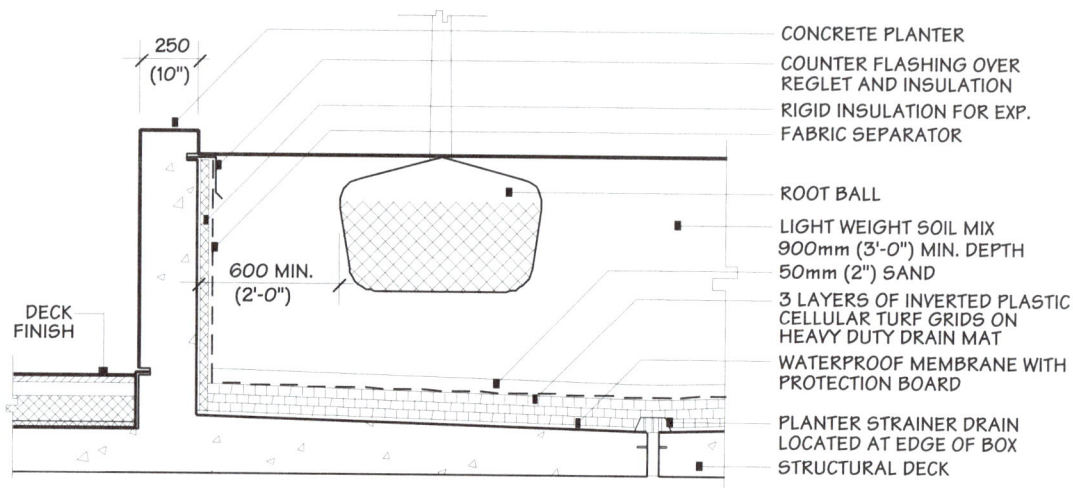

Diagram labels:

- 250 (10")
- 600 MIN. (2'-0")
- DECK FINISH
- CONCRETE PLANTER
- COUNTER FLASHING OVER REGLET AND INSULATION
- RIGID INSULATION FOR EXP.
- FABRIC SEPARATOR
- ROOT BALL
- LIGHT WEIGHT SOIL MIX 900mm (3'-0") MIN. DEPTH
- 50mm (2") SAND
- 3 LAYERS OF INVERTED PLASTIC CELLULAR TURF GRIDS ON HEAVY DUTY DRAIN MAT
- WATERPROOF MEMBRANE WITH PROTECTION BOARD
- PLANTER STRAINER DRAIN LOCATED AT EDGE OF BOX
- STRUCTURAL DECK

APPLICATION

LIGHT | MED. | HEAVY

CLIMATE

ARID | HUMID | TEMP. | COLD

SUBGRADE

PERM. | CLAY | ROOF

CSI MASTERFORMAT: 02930
DRAWING FILE: PLA10-11

- This drawing is a template for preliminary design only, and is not intended for bid purposes. It is subject to modification based on design calculations, local practices, and all applicable codes and regulations.

- This deciduous tree in planter on structure with detail is rated as heavy-duty due to the tree size and bearing capacity of inverted plastic turf grids typically associated with this structural roof deck installation. This detail may be used in all climates.

- Tree sits on prepared lightweight amended soil, sand, fabric separator, and 3 layers of inverted plastic turf grids on drain mat, protection board, and sloping waterproof membrane on structural slab.

- Tree height should be placed at or above previous existing grade as shown.

- Staking and guying are reserved for windy sites only, and should not be routinely specified. When specified, care should be taken to protect bark and wires should be removed as soon as possible.

- It is recommended that recycled and regionally available materials and products be given high priority in determining final design and specifications.

Installation Cost (per Unit)

LOW ▪▪▪▪▪ ▪▪▪▪ HIGH

$500.00

Maintenance

LOW ▪▪▪▪▪▪▪▪▪ HIGH

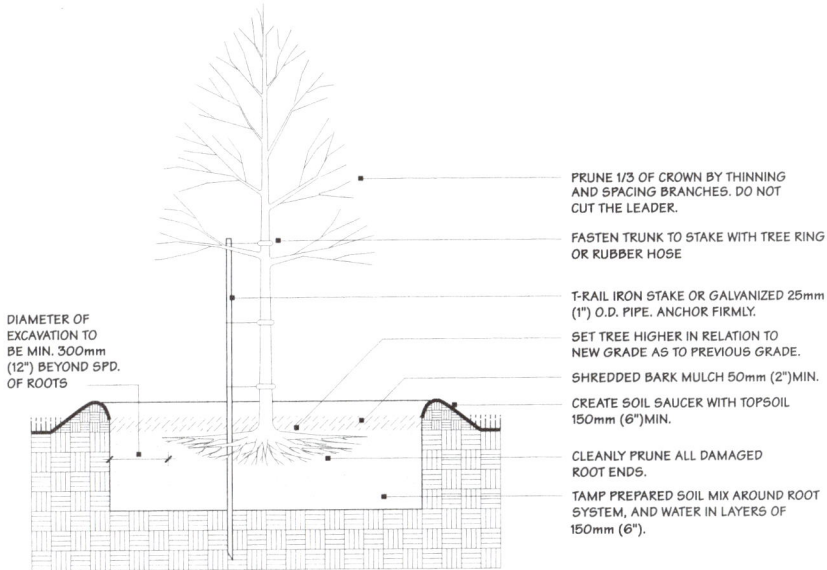

DIAMETER OF
EXCAVATION TO
BE MIN. 300mm
(12") BEYOND SPD.
OF ROOTS

PRUNE 1/3 OF CROWN BY THINNING
AND SPACING BRANCHES. DO NOT
CUT THE LEADER.

FASTEN TRUNK TO STAKE WITH TREE RING
OR RUBBER HOSE

T-RAIL IRON STAKE OR GALVANIZED 25mm
(1") O.D. PIPE. ANCHOR FIRMLY.

SET TREE HIGHER IN RELATION TO
NEW GRADE AS TO PREVIOUS GRADE.

SHREDDED BARK MULCH 50mm (2")MIN.

CREATE SOIL SAUCER WITH TOPSOIL
150mm (6")MIN.

CLEANLY PRUNE ALL DAMAGED
ROOT ENDS.

TAMP PREPARED SOIL MIX AROUND ROOT
SYSTEM, AND WATER IN LAYERS OF
150mm (6").

APPLICATION

CLIMATE

SUBGRADE

CSI MASTERFORMAT: 02930
DRAWING FILE: PLA10-10

• This drawing is a template for preliminary design only, and is not intended for bid purposes. It is subject to modification based on design calculations, local practices, and all applicable codes and regulations.

• This deciduous bare root tree planting detail is rated as light-duty due to the tree size and residential or garden location typically associated with this installation in all climates.

• Tree sits on amended soil which is firmly tamped and backfilled all around root clump. Water is used to flood air out of the hole and to moisten the roots.

• Tree should be set high to allow for settlement.

• A soil saucer filled with mulch is used to conserve water and keep roots cool during recovery period of initial growth.

• Staking and guying are reserved for windy sites only, and should not be routinely specified. When specified, care should be

taken to protect bark and wires should be removed as soon as possible. Bare root trees may need staking as shown.

• It is recommended that recycled and regionally available materials and products be given high priority in determining final design and specifications.

Installation Cost (per Unit)

LOW   HIGH

$200.00

Maintenance

LOW   HIGH

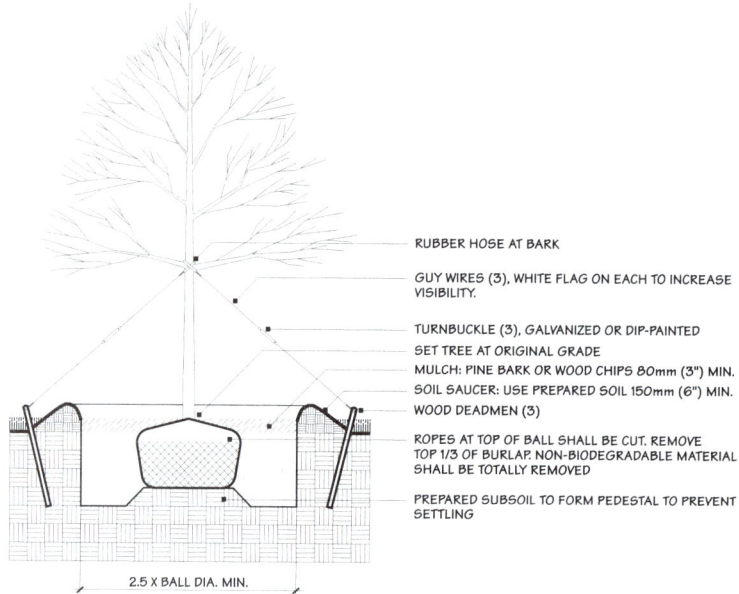

RUBBER HOSE AT BARK

GUY WIRES (3), WHITE FLAG ON EACH TO INCREASE VISIBILITY.

TURNBUCKLE (3), GALVANIZED OR DIP-PAINTED

SET TREE AT ORIGINAL GRADE

MULCH: PINE BARK OR WOOD CHIPS 80mm (3") MIN.

SOIL SAUCER: USE PREPARED SOIL 150mm (6") MIN.

WOOD DEADMEN (3)

ROPES AT TOP OF BALL SHALL BE CUT. REMOVE TOP 1/3 OF BURLAP. NON-BIODEGRADABLE MATERIAL SHALL BE TOTALLY REMOVED

PREPARED SUBSOIL TO FORM PEDESTAL TO PREVENT SETTLING

2.5 X BALL DIA. MIN.

APPLICATION

CLIMATE

SUBGRADE

CSI MASTERFORMAT: 02930
DRAWING FILE: PLA10-03

• This drawing is a template for preliminary design only, and is not intended for bid purposes. It is subject to modification based on design calculations, local practices, and all applicable codes and regulations.

• This deciduous tree planting on windy site detail is rated as heavy-duty due to the tree size and urban or institutional location typically associated with this installation in all climates.

• Tree sits on subgrade pedestal to prevent settlement and is firmly backfilled with amended soil.

• A soil saucer filled with mulch is used to conserve water and keep roots cool during recovery period of initial growth.

• Tree height should be placed at or above previous existing grade as shown.

• Staking and guying are reserved for windy sites only, and should not be routinely specified. When specified, care should be taken to protect bark and wires should be removed as soon as possible.

• It is recommended that recycled and regionally available materials and products be given high priority in determining final design and specifications.

Installation Cost (per Unit)

LOW   HIGH

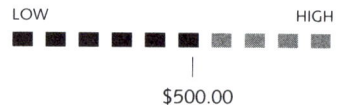

$500.00

Maintenance

LOW   HIGH

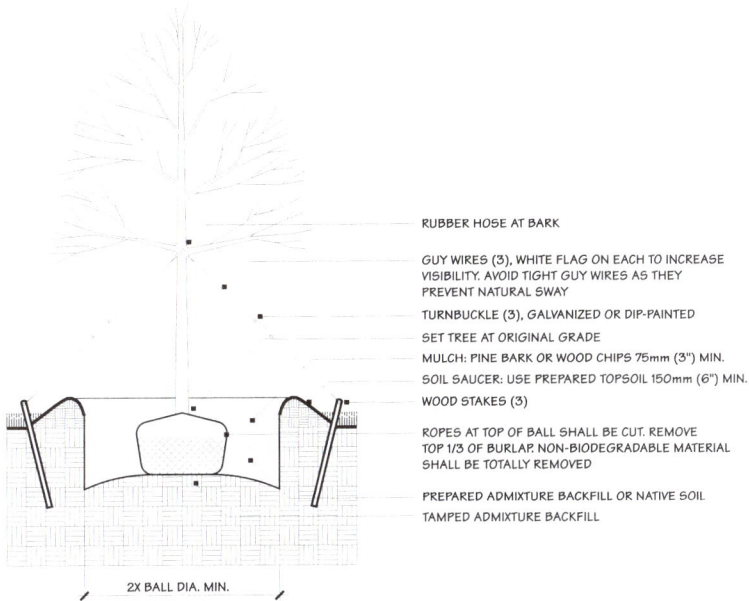

RUBBER HOSE AT BARK

GUY WIRES (3), WHITE FLAG ON EACH TO INCREASE VISIBILITY. AVOID TIGHT GUY WIRES AS THEY PREVENT NATURAL SWAY

TURNBUCKLE (3), GALVANIZED OR DIP-PAINTED

SET TREE AT ORIGINAL GRADE

MULCH: PINE BARK OR WOOD CHIPS 75mm (3") MIN.

SOIL SAUCER: USE PREPARED TOPSOIL 150mm (6") MIN.

WOOD STAKES (3)

ROPES AT TOP OF BALL SHALL BE CUT. REMOVE TOP 1/3 OF BURLAP. NON-BIODEGRADABLE MATERIAL SHALL BE TOTALLY REMOVED

PREPARED ADMIXTURE BACKFILL OR NATIVE SOIL

TAMPED ADMIXTURE BACKFILL

2X BALL DIA. MIN.

APPLICATION	CLIMATE	SUBGRADE

CSI MASTERFORMAT: 02930
DRAWING FILE: PLA10-06

• This drawing is a template for preliminary design only, and is not intended for bid purposes. It is subject to modification based on design calculations, local practices, and all applicable codes and regulations.

• This deciduous tree planting detail is rated as medium-duty due to the tree size and residential or garden location typically associated with this installation in all climates.

• Tree sits on prepared admixture pedestal to prevent settlement and is firmly backfilled with amended soil. Smaller trees with less weight may be placed on site-built mound within the hole.

• A soil saucer filled with mulch is used to conserve water and keep roots cool during recovery period of initial growth.

• Tree height should be placed at or above previous existing grade as shown.

• Staking and guying are reserved for windy sites only, and should not be routinely specified. When specified, care should be

taken to protect bark and wires should be removed as soon as possible.

• It is recommended that recycled and regionally available materials and products be given high priority in determining final design and specifications.

Installation Cost (per Unit)

LOW   HIGH

$400.00

Maintenance

LOW   HIGH

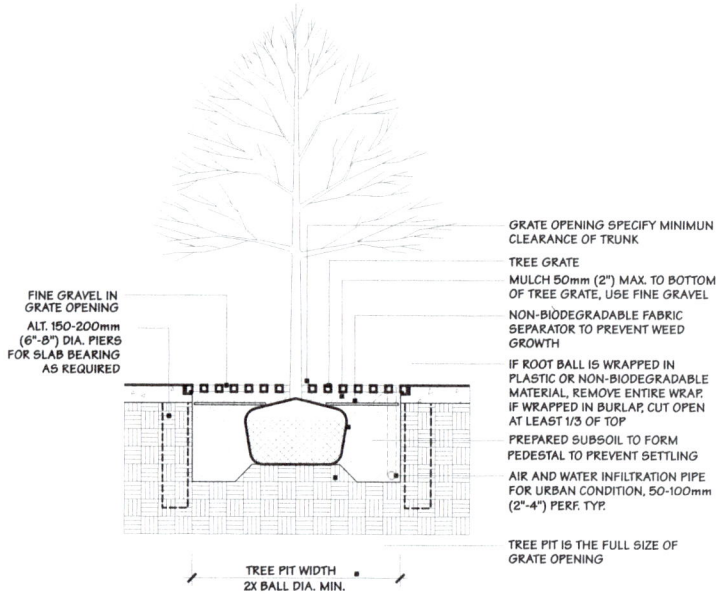

FINE GRAVEL IN GRATE OPENING

ALT. 150-200mm (6"-8") DIA. PIERS FOR SLAB BEARING AS REQUIRED

GRATE OPENING SPECIFY MINIMUN CLEARANCE OF TRUNK

TREE GRATE

MULCH 50mm (2") MAX. TO BOTTOM OF TREE GRATE, USE FINE GRAVEL

NON-BIODEGRADABLE FABRIC SEPARATOR TO PREVENT WEED GROWTH

IF ROOT BALL IS WRAPPED IN PLASTIC OR NON-BIODEGRADABLE MATERIAL, REMOVE ENTIRE WRAP. IF WRAPPED IN BURLAP, CUT OPEN AT LEAST 1/3 OF TOP

PREPARED SUBSOIL TO FORM PEDESTAL TO PREVENT SETTLING

AIR AND WATER INFILTRATION PIPE FOR URBAN CONDITION, 50-100mm (2"-4") PERF. TYP.

TREE PIT IS THE FULL SIZE OF GRATE OPENING

TREE PIT WIDTH 2X BALL DIA. MIN.

APPLICATION

CLIMATE

SUBGRADE

CSI MASTERFORMAT: 02930
DRAWING FILE: PLA10-02

• This drawing is a template for preliminary design only, and is not intended for bid purposes. It is subject to modification based on design calculations, local practices, and all applicable codes and regulations.

• This deciduous tree planting with metal grate detail is rated as heavy-duty due to the tree size and urban location typically associated with this installation in all climates.

• Tree sits on subgrade pedestal to prevent settlement and is firmly backfilled with amended soil.

• Grate is placed on embedded frame in pavement opening and pavement is sloped away from tree to avoid loading with silts, debris, and chemicals when possible.

• This detail employs a perforated pipe to connect other street trees to increase air and moisture sources for tree roots.

• Oxygen, water, and nutrient supplements are administered through vertical and lateral perforated pipes.

• Staking and guying are reserved for windy sites only, and should not be routinely specified.

• It is recommended that recycled and regionally available materials and products be given high priority in determining final design and specifications.

Installation Cost (per Unit)

LOW   HIGH

$350.00

Maintenance

LOW   HIGH

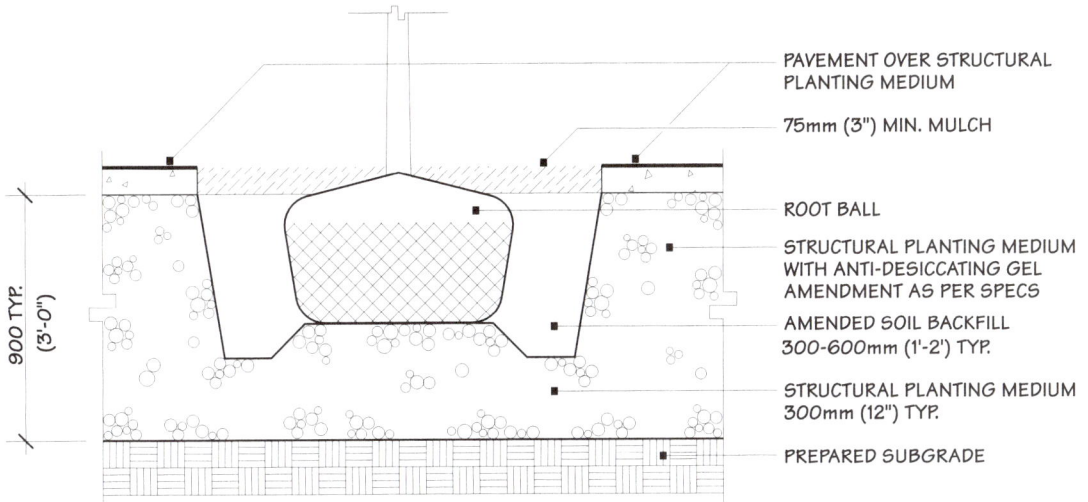

PAVEMENT OVER STRUCTURAL PLANTING MEDIUM

75mm (3") MIN. MULCH

ROOT BALL

STRUCTURAL PLANTING MEDIUM WITH ANTI-DESICCATING GEL AMENDMENT AS PER SPECS

AMENDED SOIL BACKFILL 300-600mm (1'-2') TYP.

STRUCTURAL PLANTING MEDIUM 300mm (12") TYP.

PREPARED SUBGRADE

900 TYP. (3'-0")

APPLICATION

CLIMATE

SUBGRADE

CSI MASTERFORMAT: 02930
DRAWING FILE: PLA10-18

• This drawing is a template for preliminary design only, and is not intended for bid purposes. It is subject to modification based on design calculations, local practices, and all applicable codes and regulations.

• This deciduous tree planting in structural medium detail is rated as heavy-duty due to the tree size and urban location typically associated with this installation in all climates.

• Tree sits on subgrade pedestal of structural planting medium to prevent settlement and is firmly backfilled with amended soil. Structural medium consists of specially graded stone coated with anti-desiccating gel which is placed beneath adjacent pavement to create greater root growing volume.

• Unit pavers are set on sand over fabric separator and sloped away from tree to avoid loading with silts, debris, and chemicals when possible.

• This detail employs a perforated pipe to connect other street trees to increase air and moisture sources for tree roots.

• Oxygen, water, and nutrient supplements are administered through vertical and lateral perforated pipes.

• Staking and guying are reserved for windy sites only, and should not be routinely specified.

• It is recommended that recycled and regionally available materials and products be given high priority in determining final design and specifications.

Installation Cost (per Unit)

LOW   HIGH

$550.00

Maintenance

LOW   HIGH

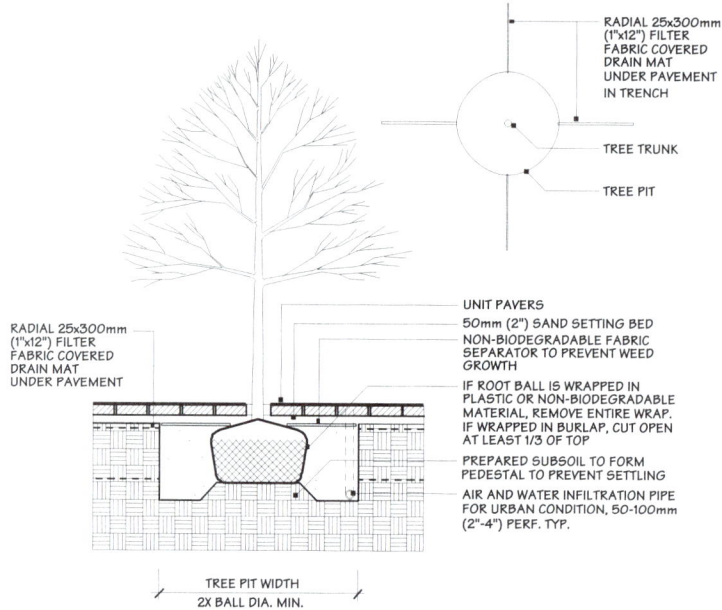

RADIAL 25x300mm (1"x12") FILTER FABRIC COVERED DRAIN MAT UNDER PAVEMENT IN TRENCH

TREE TRUNK

TREE PIT

RADIAL 25x300mm (1"x12") FILTER FABRIC COVERED DRAIN MAT UNDER PAVEMENT

UNIT PAVERS

50mm (2") SAND SETTING BED

NON-BIODEGRADABLE FABRIC SEPARATOR TO PREVENT WEED GROWTH

IF ROOT BALL IS WRAPPED IN PLASTIC OR NON-BIODEGRADABLE MATERIAL, REMOVE ENTIRE WRAP. IF WRAPPED IN BURLAP, CUT OPEN AT LEAST 1/3 OF TOP

PREPARED SUBSOIL TO FORM PEDESTAL TO PREVENT SETTLING

AIR AND WATER INFILTRATION PIPE FOR URBAN CONDITION, 50-100mm (2"-4") PERF. TYP.

TREE PIT WIDTH
2X BALL DIA. MIN.

APPLICATION

LIGHT   MED.   HEAVY

CLIMATE

ARID   HUMID   TEMP.   COLD

SUBGRADE

PERM.   CLAY   ROOF

CSI MASTERFORMAT: 02930
DRAWING FILE: PLA10-01

• This drawing is a template for preliminary design only, and is not intended for bid purposes. It is subject to modification based on design calculations, local practices, and all applicable codes and regulations.

• This deciduous tree planting in pavement detail is rated as heavy-duty due to the tree size and urban location typically associated with this installation in all climates.

• Tree sits on subgrade pedestal to prevent settlement and is firmly backfilled with amended soil.

• Unit pavers are set on sand over fabric separator and sloped away from tree to avoid loading with silts, debris, and chemicals when possible.

• This detail employs a perforated pipe to connect other street trees and radiating trenches filled with spun filament material and placed under pavement to increase air and moisture sources for tree roots.

• Oxygen, water, and nutrient supplements are administered through vertical and lateral perforated pipes.

• Staking and guying are reserved for windy sites only, and should not be routinely specified.

• It is recommended that recycled and regionally available materials and products be given high priority in determining final design and specifications.

Installation Cost (per Unit)

LOW   HIGH

$300.00

Maintenance

LOW   HIGH

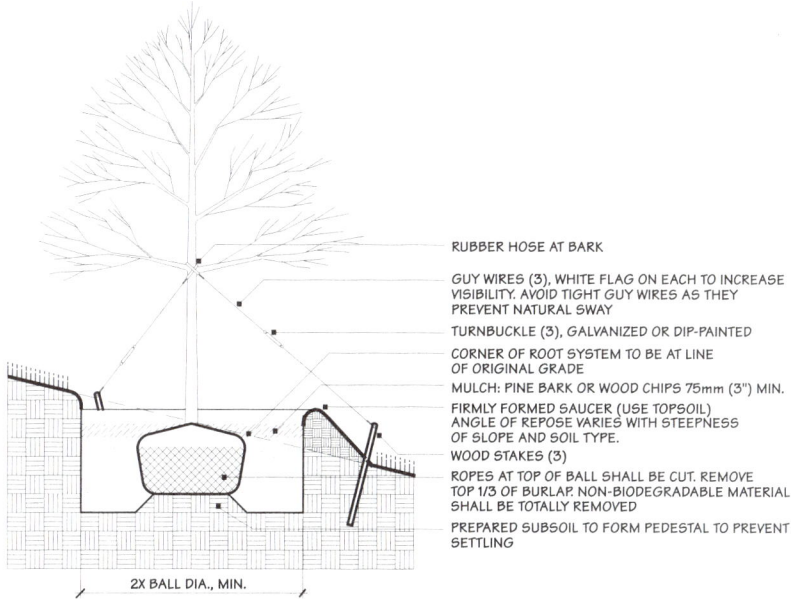

RUBBER HOSE AT BARK

GUY WIRES (3), WHITE FLAG ON EACH TO INCREASE VISIBILITY. AVOID TIGHT GUY WIRES AS THEY PREVENT NATURAL SWAY

TURNBUCKLE (3), GALVANIZED OR DIP-PAINTED

CORNER OF ROOT SYSTEM TO BE AT LINE OF ORIGINAL GRADE

MULCH: PINE BARK OR WOOD CHIPS 75mm (3") MIN.

FIRMLY FORMED SAUCER (USE TOPSOIL) ANGLE OF REPOSE VARIES WITH STEEPNESS OF SLOPE AND SOIL TYPE.

WOOD STAKES (3)

ROPES AT TOP OF BALL SHALL BE CUT. REMOVE TOP 1/3 OF BURLAP. NON-BIODEGRADABLE MATERIAL SHALL BE TOTALLY REMOVED

PREPARED SUBSOIL TO FORM PEDESTAL TO PREVENT SETTLING

2X BALL DIA., MIN.

APPLICATION

CLIMATE

SUBGRADE

CSI MASTERFORMAT: 02930
DRAWING FILE: PLA10-04

• This drawing is a template for preliminary design only, and is not intended for bid purposes. It is subject to modification based on design calculations, local practices, and all applicable codes and regulations.

• This deciduous tree planting on slope detail is rated as heavy-duty due to the tree size and urban or institutional location typically associated with this installation in all climates.

• Tree sits on subgrade pedestal to prevent settlement and is firmly backfilled with amended soil.

• A soil saucer filled with mulch is used to conserve water and keep roots cool during recovery period of initial growth.

• Tree height should be placed at or above previous existing grade as shown.

• Staking and guying are reserved for windy sites only, and should not be routinely specified. When specified, care should be taken to protect bark and wires should be removed as soon as possible.

• It is recommended that recycled and regionally available materials and products be given high priority in determining final design and specifications.

Installation Cost (per Unit)

LOW   HIGH

$400.00

Maintenance

LOW   HIGH

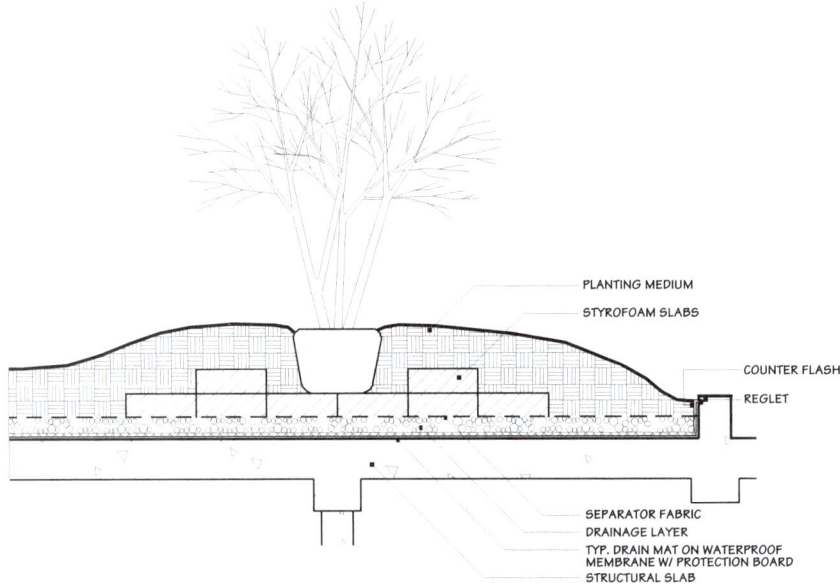

PLANTING MEDIUM
STYROFOAM SLABS
COUNTER FLASH
REGLET
SEPARATOR FABRIC
DRAINAGE LAYER
TYP. DRAIN MAT ON WATERPROOF
MEMBRANE W/ PROTECTION BOARD
STRUCTURAL SLAB

APPLICATION

CLIMATE

SUBGRADE

CSI MASTERFORMAT: 02930
DRAWING FILE: PLA10-12

• This drawing is a template for preliminary design only, and is not intended for bid purposes. It is subject to modification based on design calculations, local practices, and all applicable codes and regulations.

• This deciduous tree planting on structure with foam blocks detail is rated as medium-duty due to the tree size and weight limitations typically associated with this structural roof deck installation in all climates.

• Tree sits on prepared admixture pedestal and styrofoam blocks to raise tree ball in the mounded bed, and to lessen the weight as it bears on the structural column or slab. Alternatives include: lightweight soil and inverted plastic turf grids with fabric and sand.

• A soil saucer filled with mulch is used to conserve water and keep roots cool during recovery period of initial growth.

• Tree height should be placed at or above previous existing grade as shown.

• Staking and guying are reserved for windy sites only, and should not be routinely specified. When specified, care should be taken to protect bark and wires should be removed as soon as possible.

• It is recommended that recycled and regionally available materials and products be given high priority in determining final design and specifications.

Installation Cost (per Unit)

LOW   HIGH

$400.00

Maintenance

LOW   HIGH

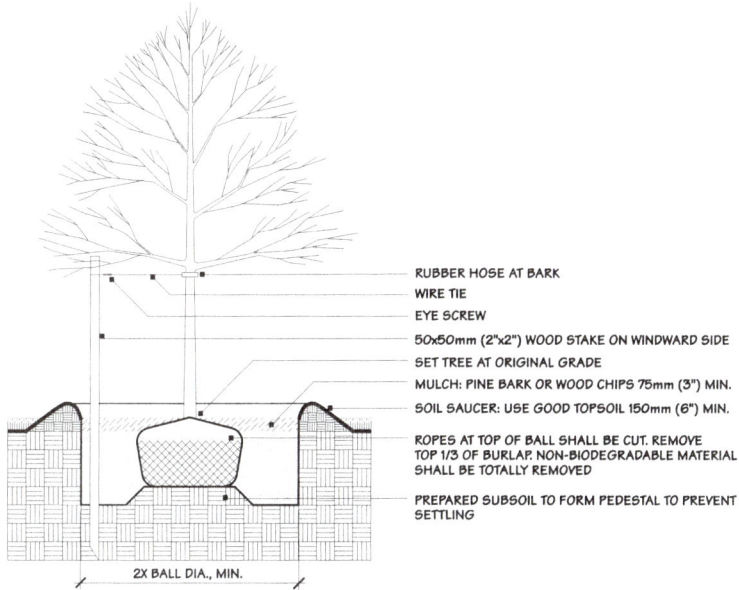

RUBBER HOSE AT BARK
WIRE TIE
EYE SCREW
50x50mm (2"x2") WOOD STAKE ON WINDWARD SIDE
SET TREE AT ORIGINAL GRADE
MULCH: PINE BARK OR WOOD CHIPS 75mm (3") MIN.
SOIL SAUCER: USE GOOD TOPSOIL 150mm (6") MIN.

ROPES AT TOP OF BALL SHALL BE CUT. REMOVE
TOP 1/3 OF BURLAP. NON-BIODEGRADABLE MATERIAL
SHALL BE TOTALLY REMOVED

PREPARED SUBSOIL TO FORM PEDESTAL TO PREVENT
SETTLING

2X BALL DIA., MIN.

APPLICATION

CLIMATE

SUBGRADE

CSI MASTERFORMAT: 02930
DRAWING FILE: PLA10-17

• This drawing is a template for preliminary design only, and is not intended for bid purposes. It is subject to modification based on design calculations, local practices, and all applicable codes and regulations.

• This deciduous tree planting with stake and wire tie detail is rated as heavy-duty due to the tree size and urban or institutional location typically associated with this installation in all climates.

• This detail shows placement of single stake on windward side of tree. If multi-directional winds prevail, select a triangular pattern for stakes.

• Tree sits on subgrade pedestal to prevent settlement and is firmly backfilled with amended soil.

• A soil saucer filled with mulch is used to conserve water and keep roots cool during recovery period of initial growth.

• Tree height should be placed at or above previous existing grade as shown.

• Staking and guying are reserved for windy sites only, and should not be routinely specified. When specified, care should be taken to protect bark and wires should be removed as soon as possible.

• It is recommended that recycled and regionally available materials and products be given high priority in determining final design and specifications.

Installation Cost (per Unit)

LOW   HIGH

$500.00

Maintenance

LOW   HIGH

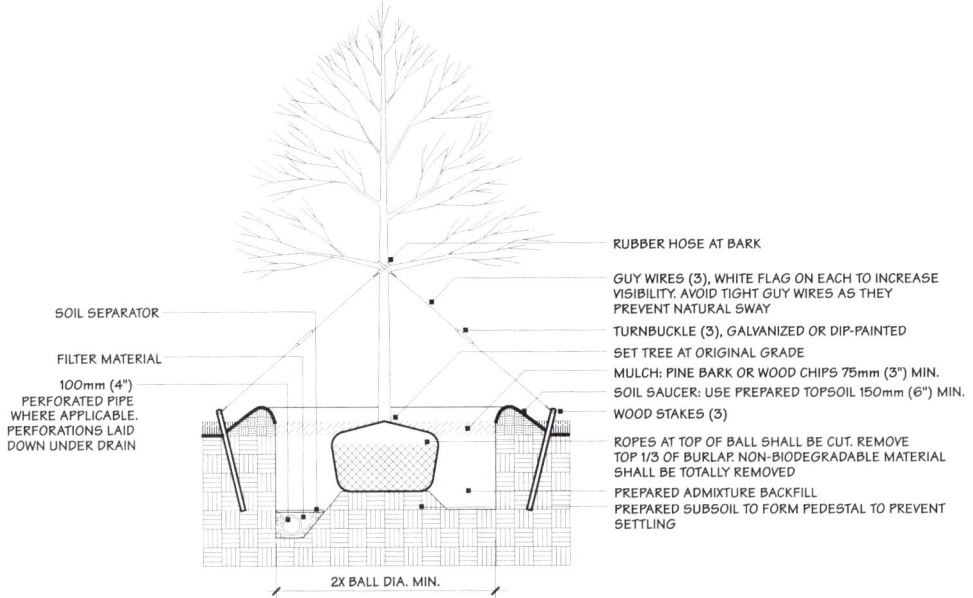

RUBBER HOSE AT BARK

GUY WIRES (3), WHITE FLAG ON EACH TO INCREASE VISIBILITY. AVOID TIGHT GUY WIRES AS THEY PREVENT NATURAL SWAY

TURNBUCKLE (3), GALVANIZED OR DIP-PAINTED

SET TREE AT ORIGINAL GRADE

MULCH: PINE BARK OR WOOD CHIPS 75mm (3") MIN.

SOIL SAUCER: USE PREPARED TOPSOIL 150mm (6") MIN.

WOOD STAKES (3)

ROPES AT TOP OF BALL SHALL BE CUT. REMOVE TOP 1/3 OF BURLAP. NON-BIODEGRADABLE MATERIAL SHALL BE TOTALLY REMOVED

PREPARED ADMIXTURE BACKFILL

PREPARED SUBSOIL TO FORM PEDESTAL TO PREVENT SETTLING

SOIL SEPARATOR

FILTER MATERIAL

100mm (4") PERFORATED PIPE WHERE APPLICABLE. PERFORATIONS LAID DOWN UNDER DRAIN

2X BALL DIA. MIN.

APPLICATION

CLIMATE

SUBGRADE

CSI MASTERFORMAT: 02930
DRAWING FILE: PLA10-05

• This drawing is a template for preliminary design only, and is not intended for bid purposes. It is subject to modification based on design calculations, local practices, and all applicable codes and regulations.

• This deciduous tree planting with drain detail is rated as heavy-duty due to the tree size and urban or institutional location typically associated with this installation in all climates.

• Tree sits on subgrade pedestal to prevent settlement and is firmly backfilled with amended soil.

• This detail shows an adaptation to wet soil or poorly drained location by means of a perforated pipe at the hole perimeter connected to other trees or daylight discharge.

• A soil saucer filled with mulch is used to conserve water and keep roots cool during recovery period of initial growth.

• Tree height should be placed at or above previous existing grade as shown.

• Staking and guying are reserved for windy sites only, and should not be routinely specified. When specified, care should be taken to protect bark and wires should be removed as soon as possible.

• It is recommended that recycled and regionally available materials and products be given high priority in determining final design and specifications.

Installation Cost (per Unit)

LOW   HIGH

$550.00

Maintenance

LOW   HIGH

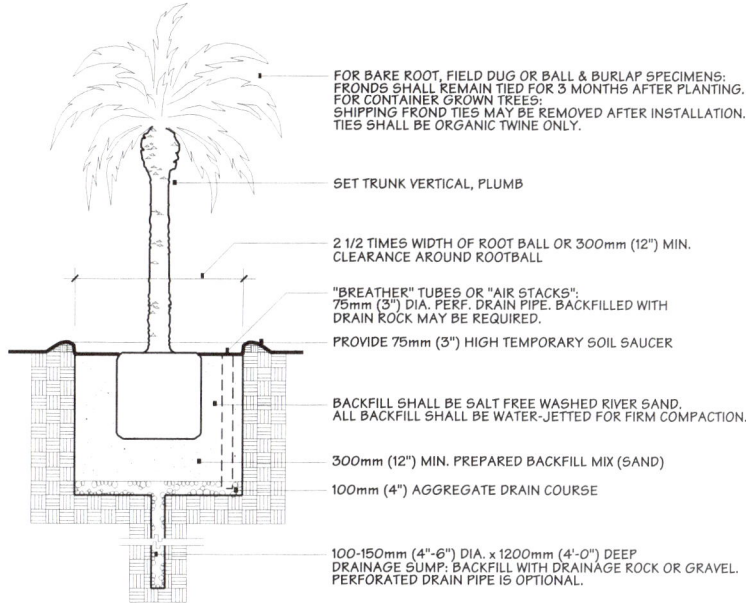

FOR BARE ROOT, FIELD DUG OR BALL & BURLAP SPECIMENS:
FRONDS SHALL REMAIN TIED FOR 3 MONTHS AFTER PLANTING.
FOR CONTAINER GROWN TREES:
SHIPPING FROND TIES MAY BE REMOVED AFTER INSTALLATION.
TIES SHALL BE ORGANIC TWINE ONLY.

SET TRUNK VERTICAL, PLUMB

2 1/2 TIMES WIDTH OF ROOT BALL OR 300mm (12") MIN.
CLEARANCE AROUND ROOTBALL

"BREATHER" TUBES OR "AIR STACKS":
75mm (3") DIA. PERF. DRAIN PIPE. BACKFILLED WITH
DRAIN ROCK MAY BE REQUIRED.

PROVIDE 75mm (3") HIGH TEMPORARY SOIL SAUCER

BACKFILL SHALL BE SALT FREE WASHED RIVER SAND.
ALL BACKFILL SHALL BE WATER-JETTED FOR FIRM COMPACTION.

300mm (12") MIN. PREPARED BACKFILL MIX (SAND)

100mm (4") AGGREGATE DRAIN COURSE

100-150mm (4"-6") DIA. x 1200mm (4'-0") DEEP
DRAINAGE SUMP: BACKFILL WITH DRAINAGE ROCK OR GRAVEL.
PERFORATED DRAIN PIPE IS OPTIONAL.

APPLICATION

CLIMATE

SUBGRADE

CSI MASTERFORMAT: 02930
DRAWING FILE: PLA10-14

• This drawing is a template for preliminary design only, and is not intended for bid purposes. It is subject to modification based on design calculations, local practices, and all applicable codes and regulations.

• This palm tree planting detail is rated as heavy-duty due to the tree size and park or urban location typically associated with this installation in all climates.

• An auger dug hole is filled with drain stone at the base of the planting hole as shown.

• Tree sits on a hydro-compacted sand amended pedestal to prevent settlement and is firmly backfilled with additional amended soil which is hydro-slurried into hole.

• This detail employs a perforated pipe to connect other street trees to increase air and moisture sources for tree roots. Oxygen, water, and nutrient supplements are administered through these pipes.

• It is recommended that recycled and regionally available materials and products be given high priority in determining final design and specifications.

Installation Cost (per Unit)

LOW   HIGH

$450.00

Maintenance

LOW   HIGH

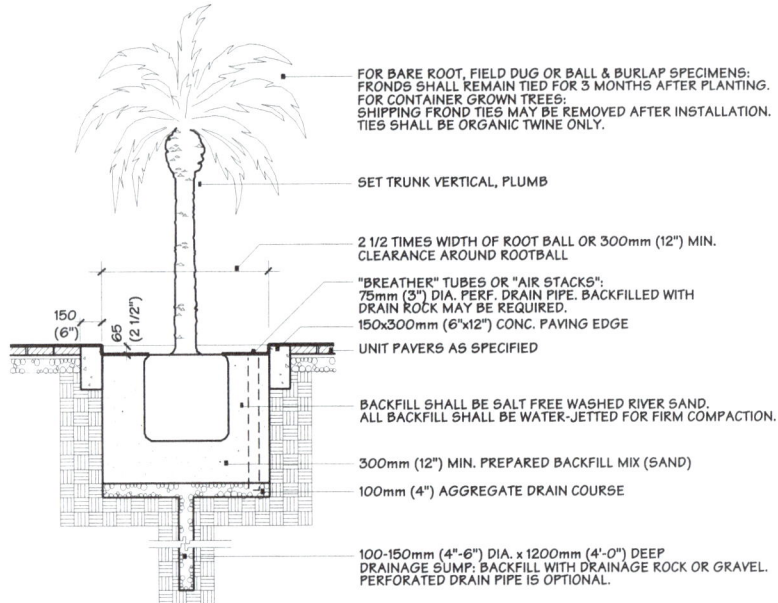

FOR BARE ROOT, FIELD DUG OR BALL & BURLAP SPECIMENS:
FRONDS SHALL REMAIN TIED FOR 3 MONTHS AFTER PLANTING.
FOR CONTAINER GROWN TREES:
SHIPPING FROND TIES MAY BE REMOVED AFTER INSTALLATION.
TIES SHALL BE ORGANIC TWINE ONLY.

SET TRUNK VERTICAL, PLUMB

2 1/2 TIMES WIDTH OF ROOT BALL OR 300mm (12") MIN.
CLEARANCE AROUND ROOTBALL

"BREATHER" TUBES OR "AIR STACKS":
75mm (3") DIA. PERF. DRAIN PIPE. BACKFILLED WITH
DRAIN ROCK MAY BE REQUIRED.
150x300mm (6"x12") CONC. PAVING EDGE

UNIT PAVERS AS SPECIFIED

BACKFILL SHALL BE SALT FREE WASHED RIVER SAND.
ALL BACKFILL SHALL BE WATER-JETTED FOR FIRM COMPACTION.

300mm (12") MIN. PREPARED BACKFILL MIX (SAND)

100mm (4") AGGREGATE DRAIN COURSE

100-150mm (4"-6") DIA. x 1200mm (4'-0") DEEP
DRAINAGE SUMP: BACKFILL WITH DRAINAGE ROCK OR GRAVEL.
PERFORATED DRAIN PIPE IS OPTIONAL.

150 (6")   65 (2 1/2")

APPLICATION

CLIMATE

SUBGRADE

CSI MASTERFORMAT: 02930
DRAWING FILE: PLA10-15

• This drawing is a template for preliminary design only, and is not intended for bid purposes. It is subject to modification based on design calculations, local practices, and all applicable codes and regulations.

• This palm tree planting in paving detail is rated as heavy-duty due to the tree size and park or urban location typically associated with this installation in all climates.

• An auger dug hole is filled with drain stone at the base of the planting hole as shown.

• Tree sits on a hydro-compacted sand amended pedestal to prevent settlement and is firmly backfilled with additional amended soil which is hydro-slurried into hole.

• This detail employs a perforated pipe to connect other street trees to increase air and moisture sources for tree roots. Oxygen, water, and nutrient supplements are administered through these pipes.

• Hole opening is edged with a concrete curb to contain pavement and to create watering recess for the tree.

• It is recommended that recycled and regionally available materials and products be given high priority in determining final design and specifications.

Installation Cost (per Unit)

LOW   HIGH

$520.00

Maintenance

LOW   HIGH

Ponds

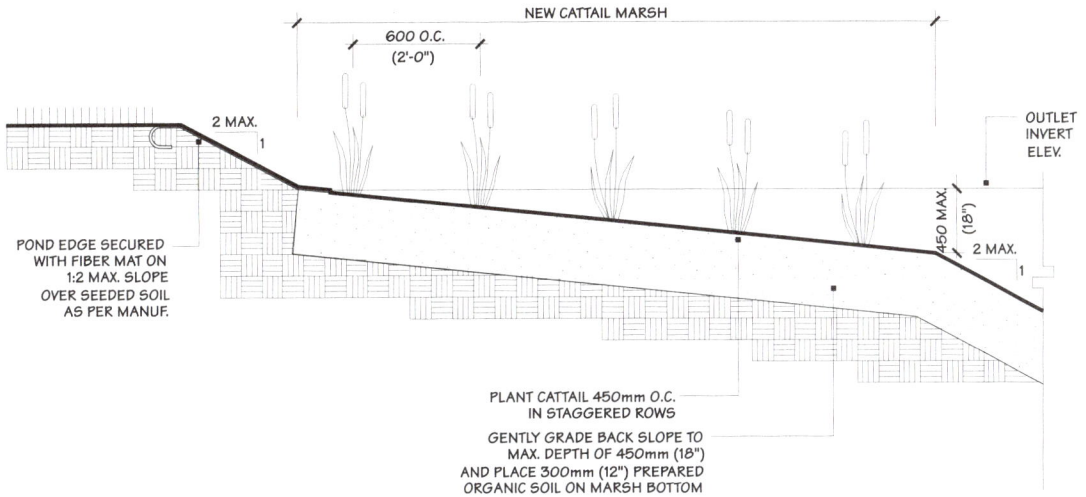

NEW CATTAIL MARSH

600 O.C.
(2'-0")

2 MAX.
1

OUTLET
INVERT
ELEV.

POND EDGE SECURED
WITH FIBER MAT ON
1:2 MAX. SLOPE
OVER SEEDED SOIL
AS PER MANUF.

450 MAX.
(18")

2 MAX.
1

PLANT CATTAIL 450mm O.C.
IN STAGGERED ROWS

GENTLY GRADE BACK SLOPE TO
MAX. DEPTH OF 450mm (18")
AND PLACE 300mm (12") PREPARED
ORGANIC SOIL ON MARSH BOTTOM

APPLICATION

CLIMATE

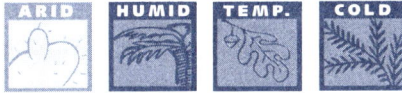

SUBGRADE

CSI MASTERFORMAT: 02670
DRAWING FILE: PND00-01

• This drawing is a template for preliminary design only, and is not intended for bid purposes. It is subject to modification based on design calculations, local practices, and all applicable codes and regulations.

• This augmented wetland pond edge detail is rated as heavy-duty due to hydraulic volume potential and typical application in commercial, institutional, and public park settings.

• This detail shows an existing wetland augmented with prepared organic soil, wetland plants for chemical balance and habitat, and fiber mat slope stabilization to heal the excavation scar.

• All wetland plants have specific soil, moisture, and depth tolerances. Use local native species for best results.

• It is recommended that recycled and regionally available materials and products be given high priority in determining final design and specifications.

Installation Cost (per Square Foot)

LOW   HIGH

$2.50

Maintenance

LOW   HIGH

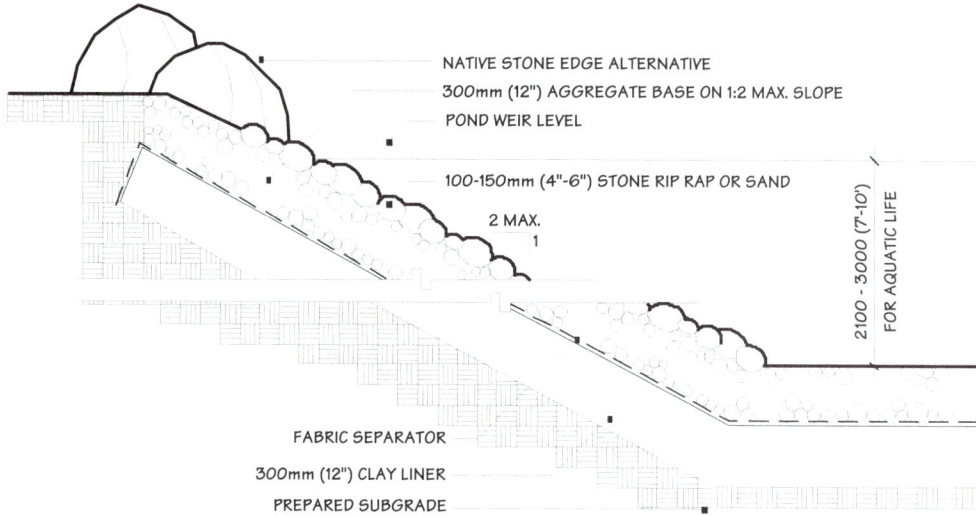

NATIVE STONE EDGE ALTERNATIVE

300mm (12") AGGREGATE BASE ON 1:2 MAX. SLOPE

POND WEIR LEVEL

100-150mm (4"-6") STONE RIP RAP OR SAND

2 MAX.
1

2100 - 3000 (7'-10')
FOR AQUATIC LIFE

FABRIC SEPARATOR

300mm (12") CLAY LINER

PREPARED SUBGRADE

APPLICATION

CLIMATE

SUBGRADE

CSI MASTERFORMAT: 02670
DRAWING FILE: PND00-05

• This drawing is a template for preliminary design only, and is not intended for bid purposes. It is subject to modification based on design calculations, local practices, and all applicable codes and regulations.

• This clay lined pond edge detail is rated as medium-duty due to hydraulic volume potential and typical application in residential, commercial, institutional, and public park settings.

• This detail shows imported clay lining placed on excavated subgrade, and covered with fabric separator to inhibit fine migration and to limit turbidity, covered by a layer of aggregate.

• Heavy stones require aggregate base at pond edge.

• Pond must achieve minimum depth for biological cycles if intended for botanical purposes.

• It is recommended that recycled and regionally available materials and products be given high priority in determining final design and specifications.

Installation Cost (per Square Foot)

LOW   HIGH

$9.50

Maintenance

LOW   HIGH

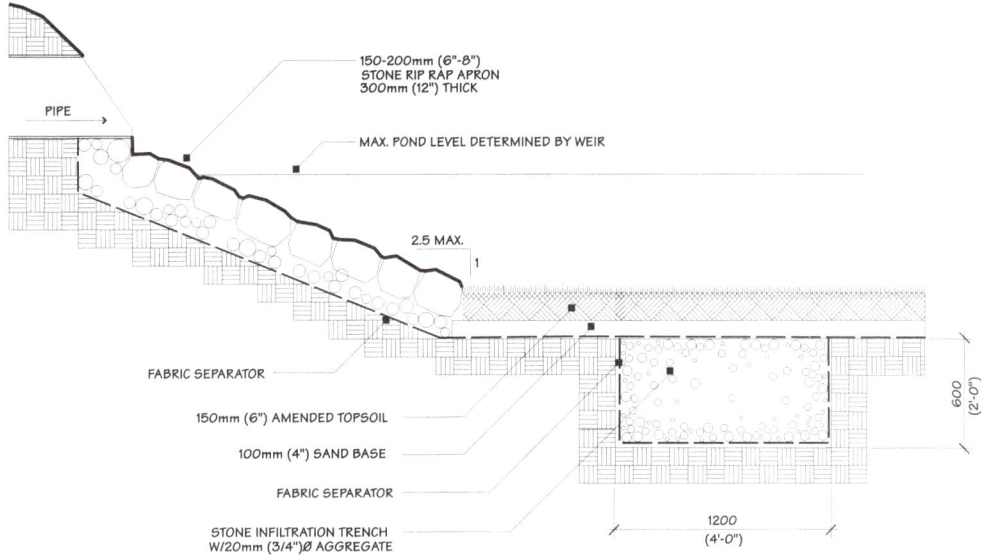

150-200mm (6"-8")
STONE RIP RAP APRON
300mm (12") THICK

MAX. POND LEVEL DETERMINED BY WEIR

PIPE

2.5 MAX.
1

FABRIC SEPARATOR

150mm (6") AMENDED TOPSOIL

100mm (4") SAND BASE

FABRIC SEPARATOR

STONE INFILTRATION TRENCH
W/20mm (3/4")Ø AGGREGATE

600 (2'-0")

1200 (4'-0")

APPLICATION

CLIMATE

SUBGRADE

CSI MASTERFORMAT: 02670
DRAWING FILE: PND00-03

• This drawing is a template for preliminary design only, and is not intended for bid purposes. It is subject to modification based on design calculations, local practices, and all applicable codes and regulations.

• This infiltration detention pond edge detail is rated as heavy-duty due to hydraulic volume potential and typical application in commercial, institutional, and public park settings.

• This detail shows a prepared horizontal dispersal basin with fabric lined stone infiltration trench to recycle site storm water. It illustrates a stone slope stabilization to dissipate energy of discharge pipe water.

• Storm water requires initial settlement before entering this re-charge basin to avoid rapid silt build-up. Soils must be moderately well drained. Maximum volume and rate must be calculated according to local soil and runoff data.

• It is recommended that recycled and regionally available materials and products be given high priority in determining final design and specifications.

Installation Cost (per Square Foot)

LOW   HIGH

$2.50

Maintenance

LOW   HIGH

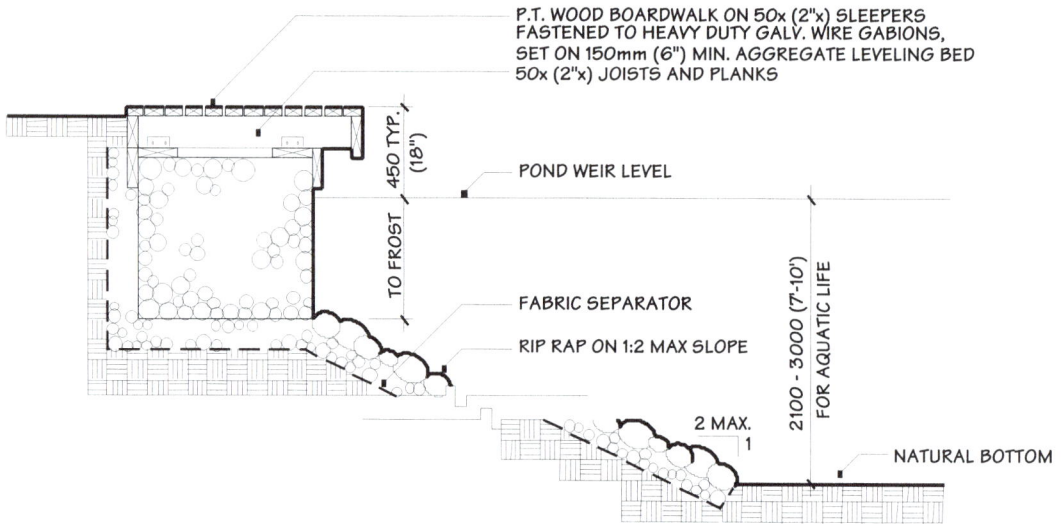

P.T. WOOD BOARDWALK ON 50x (2"x) SLEEPERS
FASTENED TO HEAVY DUTY GALV. WIRE GABIONS,
SET ON 150mm (6") MIN. AGGREGATE LEVELING BED
50x (2"x) JOISTS AND PLANKS

450 TYP. (18")

TO FROST

POND WEIR LEVEL

FABRIC SEPARATOR

RIP RAP ON 1:2 MAX SLOPE

2100 - 3000 (7'-10') FOR AQUATIC LIFE

2 MAX.
1

NATURAL BOTTOM

APPLICATION

CLIMATE

SUBGRADE

CSI MASTERFORMAT: 02670
DRAWING FILE: PND00-07

• This drawing is a template for preliminary design only, and is not intended for bid purposes. It is subject to modification based on design calculations, local practices, and all applicable codes and regulations.

• This boardwalk pond access on gabions detail is rated as heavy-duty due to hydraulic volume potential and typical application in institutional and public park settings.

• This detail shows bank of existing pond or proposed pond, augmented to allow access to water edge by means of a stone filled gabion structure on aggregate base.

• Treated or rot resistant wood deck is built as shown on the stone base using mortar shimmed sleepers to achieve level line.

• Fabric separator course helps to bind aggregate and supress migration of fines.

• Pond must achieve minimum depth for biological cycles if intended for botanical purposes.

• It is recommended that recycled and regionally available materials and products be given high priority in determining final design and specifications.

Installation Cost (per Square Foot)

LOW   HIGH

$15.00

Maintenance

LOW   HIGH

ALT. STONE EDGE ON 150mm (6") AGGREGATE BASE
PROTECTION MAT
100-150mm (4"-6") STONE AT WAVE ACTION ZONE

POND WEIR LEVEL

DRAW DOWN

2 MAX.
1

2100 - 3000 (7'-10")
FOR AQUATIC LIFE

TURN BACK LINER
AND BURY IN SOIL

SAND CUSHION
IF REQ.

150mm (6") AGGREGATE COVER
EPDM MEMBRANE / FIELD SEALED
PREPARED SUBGRADE

APPLICATION

LIGHT | MED. | HEAVY

CLIMATE

ARID | HUMID | TEMP. | COLD

SUBGRADE

PERM. | CLAY | ROOF

CSI MASTERFORMAT: 02670
DRAWING FILE: PND00-04

• This drawing is a template for preliminary design only, and is not intended for bid purposes. It is subject to modification based on design calculations, local practices, and all applicable codes and regulations.

• This stone edge at lined pond detail is rated as medium-duty due to hydraulic volume potential and typical application in residential, commercial, institutional, and public park settings.

• This detail shows a field sealed membrane placed on cushioned subgrade, and protected at embankment edges by a sandy aggregate layer, with cobble demarcating weir draw-down and wave action zone.

• Heavy stones require protection mat and aggregate base when placed within the membrane edge.

• Pond must achieve minimum depth for biological cycles if intended for botanical purposes.

• It is recommended that recycled and regionally available materials and products be given high priority in determining final design and specifications.

Installation Cost (per Square Foot)

LOW   HIGH

$12.50

Maintenance

LOW   HIGH

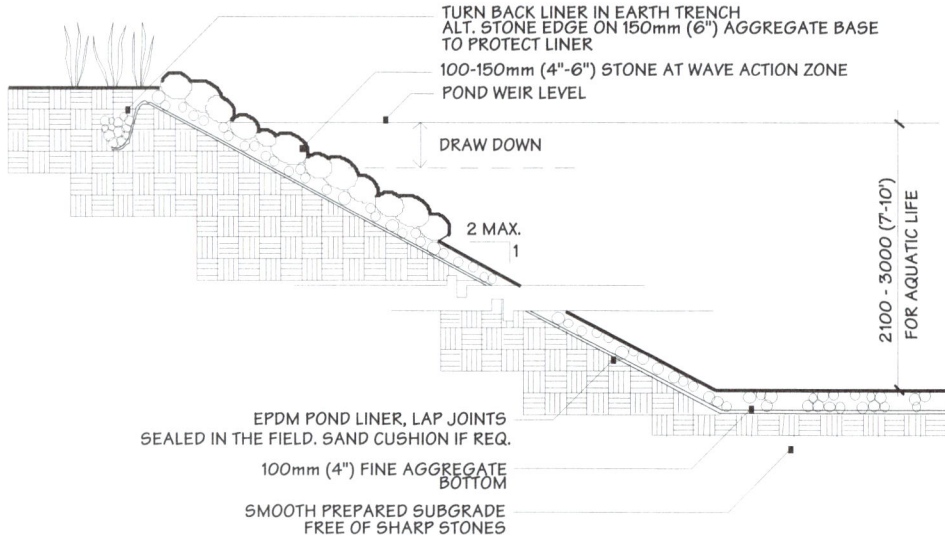

TURN BACK LINER IN EARTH TRENCH
ALT. STONE EDGE ON 150mm (6") AGGREGATE BASE
TO PROTECT LINER

100-150mm (4"-6") STONE AT WAVE ACTION ZONE
POND WEIR LEVEL

DRAW DOWN

2 MAX.
1

2100 - 3000 (7'-10')
FOR AQUATIC LIFE

EPDM POND LINER, LAP JOINTS
SEALED IN THE FIELD. SAND CUSHION IF REQ.

100mm (4") FINE AGGREGATE
BOTTOM

SMOOTH PREPARED SUBGRADE
FREE OF SHARP STONES

APPLICATION

CLIMATE

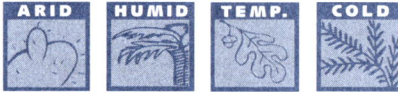

SUBGRADE

CSI MASTERFORMAT: 02670
DRAWING FILE: PND00-06

• This drawing is a template for preliminary design only, and is not intended for bid purposes. It is subject to modification based on design calculations, local practices, and all applicable codes and regulations.

• This polymer lined pond edge detail is rated as light-duty due to hydraulic volume potential and typical application in residential and public park settings.

• This detail shows a field sealed membrane placed on cushioned subgrade, and protected at embankment edges by a sandy aggregate layer, with cobble demarcating weir draw-down and wave action zone.

• Heavy stones require protection mat and aggregate base when placed within the membrane edge. Edge is treated simply with native planting and stone.

• Pond must achieve minimum depth for biological cycles if intended for botanical purposes.

• It is recommended that recycled and regionally available materials and products be given high priority in determining final design and specifications.

Installation Cost (per Square Foot)

LOW   HIGH

$10.25

Maintenance

LOW   HIGH

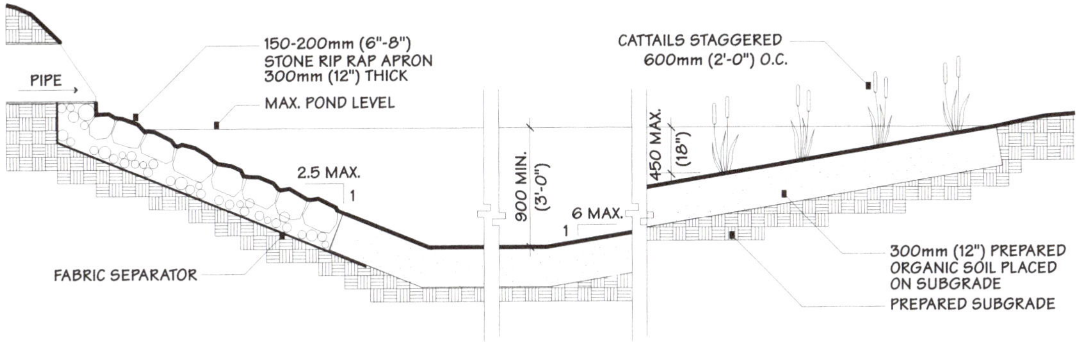

150-200mm (6"-8")
STONE RIP RAP APRON
300mm (12") THICK

MAX. POND LEVEL

PIPE

CATTAILS STAGGERED
600mm (2'-0") O.C.

2.5 MAX.
1

900 MIN.
(3'-0")

450 MAX.
(18")

6 MAX.
1

FABRIC SEPARATOR

300mm (12") PREPARED
ORGANIC SOIL PLACED
ON SUBGRADE
PREPARED SUBGRADE

APPLICATION

LIGHT | MED. | HEAVY

CLIMATE

ARID | HUMID | TEMP. | COLD

SUBGRADE

PERM. | CLAY | ROOF

CSI MASTERFORMAT: 02670
DRAWING FILE: PND00-02

• This drawing is a template for preliminary design only, and is not intended for bid purposes. It is subject to modification based on design calculations, local practices, and all applicable codes and regulations.

• This pre-treatment marsh detail is rated as medium-duty due to hydraulic volume potential and typical application in commercial, institutional, and public park settings.

• This detail shows an existing wetland augmented with prepared organic soil, wetland plants for chemical balance and habitat, and stone slope stabilization to dissipate energy of discharge pipe water.

• All wetland plants have specific soil, moisture, and depth tolerances. Use local native species for best results.

• It is recommended that recycled and regionally available materials and products be given high priority in determining final design and specifications.

Installation Cost (per Square Foot)

LOW — HIGH

$2.00

Maintenance

LOW — HIGH

Pools

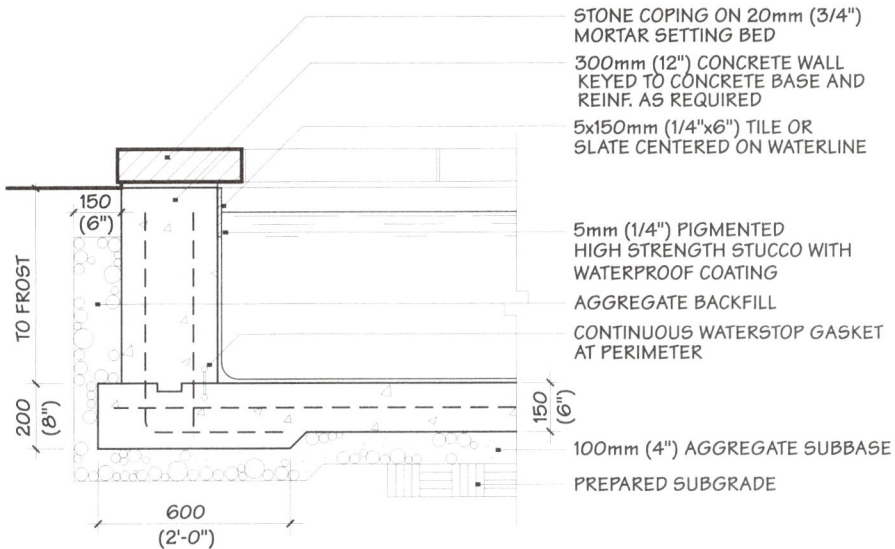

STONE COPING ON 20mm (3/4")
MORTAR SETTING BED

300mm (12") CONCRETE WALL
KEYED TO CONCRETE BASE AND
REINF. AS REQUIRED

5x150mm (1/4"x6") TILE OR
SLATE CENTERED ON WATERLINE

5mm (1/4") PIGMENTED
HIGH STRENGTH STUCCO WITH
WATERPROOF COATING

AGGREGATE BACKFILL

CONTINUOUS WATERSTOP GASKET
AT PERIMETER

100mm (4") AGGREGATE SUBBASE

PREPARED SUBGRADE

150 (6")

TO FROST

200 (8")

150 (6")

600 (2'-0")

APPLICATION

CLIMATE

SUBGRADE

CSI MASTERFORMAT: 13160
DRAWING FILE: POO02-02

• This drawing is a template for preliminary design only, and is not intended for bid purposes. It is subject to modification based on design calculations, local practices, and all applicable codes and regulations.

• This concrete garden pool is rated as medium-duty due to depth and utility of use. It is typically found in residential, garden, and park settings and used to display aquatic plants and animals, although it may be adapted to occasional human use for wading and emersion with proper filtration and circulation.

• Concrete walls are fully reinforced with steel rods as required by local conditions. Wall and base are connected by a continuous water-stop gasket. Footing should rest on frost free subgrade where required.

• This detail requires careful maintenance and monitoring of stucco lining finish and is more effective in warmer climates.

• Water requires filtering, recirculation, and careful attention to pH level to sustain life. Design may include display fountain.

• It is recommended that recycled and regionally available materials and products be given high priority in determining final design and specifications.

Installation Cost (per Square Foot)

LOW   HIGH

$20.00

Maintenance

LOW   HIGH

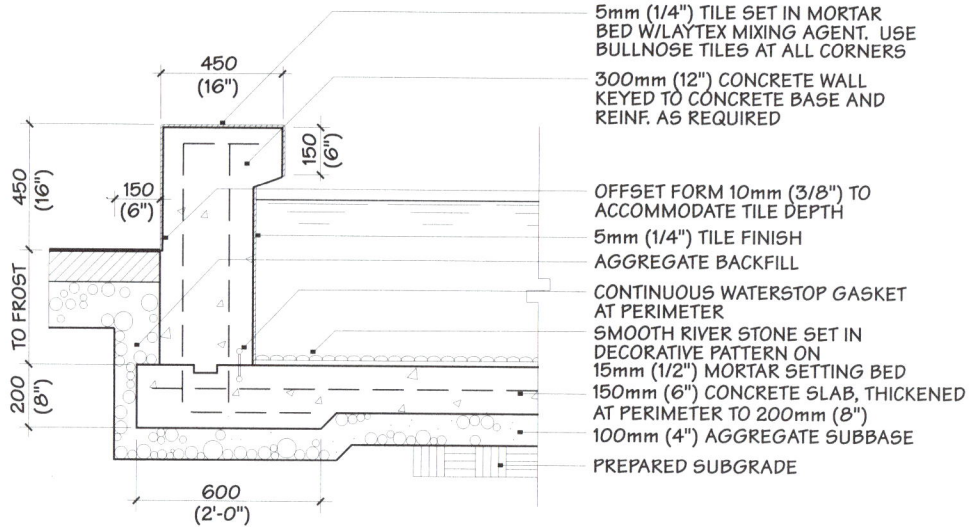

5mm (1/4") TILE SET IN MORTAR BED W/LAYTEX MIXING AGENT. USE BULLNOSE TILES AT ALL CORNERS

300mm (12") CONCRETE WALL KEYED TO CONCRETE BASE AND REINF. AS REQUIRED

OFFSET FORM 10mm (3/8") TO ACCOMMODATE TILE DEPTH

5mm (1/4") TILE FINISH

AGGREGATE BACKFILL

CONTINUOUS WATERSTOP GASKET AT PERIMETER

SMOOTH RIVER STONE SET IN DECORATIVE PATTERN ON 15mm (1/2") MORTAR SETTING BED

150mm (6") CONCRETE SLAB, THICKENED AT PERIMETER TO 200mm (8")

100mm (4") AGGREGATE SUBBASE

PREPARED SUBGRADE

APPLICATION

CLIMATE

SUBGRADE

CSI MASTERFORMAT: 13160
DRAWING FILE: POO02-06

• This drawing is a template for preliminary design only, and is not intended for bid purposes. It is subject to modification based on design calculations, local practices, and all applicable codes and regulations.

• This concrete garden pool with tile veneer detail is rated as heavy-duty due to depth and utility of use. It is typically found in residential, garden, institutional, and park settings and is used to display aquatic plants and animals, although it may be adapted to occasional human use for wading and emersion with proper filtration and circulation.

• Concrete walls are fully reinforced with steel rods as required by local conditions. Wall and base are connected by a continuous water-stop gasket. Footing should rest on frost free subgrade where required. Tile requires a concrete form inset to create a sill to set tile flush with finish.

• This detail requires careful maintenance and monitoring of tile and stone lining finish and is more effective in warmer climates.

• Water requires filtering, recirculation, and careful attention to pH level to sustain life. Design may include display fountain.

• It is recommended that recycled and regionally available materials and products be given high priority in determining final design and specifications.

Installation Cost (per Square Foot)

LOW   HIGH

$30.00

Maintenance

LOW   HIGH

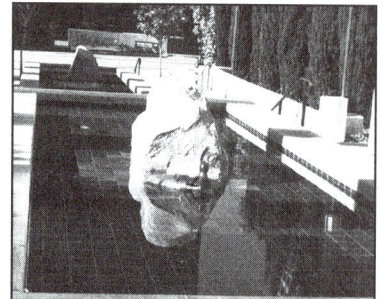

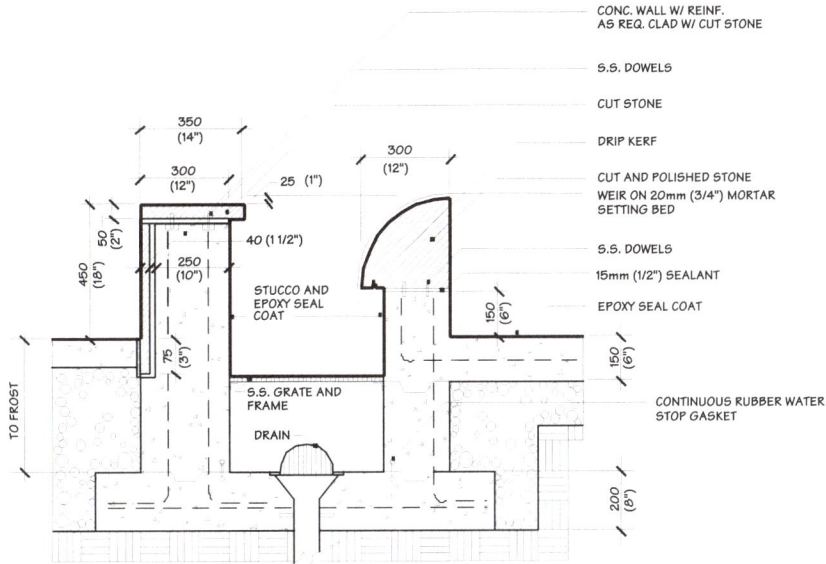

CONC. WALL W/ REINF.
AS REQ. CLAD W/ CUT STONE

S.S. DOWELS

CUT STONE

DRIP KERF

CUT AND POLISHED STONE
WEIR ON 20mm (3/4") MORTAR
SETTING BED

S.S. DOWELS

15mm (1/2") SEALANT

EPOXY SEAL COAT

CONTINUOUS RUBBER WATER
STOP GASKET

350 (14")
300 (12")
25 (1")
300 (12")
50 (2")
250 (10")
40 (1 1/2")
450 (18")
75 (3")
150 (6")
150 (6")
200 (8")
TO FROST

STUCCO AND
EPOXY SEAL
COAT

S.S. GRATE AND
FRAME

DRAIN

APPLICATION

CLIMATE

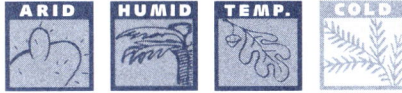

SUBGRADE

CSI MASTERFORMAT: 13160
DRAWING FILE: POO02-05

• This drawing is a template for preliminary design only, and is not intended for bid purposes. It is subject to modification based on design calculations, local practices, and all applicable codes and regulations.

• This granite weir at pool edge detail is rated as heavy-duty due to depth and utility of use. It is typically used as a display combined with large scale cooling of air conditioning water in institutional settings.

• Concrete walls are fully reinforced with steel rods as required by local conditions. Wall and base are connected by a continuous water-stop gasket. Footing should rest on frost free subgrade where required.

• This detail requires careful maintenance and monitoring of lining finish and is more effective in warmer climates. Weir requires precise positioning and maintenance to insure proper performance.

• Water requires filtering and recirculation. This pool is very expensive and requires extensive and regular maintanence.

• It is recommended that recycled and regionally available materials and products be given high priority in determining final design and specifications.

Installation Cost (per Square Foot)

LOW   HIGH

$40.00

Maintenance

LOW   HIGH

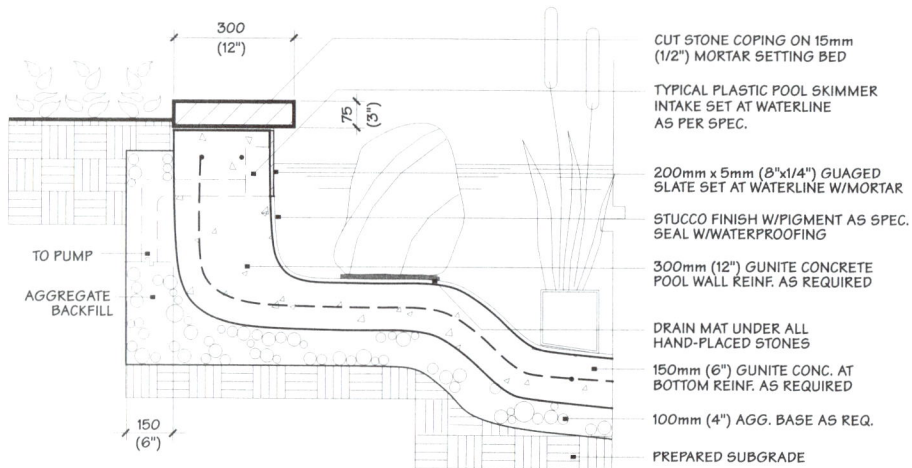

300
(12")

CUT STONE COPING ON 15mm
(1/2") MORTAR SETTING BED

75
(3")

TYPICAL PLASTIC POOL SKIMMER
INTAKE SET AT WATERLINE
AS PER SPEC.

200mm x 5mm (8"x1/4") GUAGED
SLATE SET AT WATERLINE W/MORTAR

STUCCO FINISH W/PIGMENT AS SPEC.
SEAL W/WATERPROOFING

TO PUMP

300mm (12") GUNITE CONCRETE
POOL WALL REINF. AS REQUIRED

AGGREGATE
BACKFILL

DRAIN MAT UNDER ALL
HAND-PLACED STONES

150mm (6") GUNITE CONC. AT
BOTTOM REINF. AS REQUIRED

150
(6")

100mm (4") AGG. BASE AS REQ.

PREPARED SUBGRADE

APPLICATION

CLIMATE

SUBGRADE

CSI MASTERFORMAT: 13160
DRAWING FILE: POO02-03

• This drawing is a template for preliminary design only, and is not intended for bid purposes. It is subject to modification based on design calculations, local practices, and all applicable codes and regulations.

• This gunite concrete garden pool is rated as medium-duty due to depth and utility of use. It is typically found in residential, garden, and park settings and used to display aquatic plants and animals, although it may be adapted to occasional human use for wading and emersion with proper filtration and circulation.

• Concrete shell is fully reinforced with steel rods as required by local conditions.

• This detail requires careful maintenance and monitoring of stucco lining finish and is more effective in warmer climates.

• Water requires filtering, recirculation, and careful attention to pH level to sustain life. Design may include display fountain.

• It is recommended that recycled and regionally available materials and products be given high priority in determining final design and specifications.

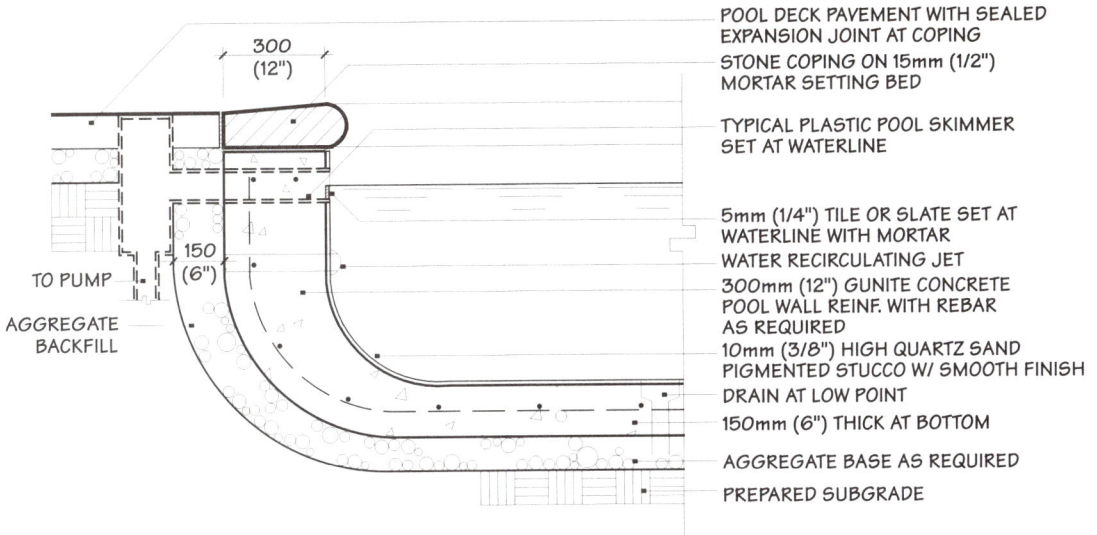

POOL DECK PAVEMENT WITH SEALED
EXPANSION JOINT AT COPING

STONE COPING ON 15mm (1/2")
MORTAR SETTING BED

TYPICAL PLASTIC POOL SKIMMER
SET AT WATERLINE

5mm (1/4") TILE OR SLATE SET AT
WATERLINE WITH MORTAR

WATER RECIRCULATING JET

300mm (12") GUNITE CONCRETE
POOL WALL REINF. WITH REBAR
AS REQUIRED

10mm (3/8") HIGH QUARTZ SAND
PIGMENTED STUCCO W/ SMOOTH FINISH

DRAIN AT LOW POINT

150mm (6") THICK AT BOTTOM

AGGREGATE BASE AS REQUIRED

PREPARED SUBGRADE

300 (12")

150 (6")

TO PUMP

AGGREGATE BACKFILL

APPLICATION

CLIMATE

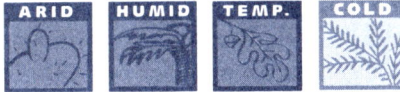

SUBGRADE

CSI MASTERFORMAT: 13160
DRAWING FILE: POO02-04

• This drawing is a template for preliminary design only, and is not intended for bid purposes. It is subject to modification based on design calculations, local practices, and all applicable codes and regulations.

• This concrete gunite pool is rated as medium-duty due to depth and utility of use. It is typically found in residential, garden, and park settings and used to display aquatic plants and animals, although it may be adapted for human use for wading and swimming with proper filtration and circulation.

• Concrete walls are fully reinforced with steel rods as required by local conditions.

• This detail requires careful maintenance and monitoring of stucco lining and slate waterline finish and is more effective in warmer climates.

• Water requires filtering, recirculation, and careful attention to pH level to sustain life, if used botanically. Design may include display fountain.

• It is recommended that recycled and regionally available materials and products be given high priority in determining final design and specifications.

Installation Cost (per Square Foot)

LOW · · · · · · · · · · · · HIGH

$30.00

Maintenance

LOW · · · · · · · · · · · · HIGH

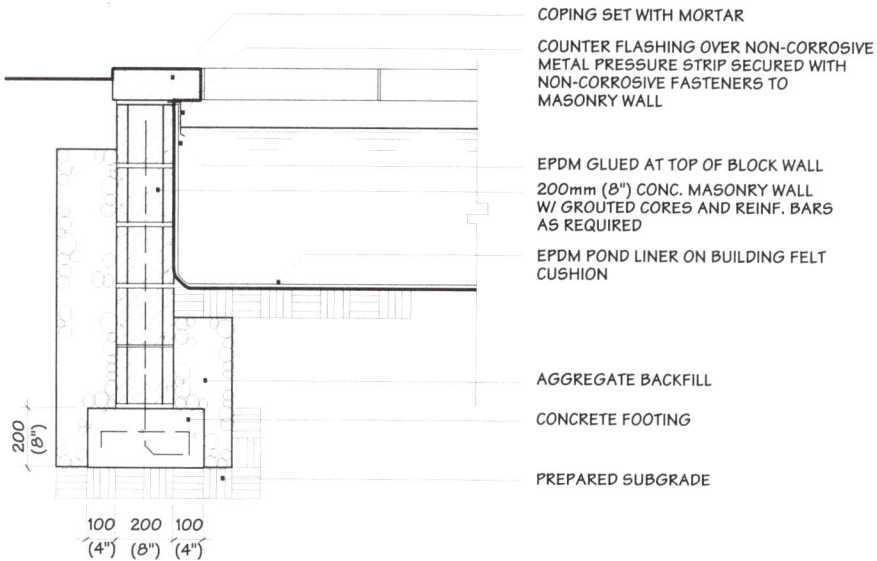

COPING SET WITH MORTAR

COUNTER FLASHING OVER NON-CORROSIVE METAL PRESSURE STRIP SECURED WITH NON-CORROSIVE FASTENERS TO MASONRY WALL

EPDM GLUED AT TOP OF BLOCK WALL

200mm (8") CONC. MASONRY WALL W/ GROUTED CORES AND REINF. BARS AS REQUIRED

EPDM POND LINER ON BUILDING FELT CUSHION

AGGREGATE BACKFILL

CONCRETE FOOTING

PREPARED SUBGRADE

200 (8")

100 (4") 200 (8") 100 (4")

APPLICATION

CLIMATE

SUBGRADE

CSI MASTERFORMAT: 13160
DRAWING FILE: POO02-01

• This drawing is a template for preliminary design only, and is not intended for bid purposes. It is subject to modification based on design calculations, local practices, and all applicable codes and regulations.

• This concrete masonry garden pool is rated as medium-duty due to depth and utility of use. It is typically found in residential, garden, and park settings and used to display aquatic plants and animals, although it may be adapted to occasional human use for wading and emersion with proper filtration and circulation.

• Concrete block walls are fully grouted and reinforced with steel rods as required by local conditions. EPDM or other membrane material is placed on sand or felt cushion and glued to upper wall perimeter and held into place with a non-corrosive pressure bar and masonry screws. Assembly is counter-flashed under stone or precast coping set with mortar.

• This detail requires careful maintenance and monitoring of membrane integrity and is more effective in warmer climates.

• Water requires filtering, recirculation, and careful attention to pH level to sustain life. Design may include display fountain.

• It is recommended that recycled and regionally available materials and products be given high priority in determining final design and specifications.

Installation Cost (per Square Foot)

LOW   HIGH

$15.00

Maintenance

LOW   HIGH

Retaining Structures

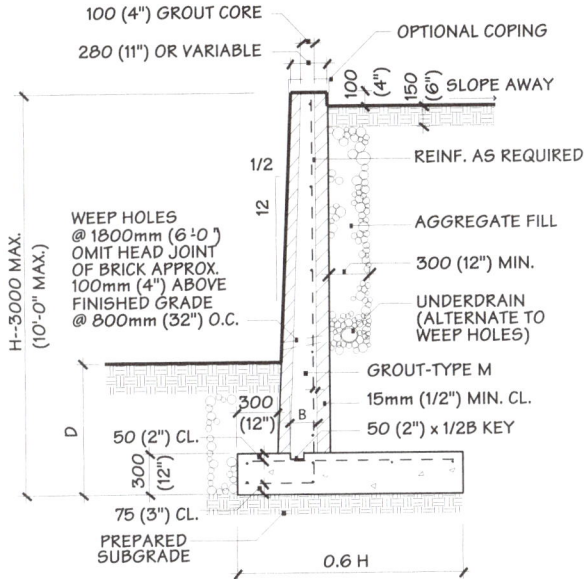

100 (4") GROUT CORE

280 (11") OR VARIABLE

OPTIONAL COPING

100 (4")

150 (6")

SLOPE AWAY

1/2

12

REINF. AS REQUIRED

AGGREGATE FILL

300 (12") MIN.

WEEP HOLES @ 1800mm (6'-0") OMIT HEAD JOINT OF BRICK APPROX. 100mm (4") ABOVE FINISHED GRADE @ 800mm (32") O.C.

UNDERDRAIN (ALTERNATE TO WEEP HOLES)

H-3000 MAX. (10'-0" MAX.)

GROUT-TYPE M

300 (12")

B

15mm (1/2") MIN. CL.

50 (2") CL.

50 (2") x 1/2B KEY

D

300 (12")

75 (3") CL.

PREPARED SUBGRADE

0.6 H

APPLICATION

LIGHT · MED. · HEAVY

CLIMATE

ARID · HUMID · TEMP. · COLD

SUBGRADE

PERM. · CLAY · ROOF

CSI MASTERFORMAT: 02830
DRAWING FILE: RET14-02

• This drawing is a template for preliminary design only, and is not intended for bid purposes. It is subject to modification based on design calculations, local practices, and all applicable codes and regulations.

• This reinforced fully grouted masonry retaining wall is rated as medium-duty due to its base to height ratio and retention capacity. It is typically used in residential, public park, and commercial settings. This wall is best used in drier well drained soils in warm and temperate climates. In heavy clays or wet soils, a base to height ratio of 0.75H is recommended.

• Reinforcing practices vary widely by region. Local codes and practices should be consulted prior to specifying any type of reinforcing.

• This wall requires weep holes and back drainage to relieve hydrostatic pressure at back of wall. In seasonal wet periods, damp proofing may be required.

• Cantilevered reinforced masonry walls are economical for heights under 3000mm (10') relative to other concrete cast-in-place systems. This wall requires less site working room due to its unitized construction.

• Footing may bear directly on prepared subgrade in well drained soils.

• Cost note: Typically calculated by square area of wall surface, measured from toe to top.

• It is recommended that recycled and regionally available materials and products be given high priority in determining final design and specifications.

Installation Cost (per Square Foot)

LOW   HIGH

$17.00

Maintenance

LOW   HIGH

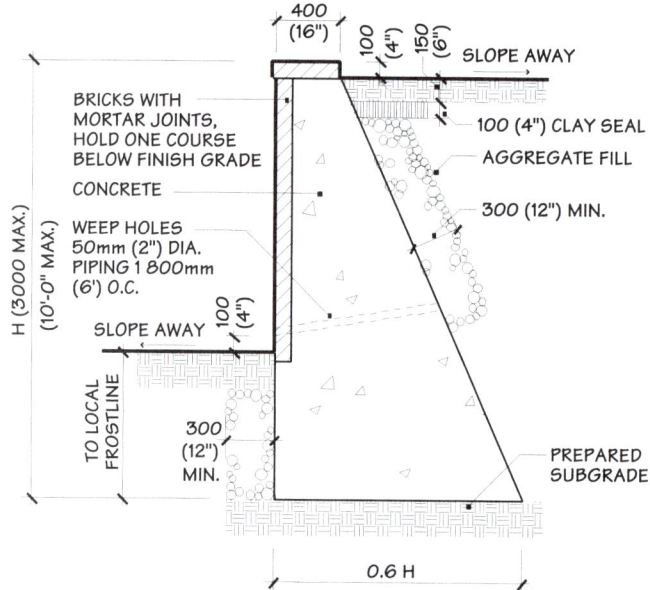

BRICKS WITH MORTAR JOINTS, HOLD ONE COURSE BELOW FINISH GRADE

CONCRETE

WEEP HOLES 50mm (2") DIA. PIPING 1 800mm (6') O.C.

SLOPE AWAY

100 (4")

H (3000 MAX.) (10'-0" MAX.)

TO LOCAL FROSTLINE

300 (12") MIN.

400 (16")

100 (4") 150 (6")

SLOPE AWAY

100 (4") CLAY SEAL

AGGREGATE FILL

300 (12") MIN.

PREPARED SUBGRADE

0.6 H

APPLICATION

CLIMATE

SUBGRADE

CSI MASTERFORMAT: 02830
DRAWING FILE: RET14-01

• This drawing is a template for preliminary design only, and is not intended for bid purposes. It is subject to modification based on design calculations, local practices, and all applicable codes and regulations.

• This concrete gravity retaining wall is rated as heavy-duty due to its base to height ratio and retention capacity. It is typically used in public park and commercial settings. In heavy clays or wet soils, a base to height ratio of 0.75H is recommended.

• It is not reinforced because it relies on compressive concrete strength and gravity to retain soil. It is dressed with a veneer of mortared bricks resting on a concrete sill and tied to the wall with metal mortar ties. Cold climates require weep holes at brick base to drain moisture. First course of brick veneer is usually below grade to achieve a finished appearance.

• This wall requires weep holes and back drainage to relieve hydrostatic pressure at back of wall. In wet conditions, damp proof-

ing and flashing may be used on upper back of wall.

• For heights over 3000mm (10'), cantilevered reinforced concrete walls may be more appropriate.

• Footing may bear directly on prepared subgrade in well drained soils.

• Cost note: Typically calculated by square area of wall surface, measured from toe to top.

• It is recommended that recycled and regionally available materials and products be given high priority in determining final design and specifications.

Installation Cost (per Square Foot)

LOW   HIGH

$25.00

Maintenance

LOW   HIGH

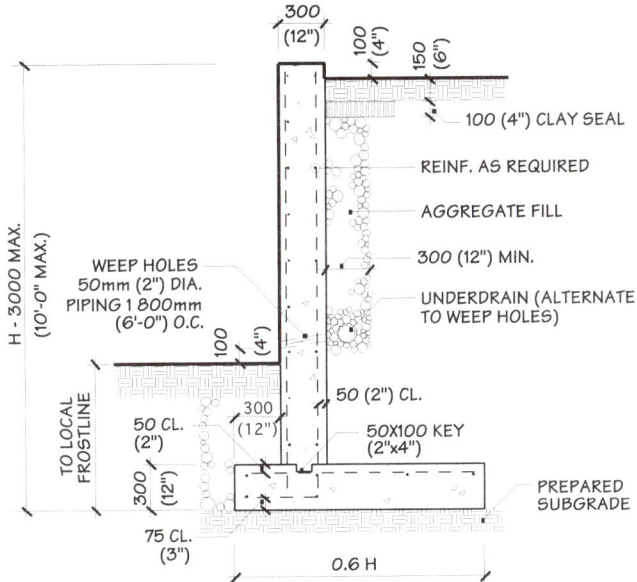

300 (12")
100 (4")
150 (6")

100 (4") CLAY SEAL

REINF. AS REQUIRED

AGGREGATE FILL

300 (12") MIN.

UNDERDRAIN (ALTERNATE TO WEEP HOLES)

H - 3000 MAX. (10'-0" MAX.)

WEEP HOLES 50mm (2") DIA. PIPING 1 800mm (6'-0") O.C.

100 (4")

50 (2") CL.

TO LOCAL FROSTLINE

50 CL. (2")

300 (12")

50X100 KEY (2"x4")

PREPARED SUBGRADE

300 (12")

75 CL. (3")

0.6 H

APPLICATION

CLIMATE

SUBGRADE

CSI MASTERFORMAT: 02830
DRAWING FILE: RET12-02

- This drawing is a template for preliminary design only, and is not intended for bid purposes. It is subject to modification based on design calculations, local practices, and all applicable codes and regulations.

- This reinforced concrete retaining wall is rated as heavy-duty due to its base to height ratio and retention capacity. It is typically used in dense residential, public park, and commercial settings. In heavy clays or wet soils, a base to height ratio of 0.75H is recommended.

- Reinforcing practices vary widely by region. Local codes and practices should be consulted prior to specifying any type of reinforcing.

- This wall requires weep holes and back drainage to relieve hydrostatic pressure at back of wall.

- Cantilevered reinforced concrete walls are economical for heights under 3000mm (10') relative to other concrete cast-in-place sys-

tems. Larger walls may require counterfort bracing.

- Footing may bear directly on prepared subgrade in well drained soils.

- Cost note: Typically calculated by square area of wall surface, measured from toe to top.

- It is recommended that recycled and regionally available materials and products be given high priority in determining final design and specifications.

Installation Cost (per Square Foot)

LOW .... HIGH

$21.25

Maintenance

LOW .... HIGH

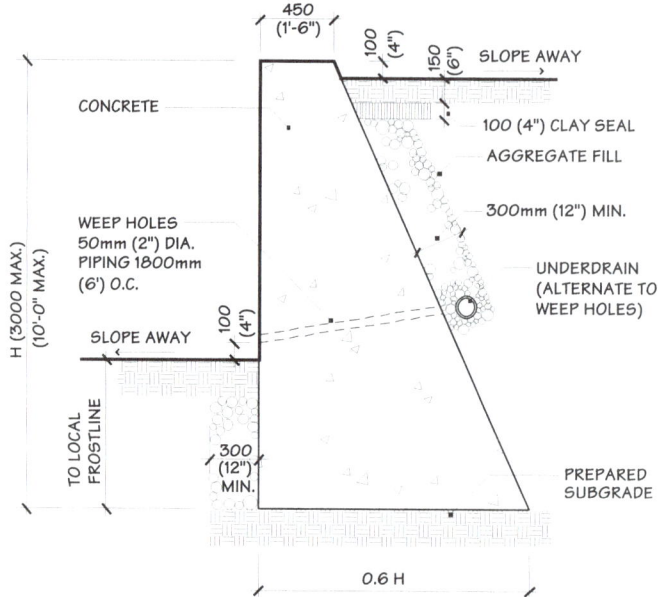

450
(1'-6")

100
(4")

150
(6")

SLOPE AWAY

CONCRETE

100 (4") CLAY SEAL

AGGREGATE FILL

WEEP HOLES
50mm (2") DIA.
PIPING 1800mm
(6') O.C.

300mm (12") MIN.

UNDERDRAIN
(ALTERNATE TO
WEEP HOLES)

H (3000 MAX.)
(10'-0" MAX.)

SLOPE AWAY

100
(4")

TO LOCAL
FROSTLINE

300
(12")
MIN.

PREPARED
SUBGRADE

0.6 H

APPLICATION

LIGHT   MED.   HEAVY

CLIMATE

ARID   HUMID   TEMP.   COLD

SUBGRADE

PERM.   CLAY   ROOF

CSI MASTERFORMAT: 02830
DRAWING FILE: RET12-01

• This drawing is a template for preliminary design only, and is not intended for bid purposes. It is subject to modification based on design calculations, local practices, and all applicable codes and regulations.

• This concrete gravity retaining wall is rated as heavy-duty due to its base to height ratio and retention capacity. It is typically used in public park and commercial settings. In heavy clays or wet soils, a base to height ratio of 0.75H is recommended.

• It is not reinforced because it relies on compressive concrete strength and gravity to retain soil.

• This wall requires weep holes and back drainage to relieve hydrostatic pressure at back of wall.

• For heights over 3000mm (10'), cantilevered reinforced concrete walls may be more appropriate.

• Footing may bear directly on prepared subgrade in well drained soils.

• Cost note: Typically calculated by square area of wall surface, measured from toe to top.

• It is recommended that recycled and regionally available materials and products be given high priority in determining final design and specifications.

Installation Cost (per Square Foot)

LOW   HIGH

$24.15

Maintenance

LOW   HIGH

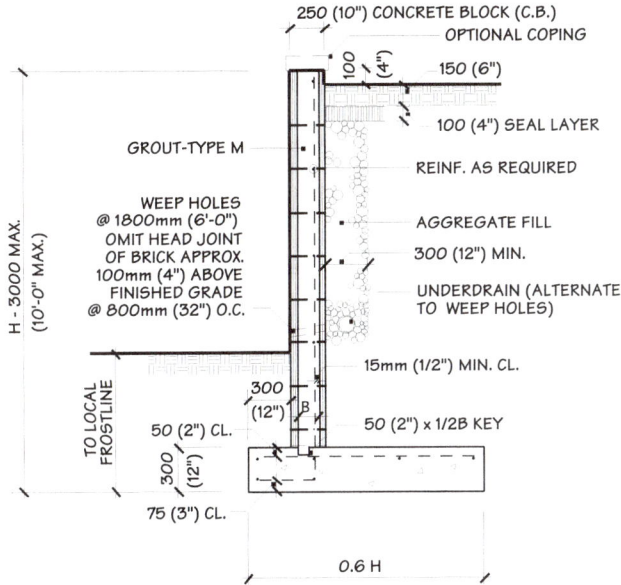

250 (10") CONCRETE BLOCK (C.B.)
OPTIONAL COPING
100 (4")
150 (6")
100 (4") SEAL LAYER
GROUT-TYPE M
REINF. AS REQUIRED
WEEP HOLES
@ 1800mm (6'-0")
OMIT HEAD JOINT
OF BRICK APPROX.
100mm (4") ABOVE
FINISHED GRADE
@ 800mm (32") O.C.
AGGREGATE FILL
300 (12") MIN.
UNDERDRAIN (ALTERNATE
TO WEEP HOLES)
H - 3000 MAX.
(10'-0" MAX.)
15mm (1/2") MIN. CL.
TO LOCAL FROSTLINE
300 (12")
50 (2") CL.
50 (2") x 1/2B KEY
300 (12")
75 (3") CL.
0.6 H

APPLICATION

CLIMATE

SUBGRADE

CSI MASTERFORMAT: 02830
DRAWING FILE: RET12-03

• This drawing is a template for preliminary design only, and is not intended for bid purposes. It is subject to modification based on design calculations, local practices, and all applicable codes and regulations.

• This reinforced fully grouted concrete masonry retaining wall is rated as medium-duty due to its base to height ratio and retention capacity. It is typically used in residential, public park, and commercial settings. In heavy clays or wet soils, a base to height ratio of 0.75H is recommended.

• Reinforcing practices vary widely by region. Local codes and practices should be consulted prior to specifying any type of reinforcing.

• This wall requires weep holes and back drainage to relieve hydrostatic pressure at back of wall.

• Cantilevered reinforced masonry walls are economical for heights under 3000mm (10') relative to other concrete cast-in-place sys-

tems. This wall requires less site working room due to its unitized construction.

• Footing may bear directly on prepared subgrade in well drained soils.

• Cost note: Typically calculated by square area of wall surface, measured from toe to top.

• It is recommended that recycled and regionally available materials and products be given high priority in determining final design and specifications.

Installation Cost (per Square Foot)
LOW   HIGH
$16.00

Maintenance
LOW   HIGH

PRECAST CONCRETE BIN RETAINING WALL

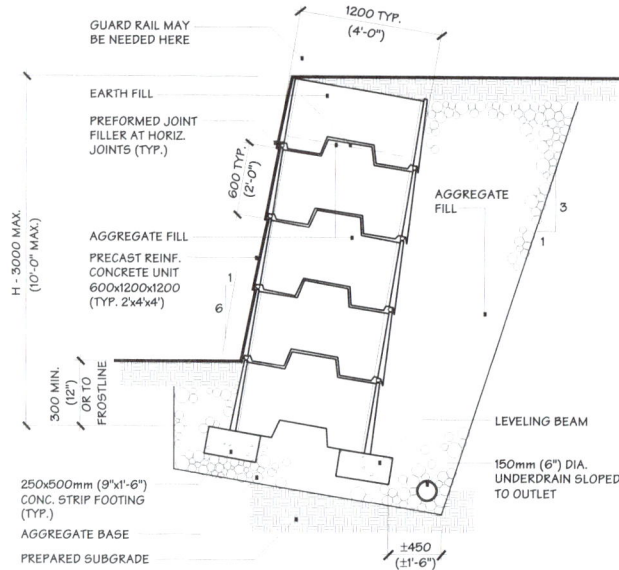

GUARD RAIL MAY BE NEEDED HERE

1200 TYP. (4'-0")

EARTH FILL

PREFORMED JOINT FILLER AT HORIZ. JOINTS (TYP.)

600 TYP. (2'-0")

AGGREGATE FILL

AGGREGATE FILL

PRECAST REINF. CONCRETE UNIT 600x1200x1200 (TYP. 2'x4'x4')

H - 3000 MAX. (10'-0" MAX.)

300 MIN. (12") OR TO FROSTLINE

LEVELING BEAM

150mm (6") DIA. UNDERDRAIN SLOPED TO OUTLET

250x500mm (9"x1'-6") CONC. STRIP FOOTING (TYP.)

AGGREGATE BASE

PREPARED SUBGRADE

±450 (±1'-6")

APPLICATION

LIGHT   MED.   HEAVY

CLIMATE

ARID   HUMID   TEMP.   COLD

SUBGRADE

PERM.   CLAY   ROOF

CSI MASTERFORMAT: 02830
DRAWING FILE: RET22-02

• This drawing is a template for preliminary design only, and is not intended for bid purposes. It is subject to modification based on design calculations, local practices, and all applicable codes and regulations.

• This precast concrete bin unit retaining wall is rated as heavy-duty due to its base to height ratio and the mechanics of its retention capacity. It is typically used in public park, highway, and commercial settings. It is not recommended for heavy clays or wet soils.

• This wall requires concrete leveling footings and can only be placed in one plane due to its interlocking design. It requires machine placement and aggregate fill to achieve its weight resistance. Batter is typically 1:6. Footing drain is recommended due to the absence of weep holes.

• For heights over 3000mm (10'), cantilevered reinforced concrete walls, or fabric reinforced masonry unit walls may be more appropriate.

• Cost note: Typically calculated by square area of wall surface, measured from toe to top.

• It is recommended that recycled and regionally available materials and products be given high priority in determining final design and specifications.

Installation Cost (per Square Foot)

LOW   HIGH

$21.00

Maintenance

LOW   HIGH

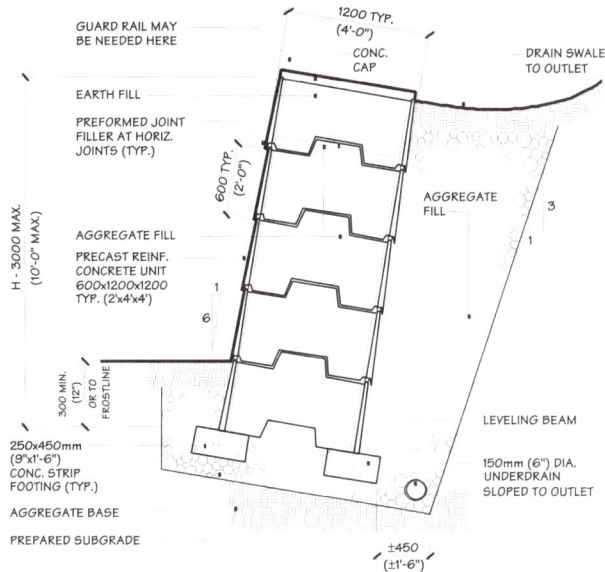

APPLICATION

CLIMATE

SUBGRADE

CSI MASTERFORMAT: 02830
DRAWING FILE: RET22-03

• This drawing is a template for preliminary design only, and is not intended for bid purposes. It is subject to modification based on design calculations, local practices, and all applicable codes and regulations.

• This precast concrete bin unit retaining wall is rated as heavy-duty due to its base to height ratio and the mechanics of its retention capacity. It is typically used in public park, highway, and commercial settings. It is not recommended for heavy clays or wet soils.

• This wall requires concrete leveling footings and can only be placed in one plane due to its interlocking design. It requires machine placement and aggregate fill to achieve its weight resistance. Batter is typically 1:6. Footing drain is recommended due to the absence of weep holes.

• Precast concrete cap limits water infiltration and provides a finished appearance at top edge.

• For heights over 3000mm (10'), cantilevered reinforced concrete walls, or fabric reinforced masonry unit walls may be more appropriate.

• Cost note: Typically calculated by square area of wall surface, measured from toe to top.

• It is recommended that recycled and regionally available materials and products be given high priority in determining final design and specifications.

Installation Cost (per Square Foot)

LOW   HIGH

$22.00

Maintenance

LOW   HIGH

1200 TYP.
(4'-0")

PRECAST REINF.
CONCRETE UNIT
(TYP.)

200 TYP. (8")

AGGREGATE FILL

HEADER

STRETCHER

AGGREGATE
FILL

H=3000 MAX.
(10'-0" MAX.)

1
6

3
1

D
300 MIN.
(1'-0")

CONCRETE
LEVELING BEAM

150mm (6") DIA.
UNDERDRAIN
SLOPED TO OUTLET

250x450mm
(9"x1'-6")
CONC. STRIP
FOOTING (TYP.)

150mm (6")
AGGREGATE BASE

±450
(±1'-6")

APPLICATION

LIGHT   MED.   HEAVY

CLIMATE

ARID   HUMID   TEMP.   COLD

SUBGRADE

PERM.   CLAY   ROOF

CSI MASTERFORMAT: 02830
DRAWING FILE: RET22-04

• This drawing is a template for preliminary design only, and is not intended for bid purposes. It is subject to modification based on design calculations, local practices, and all applicable codes and regulations.

• This precast concrete crib retaining wall is rated as medium-duty due to its base to height ratio and the mechanics of its retention capacity. It is typically used in public park, highway, and commercial settings. It is not recommended for heavy clays or wet soils.

• This wall requires concrete leveling footings and can only be placed in one plane due to its interlocking design. It requires machine placement and aggregate fill to achieve its weight resistance. Batter is typically 1:6. Footing drain is recommended due to the absence of weep holes.

• In ideal soil and climate conditions (warm, well-drained), soil backfill may be used in lower walls to support succulent plant materials.

• For heights over 3000mm (10'), cantilevered reinforced concrete walls, or fabric reinforced masonry unit walls may be more appropriate.

• Cost note: Typically calculated by square area of wall surface, measured from toe to top.

• It is recommended that recycled and regionally available materials and products be given high priority in determining final design and specifications.

Installation Cost (per Square Foot)

LOW   HIGH

$20.69

Maintenance

LOW   HIGH

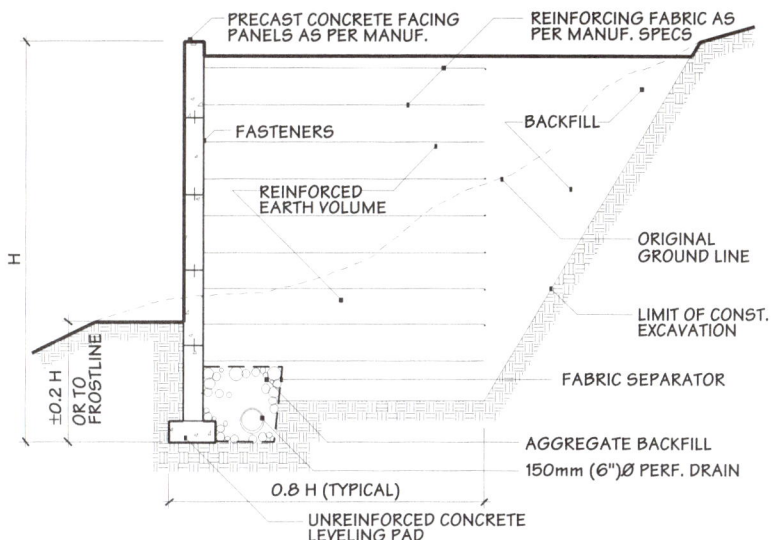

PRECAST CONCRETE FACING PANELS AS PER MANUF.

REINFORCING FABRIC AS PER MANUF. SPECS

FASTENERS

BACKFILL

REINFORCED EARTH VOLUME

ORIGINAL GROUND LINE

H

±0.2 H OR TO FROSTLINE

LIMIT OF CONST. EXCAVATION

FABRIC SEPARATOR

AGGREGATE BACKFILL
150mm (6")∅ PERF. DRAIN

0.8 H (TYPICAL)

UNREINFORCED CONCRETE LEVELING PAD

APPLICATION

CLIMATE

SUBGRADE

CSI MASTERFORMAT: 02830
DRAWING FILE: RET22-01

• This drawing is a template for preliminary design only, and is not intended for bid purposes. It is subject to modification based on design calculations, local practices, and all applicable codes and regulations.

• This concrete unit retaining wall with fabric is rated as heavy-duty due to its height and retention capacity. It is typically used in residential, public park, and commercial settings. It is not recommended for heavy clays or wet soils.

• This wall may be curved using proprietary interlocking block units.

• For heights over 3000 mm (10'), a geogrid reinforcing fabric is required every four courses for a depth of 1500-1800 (5-6') beyond rear face of wall. Backfill is placed in structural lifts for best effect.

• Footing should bear directly on prepared aggregate base in well drained soils using fabric separator and perforated subdrain pipe. Stacking batter is determined by unit type, but 6:1 is typical.

• Observation: Coastal salt spray may attack surface of split face concrete units in cold regions.

• Cost note: Typically calculated by square area of wall surface, measured from toe to top.

• It is recommended that recycled and regionally available materials and products be given high priority in determining final design and specifications.

Installation Cost (per Square Foot)

LOW   HIGH

$21.00

Maintenance

LOW   HIGH

300 (12")

150 (6")

VARIES TO 6 000 (20'-0") MAX.

DOWEL UNITS AS PER MANUF. AND PIN FABRIC TO UNITS

150 (6")

600 MIN. (2'-0")

PRECAST CAPSTONE ADHERED TO TOP UNIT AS PER MANUF.

150x300mm (6"x12") PRECAST CONC. UNITS

300mm (12") AGG. BACKFILL

SOIL BACKFILL

FABRIC REINFORCEMENT PLACED EVERY 4 UNITS FOR WALLS LESS THAN 3000 (10'). CONSULT MANUF. FOR TALLER WALLS. TYPICALLY EXTEND 1500-1800 (5'-6') BEYOND BACK OF WALL

FABRIC SEPARATOR, IF REQ.

100mm (4")∅ DRAIN PIPE PLACED ENTIRE LENGTH OF WALL

PREPARED SUBGRADE

150mm (6") AGG. BASE

300 (12") MIN. OR TO FROST

APPLICATION

LIGHT · MED. · HEAVY

CLIMATE

ARID · HUMID · TEMP. · COLD

SUBGRADE

PERM. · CLAY · ROCK

CSI MASTERFORMAT: 02830
DRAWING FILE: RET22-05

• This drawing is a template for preliminary design only, and is not intended for bid purposes. It is subject to modification based on design calculations, local practices, and all applicable codes and regulations.

• This concrete unit retaining wall with fabric is rated as heavy-duty due to its height and retention capacity. It is typically used in residential, public park, and commercial settings. It is not recommended for heavy clays or wet soils.

• This wall may be curved using proprietary interlocking block units.

• For heights over 3000 mm (10'), a geogrid reinforcing fabric is required every four courses for a depth of 1500-1800 (5-6') beyond rear face of wall. Backfill is placed in structural lifts for best effect.

• Footing should bear directly on prepared aggregate base in well drained soils using fabric separator and perforated subdrain pipe. Stacking batter is determined by unit type, but 6:1 is typical.

• Observation: Coastal salt spray may attack surface of split face concrete units in cold regions.

• Cost note: Typically calculated by square area of wall surface, measured from toe to top.

• It is recommended that recycled and regionally available materials and products be given high priority in determining final design and specifications.

Installation Cost (per Square Foot)

LOW — HIGH

$15.00

Maintenance

LOW — HIGH

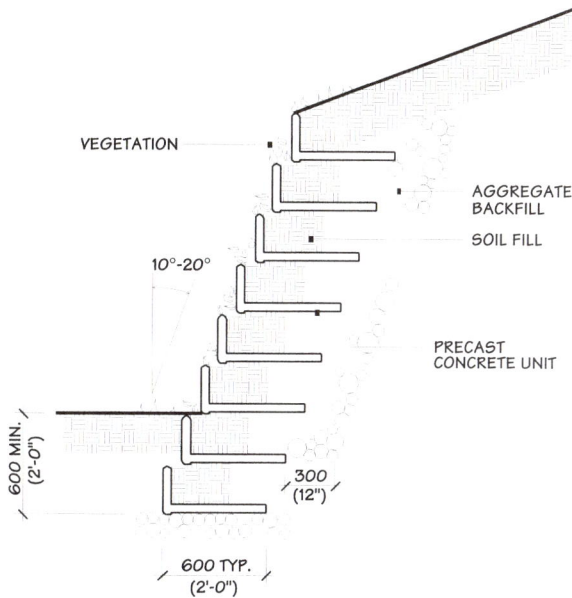

VEGETATION

AGGREGATE BACKFILL

SOIL FILL

10°-20°

PRECAST CONCRETE UNIT

600 MIN. (2'-0")

300 (12")

600 TYP. (2'-0")

APPLICATION

CLIMATE

SUBGRADE

CSI MASTERFORMAT: 02830
DRAWING FILE: RET20-01

• This drawing is a template for preliminary design only, and is not intended for bid purposes. It is subject to modification based on design calculations, local practices, and all applicable codes and regulations.

• This concrete unit vegetative retaining wall is rated as medium-duty due to its height and retention capacity. It is typically used in residential, public park, and commercial settings. It is not recommended for heavy clays or wet soils.

• This wall may easily be curved, and soil backfill allows planting of ground covers suitable to the site and soil conditions.

• For heights over 3000mm (10'), cantilevered reinforced concrete walls, or fabric reinforced masonry unit walls may be more appropriate.

• Footing should bear directly on prepared aggregate base in well drained soils. Stacking batter is typically 10-20 degrees.

• Cost note: Typically calculated by square area of wall surface, measured from toe to top.

• It is recommended that recycled and regionally available materials and products be given high priority in determining final design and specifications.

Installation Cost (per Square Foot)

LOW   HIGH

$20.00

Maintenance

LOW   HIGH

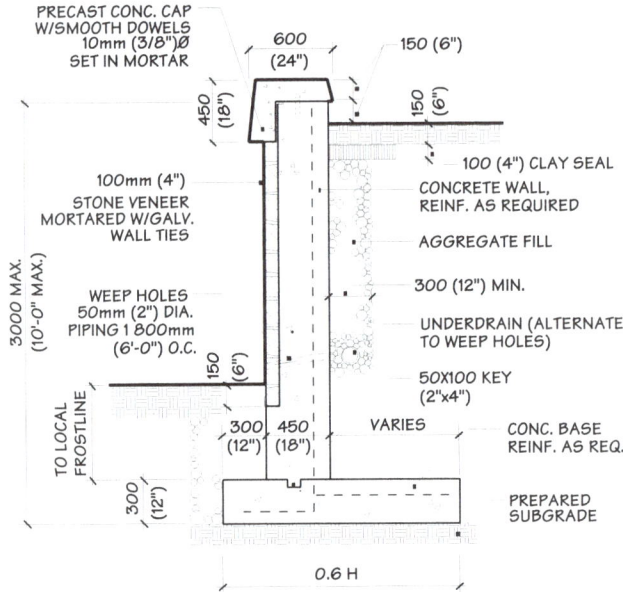

PRECAST CONC. CAP
W/SMOOTH DOWELS
10mm (3/8")Ø
SET IN MORTAR

600 (24")

150 (6")

450 (18")

150 (6")

100mm (4")
STONE VENEER
MORTARED W/GALV.
WALL TIES

100 (4") CLAY SEAL

CONCRETE WALL,
REINF. AS REQUIRED

AGGREGATE FILL

3000 MAX.
(10'-0" MAX.)

WEEP HOLES
50mm (2") DIA.
PIPING 1 800mm
(6'-0") O.C.

300 (12") MIN.

UNDERDRAIN (ALTERNATE
TO WEEP HOLES)

50X100 KEY
(2"x4")

150 (6")

TO LOCAL
FROSTLINE

300 (12")
450 (18")

VARIES

CONC. BASE
REINF. AS REQ.

300 (12")

PREPARED
SUBGRADE

0.6 H

APPLICATION

CLIMATE

SUBGRADE

CSI MASTERFORMAT: 02830
DRAWING FILE: RET12-04

• This drawing is a template for preliminary design only, and is not intended for bid purposes. It is subject to modification based on design calculations, local practices, and all applicable codes and regulations.

• This reinforced concrete retaining wall with stone veneer detail is rated as heavy-duty due to its base to height ratio and retention capacity. It is typically used in dense residential, public park, and commercial settings. In heavy clays or wet soils, a base to height ratio of 0.75H is recommended.

• Reinforcing practices vary widely by region. Local codes and practices should be consulted prior to specifying any type of reinforcing.

• This wall requires weep holes and back drainage to relieve hydrostatic pressure at back of wall. Stone veneer rests on a sill and is fastened to wall with metal mortar clips. Coping may be of cut stone or cast concrete.

• Cantilevered reinforced concrete walls are economical for heights under 3000mm (10') relative to other concrete cast-in-place systems. Larger walls may require counterfort bracing.

• Footing may bear directly on prepared subgrade in well drained soils.

• Cost note: Typically calculated by square area of wall surface, measured from toe to top.

• It is recommended that recycled and regionally available materials and products be given high priority in determining final design and specifications.

Installation Cost (per Square Foot)

LOW   HIGH

$25.00

Maintenance

LOW   HIGH

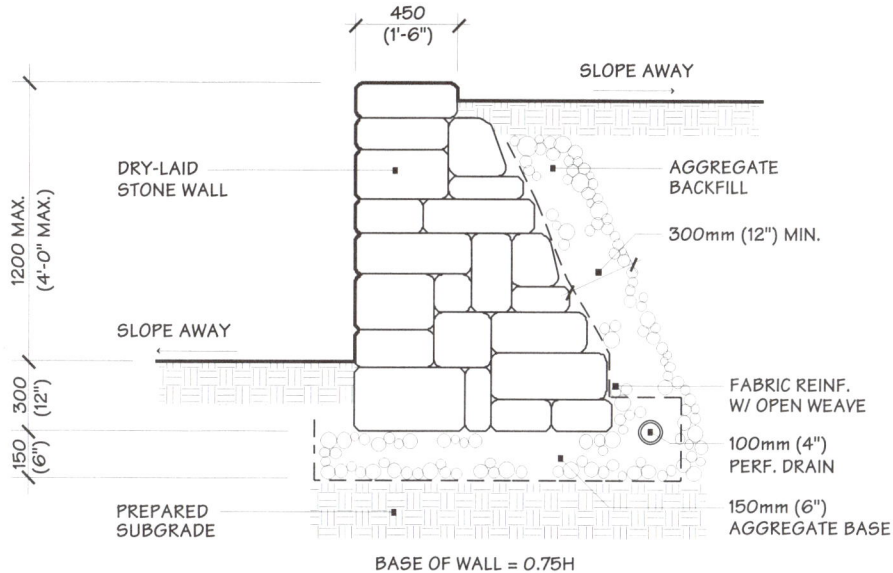

450
(1'-6")

SLOPE AWAY

DRY-LAID
STONE WALL

AGGREGATE
BACKFILL

300mm (12") MIN.

1200 MAX.
(4'-0" MAX.)

SLOPE AWAY

FABRIC REINF.
W/ OPEN WEAVE

300
(12")

100mm (4")
PERF. DRAIN

150
(6")

PREPARED
SUBGRADE

150mm (6")
AGGREGATE BASE

BASE OF WALL = 0.75H

APPLICATION

CLIMATE

SUBGRADE

CSI MASTERFORMAT: 02830
DRAWING FILE: RET23-01

• This drawing is a template for preliminary design only, and is not intended for bid purposes. It is subject to modification based on design calculations, local practices, and all applicable codes and regulations.

• This dry-laid stone gravity retaining wall is rated as heavy-duty due to its base to height ratio and retention capacity. It is typically used in residential, public park, and commercial settings. In heavy clays or wet soils, a base to height ratio of 0.75H is recommended. Footing is placed on aggregate base, bound with reinforcing fabric separator and drained with a perforated subdrain.

• It is not reinforced because it relies on the weight of the stone and gravity to retain soil. Top width can vary from 450 to 600 mm (18" to 24"), with taller walls requiring 600 mm (24") minimum top width.

• This wall requires fabric separator and aggregate backfill to insure drainage and to relieve hydrostatic pressure at rear of wall.

• For heights over 3000mm (10'), cantilevered reinforced concrete walls may be more appropriate.

• In warm climates, stone course may be keyed to a concrete slab 300 mm (12") below finished grade.

• Cost note: Typically calculated by square area of wall surface, measured from toe to top.

• It is recommended that recycled and regionally available materials and products be given high priority in determining final design and specifications.

Installation Cost (per Square Foot)

LOW   HIGH

$27.00

Maintenance

LOW   HIGH

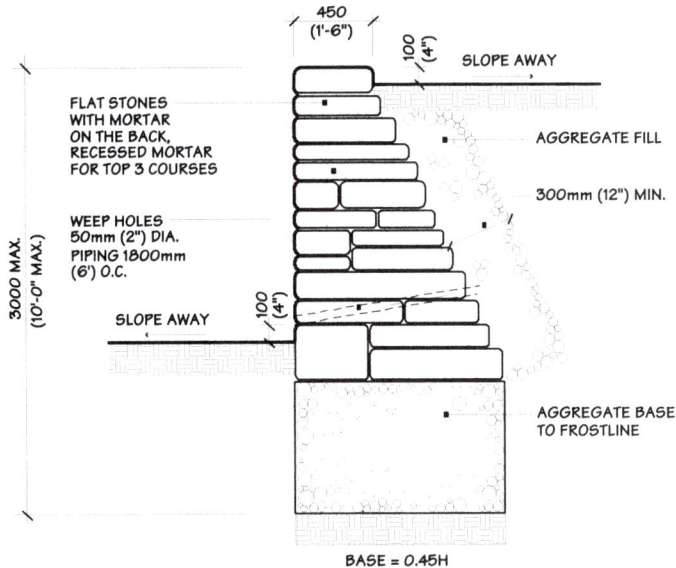

450
(1'-6")

100
(4")

SLOPE AWAY

FLAT STONES
WITH MORTAR
ON THE BACK,
RECESSED MORTAR
FOR TOP 3 COURSES

AGGREGATE FILL

300mm (12") MIN.

WEEP HOLES
50mm (2") DIA.
PIPING 1800mm
(6') O.C.

3000 MAX.
(10'-0" MAX.)

100
(4")

SLOPE AWAY

AGGREGATE BASE
TO FROSTLINE

BASE = 0.45H

APPLICATION

CLIMATE

SUBGRADE

CSI MASTERFORMAT: 02830
DRAWING FILE: RET23-02

• This drawing is a template for preliminary design only, and is not intended for bid purposes. It is subject to modification based on design calculations, local practices, and all applicable codes and regulations.

• This mortared stone gravity retaining wall is rated as light-duty due to its base to height ratio and retention capacity, and is intended for very well drained soils. It is typically used in residential, public park, and commercial settings. In heavy clays or wet soils, a base to height ratio of 0.6H to 0.75H is recommended, and the wall may require a key on the base to resist sliding.

• It is not reinforced because it relies on the weight of the stone and gravity to retain soil. Top width can vary from 450 to 600 mm (18" to 24"), with taller walls requiring 600 mm (24") minimum top width.

• This wall is "back mortared" and has the appearance of a dry-laid wall.

• This wall requires weep holes and back drainage to relieve hydrostatic pressure at back of wall.

• For heights over 3000mm (10'), cantilevered reinforced concrete walls may be more appropriate.

• A coarse graded aggregate footing may bear directly on prepared subgrade in well drained soils. In warm climates, stone course may begin 300 mm (12") below finished grade.

• Cost note: Typically calculated by square area of wall surface, measured from toe to top.

• It is recommended that recycled and regionally available materials and products be given high priority in determining final design and specifications.

Installation Cost (per Square Foot)

LOW   HIGH

$22.00

Maintenance

LOW   HIGH

450
(1'-6")

100
(4")

SLOPE AWAY

STONE
MASONRY W/
15-20mm
(1/2-3/4") JTS.

AGGREGATE FILL

300mm (12") MIN.

WEEP HOLES
50mm (2") DIA.
PIPING 1800mm
(6') O.C.

3000 MAX.
(10'-0" MAX.)

SLOPE AWAY

100
(4")

EMBED KEY STONE
50-75mm (2-3")

CONC. BASE
TO FROSTLINE

BASE = 0.5H

APPLICATION

LIGHT · MED. · HEAVY

CLIMATE

ARID · HUMID · TEMP. · COLD

SUBGRADE

PERM. · CLAY · ROOF

CSI MASTERFORMAT: 02830
DRAWING FILE: RET13-01

• This drawing is a template for preliminary design only, and is not intended for bid purposes. It is subject to modification based on design calculations, local practices, and all applicable codes and regulations.

• This mortared stone gravity retaining wall is rated as heavy-duty due to its base to height ratio and retention capacity, but is intended for very well drained soils. It is typically used in residential, public park, and commercial settings. In heavy clays or wet soils, a base to height ratio of 0.6H to 0.75H is recommended, and the wall may require a key on the base to resist sliding.

• It is not reinforced because it relies on the weight of the stone and gravity to retain soil. Top width can vary from 450 to 600 mm (18" to 24"), with taller walls requiring 600 mm (24") minimum top width.

• This wall requires weep holes and back drainage to relieve hydrostatic pressure at back of wall.

• For heights over 3000mm (10'), cantilevered reinforced concrete walls may be more appropriate.

• Footing may bear directly on prepared subgrade in well drained soils. In warm climates, stone course may be keyed to a concrete slab 300 mm (12") below finished grade.

• Cost note: Typically calculated by square area of wall surface, measured from toe to top.

• It is recommended that recycled and regionally available materials and products be given high priority in determining final design and specifications.

Installation Cost (per Square Foot)

LOW   HIGH

$22.60

Maintenance

LOW   HIGH

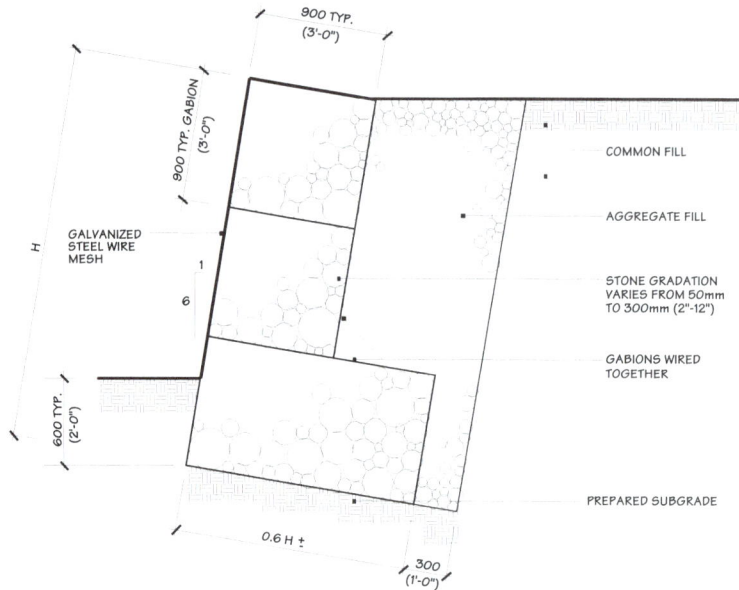

APPLICATION

CLIMATE

SUBGRADE

CSI MASTERFORMAT: 02830
DRAWING FILE: RET23-03

• This drawing is a template for preliminary design only, and is not intended for bid purposes. It is subject to modification based on design calculations, local practices, and all applicable codes and regulations.

• This stone filled wire basket gabion retaining wall is rated as heavy-duty due to its base to height ratio and retention capacity, and is adaptable to a variety of soil conditions. It is typically used in public park, highway, and commercial settings. In heavy clays or wet soils, a base to height ratio of 0.6H to 0.75H is recommended.

• It is not reinforced because it relies on the weight of the stone and gravity to retain soil. Top width can vary from 600-900 mm (24-36"), with taller walls requiring 900 mm (36") minimum top width.

• This wall is easily built in remote areas due to its unitized assembly. It is extremely flexible and does not result in a high quality finish. It is economical relative to its bulk and utility.

• This wall is porous and requires no weep holes. In wet conditions, a fabric separator at rear of wall may be used to restrict migration of fine soil particles from back to face.

• For heights over 3000mm (10'), cantilevered reinforced concrete walls may be more appropriate.

• Wire basket gabions may bear directly on prepared subgrade in well drained soils. In warm climates, stone course may begin 300 mm (12") below finished grade.

• Cost note: Typically calculated by square area of wall surface, measured from toe to top.

• It is recommended that recycled and regionally available materials and products be given high priority in determining final design and specifications.

Installation Cost (per Square Foot)

LOW   HIGH

$11.70

Maintenance

LOW   HIGH

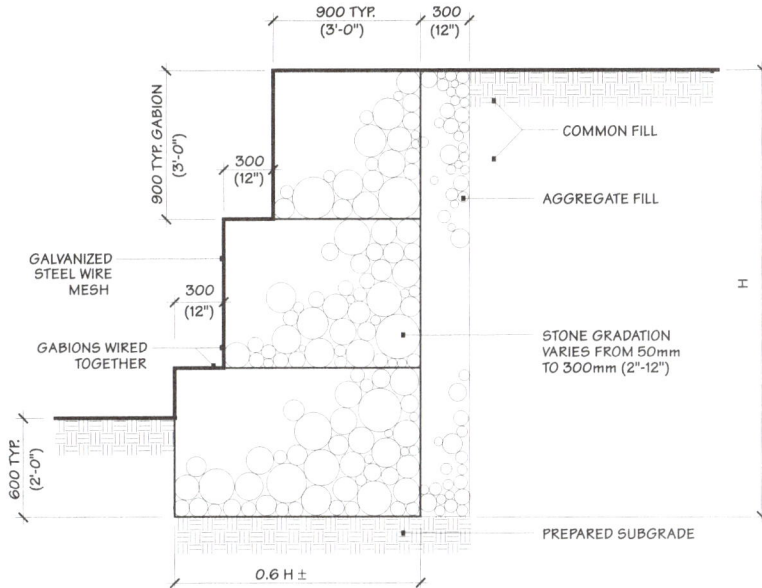

900 TYP. (3'-0")
300 (12")
900 TYP. GABION (3'-0")
300 (12")
COMMON FILL
AGGREGATE FILL
GALVANIZED STEEL WIRE MESH
300 (12")
GABIONS WIRED TOGETHER
300 (12")
STONE GRADATION VARIES FROM 50mm TO 300mm (2"-12")
600 TYP. (2'-0")
PREPARED SUBGRADE
0.6 H ±

APPLICATION

CLIMATE

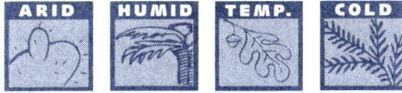

SUBGRADE

CSI MASTERFORMAT: 02830
DRAWING FILE: RET23-04

• This drawing is a template for preliminary design only, and is not intended for bid purposes. It is subject to modification based on design calculations, local practices, and all applicable codes and regulations.

• This stone filled wire basket gabion retaining wall is rated as medium-duty due to its base to height ratio and retention capacity, and is adaptable to a variety soil conditions. It is typically used in public park, highway, and commercial settings. In heavy clays or wet soils, a base to height ratio of 0.6H to 0.75H is recommended.

• It is not reinforced because it relies on the weight of the stone and gravity to retain soil. Top width can vary from 600-900 mm (24-36"), with taller walls requiring 900 mm (36") minimum top width.

• This wall is easily built in remote areas due to its unitized assembly. It is extremely flexible and does not result in a high quality finish. It is economical relative to its bulk and utility.

• Staggered face is typically used in taller installations associated with large scale road and transportation corridor construction, or river bank stabilization.

• This wall is porous and requires no weep holes. In wet conditions, a fabric separator at rear of wall may be used to restrict migration of fine soil particles from back to face.

• For heights over 3000mm (10'), cantilevered reinforced concrete walls may be more appropriate.

• Wire basket gabions may bear directly on prepared subgrade in well drained soils. In warm climates, stone course may begin 300 mm (12") below finished grade.

• Cost note: Typically calculated by square area of wall surface, measured from toe to top.

• It is recommended that recycled and regionally available materials and products be given high priority in determining final design and specifications.

Installation Cost (per Square Foot)

LOW — HIGH
$11.70

Maintenance

LOW — HIGH

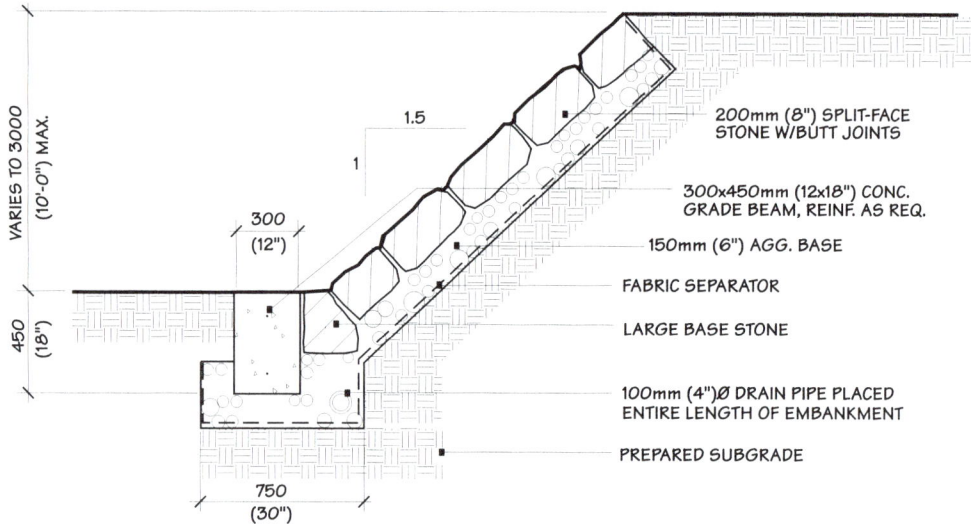

200mm (8") SPLIT-FACE
STONE W/BUTT JOINTS

300x450mm (12x18") CONC.
GRADE BEAM, REINF. AS REQ.

150mm (6") AGG. BASE

FABRIC SEPARATOR

LARGE BASE STONE

100mm (4")Ø DRAIN PIPE PLACED
ENTIRE LENGTH OF EMBANKMENT

PREPARED SUBGRADE

VARIES TO 3000 (10'-0") MAX.

1.5
1
300 (12")
450 (18")
750 (30")

APPLICATION

CLIMATE

SUBGRADE

CSI MASTERFORMAT: 02830
DRAWING FILE: RET23-05

• This drawing is a template for preliminary design only, and is not intended for bid purposes. It is subject to modification based on design calculations, local practices, and all applicable codes and regulations.

• This stone retaining embankment detail is rated as medium-duty due to its base to height ratio and retention capacity. It is typically used in residential, public park, and commercial settings. It is not recommended for heavy clays or wet soils. Footing is placed on aggregate base, bound with reinforcing fabric separator and drained with a perforated subdrain.

• Stone is placed on aggregate base reinforced with fabric separator. Large stones are typically placed at the base against the concrete grade beam base. Stone is typically 200-300 mm (8-12") thick. Igneous or metamorphic stone is preferred.

• This embankment requires fabric separator and aggregate backfill to insure drainage and to relieve hydrostatic pressure at lower 1/3 of bank.

• For heights over 3000mm (10'), cantilevered reinforced concrete walls may be more appropriate.

• It is recommended that recycled and regionally available materials and products be given high priority in determining final design and specifications.

Installation Cost (per Square Foot)

LOW   HIGH

$6.37

Maintenance

LOW   HIGH

1200 TYP.
(4'-0")

150x200 (6"x8")
TREATED TIMBER
UNITS (TYP.)
NOTCHED 1/4
OF DEPTH

AGGREGATE FILL

HEADER

STRETCHER

AGGREGATE
FILL

H - 3000 MAX.
(10'-0")

D 300 (12") MIN.
OR TO
FROSTLINE

250x450mm
(9"x1'-6")
CONC. STRIP
FOOTING (TYP.)

AGGREGATE FILL

PREPARED SUBGRADE

LEVELING BEAM

150mm (6") DIA.
UNDERDRAIN
SLOPED TO OUTLET

±450
(±1'-6")

APPLICATION

LIGHT | **MED.** | HEAVY

CLIMATE

ARID | **HUMID** | **TEMP.** | **COLD**

SUBGRADE

PERM. | CLAY | ROOF

CSI MASTERFORMAT: 02945
DRAWING FILE: RET25-01

• This drawing is a template for preliminary design only, and is not intended for bid purposes. It is subject to modification based on design calculations, local practices, and all applicable codes and regulations.

• This notched timber crib retaining wall is rated as medium-duty due to its base to height ratio and the mechanics of its retention capacity. It is typically used in public park, highway, and commercial settings. It is not recommended for heavy clays or wet soils. Its pressure treated timbers have a limited life-span.

• This wall requires concrete leveling footings and can only be placed in one plane due to its interlocking design. It requires machine placement and aggregate fill to achieve its weight resistance. Batter is typically 1:6. Footing drain is recommended.

• In ideal soil and climate conditions (warm, well-drained), soil backfill may be used in smaller walls to support succulent plant materials.

• For heights over 3000 mm (10'), cantilevered reinforced concrete walls, or fabric reinforced masonry unit walls may be more appropriate.

• Cost note: Typically calculated by square area of wall surface, measured from toe to top.

• It is recommended that recycled and regionally available materials and products be given high priority in determining final design and specifications.

Installation Cost (per Square Foot)

LOW   HIGH

$19.00

Maintenance

LOW   HIGH

200± MIN.
(8"±)

200
(8")

200x200 OR 150x150
(8"x8" OR 6"x6")
P.T. TIMBER UNIT
@ 1000mm
(3'-6") O.C.

GRANULAR
FILL

300-450
(12"-18")

150
(6")

CLAD CABLE

50 OR 80mm
(2" OR 3")
P.T. PLANKS

COURSE AGGREGATE FILL

600 MIN.
(2'-0")

1950 MAX.
(6'-6") MAX.

ANCHOR
200x200 OR 150x150x900
(8"x8" OR 6"x6"x3'-0")
TIMBER UNIT CONTINOUS

CUT LIMIT

300
(1'-0")

AGGREGATE FILL

750
(2'-6")

200 x 200mm OR 150 x 150mm
(6"x8" OR 6"x6") P.T. TIMBER UNIT

150mm (6") AGGREGATE BASE

PREPARED SUBGRADE

APPLICATION

LIGHT   MED.   HEAVY

CLIMATE

ARID   HUMID   TEMP.   COLD

SUBGRADE

PERM.   CLAY   ROOF

CSI MASTERFORMAT: 02945
DRAWING FILE: RET25-04

• This drawing is a template for preliminary design only, and is not intended for bid purposes. It is subject to modification based on design calculations, local practices, and all applicable codes and regulations.

• This vertically placed timber retaining wall is rated as medium-duty due to the mechanics of its retention capacity. It is typically used in residential, public park, and commercial settings. It is not recommended for heavy clays or wet soils. Its pressure treated timbers have a limited life-span, and total height is highly restricted.

• This wall requires an aggregate leveling bed and can only be placed in one plane due to its batter and use of structural whalers at rear of wall. Batter is typically 1:6.

• This is a utilitarian wall and has exposed vertical timbers with retaining planks fastened to the back. Stability is achieved through steel clad cable and buried anchor. For a more finished appearance, a plank cap and facia may be applied to the top of the wall.

• For heights over 900 mm (3'), other types of walls may be more appropriate.

• This wall and other wood retaining walls are best used in warm climates.

• Cost note: Typically calculated by square area of wall surface, measured from toe to top.

• It is recommended that recycled and regionally available materials and products be given high priority in determining final design and specifications.

Installation Cost (per Square Foot)

LOW   HIGH

$15.00

Maintenance

LOW   HIGH

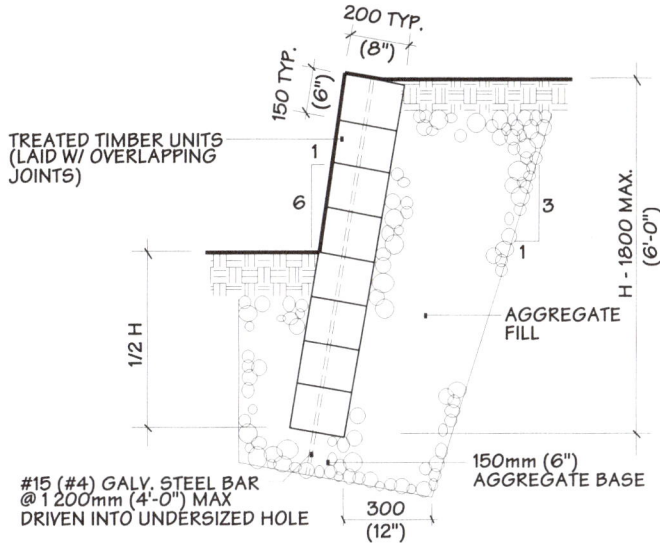

TREATED TIMBER UNITS
(LAID W/ OVERLAPPING
JOINTS)

200 TYP.
(8")

150 TYP.
(6")

1
6

3
1

H - 1800 MAX.
(6'-0")

1/2 H

AGGREGATE
FILL

150mm (6")
AGGREGATE BASE

#15 (#4) GALV. STEEL BAR
@ 1 200mm (4'-0") MAX
DRIVEN INTO UNDERSIZED HOLE

300
(12")

APPLICATION

LIGHT   MED.   HEAVY

CLIMATE

ARID   HUMID   TEMP.   COLD

SUBGRADE

PERM.   CLAY   ROOF

CSI MASTERFORMAT: 02945

DRAWING FILE: RET25-02

• This drawing is a template for preliminary design only, and is not intended for bid purposes. It is subject to modification based on design calculations, local practices, and all applicable codes and regulations.

• This stacked timber steel reinforced retaining wall is rated as light-duty due to the mechanics of its retention capacity. It is typically used in residential, public park, and commercial settings. It is not recommended for heavy clays or wet soils. Its pressure treated timbers have a limited life-span, and total height is highly restricted.

• This wall requires an aggregate leveling bed and can only be placed in one plane due to its interlocking design. Batter is typically 1:6. Footing drain is recommended.

• For heights over 900 mm (3'), other types of walls may be more appropriate.

• Cost note: Typically calculated by square area of wall surface, measured from toe to top.

• It is recommended that recycled and regionally available materials and products be given high priority in determining final design and specifications.

Installation Cost (per Square Foot)

LOW   HIGH

$13.50

Maintenance

LOW   HIGH

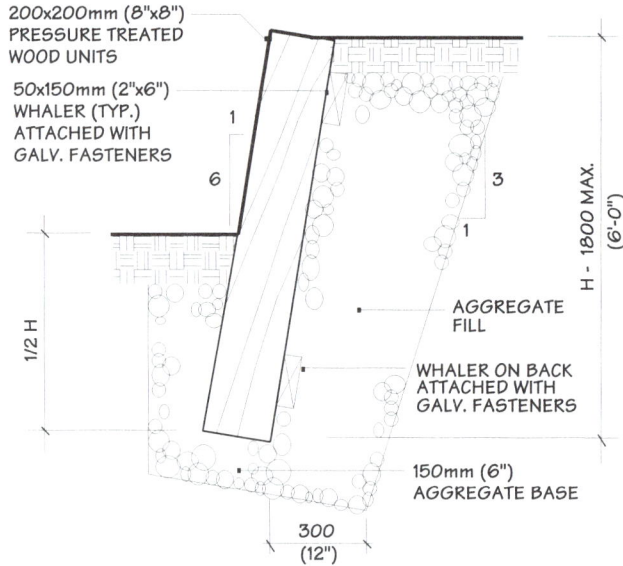

200x200mm (8"x8")
PRESSURE TREATED
WOOD UNITS

50x150mm (2"x6")
WHALER (TYP.)
ATTACHED WITH
GALV. FASTENERS

1 / 6

3 / 1

H - 1800 MAX. (6'-0")

1/2 H

AGGREGATE FILL

WHALER ON BACK
ATTACHED WITH
GALV. FASTENERS

150mm (6")
AGGREGATE BASE

300 (12")

APPLICATION

CLIMATE

SUBGRADE

CSI MASTERFORMAT: 02945
DRAWING FILE: RET25-03

• This drawing is a template for preliminary design only, and is not intended for bid purposes. It is subject to modification based on design calculations, local practices, and all applicable codes and regulations.

• This vertically placed timber retaining wall is rated as light-duty due to the mechanics of its retention capacity. It is typically used in residential, public park, and commercial settings. It is not recommended for heavy clays or wet soils. Its pressure treated timbers have a limited life-span, and total height is highly restricted.

• This wall requires an aggregate leveling bed and can only be placed in one plane due to its batter and use of structural whalers at rear of wall. Batter is typically 1:6. Footing drain is recommended. Short walls may be placed plumb and curved using structural steel whalers for added strength.

• For heights over 900 mm (3'), other types of walls may be more appropriate.

• This wall and other wood retaining walls are best used in warm climates.

• Cost note: Typically calculated by square area of wall surface, measured from toe to top.

• It is recommended that recycled and regionally available materials and products be given high priority in determining final design and specifications.

Installation Cost (per Square Foot)

LOW   HIGH

$13.67

Maintenance

LOW   HIGH

Seatwalls

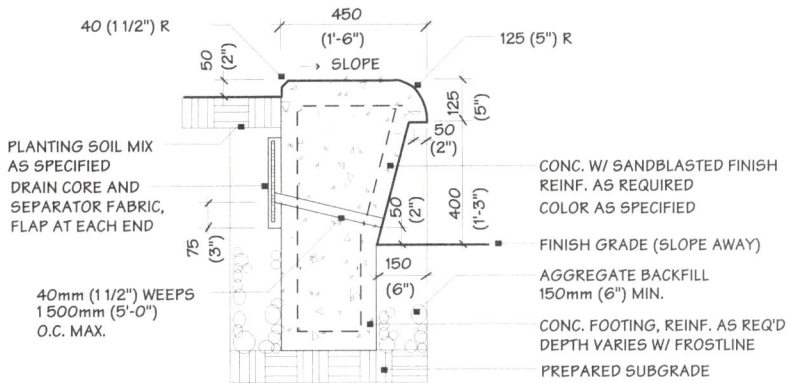

40 (1 1/2") R — SLOPE
50 (2")
450 (1'-6")
125 (5") R
125 (5")
50 (2")
50 (2")
400 (1'-3")
150 (6")
75 (3")

PLANTING SOIL MIX
AS SPECIFIED
DRAIN CORE AND
SEPARATOR FABRIC,
FLAP AT EACH END

40mm (1 1/2") WEEPS
1500mm (5'-0")
O.C. MAX.

CONC. W/ SANDBLASTED FINISH
REINF. AS REQUIRED
COLOR AS SPECIFIED

FINISH GRADE (SLOPE AWAY)

AGGREGATE BACKFILL
150mm (6") MIN.

CONC. FOOTING, REINF. AS REQ'D
DEPTH VARIES W/ FROSTLINE

PREPARED SUBGRADE

APPLICATION

CLIMATE

SUBGRADE

CSI MASTERFORMAT: 02830
DRAWING FILE: SWL02-01

• This drawing is a template for preliminary design only, and is not intended for bid purposes. It is subject to modification based on design calculations, local practices, and all applicable codes and regulations.

• This concrete seatwall is rated as heavy-duty due to its bearing capacity. It is typically found in dense residential, urban park, commercial and institutional settings.

• Concrete base is fully reinforced and typically requires back drainage to aid weep-hole drainage. Drain mat is placed against back of wall before backfilling.

• Reinforcing practices vary widely by region. Local codes and practices should be consulted prior to specifying any type of reinforcing.

• Concrete design must accommodate movement of materials by providing adequate expansion and control joints, particularly in regions of extreme temperature fluctuations. If designed for temperate or cold cli-

mates, air-entrained concrete is typically recommended due to freezing/thawing action. If longer than 7500mm (25'), sealed expansion joint will be required.

• If used in cold or temperate climate, footings must bear on subgrade below frost.

• Finish should be rubbed and sealed for best effect.

• It is recommended that recycled and regionally available materials and products be given high priority in determining final design and specifications.

Installation Cost (per Linear Foot)

LOW   HIGH

$24.00

Maintenance

LOW   HIGH

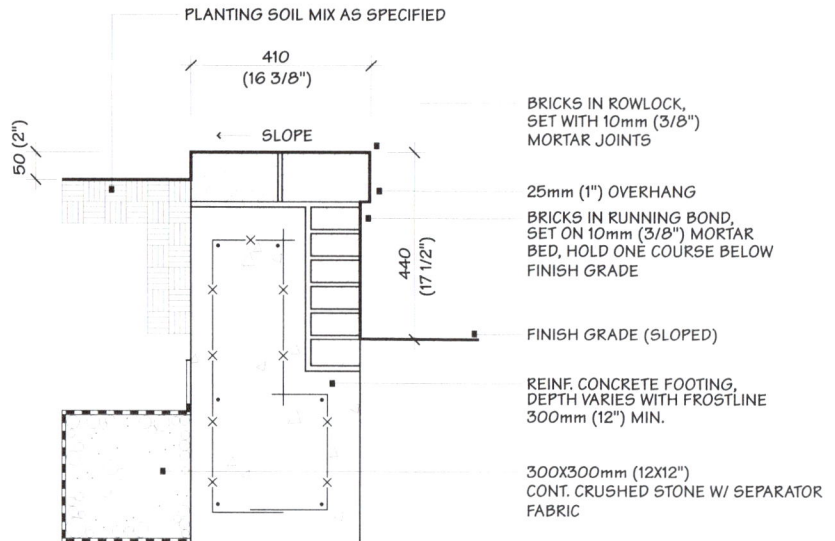

PLANTING SOIL MIX AS SPECIFIED

410 (16 3/8")

50 (2")

SLOPE

BRICKS IN ROWLOCK, SET WITH 10mm (3/8") MORTAR JOINTS

25mm (1") OVERHANG
BRICKS IN RUNNING BOND, SET ON 10mm (3/8") MORTAR BED, HOLD ONE COURSE BELOW FINISH GRADE

440 (17 1/2")

FINISH GRADE (SLOPED)

REINF. CONCRETE FOOTING, DEPTH VARIES WITH FROSTLINE 300mm (12") MIN.

300X300mm (12X12")
CONT. CRUSHED STONE W/ SEPARATOR FABRIC

APPLICATION

CLIMATE

SUBGRADE

CSI MASTERFORMAT: 02830
DRAWING FILE: SWL04-01

• This drawing is a template for preliminary design only, and is not intended for bid purposes. It is subject to modification based on design calculations, local practices, and all applicable codes and regulations.

• This brick veneered concrete seatwall is rated as heavy-duty due to its bearing capacity. It is typically found in dense residential, urban park, commercial and institutional settings.

• Concrete base is fully reinforced and typically requires back drainage due to the absence of weep-holes.

• Brick veneer is mortared to a sill and is tied to the wall with metal mortar ties. Brick seat cap may be flashed to provide damp proofing for veneer in wet conditions. Wall may require damp proofing if soil is heavily irrigated or if soil is exceptionally wet.

• Reinforcing practices vary widely by region. Local codes and practices should be consulted prior to specifying any type of reinforcing.

• Concrete design must accommodate movement of materials by providing adequate expansion and control joints, particularly in regions of extreme temperature fluctuations. If designed for temperate or cold climates, air-entrained concrete is typically recommended due to freezing/thawing action. If longer than 7500mm (25'), sealed expansion joint will be required.

• If used in cold climate, periodic re-pointing will be required.

• It is recommended that recycled and regionally available materials and products be given high priority in determining final design and specifications.

Installation Cost (per Linear Foot)

LOW   HIGH

$38.60

Maintenance

LOW   HIGH

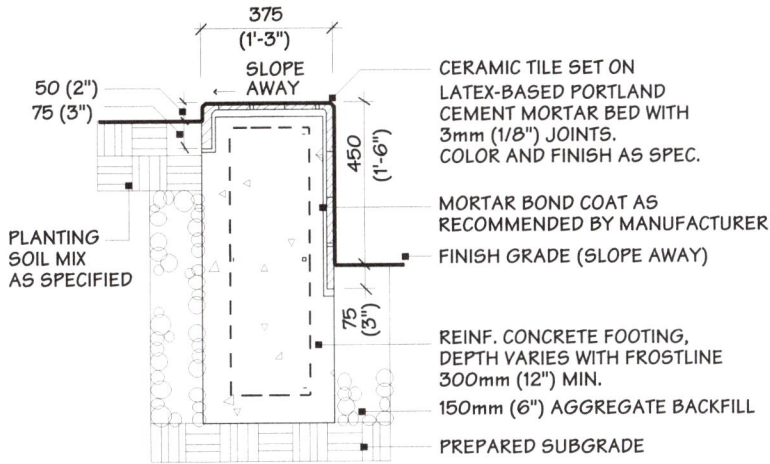

375
(1'-3")
SLOPE AWAY

50 (2")
75 (3")

450
(1'-6")

CERAMIC TILE SET ON LATEX-BASED PORTLAND CEMENT MORTAR BED WITH 3mm (1/8") JOINTS. COLOR AND FINISH AS SPEC.

MORTAR BOND COAT AS RECOMMENDED BY MANUFACTURER

FINISH GRADE (SLOPE AWAY)

PLANTING SOIL MIX AS SPECIFIED

75 (3")

REINF. CONCRETE FOOTING, DEPTH VARIES WITH FROSTLINE 300mm (12") MIN.

150mm (6") AGGREGATE BACKFILL

PREPARED SUBGRADE

APPLICATION

LIGHT   MED.   HEAVY

CLIMATE

ARID   HUMID   TEMP.   COLD

SUBGRADE

PERM.   CLAY   ROCK

CSI MASTERFORMAT: 02830
DRAWING FILE: SWL04-04

• This drawing is a template for preliminary design only, and is not intended for bid purposes. It is subject to modification based on design calculations, local practices, and all applicable codes and regulations.

• This ceramic tile veneered concrete seatwall is rated as heavy-duty due to its bearing capacity. It is typically found in dense residential, urban park, commercial and institutional settings.

• Concrete base is fully reinforced and typically requires back drainage due to the absence of weep-holes.

• Tile veneer is mortared to the wall with thin-set mortar within concrete inset. Wall may require damp proofing if soil is heavily irrigated or if soil is exceptionally wet.

• Reinforcing practices vary widely by region. Local codes and practices should be consulted prior to specifying any type of reinforcing.

• Concrete design must accommodate movement of materials by providing adequate expansion and control joints, particularly in regions of extreme temperature fluctuations. If longer than 7500mm (25'), sealed expansion joint will be required.

• It is recommended that recycled and regionally available materials and products be given high priority in determining final design and specifications.

Installation Cost (per Linear Foot)

LOW  HIGH

$26.00

Maintenance

LOW  HIGH

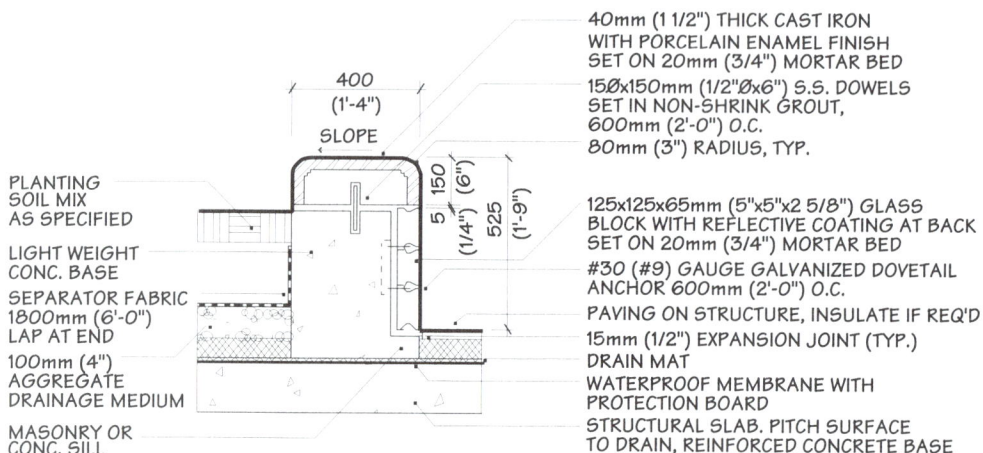

400 (1'-4")

SLOPE

5 150 (1/4") (6")

525 (1'-9")

PLANTING
SOIL MIX
AS SPECIFIED

LIGHT WEIGHT
CONC. BASE

SEPARATOR FABRIC
1800mm (6'-0")
LAP AT END

100mm (4")
AGGREGATE
DRAINAGE MEDIUM

MASONRY OR
CONC. SILL

40mm (1 1/2") THICK CAST IRON
WITH PORCELAIN ENAMEL FINISH
SET ON 20mm (3/4") MORTAR BED

15Ø x150mm (1/2"Øx6") S.S. DOWELS
SET IN NON-SHRINK GROUT,
600mm (2'-0") O.C.
80mm (3") RADIUS, TYP.

125x125x65mm (5"x5"x2 5/8") GLASS
BLOCK WITH REFLECTIVE COATING AT BACK
SET ON 20mm (3/4") MORTAR BED

#30 (#9) GAUGE GALVANIZED DOVETAIL
ANCHOR 600mm (2'-0") O.C.

PAVING ON STRUCTURE, INSULATE IF REQ'D

15mm (1/2") EXPANSION JOINT (TYP.)

DRAIN MAT

WATERPROOF MEMBRANE WITH
PROTECTION BOARD

STRUCTURAL SLAB. PITCH SURFACE
TO DRAIN, REINFORCED CONCRETE BASE

APPLICATION

CLIMATE

SUBGRADE

CSI MASTERFORMAT: 02830
DRAWING FILE: SWL09-01

• This drawing is a template for preliminary design only, and is not intended for bid purposes. It is subject to modification based on design calculations, local practices, and all applicable codes and regulations.

• This glass block-veneered seatwall with porcelain cap detail is rated as medium-duty due to its face material. It is typically found in dense residential, urban park, commercial and institutional settings on structural roof decks. This detail is limited to warm climate regions.

• Concrete base is placed directly onto heavy-duty drainage mat on sloping protection board, waterproof membrane, and structural slab.

• Reinforcing practices vary widely by region. Local codes and practices should be consulted prior to specifying any type of reinforcing.

• If designed for temperate or cold climates, air-entrained concrete is typically recommended due to freezing/thawing action.

• Glass block units are attached to concrete wall with metal mortar ties and mortared to concrete sill base.

• Porcelain seat cap is attached with dowels and mortared to concrete base, or alternately set with polymer adhesive.

• Reinforcing practices vary widely by region. Local codes and practices should be consulted prior to specifying any type of reinforcing.

• It is recommended that recycled and regionally available materials and products be given high priority in determining final design and specifications.

Installation Cost (per Linear Foot)

LOW   HIGH

$65.00

Maintenance

LOW   HIGH

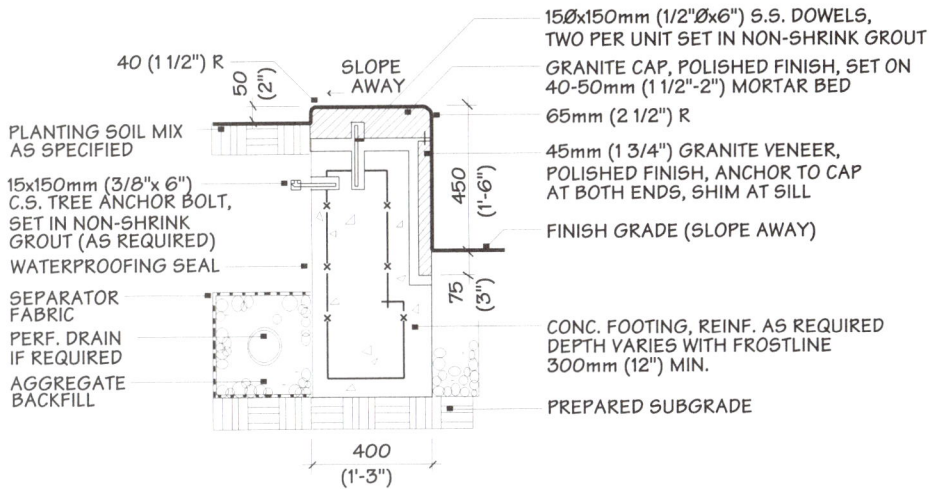

40 (1 1/2") R
50 (2")
SLOPE AWAY

150x150mm (1/2"Øx6") S.S. DOWELS, TWO PER UNIT SET IN NON-SHRINK GROUT

GRANITE CAP, POLISHED FINISH, SET ON 40-50mm (1 1/2"-2") MORTAR BED

65mm (2 1/2") R

45mm (1 3/4") GRANITE VENEER, POLISHED FINISH, ANCHOR TO CAP AT BOTH ENDS, SHIM AT SILL

FINISH GRADE (SLOPE AWAY)

450 (1'-6")

75 (3")

PLANTING SOIL MIX AS SPECIFIED

15x150mm (3/8"x 6") C.S. TREE ANCHOR BOLT, SET IN NON-SHRINK GROUT (AS REQUIRED)

WATERPROOFING SEAL

SEPARATOR FABRIC

PERF. DRAIN IF REQUIRED

AGGREGATE BACKFILL

CONC. FOOTING, REINF. AS REQUIRED DEPTH VARIES WITH FROSTLINE 300mm (12") MIN.

PREPARED SUBGRADE

400 (1'-3")

APPLICATION

CLIMATE

SUBGRADE

CSI MASTERFORMAT: 02830
DRAWING FILE: SWL03-02

• This drawing is a template for preliminary design only, and is not intended for bid purposes. It is subject to modification based on design calculations, local practices, and all applicable codes and regulations.

• This granite veneered concrete seatwall is rated as heavy-duty due to its bearing capacity. It is typically found in dense residential, urban park, commercial and institutional settings.

• Concrete base is fully reinforced and typically requires back drainage due to the absence of weep-holes. In severe conditions, a perforated drain pipe encased in washed stone and fabric separator, may be used to relieve extra hydrostatic pressure. Wall may require full damp proofing in such circumstances.

• Stone veneer is mortared to a sill and is tied to the wall with metal mortar ties. Stone seat cap is attached with stainless steel dowels and may be flashed to provide damp proofing for veneer in wet conditions. Wall

may require damp proofing if soil is heavily irrigated or if soil is exceptionally wet.

• Reinforcing practices vary widely by region. Local codes and practices should be consulted prior to specifying any type of reinforcing.

• Concrete design must accommodate movement of materials by providing adequate expansion and control joints, particularly in regions of extreme temperature fluctuations. If designed for temperate or cold climates, air-entrained concrete is typically recommended due to freezing/thawing action. If longer than 7500mm (25'), sealed expansion joint will be required.

• If used in cold climate, periodic re-pointing will be required.

• It is recommended that recycled and regionally available materials and products be given high priority in determining final design and specifications.

Installation Cost (per Linear Foot)

$38.00

Maintenance

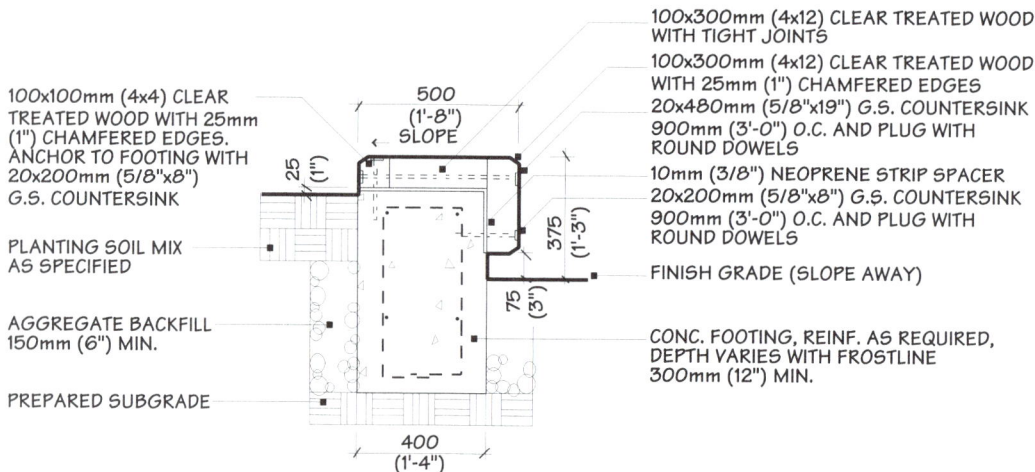

100x100mm (4x4) CLEAR TREATED WOOD WITH 25mm (1") CHAMFERED EDGES. ANCHOR TO FOOTING WITH 20x200mm (5/8"x8") G.S. COUNTERSINK

PLANTING SOIL MIX AS SPECIFIED

AGGREGATE BACKFILL 150mm (6") MIN.

PREPARED SUBGRADE

500 (1'-8") SLOPE

25 (1")

375 (1'-3")

75 (3")

400 (1'-4")

100x300mm (4x12) CLEAR TREATED WOOD WITH TIGHT JOINTS

100x300mm (4x12) CLEAR TREATED WOOD WITH 25mm (1") CHAMFERED EDGES

20x480mm (5/8"x19") G.S. COUNTERSINK 900mm (3'-0") O.C. AND PLUG WITH ROUND DOWELS

10mm (3/8") NEOPRENE STRIP SPACER

20x200mm (5/8"x8") G.S. COUNTERSINK 900mm (3'-0") O.C. AND PLUG WITH ROUND DOWELS

FINISH GRADE (SLOPE AWAY)

CONC. FOOTING, REINF. AS REQUIRED, DEPTH VARIES WITH FROSTLINE 300mm (12") MIN.

APPLICATION

CLIMATE

SUBGRADE

CSI MASTERFORMAT: 02830
DRAWING FILE: SWL05-01

• This drawing is a template for preliminary design only, and is not intended for bid purposes. It is subject to modification based on design calculations, local practices, and all applicable codes and regulations.

• This wood veneered concrete seatwall is rated as heavy-duty due to its bearing capacity. It is typically found in dense residential, urban park, commercial and institutional settings, and is appropriate for most climates.

• Concrete base is fully reinforced and typically requires back drainage due to the absence of weep-holes.

• Treated or rot resistant milled wood timbers are bolted together and in turn, bolted to the concrete with masonry screw fasteners, and are held back off of the concrete surface by gasket spacers to allow air circulation.

• Reinforcing practices vary widely by region. Local codes and practices should be consulted prior to specifying any type of reinforcing.

• Concrete design must accommodate movement of materials by providing adequate expansion and control joints, particularly in regions of extreme temperature fluctuations. If longer than 7500mm (25'), sealed expansion joint will be required.

• Wood seats may require periodic sanding and re-finishing to maintain a neat appearance.

• It is recommended that recycled and regionally available materials and products be given high priority in determining final design and specifications.

Installation Cost (per Linear Foot)

LOW   HIGH

$32.00

Maintenance

LOW   HIGH

40 (1 1/2") R

450 (1'-6")
→ SLOPE

125 (5") R

50 (2")

125 (5")

50 (2")

PLANTING SOIL MIX AS SPECIFIED

DRAIN CORE AND SEPARATOR FABRIC, FLAP AT EACH END

CONC. W/ SANDBLASTED FINISH REINF. AS REQUIRED COLOR AS SPECIFIED

50 (2")
400 (1'-3")

75 (3")

150 (6")

FINISH GRADE (SLOPE AWAY)

40mm (1 1/2") WEEPS 1 500mm (5'-0") O.C. MAX.

SEPARATOR FABRIC

AGGREGATE BACKFILL 150mm (6") MIN.

CONC. FOOTING, REINF. AS REQ'D DEPTH VARIES W/ FROSTLINE

PREPARED SUBGRADE

100 (4")

100 (4")

APPLICATION

LIGHT MED. HEAVY

CLIMATE

ARID HUMID TEMP. COLD

SUBGRADE

PERM. CLAY ROOF

CSI MASTERFORMAT: 02830
DRAWING FILE: SWL02-02

• This drawing is a template for preliminary design only, and is not intended for bid purposes. It is subject to modification based on design calculations, local practices, and all applicable codes and regulations.

• This concrete seatwall with drain is rated as heavy-duty due to its bearing capacity. It is typically found in dense residential, urban park, commercial and institutional settings.

• Concrete base is fully reinforced and typically requires back drainage to aid weep-hole drainage. Drain mat is placed against back of wall before backfilling.

• Reinforcing practices vary widely by region. Local codes and practices should be consulted prior to specifying any type of reinforcing.

• Concrete design must accommodate movement of materials by providing adequate expansion and control joints, particularly in regions of extreme temperature fluc-

tuations. If designed for temperate or cold climates, air-entrained concrete is typically recommended due to freezing/thawing action. If longer than 7500mm (25'), sealed expansion joint will be required.

• If used in cold or temperate climates, footings must bear on subgrade below frost.

• Finish should be rubbed and sealed for best effect.

• It is recommended that recycled and regionally available materials and products be given high priority in determining final design and specifications.

Installation Cost (per Linear Foot)

LOW   HIGH

$24.50

Maintenance

LOW   HIGH

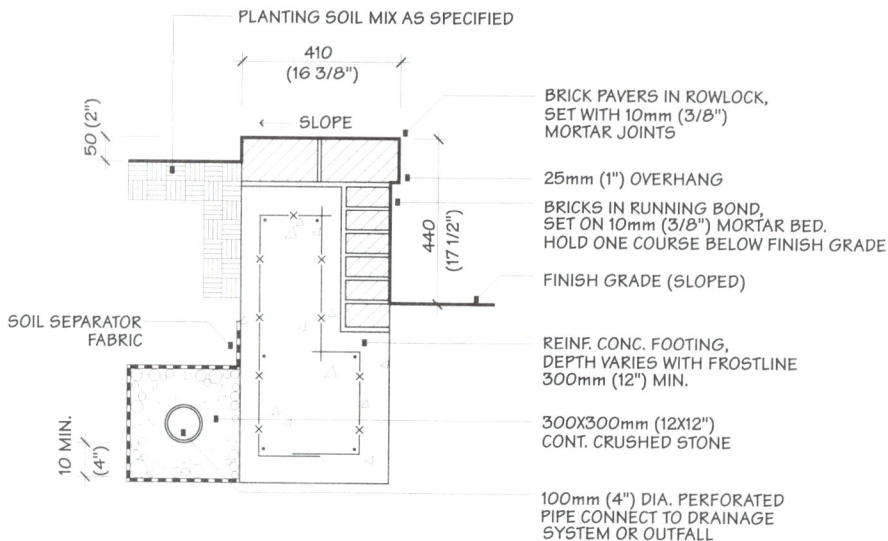

PLANTING SOIL MIX AS SPECIFIED

410
(16 3/8")

50 (2")

SLOPE

BRICK PAVERS IN ROWLOCK,
SET WITH 10mm (3/8")
MORTAR JOINTS

25mm (1") OVERHANG

BRICKS IN RUNNING BOND,
SET ON 10mm (3/8") MORTAR BED.
HOLD ONE COURSE BELOW FINISH GRADE

440
(17 1/2")

FINISH GRADE (SLOPED)

SOIL SEPARATOR
FABRIC

REINF. CONC. FOOTING,
DEPTH VARIES WITH FROSTLINE
300mm (12") MIN.

300X300mm (12X12")
CONT. CRUSHED STONE

10 MIN.
(4")

100mm (4") DIA. PERFORATED
PIPE CONNECT TO DRAINAGE
SYSTEM OR OUTFALL

APPLICATION

CLIMATE

SUBGRADE

CSI MASTERFORMAT: 02830
DRAWING FILE: SWL04-02

• This drawing is a template for preliminary design only, and is not intended for bid purposes. It is subject to modification based on design calculations, local practices, and all applicable codes and regulations.

• This brick veneered concrete seatwall is rated as heavy-duty due to its bearing capacity. It is typically found in dense residential, urban park, commercial and institutional settings.

• Concrete base is fully reinforced and typically requires back drainage due to the absence of weep-holes. In severe conditions, a perforated drain pipe encased in washed stone and fabric separator may be used to relieve extra hydrostatic pressure. Wall may require full damp proofing in such circumstances.

• Brick veneer is mortared to a sill and is tied to the wall with metal mortar ties. Brick seat cap may be flashed to provide damp proofing for veneer in wet conditions. Wall may require damp proofing if soil is heavily irrigated or if soil is exceptionally wet.

• Reinforcing practices vary widely by region. Local codes and practices should be consulted prior to specifying any type of reinforcing.

• Concrete design must accommodate movement of materials by providing adequate expansion and control joints, particularly in regions of extreme temperature fluctuations. If designed for temperate or cold climates, air-entrained concrete is typically recommended due to freezing/thawing action. If longer than 7500mm (25'), sealed expansion joint will be required.

• If used in cold climate, periodic re-pointing will be required.

• It is recommended that recycled and regionally available materials and products be given high priority in determining final design and specifications.

Installation Cost (per Linear Foot)

LOW   HIGH

$39.20

Maintenance

LOW   HIGH

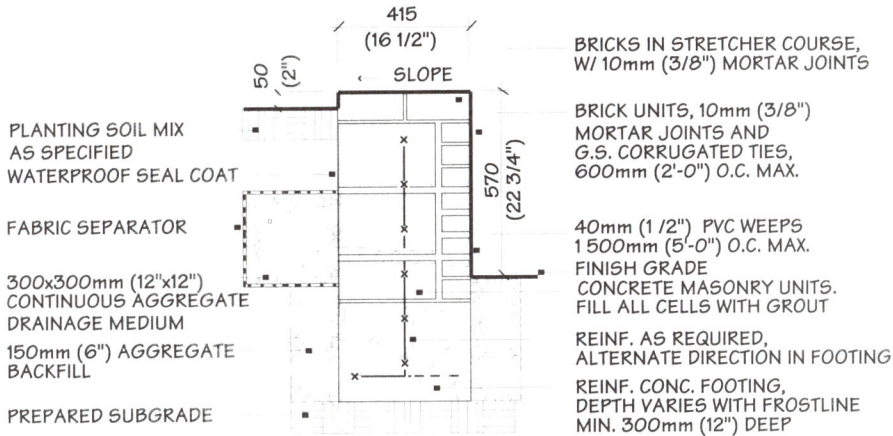

415 (16 1/2")

50 (2")

SLOPE

570 (22 3/4")

PLANTING SOIL MIX
AS SPECIFIED
WATERPROOF SEAL COAT

FABRIC SEPARATOR

300x300mm (12"x12")
CONTINUOUS AGGREGATE
DRAINAGE MEDIUM

150mm (6") AGGREGATE
BACKFILL

PREPARED SUBGRADE

BRICKS IN STRETCHER COURSE,
W/ 10mm (3/8") MORTAR JOINTS

BRICK UNITS, 10mm (3/8")
MORTAR JOINTS AND
G.S. CORRUGATED TIES,
600mm (2'-0") O.C. MAX.

40mm (1 /2") PVC WEEPS
1500mm (5'-0") O.C. MAX.
FINISH GRADE
CONCRETE MASONRY UNITS.
FILL ALL CELLS WITH GROUT

REINF. AS REQUIRED,
ALTERNATE DIRECTION IN FOOTING

REINF. CONC. FOOTING,
DEPTH VARIES WITH FROSTLINE
MIN. 300mm (12") DEEP

APPLICATION

CLIMATE

SUBGRADE

CSI MASTERFORMAT: 02830
DRAWING FILE: SWL04-03

• This drawing is a template for preliminary design only, and is not intended for bid purposes. It is subject to modification based on design calculations, local practices, and all applicable codes and regulations.

• This brick veneered masonry seatwall is rated as medium-duty due to its bearing capacity. It is typically found in dense residential, urban park, commercial and institutional settings.

• Masonry base is fully grouted and reinforced and typically requires back drainage to aid weep-hole drainage.

• Brick veneer is mortared to a sill and is tied to the wall with metal mortar ties. Brick seat cap may be flashed to provide damp proofing for veneer in wet conditions. Masonry wall may require damp proofing if soil is heavily irrigated or if soil is exceptionally wet.

• Reinforcing practices vary widely by region. Local codes and practices should be consulted prior to specifying any type of reinforcing.

• Concrete design must accommodate movement of materials by providing adequate expansion and control joints, particularly in regions of extreme temperature fluctuations. If designed for temperate or cold climates, air-entrained concrete is typically recommended due to freezing/thawing action. If longer than 7500mm (25'), sealed expansion joint will be required.

• If used in cold climate, periodic re-pointing will be required.

• It is recommended that recycled and regionally available materials and products be given high priority in determining final design and specifications.

Installation Cost (per Linear Foot)

LOW   HIGH

$39.20

Maintenance

LOW   HIGH

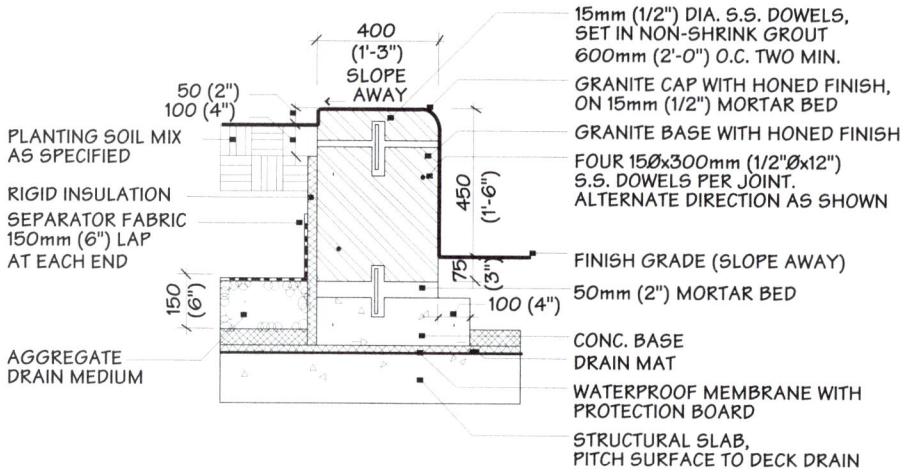

400 (1'-3")
SLOPE AWAY

50 (2")
100 (4")

PLANTING SOIL MIX AS SPECIFIED

RIGID INSULATION

SEPARATOR FABRIC 150mm (6") LAP AT EACH END

150 (6")

AGGREGATE DRAIN MEDIUM

450 (1'-6")

75 (3")
100 (4")

15mm (1/2") DIA. S.S. DOWELS, SET IN NON-SHRINK GROUT 600mm (2'-0") O.C. TWO MIN.

GRANITE CAP WITH HONED FINISH, ON 15mm (1/2") MORTAR BED

GRANITE BASE WITH HONED FINISH

FOUR 150x300mm (1/2"Øx12") S.S. DOWELS PER JOINT. ALTERNATE DIRECTION AS SHOWN

FINISH GRADE (SLOPE AWAY)

50mm (2") MORTAR BED

CONC. BASE

DRAIN MAT

WATERPROOF MEMBRANE WITH PROTECTION BOARD

STRUCTURAL SLAB, PITCH SURFACE TO DECK DRAIN

APPLICATION

CLIMATE

SUBGRADE

CSI MASTERFORMAT: 02830
DRAWING FILE: SWL03-03

• This drawing is a template for preliminary design only, and is not intended for bid purposes. It is subject to modification based on design calculations, local practices, and all applicable codes and regulations.

• This granite seatwall detail is rated as heavy-duty due to its bearing capacity. It is typically found in dense residential, urban park, commercial and institutional settings on structural roof decks.

• Concrete base is placed directly onto heavy-duty drainage mat on sloping protection board, waterproof membrane, and structural slab.

• Reinforcing practices vary widely by region. Local codes and practices should be consulted prior to specifying any type of reinforcing.

• If designed for temperate or cold climates, air-entrained concrete is typically recommended due to freezing/thawing action.

• Stone is attached with dowels and mortared to concrete base.

• Stone seat cap is attached with stainless steel dowels and mortared to granite base, or alternately set with polymer adhesive.

• Reinforcing practices vary widely by region. Local codes and practices should be consulted prior to specifying any type of reinforcing.

• It is recommended that recycled and regionally available materials and products be given high priority in determining final design and specifications.

Installation Cost (per Linear Foot)

LOW   HIGH

$80.00

Maintenance

LOW   HIGH

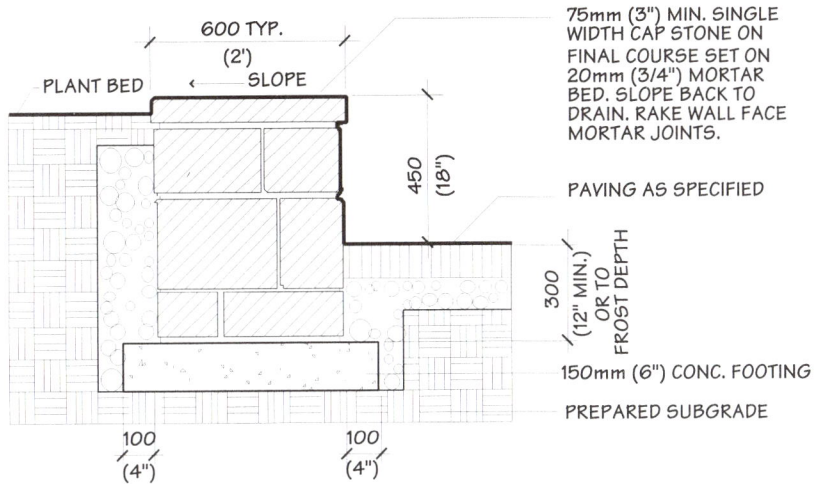

600 TYP.
(2')
SLOPE
PLANT BED

450 (18")
300 (12" MIN.) OR TO FROST DEPTH

100 (4")   100 (4")

75mm (3") MIN. SINGLE WIDTH CAP STONE ON FINAL COURSE SET ON 20mm (3/4") MORTAR BED. SLOPE BACK TO DRAIN. RAKE WALL FACE MORTAR JOINTS.

PAVING AS SPECIFIED

150mm (6") CONC. FOOTING

PREPARED SUBGRADE

APPLICATION

LIGHT   MED.   HEAVY

CLIMATE

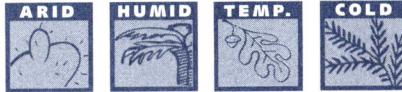

ARID   HUMID   TEMP.   COLD

SUBGRADE

PERM.   CLAY   ROOF

CSI MASTERFORMAT: 02830
DRAWING FILE: SWL03-01

• This drawing is a template for preliminary design only, and is not intended for bid purposes. It is subject to modification based on design calculations, local practices, and all applicable codes and regulations.

• This mortared stone seatwall is rated as medium-duty due to its bearing capacity and longevity. It is typically found in residential, park, commercial and institutional settings, and is appropriate for all climates.

• Wall rests on a concrete base and is back-filled with aggregate for positive drainage. Stone is mortared to base and built with raked joints. Single width cap stone is used to finish wall. Cap stone should be pitched to drain to rear of wall.

• In wet locations, a subdrain may be required at rear of wall.

• Cap stone seat may require periodic re-pointing.

• It is recommended that recycled and regionally available materials and products be given high priority in determining final design and specifications.

Installation Cost (per Linear Foot)

LOW   HIGH

$30.00

Maintenance

LOW   HIGH

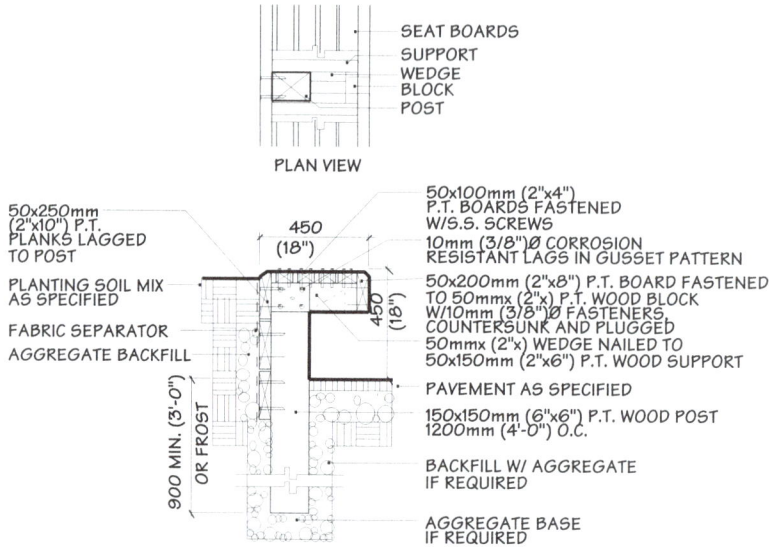

PLAN VIEW

SEAT BOARDS
SUPPORT
WEDGE
BLOCK
POST

50x250mm
(2"x10") P.T.
PLANKS LAGGED
TO POST

450
(18")

50x100mm (2"x4")
P.T. BOARDS FASTENED
W/S.S. SCREWS

10mm (3/8")Ø CORROSION
RESISTANT LAGS IN GUSSET PATTERN

PLANTING SOIL MIX
AS SPECIFIED

50x200mm (2"x8") P.T. BOARD FASTENED
TO 50mmx (2"x) P.T. WOOD BLOCK
W/10mm (3/8")Ø FASTENERS,
COUNTERSUNK AND PLUGGED

FABRIC SEPARATOR

AGGREGATE BACKFILL

50mmx (2"x) WEDGE NAILED TO
50x150mm (2"x6") P.T. WOOD SUPPORT

PAVEMENT AS SPECIFIED

150x150mm (6"x6") P.T. WOOD POST
1200mm (4'-0") O.C.

900 MIN. (3'-0")
OR FROST

BACKFILL W/ AGGREGATE
IF REQUIRED

AGGREGATE BASE
IF REQUIRED

APPLICATION

CLIMATE

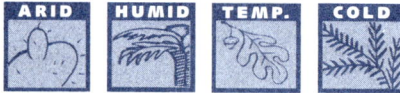

SUBGRADE

CSI MASTERFORMAT: 02830
DRAWING FILE: SWL05-03

• This drawing is a template for preliminary design only, and is not intended for bid purposes. It is subject to modification based on design calculations, local practices, and all applicable codes and regulations.

• This timber post seatwall is rated as light-duty due to its bearing capacity and longevity. It is typically found in residential, park, and garden settings, and is appropriate for all climates, but is better suited to warm climates.

• Wall posts rest on aggregate base and backfilled with aggregate for positive drainage.

• Treated wood planks are attached to treated wood posts at the rear of the wall with stainless steel fasteners. Outrigger seat supports are screwed to post and wood wedge supports to complete the seatwall frame. Sanded planks are attached to frame with stainless steel fasteners.

• Surface should slope to drain. In clay soils or frost/thaw regions, fabric separator may be required to screen fines from backfill.

• Wood seats may require periodic sanding and re-finishing to maintain a neat appearance. Post life is limited by degradation rate of buried portion.

• It is recommended that recycled and regionally available materials and products be given high priority in determining final design and specifications.

Installation Cost (per Linear Foot)

LOW   HIGH

$17.00

Maintenance

LOW   HIGH

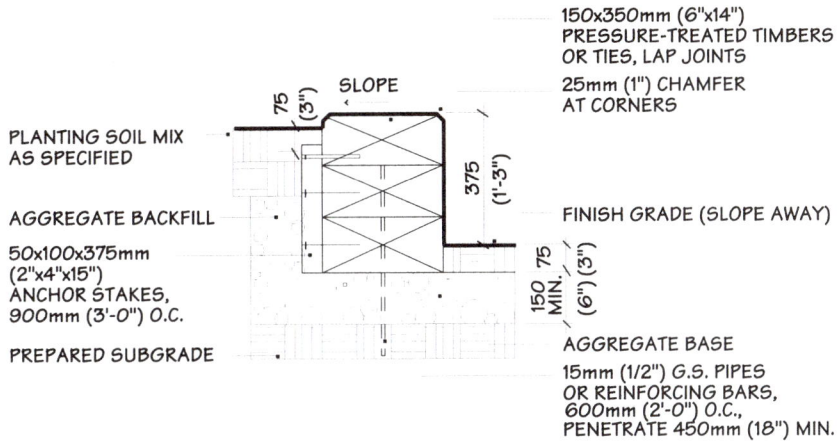

150x350mm (6"x14")
PRESSURE-TREATED TIMBERS
OR TIES, LAP JOINTS

25mm (1") CHAMFER
AT CORNERS

PLANTING SOIL MIX
AS SPECIFIED

SLOPE

75 (3")

375 (1'-3")

FINISH GRADE (SLOPE AWAY)

AGGREGATE BACKFILL

50x100x375mm
(2"x4"x15")
ANCHOR STAKES,
900mm (3'-0") O.C.

150 MIN. (6") 75 (3")

PREPARED SUBGRADE

AGGREGATE BASE

15mm (1/2") G.S. PIPES
OR REINFORCING BARS,
600mm (2'-0") O.C.,
PENETRATE 450mm (18") MIN.

APPLICATION

CLIMATE

SUBGRADE

CSI MASTERFORMAT: 02830
DRAWING FILE: SWL05-02

• This drawing is a template for preliminary design only, and is not intended for bid purposes. It is subject to modification based on design calculations, local practices, and all applicable codes and regulations.

• This wood timber seatwall is rated as light-duty due to its bearing capacity and longevity. It is typically found in residential, park, commercial and institutional settings, and is appropriate for all climates, but is better suited to warm climates.

• Wall rests on aggregate base and back-filled with aggregate for positive drainage.

• Treated milled wood timbers are attached to treated wood stakes at the rear of the wall, and the first two courses are pinned with steel rods. Surface should slope to drain. In clay soils or frost/thaw regions, fabric separator may be required to bind aggregate base and backfill, and metal pipes may be used to substitute wood stakes.

• Wood seats may require periodic sanding and re-finishing to maintain a neat appearance.

• It is recommended that recycled and regionally available materials and products be given high priority in determining final design and specifications.

Installation Cost (per Linear Foot)

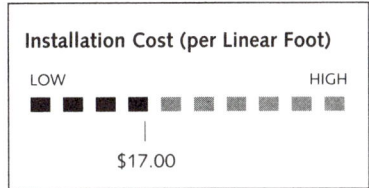

LOW   HIGH

$17.00

Maintenance

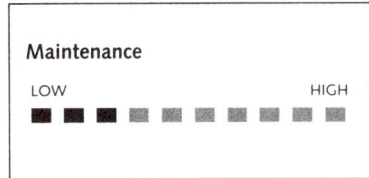

LOW   HIGH

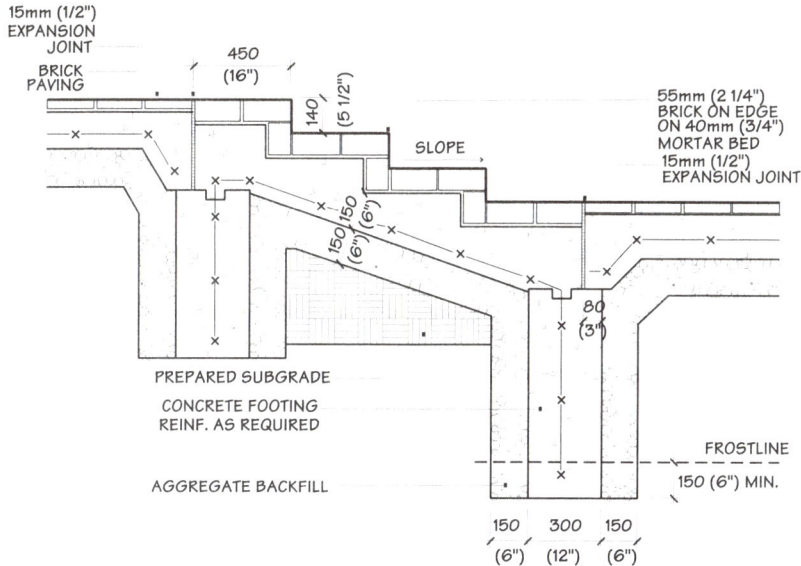

15mm (1/2")
EXPANSION JOINT

BRICK PAVING

450 (16")

140 (5 1/2")

55mm (2 1/4")
BRICK ON EDGE
ON 40mm (3/4")
MORTAR BED
15mm (1/2")
EXPANSION JOINT

SLOPE

150 (6") 150 (6")

80 (3")

PREPARED SUBGRADE

CONCRETE FOOTING
REINF. AS REQUIRED

AGGREGATE BACKFILL

FROSTLINE

150 (6") MIN.

150 (6")   300 (12")   150 (6")

APPLICATION

CLIMATE

SUBGRADE

CSI MASTERFORMAT: 02780
DRAWING FILE: STP04-01

• This drawing is a template for preliminary design only, and is not intended for bid purposes. It is subject to modification based on design calculations, local practices, and all applicable codes and regulations.

• This mortared brick veneer step detail is rated for heavy-duty applications based on thickness of concrete and aggregate base, and may support significant pedestrian loading typically associated with dense residential, public park, institutional, and commercial settings.

• Rigid pavement design must accommodate movement of materials by providing adequate expansion and control joints, particularly in regions of extreme temperature fluctuations. If designed for temperate or cold climates, air-entrained concrete is typically recommended due to freezing/thawing action.

• Reinforcing practices vary widely by region. Local codes and practices should be consulted prior to specifying any type of reinforcing.

• This detail shows footing sills for adjacent rigid pavement at top and bottom of steps. This insures precise alignment of adjacent pavements over time.

• All joints should be sealed for best performance over time, especially in frost/thaw climates. This detail is not recommended for cold climates due to mortar joints in the pavement.

• Cost note: Costs are calculated as per linear units of riser.

• It is recommended that recycled and regionally available materials and products be given high priority in determining final design and specifications.

Installation Cost (per Linear Foot)

LOW   HIGH

$58.00

Maintenance

LOW   HIGH

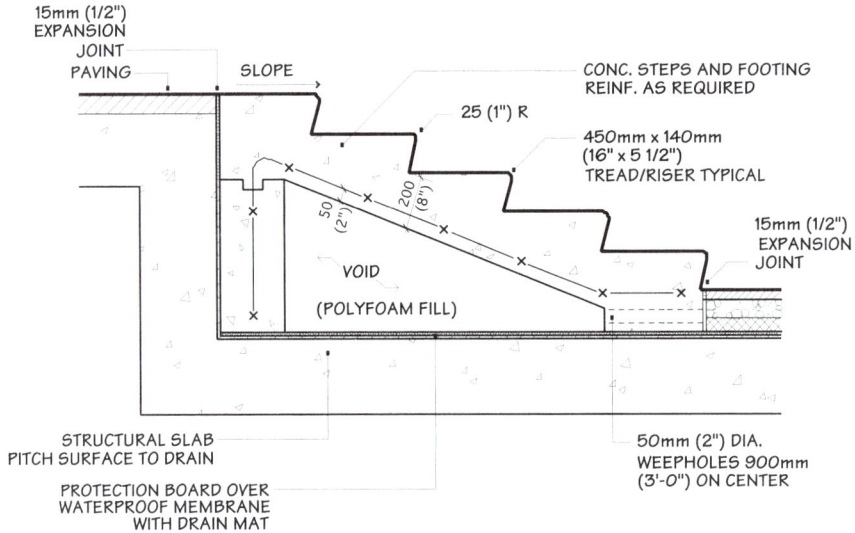

15mm (1/2")
EXPANSION
JOINT
PAVING

SLOPE

CONC. STEPS AND FOOTING
REINF. AS REQUIRED

25 (1") R

450mm x 140mm
(16" x 5 1/2")
TREAD/RISER TYPICAL

50
(2")

200
(8")

15mm (1/2")
EXPANSION
JOINT

VOID

(POLYFOAM FILL)

STRUCTURAL SLAB
PITCH SURFACE TO DRAIN

50mm (2") DIA.
WEEPHOLES 900mm
(3'-0") ON CENTER

PROTECTION BOARD OVER
WATERPROOF MEMBRANE
WITH DRAIN MAT

APPLICATION

CLIMATE

SUBGRADE

CSI MASTERFORMAT: 03300
DRAWING FILE: STP02-02

• This drawing is a template for preliminary design only, and is not intended for bid purposes. It is subject to modification based on design calculations, local practices, and all applicable codes and regulations.

• This concrete step detail is rated for heavy-duty applications based on thickness of concrete and span over polyfoam void, and may support significant pedestrian loading typically associated with structural roof deck settings.

• Rigid pavement design must accommodate movement of materials by providing adequate expansion and control joints, particularly in regions of extreme temperature fluctuations. If designed for temperate or cold climates, air-entrained concrete is typically recommended due to freezing/thawing action.

• Reinforcing practices vary widely by region. Local codes and practices should be consulted prior to specifying any type of reinforcing.

• This detail shows steps placed on heavy-duty drain mat over protection board and waterproof membrane on a structural deck. Concrete thickness must allow for void shrinkage and extent of span. Allow weep holes to drain void if required.

• Cost note: Costs are calculated as per linear units of riser.

• It is recommended that recycled and regionally available materials and products be given high priority in determining final design and specifications.

Installation Cost (per Linear Foot)

LOW   HIGH

$45.00

Maintenance

LOW   HIGH

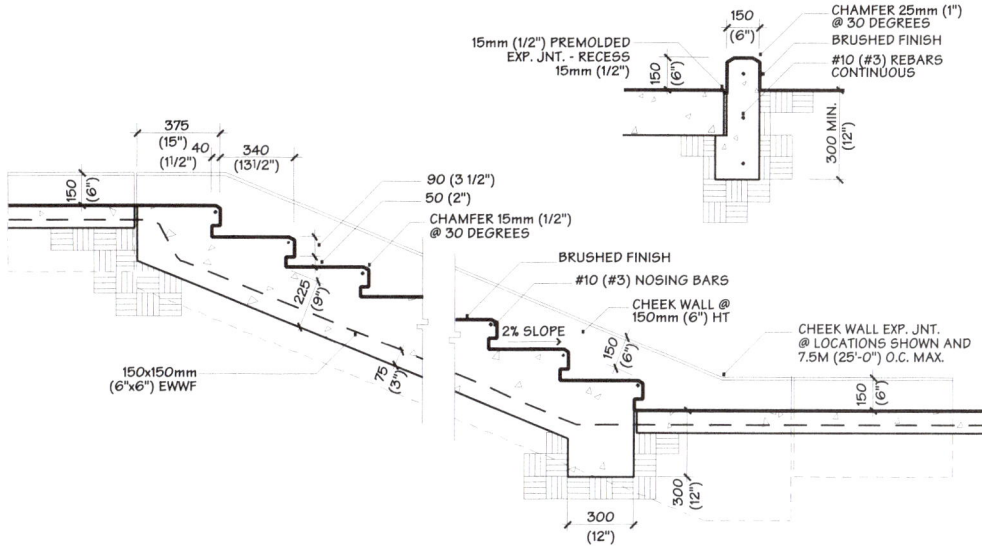

APPLICATION

LIGHT   MED.   **HEAVY**

CLIMATE

ARID   HUMID   TEMP.   COLD

SUBGRADE

PERM.   CLAY   ROOF

CSI MASTERFORMAT: 03300
DRAWING FILE: STP02-03

• This drawing is a template for preliminary design only, and is not intended for bid purposes. It is subject to modification based on design calculations, local practices, and all applicable codes and regulations.

• This concrete step detail is rated for heavy-duty applications based on thickness of concrete and aggregate base, and may support significant pedestrian loading typically associated with dense residential, public park, institutional, and commercial settings.

• Rigid pavement design must accommodate movement of materials by providing adequate expansion and control joints, particularly in regions of extreme temperature fluctuations. If designed for temperate or cold climates, air-entrained concrete is typically recommended due to freezing/thawing action.

• Reinforcing practices vary widely by region. Local codes and practices should be consulted prior to specifying any type of reinforcing.

• This detail shows concrete cheek wall for continous support of step unit. Steps rest on a sill and abut the walls with a continuous expansion joint sealed to prevent moisture penetration.

• Cost note: Costs are calculated as per linear units of riser.

• It is recommended that recycled and regionally available materials and products be given high priority in determining final design and specifications.

Installation Cost (per Linear Foot)

LOW   HIGH

$27.00

Maintenance

LOW   HIGH

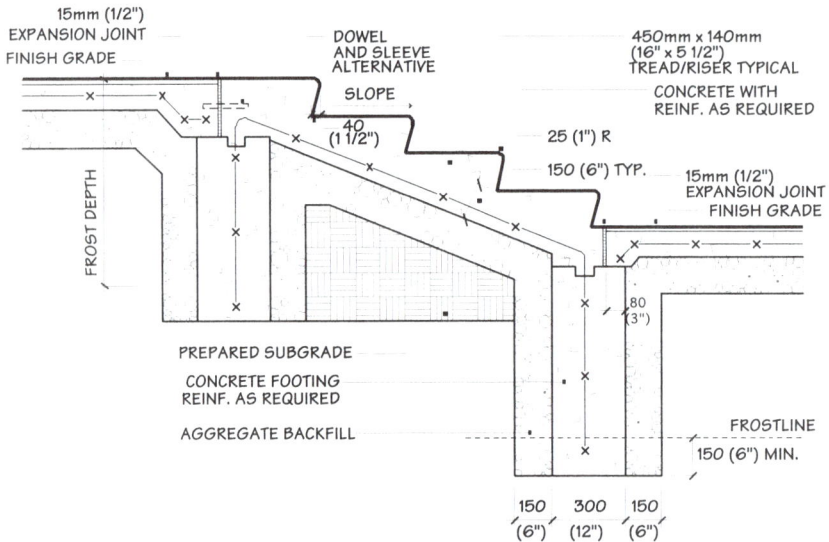

15mm (1/2")
EXPANSION JOINT
FINISH GRADE

DOWEL
AND SLEEVE
ALTERNATIVE

SLOPE

40
(1 1/2")

450mm x 140mm
(16" x 5 1/2")
TREAD/RISER TYPICAL
CONCRETE WITH
REINF. AS REQUIRED

25 (1") R

150 (6") TYP.

15mm (1/2")
EXPANSION JOINT
FINISH GRADE

FROST DEPTH

80
(3")

PREPARED SUBGRADE

CONCRETE FOOTING
REINF. AS REQUIRED

AGGREGATE BACKFILL

FROSTLINE

150 (6") MIN.

150   300   150
(6")   (12")   (6")

APPLICATION

CLIMATE

SUBGRADE

CSI MASTERFORMAT: 03300
DRAWING FILE: STP02-01

• This drawing is a template for preliminary design only, and is not intended for bid purposes. It is subject to modification based on design calculations, local practices, and all applicable codes and regulations.

• This concrete step detail is rated for heavy-duty applications based on thickness of concrete and aggregate base, and may support significant pedestrian loading typically associated with dense residential, public park, institutional, and commercial settings.

• Rigid pavement design must accommodate movement of materials by providing adequate expansion and control joints, particularly in regions of extreme temperature fluctuations. If designed for temperate or cold climates, air-entrained concrete is typically recommended due to freezing/thawing action.

• Reinforcing practices vary widely by region. Local codes and practices should be consulted prior to specifying any type of reinforcing.

• This detail shows footing sills for adjacent rigid pavement at top and bottom of steps. This insures precise alignment of adjacent pavements over time.

• Cost note: Costs are calculated as per linear units of riser.

• It is recommended that recycled and regionally available materials and products be given high priority in determining final design and specifications.

Installation Cost (per Linear Foot)

LOW   HIGH

$24.00

Maintenance

LOW   HIGH

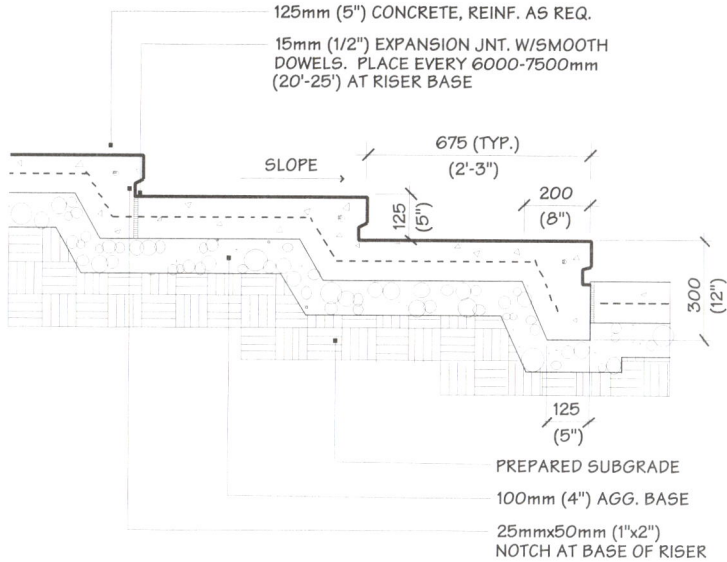

125mm (5") CONCRETE, REINF. AS REQ.

15mm (1/2") EXPANSION JNT. W/SMOOTH DOWELS. PLACE EVERY 6000-7500mm (20'-25') AT RISER BASE

SLOPE

675 (TYP.) (2'-3")

200 (8")

125 (5")

300 (12")

125 (5")

PREPARED SUBGRADE

100mm (4") AGG. BASE

25mmx50mm (1"x2") NOTCH AT BASE OF RISER

APPLICATION

CLIMATE

SUBGRADE

CSI MASTERFORMAT: 03300
DRAWING FILE: STP02-04

- This drawing is a template for preliminary design only, and is not intended for bid purposes. It is subject to modification based on design calculations, local practices, and all applicable codes and regulations.

- This concrete ramp-step detail is rated for medium-duty applications based on thickness of concrete and aggregate base, and may support significant pedestrian loading typically associated with dense residential, public park, institutional, and commercial settings.

- Rigid pavement design must accommodate movement of materials by providing adequate expansion and control joints, particularly in regions of extreme temperature fluctuations. If designed for temperate or cold climates, air-entrained concrete is typically recommended due to freezing/thawing action.

- Reinforcing practices vary widely by region. Local codes and practices should be consulted prior to specifying any type of reinforcing.

- This detail shows typical concrete ramp step. Tread width should be in multiples of natural human gait, and riser is ideally less than 150 mm (6"). Steps rest on an aggregate base and require expansion joints for long runs.

- In cold climates, a cheek wall and heating cables may be required. Stone or precast concrete edging may be placed at sides to ease maintenance.

- It is recommended that recycled and regionally available materials and products be given high priority in determining final design and specifications.

Installation Cost (per Linear Foot)

LOW   HIGH

$24.00

Maintenance

LOW   HIGH

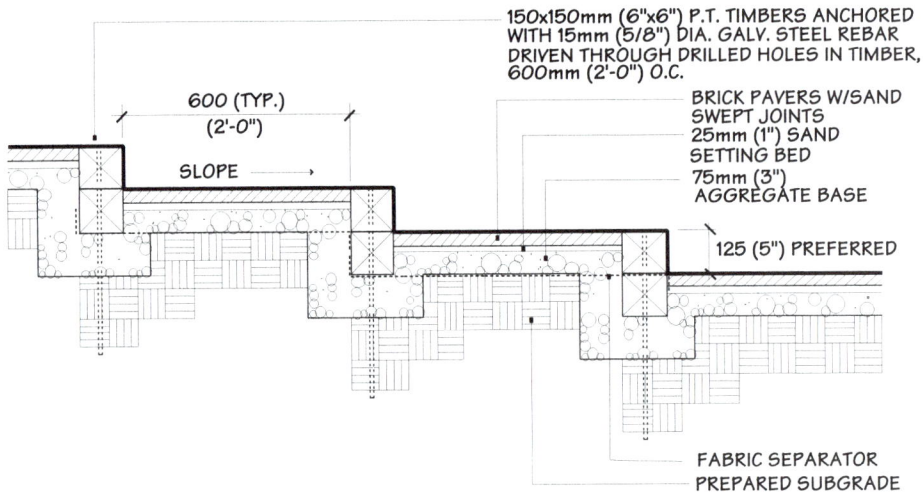

150x150mm (6"x6") P.T. TIMBERS ANCHORED WITH 15mm (5/8") DIA. GALV. STEEL REBAR DRIVEN THROUGH DRILLED HOLES IN TIMBER, 600mm (2'-0") O.C.

600 (TYP.) (2'-0")

SLOPE

BRICK PAVERS W/SAND SWEPT JOINTS
25mm (1") SAND SETTING BED
75mm (3") AGGREGATE BASE

125 (5") PREFERRED

FABRIC SEPARATOR
PREPARED SUBGRADE

APPLICATION

CLIMATE

SUBGRADE

CSI MASTERFORMAT: 02945
DRAWING FILE: STP04-02

• This drawing is a template for preliminary design only, and is not intended for bid purposes. It is subject to modification based on design calculations, local practices, and all applicable codes and regulations.

• This wood riser/ brick tread ramp step detail is as rated light-duty due to its materials and level of wear it is capable of bearing. It is typically found in residential, park, and garden settings.

• Timbers should be rot resistant or treated and be hard enough to withstand wear at tread nosing. They are secured to metal stakes through holes drilled through the timbers. This detail is recommended for frost/thaw, or clay soil regions, because metal pins lessen seasonal up-lift.

• Timbers are stacked to achieve riser installation shown and to form a stapling surface for the fabric reinforcement which binds both aggregate base and timber units.

• Edges must be contained with wood timbers, metal or plastic flanges, or wood planking set on edge to serve as a stringer trim piece to contain both riser and brick units.

• This detail requires periodic brick resetting due to heavy use and possible subgrade deformation. Total tread width should be a multiple of average stride, typically 675 mm (27").

• It is recommended that recycled and regionally available materials and products be given high priority in determining final design and specifications.

Installation Cost (per Linear Foot)

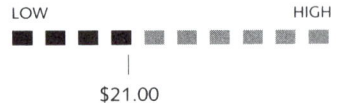

LOW   HIGH

$21.00

Maintenance

LOW   HIGH

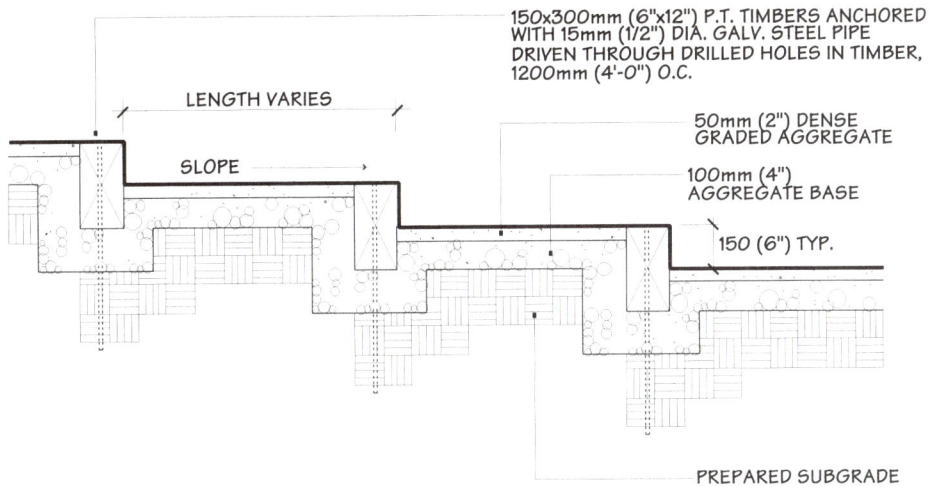

150x300mm (6"x12") P.T. TIMBERS ANCHORED WITH 15mm (1/2") DIA. GALV. STEEL PIPE DRIVEN THROUGH DRILLED HOLES IN TIMBER, 1200mm (4'-0") O.C.

LENGTH VARIES

SLOPE

50mm (2") DENSE GRADED AGGREGATE

100mm (4") AGGREGATE BASE

150 (6") TYP.

PREPARED SUBGRADE

APPLICATION

CLIMATE

SUBGRADE

CSI MASTERFORMAT: 06130
DRAWING FILE: STP07-02

• This drawing is a template for preliminary design only, and is not intended for bid purposes. It is subject to modification based on design calculations, local practices, and all applicable codes and regulations.

• This wood riser/aggregate tread ramp step detail is rated light-duty due to its materials and level of wear it is capable of bearing without significant maintenance. It is typically found in residential, park, and garden settings.

• Timbers should be rot resistant or treated and be hard enough to withstand wear at tread nosing. They are secured to metal stakes through holes drilled through the timbers. This detail is recommended for frost/thaw or clay soil regions, because metal pins lessen seasonal up-lift.

• Timbers may be one piece or stacked to achieve riser installation shown.

• Aggregate sufaces should be dense graded to achieve a smooth firm surface.

Edges must be contained with wood timbers, metal or plastic flanges, or wood planking set on edge to serve as a stringer trim piece to contain both riser and aggregate.

• This detail requires raking and replenishment of aggregate due to subgrade deformation and mechanical displacement.

• It is recommended that recycled and regionally available materials and products be given high priority in determining final design and specifications.

Installation Cost (per Linear Foot)

LOW   HIGH

$4.00

Maintenance

LOW   HIGH

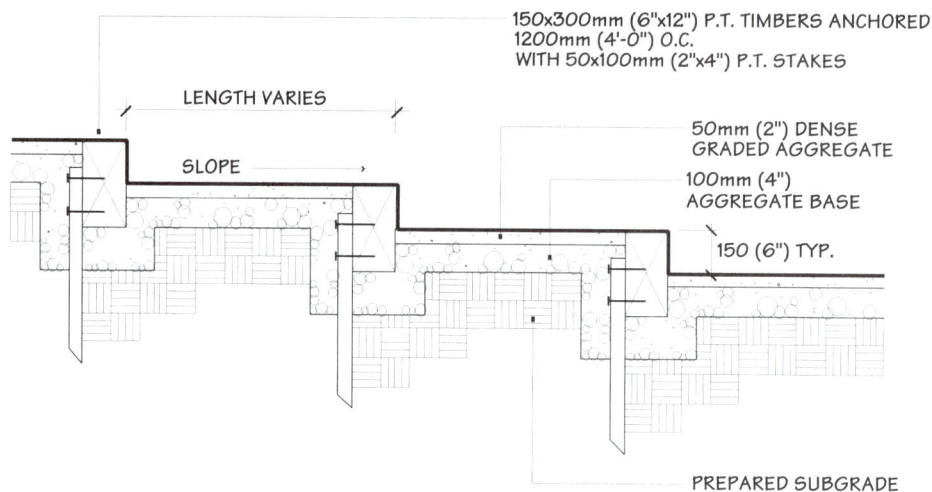

150x300mm (6"x12") P.T. TIMBERS ANCHORED
1200mm (4'-0") O.C.
WITH 50x100mm (2"x4") P.T. STAKES

LENGTH VARIES

SLOPE

50mm (2") DENSE
GRADED AGGREGATE

100mm (4")
AGGREGATE BASE

150 (6") TYP.

PREPARED SUBGRADE

APPLICATION

CLIMATE

SUBGRADE
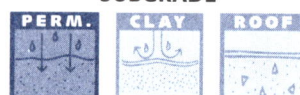

CSI MASTERFORMAT: 06130
DRAWING FILE: STP07-01

• This drawing is a template for preliminary design only, and is not intended for bid purposes. It is subject to modification based on design calculations, local practices, and all applicable codes and regulations.

• This wood riser/aggregate tread ramp step detail is rated light-duty due to its materials and level of wear it is capable of bearing without significant maintenance. It is typically found in residential, park, and garden settings.

• Timbers should be rot resistant or treated and be hard enough to withstand wear at tread nosing. They are secured to wood or metal stakes with corrosion resistant fasteners. In frost/thaw or clay soil regions, metal pins are recommended to lessen seasonal uplift.

• Aggregate sufaces should be dense graded to achieve a smooth firm surface. Edges must be contained with wood timbers, metal or plastic flanges, or wood planking set

on edge to serve as a stringer trim piece to contain both riser and aggregate.

• This detail requires raking and replenishment of aggregate due to subgrade deformation and mechanical displacement.

• It is recommended that recycled and regionally available materials and products be given high priority in determining final design and specifications.

Installation Cost (per Linear Foot)

LOW   HIGH

$4.00

Maintenance

LOW   HIGH

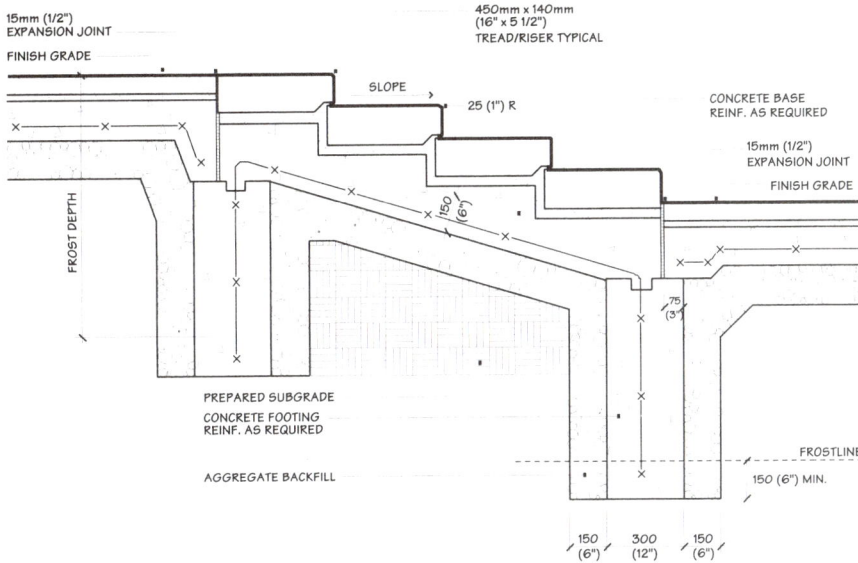

15mm (1/2")
EXPANSION JOINT

FINISH GRADE

450mm x 140mm
(16" x 5 1/2")
TREAD/RISER TYPICAL

SLOPE

25 (1") R

CONCRETE BASE
REINF. AS REQUIRED

15mm (1/2")
EXPANSION JOINT

FINISH GRADE

FROST DEPTH

150 (6")

75 (3")

PREPARED SUBGRADE
CONCRETE FOOTING
REINF. AS REQUIRED

AGGREGATE BACKFILL

FROSTLINE

150 (6") MIN.

150 (6")   300 (12")   150 (6")

APPLICATION

CLIMATE

SUBGRADE

CSI MASTERFORMAT: 04410
DRAWING FILE: STP03-01

• This drawing is a template for preliminary design only, and is not intended for bid purposes. It is subject to modification based on design calculations, local practices, and all applicable codes and regulations.

• This granite step detail is rated for heavy-duty applications based on thickness of concrete and aggregate base, and may support significant pedestrian loading typically associated with dense residential, public park, institutional, and commercial settings.

• Rigid pavement design must accommodate movement of materials by providing adequate expansion and control joints, particularly in regions of extreme temperature fluctuations. If designed for temperate or cold climates, air-entrained concrete is typically recommended due to freezing/thawing action.

• Reinforcing practices vary widely by region. Local codes and practices should be consulted prior to specifying any type of reinforcing.

• This detail shows footing sills for adjacent rigid pavement at top and bottom of steps. This insures precise alignment of adjacent pavements over time.

• All joints should be sealed for best performance over time, especially in frost/thaw climates.

• Cost note: Costs are calculated as per linear units of riser.

• It is recommended that recycled and regionally available materials and products be given high priority in determining final design and specifications.

Installation Cost (per Linear Foot)

LOW   HIGH

$70.00

Maintenance

LOW   HIGH

15mm (1/2")
EXPANSION
JOINT

PAVING

SLOPE

GRANITE TREADS 150x450mm
(6"x18") ON 40mm (1 1/2")
MORTAR BED

15 (1/2") R

RAKE JOINT, SEAL IN
FROST-THAW REGIONS

15mm (1/2")
EXPANSION
JOINT

150
(6")

VOID

(POLYFOAM FILL)

50
(2")

STRUCTURAL SLAB
PITCH SURFACE TO DRAIN

PROTECTION BOARD OVER
WATERPROOF MEMBRANE
WITH DRAIN MAT

50mm (2") DIA.
WEEPHOLES 900mm
(3'-0") ON CENTER

CONCRETE SLAB & FOOTING
REINF. AS REQUIRED

APPLICATION

LIGHT   MED.   HEAVY

CLIMATE

ARID   HUMID   TEMP.   COLD

SUBGRADE

PERM.   CLAY   ROOF

CSI MASTERFORMAT: 04410
DRAWING FILE: STP03-02

• This drawing is a template for preliminary design only, and is not intended for bid purposes. It is subject to modification based on design calculations, local practices, and all applicable codes and regulations.

• This granite step detail is rated for heavy-duty applications based on thickness of concrete and span over polyfoam void, and may support significant pedestrian loading typically associated with structural roof deck settings.

• Rigid pavement design must accommodate movement of materials by providing adequate expansion and control joints, particularly in regions of extreme temperature fluctuations. If designed for temperate or cold climates, air-entrained concrete is typically recommended due to freezing/thawing action.

• Reinforcing practices vary widely by region. Local codes and practices should be consulted prior to specifying any type of reinforcing.

• This detail shows steps placed on heavy-duty drain mat over protection board and waterproof membrane on a structural deck. Concrete thickness must allow for void shrinkage and extent of span. Allow weep holes to drain void if required.

• Cost note: Costs are calculated as per linear units of riser.

• It is recommended that recycled and regionally available materials and products be given high priority in determining final design and specifications.

Installation Cost (per Linear Foot)

LOW   HIGH

$66.00

Maintenance

LOW   HIGH

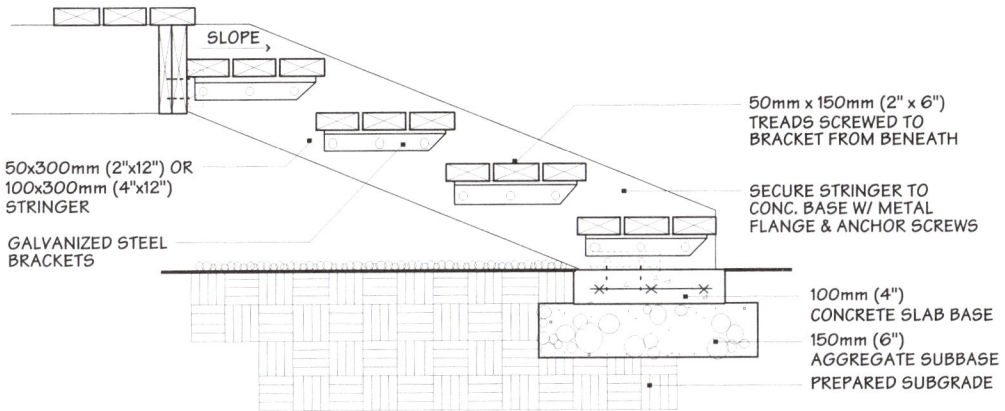

SLOPE

50mm x 150mm (2" x 6")
TREADS SCREWED TO
BRACKET FROM BENEATH

SECURE STRINGER TO
CONC. BASE W/ METAL
FLANGE & ANCHOR SCREWS

50x300mm (2"x12") OR
100x300mm (4"x12")
STRINGER

GALVANIZED STEEL
BRACKETS

100mm (4")
CONCRETE SLAB BASE

150mm (6")
AGGREGATE SUBBASE

PREPARED SUBGRADE

APPLICATION

CLIMATE

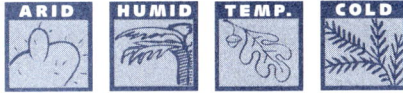

SUBGRADE

CSI MASTERFORMAT: 06110
DRAWING FILE: STP05-01

• This drawing is a template for preliminary design only, and is not intended for bid purposes. It is subject to modification based on design calculations, local practices, and all applicable codes and regulations.

• This detail is rated as light-duty due to loading potential and material longevity, and is typically found in residential and garden settings.

• Wood should be rot resistant or treated to provide reasonable length of service. For stability and moisture control, stringer should rest on metal flange or concrete as shown. All fasteners should be corrosion resistant. All surfaces should slope to drain.

• Attach stringer to deck facia with metal flange for secure assembly. In heavy-duty applications, a wood cleat sill may be required.

• It is recommended that recycled and regionally available materials and products be given high priority in determining final design and specifications.

Installation Cost (per Linear Foot)

LOW   HIGH

$16.00

Maintenance

LOW   HIGH

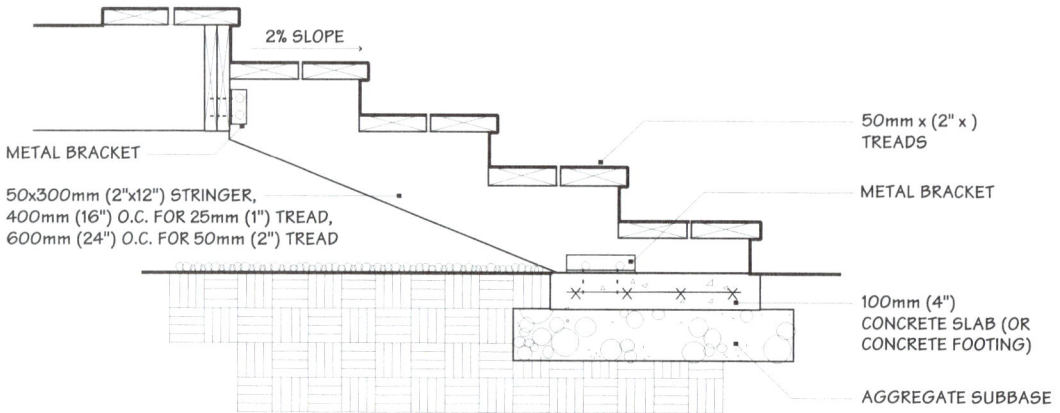

2% SLOPE

METAL BRACKET

50x300mm (2"x12") STRINGER,
400mm (16") O.C. FOR 25mm (1") TREAD,
600mm (24") O.C. FOR 50mm (2") TREAD

50mm x (2" x)
TREADS

METAL BRACKET

100mm (4")
CONCRETE SLAB (OR
CONCRETE FOOTING)

AGGREGATE SUBBASE

APPLICATION

CLIMATE

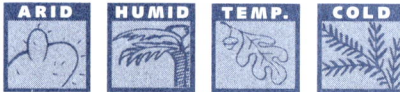

SUBGRADE

CSI MASTERFORMAT: 06110
DRAWING FILE: STP05-02

• This drawing is a template for preliminary design only, and is not intended for bid purposes. It is subject to modification based on design calculations, local practices, and all applicable codes and regulations.

• This wood step with notched stringer detail is rated as light-duty due to loading potential and material longevity, and is typically found in residential and garden settings.

• Wood should be rot resistant or treated to provide reasonable length of service. For stability and moisture control, stringer should rest on metal flange or concrete as shown. All fasteners should be corrosion resistant. All surfaces should slope to drain.

• Attach stringer to deck facia with metal flange for secure assembly. In heavy-duty applications, a wood cleat sill may be required. If facia vertical depth is insufficient to attach stringer, align first tread to be flush with deck surface, which allows space beneath stringer to attach a beveled cleat.

• It is recommended that recycled and regionally available materials and products be given high priority in determining final design and specifications.

Installation Cost (per Linear Foot)

LOW   HIGH

$15.00

Maintenance

LOW   HIGH

Walls

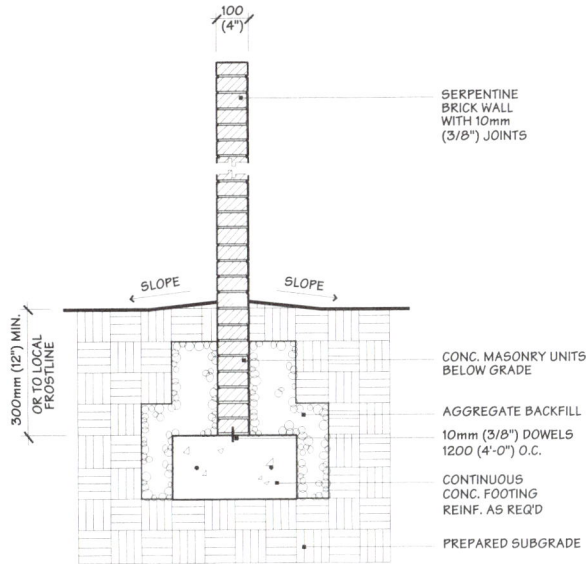

SERPENTINE BRICK WALL WITH 10mm (3/8") JOINTS

100 (4")

SLOPE ← → SLOPE

300mm (12") MIN. OR TO LOCAL FROSTLINE

CONC. MASONRY UNITS BELOW GRADE

AGGREGATE BACKFILL

10mm (3/8") DOWELS 1200 (4'-0") O.C.

CONTINUOUS CONC. FOOTING REINF. AS REQ'D

PREPARED SUBGRADE

APPLICATION

LIGHT | MED. | HEAVY

CLIMATE

ARID | HUMID | TEMP. | COLD

SUBGRADE

PERM. | CLAY | ROOF

CSI MASTERFORMAT: 03310
DRAWING FILE: WAL04-01

• This drawing is a template for preliminary design only, and is not intended for bid purposes. It is subject to modification based on design calculations, local practices, and all applicable codes and regulations.

• This single brick serpentine wall is rated medium-duty due to its height potential, strength, and durability, and is typically found in residential, park, garden, or institutional settings.

• The footing is typically reinforced and often bears on prepared subgrade in most soils. Depth is determined by frost line or local codes. Concrete masonry units are typically used below grade in areas of frost, and changed to face brick two courses below finish grade.

• This wall is best used in warmer climates, and is not recommended for cold climates. The wall derives its strength from its serpentine structure and requires precise layout for best results.

• Maintenance is moderate to heavy due to needs of pointing, and monitoring for sectional cracks.

• It is recommended that recycled and regionally available materials and products be given high priority in determining final design and specifications.

Installation Cost (per Square Foot)

LOW　　　　　　　　　　　HIGH

$9.00

Maintenance

LOW　　　　　　　　　　　HIGH

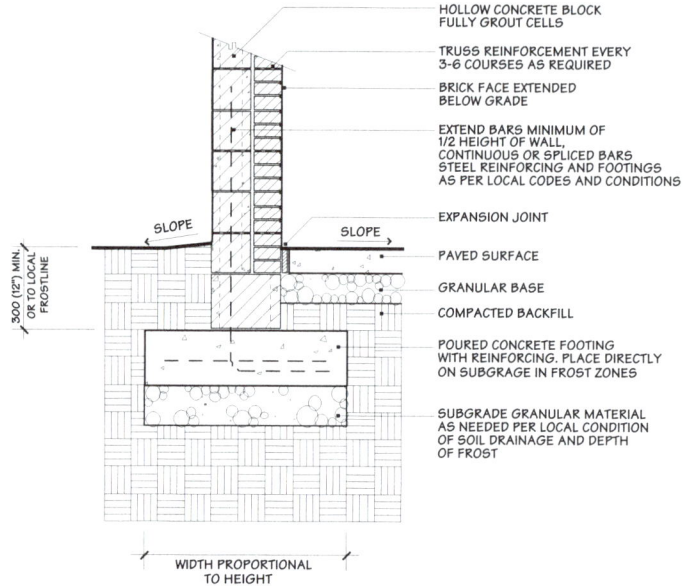

HOLLOW CONCRETE BLOCK
FULLY GROUT CELLS

TRUSS REINFORCEMENT EVERY
3-6 COURSES AS REQUIRED

BRICK FACE EXTENDED
BELOW GRADE

EXTEND BARS MINIMUM OF
1/2 HEIGHT OF WALL,
CONTINUOUS OR SPLICED BARS
STEEL REINFORCING AND FOOTINGS
AS PER LOCAL CODES AND CONDITIONS

EXPANSION JOINT

PAVED SURFACE

GRANULAR BASE

COMPACTED BACKFILL

POURED CONCRETE FOOTING
WITH REINFORCING. PLACE DIRECTLY
ON SUBGRADE IN FROST ZONES

SUBGRADE GRANULAR MATERIAL
AS NEEDED PER LOCAL CONDITION
OF SOIL DRAINAGE AND DEPTH
OF FROST

SLOPE

SLOPE

300 (12") MIN.
OR TO LOCAL
FROSTLINE

WIDTH PROPORTIONAL
TO HEIGHT

APPLICATION

CLIMATE

SUBGRADE

CSI MASTERFORMAT: 04810
DRAWING FILE: WAL04-03

- This drawing is a template for preliminary design only, and is not intended for bid purposes. It is subject to modification based on design calculations, local practices, and all applicable codes and regulations.

- This single-sided brick masonry wall detail is rated as heavy-duty due to its height potential, strength, and durability, and is typically found in commercial, urban park, or institutional settings in all climates.

- The footing is typically reinforced and often bears on prepared subgrade in most soils. Aggregate leveling course may be used in warmer climates or in finer soils. Depth and width are determined by frost line and wind loads.

- Fully grouted and reinforced concrete masonry units are mortared to the footing to act as sill for the fully grouted and reinforced concrete masonry block backer wall, and the brick veneer face. Lateral reinforcing may be required in heavy wind load circumstances and when wall is above 1800 mm (6').

- Cap may be precast concrete or cut stone, sloped to drain.

- Reinforcing practices vary widely by region. Local codes and practices should be consulted prior to specifying any type of reinforcing.

- It is recommended that recycled and regionally available materials and products be given high priority in determining final design and specifications.

Installation Cost (per Square Foot)

LOW   HIGH

$12.60

Maintenance

LOW   HIGH

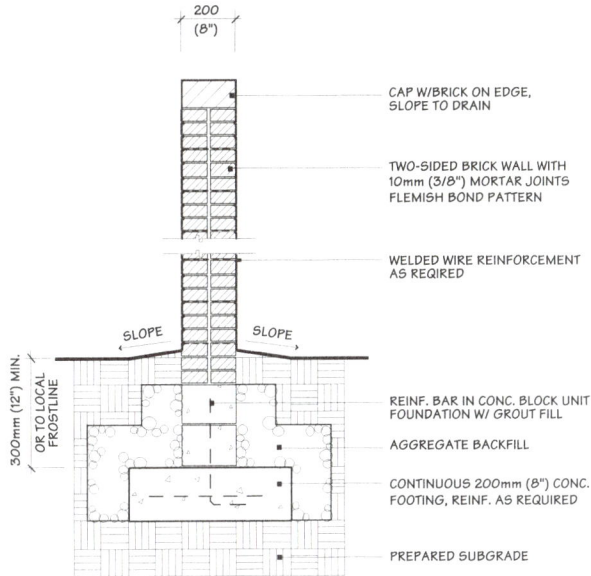

200
(8")

CAP W/BRICK ON EDGE,
SLOPE TO DRAIN

TWO-SIDED BRICK WALL WITH
10mm (3/8") MORTAR JOINTS
FLEMISH BOND PATTERN

WELDED WIRE REINFORCEMENT
AS REQIRED

SLOPE   SLOPE

300mm (12") MIN.
OR TO LOCAL
FROSTLINE

REINF. BAR IN CONC. BLOCK UNIT
FOUNDATION W/ GROUT FILL

AGGREGATE BACKFILL

CONTINUOUS 200mm (8") CONC.
FOOTING, REINF. AS REQUIRED

PREPARED SUBGRADE

APPLICATION

CLIMATE

SUBGRADE

CSI MASTERFORMAT: 04810
DRAWING FILE: WAL04-02

• This drawing is a template for preliminary design only, and is not intended for bid purposes. It is subject to modification based on design calculations, local practices, and all applicable codes and regulations.

• This two-sided brick wall is rated as medium-duty due to its height potential, strength, and durability, and is typically found in commercial, urban park, or institutional settings.

• The footing is typically reinforced and often bears on prepared subgrade in most soils. Depth is determined by frost line and wind loads.

• Fully grouted and reinforced concrete masonry units are mortared to the footing to act as sill for the Flemish bond pattern brick wall units. Lateral reinforcing may be required in heavy wind load circumstances and when wall is above 1800 mm (6').

• Cap may be brick on edge or cut stone, sloped to drain.

• Reinforcing practices vary widely by region. Local codes and practices should be consulted prior to specifying any type of reinforcing.

• It is recommended that recycled and regionally available materials and products be given high priority in determining final design and specifications.

Installation Cost (per Square Foot)

LOW   HIGH

$17.60

Maintenance

LOW   HIGH

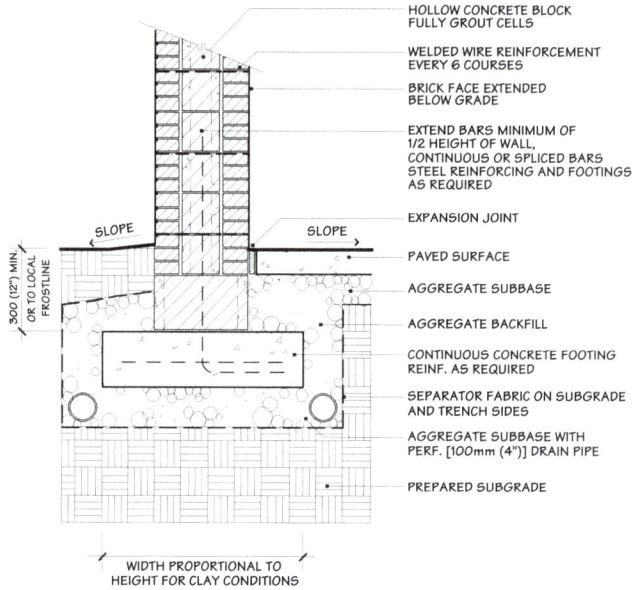

HOLLOW CONCRETE BLOCK
FULLY GROUT CELLS

WELDED WIRE REINFORCEMENT
EVERY 6 COURSES

BRICK FACE EXTENDED
BELOW GRADE

EXTEND BARS MINIMUM OF
1/2 HEIGHT OF WALL,
CONTINUOUS OR SPLICED BARS
STEEL REINFORCING AND FOOTINGS
AS REQUIRED

EXPANSION JOINT

PAVED SURFACE

AGGREGATE SUBBASE

AGGREGATE BACKFILL

CONTINUOUS CONCRETE FOOTING
REINF. AS REQUIRED

SEPARATOR FABRIC ON SUBGRADE
AND TRENCH SIDES

AGGREGATE SUBBASE WITH
PERF. [100mm (4")] DRAIN PIPE

PREPARED SUBGRADE

SLOPE   SLOPE

300 (12") MIN.
OR TO LOCAL
FROSTLINE

WIDTH PROPORTIONAL TO
HEIGHT FOR CLAY CONDITIONS

APPLICATION

CLIMATE

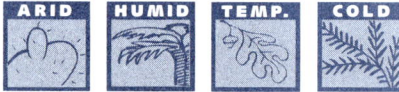

SUBGRADE

CSI MASTERFORMAT: 04810
DRAWING FILE: WAL04-04

• This drawing is a template for preliminary design only, and is not intended for bid purposes. It is subject to modification based on design calculations, local practices, and all applicable codes and regulations.

• This two-sided brick masonry wall detail is rated as heavy-duty due to its height potential, strength, and durability, and is typically found in commercial, urban park, or institutional settings in all climates.

• The footing is typically reinforced and often bears on prepared subgrade in most soils. Aggregate leveling course may be used in warmer climates or in finer soils. This detail illustrates adaptations required for clay soils by means of graded aggregate base, perforated subdrains, and fabric separator to bind aggregate and prevent fines from clogging pipes.

• Fully grouted and reinforced concrete masonry units are mortared to the footing to act as sill for the fully grouted and reinforced concrete masonry block core, and the brick veneer faces. Lateral reinforcing may be required in heavy wind load circumstances and when wall is above 1800 mm (6') to tie structure together.

• Cap may be precast concrete or cut stone, sloped to drain.

• Reinforcing practices vary widely by region. Local codes and practices should be consulted prior to specifying any type of reinforcing.

• It is recommended that recycled and regionally available materials and products be given high priority in determining final design and specifications.

Installation Cost (per Square Foot)

LOW   HIGH

$27.00

Maintenance

LOW   HIGH

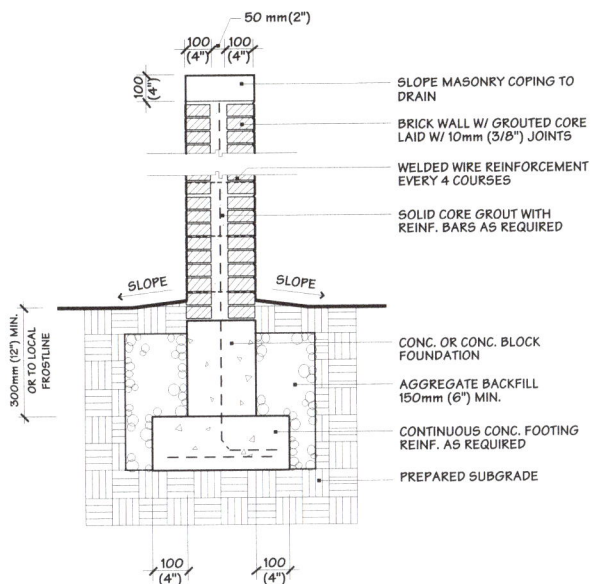

Labels on drawing:
- 50 mm(2")
- 100 (4")
- 100 (4")
- 100 (4")
- SLOPE MASONRY COPING TO DRAIN
- BRICK WALL W/ GROUTED CORE LAID W/ 10mm (3/8") JOINTS
- WELDED WIRE REINFORCEMENT EVERY 4 COURSES
- SOLID CORE GROUT WITH REINF. BARS AS REQUIRED
- SLOPE
- SLOPE
- 300mm (12") MIN. OR TO LOCAL FROSTLINE
- CONC. OR CONC. BLOCK FOUNDATION
- AGGREGATE BACKFILL 150mm (6") MIN.
- CONTINUOUS CONC. FOOTING REINF. AS REQUIRED
- PREPARED SUBGRADE
- 100 (4")
- 100 (4")

APPLICATION

LIGHT · MED. · HEAVY

CLIMATE

ARID · HUMID · TEMP. · COLD

SUBGRADE

PERM. · CLAY · ROCK

CSI MASTERFORMAT: 04810
DRAWING FILE: WAL04-05

• This drawing is a template for preliminary design only, and is not intended for bid purposes. It is subject to modification based on design calculations, local practices, and all applicable codes and regulations.

• This two-sided brick wall with grouted core detail is rated as medium-duty due to its height potential, strength, and durability, and is typically found in residential, commercial, urban park, or institutional settings in all climates.

• The footing is typically reinforced and often bears on prepared subgrade in most soils. Aggregate leveling course may be used in warmer climates or in finer soils.

• Fully grouted and reinforced concrete masonry units are mortared to the footing to act as sill for the reinforced fully grouted masonry block core, and the brick faces. This detail shows alternate solid concrete pier base. Lateral reinforcing may be required in heavy wind load circumstances and when

wall is above 1800 mm (6') to tie structure together.

• Cap may be precast concrete or cut stone, sloped to drain.

• Reinforcing practices vary widely by region. Local codes and practices should be consulted prior to specifying any type of reinforcing.

• It is recommended that recycled and regionally available materials and products be given high priority in determining final design and specifications.

Installation Cost (per Square Foot)

LOW — HIGH
$18.00

Maintenance

LOW — HIGH

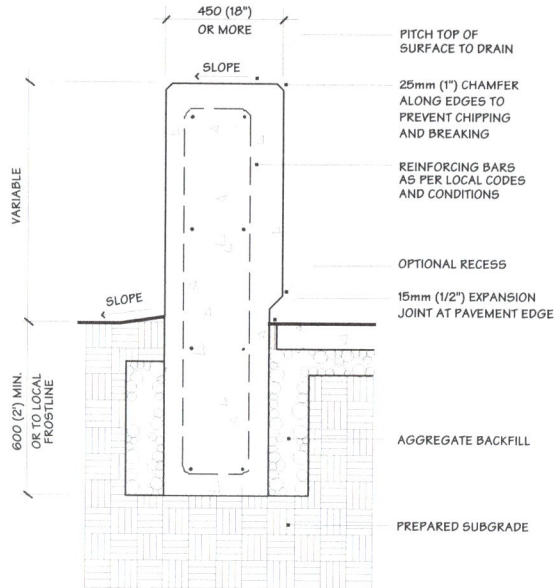

450 (18")
OR MORE

SLOPE

VARIABLE

SLOPE

600 (2") MIN.
OR TO LOCAL
FROSTLINE

PITCH TOP OF
SURFACE TO DRAIN

25mm (1") CHAMFER
ALONG EDGES TO
PREVENT CHIPPING
AND BREAKING

REINFORCING BARS
AS PER LOCAL CODES
AND CONDITIONS

OPTIONAL RECESS

15mm (1/2") EXPANSION
JOINT AT PAVEMENT EDGE

AGGREGATE BACKFILL

PREPARED SUBGRADE

APPLICATION

CLIMATE

SUBGRADE

CSI MASTERFORMAT: 03310
DRAWING FILE: WAL02-01

• This drawing is a template for preliminary design only, and is not intended for bid purposes. It is subject to modification based on design calculations, local practices, and all applicable codes and regulations.

• This concrete wall detail is rated as heavy-duty due to its height potential, strength, and durability, and is typically found in commercial, urban park, or institutional settings. This wall is appropriate for all climates, but requires well drained and high weight bearing soils as shown.

• The wall is typically fully reinforced and often bears on prepared subgrade in most soils. Depth is determined by frost line and wind loads. Many finishes and textures are possible through form work and a range of surface treatments, including sand-blasting, and retardants for washing after forms are stripped.

• Concrete design must accommodate movement of materials by providing adequate expansion and control joints, particu-

larly in regions of extreme temperature fluctuations. If designed for temperate or cold climates, air-entrained concrete is typically recommended due to freezing/thawing action.

• Reinforcing practices vary widely by region. Local codes and practices should be consulted prior to specifying any type of reinforcing.

• It is recommended that recycled and regionally available materials and products be given high priority in determining final design and specifications.

Installation Cost (per Square Foot)

LOW   HIGH

$17.00

Maintenance

LOW   HIGH

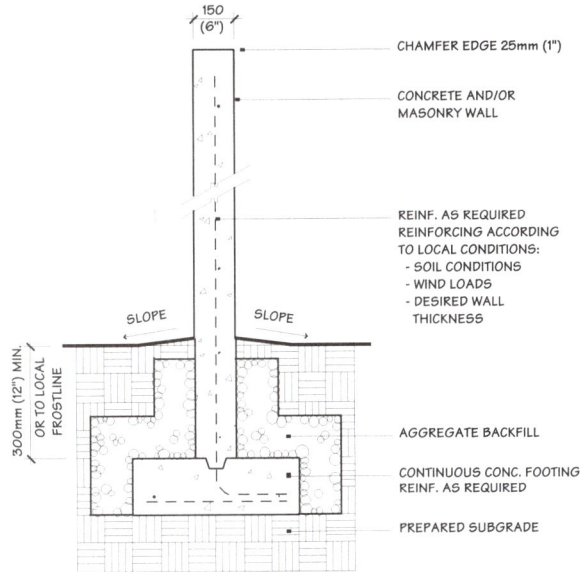

150
(6")

CHAMFER EDGE 25mm (1")

CONCRETE AND/OR
MASONRY WALL

REINF. AS REQUIRED
REINFORCING ACCORDING
TO LOCAL CONDITIONS:
- SOIL CONDITIONS
- WIND LOADS
- DESIRED WALL
  THICKNESS

SLOPE   SLOPE

300mm (12") MIN.
OR TO LOCAL
FROSTLINE

AGGREGATE BACKFILL

CONTINUOUS CONC. FOOTING
REINF. AS REQUIRED

PREPARED SUBGRADE

APPLICATION

CLIMATE

SUBGRADE

CSI MASTERFORMAT: 03310
DRAWING FILE: WAL02-02

• This drawing is a template for preliminary design only, and is not intended for bid purposes. It is subject to modification based on design calculations, local practices, and all applicable codes and regulations.

• This concrete wall is rated as heavy-duty due to its height potential, strength, and durability, and is typically found in commercial, urban park, or institutional settings.

• The footing is typically reinforced and often bears on prepared subgrade in most soils. Depth is determined by frost line and wind loads. Many finishes and textures are possible through form work and a range of surface treatments, including sand-blasting, and retardants for washing after forms are stripped.

• Rigid pavement design must accommodate movement of materials by providing adequate expansion and control joints, particularly in regions of extreme temperature fluctuations. If designed for temperate or cold climates, air-entrained concrete is typi-

cally recommended due to freezing/thawing action.

• Reinforcing practices vary widely by region. Local codes and practices should be consulted prior to specifying any type of reinforcing.

• It is recommended that recycled and regionally available materials and products be given high priority in determining final design and specifications.

Installation Cost (per Square Foot)

LOW   HIGH

$20.00

Maintenance

LOW   HIGH

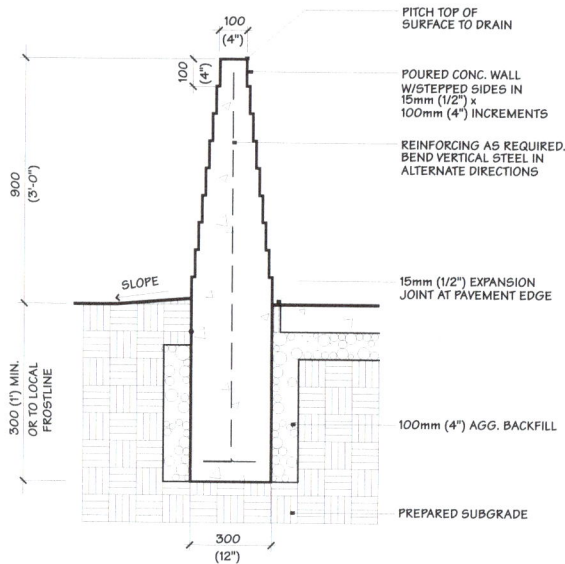

PITCH TOP OF SURFACE TO DRAIN

POURED CONC. WALL W/STEPPED SIDES IN 15mm (1/2") x 100mm (4") INCREMENTS

REINFORCING AS REQUIRED. BEND VERTICAL STEEL IN ALTERNATE DIRECTIONS

15mm (1/2") EXPANSION JOINT AT PAVEMENT EDGE

100mm (4") AGG. BACKFILL

PREPARED SUBGRADE

100 (4")

100 (4")

900 (3'-0")

SLOPE

300 (1") MIN. OR TO LOCAL FROSTLINE

300 (12")

APPLICATION

CLIMATE

SUBGRADE

CSI MASTERFORMAT: 03310
DRAWING FILE: WAL02-04

- This drawing is a template for preliminary design only, and is not intended for bid purposes. It is subject to modification based on design calculations, local practices, and all applicable codes and regulations.

- This concrete wall detail is rated as light-duty due to its height, and is typically found in commercial, urban park, or institutional settings. This wall is appropriate for all climates, but requires well drained and high weight bearing soils as shown.

- The wall is typically fully reinforced and often bears on prepared subgrade in most soils. Depth is determined by frost line and wind loads. Many finishes and textures are possible through form work and a range of surface treatments, including sand-blasting, and retardants for washing after forms are stripped.

- This detail shows staggered board form to lessen the wall mass.

- Concrete design must accommodate movement of materials by providing adequate expansion and control joints, particularly in regions of extreme temperature fluctuations. If designed for temperate or cold climates, air-entrained concrete is typically recommended due to freezing/thawing action.

- Reinforcing practices vary widely by region. Local codes and practices should be consulted prior to specifying any type of reinforcing.

- It is recommended that recycled and regionally available materials and products be given high priority in determining final design and specifications.

Installation Cost (per Square Foot)

LOW   HIGH

$19.00

Maintenance

LOW   HIGH

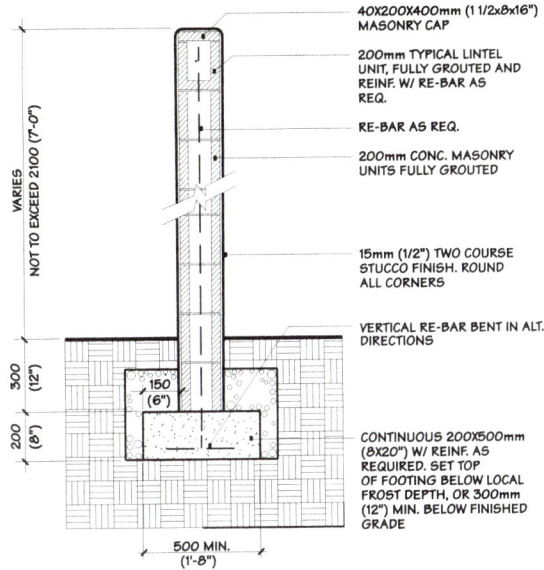

40X200X400mm (1 1/2x8x16")
MASONRY CAP

200mm TYPICAL LINTEL
UNIT, FULLY GROUTED AND
REINF. W/ RE-BAR AS
REQ.

RE-BAR AS REQ.

200mm CONC. MASONRY
UNITS FULLY GROUTED

15mm (1/2") TWO COURSE
STUCCO FINISH. ROUND
ALL CORNERS

VERTICAL RE-BAR BENT IN ALT.
DIRECTIONS

CONTINUOUS 200X500mm
(8X20") W/ REINF. AS
REQUIRED. SET TOP
OF FOOTING BELOW LOCAL
FROST DEPTH, OR 300mm
(12") MIN. BELOW FINISHED
GRADE

VARIES
NOT TO EXCEED 2100 (7'-0")

300 (12")

200 (8")

150 (6")

500 MIN. (1'-8")

APPLICATION

CLIMATE

SUBGRADE

CSI MASTERFORMAT: 04810
DRAWING FILE: WAL02-03

• This drawing is a template for preliminary design only, and is not intended for bid purposes. It is subject to modification based on design calculations, local practices, and all applicable codes and regulations.

• This concrete block masonry wall with stucco detail is rated as medium-duty due to its height potential, strength, and durability, and is typically found in commercial, urban park, or institutional settings in warm climates.

• The footing is typically reinforced and often bears on prepared subgrade in most soils. Aggregate leveling course may be used in warmer climates or in finer soils.

• Fully grouted and reinforced concrete masonry units are mortared to the footing to create the wall core. Wall is capped with reinforced and grouted lintel unit and masonry finish cap. Entire wall is finished with stucco in two coats. Lateral reinforcing may be required in heavy wind load circumstances

and when wall is above 1800 mm (6') to tie structure together.

• Other cap options must slope to drain.

• Reinforcing practices vary widely by region. Local codes and practices should be consulted prior to specifying any type of reinforcing.

• It is recommended that recycled and regionally available materials and products be given high priority in determining final design and specifications.

Installation Cost (per Square Foot)

LOW   HIGH

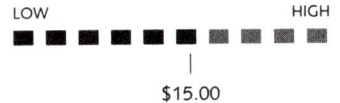

$15.00

Maintenance

LOW   HIGH

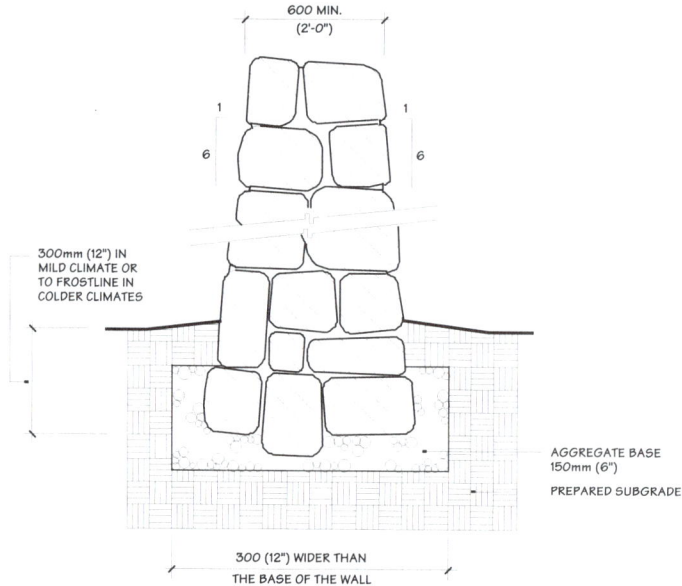

600 MIN.
(2'-0")

1
6

300mm (12") IN
MILD CLIMATE OR
TO FROSTLINE IN
COLDER CLIMATES

AGGREGATE BASE
150mm (6")

PREPARED SUBGRADE

300 (12") WIDER THAN
THE BASE OF THE WALL

APPLICATION

CSI MASTERFORMAT: 04850
DRAWING FILE: WAL03-01

• This drawing is a template for preliminary design only, and is not intended for bid purposes. It is subject to modification based on design calculations, local practices, and all applicable codes and regulations.

• This single tier dry laid stone wall detail is rated as medium-duty due to height limitations of 900-1200 mm (3-4'), although stone is a very durable material. It is found in a variety of residential, park, and garden settings in all climate zones. Dry laid walls on aggregate base are more suited to well drained soils.

• Stone is placed on an aggregate base and backfilled with aggregate material. Base should be placed below frost line for best results and lower maintenance in cold climates.

• Wall is tied together by varying coursing to include significant overlap of joints and tight fits within the wall. This wall creates an informal appearance as shown, but is able to maintain its line due to the deep footing.

CLIMATE

Wall should be battered and stones tilted inward for stability.

• It is recommended that recycled and regionally available materials and products be given high priority in determining final design and specifications.

SUBGRADE

Installation Cost (per Square Foot)

LOW   HIGH

$17.00

Maintenance

LOW   HIGH

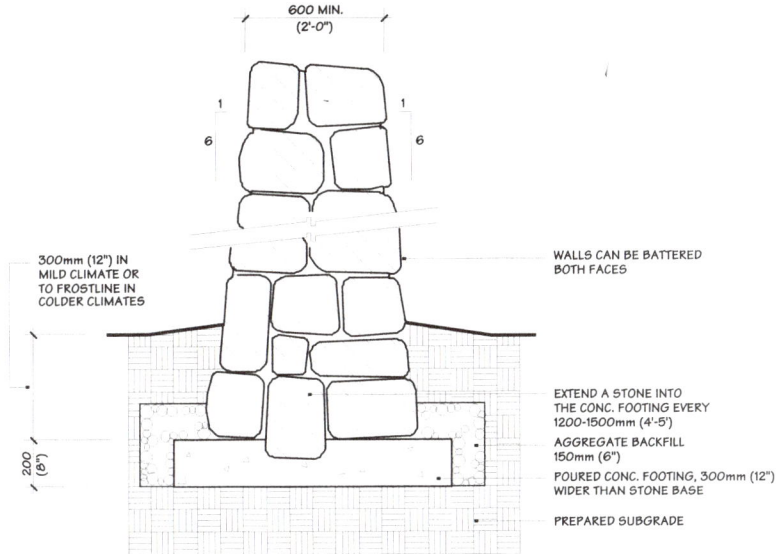

600 MIN.
(2'-0")

WALLS CAN BE BATTERED
BOTH FACES

300mm (12") IN
MILD CLIMATE OR
TO FROSTLINE IN
COLDER CLIMATES

200
(8")

EXTEND A STONE INTO
THE CONC. FOOTING EVERY
1200-1500mm (4'-5')

AGGREGATE BACKFILL
150mm (6")

POURED CONC. FOOTING, 300mm (12")
WIDER THAN STONE BASE

PREPARED SUBGRADE

APPLICATION

CLIMATE

SUBGRADE

CSI MASTERFORMAT: 04850
DRAWING FILE: WAL03-02

• This drawing is a template for preliminary design only, and is not intended for bid purposes. It is subject to modification based on design calculations, local practices, and all applicable codes and regulations.

• This single tier dry laid stone wall with concrete footing detail is rated as medium-duty due to height limitations of 900-1200 mm (3-4'), although stone is a very durable material. It is found in a variety of residential, park, and garden settings in all climate zones. Dry laid walls on aggregate base are more suited to well drained soils.

• Stone is placed on a concrete base and backfilled with aggregate material. Base should be placed below fost line for best results and lower maintenance in cold climates. Key stones may be placed in concrete footing to help secure wall plane.

• Wall is tied together by varying coursing to include significant overlap of joints and tight fits within the wall. This wall creates an informal appearance as shown, but is able to

maintain its line due to the concrete footing. Wall should be battered and stones tilted inward for stability.

• It is recommended that recycled and regionally available materials and products be given high priority in determining final design and specifications.

Installation Cost (per Square Foot)

LOW   HIGH

$18.45

Maintenance

LOW   HIGH

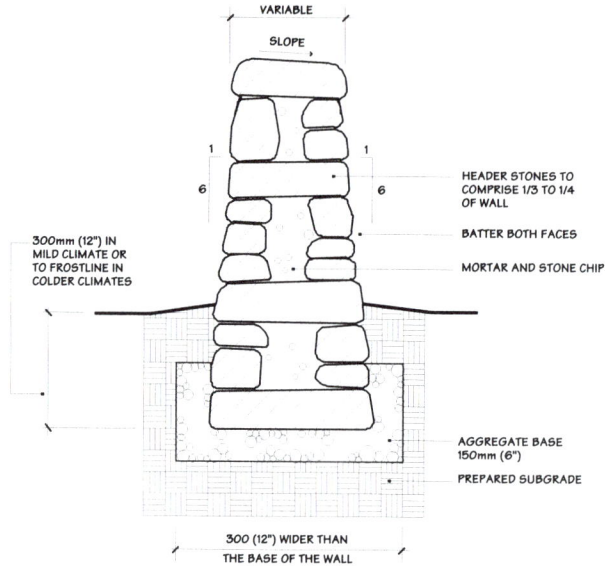

VARIABLE

SLOPE

HEADER STONES TO COMPRISE 1/3 TO 1/4 OF WALL

BATTER BOTH FACES

MORTAR AND STONE CHIP

300mm (12") IN MILD CLIMATE OR TO FROSTLINE IN COLDER CLIMATES

AGGREGATE BASE 150mm (6")

PREPARED SUBGRADE

300 (12") WIDER THAN THE BASE OF THE WALL

APPLICATION

CLIMATE

SUBGRADE

CSI MASTERFORMAT: 04850
DRAWING FILE: WAL03-03

- This drawing is a template for preliminary design only, and is not intended for bid purposes. It is subject to modification based on design calculations, local practices, and all applicable codes and regulations.

- This double tiered mortared stone wall with stone footing detail is rated as medium-duty due to height limitations of 900-1500 mm (3-5'), although stone is a very durable material. It is found in a variety of residential, park, and garden settings in most climate zones. Walls on aggregate base are more suited to well drained soils.

- Single base stone is placed on an aggregate leveling base and backfilled with aggregate material. Base should be placed below fost line for best results and lower maintenance in temperate climates. This detail is not suited for cold climates.

- Wall is tied together by single stone coursing which spans wall width and seals rubble and mortar grout layers. This wall creates a more formal appearance characterized

by distinctive horizontal banding of tie stones. Wall should be battered for stability.

- It is recommended that recycled and regionally available materials and products be given high priority in determining final design and specifications.

Installation Cost (per Square Foot)

LOW · · · · · · · · · · · · · · · · · · HIGH

$18.00

Maintenance

LOW · · · · · · · · · · · · · · · · · · HIGH

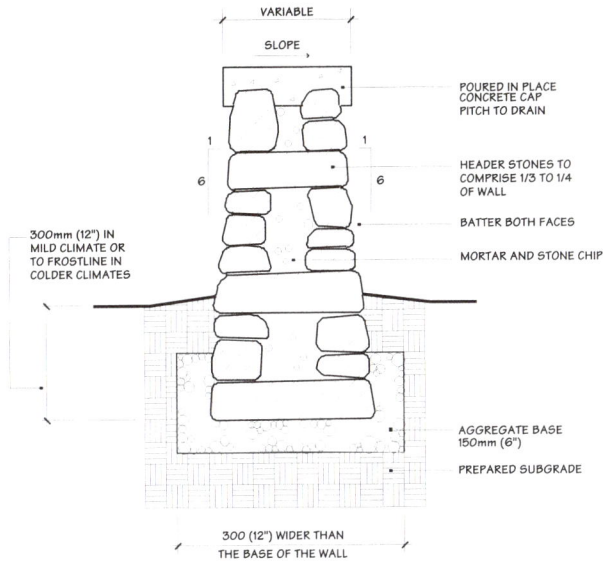

VARIABLE

SLOPE

POURED IN PLACE
CONCRETE CAP
PITCH TO DRAIN

HEADER STONES TO
COMPRISE 1/3 TO 1/4
OF WALL

BATTER BOTH FACES

MORTAR AND STONE CHIP

300mm (12") IN
MILD CLIMATE OR
TO FROSTLINE IN
COLDER CLIMATES

AGGREGATE BASE
150mm (6")

PREPARED SUBGRADE

300 (12") WIDER THAN
THE BASE OF THE WALL

APPLICATION

CLIMATE

SUBGRADE

CSI MASTERFORMAT: 04850
DRAWING FILE: WAL03-04

• This drawing is a template for preliminary design only, and is not intended for bid purposes. It is subject to modification based on design calculations, local practices, and all applicable codes and regulations.

• This double tiered mortared stone wall with concrete cap detail is rated as medium-duty due to height limitations of 900-1500 mm (3-5'), although stone is a very durable material. It is found in a variety of residential, park, and garden settings in most climate zones. Walls on aggregate base are more suited to well drained soils.

• Single base stone is placed on an aggregate leveling base and backfilled with aggregate material. Base should be placed below fost line for best results and lower maintenance in temperate climates. This detail is not suited for cold climates.

• Wall is tied together by single stone coursing which spans wall width and seals rubble and mortar grout layers. This wall creates a more formal appearance characterized by distinctive horizontal banding of tie stones. Wall should be battered for stability.

• Concrete cap is cast in place after stone wall is erected. Steel dowels may be required to tie cap to grouted core. This detail requires careful scribing of concrete form to create a clean finished edge. Cap should be pitched to drain.

• It is recommended that recycled and regionally available materials and products be given high priority in determining final design and specifications.

Installation Cost (per Square Foot)

LOW   HIGH

$18.50

Maintenance

LOW   HIGH

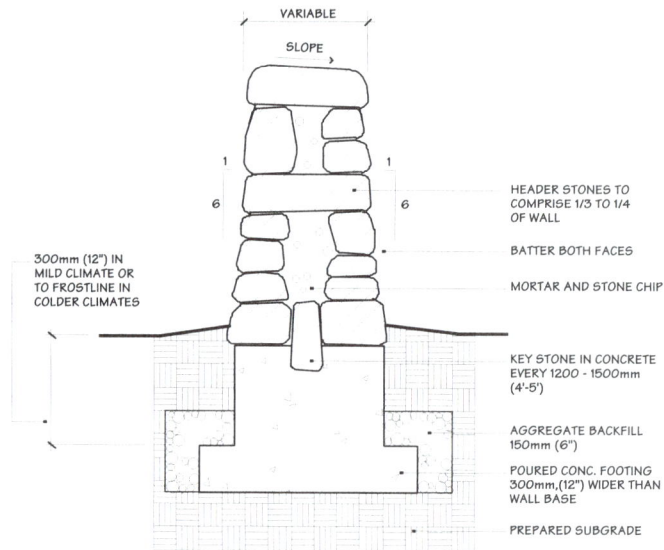

VARIABLE

SLOPE

HEADER STONES TO
COMPRISE 1/3 TO 1/4
OF WALL

BATTER BOTH FACES

MORTAR AND STONE CHIP

300mm (12") IN
MILD CLIMATE OR
TO FROSTLINE IN
COLDER CLIMATES

KEY STONE IN CONCRETE
EVERY 1200 - 1500mm
(4'-5')

AGGREGATE BACKFILL
150mm (6")

POURED CONC. FOOTING
300mm,(12") WIDER THAN
WALL BASE

PREPARED SUBGRADE

APPLICATION

CLIMATE

SUBGRADE

CSI MASTERFORMAT: 04850
DRAWING FILE: WAL03-05

• This drawing is a template for preliminary design only, and is not intended for bid purposes. It is subject to modification based on design calculations, local practices, and all applicable codes and regulations.

• This double tiered mortared stone wall on concrete footing detail is rated as heavy-duty due to height limitations of 1500-1800 mm (5-6'). It is found in a variety of residential, park, and garden settings in all climate zones.

• Base keystone is set in concrete footing and backfilled with aggregate material. Footing should be placed below fost line for best results and lower maintenance in temperate climates.

• Wall is tied together by single stone coursing which spans wall width and seals rubble and mortar grout layers. This wall creates a more formal appearance characterized by distinctive horizontal banding of tie stones. Wall should be battered for stability.

• Cap should be pitched to drain and all mortar joints should be raked for shadow effect.

• It is recommended that recycled and regionally available materials and products be given high priority in determining final design and specifications.

Installation Cost (per Square Foot)

LOW · · · · · · · · · · HIGH

$19.00

Maintenance

LOW · · · · · · · · · · HIGH

Photographic Sources

Page 4. Southwest Recreational Industries, Inc.

Page 5. Southwest Recreational Industries, Inc.

Page 10. John H. Martin, RIBA

Page 14. Theodore Osmundson, FASLA

Page 15. Theodore Osmundson, FASLA

Page 16. Berkshire Design Group, Inc.

Page 19. Safe Guard Surfacing Corp.

Page 20. Safe Guard Surfacing Corp.

Page 24. Pat Trefz, ASLA

Page 26. Lee Tennis Products

Page 33. Michael Davidsohn

Page 72. Dr. David Bloniarz

Page 76. Theodore Osmundson, FASLA

Page 114. Dr. David Bloniarz

Page 115. Dr. David Bloniarz

Page 145. MacLeod Reckord Landscape Architects

Page 146. Dr. Dwight A. Brown

Page 148. Dr. Dwight A. Brown

Page 167. Michael Davidsohn

Page 175. L.M. Scofield Company

Page 176. L.M. Scofield Company

Page 177. L.M. Scofield Company

Page 186. S.F. Concrete Technology, Inc.

Page 187. Hastings Pavement

Page 188. Hastings Pavement

Page 191. Bartron Corp.

Page 192. Dr. David Bloniarz

Page 193. Dr. David Bloniarz

Page 210. Dr. David Bloniarz

Page 212. DINOFLEX Manufacturing, ltd.

Page 213. Dr. David Bloniarz

Page 214. Dr. David Bloniarz

Page 215. Michael Davidsohn

Page 216. Michael Davidsohn

Page 218. Michael Davidsohn

Page 221. Dr. David Bloniarz

Page 249. Michael Davidsohn

Page 254. Michael Davidsohn

Page 279. Miceli, Kulik, Williams & Associates, P.C.

Page 280. Miceli, Kulik, Williams & Associates, P.C.

Page 300. Dr. David Bloniarz

Page 317. Dr. David Bloniarz

Page 330. Miceli, Kulik, Williams & Associates, P.C.

Page 331. Miceli, Kulik, Williams & Associates, P.C.

Page 359. Michael Davidsohn

Page 371. Michael Davidsohn

Page 372. Michael Davidsohn

Page 381. Michael Davidsohn

Detail Index